M000213242

# CIVIL PROCEDURE

## OBJECTIVE

## Third Edition

**LINDA S. MULLENIX**
Morris & Rita Atlas Chair in Advocacy
University of Texas School of Law
Austin, Texas

**Exam Pro** ®

WEST
ACADEMIC
PUBLISHING

*Exam Pro Series* is a trademark registered in the U.S. Patent and Trademark Office.

COPYRIGHT © 1998 WEST PUBLISHING CO.
© 2007 by THOMSON WEST
© 2016 LEG, Inc. d/b/a West Academic
    444 Cedar Street, Suite 700
    St. Paul, MN 55101
    1-877-888-1330

West, West Academic Publishing, and West Academic are trademarks of West Publishing Corporation, used under license.

Printed in the United States of America

**ISBN:** 978-1-63460-683-7

# Preface

**To the student:**

This book consists of five objective exams in civil procedure, containing a total of 125 objective questions. Each exam consists of twenty-five objective problems followed by five multiple-choice answers. Each exam is intended to take two hours. Please feel free to use the Federal Rules of Civil Procedure as you take these exams. If your instructor permits the use of other materials in taking your exam, then use these as well.

The purpose of this book is to assist first-year civil procedure students in preparing for objective multiple choice examination questions. Every first year civil procedure course is taught differently at each law school, and each professor will teach selected topics in different sequence. Almost all civil procedure courses, however, generally cover the same range of topics. Following this Preface is a **TABLE OF EXAM TOPICS** to assist you in locating procedure topics as they appear in the problems in these exams.

This is the third edition of Exam Pro in Civil Procedure. This edition reflects the typical course coverage in the now standard four credit-hour, one semester civil procedure course. The exam problems have been updated to reflect recent Supreme Court decisions on civil procedure issues, as well as recent amendments to the Federal Rules that became effective December 2015.

Each problem on the exams is based on a real case recently decided by a federal district or appellate court. The analysis and answers are derived from these judicial decisions, based on current authority and precedent. Each exam has an answer key with explanations for the *best possible answer* to the problem. The answer keys explain why other proposed answers are incorrect, or not the best possible answer. The answer keys also flag "red herring" answers that are intended to lure students into plausible-sounding but inaccurate conclusions. The problems have been chosen to test students' ability to apply doctrines and rules to actual fact patterns, and reflect settled jurisprudence. None of the problems test on issues where there currently is conflicting authority.

The exam problems cover the following topics: personal jurisdiction; subject matter jurisdiction (including federal diversity, federal question, supplemental, and removal jurisdiction); venue; transfer of venue; *forum non conveniens*; pleading (including complaint, answer, and amendment of pleadings); pre-trial Rule 12 motions; sanctions (Rule 11); joinder of parties and claims; permissive and compulsory joinder; federal discovery (including the scope, attorney-client privilege, work-product doctrine, protective orders, and sanctions); summary judgment; judgments as a matter of law (i.e., directed verdicts and judgments as a matter of law); res judicata and collateral estoppel; and applicable law.

The chief purpose of this book is to provide students with a comprehensive set of objective exam questions, to assist with exam preparation. Additionally, working through these materials should also enhance the student's understanding of civil procedure and the appropriate application of constitutional principles, case precedents, statutes, and rules as applied in actual litigation.

> Professor Linda S. Mullenix
> Morris & Rita Atlas Chair in Advocacy
> University of Texas School of Law

April 2016

# Table of Exam Topics

# Table of Contents

# CIVIL PROCEDURE

## OBJECTIVE

Third Edition

# CHAPTER 1
# EXAM #1 PROBLEMS AND QUESTIONS

Kristen Biller filed a complaint in federal district court against defendants Café Luna of Naples, Inc., Café Luna East, Edward J. Barsamian, and Shannon Radosti, on her own behalf and on behalf of other similarly situated individuals, for overtime and minimum wage compensation relief under the Fair Labor Standards Act. The defendants filed their answer and affirmative defenses.

The defendants' affirmative defenses alleged in their entirety:

- Defendants invoke the defenses, protections and limitations of the Fair Labor Standards Act.

- Plaintiff's claims are barred in whole or in part by the doctrines of waiver, estoppel or laches.

- Plaintiff's claims are barred in whole or in part by accord and satisfaction, settlement or payment and release.

- Plaintiff has failed to exhaust all administrative remedies.

- Plaintiff has failed to mitigate her alleged damages.

- Defendants reserve the right to assert further affirmative defenses as discovery proceeds.

The plaintiff moved to strike those affirmative defenses arguing that they are inadequately pled and/or were not valid defenses to an FLSA claim.

**QUESTION:**

(1) In response to the plaintiff's motion to strike the defendants' affirmative defenses, the federal district court should:

    (a) Deny the motion because the defendants have properly pled their affirmative defenses under Fed.R.Civ.P. 12(f);

    (b) Deny the motion because the defendants' affirmative defenses are listed in Fed.R.Civ.P. 8(d);

    (c) Deny the motion because the affirmative defenses gave the plaintiffs fair notice of the defenses that the defendants will assert in the action;

    (d) Grant the motion because the affirmative defenses failed to meet the pleading standards in *Twombly* and *Iqbal*;

    (e) Grant the motion because the affirmative defenses consisted of impertinent and immaterial matters.

* * *

A plaintiff filed a complaint in state court in Denver, asserting a claim against its insurer, Great American Insurance Company of New York ("Great American"), seeking indemnity for property damage to a wastewater treatment tank that the plaintiff asserted should have been covered under a building and personal property insurance policy.

The defendant removed the case to the U.S. District Court for the District of Colorado on February 12, 2015. The plaintiff also sued Matthew Gee & Associates Insurance Agency, Inc. and its principal, Matthew Gee for negligence and breaches of warranty related to the sale of the Great American insurance policy to the plaintiff. Great American answered the complaint on February 18, 2015 and Gee answered the complaint on March 13, 2015. A scheduling order set a May 1, 2015 deadline for amendment of pleadings.

The court held a settlement conference on June 2, 2015. Discovery had been open for two months, and would not end for another seven months. At the conference, the plaintiff learned of additional facts and at least one, and potentially other, witnesses supporting what it asserted were additional claims against Great American. On June 8, 2015 the plaintiff moved for leave to amend its complaint "in order to correct and clarify certain factual allegations, add additional factual allegations, and to add claims against Great American for violation of Colorado statutes and bad faith breach of insurance contract." The plaintiff asserted that its proposed amended complaint would "clarify the issues to be tried, would not burden the court, and was not prejudicial to Great American."

Great American opposed the motion because the deadline "was long past" and asserted that the plaintiff misled the court and acted in bad faith in feigning ignorance about the additional fact witness, "someone that the plaintiff was aware of all along."

**QUESTION:**

(2)   In response to the plaintiff's motion to amend its complaint, the federal district court should:

   (a)   Grant the motion under Fed.R.Civ.P. 15(a) because leave to amend should be freely given;

   (b)   Grant the motion to amend because Fed.R.Civ.P. 15(c) permits amendment of a complaint to relate back to the original filing;

   (c)   Deny the motion to amend because the defendants would be unduly prejudiced by the proposed amendments;

   (d)   Deny the motion to amend because the plaintiff had not made a mistake about the identity of one of the parties;

   (e)   Deny the motion to amend because the plaintiff's motion to amend was untimely.

* * *

Nicholas Ben filed an action in 19th Judicial District Court, East Baton Rouge Parish, Louisiana, naming as defendants Sergio Olvera-Arreola, State Auto Insurance Company ("State Auto"), and Crownson William. The plaintiff alleged that while sitting in his truck in traffic he was rear-ended by another truck driven by Mr. Olvera-Arreola. The plaintiff alleged that as a result of Mr. Olvera-Arreola's negligence, "he (the plaintiff) sustained injuries that required medical treatment." The plaintiff sought to recover past, present, and future physical pain and suffering, medical expenses, mental and emotional pain and suffering, lost wages, and loss of enjoyment of life. The plaintiff did not allege the severity of the collision or the nature of his physical injuries resulting from the collision. The plaintiff did not state whether he incurred medical and drug expenses, and did not identify the scope of the medical treatment he received or continued to receive as a result of the accident. Similarly, the plaintiff did not identify his profession or wages allegedly lost. The plaintiff did not pray for a jury trial.

State Auto removed the action alleging that the court had diversity jurisdiction pursuant to 28 U.S.C. § 1332(a). State Auto alleged that there was complete diversity because it was a citizen of Ohio, the other defendants were citizens of Arkansas, and the plaintiff was a citizen of Louisiana. State Auto further alleged that the amount in controversy requirement was satisfied based on the allegations in the petition, including the plaintiff's failure to include a general allegation that his claims did not exceed the requisite amount in controversy to establish diversity jurisdiction, his failure to enter into a binding stipulation limiting his recoverable amount, and a representation from the plaintiff's counsel that the plaintiff "had undergone an MRI on his lumbar and/or cervical spine."

The plaintiff then moved to remand on the basis that State Farm has not met its burden of proving that the amount in controversy requirement was satisfied. The plaintiff argued that the amount in controversy requirement was not facially apparent and State Auto had provided no summary judgment type evidence establishing that it was satisfied. The plaintiff noted that removal was made within 30 days of the filing of the lawsuit and there had been no discovery that would provide for summary judgment type evidence.

### QUESTION:

(3)   On the plaintiff's motion to remand the case from federal court to state court, the district court should:

   (a)   Grant the motion to remand because complete diversity was lacking;

   (b)   Grant the motion to remand because it was not facially apparent that the defendant could satisfy the requisite amount-in-controversy for federal jurisdiction;

   (c)   Grant the motion to remand because the plaintiff's claims are all state-based garden variety claims;

   (d)   Deny the motion to remand because the defendant had satisfied all the requirements for removal under 28 U.S.C. 1441(a);

(e)   Deny the motion to remand because the plaintiff's case clearly
      was worth more than $75,000.

* * *

In this same case, the plaintiff in their petition for remand also sought to
recover an award of costs and attorney's fees pursuant to 28 U.S.C. § 1447(c)
or Rule 11 of the Federal Rules of Civil Procedure, in light of the defendant's
alleged improvident removal. The plaintiff did not identify the costs and
expenses the plaintiff incurred in light of State Auto's removal and the filing
of the plaintiff's motion to remand.

QUESTION:

(4)   *For this question only*, assuming that the court ordered that the case
      should be remanded to state court, then with regard to the plaintiff's
      request for an award of costs and attorney's fees, the district court should:

      (a)   Grant the plaintiff's request for costs and attorney's fees
            pursuant to Fed.R.Civ.P. 11(c);

      (b)   Grant the plaintiff's request for costs and attorney's fees
            pursuant to 28 U.S.C. § 1927;

      (c)   Grant the plaintiff's request for costs and attorney's fees
            pursuant to 28 U.S.C. § 1447(c);

      (d)   Grant the plaintiff's request for attorney's fees under the court's
            inherent powers to supervise and discipline attorneys;

      (e)   Deny the plaintiff's request for costs and sanctions because this
            was a routine removal request and the defendant didn't do
            anything sanctionable in requesting the removal.

* * *

The plaintiffs, Heather and Glenn Farley, filed a complaint in the Federal
District Court for the Eastern District of Pennsylvania against defendants
Jeffrey Cernak and others. The complaint concerned a car accident that
occurred on December 6, 2012 on the Daniel Shays Highway at Amherst Road
in Pelham, Massachusetts. The plaintiffs filed their complaint on November 2,
2015. According to plaintiffs' complaint, all the defendants resided in
Massachusetts.

The plaintiffs alleged that due to the defendants' negligence during the car
accident the plaintiffs suffered injuries and loss of consortium, and that their
minor children also suffered injuries. In addition, other passengers in their
vehicle, Michael and Candace Harvey, suffered injuries and loss of consortium.

The defendants moved to dismiss the plaintiffs' claims pursuant to
Fed.R.Civ.P. 12(b)(6) alleging that the plaintiffs' failed to timely bring the
claims within the relevant statute of limitations. In a reply to the motion to
dismiss, the plaintiffs requested, as "alternative relief," that the matter be
transferred to the U.S. District Court for the District of Massachusetts for
improper venue.

**QUESTION:**

(5) Regarding the plaintiff's request that the matter be transferred to the District Court for Massachusetts, the federal district court in Pennsylvania should:

    (a) Grant the request because venue is improper in Pennsylvania;

    (b) Grant the request because all the defendants reside in Massachusetts;

    (c) Grant the request because Massachusetts is where the accident occurred;

    (d) Deny the request because the court gives deference to the plaintiff's choice of forum;

    (e) Deny the request because the defendant failed to raise improper venue in a responsive pleading and therefore waived any objection to venue.

* * *

In this same litigation, the defendants moved to dismiss the plaintiffs' claims alleging that the claims were barred by the relevant statute of limitations. The parties did not dispute that the plaintiffs' injuries accrued starting on the day of the incident on December 6, 2012. They disputed whether Pennsylvania's or Massachusetts's statutes of limitations should apply.

Generally, Pennsylvania courts apply the Pennsylvania statute of limitations except in cases in which the claim accrued in a foreign jurisdiction. Pennsylvania has a borrowing statute that requires that:

> The period of limitation applicable to a claim accruing outside the Commonwealth shall be either that provided or prescribed by the law of the place where the claim accrued or by the law of this Commonwealth, whichever first bars the claim.

Pennsylvania provides a two year limitation for bringing personal injury claims. Massachusetts provides a three year limitation for bringing personal injury claims.

**QUESTION:**

(6) On the defendant's motion to dismiss the claims under Fed.R.Civ.P. 12(b)(6), the federal should:

    (a) Grant the motion to dismiss because the claims were not well-pleaded;

    (b) Grant the motion to dismiss because Pennsylvania law applies to bar the claims;

    (c) Deny the motion to dismiss because Massachusetts law applies, which has a longer statute of limitations;

    (d) Deny the motion to dismiss because Pennsylvania law applies which would allow the claims to be adjudicated;

    (e)   Deny the motion because dismissal of the complaint at this early stage of the litigation would be unfair.

* * *

In civil litigation filed against CVS Caremark and other defendants in federal district court in Kentucky, the plaintiff filed a motion to compel production of two emails sent from the defendants' outside counsel to one of the defendant's employees who worked in compliance operations. The outside counsel also carbon-copied one of the two e-mails to an in-house paralegal and an in-house attorney of the defendants. The first e-mail gave outside counsel's legal analysis of facts provided by the defendants. The second e-mail appeared to contain no new information, but rather be a reply containing only copies of the communications previously sent to outside counsel. The first e-mail similarly contained copies of the prior communications from the client, albeit with additional text written by outside counsel.

**QUESTION:**

(7)   On the plaintiff's motion to compel disclosure of the content of the defendants' outside counsel emails, the federal district court should:

    (a)   Grant the plaintiff's motion to compel disclosure of the emails because the emails were sent to non-parties;

    (b)   Grant the plaintiff's motion to compel disclosure of the emails because facts are not privileged information;

    (c)   Grant the plaintiff's motion to compel disclosure of the emails because they were copied to a paralegal;

    (d)   Deny the motion to compel disclosure of the emails because these communications are protected under the attorney-client privilege;

    (e)   Deny the motion to compel disclosure of the emails because these communications are protected materials under the First Amendment.

* * *

The plaintiffs also sought the court to compel production of a case-status note that an employee of the defendant had written on a copy of a file sent to the defendants' legal department. On its privilege log, the defendants—seeking to protect the case-status note from discovery stated that the note was "regarding correspondence with Sheila Bowe, Legal Coordinator," a non-attorney member of the defendants' in-house legal team. The court reviewed the case-status note *in camera*. Upon *in camera* inspection, the case-status note revealed that the employee sent a copy of a file to the defendants' legal department. The note was not a communication with an attorney, and did not reveal the content of any communications to the legal department.

**QUESTION:**

(8) On the plaintiff's motion to compel disclosure of the defendants' case-status note, the federal district court should:

    (a) Grant the motion to compel production of the case-status note because facts are not privileged from discovery;

    (b) Grant the motion to compel production of the case-status note because the defendant has waived any privilege that might attach to the case-status note;

    (c) Grant the motion to compel production of the case-status note because the crime-fraud exception to attorney-client privilege applies to overcome the privilege;

    (d) Deny the motion to compel production to the case-status note because the file was sent to the defendants' legal department;

    (e) Deny the motion to compel production of the case-status note because attorneys' opinions are absolutely protected from disclosure.

* * *

Plaintiff Cynthia A. Henderson filed a lawsuit in the Western District of Texas federal court against defendants Boise Paper Holdings, LLC and Boise Packaging & Newsprint, LLC (collectively, Boise). She asserted a claim under the Family and Medical Leave Act (FMLA). Henderson worked for Boise as a salaried Process Improvement Facilitator in Waco, Texas from February 16, 2009 until October 13, 2011, when she was terminated for poor performance.

Henderson sued Boise on October 14, 2013, claiming her termination was not a result of poor job performance but instead in retaliation for requesting medical leave forms related to an upcoming orthopedic surgery three days earlier. Henderson claimed Boise's failure to provide such forms and her subsequent termination constituted unlawful interference with the exercise of her FMLA rights. Henderson sought unpaid wages and overtime compensation, liquidated and compensatory damages, punitive damages, and attorney's fees. She also asserted a claim for uncompensated overtime pay under the Fair Labor Standards Act.

No dispositive motions were filed and on November 2, 2015, the case went to trial. In support of her overtime claims, Henderson presented a log of the times she clocked into work in the morning and out of work in the evening, and any times she left the plant premises. Although she had intended to call a second or third witness, Henderson rested her case-in-chief at the conclusion of her own testimony.

The FMLA prohibits an employer from interfering with, restraining, or denying the exercise or attempted exercise of an employee's right to take FMLA leave. The FMLA also makes it unlawful for any employer to discharge or in any other manner discriminate against any individual for opposing the employer's unlawful FMLA practices. An employee must actually qualify for

FMLA leave or otherwise be protected under the statute in order to assert either an interference or a retaliation claim.

Under the FMLA, an eligible employee is entitled to up to twelve weeks of leave during any twelve-month period for a serious health condition that makes the employee unable to perform the functions of his or her position. A "serious health condition" is defined as "an illness, injury, impairment, or physical or mental condition that involves . . . continuing treatment by a healthcare provider." If scheduling planned medical treatment for a serious health condition, an employee must make a reasonable effort to schedule treatment so as not to disrupt the employer's operations and employees are generally expected to consult with their employers before scheduling treatment. Employees should provide at least 30 days' notice in advance of treatment, but if 30 days is not possible, notice must be given as soon as practicable. Notice need not expressly reference the FMLA, but it must indicate the request for time off is for a serious health condition and must convey the timing and duration of the leave. In addition, the FMLA does not provide for nominal damages.

At trial, Henderson testified she told her supervisor, Lena Lawrence, she would need time off for a previously scheduled neck surgery. Henderson further testified she asked an HR representative, Jennifer Crumley, for medical leave forms in passing in the parking lot while leaving work that same day. Henderson did not indicate to her employer when she would need time off of work and for how long. On cross examination, Henderson could not recall the date she was planning to have the surgery, the precise nature of her medical condition, or the name of the doctor who was scheduled to perform the procedure. Henderson presented no evidence that she actually had a serious medical condition. Henderson admitted she never went to a doctor after being terminated to follow up on her neck injury and, to date, had never actually had the surgery she was allegedly scheduled to have.

Henderson did not testify as to whether she experienced any actual damages in the form of lost wages, salary, employment benefits, or other compensation as required under the statute. Similarly, Henderson did not present any evidence of actual monetary losses sustained as a result of the alleged FMLA violations. She did argue that she was entitled to nominal damages.

**QUESTION:**

(9)  At the conclusion of the plaintiff Henderson's testimony in her case at trial, if the defendants move for judgment as a matter of law under Fed.R.Civ.P. 50(a), the federal district court should:

   (a)  Grant the defendant's motion of a judgment as a matter of law because the plaintiff was not a credible witness;

   (b)  Grant the defendants' motion for a judgment as a matter of law because no reasonable jury could find for the plaintiff based on the evidence adduced a trial;

   (c)  Deny the defendants' motion for judgment as a matter of law because the jury has not yet heard the defendants' evidence;

(d) Deny the defendant's motion for judgment as a matter of law because the jury could make a reasonable inference from the evidence that the plaintiff had suffered an injury under the FMLA;

(e) Deny the motion because taking the case from the jury after presentation only of the plaintiff's case would deny her of her Seventh Amendment right to a trial by jury.

\* \* \*

Casey Dupuis sued three defendants in Louisiana state court: LRC Energy, LLC, Erica Lisco, and Wells Fargo Bank, N.A. Dupuis's petition in state court alleged that Ms. Lisco had converted approximately $100,000 in money owed to LRC Energy, LLC. The defendant Erica Lisco removed the action to the federal district court for the Western District of Louisiana, alleging that the court has subject-matter jurisdiction over this action under 28 U.S.C. § 1332.

The state court petition did not allege Ms. Dupuis's citizenship. In the removal notice, Ms. Lisco alleged that Ms. Dupuis was a Louisiana citizen. The state court petition alleged that Ms. Lisco was a Florida resident. In the removal notice, however, Ms. Lisco alleged that she was a Florida citizen. The defendant Wells Fargo Bank, N.A. consented to the removal of the action. In its consent, it represented that it was a national bank with its main office in South Dakota. In the state court petition, it was alleged that plaintiff LRC Energy, LLC was a limited liability company incorporated in the State of Louisiana with its principal place of business in St. Landry Parish, Louisiana. Ms. Dupuis contended that she was the sole member of LRC, but Ms. Lisco contended that she was also a member of LRC. Furthermore, LRC did not consent to the removal of the action.

## QUESTION:

(10) If the plaintiff Dupuis petitions the federal district court of Louisiana to remand the case to state court, the federal district court should:

(a) Retain jurisdiction because there is valid federal diversity jurisdiction;

(b) Retain jurisdiction because there is valid "arising under" jurisdiction;

(c) Remand the case to state court because Wells Fargo Bank is a national bank with offices throughout the fifty states;

(d) Remand the case to state court because the defendant has failed to carry its burden to establish valid federal diversity of citizenship;

(e) Remand the case to state court because the requisite amount in controversy is not satisfied for the assertion of valid diversity jurisdiction.

\* \* \*

The State of Louisiana, as plaintiff, filed an action against defendants Pfizer, Inc. and Warner-Lambert Company, L.L.C. alleging that these two drug manufacturers unlawfully tried to prevent or delay entry into the market of less expensive generic equivalents to their brand name pharmaceutical product Neurontin. Neurontin is prescribed as a treatment for epilepsy and for post herpetic neuralgia. The active ingredient in Neurontin is gabapentin. Neurontin's form of gabapentin was covered by two patents which expired in 1998 and 2000. The plaintiff alleged that defendants improperly listed three additional patents in the Food and Drug Administration publication Approved Drug Products with Therapeutic Equivalents, to protect the form of gabapentin marketed as Neurontin from production as generic drug product. The plaintiff alleged that upon expiration of the original patents several generic drug manufacturers filed abbreviated new drug applications (ANDA) with the FDA seeking approval of generic gabapentin products equivalent to Neurontin.

The plaintiff alleged that the defendants responded by filing numerous sham patent infringement cases against the ANDA filers for the purpose of delaying the FDA's final approval of the pending ANDAs. The plaintiff alleged that delaying FDA approval of the generic gabapentin products caused the State of Louisiana to purchase the brand name product at inflated prices instead of spending less for a generic alternative. The plaintiff brought this action seeking restitution, penalties and attorneys' fees under provisions of the Louisiana Monopolies Act, the Louisiana Unfair Trade Practices Act, and other related state laws.

The defendants removed the case alleging subject matter jurisdiction based on federal question jurisdiction under 28 U.S.C. § 1331 and § 1338. The defendants argued that the plaintiff's claims will require an analysis of the validity and enforceability of the Neurontin patents. Specifically, the defendants asserted that the court will have to determine whether the defendants properly: (1) submitted the Neurontin patents to be listed, and (2) filed patent infringement claims in federal court against generic competitors. The defendants argued that these claims cannot be resolved without interpreting federal patent laws, including the Hatch-Waxman Act, the Federal Food, Drug, and Cosmetic Act and the accompanying FDA regulations.

The defendants argued that the federal patent issues raised are disputed and necessary to resolve the plaintiff's claims, and that these issues are sufficiently substantial to support exercising federal question jurisdiction. To demonstrate this, the defendants asserted that: (1) the plaintiff's listing allegations revolve around a pharmaceutical company's interactions with its regulator when seeking approval of a drug; (2) the federal questions raised by these claims are important because they relate to a key component of a complex federal regulatory scheme; (3) resolution of the plaintiff's listing and "sham" patent litigation allegations are determinative to the outcome; and (4) rulings on the validity and enforceability of the patent and the propriety of the listing submissions will have an impact on cases which were or could be presented in other jurisdictions.

The defendants also argued that the federal issues in this case can be heard in federal court without upsetting the balance between federal and state courts approved by Congress. Therefore, defendants argued, the plaintiff's claims invoke jurisdiction under § 1331 because they necessarily turn on substantial and disputed claims of federal law.

The plaintiff moved to remand arguing that the defendant cannot establish federal question jurisdiction. The plaintiff argued that federal patent law does not create any cause of action and any references to patent law embedded in the State's petition are not sufficiently substantial to trigger federal question jurisdiction. The plaintiff argued that its claims target the defendants' actions to block generic competition which violated state laws regarding monopolies and deceptive trade practices. The plaintiff argued that any defense raised by the defendants concerning the validity of their patents was insufficient to confer federal jurisdiction. The plaintiff also noted that its claims do not turn on any pure question of federal law and will involve a highly fact-bound and situation-specific inquiry. Finally, the plaintiff asserted that any disruption of the balance between federal and state responsibilities caused by the removal cannot be justified because it would have no precedential effect on federal patent law.

### QUESTION:

(11) On the plaintiff's motion to remand the case to Louisiana state court, the federal district court in Louisiana should:

(a) Grant the plaintiff's motion to remand the case to state court based on the Supreme Court's decision in *Grable & Sons v. Darue*, because the plaintiff's claims are not among the "special and small category" of cases in which arising under jurisdiction lies;

(b) Grant the plaintiff's motion to remand the case to state court because the federal court lacks diversity jurisdiction;

(c) Deny the plaintiff's motion to remand the case to state court because the case involves questions of patent law, for which federal courts have exclusive jurisdiction under 28 U.S.C. § 1338;

(d) Deny the plaintiff's motion to remand the case to state court in the interests of federal-state comity;

(e) Deny the plaintiff's motion to remand the case to state court because federal courts can exercise discretionary jurisdiction over state law claims.

* * *

Brookfield Relocation Services, Inc., filed a lawsuit in the federal district court for the Northern District of Ohio pursuant to the court's jurisdiction under 28 U.S.C. § 1332 to hear suits involving citizens of different states when the amount in controversy exceeds $75,000. Brookfield sued Clifford and Christine Burnley over a property transaction in they were involved.

The defendants sought to have the lawsuit dismissed dismissal on multiple grounds: lack of subject matter jurisdiction; lack of personal jurisdiction; improper venue; and the doctrine of *forum non conveniens*.

Burnley was employed by a company that obtained Brookfield Relocation Services, Inc. to manage his relocation outside of Ohio. The Burnleys were Ohio residents who owned real property located at 149 Fairway Court, Norwalk, Ohio. Brookfield and the Burnleys entered into a sales agreement. Brookfield obtained a title report and title insurance commitment. The title report reflected a single lien on the property, a mortgage held by Wells Fargo. Pursuant to the agreement, the Burnleys transferred their entire interest in the Ohio property to Brookfield. In exchange, Brookfield paid $234,240.25 to satisfy the balance remaining on the Wells Fargo Mortgage. Brookfield also paid $1,801.15 in county taxes and $1,775.00 for repairs on the property. Brookfield then listed the property for sale and accepted a third-party.

After having accepted the offer, Brookfield received an updated title report which listed a judgment lien against the property in the amount of $89,948.18, plus interest. Pursuant to their sales contract Brookfield informed the Burnleys of the defect in title and requested that they clear it within thirty (30) days. The Burnleys did not do so. The lien remained in place, but the judgment relating to that lien was on appeal when Brookfield sued the Burleys.

The Burnleys relocated to Florida and at the time of Brookfield's lawsuit, the Burnleys stated that they were Florida residents. Brookfield is a Delaware limited liability company whose principal place of business is alleged to be Burr Ridge, Illinois. Brookfield alleged that venue was proper in the Northern District of Ohio as the real property involved was located in this district and the conduct resulting in facts alleged occurred in this district. Brookfield sought various forms of relief including performance under the contract: damages for unjust enrichment and fraud; and equitable subrogation.

**QUESTION:**

(12) On the defendants' motion to dismiss the case for lack of subject matter jurisdiction, the federal district court should:

    (a)   Grant the defendants' motion to dismiss because there is no diversity of citizenship;

    (b)   Grant the defendants' motion to dismiss because the requisite amount-in-controversy is lacking;

    (c)   Grant the motion to dismiss because the case involves exclusively state-based claims;

    (d)   Deny the motion to dismiss because the court has valid diversity jurisdiction;

    (e)   Deny the motion to dismiss because the plaintiff's claims belong to that small category of important issues requiring uniform resolution by federal courts.

\* \* \*

Ohio's long-arm statute provides, at O.R.C. § 2307.382:

(A) A court may exercise personal jurisdiction over a person who acts directly or by an agent, as to a cause of action arising from the person's:

   (1) Transacting any business in this state; . . .

   (3) Causing tortious injury by an act or omission in this state;

   (4) Causing tortious injury in this state by an act or omission outside this state; . . .

   (8) Having an interest in, using, or possessing real property in this state;

   (9) Contracting to insure any person, property, or risk located within this state at the time of contracting.

   . . .

(C) When jurisdiction over a person is based solely upon this section, only a cause of action arising from acts enumerated in this section may be asserted against him.

The Brookfield plaintiff alleged that the Burnley defendants owned Ohio real property; they contracted to sell that real property to the plaintiff and then breached that contract of sale by failing to clear a defect in the title to the property created by the judgment lien issued by an Ohio court for acts or omissions that occurred in Ohio.

The Burnleys did not dispute their ownership of real property in Ohio; they did not dispute that they entered a contract with Brookfield and conveyed the real property to Brookfield; nor did they dispute that they failed to clear a defect in the title to the real property. The defendants instead contended that the fact that they relocated from Ohio to Florida extinguished the court's jurisdiction.

## QUESTION:

(13) On the defendants' motion to dismiss the case based on Fed.R.Civ.P. 12(b)(2) for a lack of personal jurisdiction, the federal district court should:

   (a) Grant the motion to dismiss the case because the defendant lacks sufficient minimum contacts with the forum state;

   (b) Grant the motion to dismiss the case because to assert personal jurisdiction over the Florida residents would offend traditional notions of fair play and substantial justice;

   (c) Grant the motion to dismiss the case because the defendants have not committed a tortious act within Ohio;

   (d) Deny the motion to dismiss the case because the Ohio court has transient jurisdiction over the defendants;

   (e) Deny the motion to dismiss the case because personal jurisdiction is supported by O.R.C. § 2307.382.

* * *

The Burnley defendants also moved to dismiss the case based on Fed.R.Civ.P. 12(b)(3), alleging improper venue. The defendants contended that venue in the Northern District of Ohio was improper because they are residents of Florida. The defendants also restated their argument concerning that the plaintiff had not satisfied the requisite amount in controversy.

Venue within the Northern District of Ohio is governed specifically by Local Rule 3.8 which divides the district into Eastern and Western Divisions, and allows "all actions brought against a resident of a county within the Eastern Divisions" to be filed "at any of the offices within the Eastern Division." Local Rule 3.8 (a) and (b). The court is situated in the Eastern Division. The real property conveyed by the Burnleys was located in the Northern District, as was the court that issued the judgment and lien against the property.

**QUESTION:**

(14) On the defendants' motion to dismiss the case pursuant to Fed.R.Civ.P. 12(b)(3), the federal district court for the Northern District of Ohio should:

  (a)  Grant the motion to dismiss because the all the defendants are located in Florida;

  (b)  Grant the motion to dismiss because the plaintiffs have not satisfied the requisite amount-in-controversy;

  (c)  Deny the motion because events giving rise to the plaintiff's claims arose in the Northern District of Ohio;

  (d)  Deny the motion because of the convenience of the parties and witnesses;

  (e)  Deny the motion because Ohio law applies to the litigation.

* * *

In the same litigation, and as an alternative to their jurisdiction and venue arguments, the Burnley defendants sought to invoke the doctrine of *forum non conveniens* because they were Florida residents. The defendants stated that continuing the matter in Ohio would present an "undue burden" on their resources. The Burnley defendants requested that the court dismiss this matter under the doctrine, and instruct plaintiff to refile in Florida.

**QUESTION:**

(15) On the defendant's motion to dismiss the case based on the doctrine forum non conveniens, the federal district court in Ohio should:

  (a)  Deny the motion to dismiss because a *forum non conveniens* dismissal is not available in domestic disputes;

  (b)  Deny the motion to dismiss because a *forum non conveniens* dismissal would work a hardship on the plaintiff;

  (c)  Grant the motion to dismiss because under the doctrine of *forum non conveniens* an adequate alternative forum is available;

    (d)   Grant the motion to dismiss because under the doctrine of *forum non conveniens* such a dismissal would be in the interests of justice;

    (e)   Grant the motion to dismiss because under the doctrine of *forum non conveniens* the public and private factors weigh in favor of such a dismissal.

* * *

The Center for Biological Diversity sued Dean Gould, the Sierra National Forest Supervisor and the United States Forest Service in federal district court for the Eastern District of California. The plaintiffs alleged that defendants violated the National Environmental Policy Act (NEPA) and the Administrative Procedure Act (APA) in approving the French Fire Recovery and Reforestation Project (French Fire Project). Sierra Forest Products sought to intervene as a defendant pursuant to Federal Rule of Civil Procedure 24(a) or, in the alternative, Rule 24(b). The plaintiffs did not oppose the motion to intervene and the defendants took no position.

The complaint was filed on August 31, 2015 and no substantive proceedings had yet occurred. Sierra Forest Products was awarded the government contract for the French Fire timber sale on September 29, 2015 and promptly filed its motion to intervene less than a month later. Sierra Forest Products agreed to follow the established summary judgment schedule.

Sierra Forest Products had contract rights; it was depending on the timber from the government contract to keep its mill fully operational through the winter. Sierra Forest Products needed to obtain timber as quickly as possible in order to keep its mill in operation through the winter and provide full-time employment for its workers. It also had a strong interest in harvesting the timber before the value of the wood is lost due to decay. The court's findings on whether the French Fire Project complied with NEPA and the APA would determine whether Sierra Forest Products contract could be executed. In addition, Sierra Forest Products alleged that any litigation that might impede its ability to obtain timber from federal lands in the future. It wanted to ensure that NEPA continued to "achieve a balance between population and resource use," and to demonstrate that this timber harvest complied with the statute.

Both Sierra Forest Products and the government were aligned to the extent they both believed the French Fire Project should proceed. The timber harvest was only one aspect of the government's project and the government must ultimately do what was best for the public interest and most in line with federal regulations. While the two interests seem to be running on parallel tracks, it is possible they could diverge as litigation proceeded.

## QUESTION:

(16)  On Sierra Forest Products' motion to intervene under Federal Rule of Civil Procedure 24(a), the federal district court should:

    (a)   Grant Sierra Forest Products' motion to intervene because it has an interest in the transaction that is the subject of the litigation;

(b)   Grant Sierra Forest Products' motion to intervene because
      courts liberally grant intervention as of right;

(c)   Deny Sierra Forest Products' motion to intervene because its
      interests will not be impaired or impeded if the court does not
      permit it to intervene;

(d)   Deny Sierra Forest Products' motion to intervene because the
      addition of Sierra Forest Products will needlessly complicate
      resolution of the litigation;

(e)   Deny Sierra Forest Products' motion to intervene because its
      motion was untimely.

* * *

Lee Hankins filed a lawsuit against Yellow Fin Marine Services LLC in the
federal district court for the Eastern District of Louisiana pursuant to the
court's maritime jurisdiction under 28 U.S.C. § 1333. Hankins, a former
employee of Yellow Fin, was working aboard vessels owned by Yellow Fin when
injured his leg, back, and body in as a result of a fall on the M/V K4, a vessel
he was asked to help prepare for voyage. While obtaining treatment for these
injuries, Hankins allegedly developed congestive heart failure. He eventually
went back to work while continuing to take heart medication.

Hankins claimed he was working on the M/V K10 when he witnessed an illegal
fuel transfer to an unaffiliated boat. Hankins claimed that the M/V K10's
captain threatened to kill him if he reported the fuel transfer. When Hankins
ultimately reported it, Yellow Fin fired the captain, which allegedly caused the
ship's crew to retaliate against Hankins. Hankins claimed that constant
harassment by the crew caused him to become "severely depressed to the point
where he required hospitalization" at River Oaks Medical Hospital. When the
plaintiff finally returned to work, he was transferred to the M/V K4 where the
harassment purportedly continued.

While working aboard the K4, one of the crew members allegedly stole
Hankins' depression, diabetes, and heart medications. Hankins claimed that
the ship did not return to port or secure delivery of replacement medications.
This lack of medication for approximately two months apparently caused
deterioration of Hankins's physical and mental health. Thereafter, the
plaintiff required implantation of a cardiac defibrillator and a pacemaker,
which prevented him from working. As a result of the above-described injuries,
Hankins sought damages for physical and mental pain and suffering, loss of
wages and earning capacity, and permanent physical disability. He also sought
maintenance and cure. Due to the allegedly willful misconduct of Yellow Fin
employees, Hankins requested punitive damages and attorney's fees.

In its answer, Yellow Fin asserted a counterclaim seeking $7,244.21 plus
interest and costs for Hankins's alleged failure to pay on a promissory in that
amount. Yellow Fin alleged that it loaned the money to Hankins to help him
deal with a number of personal issues. The defendant claimed to have lent
$1,500 to Hankins to bail him out of jail following two arrests. The first arrest
allegedly occurred because Hankins was in possession of a firearm as a

convicted felon. In connection with that arrest, the police searched Hankins's home where they apparently found human remains, which the defendant contended contributed to Hankins's mental and physical instability.

Thereafter, Hankins allegedly borrowed $500 to travel to Louisiana for work after his release from jail. When he returned to work, the defendant claimed that Hankins "was in significant distress," so Yellow Fin arranged for him to obtain medical treatment at River Oaks. The defendant then loaned him another $5,000 to pay for an attorney to help him with his legal issues. Following all of the loans, Hankins and Yellow Fin executed a promissory note evidencing the amount of money advanced to Hankins. The defendant claimed that it loaned the money to Hankins as an advance on his maritime wages, which is reflected by the fact that Hankins was required to make payments on the 5th and 20th of each month, his regularly-scheduled pay days. Moreover, Yellow Fin did not charge interest on the loans. The defendant claimed that Hankins never made any payments on the note.

### QUESTION:

(17) The plaintiff Hankins moved to dismiss the defendant Yellow Fin's counterclaim under Federal Rule of Civil Procedure 12(b)(1) because the court does not have subject matter jurisdiction over the counterclaim. On the plaintiff's motion to dismiss the counterclaim, the federal district court should:

(a) Grant the plaintiff's motion to dismiss the counterclaim because it does not arise out of the same transactions and occurrences as the plaintiff's claims;

(b) Grant the plaintiff's motion to dismiss the counterclaim because it is a permissive counterclaim and there is no independent jurisdictional basis for the counterclaim;

(c) Grant the plaintiff's motion to dismiss the counterclaim because the court does not have original jurisdiction over the plaintiff's lawsuit;

(d) Deny the plaintiff's motion to dismiss the counterclaim because it is a compulsory counterclaim and the court has supplemental jurisdiction pursuant to 28 U.S.C. § 1367;

(e) Deny the plaintiff's motion to dismiss the counterclaim because it is not well-pleaded as a counterclaim.

* * *

Heather Bostic took ondansetron, generic Zofran, to treat morning sickness during the first trimester of her pregnancy. Zofran is a drug meant to prevent nausea and vomiting caused by chemotherapy and radiation cancer treatments. Heather Bostic's daughter, D.B., was born with multiple congenital defects, including a missing kidney and a hole in her heart. When D.B. was about seven months old, she got sick and started vomiting. A doctor prescribed D.B. Zofran for her nausea, and Heather Bostic gave one dose of it to D.B. The next day, D.B. stopped breathing and died from cardiopulmonary arrest.

The plaintiffs Heather and Timothy Bostic filed a malpractice suit in Pike County Court, Kentucky, against the pediatrician who prescribed Zofran to D.B., Dr. Aaronda Wells, and Dr. Wells's employer, the East Kentucky Medical Group, P.S.C. (the Healthcare defendants). In addition, the Bostics sued three pharmaceutical companies for products liability: Zofran's manufacturer, GlaxoSmithKline LLC, and ondansetron's manufacturers and distributors, Teva Pharmaceuticals USA, Inc. and Taro Pharmaceuticals U.S.A., Inc. The Bostics also sued First DataBank, Inc. (DataBank), a company that contracts with pharmacies to provide drug information to consumers, for failure to warn.

GlaxoSmithKline removed the case to federal court, alleging diversity jurisdiction. Although the Bostics and the Healthcare Defendants are all Kentucky citizens, GlaxoSmithKline argued that the court should disregard the Healthcare defendants' citizenship because they were fraudulently misjoined to the suit. In the alternative, GlaxoSmithKline and the Pharmaceutical defendants asked the court to use Federal Rule of Civil Procedure 21 to sever the claims against the Healthcare defendants and retain jurisdiction.

The Bostics filed a motion to remand, arguing that the Healthcare defendants were properly joined and the court should not sever them from the suit.

**QUESTION:**

(18) On the plaintiff Bostics' motion to remand the case to Kentucky state court, the federal district court should:

(a)   Grant the plaintiff Bostics' motion to remand the case to state court because the Healthcare defendants were properly joined and therefore there is no diversity jurisdiction;

(b)   Grant the plaintiff Bostics' motion to remand the case to state court because the case involved only state law tort issues;

(c)   Grant the plaintiff Bostics' motions to remand the case to state court because all the defendants had not consented to the removal;

(d)   Deny the plaintiff Bostics' motion to remand the case to state court because the Healthcare defendants were fraudulently joined and therefore there is no good diversity jurisdiction;

(e)   Deny the plaintiff Bostics' motion to remand the case to state court because the litigation clearly was excess of $75,000.

* * *

Christopher Boling suffered severe burns to his right hand and a posterior dislocation of his right shoulder after vapors escaping from a gas can ignited upon coming into contact with a hot metal eye bolt. At the time of his injury, the plaintiff was married to Holly Boling. The Bolings were citizens of Kentucky.

As a result of his injuries, the Bolings filed suit against the gas can manufacturer, Blitz USA. During the course of their litigation against Blitz USA, the Bolings entered into a series of non-recourse loans with Prospect Funding Holdings, LLC and Cambridge Management Group, LLC, two out-of-state limited liability corporations, to obtain advances on his potential personal injury recovery. The Bolings received $30,000 plus fees through these loans. In entering into the loan agreements, Prospect and CMG obtained an interest in the Bolings' potential personal injury recovery the pending lawsuit against Blitz USA.

By their terms, these loans accrued interest at a rate of 4.9% per month and at the time of the suit, the total amount owed to Prospect was $340, 405.00. Boling filed a lawsuit against Prospect in the federal district court for the Eastern District of Kentucky seeking a declaratory judgment that the loan agreements were to be interpreted by and deemed unenforceable under Kentucky law. His wife was not made a party to this lawsuit. Subsequently, Prospect filed suit against the Bolings in the Superior Court of New Jersey, and Boling removed that action to the U.S. District Court for the District of New Jersey.

Kentucky has a long-arm statute that provides: courts "may exercise personal jurisdiction over a person who acts directly or by an agent, as to a claim arising from the person's . . . transacting any business in this Commonwealth. . . ."

In a motion pursuant to Federal Rule of Civil Procedure 12(b)(1), defendant Prospect moved to dismiss the case from the Kentucky federal district court for a lack of personal jurisdiction.

## QUESTION:

(19) On defendant Prospect's motion to dismiss for a lack of personal jurisdiction, the Kentucky federal court should:

    (a)    Grant the motion to dismiss because Prospect was not a citizen of Kentucky, had only very limited contact with the state through the loans to the Bolings; and assertion of personal jurisdiction would offend due process;

    (b)    Grant the motion to dismiss because Prospect had a parallel lawsuit pending in federal court in New Jersey on the same issues;

    (c)    Deny the motion to dismiss because Prospect was conducting business in the state of Kentucky and availing itself of the benefits and protections of Kentucky law;

    (d)    Deny the motion to dismiss because as a loan provider, Prospect had contacts with all fifty states;

    (e)    Deny the motion to dismiss courts generally give deference to the plaintiff's choice of forum.

\* \* \*

In the same action in Kentucky federal court, the defendant Prospect also argued that the court should dismiss Boling's complaint because Boling had failed to include his ex-wife as a party in the action because she was a necessary party. In his Kentucky declaratory judgment action, Boling sought only to litigate his claims relating to the non-recourse loans.

**QUESTION:**

(20) On defendant Prospect's motion to dismiss the lawsuit pursuant to Fed.R.Civ.P. 12(b)(7), the federal district court in Kentucky should:

(a) Grant the defendant's motion to dismiss under Fed.R.Civ.P. 12(b)(7) because Boling's wife was a necessary party and the court could accomplish a just adjudication without her;

(b) Grant the defendant's motion to dismiss under Fed.R.Civ.P. 12(b)(7) because Boling's wife was an indispensable party and the court cannot accomplish a just adjudication without her;

(c) Grant the defendant's motion to dismiss under Fed.R.Civ.P. 12(b)(7) because the joinder of Boling's wife would destroy the court's diversity jurisdiction;

(d) Deny the defendant's motion to dismiss under Fed.R.Civ.P. 12(b)(7) because the case could proceed in equity and good conscience;

(e) Deny the defendant's motion to dismiss under Fed.R.Civ.P. 12(b)(7) because Boling's wife was not an indispensable party; the defendant could attempt to enforce the loan agreements her in a subsequent separate proceeding if it so chose to do so.

* * *

National Feeds, Inc. (NFI) brought a breach of contract lawsuit in federal district court in Ohio, alleging that the defendant United Pet Foods, Inc. (UPF), produced and sold rancid mink and dog feed to the plaintiff, who then distributed the feed to its customers.

NFI's President, Edward Buschur, contacted UPF to discuss its ability to mill mink and dog feed for NFI. Buschur visited UPF's facilities in Elkhart, Indiana, and asked UPF's plant manager if UPF would produce a test run of mink feed. After the test run, Buschur drafted a proposed contract and faxed it to UPF. UPF signed the contract in Indiana and returned it to NFI in Ohio.

UPF produced its first batches of mink and dog feed for NFI. NFI arranged to ship the feed from UPF's plant in Indiana to either a distribution center in Wisconsin or directly to NFI's customers. UPF was not responsible for shipping the feed and did not sell any feed to NFI's customers.

NFI's customers began reporting problems with the feed. Mink farmers claimed the animals refused to eat the feed, while other farmers reported that animals died after eating it. Testing confirmed that the feed contained high levels of peroxide, indicating that it was rancid and did not meet quality specifications. The rancid feed caused farmers to lose upwards of whole mink herds, NFI to lose business, and NFI's insurer, plaintiff Midwestern Indemnity Company, to pay for the mink farmers' losses.

The plaintiffs filed a lawsuit in the federal district court for the Northern District of Ohio, alleging breach of contract, negligence, strict liability, statutory product liability, breach of express and implied warranty, subrogation, and contribution and indemnity.

UPF filed a motion to dismiss for a lack of personal jurisdiction, arguing that it did not transact any business in Ohio throughout its relationship with NFI and had no contacts at all with Ohio. UPF entered a general appearance and litigated the case on the merits for three years before seeking dismissal on jurisdictional grounds. By way of explanation for its delay, UPF claimed that its counsel was unaware of the ability to contest personal jurisdiction until only a few weeks before filing its motion to dismiss. UPF's counsel contended that it only recently personally learned the names and addresses of all farmers who received tainted feed. The plaintiffs asserted that UPF's conduct gave them reason to believe UPF intended to defend the case on its merits. During the three years between filing and UPF's motion to dismiss there was extensive discovery and considerable motion practice.

**QUESTION:**

(21) On the defendant UPF's motion to dismiss for lack of personal jurisdiction pursuant to Federal Rule of Civil Procedure 12(b)(2), the federal district court should:

(a) Grant the defendant's motion to dismiss because as a local Indiana company it had insufficient contacts with Ohio to support an assertion of personal jurisdiction;

(b) Grant the defendant's motion to dismiss because its contract with NFI was an insufficient basis to support an assertion of personal jurisdiction over UPF;

(c) Deny the defendant's motion to dismiss because by failing to raise the personal jurisdiction challenge earlier in the litigation, UPF waived its ability to contest personal jurisdiction after three years into the litigation;

(d) Deny the defendant's motion to dismiss because Ohio clearly can assert personal jurisdiction over UPF based on its contractual relationship with NFI;

(e) Deny the defendant's motion to dismiss because Ohio's assertion of personal jurisdiction would not offend traditional notions of fair play and substantial justice.

\* \* \*

Robert Grisset Jr. sued H.J. Baker Bros. in the federal district court for the Southern District of Alabama. His original complaint attempted to assert claims for retaliation under Title VII of the Civil Rights Act and the Occupational Safety and Health Act (OSHA), as well as state tort and contract claims. The court granted the defendant's motion to dismiss the complaint, but granted Grisset leave to file an amended complaint.

Grisset's amended complaint identified a single cause of action: a Title VII claim for hostile work environment. To plead a claim for hostile work environment a plaintiff is required to allege that: "(1) he belongs to a protected group; (2) he was subjected to unwelcome harassment; (3) the harassment was based on his membership in the protected group; (4) it was severe or pervasive enough to alter the terms and conditions of employment and create a hostile or abusive working environment; and (5) the employer is responsible for that environment under a theory of either vicarious or direct liability."

A hostile work environment claim under Title VII is established upon proof that the workplace was permeated with discriminatory intimidation, ridicule, and insult that is sufficiently severe or pervasive to alter the conditions of the victim's employment and create an abusive working environment. Failing to correct a hostile work environment that does not exist cannot itself create a hostile work environment.

Discrete acts such as termination must be challenged as separate statutory discrimination and retaliation claim and cannot be considered part of a hostile work environment claim. A plaintiff cannot complain of his termination or suspension under a hostile-work-environment rubric. Nor can he rest his claim on the allegation of forgery that allegedly prompted his termination and suspension.

Grisset's amended complaint alleged the following regarding the defendant's conduct towards the plaintiff (who is black): (1) falsely accusing him of forging and falsifying a transportation document; (2) placing him on leave (suspension) with pay; (3) terminating him (the only black office employee) and replacing him with a white male; (4) failing or refusing to take prompt remedial action in response to his complaints of being suspended and fired; and (5) failing or refusing to take prompt remedial action in response to the discrimination, hostile work environment and harassment of its managers.

**QUESTION:**

(22) On the defendant's motion to dismiss the plaintiff's case under Federal Rule of Civil Procedure 12(b)(6), the federal district court should:

   (a) Grant the defendant's motion to dismiss because the plaintiff's complaint fails to satisfy the pleading requirements under the Supreme Court's decisions in *Twombly* and *Iqbal*;

   (b) Grant the defendant's motion to dismiss because the plaintiff's complaint violates the well-pleaded complaint rule;

   (c) Grant the defendant's motion to dismiss because this is the plaintiff's second amended complaint, and the defendant should not be subjected to multiple amended pleadings;

   (d) Deny the defendant's motion to dismiss because the plaintiff's complaint is facially plausible;

    (e)  Deny the defendant's motion to dismiss because courts very rarely grant Rule 12(b)(6) dismissals early in the litigation, because of unfairness to the plaintiff.

* * *

Cory Henman was injured at a rail yard owned and operated by Indiana Harbor Belt Railroad Company (IHB). Henman, as plaintiff, field an action in the federal district court for the Northern District of Indiana under the Federal Employers' Liability Act for an injury the plaintiff sustained at the defendant's rail yard as a result of an accident. Michael Jovanovich was an employee of the defendant who was at the yard office at the time of the occurrence. He did not witness the accident or any of the train movements relating to the occurrence, but provided assistance to emergency response personnel in moving the plaintiff to an ambulance. Neither Jovanovich nor anyone else was disciplined by IHB as a result of the occurrence. Jovanovich appeared at a deposition at the plaintiff's request. The plaintiff's counsel questioned Jovanovich about his disciplinary history with IHB and Jovanovich declined to answer. The plaintiff sought to compel answers to those questions.

The plaintiff argued that if Jovanovich had received favorable treatment in his disciplinary history, he might be inclined to give testimony favorable to the defendant. The plaintiff sought information from Jovanovich about whether he had ever been disciplined by IHB for events other than those that were the subject of the lawsuit. The plaintiff argued that if any railroad witness had been given favorable treatment in discipline history, that witnesses' credibility might be affected, and that the broad scope of discovery allows for this kind of questioning. The plaintiff's lawyer admitted that he had no reason to think that there has been any exchange of favorable treatment for favorable testimony. At the deposition, Jovanovich was not asked whether there was any reason for him to give favorable testimony or if he had received any favorable treatment in exchange for his testimony; instead, the plaintiff's questions were targeted specifically to Jovanovich's discipline history and other personal employment issues.

The defendant argued that questions about any discipline unrelated to the occurrence were irrelevant to any claims or defenses in the case. The defendant argued that because the questions were a fishing expedition designed to obtain prejudicial information, the motion to compel should be denied. The defendant's counsel sought a protective order barring inquiry into unrelated disciplinary matters of IHB employees.

## QUESTION:

(23)  The plaintiff filed a motion to compel answers to deposition questions and the defendant IHB filed a response to the plaintiff's motion to compel, with a motion for a protective order. On the plaintiff's motion to compel answers to its deposition questions and the defendant's motion for a protective order, the federal district court should:

(a)  Grant the plaintiff's motion to compel answers to its deposition questions because the plaintiff has shown good cause for a need of the information requested;

(b)  Grant the plaintiff's motion to compel answers to its deposition questions because the scope of discovery is very broad and the witness's answers might lead to admissible evidence;

(c)  Deny the plaintiff's motion to compel answers to its deposition questions because a witness cannot be compelled to give testimony at a deposition;

(d)  Deny and the plaintiff's motion to compel answers to its deposition questions and grant the defendant's motion for a protective order because the defendant has satisfied the requirements of Fed.R.Civ.P. 26(c);

(e)  Deny the plaintiff's motion to compel answers to its deposition questions but also deny the defendant's motion for a protective order because there is no need for a protective order to protect any information the witness might have.

* * *

For this question only, assume in the preceding litigation that the federal district court for the Northern District of Indiana denied the plaintiff's motion to compel answers to its deposition questions and granted the defendant's motion for a protective order.

**QUESTION:**

(24) As a consequence of the court's dual rulings, which denied the plaintiff's motion to compel discovery and granted the defendant's motion for a protective order:

(a)  The plaintiff's counsel can be sanctioned under Fed.R.Civ.P. 11(b) and (c);

(b)  The plaintiff's counsel can be ordered to pay the defendant's reasonable costs and expenses under Fed.R.Civ.P. 37(a);

(c)  The plaintiff's counsel can be disciplined under 28 U.S.C. § 1927;

(d)  The plaintiff's counsel can be fined pursuant to the inherent powers of the court;

(e)  No disciplinary action can be imposed on the plaintiff's counsel because his motion to compel testimony was reasonable under the circumstances.

* * *

George Bishop commenced an action against the defendant Liberty Mutual Insurance Company in the Charleston, South Carolina County Court of Common Pleas, alleging breach of contract and bad faith refusal to pay benefits. The plaintiff alleged that the defendant issued a commercial vehicle policy covering the plaintiff's Mack truck, and that the defendant wrongfully denied the plaintiff's claim for damage to the frame of his truck.

The defendant filed a notice of removal under 28 U.S.C. § 1441, asserting that the federal court for District of South Carolina had diversity jurisdiction over the matter. The plaintiff then filed a motion to remand.

The defendant, a corporate party, failed to allege the state or states in which it was incorporated, as well as the state in which it maintained its principal place of business. The defendant's citizenship was briefly mentioned in its notice of removal and was also mentioned in the plaintiff's complaint. The defendant asserted in its notice of removal that the action was "between citizens of different states" and, "upon information and belief, exceeds the sum or value of $75,000.00, exclusive of interest and costs." The plaintiff's complaint stated that "Defendant is a corporation organized and existing under the laws of a state other than South Carolina, licensed to do business in South Carolina, solicits business in South Carolina, issue policies in South Carolina, and otherwise conducts business in South Carolina."

## QUESTION:

(25) On the plaintiff's petition to remand the case back to South Carolina state court based on 28 U.S.C. § 1447, the federal district court should:

   (a) Grant the plaintiff's petition to remand the case to state court motion because the defendant is a citizen of South Carolina;

   (b) Grant the plaintiff's petition to remand the case to state court because the defendant has not carried its burden of establishing diversity of citizenship;

   (c) Grant the plaintiff's petition to remand the case to state court because the defendant has not carried its burden of establishing the requisite amount in controversy for diversity jurisdiction;

   (d) Deny the plaintiff's petition to remand the case to state court because the federal court can determine diversity jurisdiction based on the totality of the facts;

   (e) Deny the plaintiff's petition to remand the case to state court because the court can take judicial notice that the defendant Liberty Mutual is a citizen of some other state than South Carolina.

**END OF EXAM PROBLEMS #1**

# CHAPTER 2
# EXAM #2 PROBLEMS
# AND QUESTIONS

Dr. Nami Bayan, M.D. is of Persian ancestry and Iranian national origin. He was formerly a fellow in the Geriatric Medicine Fellowship Program at the University of Connecticut School of Medicine. Dr. Gail M. Sullivan was the director of the Program.

Dr. Bayan sued Dr. Sullivan in the Superior Court of Connecticut claiming tortious interference with professional expectancies and relationships and intentional infliction of emotional distress. Dr. Bayan alleged that Dr. Sullivan terminated him from the Program, falsely and maliciously stated that he was unprofessional and inappropriate in his relationships with colleagues, and refused to respond to inquiries seeking clarification of her opinions. The complaint stated that Dr. Sullivan was being sued in her individual capacity. Dr. Sullivan moved to dismiss on the ground that the court lacked subject matter jurisdiction because Dr. Bayan's claims were barred by sovereign immunity.

Before the court ruled on Dr. Sullivan's motion to dismiss, Dr. Bayan filed a federal lawsuit in the federal district court for the District of Connecticut, alleging disparate treatment on the basis of his ancestry and national origin in violation of the Equal Protection Clause of the Fourteenth Amendment as enforced through 42 U.S.C. § 1983. The complaint in this action was substantially similar to the complaint in the state court action in both form and substance, centering on the same allegations that Dr. Sullivan terminated Dr. Bayan from the Program, falsely and maliciously stated that he was unprofessional and inappropriate in his relationships with colleagues, and refused to respond to inquiries requesting clarification of her opinions. However, the complaint in the federal action added allegations to support the § 1983 claim, including allegations that Dr. Sullivan believed that Dr. Bayan was Muslim, and asserted that another fellow in the Program was superior to Dr. Bayan because he was of Eastern European heritage.

The state Superior Court granted Dr. Sullivan's motion to dismiss the state court action and entered a judgment of dismissal. The entire substance of the court's order read as follows: "Granted on the basis of statutory and sovereign immunity."

In the federal court action, Dr. Sullivan moved for judgment on the pleadings under Fed.R.Civ.P. 12(c) on the ground that Dr. Bayan's current § 1983 claim was barred by *res judicata* because it could have been brought in the state court action.

**QUESTION:**

(1) On a motion for a judgment on the pleadings pursuant to Fed.R.Civ.P. 12(c), a federal district court:

   (a) The standard of review is the same as a motion to dismiss for failure to state a claim under Fed.R.Civ.P. 12(b)(6);

   (b) The court must draw all inferences in the moving party's favor;

   (c) The court must not accept all the allegations in the complaint as true, but must probe beyond the pleadings to understand the actual nature of the case;

   (d) The court may not consider affirmative defenses;

   (e) The court should not dismiss a case on the pleadings because to do so early in the litigation would violate the plaintiff's due process and jury trial rights.

**QUESTION:**

(2) In response to the defendant Sullivan's motion to dismiss the case pursuant to Fed.R.Civ.P. 12(c), the federal district court should:

   (a) Grant the defendant's motion to dismiss the case because the plaintiff Bayan's § 1983 claim could have been brought in his state court action and therefore it was barred by the doctrine of res judicata;

   (b) Grant the defendant's motion to dismiss the case because the plaintiff Bayan was blatantly forum-shopping, which is disfavored by the courts;

   (c) Grant the defendant's motion to dismiss because the plaintiff Bayan should be permitted to have "two bites at the apple";

   (d) Deny the motion to dismiss because res judicata cannot be raised on a Rule 12(c) motion;

   (e) Deny the motion to dismiss because the state court dismissal was on jurisdictional grounds and not a judgment on the merits.

\* \* \*

Tricia Basch, through her attorney Jeffrey S. Burg, filed a multi-claim lawsuit in the federal district court for the Western District of Michigan against the defendant Knoll, Inc. The plaintiff's complaint asserted nine claims of employment discrimination and retaliation based on disability, gender, age, and the Family Medical Leave Act (FMLA). At the close of discovery, the defendant sent the plaintiff a safe-harbor letter and a proposed motion for Rule 11 sanctions, demanding that plaintiff withdraw her complaint. Plaintiff had an arguable basis for proceeding on her FMLA and disability claims. However, even under a most generous view of the pleadings, there were no factual allegations in the complaint with respect to the plaintiff's age and gender claims. The plaintiff's age and gender claims lacked any arguable evidentiary support.

The plaintiff did not withdraw her complaint, nor did she withdraw any of her individual claims. The defendant subsequently filed a motion for summary judgment on all nine claims. In its brief on summary judgment, the defendant argued that all of the plaintiff's discrimination and retaliation claims were deficient because the plaintiff failed to show an adverse employment action, because she failed to establish a prima facie case, and because she did not rebut the defendant's legitimate non-discriminatory reason for her termination. The defendant did not independently analyze the plaintiff's age and gender claims.

In response to the summary judgment motion, the plaintiff only defended her claim under the FMLA. With respect to her eight remaining claims alleging disability, gender, and age discrimination and retaliation under federal and state law, the plaintiff stated that she did not abandon her arguments, but was unable to complete them at that time. She further asserted that she would move for leave to supplement her brief. The court previously had granted the plaintiff two extensions of time to respond to the defendant's motion and had indicated that no further extensions would be granted. The plaintiff never moved to supplement her response to the defendant's motion for summary judgment, and the court ultimately found that the defendant was entitled to summary judgment on all nine of the plaintiff's claims. The plaintiff only appealed the ruling with respect to her FMLA retaliation claim, and that ruling was affirmed on appeal.

The defendant requested sanctions against the plaintiff and/or her attorney under Rule 11 and under 28 U.S.C. § 1927.

**QUESTION:**

(3) On the defendant's motion for sanctions against the plaintiff and/or her attorney under Rule 11 and 28 U.S.C. § 1927, the federal district court should:

   (a) Deny the defendant's motion for Rule 11 sanctions against the plaintiff because her attorney had a good faith basis for pursuing all the claims;

   (b) Deny the defendant's motion for Rule 11 sanctions against the plaintiff because the defense counsel failed to comport with the proper procedures for filing a Rule 11 motion;

   (c) Deny the defendant's motion for sanctions against the plaintiff under 28 U.S.C. § 1927 because the plaintiff's counsel was merely zealously representing the interests of his client;

   (d) Grant the defendant's motion for sanctions under Rule 11 and 28 U.S.C. § 1927 because the plaintiff's counsel used a shot-gun approach in the complaint and failed to review the viability of the claims after the close of discovery;

   (e) Grant the defendant's motion for sanctions under Rule 11 and 28 U.S.C. § 1927 because the court granted the defendant summary judgment for the defendant on all the plaintiff's claims.

* * *

Tyrese Doughty filed a single-count complaint against the defendant Washington Metropolitan Area Transit Authority ("WMATA") in the federal district court for the District of Maryland, contending that she incurred personal injuries as a result of the defendant's negligence. Specifically, the plaintiff claimed that she was walking at the defendant's Rosslyn Metro Station when she fell as a result of a "black oily substance" on the escalator. The defendant moved for summary judgment on the complaint.

In Maryland, the duty that an owner or occupier of land owes to persons entering onto the land varies according to the visitor's status as an invitee (i.e., a business invitee), a licensee by invitation. The highest duty is owed to a business invitee, defined as "one invited or permitted to enter another's property for purposes related to the landowner's business." Storekeepers, such as the defendant, owe their business invitees or customers a duty of ordinary and reasonable care to maintain their premises in a reasonably safe condition. The customer is entitled to assume that the storekeeper will exercise reasonable care to ascertain the condition of the premises, and, if he discovers any unsafe condition, he will either take such action as will correct the condition and make it reasonably safe or give a warning of the unsafe condition. The duties of a storekeeper thus include the obligation to warn customers of known hidden dangers, a duty to inspect, and a duty to take reasonable precautions against foreseeable dangers.

Nevertheless, storekeepers are not insurers of their customers' safety, and no presumption of negligence arises merely because an injury was sustained on a storekeeper's premises. A storekeeper's liability under negligence principles for a customer's injuries arises only from a failure to observe the duty of ordinary and reasonable care.

The defendant's motion set forth record evidence regarding the circumstances of the plaintiff's injury, which evidence was provided exclusively from the transcript of the plaintiff's testimony during her deposition. In pertinent part, the defendant stated the following from the deposition:

> The plaintiff slipped and fell while walking up a moving escalator. Deposition of Tyrese Doughty ("Doughty Dep."), pp. 16:17–17:2.

> It was not raining, but it had snowed the night before. *Id.* at 14:13–14.

> The plaintiff does not recall for sure that she was holding the handrail. *Id.* at 17:3–7.

> The escalator made no movements that caused her to slip. *Id.* at 18:1–3.

> The plaintiff believed that an oily substance caused her to fall, based on the fact that there was an oily substance on her coat. She did not notice the substance until she arrived at her office. *Id.* at 18:4–18.

> The plaintiff has no information that the defendant was aware of the substance and she does not know how long the substance had been there. *Id.* at 24:4–12.

The plaintiff's opposition to the summary judgment motion, in its entirety, was limited to two pages. While the opposition set forth several additional "facts," the plaintiff did not direct the court to any support in the record, nor did the plaintiff provide a supporting affidavit. The plaintiff provided four photographs of the coat she was wearing at the time.

## QUESTION:

(4) On the defendant's motion for summary judgment pursuant to Fed.R.Civ.P. 56 against the plaintiff's once-count complaint, the federal court should:

   (a) Deny the defendant's motion to dismiss the case under Rule 56 because the defendant, as the moving party, has failed to satisfy its initial burden of production;

   (b) Deny the defendant's motion to dismiss the case under Rule 56 because there is a genuine issue of material fact as to whether an oily substance caused the plaintiff's fall;

   (c) Grant the defendant's motion to dismiss the case under Rule 56 because the plaintiff has failed to adduce evidence demonstrating a triable issue of fact;

   (d) Grant the defendant's motion to dismiss the case under Rule 56 because the plaintiff's photographs of her coat were self-serving;

   (e) Before issuing a ruling on the summary judgment motion, permit the plaintiff to conduct additional discovery in response to the defendant's motion for summary judgment.

* * *

Otis Allen initially brought an action in the federal court for the Eastern District of Louisiana seeking relief under 42 U.S.C. § 1983 against James Pohlmann, Sheriff of the St. Bernard Parish Sheriff's Office, and Karl Bartholomew, individually and in their official capacities. The plaintiff also sought relief under state law against R & S Towing, Inc. of Chalmette (R & S Towing). The court continued the trial dates noting that R & S Towing had only recently made an appearance in the case. Soon after, the court granted the plaintiff's motion to voluntarily dismiss the defendants Karl Bartholomew and James Pohlmann in light of a settlement between the plaintiff and those defendants.

The plaintiff subsequently moved for leave to file an amended complaint. The plaintiff's proposed amendment named both state actors and R & S Towing as defendants. The plaintiff was granted leave to file an amendment, but only as to R & S Towing, because all claims against the named state actors had been settled. In pertinent part, the plaintiff alleged that R & S Towing towed the plaintiff's vehicle. At some point thereafter and while the plaintiff was incarcerated, the plaintiff's family attempted to pay R & S Towing the fees necessary to recover the vehicle; however, R & S Towing rejected the family members' offer and instead sold the plaintiff's vehicle without providing proper notice under the Louisiana Towing and Storage Act. R & S Towing had not participated in discovery, any negotiations, and did not participate in conference calls in the matter.

With no remaining federal claims the court ordered the parties to brief the issue of whether the Court should continue to exercise its supplemental jurisdiction. R & S Towing filed a motion to dismiss for lack of jurisdiction over the remaining state law claims in the case. The essence of R & S Towing's argument was that the court should allow a state court to decide the matter because the court had not yet become familiar with the facts of the case or reached the merits of any argument. The plaintiff filed its support of continued jurisdiction.

**QUESTION:**

(5)   On the defendant R & S Towing's motion to dismiss for lack of jurisdiction, the federal district court should:

   (a)   Grant the defendant's motion to dismiss under 28 U.S.C. § 1367(c) because the court has discretion to dismiss state law claims when no federal claims remain;

   (b)   Grant the defendant's motion to dismiss because the court never had good jurisdiction over the claims under 28 U.S.C. § 1367(a);

   (c)   Grant the defendant's motion to dismiss because federal courts are courts of limited jurisdiction and do not adjudicate state law claims;

   (d)   Deny the defendant's motion to dismiss because the state law claims against R & S Towing were properly in the court's supplemental jurisdiction over the plaintiff's original federal claims;

   (e)   Deny the defendant's motion to dismiss because it doesn't make a difference to the federal court's jurisdiction that the plaintiff's original federal claims were settled.

* * *

Nelcia Collins was employed with the Department of Defense Education Activity ("DoDEA") as a special education assessor in Okinawa, Japan. Collins claimed that "she felt as though she was singled out and treated different from peers who worked in a similar capacity," and that she "was subject to harassment and intimidation throughout the course of her employment." She reported her treatment to Diversity Management & Equal Opportunity within the DoDEA.

Stan Hays, the principal of the school where she worked and her immediate supervisor, subsequently sent Collins a termination letter that pointed out problems with her work performance, conduct and "general character traits," and stated that based upon his review, he concluded that her performance warranted her termination. Collins asserted that she "was not provided any performance evaluations throughout the year to substantiate or validate Hays' assessment."

Collins filed a complaint in the federal district court for the Northern District of Georgia, suing Chuck Hagel, the Secretary of Defense and Marlee Fitzgerald, the Director of the DoDEA. Collins alleged that the defendants discriminated against her because of her race (African American), gender (female), and national origin (West Indies), in violation of Title VII of the Civil Rights Act of 1964, 42 U.S.C. § 2000e, *et seq.* In paragraph five of her complaint, the plaintiff asserted that "all actions/inaction by Defendants, as alleged, occurred by officers/employees of the United States. As such, Plaintiff contends that venue in this district is proper for the Defendants pursuant to 28 U.S.C. § 1391(e)."

The defendants filed their answer. The defendants asserted that the plaintiff had not alleged a proper basis for venue in the district court, and "with respect to the allegations in paragraph 5 of the Complaint, Defendants admit that the named defendants are employees of the United States. Defendants deny that venue is determined by 28 U.S.C. § 1391(e) but rather by the specific venue provisions of Title VII of the Civil Rights Act."

42 U.S.C. § 2000e–5(f)(3) provides, in relevant part, that the appropriate venue for a Title VII claim is:

> (1) in any judicial district in the State in which the unlawful employment practice is alleged to have been committed, (2) in the judicial district in which the employment records relevant to such practice are maintained and administered, or (3) in the judicial district in which the aggrieved person would have worked but for the alleged unlawful employment practice, but (4) if the respondent is not found within any such district, such an action may be brought within the judicial district in which the respondent has his principal office. For purposes of sections 1404 and 1406 of Title 28, the judicial district in which the respondent has his principal office shall in all cases be considered a district in which the action might have been brought.

The plaintiff worked at Kadena Elementary School in Okinawa, Japan. The claimed Title VII violations occurred in Okinawa, Japan, and she would have continued to work in Okinawa, Japan, if the alleged discrimination had not occurred. The plaintiff's employment records were maintained by the DoDEA Human Resources Directorate, located in Alexandria, Virginia. The principal office of defendant Marilee Fitzgerald, the Director of DoDEA, was in Alexandria, Virginia, and the principal office of the defendant Chuck Hagel, the Secretary of Defense, was located at the Pentagon in Arlington, Virginia. Both Alexandria and Arlington, Virginia, are located within the Eastern District of Virginia.

**QUESTION:**

(6) On the defendants' motion to dismiss for improper venue pursuant to Fed.R.Civ.P. 12(b)(3), the federal district court for the northern District of Georgia should:

   (a) Grant the defendants' motion to dismiss for improper venue because the Secretary of Defense is not subject to suit in federal court;

   (b) Grant the defendant's motion to dismiss for improper venue because the proper venue is in Japan;

   (c) Grant the motion to dismiss for improper venue because the Title VII special venue provision supersedes the general venue provision under 28 U.S.C. § 1391(e);

   (d) Deny the motion to dismiss for improper venue because venue is proper under 28 U.S.C. § 1391(e), because the plaintiff resides in Georgia;

   (e) Deny the motion to dismiss for improper venue because the court should defer to the plaintiff's choice of forum in a Title VII civil rights case.

* * *

James R. Hausman filed a negligence action in the federal district court for the Western District of Washington against Holland America Line-U.S.A., a cruise company, and other related corporate entities. The plaintiff alleged that while traveling as a passenger on the defendants' cruise ship—the MS AMSTERDAM, an automatic sliding glass door improperly closed, striking his head and causing him injury. After a two week jury trial, the jury rendered a verdict in favor of the plaintiff, awarding five million in compensatory damages and 16.5 million in punitive damages. The court entered judgment in favor of the plaintiff.

Thereafter the defendants filed a motion to vacate the judgment and for dismissal, or alternatively, a motion to vacate the judgment and for a new trial based on the plaintiff's fraud on the court, willful violation of the court's discovery order, intentional destruction of evidence, and witness tampering. The defendants based the motion to vacate, in part, on the declaration of Amy Mizeur, a former employee of the plaintiff. The defendants contended that after the jury's verdict was rendered, Mizeur contacted the defendants' counsel and reported that, prior to trial, the plaintiff had "willfully and systematically destroyed evidence" in violation of the court's order, "fabricated evidence," and "tampered with at least one witness."

The plaintiff's filed a motion to compel production of any records the defendants have of contact with the witness Mizeur. Specifically, the plaintiff sought a copy of notes the defense paralegal Ellen Roberts took during an interview she conducted of Mizeur before the trial as part of the defendants' trial preparation.

The plaintiff argued that he was entitled to a copy of Roberts' notes from her pre-trial interview of Mizeur. The plaintiff claimed that he was entitled to the notes because the defendants' motion to vacate was based solely on what the defendants alleged to be newly discovered evidence from Mizeur. According to the plaintiff, because the defendants implied that Mizeur lied to the defendants when they interviewed her before trial, the defendants had placed at issue the content of any interview the defendants had with her. The plaintiff argued that the defendants must establish that Mizeur actually lied to them. That required a comparison between what she actually told them and what she then claimed to be the truth. As a result, the plaintiff alleged that any notes, recording, transcript, or other records of the defendants' contacts should be produced.

The defendants opposed the plaintiff's request, arguing that the notes were protected attorney opinion work-product.

### QUESTION:

(7)  On the plaintiff's motion to compel production of the any record of the defendant's contacts with witness Mizeur, the federal district court should:

(a)  Grant the motion to compel production because the defendant has placed Mizeur's veracity in issue;

(b)  Grant the motion to compel production because the materials requested are ordinary work product, and the plaintiff cannot obtain these materials by other means;

(c)  Grant the motion to compel production because the materials requested are not protected attorney work product;

(d)  Deny the motion to compel production because the materials requested are protected opinion work product;

(e)  Deny the motion to compel because the plaintiff had committed fraud.

\* \* \*

The Sinclair Cattle Company (SCC) filed a federal diversity lawsuit in the Middle District of Pennsylvania against Jeffery and Rebecca Ward. The court had valid diversity jurisdiction pursuant to 28 U.S.C. § 1332. The plaintiff SCC ran a Black Angus cattle farming business that conducted operations including the purchase, breeding, and selling of cattle. The defendant Jeffrey Ward was an employee of SCC from 1996 until 2013 and served as its president, treasurer, and acting chief executive officer. His wife, defendant Rebecca Ward, also worked at SCC and performed office management duties between 1998 and 2013.

SCC filed a complaint against the Wards alleging breach of fiduciary duty and claims sounding in fraud. The Wards filed an answer. In numerous paragraphs of their answer, the Wards generally denied the allegations and also attached the following qualifier:

. . . except those allegations constituting admissions against the interests of Sinclair Cattle and Smith, and each of them . . .

SCC filed a motion to strike the Wards' answer in its entirety or to the extent that it did not conform to Federal Rule of Civil Procedure 8(b)–(c), pursuant to Federal Rule of Civil Procedure 12(f). Specifically, SCC averred that the Wards' answer was replete with responses that did not comply with Rule 8(b). The Wards replied that their answer complied with Rule 8(b), and therefore should not be stricken.

## QUESTION:

(8)  On SCC's Fed.R.Civ.P. 12(f) motion to strike the defendants' answers to the plaintiff's complaint, the federal district court should:

  (a)  Grant the plaintiff's motion to strike because the federal rules do not permit a defendant to issue a general denial;

  (b)  Grant the plaintiff's motion to strike because the defendant's answers do not fairly respond to the substance of the plaintiff's allegations;

  (c)  Deny the plaintiff's motion to strike because the defendants have sufficiently pleaded answers to the plaintiff's allegations under Fed.R.Civ.P. 8(b);

  (d)  Deny the plaintiff's motion to strike because the form of defendants' answer admitted the parts that were true and denied the rest;

  (e)  Deny the plaintiff's motion to strike because Fed.R.Civ.P. 12(f) does not apply to provide relief from pleading defects.

* * *

In the same case, the Wards in their answer to the plaintiffs' complaint further asserted thirteen affirmative defenses, including failure to state a claim, statute of limitations, laches, estoppel and waiver, and unclean hands. The Wards' thirteenth affirmative defense stated that the defendants "reserved the right to assert further defenses as discovery warranted." SCC also moved to strike the Ward's affirmative defenses pursuant to Fed.R.Civ.P. 12(f). SCC argued that the Wards contravened the pleading requirements of Rule 8(c) by presenting a laundry list of boilerplate, conclusory affirmative defenses that failed to provide fair notice. The Wards contended that their affirmative defenses satisfied the fair notice standard because they were "logically related" to the litigation, and should therefore not be stricken.

## QUESTION:

(9)  In response to SCC's motion to strike the defendants' affirmative defenses pursuant to Fed.R.Civ.P. 12(f), the federal district court should:

  (a)  Grant the motion to strike the affirmative defenses because they are conclusory;

(b) Grant the motion to strike the affirmative defenses because they do not give the plaintiff a fair notice of the affirmative defenses;

(c) Grant the motion to strike the affirmative defenses because they set forth matter that is impertinent and immaterial to the litigation;

(d) Deny the motion to strike the affirmative because Rule 12(f) is not the appropriate federal rule for addressing pleading defects in affirmative defenses;

(e) Deny the motion to strike the affirmative defenses because the affirmative defenses are logically within the ambit of the plaintiff's claims and therefore give fair notice of the affirmative defenses.

\* \* \*

Ray Watts brought an action for damages against the defendants Smoke Guard, Inc., Powers Products Co., the Residences at Little Nell Development, LLC, and SimplexGrinnell, LP in the federal district court for Colorado. He filed his original complaint on July 9, 2014. The lawsuit related to serious injuries sustained by Watts on June 14, 2012 when he was struck on the head by a smoke detector in an elevator at the Residences at the Little Nell in Aspen, Colorado.

On July 15, 2015, Watts filed a third amended complaint in which he added defendant Little Nell Condominium Association, Inc. (LNA) to the lawsuit, alleging a claim of negligence arising out of the same June 14, 2012 incident that caused the plaintiff's injuries. Under Colorado law, the applicable statute of limitations for a negligence claim is two years. In the original and amended complaints the plaintiff asserted various negligence claims arising out of the incident where he was hit on the head by a falling smoke detector.

LNA moved to dismiss the complaint based on the expiration of the applicable statute of limitations.

In opposition to the motion to dismiss, the plaintiff stated that LNA's knowledge and notice of the negligence claim was shown by the proximity and connection between LNA and an already named defendant, Little Nell Development ("LND"). The defendant LNA's Articles of Incorporation show Brooke Peterson, as one of three members serving on the "Executive Board" of Little Nell Association. This same individual, as indicated by the Colorado Secretary of States' online website, served as the registered agent for Defendant LND when the action was commenced, and served as the registered agent for Defendant LNA. Peterson served as the registered agent for LND at the same time that she served for LNA as both its registered agent and Executive Board member. LNA did not filed any opposition to the plaintiff's argument.

QUESTION:

(10) On the defendant LNA's motion to dismiss Watt's negligence claim against it as a party newly added to the third amended complaint, the federal district court should:

(a) Grant the defendant LNA's motion to dismiss it from the case because the statute of limitations has run;

(b) Grant the defendant LNA's motion to dismiss it from the case because the plaintiff's lawyer made a mistake in failing to properly investigate the parties prior to filing its original complaint;

(c) Grant the defendant LNA's motion to dismiss because allowing the lawsuit to proceed against LNA would be an injustice;

(d) Deny the defendant LNA's motion to dismiss because Fed.R.Civ.P. 15(c) permits Watts' amendment adding LNA to relate back to the original pleading;

(e) Deny the defendant LNA's motion to dismiss because Fed.R.Civ.P. 15(a) permits liberal amendment of pleadings when a plaintiff has made a mistake of identity.

* * *

Amanda Zabic, who was 18 at the time, sought to upgrade her cellular telephone at a Verizon store in Bartow, Florida. A Verizon employee, Joshua Stuart, provided Zabic with a new phone and assisted her in transferring data which had been electronically stored in Zabic's old cellular phone to a new cellular phone. The electronically stored data included photographs of Zabic in an undressed, or semi-dressed state. According to Zabic, Verizon promised and repeatedly assured that all data would be transferred from her old phone to the new unit without the necessity of displaying any of the photographs and without the photographs or other personal information being seen or viewed by Verizon employees or anyone else. Despite these assurances, Zabic contended that Verizon employees, including Stuart and another employee viewed the nude photographs of her, saved the photographs to their personal cellular phones, and then shared those images with others. Specifically, Zabic alleged that when one of her acquaintances, Joshua Wingate, came to the same Bartow, Florida Verizon store, Verizon employees showed Wingate photographs of a nude, semi-nude and partially clothed Zabic. Wingate advised Zabic that Verizon employees were displaying her nude photos and Zabic contacted law enforcement.

Zabic filed a complaint against Verizon Wireless Services, LLC and Cellular Sales of Knoxville, Inc. in the Circuit Court of the Thirteenth Judicial Circuit for Hillsborough County, Florida, bringing the following counts: negligence, invasion of privacy, public disclosure of private facts, theft and conversion, civil remedies for criminal practices, intentional infliction of emotional distress, respondeat superior, and vicarious liability.

The defendants removed action to the federal district court for the Middle District of Florida on the basis of the court's diversity jurisdiction. Thereafter, Zabic filed an amended complaint naming Cellco Partnership d/b/a Verizon Wireless and Cellular Sales of Knoxville, Inc. as the defendants. The defendants provided detailed information about their citizenship, and the court was satisfied that the parties were completely diverse.

The plaintiff filed for remand to state court, alleging that the defendant failed to demonstrate the requisite amount in controversy to establish diversity jurisdiction. In both the initial and amended complaints Zabic alleged damages "in excess of $15,000." In the notice of removal, the defendants indicated: "Plaintiff's counsel has demanded $150,000 to settle the case" and "therefore, the amount in controversy exceeds $75,000.00, exclusive or interest and costs, as required for diversity jurisdiction in federal court."

Zabic's counsel had sent a demand letter to the defendants' counsel that was factually detailed, but contains no analysis of why her claim is worth $150,000.00, or any other amount. Zabic's counsel indicated in the demand letter: "This is not a claim in which the loss and damages suffered by Ms. Zabic can be quantified with any degree of precision." Zabic's counsel discussed only one other case:

> With respect to damages and what constitutes a reasonable amount, I commend your attention to the reported case styled *In re Thomas*, 254 B.R. 879 (S.C. Dist. Bkrtcy Ct.1999), a case arising in the context of a bankruptcy proceeding in which the debtor's finance (sic)—both private, non-celebrity citizens—was awarded $300,000 in compensatory damages, together with an additional $125,000 in punitive damages for the mailing of private, sexually explicit photographs of a girlfriend and the threat of publication.

In the *Thomas* case, Hardy had a sexual relationship with Thomas and allowed Thomas to take photographs during various sexual acts. Hardy ended the relationship with Thomas and began a new romantic relationship with Mr. Prezioso, which led to an engagement to be married. Thereafter, Thomas mailed a copy of some of the sexually explicit photographs of Hardy to Prezioso and demanded money from Prezioso as well as the opportunity to have sex with Hardy once again. Unless these conditions were met, Thomas threatened to send the sexually explicit photos to Hardy's employer. Thomas was found guilty of criminal extortion and, in a trial brought by Prezioso, the court awarded $300,000 for intentional infliction of emotional distress as well as punitive damages.

**QUESTION:**

(11) On the plaintiff's motion to remand her case back to state court based on 28 U.S.C. § 1447(c), the federal district court should:

    (a) Grant the plaintiff's motion to remand the case back to state court because her claims involve only garden-variety state-based claims;

(b)  Grant the plaintiff's motion to remand the case back to state court because the defendant has not carried its burden of demonstrating that the case exceeds $75,000 in damages;

(c)  Deny the plaintiff's motion to remand the case back to state court because the court determined there was valid diversity of citizenship;

(d)  Deny the plaintiff's motion to remand the case back to state court because the defendant has established the requisite amount in controversy for federal diversity jurisdiction through the plaintiff's settlement demand;

(e)  Deny the plaintiff's motion for remand to state court because the defendant has established the requisite amount in controversy through the plaintiff's demand letter and citation to the *Thomas* case.

* * *

D & S Marine Transportation, L.L.C., as plaintiff, sued the defendants S & K Marine, L.L.C., Ben Strafuss, and BJS Blessey, L.L.C. in the Thirty-Second Judicial District Court, Parish of Terrebonne, Louisiana. D & S Marine was a marine transportation company that operated a fleet of tow boats that moved barges. On August 11, 2014, D & S Marine filed an action against the defendants alleging that the defendants breached a bareboat charter agreement entered into between D & S Marine and S & K Marine. D & S Marine also alleged that the defendants breached that contract in bad faith, that Strafuss committed an intentional interference with contractual relations, and that defendants were liable for detrimental reliance. The defendants removed the action to the United States District Court for the Eastern District of Louisiana. The defendants filed a motion to dismiss under Rule 12(b)(6) of the Federal Rules of Civil Procedure arguing that D & S Marine failed to state any viable claims under either Louisiana law or the general maritime law.

Applying Louisiana law, the court denied the motion to dismiss as to D & S Marine's breach of contract, bad faith breach of contract, and detrimental reliance claims against S & K Marine, and its tortious interference with contractual relations claim against Strafuss. The court found that the parties contemplated that the final bareboat charter agreement would be in writing and signed by the parties, which did not occur. However, the court also found that by alleging that it "undertook a significant amount of work with the shipyard to modify the vessel under construction to meet the configurations required and used in its fleet," D & S Marine alleged that it began performance under the bareboat charter agreement by spending money to make modifications to the vessel while it was under construction.

Thus, the court found that this was sufficient for D & S Marine to state claims for breach of contract and bad faith breach of contract against S & K Marine, and for tortious interference with contractual relations against Strafuss. Further, the court found that D & S Marine sufficiently stated a claim for detrimental reliance against S & K Marine, because it alleged that it relied on S & K Marine's word and conduct regarding the formation of the charter party, and alleged that S & K Marine changed its position to D & S Marine's detriment by spending money to modify the vessel under construction and by entering into a sub-charter agreement with one of its customers.

Thereafter, S & K Marine and Strafuss filed a motion for summary judgment arguing that all claims against them must be dismissed because D & S Marine did not spend any money modifying the vessel. The court denied the motion finding that there were disputed issue of material fact that precluded summary judgment.

On May 29, 2015, D & S Marine filed a motion to for leave of court to file a second supplemental and amending complaint that sought to bring claims under the Louisiana Unfair Trade Practices Act (LUTPA) against Strafuss. D & S Marine contended that an email to Strafuss from his business partner, Calvin Klotz, dated February 17, 2014, which was produced during discovery, provided a basis for such claims.

The defendants argued that the amendment was futile because the claims were preempted under LUTPA's one-year preemption period. Louisiana law provides that an action under LUTPA "shall be prescribed by one year running from the time of the transaction or act which gave rise to the right of action." This is a preemptive period.

In construing LUPTA, the Supreme Court of Louisiana has held that preempted claims cannot relate back to the filing of the original petition under the Louisiana Code of Civil Procedure. The Supreme Court of Louisiana also has stated that preemption is not merely a procedural bar to litigation, but that it destroys the existence of a substantive right.

The United States magistrate judge granted D & S Marine's motion adding LUTPA claims against Strafuss. While she recognized that the LUTPA claims were technically preempted, the magistrate judge ruled that under Rule 15(c) of the Federal Rules of Civil Procedure, the LUTPA claims against Strafuss related back to the filing of the original petition because they arose out of the same conduct, transaction or occurrence as the allegations in the original complaint.

The defendants filed an appeal of the magistrate judge's ruling, arguing that the finding was contrary to law. The defendants argued that a preemptive period was a substantive right under Louisiana state law, and the Rules Enabling Act, 28 U.S.C. § 2072, prohibited using Rule 15(c) to enlarge a substantive right. D & S Marine argued that the magistrate judge's order was correct because she applied the federal procedural rules.

**QUESTION:**

(12) On appeal from the magistrate judge's order permitting the plaintiff's amendment to add LUPTA claims against the defendant Strafuss, the federal district court should:

    (a)   Uphold the magistrate judge's ruling because the Federal Rules of Civil Procedure apply in diversity cases;

(b) Uphold the magistrate judge's ruling because federal common law applies to determine whether the amendment should be allowed;

(c) Uphold the magistrate judge's ruling because application of Fed.R.Civ.P. 15(c) is consistent with the mandate of the Rules Enabling Act;

(d) Overrule the magistrate judge's ruling because the preemptive period is substantive under Louisiana law, which the federal court must follow in a diversity case;

(e) Overrule the magistrate judge's ruling because the Louisiana Supreme Court has held that a plaintiff cannot amend its complaint under the Louisiana Code of Civil Procedure after the preemptive period has run.

\* \* \*

Marc Wichansky sued David Zowine in the federal district court for the District of Arizona. Wichansky sent various email communications to his father-in-law, George Prussin, communications that also included the plaintiff's litigation counsel. The emails were sent to Wichansky in anticipation of his lawsuit against Zowine. In the emails, Prussin discussed litigation strategy with Wichansky and his counsel. There was no agreement with Prussin that he would act as a paid consultant or advisor.

**QUESTION:**

(13) The defendant filed a motion to compel discovery of the plaintiff Wichansky's emails, and the plaintiff opposed disclosure, relying on the attorney-client privilege. In response to the plaintiff's invocation of attorney-client privilege to protect the mails from disclosure, the federal district court should rule:

(a) The plaintiff's emails are protected by attorney-client because they were communicated to Prussin as well as Wichansky's attorney;

(b) The plaintiff's emails are protected by attorney-client privilege because they contain litigation strategy;

(c) The plaintiff's emails are protected by attorney-client privilege because the privilege belongs to the client Wichansky;

(d) The plaintiff's emails are not protected by the attorney-client privilege because email communications are not encompassed by the scope of matters protected by the privilege;

(e) The plaintiff's emails are not protected by attorney-client privilege because they were communicated to a third-party not an attorney.

QUESTION:

(14) In the same case in which the defendant sought disclosure of the plaintiff's emails, the plaintiff further invoked the doctrine of work product immunity in order to prevent disclosure of the emails. In response to the plaintiff's reliance on the doctrine of work product immunity to prevent disclosure of the emails, the federal district court should:

(a) Allow disclosure of the plaintiff's emails because they do not constitute attorney work product subject to the immunity;

(b) Allow disclosure of the plaintiff's emails because the content was disclosed to a non-party third person;

(c) Allow disclosure of the plaintiff's emails because they constitute ordinary work product and the defendant has overcome the immunity by showing a need for the documents;

(d) Deny disclosure of the plaintiff's emails because they were prepared in anticipation of litigation and therefore come within the scope of the work product immunity;

(e) Deny disclosure of the emails plaintiff's because disclosure would unfairly prejudice the plaintiff in preparation of his case.

\* \* \*

Kia Song Tang sued her former employer, Glocap Search LLC, and its principal, Adam Zoia, in the federal district court for the Southern District of New York. She alleged that the defendants discriminated against her when she became pregnant and then fired her when she complained about that discrimination. She brought discrimination and retaliation claims pursuant to Title VII of the Civil Rights Act of 1964, as well as New York City and State anti-discrimination laws. After five days of trial, a jury rendered a verdict in the defendants' favor on all claims. The plaintiff moved for judgment as a matter of law on her city-law retaliation claim or, in the alternative, a new trial on all of her retaliation claims.

To prevail on her retaliation claim under the New York City Human Rights Law, the plaintiff was required to show, among other things, that she engaged in a protected activity. There is no dispute that an employee's complaint about pregnancy discrimination—whether formal or informal—can constitute protected activity. For a complaint to qualify, however, the employee must also show that she had "a good faith, reasonable belief that the underlying challenged actions of the employer violated the law." That showing involves two components: first, that the plaintiff had subjective good faith belief that her employer had violated the law and, second that the complaint was objectively reasonable. Thus, if a plaintiff complained, not in good faith, but rather to protect her job or extort money from her employer, the activity was not protected under the statute.

The plaintiff had complained to Zoia that she was subject to pregnancy discrimination. The defendants admitted, by failing to respond to the plaintiff's requests for admissions, that in the weeks after the plaintiff revealed her pregnancy to Zoia, he excluded her from certain discussions and decisions, reassigned some of her responsibilities to others, and asked her to transition to a compensation structure that would not include maternity leave.

At the trial, the plaintiff testified that she continued to stay at his home while she was in New York, even after Zoia purportedly reacted negatively to news of her pregnancy and asked her to take a pay cut. Three weeks after Zoia began treating the plaintiff differently, she generated a paper trail to support a later claim of discrimination by directing a subordinate who had called to ask why Zoia had reassigned some of the plaintiff's responsibilities to write her an e-mail as if they had not spoken and then responded by e-mail, again with no reference to their prior conversation, that she believed that Zoia was discriminating against her.

The plaintiff contended that Zoia himself admitted that the plaintiff had subjectively believed that she was being treated differently because of her pregnancy, pointing to his testimony that the plaintiff "felt she was being excluded from things" and that the email in which she complained to him about discrimination represented "a continuation of the sort of strange lack of understanding of what was really happening."

Zoia testified at trial that he was "very happy for the plaintiff" when he heard that she was pregnant and enthusiastically congratulated her. The defendant argued at trial was that the plaintiff's complaint was made in bad faith: that she knew her job was on the line after her allegedly tepid response to a "crisis" at the company—a crisis that highlighted the problems of having a highly paid chief operating officer working from a different city—and that, days later, she told Zoia she was pregnant (despite not yet showing) and ultimately complained in a cynical effort to either keep her job or (in Zoia's words) "position" herself to file a lawsuit. Zoia never linked the plaintiff's feelings to any perceived or actual discrimination. To the contrary, he explicitly testified that, upon receiving the plaintiff's alleged complaint of discrimination, he came to the conclusion that she was merely "positioning" to "protect her job."

## QUESTION:

(15) On the plaintiff's motion for a judgment notwithstanding the jury verdict under Fed.R.Civ.P. 50(b), the federal district court should:

   (a) Deny the plaintiff's Rule 50(b) motion because the jury was entitled to find that the plaintiff did not have a subjective good faith belief that the defendants had engaged in discrimination and therefore did not engage in protected activity;

   (b) Deny the plaintiff's Rule 50(b) motion because that plaintiff failed to move for a directed verdict at the close of her case;

   (c) Deny the plaintiff's Rule 50(b) motion because to grant it would deny the defendants of their Seventh Amendment to a jury trial;

   (d) Grant the plaintiff's Rule 50(b) motion because no reasonable jury could conclude on the evidence that the defendants had not engaged in discrimination against her;

(e)  Grant the plaintiff's Rule 50(b) motion because, allowing for all reasonable inferences from the testimony, the plaintiff was entitled to the judgment.

\* \* \*

Torrey Harrison, a social worker, filed a lawsuit in Maine Superior Court against her employer Granite Bay Care, Inc. alleging that Granite Bay illegally fired her in violation of Maine's Whistleblower Protection Act. Her theory was that Granite Bay was getting back at her for reporting what she considered to be violations of state employment law to her supervisor and, later, to Maine's Department of Health and Human Services.

Harrison, a Maine citizen, filed her suit (which raised state law claims only) in Maine Superior Court. Granite Bay preferred to be in federal court and, invoking federal diversity jurisdiction, removed the action to the Maine district court. In doing so, Granite Bay held itself out as a New Hampshire corporation with a principal place of business in Concord, New Hampshire.

The court *sua sponte* raised a question raised a question as to whether Granite Bay was a citizen of both New Hampshire and Maine, which would render diversity jurisdiction invalid. Granite Bay ran group homes and provided services for adults who have cognitive or physical disabilities. Granite Bay was a New Hampshire corporation and it maintained its corporate headquarters in Concord, New Hampshire. Nevertheless, its group homes were all in Maine and all of its clients were Maine residents. In addition to its Concord headquarters, Granite Bay had an administrative office in Portland, Maine.

Granite Bay was owned by two individuals, Kasai Mumpini and Caroletta Alicea, both of whom worked out of Concord. Mumpini has served as the corporation's President, with Alicea as its Vice President. Mumpini and Alicea were Granite Bay's only two officers and corporate directors. Their role was to maintain a vision for the company and to set overall corporate policies.

Granite Bay's day-to-day operations—things like providing care to its clients and hiring, training, and supervising employees—were handled out of the Portland, Maine office. An employee with the title of state director ran the operation in Maine. There have been two state directors, Gregory Robinson and Ken Olson, and there were no significant differences between how each one went about the job. Olson, the current state director, divided his work week between the offices in Portland and Concord.

Although he had significant flexibility in managing Granite Bay, Olson nevertheless reported to Mumpini and Alicea. He communicated with them daily and met with them in person at least once per week. Olson kept the owners updated as to how Granite Bay was doing, and the owners directed him on the overall strategy he was to employ in working towards the company's future goals. Furthermore, they gave Olson general financial parameters in which to operate, and they gave him different objectives to accomplish. The previous state director, Robinson, held that position for about seven years before becoming Granite Bay's Chief Operations Officer.

**QUESTION:**

(16) With regard to whether the Federal District Court of Maine had good diversity jurisdiction over the parties to Harrison's' lawsuit, the federal court should hold that:

(a) There was valid diversity jurisdiction because Harrison was a citizen of Maine and Mumpini and Alicea were citizens of New Hampshire;

(b) There was valid diversity jurisdiction because evidence in the record established that Granite Bay's principal place of business was in Concord, not Portland;

(c) There was no valid diversity jurisdiction because all of Granite Bay's group homes and clients were located in Maine;

(d) There was no valid diversity jurisdiction because the nerve center of Granite Bay's operations was actually in Maine;

(e) There was no valid diversity jurisdiction because Granite Bay's principal place of business was Maine.

\* \* \*

Freda Troyer, and Ohio citizen, filed a complaint against the defendants, Verba J. Johnson and United Financial Casualty Company, in the Circuit Court of Kanawha County, West Virginia. Johnson was a citizen of Ohio, and United Financial was an Ohio corporation with it principal place of business in Ohio. The plaintiff alleged she sustained personal injuries and economic and non-economic damages as a result of Johnson's negligence. The plaintiff claimed she was part of a group that hired Johnson—who was in the "business of transporting passengers for hire"—to drive them to Myrtle Beach, South Carolina. During the trip, Johnson "ran off of the edge of the roadway, crossed the median, and struck a concrete barrier while traveling south on Interstate 77" in West Virginia, resulting in the plaintiff's injuries and damages. In addition to compensatory damages, the plaintiff sought a declaratory judgment that United Financial was "obligated to provide at least $1.5 million in public liability insurance" under the policy issued to Johnson because "the covered vehicle was a commercial motor vehicle designed and used to transport 9 to 15 passengers, and engaged in the interstate transportation of passengers for compensation."

United Financial removed the case to federal court based on federal question jurisdiction. The plaintiff filed a motion to remand. United Financial claimed removal was appropriate and the court could exercise jurisdiction because the complaint raised a federal question, vesting the court with original jurisdiction under 28 U.S.C. § 1331. The defendant stated that the case implicated the federal Motor Carrier Safety Act and its attendant regulations, 49 U.S.C. § 387. This Act provides for civil penalties for violations of the Act, but does not provide a route for private enforcement. United Financial argued the case presented a substantial question of federal law because resolution of whether a federal regulation (i.e., 49 U.S.C. § 387) applied would resolve this case and might control the application of § 387 in other cases. Neither United Financial nor Johnson nor the plaintiff asked the court to interpret § 387.

**QUESTION:**

(17) On the plaintiff's motion to remand the case to state court, the federal district court should:

    (a)  Grant the plaintiff's motion for a remand to state court because there is no valid federal question jurisdiction under 28 U.S.C. § 1331;

    (b)  Grant the plaintiff's motion for remand to state court because federal courts disfavor implied rights of action in federal statutes;

    (c)  Deny the plaintiff's motion for remand to state court because there is valid federal question jurisdiction conferred by the federal Motor Carrier Safety Act;

    (d)  Deny the plaintiff's motion for remand to state court because federal courts have an interest in uniform interpretations of the federal Motor Carrier Safety Act;

    (e)  Deny the plaintiff's motion for remand to state court in the interests of inter-system comity.

* * *

OKS Group, LLC, sued Axtria Inc. in the federal district court for New Jersey. OKS and Axtria were global consulting firms. OKS' principal place of business was in Bala-Cynwyd, Pennsylvania, while the defendant Axtria's principal place of business was in Berkeley Heights, New Jersey. The plaintiff provided outsourcing services to BSI Financial Services, Inc. (BSI). The plaintiffs' work for BSI included data and information management involving proprietary work processes. In its complaint, the plaintiff contended that these proprietary work processes played a key role in the services it provided and that they constituted trade secrets. OKS stated that it entered into an oral agreement to lease an office space in Okhla, India to BSI, to be used by a combination of BSI employees and employees of the plaintiff who performed work for BSI.

BSI informed the plaintiff that it had retained the defendant Axtria to analyze and improve work flow and automate functions. The plaintiff contended that a BSI employee represented that the Axtria's role would increase the plaintiff's work for BSI. The plaintiff alleged that, based upon this representation, it gave the Axtria access to its proprietary work processes.

Instead of increasing plaintiffs' work for BSI, however, the plaintiff asserted that the defendant stole its proprietary work processes and displaced the plaintiff in performing data management services that it had previously rendered for BSI. The plaintiff alleged that the defendant convinced a key employee of the plaintiff, Niraj Jha, to spread rumors that created labor problems and that, after Jha's termination, Axtria hired him for his knowledge of the plaintiff's trade secrets. The plaintiff also contended that the defendant attempted to poach the plaintiff's employees and successfully induced BSI to renege on its agreement to rent the Okhla office space.

The plaintiff's complaint alleged claims against the defendant for fraud, negligent misrepresentation, misappropriation of trade secrets in violation of the Trade Secrets Act, common-law misappropriation of confidential information, intentional interference with contract, tortious interference with prospective economic advantage, and unjust enrichment. The defendant answered the complaint and filed a motion to dismiss the action on the basis of *forum non conveniens.*

The defendant moved to dismiss for *forum non conveniens,* arguing that the action would be better heard by the courts of India. It argued that the acts underlying the complaint occurred in India and that most or all relevant witnesses and evidence were located there. The Indian courts were an adequate forum, the defendant argued, because its Indian subsidiary, Axtria India Pvt. Ltd., which it characterized as "the party who is alleged to have committed the complained-of conduct," was subject to jurisdiction there. The defendant stressed that the plaintiff's Indian subsidiary, OKS Group International Pvt. Ltd., already has commenced proceedings against Axtria India in the Indian courts, asserting claims similar to those alleged in this action and based upon the same general set of facts. The defendant supported its motion with the certified statement of the lawyer representing Axtria India in the litigation with OKS India, who opined that the underlying conflict would be best resolved in that action before the Indian courts. The defendant further argued that, while deference was usually afforded to a plaintiff's choice of forum, such deference was reduced where the chosen forum was not the plaintiff's home forum.

The plaintiff, in opposition to the motion, contended that the defendant failed to demonstrate that India constituted an adequate alternative forum or that it would be more convenient than the New Jersey federal court, particularly considering that the defendant maintained its corporate headquarters in New Jersey. The defendant had not demonstrated that it was subject to service of process in India and had indicated that it would not consent to such service. The plaintiff argued that much of the underlying evidence was maintained electronically and thus would not be difficult to produce in the New Jersey forum. It contended, in any case, that ongoing arbitration between itself and BSI in the United States meant that many key documents already had been produced within this country. The plaintiff contested the defendant's assertion that all witnesses were Axtria India employees located in India, because the acts underlying the complaint were directed by the defendant's management in the United States.

### QUESTION:

(18) On the defendant's motion to dismiss on the grounds of *forum non conveniens*, the federal district court in New Jersey should:

    (a)   Grant the defendant's motion to dismiss on the grounds of *forum non conveniens* because most the events underlying the plaintiff's claims occurred in India;

(b) Grant the defendant's motion to dismiss on the grounds of *forum non conveniens* for the convenience of the parties and in the interests of justice;

(c) Grant the defendant's motion to dismiss on the grounds of *forum non conveniens* because the defendant demonstrated that India was an adequate alternative forum;

(d) Deny the defendant's motion to dismiss on the grounds of *forum non conveniens* because less favorable Indian law would apply to the plaintiff's detriment;

(e) Deny the defendant's motion to dismiss on the grounds of *forum non conveniens* because the defendant failed to show that India was an adequate alternative forum.

\* \* \*

Scott McCormick, as plaintiff, filed a state court action in Davidson County Circuit Court, Tennessee against Maquet Cardiovascular U.S. Sales, LLC. In his complaint, McCormick alleged employment discrimination claims. The defendant then removed the case to the federal district court for the Middle District of Tennessee. The parties did not dispute that the plaintiff's employment agreement with the defendant contained a choice of law provision and a forum selection clause through which the parties had agreed that exclusive personal jurisdiction and venue of any disputes would be in New Jersey.

After the removal of the case, to the federal court, the defendant moved to dismiss the plaintiff's case pursuant to Fed.R.Civ.P. 12(b)(3), or in the alternative Fed.R.Civ.P. 12(b)(6). Instead, the plaintiff moved to transfer venue under 28 U.S.C. § 1404(a).

**QUESTION:**

(19) In response to the defendant's motion to dismiss under Fed.R.Civ.P. 12(b)(3) or 12(b)(6), the federal court should:

(a) Grant the defendant's motion to dismiss under Fed.R.Civ.P. 12(b)(3) because venue was improper in the federal court in Tennessee;

(b) Grant the defendant's motion to dismiss under Fed.R.Civ.P. 12(b)(6), because a 12(b)(6) motion was the correct way to enforce a forum selection clause;

(c) Grant the defendant's motion to dismiss under both Fed.R.Civ.P. 12(b)(3) and Fed.R.Civ.P. 12(b)(6);

(d) Deny the defendant's motions and grant the plaintiff's motion to transfer the case to New Jersey, for the convenience of the parties and in the interests of justice;

(e) Deny the defendant's motion to dismiss because the forum selection clause in the plaintiff's employment contract was unconscionable and unenforceable.

\* \* \*

A dispute arose over the government's processing of drilling permit applications for wells in Osage County, Oklahoma. To drill a new well in Osage County, an oil and gas operator had to obtain a permit from the Superintendent of the Osage Agency within the Bureau of Indian Affairs (BIA). The Osage Producers Association (OPA) brought an action pursuant to the Administrative Procedure Act against several governmental defendants, alleging that the government had unreasonably delayed issuing drilling permits and that, in doing so, had tacitly denied each and every permit currently pending before the Superintendent.

David Hayes filed a motion to intervene. Hayes owned property in Osage County which, he contended, might be affected by the court's ruling in this case. Hayes asserted a right to intervene in the case and, in the alternative, requested permission to intervene. Both the plaintiff and defendants opposed the intervention. Hayes claimed an interest in the litigation based on the land "he owned in Osage County and the potential environmental harm that could" occur to his property as a result of this litigation. In particular, he contended that the government's failure to timely approve drilling permits was the result of BIA's efforts to comply with the National Environmental Policy Act, and that a ruling in OPA's favor could cause the government to shirk its duties under the statute. This interest, Hayes contended, was not adequately represented by the government because "the BIA could put up a weak defense to this action" so as to avoid complying with NEPA.

In response, the existing parties submitted that the case is about the government's alleged failure to approve drilling permits and that Hayes has failed to plead facts tying this dispute to the property in which he claimed an interest. In particular, the government contended that this case only concerns portions of the Osage Mineral Estate that were subject to pending permit applications and that Hayes had not shown that his property was so affected. Hayes did not allege, nor was there any indication in the record, that his property was subject to a pending permit application. Further, the parties asserted this action could not impair Hayes's interest in ensuring NEPA compliance on his land because, regardless of the outcome here, the government must comply with NEPA.

**QUESTION:**

(20) On Hayes' motion to intervene as of right under Fed.R.Civ.P. 24(a), the federal district court should:

    (a)    Grant the motion to intervene because Hayes demonstrated a generalized interest in preventing environmental harm to properties involved in the litigation;

    (b)    Grant the motion to intervene because Hayes had property interest that was the subject of the litigation between the parties;

    (c)    Deny the motion to intervene because Hayes did not have an interest that would be impaired by the litigation;

(d) Deny the motion to intervene because both the plaintiff and the defendant opposed the intervention;

(e) Deny the motion to intervene because Hayes's participation as a party-intervenor was untimely.

\* \* \*

In the same litigation, Hayes moved in the alternative to permissively intervene pursuant to Fed.R.Civ.P. 24(b). Hayes asserted that he "had claims and defenses relating to NEPA that he wished to present in the instant action" and that such "NEPA-related issues were central to the disposition of the case."

QUESTION:

(21) On Hayes motion to intervene permissively under Fed.R.Civ.P. 24(b), the federal district court should:

(a) Grant the motion to permissively intervene because the standard for intervention is much more liberal under Fed.R.Civ.P. 24(b) than under Fed.R.Civ.P. 24(a);

(b) Grant the motion to permissively intervene because it is in the court's discretion to grant the intervention and courts liberally grant this;

(c) Deny the motion to permissively intervene because Hayes did not demonstrate that he had claim and defenses that shared a common question of law or fact with the main action;

(d) Deny the motion to permissively intervene because Hayes's interests were adequately represented;

(e) Deny the motion to permissively intervene because the court could just as easily have granted Hayes status as an *amicus curiae*.

\* \* \*

Robin Poehler was a former employee of Cleaning Solution Service LLC and Debra Fenwick. She worked as a cleaner with CSS and filed a lawsuit against CSS and Fenwick for violations of the federal Fair Labor Standards Act (FLSA) and Arizona's state minimum wage law in Arizona state court.

Poehler alleged that she was not paid for overtime and that the defendants made illegal deductions of pay and hours worked that caused her compensation to fall below the minimum wage. The defendants removed the case to Arizona federal court. After the case was removed, the defendants filed counterclaims against Poehler for breach of contract and breach of fiduciary duty. The allegations in the counterclaims involved the plaintiff's allegedly wrongful competition with CSS.

Poehler argued that these state law counterclaims were not sufficiently related to her wage claims to allow the court to exercise supplemental jurisdiction over them pursuant to 28 U.S.C. § 1367(a), or, alternatively, she argued the court should decline to exercise supplemental jurisdiction over the counterclaims under § 1367(c)(4).

The parties agreed that the defendants' counterclaims were state law claims and were permissive, not compulsory, under Rule 13 of the Federal Rules of Civil Procedure. That is, the defendants conceded that their counterclaims for breach of contract and breach of fiduciary duty did not arise out of the same transaction or occurrence as the plaintiff's wage claims. However, the defendants argued the two sets of claims shared a common nucleus because they both stemmed from "alleged monies owed to one another for one another's conduct during employment" and they both required common witnesses.

Poehler moved to dismiss the defendants' counterclaims pursuant to Fed.R.Civ.P. 12(b)(1) for lack of subject matter jurisdiction.

### QUESTION:

(22) On the plaintiff's motion to dismiss the defendants' counterclaims under Fed.R.Civ.P. 12(b)(1), the federal district court should:

    (a)   Grant the plaintiff's motion to dismiss for a lack of subject matter jurisdiction because the defendants' counterclaims did not share a common nucleus of operative fact with the plaintiff's federal wage claims;

    (b)   Grant the plaintiff's motion to dismiss for a lack of subject matter jurisdiction because the court lacked federal question jurisdiction;

    (c)   Deny the plaintiff's motion to dismiss for a lack of subject matter jurisdiction because the parties agreed that the counterclaims were permissive under Fed.R.Civ.P. 13(b);

    (d)   Deny the plaintiff's motion to dismiss for a lack of subject matter jurisdiction in the interest of judicial economy, convenience, and fairness;

    (e)   Deny the plaintiff's motion to dismiss because the court had automatic supplemental jurisdiction over the defendants' counterclaims.

*　*　*

Thorpe Design Inc., a California corporation, filed suit against The Viking Corporation, a Michigan corporation, in Contra Costa, California Superior Court. The complaint also named "Does 41 through 1000." The defendants timely removed the complaint to the federal district court for the Northern District of California on the basis of diversity.

The complaint alleged that the plaintiff was engaged in the business of installation of fire sprinkler systems, and "began purchasing fire sprinkler systems designed, manufactured, and/or supplied by the defendants, including the Viking 457" approximately five years ago. According to the complaint, the plaintiff properly installed the fire sprinkler systems, but the fire sprinkler systems were defective. When the fire sprinklers failed and improperly discharged, it resulted in damages and costs to the plaintiff, including future damages, economic losses, and lost profits. The plaintiff further alleged that the defendants knew or should have known that the defective fire sprinklers would be installed without inspection and, if defective, would expose the plaintiff to claims by homeowners and others.

Doe defendants 41 through 1000 were "residents of the State of California and homeowners or occupiers of homes in which there are or were defective Viking sprinklers and/or representatives of said homeowners and/or occupiers, who now have, or may have in the future claims against the plaintiff by and for the reasons alleged herein, including indemnity or subrogation claims." Based on these general allegations, the plaintiff brought claims for negligence, products liability, unfair business practices, breach of the implied warranties of merchantability and fitness for a particular purpose, implied indemnity, and declaratory and injunctive relief.

The defendants moved to dismiss the complaint in its entirety pursuant to Federal Rules of Civil Procedure 12(b)(6) and 12(b)(7).

To state a claim for products liability against a manufacturer or supplier of a defective product, a plaintiff must allege that defendant placed the product on the market in the ordinary course of business, defendant knew the product was to be used without inspection for defects, the product was defective, the plaintiff was injured by the product as a proximate result of the defect and the plaintiff sustained injuries compensable in money. The defendants argued that the plaintiff's complaint failed to state a product liability or negligence claim because it did not identify which fire sprinkler product, part, component, system or model allegedly failed due to a defect in design or manufacture. The defendants argued that they designed and manufactured a number of different components and parts, and the vague allegations relating to the failure of a "fire sprinkler system" or "fire sprinkler" were insufficient to allow it to determine its applicable defenses.

The plaintiff countered that it did not need to identify the specific component or model of the allegedly defective product, and that in any event the defendants had fair notice of the claims against them in light of paragraph 6, which stated: "Approximately five (5) years ago, Plaintiff began purchasing fire sprinkler systems designed, manufactured, and/or supplied by Defendants . . . including the Viking 457." Paragraph 31 of the complaint also mentioned the "Viking 457" but did not provide any explanation as to how or why it was defective.

**QUESTION:**

(23) On the defendant's removal of the litigation to the federal district court for the Northern District of California, the federal district court should:

    (a) Remand the case back to California state court because there was no federal question jurisdiction;

    (b) Remand the case back to state court because the amount in controversy was not satisfied;

(c) Remand the case back to state court because there was no complete diversity of citizenship between the plaintiff and the defendants;

(d) Retain federal jurisdiction based on the court's supplemental jurisdiction under 28 U.S.C. § 1367(a) and discretionary jurisdiction under 28 U.S.C. § 1367(c);

(e) Retain federal jurisdiction because courts can disregard the citizenship of Doe defendants on federal removal.

**QUESTION:**

(24) On the defendant's motion to dismiss the plaintiff's products liability claim pursuant to Fed.R.Civ.P. 12(b)(6), the federal district court should:

(a) Grant the defendant's motion to dismiss the plaintiff's liability claim because there was no basis in law for the claim;

(b) Grant the defendant's motion to dismiss the plaintiff's liability claim because the complaint is overly vague as to what product was at issue;

(c) Deny the defendant's motion to dismiss the plaintiff's liability claim because the court in deciding a Fed.R.Civ.P. 12(b)(6) must take the plaintiff's allegations as true;

(d) Deny the defendant's motion to dismiss the plaintiff's liability claim because the court must draw all inferences favorable to the non-moving party;

(e) Deny the defendant's motion to dismiss the plaintiff's liability claim because the plaintiff has properly pleaded the products liability claim under *Twombly* and *Iqbal*.

* * *

In the same litigation, the defendants also moved to dismiss the complaint in its entirety pursuant to Federal Rule of Civil Procedure 12(b)(7) for failure to join parties under Rule 19. According to the defendants, the unnamed homeowners were deliberately not named in the litigation, but that they were necessary parties because there could be a final determination of rights and there was a substantial risk of multiple liability or inconsistent obligations if the homeowners were not joined because they might try to recover overlapping damages from the defendants.

**QUESTION:**

(25) On the defendants' motion to dismiss the complaint in its entirety pursuant to Fed.R.Civ.P. 12(b)(7), the federal district court should:

(a) Grant the defendant's motion to dismiss under Fed.R.Civ.P. 12(b)(7) because the homeowners are necessary parties and the court could not effectuate a just adjudication without them in the litigation;

(b) Grant the defendant's motion to dismiss under Fed.R.Civ.P. 12(b)(7) because the homeowners are indispensable parties and the court could not effectuate a just adjudication without them in the litigation;

(c) Deny the defendant's motion to dismiss under Fed.R.Civ.P. 12(b)(7) because joining the homeowners was not feasible because their presence would destroy diversity jurisdiction;

(d) Deny the defendant's motion to dismiss under Fed.R.Civ.P. 12(b)(7) because in equity and good conscience the court could allow the case to go forward without the homeowners;

(e) Deny the defendant's motion to dismiss under Fed.R.Civ.P. 12(b)(7) in the interests of judicial efficiency and economy.

**END OF EXAM PROBLEMS #2**

# CHAPTER 3
# EXAM #3 PROBLEMS AND QUESTIONS

Eve Kleinfeld commenced an action against Marnin Rand in New York state court to recover pursuant to a promissory note and accompanying guaranty.

The plaintiff alleged that pursuant to a promissory note, three entities 128 22nd Street Associates, LLC, Mag Builders, LLC and 259 Garside Associates, LLC borrowed $300,000 from the plaintiff. The note and alleged guaranty were both executed in New Jersey, and both the defendant and the borrowers were New Jersey residents. The plaintiff further alleged that the defendant personally executed the note as a guarantor and that the borrowers and the defendant defaulted under the note by failing to make payment when it became due. Thus, plaintiff commenced the action against defendant, as guarantor, seeking to recover the amount outstanding under the note.

The defendant, a New Jersey resident, moved to dismiss the action on the ground that the New York court lacked personal jurisdiction over him. In opposition, the plaintiff contended that jurisdiction over defendant was proper pursuant to both New York Civil Practice Law & Rules (CPLR) §§ 301 and 302(a)(1).

CPLR § 301, which is the codification of the common law concept of general personal jurisdiction, provides that "a court may exercise such jurisdiction over person, property, or status as might have been exercised heretofore." A defendant is subject to general personal jurisdiction in New York when it is "engaged in such a continuous and systematic course of 'doing business' here as to warrant a finding of its 'presence' in this jurisdiction."

CPLR § 302(a)(1) provides in relevant part:

> As to a cause of action arising from any of the acts enumerated in this section, a court may exercise personal jurisdiction over any non-domiciliary, or his executor or administrator, who in person or through an agent:
>
> 1.  transacts any business within the state or contracts anywhere to supply goods or services in the state

Whether a non-domiciliary is transacting business within the meaning of CPLR 302(a)(1) requires a finding that the non-domiciliary's activities were purposeful and established "a substantial relationship between the transaction and the claim asserted." "Purposeful activities are volitional acts by which the non-domiciliary 'avails itself of the privilege of conducting activities within the forum State, thus invoking the benefits and protections of its laws.'" "More than limited contacts are required for purposeful activities sufficient to establish that the non-domiciliary transacted business in New York."

The plaintiff contended that the defendant was subject to general jurisdiction in New York as the defendant made numerous visits over the years to BNB bank's offices in Manhattan to obtain financing for his real estate business. The plaintiff asserted that defendant's attendance at two, perhaps three, meetings in New York to negotiate the essential terms of the note, including defendant's personal guaranty, was sufficient to confer jurisdiction over defendant to recover pursuant to the guaranty.

**QUESTION:**

(1)  On the defendant's motion to dismiss the plaintiff's complaint for a lack of personal jurisdiction, the New York State court should:

   (a)  Grant the defendant's motion to dismiss for a lack of personal jurisdiction because New York assertion of personal jurisdiction over the defendant would violate the Full Faith and Credit Clause of the U.S. Constitution;

   (b)  Grant the defendant's motion to dismiss for a lack of personal jurisdiction because New York state court lacks general jurisdiction over the defendant;

   (c)  Deny the defendant's motion to dismiss for a lack of personal jurisdiction because the litigation involves a contractual relationship between the plaintiff and the defendants;

   (d)  Deny the defendant's motion to dismiss for a lack of personal jurisdiction because New York has an interest in protecting its citizens from parties who default on loan agreement;

   (e)  Deny the defendant's motion to dismiss for a lack of personal jurisdiction because banking is a highly regulated industry in New York, and therefore New York has an interest in the litigation sufficient to assert personal jurisdiction over the defendant.

\* \* \*

Susan F. Mikan sued Arbors at Fairlawn Care LLC in the federal district court for the Northern District of Ohio. She sued Arbors for wrongful discharge and emotional distress in conjunction with her claims under the Family Medical Leave Act (FMLA). The plaintiff was employed by Arbors' nursing facility in Fairlawn, Ohio, as a registered nurse for more than ten years. She was placed on administrative leave by her employer due to a pending investigation into a patient's fall. The plaintiff stated that she was aware she would need to request FMLA leave prior to being placed on administrative leave. However, she did not inform her employer of the need until she requested FMLA paperwork ten days after she was placed on administrative leave. According to the plaintiff, she was told the human resources department would respond to her FMLA request with the necessary paperwork. Instead, the plaintiff stated, she was terminated by human resources about an hour later that same day.

The plaintiff alleged that her employment was terminated in violation of the FMLA (Count One), that her termination was wrongful, in violation of public policy (Count Two), and that her termination resulted in emotional distress (Count Three).

In response to the plaintiff's complaint, the defendant sought dismissal pursuant to Fed.R.Civ.P. 12(b)(6) of the plaintiff's wrongful discharge and emotional distress claims, presented as Counts Two and Three of the complaint.

Ohio employment law does not recognize a separate cause of action for wrongful termination in violation of public policy if the statute establishing the policy contains its own remedy. The Ohio Supreme Court states: "Simply put, there is no need to recognize a common-law action for wrongful discharge if there already exists a statutory remedy that adequately protects society's interests." The plaintiff's count two was predicated on the same facts as count one, the FMLA claim.

## QUESTION:

(2)   In response to the defendant's motion to dismiss the plaintiff's Count Two pursuant to Fed.R.Civ.P. 12(b)(6), the federal district court should:

(a)   Grant the defendant's motion to dismiss Count Two pursuant to Fed.R.Civ.P. 12(b)(6) because Ohio law does not recognize the plaintiff's claim as she pleaded it in her complaint;

(b)   Grant the defendant's motion to dismiss Count Two pursuant to Fed.R.Civ.P. 12(b)(6) because there is no set of facts upon which the plaintiff could prevail at trial;

(c)   Deny the defendant's motion to dismiss Count Two pursuant to Fed.R.Civ.P. 12(b)(6) because the federal court has supplemental jurisdiction over the plaintiff's state law claims;

(d)   Deny the defendant's motion to dismiss Count Two pursuant to Fed.R.Civ.P. 12(b)(6) because such a dismissal would prejudicially frustrate the plaintiff's ability to pursue her claim;

(e)   Deny the defendant's motion to dismiss Count Two pursuant to Fed.R.Civ.P. 12(b)(6) because courts rarely grant Rule 12(b)(6) motions so early in litigation.

\* \* \*

Count Three of the plaintiff's complaint made a generic claim for emotional distress without specifying the defendant's conduct or actions directed at her. Court Three did not identify outrageous behavior or state whether the cause was deliberate, intentional, reckless and/or negligent.

Ohio law recognizes two emotional distress torts: intentional infliction of emotional distress and negligent infliction of emotional distress. The plaintiff did not state whether she was claiming negligent or intentional infliction of emotional distress, but made an attempt to cover the elements of both offenses in her pleading. Ohio courts do not recognize a separate tort for negligent infliction of emotional distress in the employment context.

The Ohio Supreme Court has characterized intentional infliction of emotional distress as involving "one who by extreme and outrageous conduct intentionally or recklessly causes serious emotional distress to another." The Ohio Supreme Court has identified three elements of an intentional infliction of emotional distress claim:

(1) That the defendant intended to cause the plaintiff serious emotional distress,

(2) That the defendant's conduct was extreme and outrageous, and

(3) That the defendant's conduct was the proximate cause of the plaintiff's serious emotional distress

Liability can only be found where conduct is "so outrageous in character, and so extreme in degree, as to go beyond all possible bounds of decency, and to be regarded as atrocious, and utterly intolerable in a civilized community."

## QUESTION:

(3) In response to the defendant's motion to dismiss the plaintiff's Count Three pursuant to Fed.R.Civ.P. 12(b)(6), the federal district court should:

(a) Grant the defendant's motion to dismiss Count Two pursuant to Fed.R.Civ.P. 12(b)(6) only as to the claim of negligent infliction of emotional distress;

(b) Grant the defendant's motion to dismiss Count Two pursuant to Fed.R.Civ.P. 12(b)(6) only as to the claim of intentional infliction of emotional distress;

(c) Grant the defendant's motion to dismiss Count Two pursuant to Fed.R.Civ.P. 12(b)(6) as to both the claims of negligent and intentional infliction of emotional distress;

(d) Deny the defendant's motion to dismiss Count Two pursuant to Fed.R.Civ.P. 12(b)(6) because the plaintiff plausibly pleaded claims for emotional distress;

(e) Deny the defendant's motion to dismiss Count Two pursuant to Fed.R.Civ.P. 12(b)(6) because the plaintiff should be permitted further discovery to develop her emotional distress claims.

\* \* \*

Michael Matysik sued Judd Transportation LLC and Brett Larsen in the federal district court for the Southern District of Indiana for injuries resulting from an accident in which a Judd Transportation truck hit Matysik's automobile. The truck was driven and operated by Judd's employee Larsen. Matysik contended that Larsen suffered from a condition that caused him to fall asleep at the wheel. The plaintiff issued discovery requests to defendant Larsen, seeking the identification of pharmacies at which Larsen filled any prescription, and Larsen's execution of an authorization for release of medical information.

Previously, the defendants moved to quash subpoenas issued to Dr. Paula Robinson, Estill Medical Clinic, and North Toledo Urgent Care, which subpoenas sought Larsen's Department of Transportation (DOT) physical exam files. The motion to quash was denied by the District Court for the Northern District of Indiana. DOT physical examination records for purposes of meeting federal regulatory requirements and not for purposes of diagnosis and treatment are not protected by the physician-patient privilege. However, the privilege extends to other medical records. The judge's opinion noted that the information sought was relevant and discoverable and that the nonparties had already complied with the subpoenas.

The defendants' moved for a protective order against discovery into Brett Larsen's medical history. The defendants' motion for protective order stated that they sought "to claw back any of Larsen's medical records which have already issued. . . ." A "claw back" generally relates to inadvertent disclosure or production of privileged or otherwise protected material. Larsen claimed no personal injury and he did not raised his medical condition or health as a defense.

## QUESTION:

(4)  On the defendant's motion for a protective order against the plaintiff's discovery into Larsen's medical history, the federal district court should:

(a)  Grant the defendant's motion for a protective order against the plaintiff's discovery into Larsen's medical history because granting the discovery request would violate Larsen's privacy rights;

(b)  Grant the defendant's motion for a protective order against the plaintiff's discovery into Larsen's medical history because Larsen had not placed his medical condition in issue;

(c)  Deny the defendant's motion for a protective order against the plaintiff's discovery into Larsen's medical history because Larsen waived the physician-patient privilege by the previous disclosures;

(d)  Deny the defendant's motion for a protective order against the plaintiff's discovery into Larsen's medical history because Larsen's medical condition was at issue;

(e)  Deny the defendant's motion for a protective order against the plaintiff's discovery into Larsen's medical history because the plaintiff had shown good cause for a need for the information.

\* \* \*

Elizabeth Omutiti and Rima Chemali, citizens of Texas, were employed by Macy's as sales associates at its store in Greenspoint Mall in Houston, Texas. Macy's is a New York corporation with its principal place of business in Ohio.

Omutiti was terminated by Macy's. She alleged that after Macy's terminated her employment, its employees told customers that she was terminated for misconduct. Omutiti alleged that, while employed at Macy's, she complained about age and national origin discrimination against her, and about mold in the building creating an unsafe work environment.

Chemali alleged the when she returned to work following surgery, she was required to perform heavy duty tasks such as scrubbing the floor and lifting heavy objects. Chemali alleged that she was sexually harassed by her manager, that Macy's stopped paying her medical bills incurred in connection with an on-the-job injury to her back, and that Macy's terminated her employment.

Omutiti and Chemali filed a lawsuit against Macy's in Texas state court. In the original petition, Omutiti asserted causes of action for false imprisonment, intentional infliction of emotional distress, defamation, defamation per se, and violation of the Fair Labor Standards Act (FLSA) and the Texas Labor Code. Chemali asserted causes of action for false imprisonment and intentional infliction of emotional distress. The plaintiffs sought monetary relief, including exemplary damages. Specifically, Chemali sought to recover up to $200,000.00, and Omutiti sought to recover over $200,000.00, but less than $1,000,000.00. In their amended petition, filed in Texas state court, the plaintiffs asserted the same causes of action, including Omutiti's FLSA claim, and requested the same amounts of monetary relief.

Macy's filed a timely notice of removal in the federal district court for the Southern District of Texas. Macy's asserted that the court had subject matter jurisdiction based both on federal question and on diversity of citizenship. The plaintiffs filed their motion for remand, to which they attached a second amended petition. The unfiled second amended petition did not contain the FLSA claim, and each plaintiff stated that she was seeking $74,899.00 in damages. The plaintiffs continued to seek exemplary damages and attorney's fees. The plaintiffs' argued that they inadvertently included the FLSA claim in their petitions, and that Macy's was a Texas corporation because it did business in Texas at several stores located in Houston, Dallas, San Antonio, and Austin.

**QUESTION:**

(5) On the plaintiff's petition to remand the case back to Texas state court, the federal district court should:

(a) Grant the plaintiff's petition to remand the case back to Texas state court because there is no federal question jurisdiction without the FSLA claim;

(b) Grant the plaintiff's petition to remand the case back to Texas state court because there is no valid diversity jurisdiction because the amount in controversy is less than $75,000;

(c) Grant the plaintiff's petition to remand the case back to Texas state court because Macy's is a citizen of Texas because it conducts systematic and continuous business within the state;

(d) Deny the plaintiff's petition to remand the case back to Texas state court because the court has both valid federal question and diversity jurisdiction;

(e) Deny the plaintiff's petition to remand the case back to Texas state court because the FSLA raises issues of substantial federal interest for which federal courts desire to provide uniform interpretation.

\* \* \*

Paul Jones financed the purchase of a home at 572 Park Street in Stoughton, Massachusetts, by executing a promissory note in exchange for a loan from Optima Mortgage Corporation. The note was secured by a mortgage to Mortgage Electronic Registration System, Inc., as nominee for Optima and its successors and assigns. The mortgage was later assigned to the Bank of New York, as trustee, and the plaintiff defaulted on the loan. The Bank of New York foreclosed on the property. BANA, as the mortgage servicer, was the Bank of New York's agent with regard to the mortgage at issue.

Jones unsuccessfully sued Bank of New York in Massachusetts state court, challenging the assignment and foreclosure in state court. In his state court action, Jones contested the foreclosure sale on the theory that the assignment of his mortgage to Bank of New York was invalid, rendering the foreclosure improper. The Superior Court granted summary judgment for the Bank of New York, concluding that Jones's argument failed as a matter of law. That judgment was affirmed on appeal. Despite the foreclosure sale, the plaintiff continued to reside at the property.

Jones then brought a lawsuit in federal district court for Massachusetts. In his first federal action, the plaintiff sued Bank of New York and BANA, among others, challenging the assignment of the mortgage, the foreclosure sale, and debt collection practices. The plaintiff brought causes of action under the Fair Debt Collection Practices Act (FDCPA), the Real Estate Settlement Procedures Act (RESPA), the Truth in Lending Act (TILA), and state unfair or deceptive practices laws, as well as a claim against BANA alone for violations of the FCRA. The district court dismissed Jones's federal claims under theories of collateral estoppel, failure to state a claim, time bar, and lack of jurisdiction. The plaintiff's appeal of that decision to the First Circuit remained pending.

The plaintiff then filed a second federal lawsuit against numerous defendants including BANA. In his first amended complaint, the plaintiff accused BANA of violating the Fair Debt Collection Practices Act, the Telephone Communications Act, the Massachusetts Debt Collection Regulation Act, and the Fair Credit Reporting Act by its conduct in attempting to collect the balance due on the defaulted loan, and in reporting the default and foreclosure to consumer reporting agencies. In his amended complaint, the plaintiff based his claims on the premise that Bank of New York lacked the authority to foreclose, and that the debt he allegedly owed BANA was "nonexistent." His entire claim under the FCRA was based on the premise that the foreclosure was invalid.

In Jones's second federal lawsuit, BANA filed a motion to dismiss the plaintiff's first amended complaint pursuant to Fed.R.Civ.P. 12(b)(6), arguing that because of the rulings that courts made in his previous state and federal lawsuits, Jones' claims were barred by the doctrine of res judicata.

Massachusetts res judicata law makes a valid, final judgment conclusive on the parties and their privies, and prevents relitigation of all matters that were or could have been adjudicated in the action. In Massachusetts, res judicata requires three elements: (1) the identity or privity of the parties to the present and prior actions, (2) identity of the cause of action, and (3) prior final judgment on the merits.

**QUESTION:**

(6) With regard to the defendant BANA's motion to dismiss pursuant to Fed.R.Civ.P. 12(b)(6) based on res judicata, the federal district court should:

   (a) Grant the defendant BANA's motion to dismiss based on res judicata because the second federal action shared a common nucleus of common facts with the state and first federal action;

   (b) Grant the defendant BANA's motion to dismiss based on res judicata because the plaintiff Jones's second federal complaint was frivolous;

   (c) Deny the defendant BANA's motion to dismiss based on res judicata because the parties to the state and federal actions were not in privity;

   (d) Deny the defendant BANA's motion to dismiss based on res judicata because Jones's judgment in the first federal action was still on appeal when he filed his second federal action;

   (e) Deny the defendant BANA's motion to dismiss based on res judicata because Jones raised different claims and theories in his various lawsuits.

* * *

Darren Handy initiated an action in the federal district court for the Eastern District of California this action by filing a class action complaint challenging the defendant's Logmein, Inc.'s misleading business practices that allegedly caused the plaintiff damages. The plaintiff stated that he purchased an application called Ignition from the defendant for $29.99. According to the plaintiff, the defendant advertised Ignition as "One app to control all your information," manage files, expand an iPad's possibilities, and "to be more productive." The plaintiff alleged the advertising explained: "With one touch, you can directly control all of your computers from your iPad or iPhone. It's anywhere, anytime access to everything on your PC or Mac—all your files, applications and desktops—right at your fingertips."

Handy alleged that the "Defendant abruptly informed consumers . . . that consumers would no longer be able to utilize Ignition the functions for which consumers previously paid $29.99. The plaintiff alleged that the defendant stated that customers who "desired to continue using Ignition were required to purchase an account-level subscription of LogMeIn Pro," which ranged in an annual cost from $99.00 for an individual to $449.00 for small businesses. The plaintiff asserted that when induced to purchase Ignition, the "Defendant did not inform Plaintiff that additional fees beyond the $29.99 already paid to download the app would ever be required to continue usage of Ignition." The plaintiff alleged that he could "no longer utilize Defendant's app without paying an undisclosed fee now required by Defendant." Based upon these allegations, the plaintiff asserted that the defendant was liable for violations of California Business & Professions Code Section 17200, which prohibits unfair, unlawful, and fraudulent business practices.

The defendant waived service of the complaint on December 1, 2014. The defendant then served the plaintiff with a draft of the motion for sanctions on January 9, 2015, pursuant to Rule 11(c)(2) of the Federal Rules of Civil Procedure. The defendant filed the motion with the court, as well as a motion to dismiss the complaint, on January 30, 2015. The plaintiff filed a first amended complaint on February 17, 2015. Accordingly, the defendant withdrew the motion to dismiss. However, the amended pleading, which was filed beyond the safe harbor period, did not render the motions for Rule 11 sanctions moot.

The defendant argued that the plaintiff's initial complaint lacked any objective factual basis. According to the defendant, the plaintiff's entire theory of liability rested upon the demonstrably false factual allegation that users who purchased the App no longer had access to it without paying an additional subscription fee. The defendant maintained that, contrary to the plaintiff's allegations, all App users still had full access to the App without paying any additional subscription fees. The defendant asserted that the subscription fee applied to LogMeIn's separate and distinct premium service, LogMeIn Pro.

The defendant further argued that the plaintiff's counsel failed to make a reasonable inquiry into the relevant facts prior to filing suit. The defendant asserted that it appeared that the plaintiff relied entirely upon a blog posted by LogMeIn on January 21, 2014, which merely provided notice of upcoming changes to LogMeIn's suite of products, namely LogMeIn Pro, and alerted users to potential future developments, the details of which would be communicated to users in future messages. The defendant contended that even the most cursory investigation by the plaintiff at any point in time prior to the filing of the complaint would have revealed that users could still access the App without paying any additional subscription fees.

The plaintiff's counsel, Matthew Loker, reported that he spoke extensively with the plaintiff prior to filing the action, and the plaintiff informed Loker that the plaintiff was no longer able to use the defendant's App despite paying $29.99 for the App. Loker asserted that he also conducted research regarding the defendant's App by visiting the defendant's website and reading online forums regarding the App. Loker reviewed the "FAQ about Changes to LogMeIn Free" prepared by the defendant, which stated in relevant part:

**Q:  How do I continue using remote access?**

**A:**  To continue using remote access, you will need to purchase an account-level subscription of LogMeIn Pro that meets your needs based on the number of computers you want to access. Log in at LogMeIn.com to see pricing details and a link to purchase.

**Q:  What happens if I do not purchase an account-level subscription of LogMeIn Pro?**

**A:**  Once your 7-day grace period is over, you will no longer be able to remotely access your Free-enabled computers. In order to access them, you will need to purchase an account-level subscription of LogMeIn Pro and choose a package that covers all the computers you want to access.

In addition, the plaintiff gave Mr. Loker a screenshot after attempting to login to the App which stated:

**You no longer have access to your computers.**

In order to continue using remote access, you'll need to purchase an account subscription of LogMeIn Pro. But you can still take advantage of discounted introductory pricing, with packages starting at **$49/year for two computers.**

Notably, this language was not restricted only to remote access from a non-mobile device and Loker declared that it was provided by the plaintiff as to the Ignition App.

Further, Loker asserted that before filing the original pleading he "found thousands of complaints by consumers on online forums." Loker determined "consumers were . . . quite dissatisfied with the forced migration and the effect it had on their ability to meaningfully utilize the Ignition App." Based upon his review of the websites and the screenshot provided by the plaintiff, Loker concluded the "pre-filing research established a violation of Cal. Bus. & Prof.Code § 17200."

**QUESTION:**

(7)  With regard to the defendant's motion asking the court to impose sanctions on the plaintiff and his attorney pursuant to Fed.R.Civ.P. 11(c), the federal district court should:

(a)  Grant the motion to impose Rule 11 sanctions because attorney Loker relied on his client's rendition of facts;

(b)  Grant the motion to impose Rule 11 sanctions because conducting research of online web pages does not constitute a reasonable inquiry prior to filing a federal lawsuit;

(c)  Grant the motion to impose Rule 11 sanctions because the plaintiff's complaint was patently frivolous;

(d)  Deny the motion to impose Rule 11 sanctions because the attorney's investigation was reasonable under the circumstances;

(e) Deny the motion to impose Rule 11 sanctions because the defendant failed to comply with the requirements of Rule 11 in seeking sanctions.

* * *

Cheese Depot, Inc. and Defendant Sirob Imports, Inc. manufactured and distributed cheese. Cheese Depot sued Sirob Imports in the federal district court for the Northern District of Illinois. Cheese Depot contended that Sirob was liable for money damages based on Sirob's alleged breach of contract for the sale of property in Romania.

Cheese Depot was an Illinois citizen and Sirob was a citizen of New York. Cheese Depot entered into an agreement to sell or otherwise transfer ownership of certain real estate and equipment located in Romania to Sirob. The Chicago agreement was negotiated in Chicago, executed in Chicago, and that payments were sent to Chicago, The parties' agreement also governed the sale of certain inventory located within the Romanian property. The Chicago agreement provided, in full, as follows:

> This agreement, made in Chicago, Illinois, July 24, 2007, is between Nick Boboris and John Livadatis. In this agreement Nick Boboris, President, DBA Sirob Imports, 21 Gear Avenue, Lindenhurst, NY 11757, is referred to as NB. John Livaditis, Director, DBA Lacto Baneasa, Cheese Factory, 16 E. Old Willow Road, Prospect Heights, IL, 60070, who has the power to enter into contracts on behalf of Cheese Factory, is referred to as JL.
>
> JL agrees to sell to NB 75% of the Lacto Baneasa building and equipment for $810,000.00 with a $10,000.00 down payment on signing of the contract. The balance is to be paid within 8 years with 7% interest. Interest only payment will start on January 1, 2008. The principal balance will be reduced by $30,000.00 annually by December 31st each with the balance due on September 1, 2015, or sooner.
>
> INVENTORY:
>
> NB will buy the inventory of the 2007 season; estimated amount is 85,000 kg of Feta and 5,000 kg of Hard Cheese. After he checks the quality at the factory, he will make a commitment to buy it or not to buy. Also all the new plastic containers ordered for the season 2008 will pay cost. The price of the Feta will be $3.85 per kg. plus shipping costs. The price of the Hard Cheese will be $4.85 per kg. plus shipping costs. The terms for the inventory will be 120 days, paying weekly, as he collects money for sales.
>
> SIROB IMPORTS, INC.
> Accepted by:
> _____ /s/ _____
> Nick Boboris, President

CHEESE FACTORY
Accepted by:
_____ /s/ _____
John Livaditis

Cheese Depot alleged that it transferred the property to Sirob's designated agent in Romania in 2007. After the transfer agreement was finalized, Sirob timely made its initial $10,000 payment to Cheese Depot. In 2008, Sirob complied with the terms of the Chicago agreement by making all interest payments to Cheese Depot in the amount of $56,000 and by reducing the principal balance by the agreed-upon amount of $30,000. Sirob fulfilled its obligations under the agreement again in 2009, but made an incomplete payment in 2010. There were no payments at all in 2011, and another incomplete payment in 2012. The payments stopped entirely after 2012. Cheese Depot made multiple demands upon Sirob to repay the amounts due and overdue, but Sirob did not complied. As of April 30, 2015, Sirob owed to Cheese Depot $725,414.08 in unpaid principal balance, and $226,000 in past due interest.

Sirob sought to dismiss the original complaint filed by Cheese Depot on the basis that, after the parties signed the Chicago agreement, Nick Boboris (Sirob's President) and John Livaditis (Cheese Depot's owner), in their individual capacities, executed a contract governing the sale of the Romanian property in Romania and that the Romanian agreement, not the Chicago agreement, governed the sale of the property at issue. Sirob argued that Cheese Depot's complaint failed to state a claim since the Chicago agreement was only a letter of intent and not the contract at issue. Sirob further argued that venue in this district was improper as Boboris, who signed the Romanian agreement in his individual capacity, was the proper defendant and that, since Boboris was a New York Citizen, Illinois he had no connection to the Romanian agreement.

This court, in denying Sirob's original motion to dismiss, decided that Cheese Depot's interpretation that the Chicago agreement reflected the parties' intent to transfer the land to Sirob and that the Romanian agreement merely set forth when Sirob's payment obligations would begin was plausible. After Sirob's motion to dismiss Cheese Depot's original complaint was denied, Sirob filed a motion for more definite statement. Sirob sought clarification regarding whether Cheese Depot was seeking damages under the Chicago agreement pertaining to the sale of the Romanian property or the sale of the inventory contained therein. Cheese Depot filed its amended complaint and made clear that it was seeking damages pursuant to a breach of the Chicago agreement for non-payment for the transfer of the Romanian property.

In response to the amended complaint, Sirob filed a motion to dismiss for improper venue pursuant to Fed.R.Civ.P. 12(b)(3).

**QUESTION:**

(8) On the defendant Sirob's motion to dismiss for improper venue pursuant to Fed.R.Civ.P. 12(b)(3), the federal district court should:

    (a) Grant the defendant's motion to dismiss for improper venue pursuant to Fed.R.Civ.P. 12(b)(3) because the property at issue was in Romania;

    (b) Grant the defendant's motion to dismiss for improper venue pursuant to Fed.R.Civ.P. 12(b)(3) because the equipment and cheese inventory at issue was in Romania;

    (c) Grant the defendant's motion to dismiss for improper venue pursuant to Fed.R.Civ.P. 12(b)(3) because the Romanian contract governed the sale;

    (d) Deny the defendant's motion to dismiss for improper venue pursuant to Fed.R.Civ.P. 12(b)(3) because Illinois can assert personal jurisdiction over the non-resident defendant;

    (e) Deny the defendant's motion to dismiss for improper venue pursuant to Fed.R.Civ.P. 12(b)(3) because the events giving rise to the litigation occurred in Chicago.

\* \* \*

In the same litigation, after the filing his Rule 12(b)(3) motion, the defendant Sirob then also sought to dismiss Cheese Depot's amended complaint pursuant to Rule 12(b)(6), arguing that Cheese Depot was not the proper party to enforce the Chicago agreement. Sirob argued that the Chicago agreement was entered into by Nick Boboris and Nick Livaditis on behalf of an entity called "Cheese Factory." Cheese Depot argued that Federal Rule of Civil Procedure 12(g) barred Sirob from presenting this defense as Sirob failed to raise it in its original motion to dismiss.

**QUESTION:**

(9) On the defendant Sirob's Fed.R.Civ.P. 12(b)(6) motion to dismiss the plaintiff's complaint, the federal district court should:

    (a) Grant the defendant's motion to dismiss pursuant to Fed.R.Civ.P. 12(b)(6) because the plaintiff's pleading fails to satisfy the pleading standards of *Twombly* and *Iqbal*;

    (b) Grant the defendant's motion to dismiss pursuant to Fed.R.Civ.P. 12(b)(6) because the "Cheese Factory" is not a proper party;

    (c) Deny the defendant's motion to dismiss pursuant to Fed.R.Civ.P. 12(b)(6) because the defendant failed to consolidate all his Rule 12 motions;

    (d) Deny the defendant's motion to dismiss pursuant to Fed.R.Civ.P. 12(b)(6) because this rule is not the appropriate basis for challenging a plaintiff's misnomer;

(e)   Deny the defendant's motion to dismiss pursuant to Fed.R.Civ.P. 12(b)(6) because granting the motion would violate the plaintiff's right to a trial by jury.

* * *

Dr. Dawn B. McLin was an associate professor at Jackson State University (JSU). She filed a lawsuit against the university in the federal district court for the Southern District of Mississippi. She originally contended that JSU discriminated against her based on race and gender. But following the court's ruling on JSU's motion to dismiss, the only remaining claim was for Title VII gender discrimination. More particularly, McLin contended that JSU promoted a male counterpart, Dr. Bryman Williams, to be the Director of Clinical Training Ph.D. Program without posting the position. McLin insisted that she should have received the appointment. JSU sought summary judgment on the failure-to-promote claim asserting that it was undisputed that the position was advertised, McLin knew about it, and she never applied.

Title VII of the Civil Rights Act of 1964 prohibits discrimination based on gender. Generally speaking, plaintiffs seeking recovery under a failure-to-promote claim must demonstrate that (1) she was a member of a protected class; (2) she sought and was qualified for an available employment position; (3) she was rejected for that position; and (4) the employer continued to seek applicants with the plaintiff's qualifications.

McLin originally contended that JSU did not post the position of the Director of Clinical Training Ph.D. program before selecting Dr. Williams. On that basis that the court allowed the claim to survive JSU's motion to dismiss. JSU subsequently submitted competent record evidence that it had advertised the position, McLin was aware of it, and she did not apply. McLin essentially conceded these facts in her response to the summary judgment motion and supporting affidavit. But she raised two arguments to avoid summary judgment. First, she contended that she did not apply for the disputed position because it would have been futile. Second, she sought additional discovery.

In the Fifth Circuit, a plaintiff need not prove she applied for the position if doing so would have been a "futile gesture." McLin contended that she was deterred from applying based on JSU's history of systemically denying employment opportunities to women. In her original *and* amended complaints, McLin premised her claim on the assertion that JSU never posted the disputed position. Faced with evidence to the contrary in JSU's summary-judgment motion, McLin pivoted to the futility claim.

Citing Fed.R.Civ.P. 56(d), McLin also contended that "if allowed to conduct discovery, she can establish a *prima facie* case," without explaining the discovery she sought or how it would create a genuine fact issue. McLin asserted that she "should be allowed to conduct discovery and complete the presentation of her case against JSU's motion for summary judgment."

QUESTION:

(10) On the defendant JSU's motion for summary judgment on the plaintiff's gender discrimination claim, pursuant to Fed.R.Civ.P. 56, the federal district court should:

(a) Grant the defendant JSU's motion for summary judgment pursuant to Fed.R.Civ.P. 56 because there is no genuine issue of material fact and in its discretion the court can deny the plaintiff further discovery under Fed.R.Civ.P. 56(d);

(b) Grant the defendant JSU's motion for summary judgment pursuant to Fed.R.Civ.P. 56 because the plaintiff's claim of gender discrimination is frivolous;

(c) Deny the defendant JSU's motion for summary judgment pursuant to Fed.R.Civ.P. 56 because there is a genuine issue of material fact whether the university's failure to promote McLin was based on gender;

(d) Deny the defendant JSU's motion for summary judgment pursuant to Fed.R.Civ.P. 56 because there was a genuine issue of material fact whether McLin's attempt to apply for the position would have been futile;

(e) Deny the defendant JSU's motion for summary judgment pursuant to Fed.R.Civ.P. 56 because the plaintiff McLin is entitled to additional discovery under Fed.R.Civ.P. 56(d).

\* \* \*

Ned Tolliver, a police officer employed by the City of New Roads for approximately 12 years, filed a petition for declaratory judgment and injunctive relief, compensation and damages in the 18th Judicial District Court for the Parish of Pointe Coupee, Louisiana, naming as defendants the City of New Roads, Kevin McDonald, and Robert Myer. The plaintiff alleged that he attended a monthly meeting of the New Roads Police Department and was accused by another officer, Shane Fabre, of being intoxicated. The plaintiff alleged that he was ordered to attend a meeting at the chief's office in which he was told that he was being terminated for spreading a rumor that Mr. Fabre was having an affair with a newly hired female officer and for uttering disparaging remarks about him. The plaintiff alleged that he was then placed on suspension "per an inapplicable city grievance procedure."

The plaintiff's state court petition alleged five causes of action: (1) recovery of unpaid wages and accrued benefits pursuant to the Louisiana Wage Payment Act (LWPA); (2) a declaration that the termination was an absolute nullity pursuant to the Police Officers Bill of Rights (POBR); (3) injunctive relief for reinstatement of his employment; (4) damages under the Louisiana Civil Code; and (5) declaratory, injunctive, and monetary recovery pursuant to 42 U.S.C. § 1983 based on the alleged deliberate indifference and reckless disregard of the defendants for the plaintiff's constitutional rights under the Fourteenth Amendment.

The defendants removed the action to federal court for the Eastern District of Louisiana on the basis of federal question jurisdiction pursuant to 28 U.S.C. § 1331. More specifically, the defendants asserted that the plaintiff has alleged claims that arise under federal law, "including claims that defendants engaged in conduct in violation of the Fourteenth Amendment of the United States Constitution, and the Civil Rights Act, 42 U.S.C. §§ 1983–1988." The defendants further asserted that the court had supplemental jurisdiction over the plaintiff's state law claims pursuant to 28 U.S.C. § 1367.

The plaintiff filed a motion to remand, which sought remand of the entire action or, in the alternative, for the court to decline to exercise supplemental jurisdiction over the state law claims.

In support of remand, the plaintiff did not dispute that the court had federal question jurisdiction pursuant to 28 U.S.C. § 1331 over the plaintiff's cause of action under 42 U.S.C. § 1983 or that the court could exercise supplemental jurisdiction over the plaintiff's state law claims pursuant to 28 U.S.C. § 1367. The plaintiff, however, argued that he was entitled to expedited adjudication of his claims under Louisiana law, and the exercise of jurisdiction by the federal court over all of his claims would substantially prejudice him in violation of his rights under state law. The plaintiff further argued that there is a "substantial likelihood that consideration of the constitutional question may be avoided under the procedures afforded by Louisiana law" and remand of the action would alleviate substantial prejudice to him "as well as serve the interests of judicial efficiency and economy." The plaintiff did not, however, argue that his claims made pursuant to Louisiana law raised any novel or complex issues of state law or substantially predominated over the Section 1983 claims.

In opposition, the defendants argued that the action was properly removed and there was no basis for remand. First, the defendants argued that there is no basis for severing and remanding the state law claims pursuant to 28 U.S.C. § 1441(c). Second, the defendants contended that the plaintiff's arguments did not provide good grounds for declining supplemental jurisdiction pursuant to 28 U.S.C. § 1367 because his LWPA claim was premature as he was on suspension and not terminated, the court could award the plaintiff the relief he sought if warranted, the exercise of jurisdiction would not violate the plaintiff's rights under the Louisiana constitution, and the court was well suited to adjudicate the plaintiff's POBR claims. The defendants further argued that the court should exercise supplemental jurisdiction as a matter of judicial efficiency.

**QUESTION:**

(11) On the plaintiff's motion to remand the litigation pursuant to 28 U.S.C. § 1367(c), the federal district court should:

   (a)  Grant the plaintiff's motion to remand the case to state court pursuant to 28 U.S.C. § 1367 because the case involves mostly Louisiana state-based claims;

(b) Grant the plaintiff's motion to remand the case to state court pursuant to 28 U.S.C. § 1367 because of the exceptional circumstances presented by the state claims;

(c) Retain the federal constitutional and civil rights claims, but sever the state claims and remand the state claims to state court;

(d) Deny the plaintiff's motion to remand the case to state court pursuant to 28 U.S.C. § 1367 because the federal court was capable of adjudicating the state-based claims;

(e) Deny the plaintiff's motion to remand the case to state court pursuant to 28 U.S.C. § 1367 because the plaintiff pleaded two federal question claims.

\* \* \*

Northeast Landscape & Masonry Associates, Inc. is a business corporation operating in the County of Westchester, New York. The State of Connecticut Department of Labor (CTDOL) is an executive agency in Connecticut responsible for overseeing matters pertaining to workers and employers operating within the State of Connecticut. Sharon Palmer was the Commissioner of CTDOL, and Mary Toner was a wage enforcement officer employed by CTDOL.

Northeast Landscape was hired to perform general labor and masonry-related work on three projects located in Connecticut. All three projects were "prevailing wage jobs," for which the Rizzo Corporation (Rizzo) served as the general contractor. Toner informed Rizzo of an investigation by CTDOL to determine Northeast Landscape's compliance with Connecticut's prevailing wage law. The letter advised Rizzo "that until . . . CTDOL concluded its investigation, Rizzo should 'withhold any funds or retainage payable to Northeast Landscape in connection with the projects." In response to an email from Northeast Landscape's counsel demanding "the release of any funds" and "an update on the status of CTDOL's investigation," Toner "advised that a preliminary review of records received showed violations" though "no formal investigation had been conducted". She further advised Northeast Landscape that Rizzo would continue to withhold the funds in dispute until CTDOL had completed its investigation but "did not provide any timetable for the conclusion of the investigation."

Northeast Landscape filed a complaint against CTDOL, Palmer, and Toner, in the federal district court for the Southern District of New York, seeking declaratory and injunctive relief. The plaintiff alleged that the defendants had failed to diligently undertake any investigation relating to purported violations of prevailing wage law, thereby depriving the plaintiff of rights and property for an *indeterminable* period of time into the future without any means of recourse. Accordingly, the plaintiff specifically asked the court to order "the immediate release of all funds subject to the CTDOL withholdings," and to issue a "declaratory judgment that the plaintiff fully complied with all Connecticut prevailing wage laws."

The defendants moved to dismiss the complaint pursuant to Federal Rule 12(b)(3) on the basis that none of the requirements for venue in 28 U.S.C. § 1391 were met.

The defendants contended that the prevailing wage investigation and withholding of funds arose out of projects in Danbury, Connecticut, such that "the entirety of the property subject to this action were located in the District of Connecticut." The plaintiff, on the other hand, countered that the plaintiff's time and payroll records were kept in New York and those record-keeping practices and the information contained in the plaintiff's records were the root of the controversy. The plaintiff also alleged that the economic effect of the failure to be paid was felt by it in New York.

**QUESTION:**

(12) On the defendant's motion to dismiss for improper venue pursuant to Fed.R.Civ.P. 12(b)(3), the federal district court in the Southern District of New York should:

(a) Grant the defendant's motion to dismiss the case from the Southern District of New York because all the defendants are located in Connecticut;

(b) Grant the defendant's motion to dismiss because the federal court in Connecticut had personal jurisdiction over all the defendants;

(c) Grant the defendant's motion because venue in the Southern District of New York is improper, but transfer the case to Connecticut pursuant to 28 U.S.C. § 1406(a);

(d) Deny the defendant's motion to dismiss because the economic effects of the defendant's conduct were felt by the plaintiff in New York;

(e) Deny the defendant's motion to dismiss in deference to the plaintiff's choice of forum.

*    *    *

Steven Peterson filed an action in the Iowa state district court for Worth County. His state court petition included claims brought under state and federal law based on allegations of discrimination and retaliation. The defendants include his former employer, Martin Marietta Materials, Inc. (MMM), and two individuals who were alleged to have been managerial employees of MMM. The defendants filed a notice of removal to the federal district court for the Northern District of Iowa, and then filed an answer in which they denied liability to Peterson and raised various defenses.

Peterson served his initial disclosures on the defendants. His description of the documents or other evidentiary materials in his possession, custody, or control that he might use to support his claims included the following:

Recording from coworker from attorney investigating Petition about questions being asked of employees, fear of retaliation or being "black balled" for answering questions, that Plaintiff warned the water pump area was a safety hazard, that the accident occurred, and that then management cleaned it up, took pictures and then fired Plaintiff. ("Voicemail Message")

MMM later served interrogatories on Peterson, including Interrogatory No. 24, which read as follows:

Identify each Document and tangible item requested in the document request not produced in response thereto, including the date, author, addressee(s), all recipient(s), and subject matter of the Document and tangible item and the basis for withholding the Document and tangible item.

Peterson's initial answer stated:

A voicemail message from a current employee is being withheld as attorney work product and also based on the fear of employee's retaliation.

Peterson later supplemented his answer to add the following statement:

The message left by an employee of Martin Marietta was created in anticipation of litigation. Litigation was already pending and he understood that the message would likely be transmitted to Plaintiff's counsel and used by the Plaintiff and/or his counsel in preparation for litigation and/or trial.

MMM also served document requests that sought production of the Voicemail Message. Peterson objected on grounds that he "has determined that the recording from a co-worker constituted the Plaintiff's work-product and disclosure to the defendants would risk retaliation of the coworker."

The counsel for MMM then made informal attempts to resolve the situation by asking Peterson's counsel to reconsider the refusal to produce the Voicemail Message. MMM filed a motion to compel disclosure of the Voicemail Message after those efforts were unsuccessful.

**QUESTION:**

(13) On the defendant MMM's motion to compel disclosure of the Voicemail Message from the plaintiff, the federal district court should:

   (a)   Grant the defendant MMM's motion to compel disclosure of the Voicemail Message from the plaintiff because MMM has demonstrated a need for the material;

   (b)   Grant the defendant MMM's motion to compel disclosure of the Voicemail Message from the plaintiff because the Voicemail Message is not ordinary work product;

   (c)   Deny the defendant MMM's motion to compel disclosure of the Voicemail Message from the plaintiff because the Voicemail Message is protected opinion work product;

(d) Deny the defendant MMM's motion to compel disclosure of the Voicemail Message from the plaintiff because disclosure would violate the plaintiff's constitutional privacy rights;

(e) Deny the defendant MMM's motion to compel disclosure of the Voicemail Message from the plaintiff because disclosure might cause harm to a non-party.

\* \* \*

In the same litigation, the plaintiff Peterson alternatively argued that he wished to withhold disclosure of the Voicemail Message because its disclosure to MMM would create a risk that MMM would retaliate against the employee who left the message. Therefore, Peterson requested entry of a protective order pursuant to Fed.R.Civ.P. 26(c)(1) to protect that employee from annoyance, embarrassment, and oppression.

**QUESTION:**

(14) On the plaintiff Peterson's request for entry of a protective order pursuant to Fed.R.Civ.P. 26(c)(1), the federal district court should:

(a) Grant the plaintiff's motion for a protective order pursuant to Fed.R.Civ.P. 26(c)(1) because the plaintiff has shown good cause for issuance of a protective order;

(b) Grant the plaintiff's motion for a protective order pursuant to Fed.R.Civ.P. 26(c)(1) because a non-party to the litigation should be protected from harm through the discovery process;

(c) Grant the plaintiff's motion for a protective order pursuant to Fed.R.Civ.P. 26(c)(1) because the defendant MMM's discovery request violates the privacy rights of a non-party to the litigation;

(d) Deny the plaintiff's motion for a protective order pursuant to Fed.R.Civ.P. 26(c)(1) because the plaintiff's claim of retaliation against an unnamed employee is speculative;

(e) Deny the plaintiff's motion for a protective order pursuant to Fed.R.Civ.P. 26(c)(1) because the non-party did not request the protective order.

\* \* \*

J & J Sports Productions, Inc., owned the exclusive rights to distribute "The Clash in Cotai", a boxing match between Manny Pacquiao and Brandon Rios. On November 23, 2014, the fight was broadcast across the United States. J & J Sports filed a lawsuit in the federal district court for the Southern District of California against Jose Olivo and Juan Martinez, both individually and doing business as Club Caribe, and other defendants. In the complaint, the plaintiff alleged and identified Martinez and Olivo as the owners on the liquor license issued to Club Caribe. The plaintiff alleged that the defendants knowingly intercepted and showed the fight without the plaintiff's permission, in violation of the Telecommunications Act of 1996, the Cable Television

Consumer Protection and Competition Act of 1992 and the California Business and Professional Code. The plaintiff also alleged a common law claim of conversion. The defendants denied all allegations and raised fifteen enumerated affirmative defenses.

The plaintiff brought a motion to strike the defendants' answers and affirmative. The plaintiff's motion to strike argued both that the defendants' answers (*i.e.,* responses to the allegations enumerated in the complaint) were invalid, and the defendants' affirmative defenses were not legally sufficient.

The plaintiff's complaint contained forty-eight allegations and included four separate counts. The first nineteen allegations addressed jurisdiction and the parties to the matter, as well as other allegations general to all counts. Beginning with the twentieth allegation, the complaint was broken into four counts, with all preceding allegations reincorporated into each count. In their answer to the complaint, the defendants listed the four counts but merely stated that "Defendant denies each and every allegation of the complaint" by means of response to each of the counts.

## QUESTION:

(15) On the plaintiff's motion to strike the defendant's answers to its complaint, the federal district court should:

    (a)  Grant the plaintiff's motion to strike the defendant's answers to its complaint because the federal rules do not permit general denials;

    (b)  Grant the plaintiff's motion to strike the defendant's answers to its complaint because the defendant has not complied with Fed.R.Civ.P. 11;

    (c)  Grant the plaintiff's motion to strike the defendant's answers to its complaint, but grant leave to the defendant to amend its answers;

    (d)  Deny the plaintiff's motion to strike the defendant's answers to its complaint because the federal rules permit a defendant to respond with a general denial;

    (e)  Deny the plaintiff's motion to strike the defendant's answers to its complaint, because a Rule 12(e) motion to strike is not the proper procedural means for challenging a defendant's answers.

\* \* \*

Gabriel Dominguez fell 35 feet from the top of a shelving unit on which he was working and sustained permanent brain injuries. The accident occurred on April 11, 2012. Due to his injuries, he has been unable to communicate since the date of the accident. On April 4, 2014, Dominguez and Silvia Cuevas—Dominguez's wife—filed suit in California state court against defendants Crown Equipment Corporation; DB Industries, LLC; and Does 1–60. Even though the plaintiffs were represented by counsel, the complaint was filed on a pre-made form with boxes to check off and small sections in which to add a narrative. In their complaint, the plaintiffs asserted claims for strict liability, negligence, and breach of warranty. They asserted that Dominguez's injuries were caused by a "truck lift," retractable safety line, and safety belt.

On October 14, 2014, the defendants removed the action to the federal district court for the Central District of California. On March 26, 2015, the plaintiffs moved to amend the complaint and to remand to state court. The plaintiffs sought leave to amend the complaint by: (1) adding Cuevas as Dominguez's guardian *ad litem*; (2) adding several diverse defendants who designed, manufactured, or sold components of the allegedly defective safety equipment; (3) by adding claims against Crown pertaining to the allegedly defective shelving unit/rack; and (4) by joining nondiverse defendants which allegedly "designed, manufactured, fabricated, assembled, tested, marketed, installed, maintained, repaired, and/or sold" the purportedly defective shelving unit/rack. The plaintiffs did not assert any claim against Dominguez's employer, and Dominguez's employer had moved to a new warehouse facility. Thus the facility where Dominguez's accident occurred was apparently no longer in existence (at least not in the condition in which it existed at the time of the accident).

Crown did not object to adding the diverse defendants who were involved in making and selling the allegedly defective safety equipment. Instead, Crown objected to the assertion of a new shelving unit/rack claim against Crown and to the addition of the nondiverse defendants.

The plaintiffs claimed that they did not discover the shelving unit/rack defect until February 20, 2015—when Dominguez's coworker informed them in deposition that a piece of plywood seen in photographs of the accident site wasn't added until after the accident. The coworker told the plaintiffs' counsel that this plywood blocks a roughly 40-foot hole through which Dominguez fell. Crown asserted that the plaintiffs were on notice about the factual basis for the shelving unit/rack claim as of December 2014, and thus unreasonably delayed bringing this claim because they did not move to amend until March 2015. According to Crown, not only was the relevant factual information contained in the OSHA report produced at the end of October 2014, but plaintiffs' counsel interviewed Dominguez's coworker in December 2014 (before the coworker's deposition) and then learned of the relevant facts. Both sides also accused each other of improperly withholding relevant information or evidence during discovery.

In California, there is a two year statute of limitations for personal injury actions. The time for Dominguez to file a claim arising from his April 11, 2012 accident expired in April 2014—roughly one week after Dominguez filed his complaint in state court. The plaintiffs asserted that the claims against the nondiverse defendants related back because the plaintiffs originally named those defendants as Does in the original complaint. California law generally does not allow relation back of an amendment adding a party not named in the original complaint. However, where an amendment does not add a new defendant, but simply corrects a misnomer by which an old defendant was sued, case law recognizes an exception to the general rule of no relation back. Thus, California Civil Procedure Code allows plaintiffs to substitute a fictional

'Doe' defendant in a lawsuit with a named defendant, so long as the plaintiff was unaware of the defendant's true identity at the time the prior complaint was filed. The relation-back doctrine applies even if the plaintiff's ignorance was the result of her own negligence.

The original complaint named Does 1–60, but it did not describe any of the Doe defendants as being a designer, manufacturer, or installer of the shelving unit/rack. The plaintiffs did not assert that the nondiverse proposed defendants received notice within the time for serving the complaint, and there was nothing about allegedly defective safety equipment that would alert them to a defect in their shelving unit/rack. Additionally, though the original complaint describes Dominguez's injuries as being caused by a fall, it did not allege any facts pertaining to a hole or other defect in the shelving unit/rack. The plaintiffs' original complaint did not assert any claim based on the shelving rack/unit.

The plaintiffs also argued that under California Code of Civil Procedure liability for non-economic damages is several. Thus, the failure to include the nondiverse defendants might prejudice the plaintiffs by preventing them from obtaining a full recovery. Additionally, in their motion to amend and remand, the plaintiffs admitted that the nondiverse defendants were named on publicly recorded permit documents.

### QUESTION:

(16) On the plaintiff's motion to amend its complaint to add the non-diverse designers, manufacturers, or installers of the shelving unit/rack, the federal district court should:

(a) Grant the plaintiff's motion to amend its complaint to add the additional non-diverse defendants because Fed.R.Civ.P. 15(c) permits relation-back of the complaint to these parties;

(b) Grant the plaintiff's motion to amend its complaint because the failure to permit the amendment would cause prevent them from recovering non-economic damages;

(c) Grant the plaintiff's motion to amend because its failure to name the additional non-diverse defendants was due to a reasonable mistake;

(d) Deny the plaintiff's motion to amend because the plaintiff because its failure to name the additional non-diverse defendants was due to the plaintiff's own negligence in conducting a proper pre-filing investigation;

(e) Deny the plaintiff's motion to amend its complaint to add the additional non-diverse defendants because the requirements for permitting relation-back under Fed.R.Civ.P. 15 were not satisfied.

\* \* \*

Trielle Lewis filed a complaint in the Superior Court of the State of California for the County of Los Angeles against defendants Chubb & Son Inc., Dale Pringle, and Does 1 through 25, based on an employment dispute. Lewis resigned from Chubb's employment. In her complaint, Lewis sought compensatory damages, damages for emotional distress, and punitive damages. Lewis also sought attorney fees.

Chubb removed that action to the federal district court for the Central District of California on diversity jurisdiction grounds pursuant to 28 U.S.C. §§ 1332 and 1441. Lewis petitioned the court for remand to state court, alleging that the federal court lacked diversity jurisdiction. Lewis's allegations indicated that the plaintiff and defendants were citizens of different states, but the complaint did not set forth a specific amount that she sought in her action.

Chubb contended that the amount in controversy threshold was met because at the time of plaintiff's resignation, plaintiff's hourly rate was $17.00, and calculating plaintiff's "lost income, earnings, and benefits on an annualized basis . . . Plaintiff sought to recover $35,360 per annum, and when considering the date of any trial, "Plaintiff's unmitigated lost wages could amount to at least $88,400." A declaration by a corporate representative filed in support of the defendant's removal petition did not indicate the number of hours a week the plaintiff worked, and whether she worked the same hours every week. The defendant also contended that Lewis's request for emotional distress damages, punitive damages, and attorney fees cumulatively demonstrated that the amount in controversy met and exceeded the jurisdictional threshold for diversity jurisdiction.

**QUESTION:**

(17) On the plaintiff Lewis's petition for remand of her case back to state court for a lack of diversity jurisdiction, the federal district court should:

   (a) Grant the plaintiff's motion to remand the case back to state court because the defendant failed to carry its burden of demonstrating that the amount-in-controversy exceeds $75,000;

   (b) Grant the plaintiff's motion to remand the case back to state court because complete diversity was lacking;

   (c) Deny the plaintiff's motion to remand the case back to state court because the defendant's valuation of the plaintiff's lost wages satisfied the threshold amount-in-controversy requirement;

   (d) Deny the plaintiff's motion to remand the case back to state court because the claims for emotional distress, punitive damages, and attorney fees satisfied the threshold amount-in-controversy requirement;

   (e) Deny the plaintiff's motion to remand the case back to state court because the defendant should not be barred from federal jurisdiction merely because the plaintiff failed to state an amount of damages in her state complaint.

\* \* \*

Guy Anderson owned sixteen mining claims in Arizona's Copper Mountain Mining District. Upon his death, he bequeathed them to his six children, with each child receiving an undivided one-sixth interest in each mining claim. Five of Guy's children wished to sell their interests in the mining claims to Freeport-McMoRan Morenci Inc., the owner of an open-pit copper mine operating on adjacent property. Guy's remaining child, John H. Anderson, did not want to sell his interest in the mining claims. Those who wished to sell formed the entity Cuprite Mine Partners, LLC, which filed a partition action against John in the federal district court of the District of Arizona. In the original complaint, Cuprite prayed alternatively for partition in kind or partition by sale.

Shortly after the complaint was filed, John executed a series of quitclaim deeds in which he granted his interest in twelve of the mining claims to his four children. Each child received three of the mining claims, and John kept four for himself. He apportioned the claims among his children in such a way that no single owner would have an interest in contiguous claims.

After John executed the quitclaim deeds, Cuprite filed an amended complaint to add John's children as additional defendants. Instead of requesting either partition in kind or partition by sale, the amended complaint requested only partition by sale. Cuprite alleged that because the quitclaim deeds diffused John's interest over multiple non-contiguous tracts of land, the property could no longer be realistically partitioned in kind without depreciating its value, and that partition by sale would be more beneficial.

Cuprite moved for summary judgment, arguing that no material facts were in dispute, and that as a matter of law it was entitled to judgment ordering partition by sale. The district court granted summary judgment to Cuprite. The court appointed a commissioner to execute the sale of the property, and directed the commissioner to sell the property on terms "at least as favorable" as the terms outlined in an outstanding offer letter from Freeport. The commissioner was instructed not to sell the property for sixty days following the entry of the order, during which time any party could procure and present a better offer to purchase the property. The commissioner was ordered to proceed with whatever offer he believed to be the most favorable after the sixty-day period had passed.

By the end of the sixty-day period, no one but Freeport had submitted an offer to purchase the property. On April 24, 2014, the district court approved the sale of the property to Freeport. The defendants appealed. On appeal, the defendants asserted that the district court erred by ordering the sale on a summary judgment motion instead of after a trial. The defendants contended that the summary judgment order should be reversed because a trial is required in an Arizona partition action.

Section 12–1218(B) of the Arizona Code contemplates partition of land by sale "on the trial of the action." It is not clear whether this language means that summary judgment is never appropriate in a partition action under Arizona law. Like the federal rules, the Arizona rules of procedure allow for summary judgment when there are no genuine disputes of material fact. Ariz. R. Civ. P.

56(a). The partition statute states that the rules of procedure "which govern all other civil actions shall govern actions for partition when not in conflict with the proceedings provided by this article." Ariz. Rev. Stat. § 12–1224(B). The defendants argued that the "trial" language from section 12–1218(B) conflicted with Rule 56, making it inapplicable to partition actions. In a prior case, the Arizona Supreme Court held that it was appropriate to order partition by sale on summary judgment, but the Court did not specifically addressing the "trial" referenced in section 12–1218(B).

**QUESTION:**

(18) On the defendant's appeal of the federal district court's order of partition by sale of the land based on a summary judgment, the appellate court should:

    (a)  Reverse the district court's summary judgment order of partition by sale because Arizona law applied to require a trial on the issue of a partition by sale of property;

    (b)  Reverse the district court's summary judgment order of partition by sale because the summary judgment order denied the defendants of their jury trial right;

    (c)  Reverse the district court's summary judgment order of partition by sale because an Arizona jury might have found in favor of the defendants, which would have defeated the plaintiffs' attempts to force the sale of the land;

    (d)  Affirm the district court's summary judgment order of partition by sale because Fed.R.Civ.P. 56 applied and the district court legitimately issued the order for the sale;

    (e)  Affirm the district court's summary judgment order of sale because the requirement for a trial in a suit for partition by sale was substantive in nature.

* * *

Cedric Gillespie filed suit against his employer, Charter Communications, and his supervisors Robert Sewell and Richard Sturck, in the federal district court for the Eastern District of Missouri, alleging that he was discriminated against on the basis of his race and his membership in the military. The plaintiff initially filed his petition in state court, stating claims for racial discrimination and retaliation under the Missouri Human Rights Act, and for prejudicial employment actions based on the plaintiff's membership in the military under the Uniformed Services Employment and Reemployment Rights Act. Charter removed the action pursuant to this Court's federal question jurisdiction, under 28 U.S.C. § 1331. In its notice of removal, Charter asserted that the court had supplemental jurisdiction over the plaintiff's state law MHRA claims, pursuant to 28 U.S.C. § 1367.

The parties filed a joint motion for a protective order and the court entered the consent protective order. The protective order permitted parties to mark documents they produce as "confidential" if they had a good faith belief that the documents contained either trade secrets, or proprietary or sensitive business, personal, or financial information. Documents marked as "confidential" could only be disclosed to parties' counsel, agents and employees of Charter, the plaintiff, the court and its staff, relevant witnesses, court reporters employed for the purposes of recording depositions, and the jury.

During discovery, the plaintiff requested information and documents relating to internal complaints filed within Charter, alleging that Charter or any defendant discriminated or retaliated against an employee on the basis of race or membership in the military. Charter identified two documents responsive to the plaintiff's requests. One was a document detailing an anonymous complaint made to Charter's EthicsPoint system, which allows employees to report unethical or illegal conduct they observed. The complaint related to alleged prior racial discrimination by the defendant Robert Sewell. The other document identified by Charter was an internal "Incident Investigation Report," which detailed Charter's investigation of the claims made in the EthicsPoint complaint.

Charter indicated that it would produce these two documents only if the plaintiff agreed to stipulate that the production would not constitute a waiver of Charter's attorney-client or work product privileges, and only if Plaintiff agreed to the documents being produced with an "Attorneys' Eyes Only" designation. Charter claimed that the attorney-client and work product privileges applied to the documents because they were prepared at the direction of Charter's counsel. Charter subsequently communicated to the plaintiff that it sought the "Attorneys' Eyes Only" designation because it was Charter's policy to keep the persons involved in, and the contents of, any EthicsPoint complaint confidential, and that Charter had concerns about maintaining this confidentiality as the plaintiff was currently employed by Charter.

The plaintiff then filed a motion to compel Charter to produce the two documents it identified, without an "Attorneys' Eyes Only" designation. The plaintiff argued that the documents in question were not protected by the attorney-client privilege. The plaintiff cited state and federal cases for the proposition that internal investigative reports are not protected by the attorney-client privilege just because legal counsel was involved in the investigation. The plaintiff argued that Charter's investigation was done in the ordinary course of business and was not prepared for the purpose of seeking legal advice.

Likewise, the plaintiff argues that the documents do not constitute work product protected by Federal Rule of Civil Procedure 26(b)(3), because they were prepared in the ordinary course of business rather than in anticipation of litigation or for trial. The plaintiff also argued that the documents in question did not contain any attorney mental impressions or similar notes. Further, the plaintiff argued that, even if the court found that the documents constituted protected work product, the plaintiff had made the required showing that he has a substantial need for the documents to demonstrate that Charter had a pattern and practice of discrimination, and that the plaintiff could obtain the substantial equivalent of this material through other means.

The plaintiff contended that the subject matter of the EthicsPoint complaint was nearly identical to the plaintiff's claims in the case, and that his need for such relevant information should overcome any alleged work product privilege.

Finally, the plaintiff argued that Charter's designation of the documents as "Attorneys' Eyes Only" was unnecessary, in light of the protective order already entered in this case, and would prejudice the plaintiff's ability to prosecute his claims. Specifically, the plaintiff argued that the "Attorneys' Eyes Only" designation was generally only used in the context of patent, trademark, or copyright infringement cases, to protect a party from inadvertent disclosure of confidential information that would impact the party's commercial competitive advantage. Here, the plaintiff argued that the information at issue was not of the type generally protected by such a designation, and that Charter might instead label the documents "confidential," which would adequately protect them from disclosure or use outside the scope of the present litigation. The plaintiff argued that only allowing his counsel to view these documents would prevent them from conferring about the contents of the documents to prepare for deposition and trial, impairing the plaintiff's ability to prosecute his case.

In response, Charter contended that it is not withholding the documents at issue, since it had agreed to produce them with an "Attorneys' Eyes Only" designation. Charter argued that the incident report was privileged because it was created by Charter's Director of Human Resources at the direction of, and following a process instituted by, Charter's compliance team, which included three in-house attorneys. Charter provided no facts as to the overall size of the compliance team, nor to the composition of its remaining members.

Finally, Charter argued that the "Attorneys' Eyes Only" designation was necessary to protect the confidentiality of both the EthicsPoint complaint and the incident report. If this confidentiality were breached, Charter argued, it would frustrate the purpose of the EthicsPoint reporting program, as employees would no longer feel safe to report violations they encounter. Charter also alleged that it had learned that the plaintiff had discussed the claims in his case with his coworkers, which Charter asserted raised the concern that the plaintiff might have breached the confidentiality required by the protective order.

**QUESTION:**

(19) On the plaintiff's motion to compel production of the two documents without an "Attorney Eyes-Only" designation, contending that the documents are not protected by attorney-client privilege, the federal district court should:

(a) Grant the plaintiff's motion to compel production of the documents because Charter had waived any privilege relating to the documents;

(b) Grant the plaintiff's motion to compel production of the documents because Charter failed to show that the incident report was created to obtain legal advice;

(c) Grant the plaintiff's motion to compel production of the documents because the "Attorney Eyes Only" designation was being used by the defendant to defeat the plaintiff's ability to prepare his case;

(d) Deny the plaintiff's motion to compel production of the documents because the privilege for corporate communications applied;

(e) Deny the plaintiff's motion to compel production of the documents because the plaintiff contravened the court's earlier protective order.

\* \* \*

In response to the plaintiff's motion to compel production of the two documents in this same litigation, the defendant Charter also contended that the documents were protected from disclosure by the attorney-work product doctrine. Charter further explained that the company's EthicsPoint reporting system, and the process of investigating claims made within this system, were part of an ongoing compliance program instituted by Charter. It was undisputed that the incident report contained no opinions or mental impressions of Charter's attorneys and that the documents in question were not prepared in anticipation of litigation, but were rather generated in the ordinary course of Charter's business through its EthicsPoint system.

### QUESTION:

(20) In response to the plaintiff's motion to compel production of the two documents, and in response to the defendant's contention that attorney-work product shielded those documents from production, the federal district court should:

(a) Grant the plaintiff's motion to compel production of the documents because the crime/fraud exception overrode the defendant's work product immunity;

(b) Grant the plaintiff's motion to compel production of the documents because the documents did not constitute attorney-work product subject to immunity;

(c) Deny the plaintiff's motion to compel production of the documents because the documents eventually were reviewed by attorneys;

(d) Deny the plaintiff's motion to compel production of the documents because the documents constituted ordinary work product subject to protection;

(e) Deny the plaintiff's motion to compel production of the documents because disclosure would subvert the defendant's ongoing EthicsPoint compliance program.

\* \* \*

Kathleen Destefano was an Orange County, Florida deputy sheriff and married to Dennis Ela, also a deputy sheriff. Before marrying Destefano, Dennis was married to Theresa Ela. Knowing it to be illegal and in violation of the sheriff's policy, Destefano used her authority as a deputy sheriff to access Ela's personal information contained in law enforcement databases. The plaintiff first learned of Destefano's actions when she made a public records request with the Florida Department of Law Enforcement. When Ela discovered this conduct, she sued Destefano federal district court for the Middle District of Florida, in her individual capacity under the Driver's Privacy Protection Act (DPPA) and 42 U.S.C. § 1983. Ela also sued sheriff Jerry Demings in his official capacity under § 1983.

In her capacity as an officer with the Orange County Sheriff's Office, Destefano had access to databases used by law enforcement agencies, including the Driver and Vehicle Information Database (DAVID), the Florida Crime Information Center database, and the National Crime Information Center database. These databases contain information about individuals, including photographs, addresses, vehicle information, and emergency contacts.

In her amended complaint, the plaintiff sued Destefano under the DPPA (Count I) and 42 U.S.C. § 1983 (Count II); and the sheriff under § 1983 for failure to supervise and train its employees on the proper use of DAVID (Count III).

Congress enacted the DPPA in reaction to the ability of wrongdoers to easily use and distribute drivers' personal information in furtherance of criminal conduct and marketing schemes. In determining remedies available to drivers whose personal information is compromised, "Congress clearly contemplated that in most cases, a defendant who obtained motor vehicle information would put it to some use." The DPPA created a statutory right to privacy that is enforceable under § 1983. It generally provides that except when carrying out an official governmental or law enforcement function "a person who knowingly obtains, discloses or uses personal information, from a motor vehicle record shall be liable to the individual to whom the information pertains." To "obtain" personal information under the DPPA, a defendant need only access and observe the data. Also, each "access" of a person's personal information is a separate "obtainment" and thus an additional violation of the DPPA.

The case proceeded to trial on Counts I, II, and III. At trial, Destefano was contrite. She admitted that she viewed the plaintiff's personal information on the databases without a legitimate law enforcement purpose many times, almost always using DAVID to do so. Destefano admitted that while she was on duty as a law enforcement officer she accessed driver's license databases to view the plaintiff's personal information. She admitted she had "no good explanation" for accessing the plaintiffs personal information, that "it was a mistake," and that she was "sorry." She further admitted that she did not have a legitimate law enforcement purpose for accessing the information. As a result of her conduct, the sheriff suspended Destefano for sixty hours without pay and placed her on disciplinary probation for six months. As additional punishment, the sheriff prohibited Destefano from driving a patrol car to and from her home and from participating in off-duty private employment ordinarily available to sheriff's deputies.

At the conclusion of the plaintiff's case-in-chief, each party moved for judgment as a matter of law pursuant to Federal Rule of Civil Procedure 50(a). The plaintiff and Destefano both moved for judgment as to the DPPA and § 1983 claims against Destefano.

**QUESTION:**

(21) On the plaintiff's motion for judgment as a matter of law against Destefano under Fed.R.Civ.P. 50(a), the district court judge should:

- (a) Grant the plaintiff's motion for a judgment as a matter of law under Fed.R.Civ.P. 50(a) because the plaintiff's evidence demonstrated that she should prevail on her claim;

- (b) Grant the plaintiff's motion for a judgment as a matter of law under Fed.R.Civ.P. 50(a) because of the egregious violation of the DPPA statute;

- (c) Deny the plaintiff's motion for a judgment as a matter of law under Fed.R.Civ.P. 50(a) because there was a genuine issue of material fact that a jury should determine;

- (d) Deny the plaintiff's motion for a judgment as a matter of law under Fed.R.Civ.P. 50(a) because the defendant Destefano should have had the opportunity to present her case-in-rebuttal;

- (e) Deny the plaintiff's motion for a judgment as a matter of law under Fed.R.Civ.P. 50(a) because the court failed to dismiss the case on summary judgment prior to trial.

\* \* \*

In the same case, the plaintiff (in Count III) attempted to hold the sheriff accountable in his official capacity for Destefano's conduct under § 1983 based on inadequate training or supervision. A municipality may only be liable under § 1983 if its policy directly causes a violation. The plaintiff did not claim the sheriff's policy on its face violated federal law or that it directed its employees to do so. To prove that the sheriffs' office caused a violation, a plaintiff must show that the sheriff had in place a policy or custom that amounted to a deliberate indifference to the plaintiff's rights. This requires evidence that the sheriff had notice of a need to train or supervise his employees. The notice requirement can be satisfied by a pattern of similar constitutional violations by untrained employees or through a single prior incident. The plaintiff had to establish that, once the sheriff had notice of a violation, he made a deliberate choice not to train his employees.

At the trial, the plaintiff did not present evidence of a prior violation of the DPPA by a sheriff's employee, or evidence that misuse of law enforcement databases was widespread. One of the sheriff's employees testified that there may have been one or two investigations per year into instances of improper use of DAVID, but he could not recall the specifics of a single such investigation, nor could he identify a single violation of the DPPA on the part of the sheriff's employees. Toni Dow, the terminal agency coordinator in charge of DAVID user management, testified that she was unaware of any sheriff's employee misusing the DAVID system. There was no evidence in the record to the contrary.

There was no evidence that the sheriff made a deliberate choice not to train or supervise his employees. Evidence was presented that the Sheriff ensured that his employees understood that the databases were to be used only for law enforcement purposes. As a condition for use of DAVID, deputies were required to sign an acknowledgment of the Memorandum of Understanding making it clear that DAVID was to be used only for official law enforcement purposes. The acknowledgment also put deputies on notice that unauthorized use could result in criminal and civil liability.

Additionally, deputies were reminded each time they accessed the DAVID database that their use was authorized only for law enforcement purposes. Both the current and former terminal agency coordinators, testified that before each separate access of DAVID, officers were required to enter through the criminal justice information system portal, which prompted the user to agree to use the database solely for law enforcement purposes. If an officer did not register agreement, he or she was denied access to the system. Destefano testified that each time she accessed the plaintiff's personal information she knew she was misusing DAVID in violation of the Sheriff's policy, but she did so anyway.

### QUESTION:

(22) At the conclusion of the plaintiff's case-in-chief at the trial, the defendant sheriff's moved for a judgment as a matter of law under Fed.R.Civ.P. 50(a) on the § 1983 claim against him. On this motion, the federal district judge should:

    (a) Grant the sheriff's motion for a judgment as a matter of law under Fed.R.Civ.P. 50(a) on the § 1983 claim against him because as a municipal employee the sheriff was entitled to immunity from suit;

    (b) Grant the sheriff's motion for a judgment as a matter of law under Fed.R.Civ.P. 50(a) on the § 1983 claim against him because the plaintiff failed to present evidence upon which a reasonable jury could infer that the sheriff had a policy indifferent to rights established by the DPPA and therefore the sheriff was not liable to the plaintiff under § 1983;

    (c) Deny the sheriff's motion for a judgment as a matter of law under Fed.R.Civ.P. 50(a) on the § 1983 claim against him because there was a genuine question whether the plaintiff had presented sufficient evidence that would allow the jury to conclude that there was a direct causal connection between the sheriff's policy and the alleged violation;

(d)  Deny the sheriff's motion for a judgment as a matter of law under Fed.R.Civ.P. 50(a) on the § 1983 claim against him because granting the motion would deny the plaintiff of her right to a jury determination of the sheriff's liability under § 1983;

(e)  Grant the sheriff's motion for a judgment as a matter of law under Fed.R.Civ.P. 50(a) on the § 1983 claim against him because there was testimony of prior misuse of the DAVID databases sufficient to send the case to the jury.

\* \* \*

Dr. Lee R. Turner was a dentist for over twenty years. He obtained a life-insurance policy from Defendant Paul Revere Life Insurance Company (Paul Revere). The life-insurance policy provided coverage for loss due to injury or sickness.

Dr. Turner became ill and was unable to work. Paul Revere began paying disability insurance benefits provided by the policy, but subsequently stopped paying those benefits. Turner appealed Paul Revere's decision to deny his claim, and prevailed; the company agreed to issue back payments. Four days later, Dr. Turner was severely injured in a car accident and hospitalized. At the time of the accident, he was uninsured.

Turner sued Paul Revere in the federal district court for the District of Nevada, claiming that Paul Revere breached his contract and engaged in bad-faith insurance because he could not reinstate his medical or life-insurance policies before the accident on account of Paul Revere's failure to issue the back pay until after the accident occurred. The gravamen of Dr. Turner's complaint was that Paul Revere failed to honor its policy when it should have.

In the litigation, Dr. Turner's attorney filed a motion to compel seeking production of four categories of information: (1) prior testimony/deposition transcripts and/or affidavits from employees who handled the plaintiff's claim; (2) employee training documents from the defendant's training session entitled "Defining the Scope of the Insured's Own or Regular Occupation;" (3) employee performance reviews from employees who handled the plaintiff's claims; and (4) the defendant's corporate ethics manual.

Prior to the plaintiff's motion to compel discovery, Paul Revere had provided the plaintiff with its employee Code of Conduct and a Benefits Center Manual. In its motion to compel, the plaintiff did not argue that good cause existed for expanding the scope of discovery. The defendant Paul Revere opposed the motion to compel discovery.

**QUESTION:**

(23)  On the plaintiff's motion to compel discovery of the four categories of information from the defendant, the federal district court should:

(a)  Grant the plaintiff's motion to compel disclosure of all four categories of information, because the materials sought were in the scope of discovery under Fed.R.Civ.P. 26(b);

(b)  Grant the plaintiff's motion to compel disclosure of all four categories of information, because none of the materials sought were subject to a privilege or immunity;

(c)  Deny the plaintiff's motion to compel disclosure of all four categories of information, because the discovery requests were burdensome;

(d)  Deny the plaintiff's motion to compel disclosure of all four categories of information, because the requests were made for the purpose of harassment;

(e)  Deny the plaintiff's motion to compel disclosure of categories (1), (2), and (4), but grant the motion to compel disclosure of category (3).

* * *

Phillip Stringer filed a lawsuit against defendants Volkswagen Group of America, Inc., Volkswagen AG, and Audi AG in the federal district court for the Southern District of Alabama. The complaint was filed pursuant to the court's jurisdiction under 28 U.S.C. § 1332(c). In his complaint, Stringer alleged that he was a "resident of the state of Alabama." He further alleged that Volkswagen Group of America, Inc. was incorporated in New Jersey and had its principal place of business in Virginia. As to Volkswagen AG and Audi AG, the complaint stated that each of them was "a corporation created and existing pursuant to the laws of the nation of Germany." The plaintiff claimed that the damages sought were "in excess of $75,000 exclusive of interest and costs."

## QUESTION:

(24)  The federal district court judge *sua sponte* questioned whether the court had proper jurisdiction under 28 U.S.C. § 1332(c). In assessing whether the federal court had valid jurisdiction, the court should conclude:

(a)  Federal court jurisdiction was improper because of a lack of complete diversity pursuant to the Supreme Court's complete diversity rule in *Strawbridge v. Curtiss*;

(b)  Federal court jurisdiction was improper because foreign corporate defendants are not subject to federal court jurisdiction;

(c)  Federal court jurisdiction could not be established because, based on the plaintiff's complaint, the court could ascertain the citizenship of the parties;

(d)  Federal court jurisdiction existed because there was diversity of citizenship between the plaintiff and the defendants;

(e)  Federal court jurisdiction existed because the court could exercise pendant party jurisdiction over Volkswagen AG and Audi AG.

* * *

Christiana Trust sued Cyndi L. Staab and Jay R. Staab in the Riverside County Superior Court, California, in an unlawful detainer action. An unlawful detainer action is an action wherein a plaintiff alleges that some party has retained their property without a legal right to do so. After Trust field her complaint, the Staabs then filed a notice of removal to the federal district court for the Central District of California under 28 U.S.C. § 1441, on the basis of federal question jurisdiction. The Staabs asserted that the federal court had jurisdiction under 28 U.S.C. § 1331, because they had a defense under the federal Troubled Asset Relief Program (TARP), 12 U.S.C. § 5201. Trust petitioned the federal court for a remand of her case back to state court.

**QUESTION:**

(25) On the plaintiff's petition for remand of her case back to state court, the federal district court should:

    (a)  Grant the plaintiff's petition for a remand of her case back to state court because the case involves only a single state law claim;

    (b)  Grant the plaintiff's petition for a remand of her case back to state court because the existence of a defense in federal law does not create federal question jurisdiction;

    (c)  Deny the plaintiff's petition for a remand of her case back to state court because the court has supplemental jurisdiction over the defendant's federal defense under TARP;

    (d)  Deny the plaintiff's petition for a remand of her case back to state court because the removal satisfies the well-pleaded complaint rule;

    (e)  Deny the plaintiff's petition for a remand of her case back to state court under 28 U.S.C. § 1441(c).

**END OF EXAM PROBLEMS #3**

# CHAPTER 4
# EXAM #4 PROBLEMS AND QUESTIONS

Janet S. Kellerman and her spouse, Gregory K. Kellerman, commenced an action against Inter-Island Launch d/b/a Prince of Whales Whale Watching (Inter-Island) and Bo J. Garrett in the federal district court for the Western District of Washington (located in Seattle). The plaintiffs claimed that Ms. Kellerman sustained injuries during a whale watching tour that departed from Victoria, British Columbia. The defendants moved to dismiss for improper venue arguing that the plaintiffs signed a release containing a forum selection clause and choice of law provision requiring that any suit arising from the tour be brought in British Columbia. The plaintiffs claimed that they never signed such a release.

The defendants brought a motion pursuant to Fed.R.Civ.P. 12(b)(3) to enforce a forum selection clause that they claim the plaintiffs signed. The plaintiffs purchased tickets for a three-hour whale watching tour on Inter-Island's vessel, the *Countess*. Defendant Garrett, the skipper and guide for the *Countess*, intended to depart from Victoria and return to Victoria with no stops at any other ports. However, the *Countess* made an unanticipated stop at a dock in San Juan County, Washington after Ms. Kellerman sustained injuries. According to the plaintiffs, Ms. Kellerman's injuries occurred after the Garrett turned toward the wake of a large yacht. Once the *Countess* docked in San Juan County, Ms. Kellerman was airlifted to Harborview Medical Center in Seattle and treated for her injuries.

The plaintiffs initiated a tort action against the defendants in the Western District of Washington. However, the defendants argued that the plaintiffs had signed a release, which required that any suit resulting from the whale watching tour be brought in British Columbia. According to the defendants, all guests, including the plaintiffs, were required to review, complete, and sign a "Participant Agreement, Release, and Acknowledgement of Risk." The defendants describe this document as a single-spaced document, printed with twelve-point Times New Roman font on a single 11″ x 17″ sheet that is folded over like a booklet.

The first page of the booklet included the title "Participant Agreement, Release, And Acknowledgement of Risk," the acknowledgment and assumption of risk clauses, and a release of liability clause. The second page of the booklet contained an indemnification clause, an insurance clause, a forum selection clause, a choice of law provision, and a waiver clause. Neither the first nor the second page required a passenger's signature or initials.

The third page of the booklet required passengers to do the following in the order listed: disclose any pre-existing medical conditions; sign their name;

print their name, address and telephone number; date the waiver; and fill out an indemnification section if a participant was under the age of nineteen. The signature block is in the middle of the third page. Unlike pages one and two, the third page had no pagination; nor does it have any carry-over sentences or references to pages one or two.

Inter-Island insisted that it had a policy that required all employees to physically open all pages of the booklet, and to explain to passengers that they should read the entire booklet before signing it. Inter-Island also stated that passengers were permitted to sign the booklet at the front desk or take it and return it before the trip departed.

According to the plaintiffs, the Inter-Island office was crowded and hectic when they arrived for their tour. They contended that they were given a one-page document to sign (later identified as the third page of the booklet) and no one from Inter-Island discussed the one-page document with them other than to tell them to sign it. In addition, the plaintiffs alleged that the document did not contain a release or waiver at the time they signed it.

Ms. Kellerman stated that she signed the document on a desktop surface and Mr. Kellerman stated he signed it on a clipboard. They also claimed that the document took less than one minute to complete. To corroborate their description of the one-page document that they alleged they signed, the plaintiffs offered the declarations of three of the other seven passengers on their tour that day. All of these passengers recalled that they signed a single page document, and that no one explained the document to them.

The plaintiffs contended they were never shown the forum selection clause because it was not included on the one-page document they alleged they signed. The plaintiffs believed they were signing a single page disclosure of medical conditions and contact information (page three of the booklet). The plaintiffs argued that page three of the booklet reasonably appeared to be a stand-alone document because it did not include references to prior pages nor did it have any pagination to indicate it was the third page of a three-page document.

In their reply, the defendants contended that the one-page document signed by the plaintiffs did refer to the booklet's prior pages. More specifically, the defendants noted that the bottom of page three included an indemnification clause for the parents/guardians of children which contained an acronym that was earlier defined on page one of the booklet. Additionally, the defendants insisted that the passengers' decision to complete the waiver quickly should not invalidate the enforceability of the waiver.

**QUESTION:**

(1) On the defendant's motion to dismiss for improper venue under Fed.R.Civ.P. 12(b)(3), the federal district court in Washington should:

    (a) Grant the defendant's motion to dismiss for improper venue under Fed.R.Civ.P. 12(b)(3) because Inter-Island's Participant Agreement contained a valid forum selection clause;

    (b)   Grant the defendant's motion to dismiss for improper venue under Fed.R.Civ.P. 12(b)(3) because Inter-Island's Participant Agreement contained a choice of law provision which should have put the plaintiffs on notice they were subject to suit in British Columbia;

    (c)   Grant the defendant's motion to dismiss for improper venue under Fed.R.Civ.P. 12(b)(3) because the plaintiffs' signatures on the third page of the booklet indicated that they understood and agreed to the entire booklet, including the forum selection clause;

    (d)   Deny the defendant's motion to dismiss for improper venue under Fed.R.Civ.P. 12(b)(3) because the plaintiffs were not bound by the forum selection clause as it was not included on the one-page document they signed and they therefore did not manifest their assent to the clause;

    (e)   Deny the defendant's motion to dismiss for improper venue under Fed.R.Civ.P. 12(b)(3) because Inter-Island's employees did not explain the Participant Agreement to them.

* * *

In the same litigation, the defendants asked the court, in the alternative, to dismiss the case based on the doctrine of *forum non conveniens*.

The parties and the witnesses were located in two countries. The defendants resided in Canada, whereas the plaintiffs resided in the United States. The witnesses resided in various provinces throughout Canada. The cost of flying witnesses for depositions or flying them to trial was relatively the same whether the trial was held in Victoria, British Columbia or Seattle, Washington, given that the two cities are not far from one another. Moreover, there was no indication that there would be unwilling witnesses requiring a court's subpoena power in order to compel testimony.

The defendants argued that the defendants, witnesses, and the evidence were located in British Columbia, making travel to that forum more convenient and less costly. The plaintiffs argued that, as plaintiffs, they had the right to choose the forum within which to bring their case and Washington was no less convenient as a forum than British Columbia. The plaintiffs urged that a judgment secured in the Western District of Washington would be readily enforced in Canada. With respect to the location of evidence, the plaintiffs indicated that the only evidence they intended to present were documents. The defendants raised the possibility that the *Countess* would need to be inspected, but the plaintiffs assured the court that they had no desire to inspect the *Countess*.

The defendants further argued that Washington's interest in resolving the dispute was minimal, the burden on juries would be great, the Western District of Washington had a full docket, and the Washington federal court did not regularly preside over Canadian maritime law. The defendants argued that Canada was an adequate alternative forum because the defendants were amenable to service of process there and the plaintiffs could still pursue their claims under Canadian law. The plaintiffs countered that Canada was not an adequate alternative forum and emphasized that Washington and the people in the Seattle community were interested in resolving tort actions where the alleged accident and treatment occurred in Washington.

**QUESTION:**

(2) For the purpose of this question only, assuming that the court did not enforce Inter-Island's forum selection clause, on the defendant's alternative motion to dismiss the case on the grounds of *forum non conveniens*, the federal district court should:

(a) Grant the defendant's motion to dismiss on the grounds of *forum non conveniens* because the events giving rise to the plaintiff's injuries occurred in Canada;

(b) Grant the defendant's motion to dismiss on the grounds of *forum non conveniens* because Canada was an adequate alternative forum;

(c) Grant the defendant's motion to dismiss on the grounds of *forum non conveniens* because British Columbia was only 180 miles from Seattle;

(d) Deny the defendant's motion to dismiss on the grounds of *forum non conveniens* because the private and public factors weigh in favor of a lawsuit in Seattle;

(e) Deny the defendant's motion to dismiss on the grounds of *forum non conveniens* because courts should favor a plaintiff's choice of forum.

* * *

Virginia Uranium, Inc., Coles Hill, LLC, Bowen Minerals, LLC, and Virginia Energy Resources, Inc., as plaintiffs sued Virginia's Governor, Secretary of Commerce and Trade, Secretary of Natural Resources, and various officials affiliated with the Department of Mines, Minerals, and Energy or the Department of Environmental Quality. The plaintiffs were entities that either owned the land above, or had mining rights to, a large uranium deposit in Pittsylvania County, Virginia. The plaintiffs alleged that the defendants were responsible for implementing a Virginia statute that provided:

> Notwithstanding any other provision of law, permit applications for uranium mining shall not be accepted by any agency of the Commonwealth prior to July 1, 1984, and until a program for permitting uranium mining is established by statute. For the purpose of construing this statute, uranium mining shall be deemed to have a significant effect on the surface.

The plaintiffs filed suit for a declaration that the Atomic Energy Act of 1954 preempted the Virginia statute and for an injunction forbidding the defendants from following requiring them to process applications to mine uranium. The

Office of the Attorney General of Virginia represented the defendants, who moved to dismiss. The plaintiffs moved for summary judgment. The parties fully briefed these motions, either of which could dispose of the suit.

The Dan River Basin Association and the Roanoke River Basin Association, by common counsel from the Southern Environmental Law Center, moved to intervene as parties. The plaintiffs opposed, but the defendants did not.

The basin associations are nonprofit organizations, and their members included Virginia and North Carolina "local governments, non-profit, civic and community organizations, and regional governmental entities," as well as individual citizens. They claimed to have, on their members' behalf, "a clearly defined interest in the preservation and promotion of . . . natural and aquatic resources" that, they asserted, would be harmed by runoff from the plaintiffs' potential uranium-mining site. The basin associations had missions "to protect, preserve, and enhance" these resources, and they did so through various environmental, recreational, and educational activities in their respective regions.

The basin associations claimed that their interests in the litigation differ from the defendants. They added that the plaintiffs' "requested injunctive relief seeks to commandeer state agencies to engage in a permitting process, at which point the interests of the defendants and those of the basin associations may diverge." If made parties, they would move to dismiss on the grounds that the AEA does not preempt the Virginia statute and that injunctive relief would reflect an unconstitutional federal commandeering of the defendants.

Although their respective motions to dismiss oppose injunctive relief, the defendants have not briefed the subject to the same extent, or along the same argument, that the basin associations did. The defendants were diligently and zealously defending against the suit.

**QUESTION:**

(3) On the river basin associations' motion to intervene under Fed.R.Civ.P. 24(a), the federal district court should:

(a) Grant the association's motion to intervene under Fed.R.Civ.P. 24(a) because the associations had a property interest in the litigation;

(b) Grant the association's motion to intervene under Fed.R.Civ.P. 24(a) because the associations interests were not adequately protected by the defendants;

(c) Grant the association's motion to intervene under Fed.R.Civ.P. 24(a) because the defendants did not object to the intervention;

(d) Deny the association's motion to intervene under Fed.R.Civ.P. 24(a) because the plaintiffs opposed the intervention;

(e) Deny the association's motion to intervene under Fed.R.Civ.P. 24(a) because the defendants adequately represented the basin associations' interests and the basin associations' motion to dismiss merged, in substance, with the defendants'.

* * *

Francisco Espinoza and Laura Perez were former employees of the Mex-Am Café. They filed a lawsuit in the federal district court for the Middle District of North Carolina, complaining that the defendants "failed to compensate them at their promised rate at or above the statutory minimum wage, failed to pay overtime compensation for hours worked in excess of 40 per week, and failed to pay wages when due on their regular scheduled payday" in violation of the Fair Labor Standards Act and the North Carolina Wage and Hour Act. In other words, the plaintiffs complained that the "Defendants willfully violated the FLSA and the NCWHA by not compensating Plaintiffs for any hours worked generally." The defendants filed an answer, counterclaim, and third party complaint; and a motion to dismiss the complaint. The counterclaims against Espinoza were for alleged breach of contract and conversion. In response, the plaintiffs filed a motion to dismiss the defendants' counterclaims and third-party complaint.

The defendants alleged that Galvan, Espinoza, and Casares entered into an agreement to operate the restaurant as partners and held interests of 70%, 15% and 15%, respectively. Subsequently, Espinoza severed all ties with the restaurant. Espinoza and Casares failed to contribute their proportional share of the debts of Mex-Am, forcing Galvan to incur the costs of all debts owed by Mex-Am.

The defendants alleged that, Espinoza returned to the restaurant and, without authorization from Galvan or Casares, removed three plasma televisions and plants from the restaurant. According to the defendants, "the facts involved in determining whether Espinoza was the owner of the plasma televisions and plants largely related to whether Espinoza was an owner or member/manager of Mex-Am or an employee." Espinoza's removal of the items from the restaurant might not amount to conversion if he was deemed a member/manager because Espinosa might then have had an interest in the restaurant's fixtures in the restaurant.

The plaintiffs contended that the defendants' counterclaims were permissive counterclaims that relied solely on issues involving state law and lacked an independent jurisdictional basis and had to be dismissed pursuant to Fed.R.Civ.P. 12(b)(1). The plaintiffs further argued that, even if the defendants' counterclaims were deemed compulsory, they should be dismissed because they were an inappropriate effort to seek recoupment from FLSA-owed wages or because they were nothing more than a veiled attempt to retaliate against the plaintiffs. The defendants responded that their counterclaims were compulsory or, at minimum, satisfy the requirements for supplemental jurisdiction of 28 U.S.C. § 1367(a) and thus should proceed.

**QUESTION:**

(4) On the plaintiff's motion to dismiss the defendants' counterclaims pursuant to Fed.R.Civ.P. 12(b)(1), the federal district court should:

   (a) Grant the plaintiff's motion to dismiss the defendants' counterclaims because the counterclaims are permissive under Fed.R.Civ.P. 13(b);

   (b) Grant the plaintiff's motion to dismiss the defendants' counterclaims because there is no jurisdictional basis for the counterclaims;

   (c) Grant the plaintiff's motion to dismiss because the defendants' counterclaims are state-based claims asserted to retaliate against the plaintiff's federal hour and wage claim against the defendants;

   (d) Deny the plaintiff's motion to dismiss the defendants' counterclaims because the counterclaims are compulsory under Fed.R.Civ.P. 13(a);

   (e) Deny the plaintiff's motion to dismiss the defendants' counterclaims because they were asserted in good faith and not for a retaliatory purpose.

\* \* \*

Laura Broadstone, Julie Boesch, and Renee Boesch filed a lawsuit against Sherman's Place, Inc. in the federal district court for the Central District of Illinois. Count I of the complaint detailed the events surrounding Laura Broadstone's employment as salesperson at the Sherman's store in Peoria, Illinois. Broadstone alleged that she complained to the store manager, Tony Hnilicka of sex discrimination in payment of commissions, and that she complained of sex discrimination to the assistant manager, Dan Stein. Broadstone also alleged that she was told by Hnilicka and Renee Boesch that her employment was terminated because she had sold a clearance mattress falsely telling the customer it had never been used.

Count 2 of the complaint detailed the events surrounding Julie Boesch's employment as salesperson at the Sherman's store in Peoria, Illinois. Julie Boesch alleged that she complained various times to Jim Torok, Sales Manager and her supervisor, that male salespersons were being treated more favorably than she as the only female salesperson. She alleged that Paul Sherman telephoned her and told her she was terminated for breaking "Core Values."

Count 3 of the complaint detailed the events surrounding Renee Boesch's employment as Human Resources Manager at Sherman's in Peoria, Illinois. She alleged that Paul Sherman told her that he would have to demote her several levels in the company if she were ever to date a Sherman's employee again after she ended her engagement to the Sherman's Electronics Merchandiser David Weiss, who was also Paul Sherman's nephew; such a policy was never applied to males. She also alleged that because she felt unsafe at work and after the bad evaluations by Paul Sherman, she resigned her position.

Each of the plaintiffs brought their claims pursuant to Title VII of the federal civil rights employment discrimination statute, for sex discrimination and retaliation for complaining of sex discrimination. Broadstone and Julie Boesch also brought claims pursuant to the Illinois Sales Representative Act. All three of the plaintiffs requested compensatory damages and attorney's fees, expenses, and costs. Broadstone and Julie Boesch also requested treble damages pursuant to the Illinois Sales Representative Act.

The defendant filed a motion to sever the plaintiffs for misjoinder, arguing that the plaintiffs' claims did not satisfy the requirements for permissive joinder under Federal Rule of Civil Procedure 20(a) and that joinder of their claims would not increase judicial economy or avoid prejudice. The defendant requested that the court remedy the plaintiffs' misjoinder by severing the claims of Julie Boesch and Renee Boesch, assigning them new docket numbers, leaving the first-named plaintiff Laura Broadstone as the only plaintiff in the case, and requiring all the plaintiffs to file separate amended complaints containing only their claims.

**QUESTION:**

(5)   On the defendant's motion to sever the claims of Julie and Renee Boesch, the federal district court should:

(a)   Grant the defendant's motion to sever the claims of Julie and Renee Boesch because the women's claims did not arise out of the same transactions or occurrences;

(b)   Grant the defendant's motion to sever the claims of Julie and Renee Boesch because the women's claims did not assert any right to relief jointly;

(c)   Deny the defendant's motion to sever the claims of Julie and Renee Boesch because the differences among the claims were not so distinct or significant to preclude a finding that the claims arose out of the same transaction, occurrence, or series of transactions or occurrences;

(d)   Deny the defendant's motion to sever the claims of Julie and Renee Boesch because the defendant through the severance sought to needlessly multiply lawsuits;

(e)   Deny the defendant's motion to sever the claims of Julie and Renee Boesch because severance would unfairly prejudice the plaintiffs' ability to recover on the merits.

\* \* \*

Megan and Samuel Giampietro lived in Cheltenham, Pennsylvania. Viator, Inc. and TripAdvisor LLC "were corporations engaged in the business of providing travel related services and tours through their websites which also include reviews of travel related destinations and tours." The Giampietros sued Viator and TripAdvisor in connection with a scooter accident that happened while they were on vacation in Italy. They brought suit in the federal district court for the Eastern District of Pennsylvania, pursuant to 28 U.S.C. § 1332.

In their complaint, the Giampietros alleged that the defendants' "business model was an internet based travel services company whose services were sold to customers wherein the point of sale was at the customer's location," and that the defendants "provided side tours in various locations throughout the world, including the placement of its customers with tour operators." The Giampietros booked a vacation to Italy through Viator. At Viator's "suggestion/recommendation," they also booked the "Chianti Small Group Vespa Tour." Viator's advertisement for this tour stated that it would have no more than ten people, involved travel on quiet and scenic roads, and began with a thirty minute orientation session on how to safely ride a Vespa.

The Giampietros began their Vespa tour in Florence, Italy. Florencetown Vespa ran the tour. The tour was not as advertised—there were in fact about twenty people, travel was mainly on busy roads with heavy two-way traffic and no shoulders, and the orientation lasted only ten minutes. While on the tour, Megan's Vespa stalled twice, but the tour conductor told her that her Vespa "would be okay" and that she should continue to use it. When Megan's Vespa stalled a third time, she fell and sustained serious injuries, including third degree burns, a loss of consciousness, injuries to her lips and eyes, and a concussion.

About one year after Megan's accident, TripAdvisor purchased Viator. The Giampietros alleged that this purchase subjected TripAdvisor to "successor liability." The Giampietros also alleged that Viator and, by dint of successor liability, TripAdvisor, were liable for Megan's injuries, and Samuel's concomitant loss of consortium, because they failed to use reasonable care in selecting local tour providers; failed to warn the Giampietros of the unsafe conditions and dangers of the Vespa tour; failed to select a competent tour provider; negligently misrepresented the tour; failed to provide proper control and supervision of the tour; negligently selected Florencetown Vespa as the tour provider; failed to investigate the operations and conduct of the tour provider; and continued to place customers with Florencetown Vespa operators even after learning of problems with its scooters and that the tours were conducted on heavily trafficked roads.

Trip Advisor and Viator filed a motion to dismiss. Among many reasons requesting the dismissal, the defendants alleged that the Giampietros had failed to join two indispensable parties. TripAdvisor and Viator contended that Florencetown Vespa, the tour operator, and Piaggio & C. S.p.a., the manufacturer of Vespa, were indispensable parties whom the Giampietros failed to join. The Giampietros responded that the defendants' advertisements and solicitations for the tour did not mention either Florencetown Vespa or Piaggio.

In their complaint, Megan Giampietro alleged that "As a result of the stalled Vespa, Plaintiff sustained various burns, injuries and damages as set forth below." The "Plaintiff's burns, injuries and damages were the direct and proximate result of Defendants' (Viator and TripAdvisor) negligence." That was the extent of Megan Giampietro's complaint about the Vespa. There were no allegations of defective design or manufacture implicating the Vespa's manufacturer. In its answer, Viator and TripAdvisor alleged that "it was clear that a defective part or manufacturing process by the Vespa manufacturer might have jointly or proximately caused or could be the superseding/intervening cause of Plaintiff's injuries and resulting damages."

Count I was Megan Giampietro's negligence claim against TripAdvisor and Viator and Count II was Samuel Giampietro's derivative claim for loss of consortium. Megan Giampietro alleged that Viator and TripAdvisor were negligent for failing to use reasonable care in selecting a local tour provider; failing to warn her of the unsafe conditions and dangers of the tour; failing to select a competent provider for the tour; negligent misrepresentation; failing to provide proper control and supervision of the tour; failing to exercise reasonable care under the circumstances; negligently selecting Florencetown Vespa as the tour provider; failing to investigate the operations and conduct of the tour provider; and continuing to place its customers with the tour provider after learning of problems with its operations, vehicles, and where the tour was conducted.

The defendants argued that Florencetown Vespa was a necessary party because the Giampietros "must first prove as a threshold matter that it was the negligence or carelessness of Florencetown Vespa that proximately caused her injuries."

## QUESTION:

(6)  On the Viator and TripAdvisor's motion to dismiss the Giampietros' complaint for failure to join parties needed for a just adjudication under Fed.R.Civ.P. 19, the federal district court should:

   (a)  Grant Viator and TripAdvisor's motion to dismiss pursuant to Fed.R.Civ.P. 19 because Piaggio and Florencetown Vespa were necessary parties;

   (b)  Grant Viator and TripAdvisor's motion to dismiss pursuant to Fed.R.Civ.P. 19 because Piaggio and Florencetown Vespa were indispensable parties;

   (c)  Grant Viator and TripAdvisor's motion to dismiss pursuant to Fed.R.Civ.P. 19 because it was be feasible to join Piaggio and Florencetown Vespa;

   (d)  Deny Viator and TripAdvisor's motion to dismiss pursuant to Fed.R.Civ.P. 19 because Piaggio and Florencetown Vespa needed to be joined in the litigation;

   (e)  Deny Viator and TripAdvisor's motion to dismiss pursuant to Fed.R.Civ.P. 19 because Piaggio and Florencetown Vespa were not necessary parties.

* * *

Louis Cappelli was the officer and a principal shareholder of Helios Yachting Services, Ltd. (Helios). Anthony Pullar worked as captain of the S/Y Atlanta, a 121-foot sailboat owned and operated by Helios, and was paid $12,500 per month for his services as captain. Pullar filed a seven-count complaint against Cappelli in Newport County Superior Court, Rhode Island, based on the Cappelli's refusal to pay a $150,000 bonus. The plaintiff's complaint included counts for breach of contract, breach of the covenant of good faith and fair dealing, and fraud. He also sought to recover on theories of unjust enrichment, *quantum meruit*, and equitable estoppel. Moreover, he sought specific performance from the defendant.

The plaintiff alleged that the he and the defendant negotiated a one-year contract to work as captain of the sailboat in the State of New York. The defendant suggested that the contract be made for three years and that if the plaintiff accepted the position for three years he would be awarded a bonus of one additional year's salary, totaling $150,000. As part of this oral contract, the plaintiff's employment could only be terminated with good cause. The plaintiff accepted these terms. At that time, the Atlanta was located in Rhode Island. The plaintiff worked as captain of the Atlanta until he was terminated one month shy of reaching the three years required for the bonus. The plaintiff alleged that he was terminated without cause and with the sole purpose of not having to pay him the bonus. The plaintiff claimed that the parties subsequently met and agreed that the outstanding $150,000 bonus would be paid off at a rate of $10,000 per month. However, the plaintiff asserted that the defendant failed to make any bonus payments.

The defendant filed an answer denying all the allegations in the complaint and asserted several affirmative defenses, including lack of personal jurisdiction, insufficiency of service of process, statute of frauds, and failure to state a claim with respect to all counts. In support of his motion to dismiss for a lack of personal jurisdiction, the defendant filed a sworn affidavit asserting that he was a resident of White Plains, New York who had never lived in Rhode Island; and that he had not transacted business in Rhode Island. He admitted to visiting Rhode Island on several occasions, but claimed that these visits were only for recreational purposes.

The defendant attested that he never personally employed the plaintiff, and that he did not own the sailboat in his individual capacity. Instead, not only was the plaintiff hired, paid and employed by Helios, but Helios owned the sailboat. The defendant admitted that he made the decision to hire the plaintiff in his capacity as an officer and principal shareholder of Helios, but insisted that all crewmembers, including the plaintiff, were "at will" employees, who were compensated by Helios directly. He also maintained that there was never a discussion regarding a three-year contract or bonus. He also denied the subsequent agreement to pay the bonus in monthly installments.

The defendant further contended that Helios was a Cayman Islands corporation and had offices at 115 Stevens Ave., Valhalla, New York. He asserted that Helios purchased the Atlanta before hiring the plaintiff and noted that the Atlanta required a full-time captain and approximately five crew members. The defendant claimed that Helios paid for all costs and expenses for the ownership and operation of the Atlanta. All licenses and insurance pertaining to the Atlanta were obtained by, issued to, and held by Helios. Likewise, all maintenance and repair costs for the sailboat were paid by Helios. Additionally, the Atlanta was a British registered vessel that was kept in the Caribbean approximately six months of the year, and in Sag Harbor and Newport for parts of the year. Helios docked the Atlanta in Rhode Island for a few months in the year and had some maintenance work done to the sailboat in Rhode Island.

In further support of his motion, the defendant submitted portions of the plaintiff's deposition. In the deposition, the plaintiff conceded that all payments he received during the time that he was employed were made by Helios and never by the defendant individually. He also acknowledged that all repairs and maintenance to the vessel were paid for by Helios. During the deposition, the plaintiff stated that he did not know of any other substantial business the defendant had in Rhode Island, besides for the Atlanta. He also admitted that because he was serving as captain for the Atlanta, he was really working for Helios and that any compensation for that work would be owed to him by Helios.

The defendant argued that the Rhode Island court had no personal jurisdiction over him because he, in his individual capacity, did not have sufficient contacts with Rhode Island. The defendant insisted that the only contacts with Rhode Island related to Helios as a corporation. However, since Helios was not a party to this suit, nor had an alter-ego form of liability been pled in the complaint, Helios's contacts with Rhode Island could not be imputed to the defendant personally. Additionally, the defendant argued that the plaintiff could not obtain personal jurisdiction over the defendant through invocation of the alter-ego doctrine when he had not named Helios as a defendant nor even alleged the existence of personal jurisdiction over Helios.

The plaintiff countered that the defendant waived personal jurisdiction by failing to raise the issue in a timely manner, waiting until discovery was completed and the plaintiff had requested that the case be set for a trial. The plaintiff argued that the issue of personal jurisdiction had been waived. Alternatively, the plaintiff argued that the contacts of Helios should be attributed to the defendant. The plaintiff insisted that Helios was the defendant's alter-ego, justifying the piercing of its corporate veil and imputing the contacts of Helios with Rhode Island to the defendant. Neither party disputed that the court did not have personal jurisdiction over the defendant as an individual.

Rhode Island's long-arm statute, provides in part that:

> "every foreign corporation, every individual not a resident of this state ... and every partnership or association, composed of any person or persons not such residents, that shall have the necessary minimum contacts with the state of Rhode Island, shall be subject to the jurisdiction of the state of Rhode Island ... in every case not contrary to the provisions of the constitution or laws of the United States."

The Rhode Island Supreme Court has interpreted its long-arm statute to permit the exercise of jurisdiction over nonresident defendants to the fullest extent allowed by the United States Constitution.

In addition, the forum-state contacts of a corporation may be attributed to an individual who is an officer, director, or shareholder of the corporation when evidence is presented that shows that the corporation is the alter ego of the individual, or where other circumstances permit the court to pierce the corporate veil. In Rhode Island, to invoke the equitable alter-ego doctrine "there must be a concurrence of two circumstances: (1) there must be such a unity of interest and ownership that the separate personalities of the corporation and the individual no longer exist, viz., the corporation is, in fact, the alter ego of one or a few individuals; and (2) the observance of the corporate form would sanction a fraud, promote injustice, or an inequitable result would follow."

## QUESTION:

(7) In response to the defendant Cappelli's motion to dismiss for a lack of personal jurisdiction, the plaintiff Pullar contended that the court should deny the motion because it was not timely filed. In response to the plaintiff's challenge based on a lack of timeliness, the court should:

(a) Determine that the defendant's motion to dismiss for a lack of personal jurisdiction was timely because a motion to dismiss for a lack of personal jurisdiction may be raised at any time;

(b) Determine that the defendant's motion to dismiss for a lack of personal jurisdiction was timely because the defendant first raised this issue as an affirmative defense in his answer;

(c) Determine that the defendant's motion to dismiss for a lack of personal jurisdiction was not timely because the defendant waited until after discovery to raise this issue;

(d) Determine that the defendant's motion to dismiss for a lack of personal jurisdiction was not timely because the defendant waited until trial was set to raise this issue;

(e) Determine that the defendant's motion to dismiss for a lack of personal jurisdiction was not timely because the defendant failed to consolidate all his motions to dismiss.

## QUESTION:

(8) In the same litigation, and *assuming for this problem only* that the court determined that the defendant's motion to dismiss for a lack of personal jurisdiction was timely, on the merits of the defendant's motion to dismiss, the court should:

(a) Grant the defendant's motion to dismiss for a lack of personal jurisdiction because the plaintiff failed to plead a theory of alter-ego in his complaint;

(b)  Grant the defendant's motion to dismiss for a lack of personal jurisdiction because the case was subject to maritime jurisdiction;

(c)  Deny the defendant's motion to dismiss for a lack of personal jurisdiction because the court had general jurisdiction over Cappelli;

(d)  Deny the defendant's motion to dismiss for a lack of personal jurisdiction because the court had specific jurisdiction over Cappelli;

(e)  Deny the defendant's motion to dismiss for a lack of personal jurisdiction because Helios was the alter-ego of Cappelli.

\* \* \*

Daniel Strizic, a Montana citizen and a former employee of Northwestern Corporation, brought a breach of contract and unfair trade practices action in Montana state court. He sued Northwestern, the Standard Insurance Company, and Peggy Lowney, a Northwestern employee. The plaintiff alleged that Northwestern breached its contract with him by denying his claim for short-term disability payments. Northwestern's disability income plan was self-funded and administered by Standard Insurance Company. Strizic alleged in the complaint that "Defendant Peggy Lowney was the Director of Compensation and Benefits at Northwestern's operations in Montana, and is a citizen and resident of Montana." Strizic further alleged that defendant Lowney acted as agent of Northwestern and provided "inaccurate information" to Standard because "she desired to prevent Strizic from obtaining disability benefits." Northwestern and Standard both were corporations, with their place of incorporation and principal places of business outside Montana.

In addition to his breach of contract claim, the plaintiff's unfair trade practices claim alleged that the defendants "misrepresented pertinent facts and policy provisions relating to coverages at issue, failed to conduct a reasonable investigation before denying Strizic's claim and neglected to attempt in good faith to settle Strizic's claim promptly, fairly, and equitably when liability was clear."

The defendants removed the case to federal court, alleging that the court had jurisdiction under both the diversity of citizenship statute, 28 U.S.C. § 1332, and the removal statute, 28 U.S.C. § 1441. After removal, the defendants moved to dismiss Lowney. The plaintiff petitioned for remand to state court. The defendants asserted that the plaintiff had fraudulently joined Lowney as a party for the purpose of defeating diversity jurisdiction.

Although Strizic's short-term disability benefits (had they been paid) were apparently worth $50,079.58, neither the defendants nor the plaintiff addressed whether the defendants demonstrated that the $75,000 amount in controversy requirement was met. Strizic's complaint sought the benefits owed to him under the short-term disability income plan, prejudgment interest on all overdue payments, consequential economic damages, general damages, punitive damages, and attorneys' fees and costs. The defendants averred that there was more than $75,000 in dispute.

The defendants asserted that the plaintiff failed to state a claim against Lowney upon which relief could be granted. Under Montana law, a corporation's employees are not personally liable for acts taken on behalf of the corporation. Strizic had no contract with Lowney, and did not make any specific allegation of unfair trade practices against Lowney. His punitive damages claim was not a stand-alone claim against her. The plaintiff did not allege that Lowney was a claims adjuster, and there was no privity of contract between Lowney and Strizic. An unfair trade practices violation against an individual must be pleaded that it was done with such frequency as to indicate a general business practice. The plaintiff did not plead that Lowney's acts were of such frequency as to indicate a general business practice.

In opposing the motion to dismiss, the plaintiff's counsel informed the court that Strizic might amend the complaint to allege a negligence claim against Lowney. The attorney intended to wait until the case was remanded to state court to so amend, so as to take advantage of a more lenient state pleading requirement.

### QUESTION:

(9)   On the defendant's motion to dismiss Lowney from the action, pursuant to Fed.R.Civ.P. 12(b)(6) for failure to state a claim, the federal district court should:

(a)   Grant the defendant's motion to dismiss pursuant to Fed.R.Civ.P. 12(b)(6) because Lowney was fraudulently joined;

(b)   Grant the defendant's motion to dismiss pursuant to Fed.R.Civ.P. 12(b)(6) because there was no possibility that the plaintiff Strizic could recover from Lowney;

(c)   Deny the defendant's motion to dismiss pursuant to Fed.R.Civ.P. 12(b)(6) because, taking all the plaintiff's allegations as true, there was at least a possibility that the plaintiff could recover against Lowney;

(d)   Deny the defendant's motion to dismiss pursuant to Fed.R.Civ.P. 12(b)(6) because, taking all the plaintiff's allegations as true, there was at least a plausible chance that the plaintiff could recover against Lowney;

(e)   Deny the defendant's motion to dismiss pursuant to Fed.R.Civ.P. 12(b)(6) because the defendant should have the opportunity to conduct additional discovery with regard to his claims of breach of contract and the defendant's unfair trade practices.

* * *

In the same litigation, the plaintiff petitioned the court for a remand to Montana state court. Strizic's motion for remand asserted that the plaintiff properly joined Lowney as a defendant because there was a possibility that an unfair trade practices claim could be proven against Lowney. Strizic alleged that Lowney was doing her job for Northwestern when she provided inaccurate information to Standard.

**QUESTION:**

(10) On the plaintiff's petition for remand of the case to Montana state court, the federal district court should:

   (a)  Grant the plaintiff's motion to remand the case to state court because Lowney's citizenship was not diverse from the plaintiff Strizic's citizenship;

   (b)  Grant the plaintiff's motion to remand the case to state court because the plaintiff should have the opportunity to add a negligence claim against Lowney under Montana law;

   (c)  Grant the plaintiff's motion to remand the case to state court to allow the plaintiff to take advantage of the state's more liberal pleading rules;

   (d)  Deny the plaintiff's motion to remand the case to state court if the court determined that Lowney was fraudulently joined;

   (e)  Deny the plaintiff's motion to remand the case to state court because the federal court had supplemental jurisdiction over the claims against Lowney;

* * *

PPG Industries, a non-party intervenor, filed a motion for a protective order in a litigation that was proceeding in the federal district court for the Northern District of Illinois. In the underlying litigation, The Boyd Group Inc. sued Roger D'Orazio. During the course of discovery, the defendant D'Orazio requested discovery from Boyd, which would have required Boyd to produce documents relating to PPG's business relationship with Boyd.

PPG filed the its protective order motion as a non-party intervenor in this action, seeking an "attorneys' eyes only" designation over: (1) the paint supply contract that PPG entered into with Boyd, (2) drafts of that contract, and (3) "a small set of documents that reflect highly confidential and proprietary terms of the PPG-Boyd Contract." PPG argued that disclosure of these documents to its customers or competitors in "the auto collision refinish business posed serious and irreparable risks of economic harm to PPG," because those customers and competitors could glean proprietary information about PPG's pricing and business model. According to PPG, D'Orazio was involved in the relevant industry "for decades, and undoubtedly had frequent contact with participants to whom such disclosure could be made, whether inadvertently or otherwise." PPG's urged the court that granting its motion was "proper and reasonable regardless of whether specific evidence presently existed that disclosure of this information to D'Orazio would, or even might, result in disclosure to participants in the broader North American automotive refinish industry, including PPG's customers and/or competitors."

D'Orazio was not a competitor of PPG. PPG asserted that D'Orazio was once a customer of PPG, but that was no longer true. D'Orazio's sale of his company and subsequent exit from the industry was what gave rise to the underlying suit. PPG simply asserted that D'Orazio was involved in the relevant industry for a long time and "undoubtedly" had contact with participants in the industry. PPG did not identify who these participants were, or provide evidence that D'Orazio was, in fact, in contact with them.

QUESTION:

(11) On PPG's motion for a protective order under Fed.R.Civ.P. 26(c), the federal district court should:

    (a) Grant PPG's motion for a protective order pursuant to Fed.R.Civ.P. 26(c) because PPG sought to protect propriety information;

    (b) Grant PPG's motion for a protective order pursuant to Fed.R.Civ.P. 26(c) because disclosure of the information might harm PPG's competitiveness in the auto collision refinishing industry;

    (c) Deny PPG's motion for a protective order pursuant to Fed.R.Civ.P. 26(c) because PPG had not shown a clearly defined and serious injury to its business;

    (d) Deny PPG's motion for a protective order pursuant to Fed.R.Civ.P. 26(c) because as an intervenor, PPG was not entitled to a protective order;

    (e) Deny PPG's motion for a protective order pursuant to Fed.R.Civ.P. 26(c) because the plaintiff Boyd could adequately protect PPG's interests in the documents.

\* \* \*

Tracy Green was a former owner of real property located in Columbia County, Georgia. American Homes 4 Rent Properties Eight, LLC purchased the property at a foreclosure sale. American Homes, as plaintiff, later initiated dispossessory eviction proceedings in the Magistrate Court of Columbia County against Green and all other occupants of the property.

The defendant Green removed the case to the federal district court for the Southern District of Georgia. In its petition for removal, the defendant alleged violations of three federal provisions: 15 U.S.C. § 1692, Federal Rule of Civil Procedure 60, and the Due Process Clause of the Fourteenth Amendment. The defendant did not allege either party's citizenship, or the citizenship of the members of American Homes Limited Liability Corporation. The record contained no evidence that defendant was a citizen of another state, and the defendant's address for service—a Georgia address—was the same address for the premises at issue here. Under Georgia law, a dispossessory claim seeking ejectment cannot be reduced to a monetary sum.

The plaintiff filed a motion to remand arguing that the court lacked subject matter jurisdiction pursuant to 28 U.S.C. 1332.

**QUESTION:**

(12) On the plaintiff's motion to remand the case to the Georgia state court, the federal district court should:

   (a)   Grant the plaintiff's motion to Georgia state court for remand because the defendant was a citizen of the state of Georgia;

   (b)   Grant the plaintiff's motion to Georgia state court for remand because dispossessory eviction claim was a matter of purely local state law;

   (c)   Deny the plaintiff's motion to Georgia state court for remand because the defendant pleaded federal and constitutional claims and defenses;

   (d)   Deny the plaintiff's motion to Georgia state court for remand because the court might exercise supplemental jurisdiction over the state-based claims;

   (e)   Deny the plaintiff's motion to Georgia state court for remand because the court had valid diversity jurisdiction.

\* \* \*

Lightning Energy Services, LLC hired Aaron Horne as its Chief Operating Officer. Lightning Energy subsequently placed Horne in operational control of Lightning Trucking Services, LLC, an LLC of which Lightning Energy is the sole member. Subsequently, Lightning Energy and Lightning Trucking terminated Horne's employment. Horne claimed he was owed $36,000 in compensation. The West Virginia Unemployment Compensation Commission (WVUCC) reviewed Horne's termination and determined that he had not been terminated for good cause. Further, Horne contended that, after his termination, Tracy Turner reported him to law enforcement for embezzlement of assets and property of Lightning Energy and Lightning Trucking.

In January 2014, Horne filed suit in the Circuit Court of Harrison County, West Virginia, against Lightning Energy, Lightning Trucking, Charles Hamrick, August Schultes, and Tracy Turner, alleging abuse of process, defamation, and violation of the WVUCC. The defendants filed a motion for summary judgment as to all claims, and a motion to dismiss Tracy Turner for improper service of process.

On March 15, 2015, the Circuit Court judge, dismissed the motion for summary judgment as to the abuse of process claim, but granted the motion to dismiss and dismissed Tracy Turner with prejudice because Horne had not perfected service upon Turner. The trial as to the remaining defendants began on April 14, 2015, and concluded on April 22, 2015 with a jury verdict of no liability.

On April 14, 2015, Horne filed a second lawsuit in the Circuit Court of Harrison County against Lightning Energy, Lightning Trucking, and Turner, alleging claims of defamation, abuse of process, and a violation of the WVWPCA. The complaint included an *ad damnum* clause, which stated that "the total damages sought by the plaintiff inclusive of all interest, costs, attorney fees and punitive damages does not exceed $75,000.00." On April 15, 2015, while Turner was waiting in the Harrison County courthouse to testify in the first state court action, Horne's counsel served Turner with the summons and complaint in this case.

On May 15, 2015, the defendants filed a notice of removal to the federal district court for the Northern District of West Virginia, invoking the court's diversity jurisdiction. Horne was a citizen of West Virginia. Turner was a citizen of Texas. Lightning Trucking was a Delaware limited liability company whose sole member was Lightning Energy, which was also a Delaware limited liability company. In paragraph 10 of the notice of removal, Turner listed the members of Lightning Energy, asserting that "none . . . were citizens of West Virginia." Turner, however, then stated that "defendant Lightning Energy . . . had a member who owned a minority interest and was a citizen of West Virginia." On August 3, 2015, the defendants clarified that none of the four LLCs that were members of Lightning Energy was a citizen of West Virginia, but that an individual member, Charles Hamrick, owned a minority interest and was a citizen of West Virginia.

On May 15, 2015, Turner filed a motion to dismiss, arguing that the second action was identical to the first action from which he was dismissed with prejudice prior to trial, and which ultimately resulted in a jury verdict against Horne on all counts. On June 12, 2015, Horne filed a motion to remand, contending that he had limited the amount in controversy to $75,000 or less. On July 17, 2015, the defendants responded, arguing that Horne had not successfully limited his recovery and that, more likely than not, were he to prevail in his suit, Horne would recover more than $75,000.

Turner contended that if either Lightning Trucking or Lightning Energy had West Virginia citizenship due to Hamrick's minority interest, the citizenship of Lightning Trucking and Lightning Energy should be disregarded under the doctrine of fraudulent joinder because (1) Horne's defamation claim was barred by the statute of limitations, and (2) the same claims have been tried already, resulting in a verdict against Horne.

QUESTION:

(13) On the plaintiff Horne's motion to remand the case back to West Virginia state court, the federal district court should:

(a) Find that there was complete diversity of citizenship because the plaintiff was from West Virginia and the corporate and individuals were all from other states;

(b) Find that there was complete diversity of citizenship because none of the four LLCs that were members of Lightning Energy was a citizen of West Virginia;

(c) Find that complete diversity of citizenship because Hamrick's minority ownership of Lightning Energy could be disregarded in determining diversity jurisdiction;

(d)  Find that complete diversity of citizenship was lacking because Hamrick's minority ownership of Lightning Energy defeated diversity jurisdiction;

(e)  Find that diversity jurisdiction was lacking because a plaintiff cannot artificially limit the amount in controversy in a state court action to less than $75,000.

* * *

In the same action, the defendants argued, in the alternative, that the court should disregard the West Virginia citizenship of Lightning Energy and Lightning Trucking under the doctrine of fraudulent joinder, and therefore retain jurisdiction of the case. Assuming that the federal court applied the doctrine of fraudulent joinder and retained removal jurisdiction, Turner and the defendants moved to dismiss the case on the grounds that res judicata precluded Horne from bringing his claims based on his prior action against the defendants in West Virginia court.

**QUESTION:**

(14)  On the defendant's motion to dismiss the case based on application of the doctrine of res judicata to preclude Horne from bringing his claims based on the prior action against the defendants in West Virginia court, the federal district court should:

(a)  Grant the defendant's motion to dismiss based on res judicata because the two cases were the same causes of action and the parties or their privies were the same in both actions;

(b)  Grant the defendant's motion to dismiss based on res judicata in the interests of judicial efficiency and economy;

(c)  Deny the defendant's motion to dismiss based on res judicata because there was no adjudication on the merits in Horne's first action;

(d)  Deny the defendant's motion to dismiss based on res judicata because the claims in the two actions were not identical;

(e)  Deny the defendant's motion to dismiss based on res judicata because the parties or their privies were not the same in the two cases.

* * *

Gregory Bodenheimer filed suit in the federal district court for the Eastern District of Louisiana, pursuant to 28 U.S.C. § 1332. In his original complaint, the plaintiff alleged various claims under Louisiana law, including fraud, breach of contract, unfair and deceptive practices. The defendant, Luther Speight, III, was served and the court granted an extension of time to serve the remaining two defendants, Luther Speight & Company, LLC, and Terry Williams. The plaintiff thereafter served Luther Speight & Company and Williams.

Subsequently the court issued an order to show cause why the plaintiff's claims should not be dismissed for the plaintiff's failure to prosecute as no record of an appearance had been made by any defendant nor had the plaintiff moved for entry of default. On the same day, the plaintiff filed a motion for entry of default, which the clerk of court granted. The defendants then filed a motion to set aside the entry of default and two motions to dismiss. The defendants filed a motion for sanctions pursuant to 28 U.S.C. § 1927.

The defendants' contended that the plaintiff's counsel knowingly or recklessly advanced frivolous claims in violation of Fed.R.Civ.P. 11(b)(2). Specifically, the defendants' claimed that the plaintiff's counsel "had to have known" that, from the face of the complaint, each of his claims were prescribed under Louisiana law. Because the defendants alleged that the plaintiff's counsel should have known that the claims were time-barred, the defendants contended that the plaintiff's counsel made groundless claims and was subject to Rule 11 sanctions. The defendants acknowledged that any Rule 11 argument was not yet ripe under the safe-harbor provision in Rule 11. Nevertheless, the defendants argued that, by virtue of 28 U.S.C. § 1927, the court may award the defendants excess fees as the plaintiff's counsel acted in bad faith by persisting in pursuing meritless claims.

The defendants' counsel had informed the plaintiff's counsel that the plaintiff's claims were prescribed, but the plaintiff's counsel refused to withdraw the complaint and granted the defendants an informal extension of time to file responsive pleadings. After months of inactivity and the issuance of a call docket ordering the plaintiff to show cause why his claim should not be dismissed for inaction, the plaintiff's counsel moved for entry of preliminary default. The defendants asserted that, while no rule required the plaintiff's counsel to provide the defense counsel with notice prior to moving for entry of preliminary default, professional courtesy dictated that after granting an informal extension of time to file responsive pleadings such an action would have been appropriate.

The plaintiff's counsel argued that by seeking sanctions under § 1927, which was within the court's inherent powers to grant, the defendants' motion sought to circumvent the safe-harbor provision in Rule 11. The plaintiff's counsel noted that he had reformed the complaint, clarifying previously alleged facts and alleged new facts refuting the defendants' claims that the plaintiff's claims were prescribed and had withdrawn opposition to the defendants' motion setting aside entry of default. The plaintiff's counsel argued that he had complied with the safe-harbor provision of Rule 11. The plaintiff's counsel argued that he did not take these actions in bad faith or in abuse of the judicial process; he believed his client was entitled to relief and had not taken actions to harass the defendants.

**QUESTION:**

(15) On the defendant's motion for sanctions pursuant to 28 U.S.C. § 1927 the federal district court should:

    (a)   Grant the defendant's motion for sanctions under 28 U.S.C. § 1927 because the plaintiff's counsel had multiplied the proceedings in the case unreasonably and vexatiously;

    (b)   Grant the defendant's motion for sanctions under 28 U.S.C. § 1927 because the plaintiff's counsel had acted in bad faith;

    (c)   Grant the defendant's motion for sanctions under 28 U.S.C. § 1927 because the defense counsel had communicated with the plaintiff's counsel alerting him to the pleading defects in the plaintiff's complaint;

    (d)   Deny the defendant's motion for sanctions under 28 U.S.C. § 1927 because the plaintiff's counsel acted within the scope of the Rule 11 safe-harbor provision in amending the complaint;

    (e)   Deny the defendant's motion for sanctions under 28 U.S.C. § 1927 because the Rule 11 motion for sanctions was not yet ripe.

\* \* \*

Keagan R. Allen commenced an action in the federal district court for the Southern District of New York, alleging constitutional law claims arising under 42 U.S.C. §§ 1983 and 1985 against various Dutchess County and New York State employees. Allen also brought a legal malpractice claims against the county defendants who were attorneys and against Del Atwell. The court dismissed all claims asserted by the plaintiff, except the legal malpractice claim asserted against Atwell.

The plaintiff's lawsuit stemmed from an alleged illegal vehicle stop in Dutchess County conducted by New York State troopers, which resulted in the discovery of a firearm, ammunition, and other contraband. The plaintiff was arrested, prosecuted, convicted following a guilty plea, and ultimately sentenced to a period of three and one-half years of incarceration, to be followed by three years of post-release supervision (PRS). Allen appealed. He was eventually released to the supervision of the New York State Division of Parole, having completed his sentence.

The state appellate division assigned Atwell to handle the appeal, which division vacated Allen's conviction. Subsequently, the Dutchess County clerk received a certified copy of the appellate division's order reversing the judgment of conviction, and ordering that the indictment be dismissed. The plaintiff Allen alleged that he was not notified that his conviction had been reversed, and he continued to serve his PRS term. The state applied for leave to appeal order, which was granted.

The plaintiff then failed a drug test, in violation of the terms of his PRS. He was arrested by the Division of Parole and admitted to the violation of his PRS terms. The plaintiff's newly-retained parole defense counsel discovered that the plaintiff's judgment of conviction had been reversed. He contacted the clerk for the Court of Appeals and learned that the Dutchess County district attorney had never perfected the appeal, so he sought dismissal of the abandoned appeal. The Court of Appeals dismissed the state's appeal *sua sponte* for failure to prosecute. The plaintiff's retained attorney next filed a motion in the Dutchess County court seeking termination of Allen's post-release supervision, and the plaintiff's PRS was terminated.

The plaintiff filed this lawsuit and alleged that he was unjustifiably incarcerated and/or under the control of the state corrections and parole services due at least in part to professional malpractice by Atwell. Specifically, the plaintiff alleged that Atwell, after prevailing in the appeal of the plaintiff's conviction, failed to notify the plaintiff and the appropriate governmental entities of the reversal and dismissal of the conviction, and that these delays in notifying law enforcement agencies following the successful appeal postponed his release from custody and freedom from governmental control.

The plaintiff's complaint alleged claims against the various defendants for false arrest, search and seizure, false imprisonment, malicious prosecution, abuse of process, assault and battery, unjust conviction, and conspiracy pursuant to 42 U.S.C. §§ 1983 and 1985, as well as state law claims for legal malpractice, breach of fiduciary duty, negligence, and violations of the New York Civil Rights Law and the New York state constitution. The defendants moved, pursuant to Rule 12(b)(6), to dismiss the complaint. The court dismissed all the plaintiff's claims, except the legal malpractice claim against Atwell.

The defendant Atwell moved for judgment on the pleadings pursuant to Rule 12(c), and/or to convert his Rule 12(c) motion into a Rule 56 motion for summary judgment, asserting there was no genuine dispute of material fact and the defendant was entitled to judgment on the plaintiff's legal malpractice claim as a matter of law.

The defendant presented matters outside the pleadings, and the plaintiff was timely apprised of the possibility that the motion could be treated as a motion for summary judgment. The plaintiff had the opportunity to present supporting material.

## QUESTION:

(16) On the defendant Atwell's motion for a judgment on the pleadings pursuant to Fed.R.Civ.P. 12(c), the federal district court should:

    (a) Construe the allegations in the complaint most favorably to the defendant as the party moving for the judgment on the pleadings;

    (b) Construe the allegations in the complaint most favorably to the plaintiff as the party opposing the judgment on the pleadings;

    (c) Convert the motion for a judgment on the pleadings to a summary judgment pursuant to Fed.R.Civ.P. 12(d);

(d)  Decline to convert the motion the motion for a judgment on the
     pleadings to a summary judgment because this would impose a
     higher burden on the non-moving party;

(e)  Decline to convert the motion for a judgment on the pleadings to
     a summary judgment because this would result in prejudice to
     the plaintiff.

*  *  *

In the same litigation, in order to prove a claim for legal malpractice under
New York law, a plaintiff must establish: (1) an attorney-client relationship,
(2) attorney negligence, (3) that the attorney's negligence was the proximate
cause of plaintiff's loss or injury, and (4) actual damages. The rule in a legal
malpractice action is that a plaintiff must demonstrate not only that actual
damages have been sustained, but also that counsel's negligence was the
proximate cause of the loss. To prove the proximate cause element, a plaintiff
must demonstrate that but for the attorney's negligence, she would have
prevailed in the underlying matter or would not have sustained any
ascertainable damages. Where the record in a professional malpractice case
demonstrates that an intervening cause was responsible for the injury,
summary judgment will be granted to the defendant.

New York law provides that:

> Upon the termination of a criminal action or proceeding against a
> person in favor of such person . . . , the record of such action or
> proceeding shall be sealed and the clerk of the court wherein such
> criminal action or proceeding was terminated shall immediately
> notify the commissioner of the division of criminal justice services
> and the head of all appropriate police departments and other law
> enforcement agencies that the action has been terminated in favor of
> the accused, and unless the court has directed otherwise, that the
> record of such action or proceeding shall be sealed.

The plaintiff alleged that Atwell's failure occurred after he actually secured a
reversal of the plaintiff's conviction, when he allegedly failed to notify the
plaintiff that his conviction was vacated and failed to follow up to ensure that
his rapsheet was cleared.

### QUESTION:

(17) For the purposes of this question only, assuming that the federal court
     converted the defendant Atwell's motion for a judgment on the pleadings
     to a motion for summary judgment, the federal district court should:

(a)  Grant the defendant's motion for summary judgment because
     there was no genuine issue of material fact whether Atwell's
     negligence was the proximate cause of the plaintiff's injuries;

(b)  Grant the defendant's motion for summary judgment because
     the defendant had previously moved for a judgment on the
     pleadings pursuant to Fed.R.Civ.P. 12(c);

(c) Deny the defendant's motion for summary judgment because a jury should be able to determine whether Atwell committed legal malpractice;

(d) Deny the defendant's motion for summary judgment because the defendant Atwell's credibility was at issue;

(e) Deny the defendant's motion for summary judgment because a jury should be permitted to draw all reasonable inferences from the evidence as to Atwell's alleged malpractice.

\* \* \*

Lauren Hooks sued Auto Field Corp. in the federal district court for the Eastern District of New York. Her complaint contained nine claims for relief. The first alleged that when the plaintiff purchased a used BMW from the defendant automobile dealer, the defendant understated the applicable interest rate by .135%, causing plaintiff to pay an extra $198. The plaintiff alleged that this violated the disclosure requirements of the federal Truth in Lending Act (TILA) and accompanying federal regulations.

The remaining eight claims for relief all arose under state law, and all but one of them have nothing to do with financing or federally required disclosures. The claims sought damages for violation of the New York Lemon Law, breach of express warranty and breach of the implied warranty of merchantability under the New York Uniform Commercial Code; revocation of acceptance under the New York Uniform Commercial Code; violation of the duty of good faith and fair dealing under New York Uniform Commercial Code; a violation of the warranty of serviceability under the New York Vehicle and Traffic Law; engaging in Deceptive Sales Practices under the New York General Business Practices Code; and common law fraud.

The common law fraud claim alleged that but for the $198 overcharge, the plaintiff would not have purchased the vehicle (the total financed cost was over $45,000). The other state law claims arose out of allegations that after purchasing the car, the plaintiff encountered a series of mechanical problems, which were set forth in great detail in the complaint. The plaintiff alleged that defendant refused to perform any repairs on the vehicle, and that she was forced to take it to an authorized BMW dealership to have it repaired at great expense. The plaintiff further alleged that even the authorized BMW dealership was unable to repair the car and that she was unable to drive it. She also alleged that defendant never gave her the key to the wheel locks and thus she cannot replace the worn out tires on it.

The defendant sharply disputed the facts giving rise to plaintiff's state law claims. It contended that plaintiff only brought the car back to defendant for repairs on one occasion, and thereafter, without giving defendant a reasonable opportunity to effect the repairs, brought it to the BMW dealership, which apparently botched the repairs. The defendant pointed out that while the plaintiff exhibited extensive records of the repairs attempted by the BMW dealership, neither the defendant nor the plaintiff had any documents showing that defendant was given an opportunity to work on the vehicle.

The defendant moved the federal court to dismiss all the state law claims pursuant to 28 U.S.C. § 1367.

**QUESTION:**

(18) On the defendant's motion to dismiss the plaintiff's state law claims pursuant to 28 U.S.C. § 1367, the federal district court should:

    (a)   Grant the defendant's motion pursuant to 28 U.S.C. § 1367 and dismiss the entire case;

    (b)   Grant the defendant's motion pursuant to 28 U.S.C. § 1367 as to the state law claims, but retain the TILA claim;

    (c)   Deny the defendant's motion pursuant to 28 U.S.C. § 1367(a) because the federal TILA claim and the state law claims constitute one constitutional case;

    (d)   Deny the defendant's motion pursuant to 28 U.S.C. § 1367(c) because the court has discretion to exercise jurisdiction over the state law claims;

    (e)   Deny the defendant's motion pursuant to 28 U.S.C. § 1367 in deference to the plaintiff's choice of forum.

\* \* \*

Dr. Emmanuel Okereke, brought an action in the federal district court for the Southern District of New York against his former attorney, John Charles Allen, Esq., asserting a claim of legal malpractice. Allen moved to dismiss the complaint under Rule 12(b)(3) of the Federal Rules of Civil Procedure on the ground that venue was not proper

Dr. Okereke had retained Mr. Allen to represent and counsel him in connection with a legal action involving Ross University School of Medicine (RUSM) in New Jersey. Mr. Allen was licensed to practice law in New Jersey and his practice was confined to that state. Allen commenced an action on Dr. Okereke's behalf against RUSM in the Superior Court of New Jersey, Middlesex County. The complaint alleged discrimination, tortious interference with contract, damage to reputation, and breach of contract. While the exact goals of the underlying litigation against RUSM remained in dispute, Dr. Okereke alleged in his lawsuit against Allen that in his lawsuit against RUSM he sought to be reinstated as a student, to pursue monetary damages, to be permitted to sit for the United States medical licensing exam to acquire a Doctor of Medicine (M.D.) degree, and to begin a paid residency in a United States hospital. The action against RUSM was dismissed with prejudice due to the plaintiff's failure to provide responsive answers to interrogatories and document demands.

After the dismissal of his lawsuit against RUSM, Dr. Okereke filed his action against Allen. At that time, Okereke resided in Armonk, New York and Allen lived in New Brunswick, New Jersey. Okereke alleged that Mr. Allen acted negligently, improperly and without reasonable skill, diligence, and knowledge in representing him in the action against RUSM. Furthermore, Okereke asserted that Allen's malpractice resulted in damages including financial loss, anguish, and aggravation.

The clerk of the court issued a certificate of default when Allen failed to answer or otherwise move with respect to the complaint. Thereafter, the Allen submitted a motion to vacate the default and dismiss the complaint. He alleged that the default judgment needed to be vacated and the case dismissed because the federal court lacked proper venue.

**QUESTION:**

(19) On the defendant Allen's motion to dismiss because of improper venue pursuant to Fed.R.Civ.P. 12(b)(3), the federal district court should find that:

   (a) Venue was proper in the Southern District of New York because the plaintiff resided in New York;

   (b) Venue was proper in New York because the events or transactions giving rise to the malpractice litigation occurred in New York;

   (c) Venue was proper in New York because Allen was subject to personal jurisdiction in New York;

   (d) Venue was improper in New York because the defendant resided in New Jersey;

   (e) Venue was improper in New York because the plaintiff's activities could not serve as a basis for determining proper venue.

* * *

Thai Le was employed by Nice Glide Fishing LLC, Inc. as a crew member aboard the F/V Diligence, a scallop vessel owned and operated by Diligence, Inc. He sued Nice Glide Fishing and Diligence Inc. in the federal district court for the District of Massachusetts, for injuries Le received while during his employment on the boat. During the course of discovery, Le filed a motion to compel a second deposition of boat captain Scott Larsen, and the production of fourteen photographs of the F/V Diligence.

The plaintiff propounded interrogatories and document requests on both defendants requesting, among other things, maintenance records of the F/V Diligence. The defendants responded jointly with 65 pages of documents. The plaintiff took the deposition of Captain Larsen, as the 30(b)(6) designee of both the defendants. The plaintiff subsequently learned more information about the condition of the "wind station" aboard the vessel at the time of the incident. After prompting by the plaintiff to supplement discovery, the defendants produced an additional 1,089 responsive documents relating to maintenance of the vessel during the relevant time period. These records indicated that the wind station may have been removed from the F/V Diligence and replaced after the plaintiff's injury. Based on that newly-revealed discovery and facts gleaned from other depositions, the plaintiff then sought to conduct a second 30(b)(6) deposition of Captain Larsen.

The defendants opposed a second deposition of Captain Larsen, arguing that a second deposition would be cumulative and duplicative because the plaintiff's counsel questioned Captain Larsen about the wind station during the first deposition. The transcripts of the first deposition showed the following line of questioning:

**Q:** Do you have one of those wind gauges?

**A:** I do.

**Q:** Do you ever use it?

**A:** I do, yeah.

**Q:** Do you remember whether—was that typically how you figured out what the wind outside, or would you more do it by feel?

**A:** Well, yeah, I look at that, but it's not in a position where I see it all the time, and I don't even know how accurate it is, but—well, I do have a wind gauge on the boat though. I'm sure I looked at it, you know, but that might have been where I came up with the 25 (knots estimate), you know.

**Q:** Typically would you come up—like typically would you look at the wind gauge or

**A:** Yeah.

**Q:** Do you think you probably did look at the wind gauge?

**A:** I think I did.

At the time of this deposition, the plaintiff's counsel did not have access to the maintenance invoices provided in the defendants' supplemental discovery response. He was unaware that the weather sensor malfunctioned and was removed after the accident, that a new upgraded weather sensor was installed after the accident, and that within a month after the accident a technician might have performed work on the electronic connection between the weather sensor and the display in the wheelhouse.

**QUESTION:**

(20) On the plaintiff Le's motion to take a second Rule 30(b)(6) deposition of Captain Larsen, the federal district court should:

(a) Grant the motion for a second deposition of Captain Larsen because of the newly discovered evidence;

(b) Grant the motion for a second deposition of Captain Larsen because the plaintiff would be prejudiced by barring Le from conducting the second deposition;

(c) Deny the motion for a second deposition of Captain Larsen because a second deposition of Larsen would be needlessly duplicative and cumulative of his earlier deposition;

(d) Deny the motion for a second deposition of Captain Larsen because Fed.R.Civ.P. 30 limits deposition testimony of any deponent to seven hours;

(e) Deny the motion for a second deposition of Captain Larsen because the plaintiff's counsel should have conducted a more thorough investigation prior to taking the first deposition of Captain Larsen.

\* \* \*

In the same litigation, the plaintiff Le sought discovery of fourteen photographs of the F/V Diligence taken by the defendants two days after the plaintiff's injuries. Those photographs showed the condition of the vessel at the time of the incident, before later structural changes were made.

The defendants opposed production of the photos, contending that the photographs fell into the work-product exception to the discovery rules. The defendants argued that the photographs were taken in anticipation of litigation, and are therefore exempt from discovery as work product. The defendants included an affidavit from counsel asserting that none of the photographs show a location where the wind station would have been visible. The plaintiff responded that it had substantial need for the photographs and no means of obtaining equivalent images.

**QUESTION:**

(21) On the plaintiff Le's request for production of the fourteen requested photographs, the federal district court should:

(a) Grant the plaintiff's motion for production of the fourteen photographs because the photographs were ordinary work product and the plaintiff might be able to use the photographs to question witnesses, seek expert opinions, or pursue alternate theories of his case;

(b) Grant the plaintiff's motion for production of the fourteen photographs because the plaintiff was entitled to all materials relating to the accident in the defendant's possession and control;

(c) Deny the plaintiff's motion for production of the fourteen photographs because the photographs were protected from production as ordinary work product;

(d) Deny the plaintiff's motion for production of the fourteen photographs because the photographs were the defense attorney's opinion work product, which materials was absolutely protected from discovery;

(e) Deny the plaintiff's motion for production of the fourteen photographs because the photographs did not contain any useful information for the plaintiff's development of his case.

\* \* \*

The trustee of a revocable living trust sued the Lake Erie Utilities Company in the federal district court for the Northern District of Ohio. The plaintiff moved for a judgment on the pleadings or in the alternative, to strike the defendant's answers. The defendants filed an opposition to the plaintiff's motions.

In their answer to the plaintiff's complaint, the defendants answered with only one of two responses to each allegation in which they either: (1) denied the allegations of a particular paragraph "in the manner and form alleged;" or (2) "neither admit nor deny the allegations," leaving the plaintiff "to his strict proofs thereof."

The plaintiff argued that the federal rules do not permit these types of responses to a plaintiff's allegations and that the responses should be construed as admissions. The plaintiff requested that the court deem the allegations in the complaint admitted, and enter judgment on the pleadings pursuant to Rule 12(c). In the alternative, and for the same reasons, the plaintiff requests these answers be stricken pursuant to Rule 12(f).

The defendants responded that their answers were "more than sufficient to meet the federal notice pleading standards that require parties to plead claims and defenses in a simple, concise, and direct manner."

**QUESTION:**

(22) In response to the plaintiff's motion to strike the defendant's answers pursuant to Fed.R.Civ.P. 12(f) and to grant a judgment on the pleadings pursuant to Fed.R.Civ.P. 12(c), the federal district court should:

  (a)  Grant judgment on the pleadings to the plaintiff because the defendant's responses did not follow the form required in Fed.R.Civ.P. 8(b) and (d);

  (b)  Grant judgment on the pleadings to the plaintiff and sanction the defense attorney pursuant to Fed.R.Civ.P. 11;

  (c)  Deny the plaintiff's motion for a judgment on the pleadings pursuant to Fed.R.Civ.P. 12(c), but grant the plaintiff's motion to strike pursuant to Fed.R.Civ.P. 12(f);

  (d)  Deny the plaintiff's two motions because the federal rules permit defendants to respond with general denials and the defendant's answers are simple, concise, and direct;

  (e)  Hold that the defendants answers failed to comport with the requirements of Fed.R.Civ.P. 8(b) and (d), but grant the defendant leave to amend his answers pursuant to Fed.R.Civ.P. 15.

* * *

George Wadis, a state prisoner proceeding *pro se*, filed suit in the federal district court for the Eastern District of Pennsylvania under 42 U.S.C. § 1983 against the Norristown State Hospital and two individuals identified only as "Theodore" and "Isaiah." He alleged that he had been beaten by those individuals and he sought three million dollars in damages. The Hospital failed to enter an appearance and file an answer, and Wadis moved for a default judgment. After a hearing on the motion, the district court dismissed Wadis' complaint for failure to state a claim upon which relief could be granted. The court concluded that the Hospital was not a "person" within the meaning of 42 U.S.C. § 1983 and that Wadis had not identified or served the other defendants.

About two weeks later, Wadis filed a motion for leave to file an amended complaint, seeking to add new defendants and expand his claims. Wadis named eighteen additional defendants in his amendment, all of whom he alleged were employees of the Hospital. Wadis stated that he could not discover the last names of "Theodore" and "Isaiah"—the Hospital employees alleged to have beaten him—so he sought to add numerous other individuals who he claimed worked in the building where he was attacked. He claimed that these defendants were part of an ongoing conspiracy to victimize him by tampering with his food, forcing drugs on him, and stealing his mail. He also alleged that he was subject to "serious life threatening abuses" within the Philadelphia prison system. Wadis' allegations of new abuses did not appear to arise out of the 2012 beating at the Hospital, and at least one of them did not concern the Hospital. There is no evidence that the new defendants received notice of the lawsuit or had reason to believe that Wadis intended to sue them.

The statute of limitations for § 1983 claims arising in Pennsylvania is two years. The incident and injury Wadis complained of occurred on May 16, 2012, whereas his motion to amend the complaint was signed on August 26, 2014, and filed on September 4, 2012, more than two years later. Wadis argued that the statute of limitations should have been be tolled until his release from prison, but courts generally recognize that a state's statute of limitations for personal injury tort claims—and its tolling principles—generally govern § 1983 claims. Pennsylvania does not have a provision that tolls the limitations period during an inmate's incarceration.

The district court denied the motion, noting briefly that the statute of limitations had expired and that Wadis had shown no basis for the proposed amendment to relate back to the original complaint under Rule 15(c) of the Federal Rules of Civil Procedure. Wadis then appealed to the United States Court of Appeals for the Third Circuit.

QUESTION:

(23) On the plaintiff's appeal from the district court's denial of leave to amend his complaint, the Third Circuit Court of Appeal should:

    (a) Reverse the district court's denial of the plaintiff's amendment because courts generally liberally grant leave to amend pursuant to Fed.R.Civ.P. 15(a);

    (b) Reverse the district court's denial of the plaintiff amendment because the plaintiff Wadis was unable to properly identify his assailants at the time of his assault and injury;

(c)   Reverse the district court's denial of the plaintiff's amendment
      because his amendment related back to the original complain
      under Fed.R.Civ.P. 15(c);

(d)   Affirm the district court's denial of the amendment because the
      statute of limitations had expired and his amendment could not
      relate back to the original complaint;

(e)   Affirm the district court's denial of the amendment because
      Wadis should not be permitted to conform his pleadings to this
      proof under Fed.R.Civ.P. 15(b).

* * *

Ronald T. Squyres filed a lawsuit in the 19th Judicial District Court in East
Baton Rouge Parish, Louisiana, against United Airlines, Inc. The plaintiff
alleged that he boarded United Airlines Flight in Phoenix, Arizona to return
to his home in Baton Rouge, Louisiana. He alleged that because he suffered
from fibromyalgia, a painful nerve disease, he upgraded to a first-class seat . . .
Before takeoff, the plaintiff went to the restroom. As he was returning to his
seat, he was asked by a security person from United Airlines to leave the flight
because a flight attendant saw him stumble getting on to the airplane and
thought he was drunk. The plaintiff informed the security person that he was
not drunk, but after the flight attendant insisted he leave, the plaintiff got off
of the airplane in fear of arrest. The plaintiff stayed in Phoenix for an
additional two days before he could return home to Baton Rouge.

In his state court complaint, the plaintiff alleged that as a result of the incident
he "suffered increased paranoia and nervousness." He sought damages for the
following categories of injuries: (a) severe mental anguish and distress; (b)
severe paranoia; (c) airline ticket expenses; (d) hotel expenses; and (e) other
damages which may be shown at the trial. The plaintiff specifically alleged
that his "cause of action did not exceed fifty thousand dollars exclusive of
interest and costs." In Louisiana state court, plaintiffs are prohibited from
alleging a specific monetary amount of damages sought in their petitions and
the plaintiff indicated he did not specify and amount of damages because he
was not seeking a jury trial.

The defendant removed the action, alleging that the court had diversity
jurisdiction pursuant to 28 U.S.C. § 1332. The defendant alleged that despite
the statement in the petition that the plaintiff's cause of action "did not exceed
fifty thousand dollars exclusive of interest and costs," removal was appropriate
because the plaintiff "did not affirmatively and unequivocally stipulate that he
renounces a damages award in excess of $75,000.00." The defendant claimed
that the amount in controversy exceeded $75,000.00 for the purpose of
diversity jurisdiction solely because the plaintiff did not affirmatively seek "to
preclude" removal by stipulating that the jurisdictional amount was not
satisfied. The defendant did not discuss in the notice of removal whether the
amount in controversy was facially apparent or otherwise present any facts in
controversy or summary judgment type evidence in support of a finding that
the amount in controversy requirement was satisfied.

The plaintiff filed a motion to remand, arguing that the amount in controversy requirement was not satisfied.

**QUESTION:**

(24) In response to the plaintiff's petition for remand to state court for lack of diversity jurisdiction with regard to the amount in controversy, the federal district court should:

    (a) Grant the plaintiff's motion to remand the case to state court because the jurisdictional amount was not facially apparent and the defendant did not otherwise prove that the plaintiff's claim exceeded the jurisdictional amount;

    (b) Grant the plaintiff's motion to remand the case to state court because there was a lack of diversity of citizenship;

    (c) Deny the plaintiff's motion to remand the case to state court because the plaintiff refused to submit to a binding stipulation precluding recovery in exceeding the jurisdictional amount;

    (d) Deny the plaintiff's motion to remand the case to state court because common sense supported the conclusion that the amount in controversy exceeds $75,000;

    (e) Deny the plaintiff's motion to remand the case to state court because the plaintiff had failed to carry its burden regarding an allegation of the amount in controversy.

* * *

Shao Ying Sun sued Ikea U.S. West, Inc. in the federal district court for the Northern District of California. The plaintiff alleged that while standing at the check-out counter at the defendant's Emeryville, California location, an employee negligently set a "low-pallet-type cart" in motion. The plaintiff contended the cart struck her, causing serious injuries.

The plaintiff served a request for production of documents on the defendant for "any and all documents pertaining to the incident, including any investigation of the incident." The defendant initially objected to the request in its entirety as "vague and ambiguous," but agreed to produce responsive documents in its possession. Subsequently, the defendant's counsel informed the plaintiff that the defendant was unable to locate the incident report but would continue its search. The defendant was five days late in its initial response to the plaintiff's request for the incident report, and explained it was unable to locate the report "after performing a reasonable and diligent search," but would continue to search.

Once the defendant located the incident report, the defendant's counsel informed the plaintiff that an amended response would be sent, including additional objections. The defendant served an amended response thirty-three days after the plaintiff first was alerted that the incident report was not included in the initial request. The defendant subsequently served an amended response, objecting to production of the incident report "to the extent it calls for information under attorney-client privilege and attorney work-product doctrine."

The plaintiff rejected the defendant's explanation, arguing that the defendant produced extensive documentation of company policies and procedures regarding the preparation of incident reports. The plaintiff added that the defendant's employee manual provided eight pages on the company's incident reporting system, as well as a sample incident report. The plaintiff argued these policies, along with the fact that the plaintiff remained on the store floor after the incident until paramedics arrived, made it reasonably apparent that an incident report likely existed. The plaintiff did not argue that she suffered prejudice as a result of the delay.

After attempting to resolve their dispute informally, the plaintiff filed a motion to compel production of the documents, including the incident report. The plaintiff argued that the defendant failed to raise a timely objection to the request for production of documents and therefore waived any objections. Alternatively, the plaintiff argued the defendant failed to meet its burden of proving the incident report was protected under attorney work-product doctrine and attorney-client privilege. In response, the defendant maintained its objections were timely since it did not know the incident report existed "after performing a reasonable and diligent search." The defendant claimed to have acted in good faith by immediately notifying the plaintiff's counsel once it located the document. The defendant also maintained the incident report was protected by attorney work-product doctrine and attorney-client privilege because it was "submitted to the defendant's counsel and risk management department for the purpose of evaluating the potential litigation claim."

**QUESTION:**

(25) With regard to the plaintiff's contention that the defendant had waived any right to contest production of documents, the federal district court should rule that:

(a)   The defendant had waived any objections to the plaintiff's discovery requests because it acted in bad faith in responding to the plaintiff's initial request for production;

(b)   The defendant waived any objections to the plaintiff's discovery requests because the defendant's response to the plaintiff's initial request was untimely;

(c)   The defendant waived any objections to the plaintiff's discovery requests because it previously had turned over various company manuals and other materials;

(d)   The defendant had not waived any objections to the plaintiff's discovery requests because it had reasonably complied with the plaintiff's initial requests for production;

(e)   The defendant had not waived any objections to the plaintiff's discovery requests because parties cannot waive objections to discovery requests.

# CHAPTER 5
# EXAM #5 PROBLEMS AND QUESTIONS

Following a five-day trial held in the federal district court for the Northern District of Illinois, a jury found for the defendants City of Chicago, Nicholas Cervantes, John Frano, and Wayne Frano, Jr. and against the plaintiffs Anthony Bennett, Jeffery Brown, James Mustafa, and Randell Williams. The plaintiffs had alleged Fourth Amendment claims of excessive force, false arrest, unlawful search and seizure, and conspiracy. The court entered judgment in favor of the defendants. The plaintiffs Brown and Mustafa then moved, pursuant to Fed.R.Civ.P. 50(b) and 59, for judgment as a matter of law in their favor or, alternatively, for a new trial.

During the trial, Brown's failed to first raise his arguments for a judgment as a matter of law pursuant to a Rule 50(a) motion, prior to submission of the case to the jury. On his Rule 50(b) motion, Brown asserted that the language of Rule 50 need not be applied rigidly where the moving party made its arguments clear in previously presented documents, such as motions *in limine* and trial briefs, which he claimed he had done.

QUESTION:

(1) As a threshold matter, on Brown's Rule 50(b) motion for a judgment as a matter of law, the federal district court should:

   (a) Consider Brown's Rule 50(b) motion, because Fed.R.Civ.P. 50(b) does not require that a party seeking a judgment as a matter of law at the conclusion of a trial have previously sought a judgment as a matter of law earlier in the case;

   (b) Consider Brown's Rule 50(b) motion, because Brown effectively had called the court's attention to evidentiary deficiencies in its earlier motions *in limine* and trial briefs;

   (c) Consider Brown's Rule 50(b) motion, because Brown should be able to challenge the jury's verdict post-trial;

   (d) Decline to consider Brown's Rule 50(b) motion, because he failed to make a prior Rule 50(a) motion;

   (e) Decline to consider Brown's Rule 50(b) motion, because this would unfairly prejudice the defendants who had already won a jury verdict.

* * *

For the purpose of this question only, assume that the court decided to adjudicate Brown's Rule 50(b) motion for a judgment as a matter of law.

At the time of the search, the police officers were searching for marijuana in the second floor apartment when Brown was found; at the same time, officers were searching for weapons in the basement apartment of the same building. In his motion for judgment as a matter of law, Brown asserted that the defendants violated his Fourth Amendment right to be free from unreasonable search and seizures. He contended that the search of his body and subsequent handcuffing was unreasonable as a matter of law because he did not live in either of the apartment building units identified in the defendants' search warrant; he could not reasonably have been mistaken for the target of the warrant of the second floor apartment (a middle-aged woman named Jacqueline Williams); he posed no threat to the defendants; he was handcuffed for an excessive amount of time (approximately two hours); and he was made to sit in his boxer shorts and was not allowed to pull up his pants during much of the time he spent handcuffed.

Brown contended that it was unreasonable of the defendants to force him to sit handcuffed in his boxer shorts for what he says was two hours. At trial, Brown testified that he was not an occupant of the apartment being searched, but that he was present at the apartment during the search because he was thirsty and had come over that night for a glass of water Brown testified that he was pulled onto the ground by police officers because he had his back to the officers when they first entered the upstairs apartment. He testified that a police officer—he did not identify which one—pulled his boxer shorts down, searched both his boxer shorts and his private parts, and then pulled his boxer shorts back up. Brown stated that he was repeatedly punched and kicked by various police officers, and he specifically identified defendant Nicholas Cervantes as the officer who punched him in the face—an assertion that Officer Cervantes denied. The jury also heard testimony from Officer Michael Napoli—the officer who "breached" the upstairs apartment door with a battering ram (and was thus the first person into the upstairs apartment and who remained there throughout the search)—that he never saw any police officers put their hands on Mr. Brown or struggle with him in any way. Brown stated that he never sought medical care for the beating he said he suffered at the hands of the police.

Brown testified that after he had been beaten and searched, various officers put him on his feet and placed him on the living room couch, although they left his pants down around his ankles. Brown gave testimony, frequently at odds with his deposition testimony, as to his ability to identify the officers responsible for his search and detention. Takeyla Williams, who was in the second floor apartment during the entirety of the search, stated that Brown's pants fell down during the search because he wears his pants "low." Takeyla Williams, who arrived at the second floor apartment while the search was in progress, stated that she saw Brown's pants around his ankles, that Brown asked to pull them up, and that police officers "eventually" allowed him to pull his pants back up.

With the exception of conflicting testimony regarding Officer Cervantes having hit Brown in the face, the jury heard no testimony from Brown specifically identifying John Frano, Wayne Frano, and/or Nicholas Cervantes as the officers who searched his body and then handcuffed him.

The test of reasonableness under the Fourth Amendment is an objective one and requires a careful balancing of the specific facts and circumstances underlying the case, including "the severity of the crime at issue, whether the suspect poses an immediate threat to the safety of the officers or others, and whether he is actively resisting arrest or attempting to evade arrest by flight." In considering whether actions taken were unreasonable, the interests of law enforcement must be considered, as well, including the "interest in preventing flight in the event that incriminating evidence is found. Less obvious, but sometimes of greater importance, is the interest in minimizing the risk of harm to the officers." Even under circumstances where there is no direct evidence of enhanced danger to the police, "the execution of a warrant to search for narcotics is the kind of transaction that may give rise to sudden violence or frantic efforts to conceal or destroy evidence, and the risk of harm to both the police and the occupants is minimized if the officers routinely exercise unquestioned command of the situation."

At the end of the trial, the jury was instructed that in order for Brown to prevail, he needed to show that one or more the defendants (meaning, specifically, John Frano, Wayne Frano, or Nicholas Cervantes) detained him, and that the detention was unreasonable. In determining whether Mr. Brown's detention was unreasonable, the jury was instructed to consider: (1) the severity of the suspected crime or other circumstances that led to the search warrant; (2) whether Brown was the subject of the investigation; (3) whether Brown posed a threat to the safety of the defendants or to others or to the ability of the defendants to conduct the search; (4) whether Brown was actively resisting arrest or attempting to flee; and (5) whether Brown's detention was unnecessarily painful, degrading, prolonged, or involved an undue invasion of privacy. The jury returned a verdict in favor of the defendants as to Brown's Fourth Amendment claim and conspiracy claim.

### QUESTION:

(2) Assuming for the purpose of this question only that the court permitted Brown's Role 50(b) motion for a judgment as a matter of law to be adjudicated on its merits, the federal district court should:

    (a) Grant Brown's Rule 50(b) motion for a judgment as a matter of law because no reasonable jury could have found for the defendants;

    (b) Grant Brown's Rule 50(b) motion because the police officers' credibility was in question;

    (c) Deny Brown's Rule 50(b) because the jury rationally could have concluded that the detention of Brown was neither degrading nor unduly prolonged;

    (d) Deny Brown's Rule 50(b) motion because granting his motion this would usurp the province of the jury as fact-finder;

(e)   Deny Brown's Rule 50 (b) motion because there was conflicting
      testimony between his prior deposition testimony and his trial
      testimony.

* * *

Danny J. Wertz brought an action in the federal district court for the Middle
District of Pennsylvania, arising out of the termination of his employment with
GEA Heat Exchangers, Inc. Wertz alleged that he was terminated in violation
of the federal Family and Medical Leave Act (FMLA), Americans with
Disabilities Act, and the Pennsylvania Human Relations Act. The defendants
maintained that they did not discriminate or retaliate against the plaintiff.

A discovery dispute arose among the parties. Wertz sought to take eleven
depositions, one deposition in excess of the ten permitted in the court's case
management order, including the depositions of Tim Ambrose, Sandra Shirey
and Dave Stauch. The defendants opposed any deposition in excess of ten, and
further opposed the depositions of Shirey and Stauch on the basis that the
depositions were disproportionate to the needs of the case.

Wertz made a particularized showing to the court as to why additional
depositions were reasonable and necessary, averring that the case was
complex so as to justify deviation from the presumptive number of depositions.
The plaintiff argued that the information sought through the proposed
deposition of Ambrose was information only in the defendants' possession, as
Ambrose was a current employee of the defendant. Wertz's attorney
represented to the court that they expected the deposition to be limited to two
hours.

The plaintiff also sought to take the depositions of Shirey and Stauch, and the
defendants objected. The plaintiff submitted that Shirey's deposition was
relevant to impeach defendant Brubaker's testimony, because she worked on
the plaintiff's FMLA requests, attendance tracking, and re-certification under
Brubaker's supervision. The plaintiff additionally submitted that the Stauch's
deposition was relevant to whether defendants Lutz and Lee were aware of the
plaintiff's reading disability.

The defendants objected to these depositions as speculative. The defendants
further submitted that these depositions were disproportionate to the needs of
the case, and that the burden and the expense of the depositions outweighed
any relevance they might have.

**QUESTION:**

(3)   On the plaintiff's request to take in excess of the ten depositions permitted
      by the discovery rules and the court's case management order, the federal
      district court should:

      (a)   Grant the plaintiff's request to take additional depositions
            because the proposed depositions would not be unduly
            burdensome to the defendant and that the information sought
            was important to the issues at stake in the case;

(b)  Grant the plaintiff's request to take additional depositions because the proposed depositions were within the scope of permissible discovery under Fed.R.Civ.P. 26(b);

(c)  Deny the plaintiff's request to take additional depositions because the plaintiff's request was not proportional to the needs of the case;

(d)  Deny the plaintiff's request to take additional depositions because the additional depositions were unduly burdensome and would increase the cost of the litigation;

(e)  Deny the plaintiff's request to take additional depositions because the proposed depositions were cumulative of other testimony and unnecessary.

\* \* \*

OHM Hotel Group, LLC (OHM) initially filed suit in the Circuit Court of St. Louis County, State of Missouri against Dewberry Consultants, LLC. The plaintiff's petition alleged a state law claim for breach of contract. Dewberry removed the action to the federal district court for the Eastern District of Missouri based on diversity of citizenship pursuant to 28 U.S.C. §§ 1332(a), 1441(b) and 1446.

Both the plaintiff and defendant were limited liability companies. The petition alleged only that plaintiff OHM was a Missouri limited liability company and that the defendant Dewberry was a Virginia limited liability company. Dewberry's removal notice alleged that plaintiff OHM was an LLC organized under Missouri law, and alleged "on information and belief" that OHM's principal place of business was in Missouri and that none of its members were citizens of Virginia. With respect to Dewberry's own citizenship, the notice of removal alleged Dewberry was a limited liability company organized under the laws of Virginia with its principal place of business in Virginia, and that its sole member was The Dewberry Companies, LLC, also a limited liability company organized under the laws of Virginia.

## QUESTION:

(4)  In evaluating whether the federal court has valid removal jurisdiction, the federal district court should determine that:

(a)  The federal court had valid removal jurisdiction because the plaintiff was a citizen of Missouri and the defendant was a citizen of Virginia;

(b)  The federal court had valid removal jurisdiction because OHM's principal place of business was in Missouri and none of its members were citizens of Virginia;

(c)  The federal court had valid removal jurisdiction because Dewberry was a limited liability company organized under the laws of Virginia with its principal place of business in Virginia;

(d)  The federal court did not have valid removal jurisdiction because OHM pleaded a single breach of contract claim in its state court petition;

(e)  The federal court could not determine whether it had valid removal jurisdiction because the court could not determine the citizenship of the parties based on the notice of removal.

\* \* \*

Scott Tanner filed an action against Kaiser Foundation Health Plan, Inc., the Kaiser Foundation Hospitals, and The Permanente Medical Group, Inc. in California state court. The defendants removed the action to the federal district court for the Northern District of California based on federal-question jurisdiction.

Tanner began working for the Kaiser Permanente Pharmacy Department, serving as a staff pharmacist, a lead pharmacist, and finally, a pharmacist supervisor at Kaiser's Manteca location. In a 70-page complaint, Tanner alleged that he was subject to harassment, discrimination, and retaliation at work beginning. The plaintiff was a white male, over the age of 40, with an undisclosed "physical disability/physiological health condition." According to the plaintiff, Kaiser's pharmacy staff in Manteca was 85–90% Asian, 85–90% female, and 90–100% under the age of forty. The plaintiff asserted that he suffered adverse employment consequences based on his color, gender, and age, as well as his disability, for which the defendants allegedly failed to provide adequate accommodation. The plaintiff further asserted that he suffered retaliation based on these same factors, as well as for reporting the defendants' misconduct affecting patient safety and care.

Tanner was suspended from work at Kaiser. According to the plaintiff, the defendants explained the basis for his suspension. The plaintiff executed a separation agreement and separated from Kaiser. He alleged that he executed the separation agreement under duress, and was therefore entitled to rescind it. He further alleged that the defendants constructively discharged him in violation of public policy.

Tanner sought an array of damages, costs, and an order permanently enjoining Kaiser from committing certain further acts of retaliation and discrimination.

Tanner filed suit in the Alameda County Superior Court, alleging causes of action for: (1) unlawful attainment of invalid separation agreement; (2) age discrimination in violation of the ADEA and the FEHA; (3) disability discrimination in Violation of ADA and FEHA; (4) race, color, gender, and national origin discrimination in violation of Title VII of the Civil Rights Act and FEHA; (5) failure to accommodate disability; (6) retaliation; (7) failure to prevent discrimination, harassment or retaliation; (8) unlawful business practices; and (9) constructive discharge in violation of public policy. The majority of the plaintiff's claims alleged violations of both state and federal law.

The defendants removed the action to federal court. The notice of removal averred that the court has jurisdiction pursuant to 28 U.S.C. § 1331 because the "Plaintiff specifically and unambiguously alleges claims arising under federal law in his Second, Third, Fourth, Fifth, Sixth, and Seventh Causes of Action." The plaintiff filed a motion to remand, arguing that removal was "procedurally defective" and that "exclusive federal question jurisdiction" was lacking.

## QUESTION:

(5) On the Plaintiff's petition for remand of his case back to California state court, the federal district court should:

(a) Grant the plaintiff's motion for remand to state court because removal statutes are strictly construed against removal;

(b) Grant the plaintiff's motion for remand to state court because there is a presumption against removal;

(c) Grant the plaintiff's motion for remand to state court because the plaintiff has pleaded causes of action sounding in both state and federal law;

(d) Deny the plaintiff's motion for remand to state court because the plaintiff's case was within the court's concurrent federal question jurisdiction;

(e) Deny the plaintiff's motion for remand to state court because any doubts about removal should be decided in favor of the removing defendant.

\* \* \*

Patti and Michael Wenzel, who lived in New York City, vacationed in Aruba at a Marriott International resort. Patti had an accident there and was injured during her stay at the Marriott Aruba property. Her injuries were treated in New York City. The Wenzels subsequently filed a lawsuit against Marriott International, Inc., alleging negligence among other claims, in the federal district court for the Southern District of New York. The defendant filed a motion to dismiss on the grounds of *forum non conveniens*, which the district court granted.

On the motion to dismiss on the grounds of *forum non conveniens*, the Wenzels had argued that Aruba was an inadequate forum because tort cases there are decided by judges, pretrial discovery was more limited, and the potential recovery was less than if the case proceeded in the United States. They noted that Patti Wenzel's injuries had been treated at New York City medical facilities, and that they resided in New York.

In support of the *forum non conveniens* dismissal, the defendant contended that the premises, equipment, employees, and other sources of proof relevant to establishing liability were, with the exception of the plaintiffs themselves, located entirely in Aruba. The defendant also identified a busy Southern District of New York docket, the difficulty of applying foreign law, and the importance of the hotel and tourism industry to Aruba supported Aruba as the forum for the litigation. The district court concluded that service of process on the defendants was possible if the Wenzels brought their suit in Aruba, and litigation of this sort was permitted in that jurisdiction.

QUESTION:

(6) On appeal from the district court's grant of dismissal based on the doctrine of forum non conveniens, the Second Circuit Court of Appeals should:

    (a) Affirm the district court's dismissal based on *forum non conveniens* because plaintiffs cannot forum shop for their own litigation advantage;

    (b) Affirm the district court's dismissal based on *forum non conveniens* because Aruba was an adequate alternative forum;

    (c) Reverse the district court's dismissal based on *forum non conveniens* because Aruba's procedural law was less favorable to the plaintiff;

    (d) Reverse the district court's dismissal based on *forum non conveniens* because underlying tort law was less favorable to the plaintiffs;

    (e) Reverse the district court's dismissal based on *forum non conveniens* for the convenience of the witnesses and the parties, and in the interest of justice.

* * *

Jobe Danganan brought a class action against Guardian Protection Services in the Court of Common Pleas of Philadelphia County, in which he challenged the legality of its home security protection services agreements with its customers. The complaint alleged violations of the Pennsylvania Unfair Trade Practices and Consumer Protection Law and the Pennsylvania Fair Credit Extension Uniformity Act. The action was timely removed to the federal district court for the Eastern District of Pennsylvania on the basis of diversity of citizenship.

Guardian moved to transfer venue to the United States District Court for the Western District of Pennsylvania pursuant to 28 U.S.C. § 1404(a). The motion to transfer was grounded on a forum selection clause allegedly found in all the agreements. It read in relevant part:

> Each party hereby irrevocably agrees that any suit, action or other legal proceeding ("suit") arising out of or from, in connection with or as a result of this Agreement shall be brought by such party exclusively in the state courts of record or the courts of the United States located in the district or county where the other party's residence or principal place of business is located. Each party consents to the exclusive jurisdiction and venue of each such court in any such suit and waives any objection that it may have to Jurisdiction of venue of any such suit.

It was undisputed that Guardian's principal place of business was located in Allegheny County, Pennsylvania. Allegheny County lies within the Western District of Pennsylvania. Guardian argued the lawsuit belonged in that district pursuant to the forum selection clause. The plaintiff countered that the forum selection clause should not be honored because the agreements with Guardian's customers were contracts of adhesion.

The plaintiff argued that this court should apply the usual balancing of interests under § 1404(a) because the plaintiff here was a consumer who signed a form contract and realistically had no opportunity to negotiate over its terms. The plaintiff alleged that the forum selection clause was the product of fraud or overreaching, but did not offered supporting evidence. The forum selection clause contained reciprocal terms. When a customer initiates suit, the clause required that suit be brought in the place encompassing Guardian's principal place of business. However, if Guardian initiated suit, the clause required the suit to be brought in a forum where the customer resided.

## QUESTION:

(7) On the defendant Guardian's motion to transfer the litigation to the Western District of Pennsylvania, the federal district court should:

(a) Grant the motion to transfer to the Western District of Pennsylvania based on the authority of *Carnival Cruise Lines v. Shute*;

(b) Grant the motion to transfer to the Western District of Pennsylvania because the contracting parties were sophisticated entities;

(c) Deny the motion to transfer to the Western District of Pennsylvania because the forum selection clause was clearly unconscionable;

(d) Deny the motion to transfer to the Western District of Pennsylvania because courts should pay deference to a plaintiff's choice of forum;

(e) Deny the motion to transfer to the Western District of Pennsylvania because the forum selection clause unfairly favored the corporate defendant.

\* \* \*

Lois Breech brought an action against Defendant Liberty Mutual Insurance Company, asserting breach of contract and bad faith arising from a disputed insurance claim. Non-party Finnicum Adjusting Company moved to intervene in the litigation. Finnicum was corporation organized under the laws of Ohio with its principal place of business in Ohio. Breech was a citizen of Ohio. Liberty Mutual was a company organized under the laws of Wisconsin with its principal place of business in Massachusetts.

Breech purchased a homeowner's insurance policy from Liberty Mutual. After damage occurred to the structure, the plaintiff pursued a claim under her policy in the federal district court for the Southern District of Ohio. Finnicum entered into a contract with Breech, under which Finnicum was apparently entitled to fourteen percent of any proceeds the plaintiff might eventually receive from her disputed claim with Liberty Mutual.

In its motion to intervene, Finnicum argued that it had a substantial legal interest in any award that the plaintiff might receive in the underlying insurance litigation. According to Finnicum, it could only protect that interest by intervening and filing as a third-party plaintiff. Although styled as a motion to intervene, Finnicum's filing also argued for its joinder as a required party under Fed.R.Civ.P. 19. Breech opposed the intervention and argued that Finnicum did not have a substantial legal interest in this matter.

## QUESTION:

(8) On Finnicum's motion to intervene as of right pursuant to Fed.R.Civ.P. 24(a), the federal district court should:

   (a) Grant the motion to intervene as of right because the movant had a property interest in the underlying insurance litigation;

   (b) Grant the motion to intervene as of right because the movant's interest would not be adequately protected by the plaintiff in the litigation;

   (c) Deny the motion to intervene because the movant's contract with the plaintiff has nothing do with the underlying insurance litigation;

   (d) Deny the motion to intervene because the movant's presence in the litigation will needlessly complicated the proceedings;

   (e) Deny the motion to intervene as of right, but permit the movant to intervene permissively under Fed.R.Civ.P. 24(b).

## QUESTION:

(9) In the same litigation, Finnicum alternatively argued that its joinder was required under Fed.R.Civ.P. 19. Construing Finnicum's motion alternatively as a motion for joinder under Fed.R.Civ.P. 19, the federal district court should:

   (a) Order that Finnicum be joined because the company was a necessary party to the litigation;

   (b) Order that Finnicum be joined because the company was an indispensable party to the litigation;

   (c) Deny Finnicum's request to be joined because the company was neither a necessary nor an indispensable party the litigation;

   (d) Deny Finnicum's request to be joined because even though Finnicum had an interest in the outcome of the underlying litigation, the court could allow the case to go forward without Finnicum in equity and good conscience;

(e) Deny Finnicum's request to be joined because this would destroy the court's diversity jurisdiction.

\* \* \*

Gregory Nehrlich worked for JLW-TW Corp. dba Suntan Supply (Suntan), but he subsequently resigned. He filed a notice of claim with the California Labor Commissioner asserting that Suntan failed to pay him wages owed in the total amount of $13,446.54 and reimbursable business expenses in the amount of $672.85.

Thereafter Suntan sued Nehrlich in the Court of Common Pleas in Lorain County, Ohio, alleging false representations, breach of employment contract, tortious interference with business relations, and defamation. In the Ohio action, Suntan alleged that Nehrlich made false representations to the California Labor Commission, which he then copied to JK Group, a company with which Suntan had a substantial business relationship, thereby defaming Suntan and harming Suntan's business relationship with the JK Group. Suntan further alleged that Nehrlich violated his employment agreement with Suntan by leaving Suntan to work for a competitor, taking confidential information with him, and using this confidential information to steer business to the competitor.

Nehrlich then sued Suntan in California Superior Court alleging wrongful constructive termination in violation of public policy, intentional misrepresentation, negligent misrepresentation, and breach of contract. In this lawsuit, Nehrlich alleged that Suntan violated his employment agreement, failed to follow through on promises inherent in the agreement, and forced him to resign when it failed to pay taxes as required. Suntan removed the action to federal court for the Southern District of California based diversity jurisdiction and moved to dismiss the case pursuant to Federal Rule of Civil Procedure 12(b)(6).

Suntan moved to dismiss on the grounds the plaintiff's claims were "barred because they constituted compulsory counterclaims which had not been asserted in state court litigation pending in Ohio involving the subject matter of this dispute."

The Ohio rule governing compulsory counterclaims, Ohio Civ. R. 13, which was modeled on Rule 13 of the Federal Rules of Civil Procedure, states, in relevant part:

> A pleading shall state as a counterclaim any claim which at the time of serving the pleading the pleader has against any opposing party, if it arises out of the transaction or occurrence that is the subject matter of the opposing party's claim and does not require for its adjudication the presence of third parties of whom the court cannot acquire jurisdiction. But the pleader need not state the claim if (1) at the time the action was commenced the claim was the subject of another pending action, or (2) the opposing party brought suit upon his claim by attachment or other process by which the court did not

acquire jurisdiction to render a personal judgment on that claim, and the pleader is not stating any counterclaim under this Rule 13.

Ohio Civ. R. 13(A). The Supreme Court of Ohio applies a two-prong test for determining whether there is a compulsory counterclaim: (1) does the claim exist at the time of serving the pleading; and (2) does the claim arise out of the transaction or occurrence that is the subject matter of the opposing claim.

## QUESTION:

(10) On the defendant's Suntan's motion to dismiss the plaintiff's claims because those claims were compulsory counterclaims in the Ohio action, the federal district court should:

(a) Grant the defendant's motion to dismiss the plaintiff's claims because they were compulsory counterclaims in the Ohio action;

(b) Grant the defendant's motion to dismiss the plaintiff's claims because were redundant of the Ohio litigation;

(c) Deny the defendant's motion to dismiss the plaintiff's claims because the Ohio state court action had no relevance to the plaintiff's federal action;

(d) Deny the defendant's motion to dismiss the plaintiff's claims because Ohio state law cannot determine federal proceedings in California federal court;

(e) Deny the defendant's motion to dismiss the plaintiff's claims because the plaintiff can choose to litigate his claims solely in California court.

\* \* \*

SPM Thermo-Shield, Inc. (SPM) filed a four-count complaint against SICC GmbH (SICC) and Waldemar Walczok in the federal district court for the Middle District of Florida, alleging that the defendants impermissibly used test results, certifications, photographs, and other materials belonging to the plaintiff to advertise and market SICC's products.

SPM was a Florida corporation in the business of marketing and selling energy-efficient paint and coating materials. SICC, a German corporation, was a competitor in the coating materials business. Walczok was the Managing Director of SICC. According to SPM, SICC made multiple sales and marketing presentations in which SICC used SPM's studies, test results, certifications, and photographs to tout SICC products. For example, SPM alleged that multiple SICC presentations used photographs of buildings coated with SPM's products while misrepresenting that the buildings were coated with SICC's products. SPM further alleged that SICC's publicly-available website similarly misappropriated SPM's marketing materials. Based on these allegations, SPM brought causes of action against the defendants for misleading advertising in violation of Florida law (Count I), false advertising in violation of the Lanham Act (Count II), common law unfair competition (Count III), and deceptive and unfair trade practices in violation of statutes (Count IV). The defendants now moved to dismiss the complaint in its entirety for lack of personal jurisdiction.

Walczok argued that the complaint had to be dismissed as to him because the court lacked personal jurisdiction. Walczok was a German citizen and a non-resident of Florida. The complaint did not contain any specific allegation concerning personal jurisdiction over Walczok, although it alleged that Walczok "directed, controlled, ratified, participated in or was the moving force behind SICC's wrongful activity," and that SPM was harmed in Florida as a result. The complaint alleged that Walczok was subject to personal jurisdiction via Florida's long-arm statute as a result of the alleged "wrongful activity" he committed against SPM, a Florida corporation. The defendants argued that neither Walczok nor SICC had Florida contacts sufficient to permit the exercise of long-arm personal jurisdiction.

In its response to the motion to dismiss, SPM eschewed that argument and instead contended that the court has personal jurisdiction over Walczok because he was personally served in Naples as he was leaving a business meeting with SPM.

The parties have each submitted affidavits concerning the events surrounding the business meeting that brought Walczok to Florida. In early 2015 SPM commenced a trademark infringement lawsuit against SICC in Turkey. On July 3, 2015, an SICC employee emailed Peter Spiska, President of SPM, regarding the Turkish lawsuit and suggested that Spiska and Walczok meet in New York "to discuss the possibilities of a peaceful co-existence and successful business development in the future." In reply, Spiska expressed interest in meeting with Walczok and offered to host the meeting in Naples, Florida at his country club. SICC accepted the offer and the parties agreed to meet in Naples on July 23rd. Walczok averred that the sole reason he entered Florida was to attend the meeting and that he would not have attended had he known SPM intended to serve him while he was in Florida.

On July 22nd, the day before the meeting, SPM commenced this lawsuit. The summons issued in connection with the lawsuit listed SICC's address as 4784 Naples Lake Boulevard, which was the address of Spiska's country club. The meeting took place at the country club on July 23rd as planned. According to Walczok, while the meeting was ongoing "it appeared that SPM's representatives received a text message and immediately after receiving this alert they suddenly terminated the meeting and left the room." Walczok then left the meeting room and was served with process in the parking lot of the country club as he was walking to his car. Although Spiska averred that he "entered the meeting in good faith, but realistic of the potential that out disputes would not be resolved," neither he nor SPM took issue with Walczok's description of the events immediately preceding service of process.

**QUESTION:**

(11) With regard to whether the Florida federal court may assert personal jurisdiction over Walczok, the federal district court should find that:

    (a)   The court may assert personal jurisdiction over Walczok because he made a voluntary appearance in the jurisdiction;

   (b)   The court may assert personal jurisdiction over Walczok because he was "tagged" with service of process while in the jurisdiction;

   (c)   The court may assert personal jurisdiction over Walczok because by travelling to the meeting in Florida, he consented to the jurisdiction of the court;

   (d)   The court may not assert personal jurisdiction over Walczok because he was enticed into the jurisdiction under false pretenses;

   (e)   The court may not assert personal jurisdiction over Walczok because he made a special appearance in the jurisdiction, which cannot confer general jurisdiction for all issues.

* * *

In the same litigation, the plaintiff SPM further alleged that the court had personal jurisdiction over the defendant SICC because SICC's misleading advertising, Lanham Act violations, unfair competition, and deceptive and unfair trade practices were committed in Florida. In relevant part, Florida's long-arm statute provides for personal jurisdiction over defendants who commit "a tortious act" within Florida. Florida courts have interpreted this provisions expansively, concluding that it encompasses a "nonresident defendant who commits a tort outside of the state that causes injury inside the state." Furthermore, an out-of-state defendant's physical presence in Florida is not necessarily required. Rather, a nonresident defendant can commit a tortious act in Florida "through the nonresident defendant's telephonic, electronic, or written communications into Florida," as long as the cause of action arises from those communications.

SPM alleged that SICC knowingly and intentionally misappropriated SPM's studies, test results, certifications, and photographs. SPM further alleged that SICC used those marketing materials to tout SICC's competing products on SICC's publicly-available website and in sales presentations given in the United States. Finally, SPM alleged that its products competed with SICC's in the United States and, therefore, SICC's alleged misappropriation of SPM's marketing materials caused SPM injury in Florida.

In cases involving intentional torts, a defendant will be found to have constitutionally significant contact with a forum state if he "(1) committed an intentional tort (2) that was directly aimed at the forum, (3) causing an injury within the forum that the defendant should have reasonably anticipated."

### QUESTION:

(12) With regard to the defendant SICC motion to dismiss for a lack of personal jurisdiction pursuant to Fed.R.Civ.P. 12(b)(2), the federal district court should:

   (a)   Grant the defendant's motion to dismiss for a lack of person jurisdiction over SICC because SICC had not committed a tortious act in Florida;

(b) Grant the defendant's motion to dismiss for a lack of personal jurisdiction over SICC because the German defendant could not reasonably have anticipated that it would be haled into Florida court to answer to a lawsuit;

(c) Grant the defendant's motion to dismiss for a lack of personal jurisdiction over SICC because assertion of personal jurisdiction over the German corporation would offend traditional notions of fair play and substantial justice;

(d) Deny the defendant's motion to dismiss for a lack of person jurisdiction over SICC because the corporation had a contractual relationship with the plaintiff which supported the assertion of personal jurisdiction;

(e) Deny the defendant's motion to dismiss for a lack of personal jurisdiction because Florida had an interest in resolving the alleged misappropriation of a Florida company's trademarks and marketing materials.

\* \* \*

Lisa Zemba sued Integrated Tech Group, LLC (ITG) and Comcast Corporation, a joint venture, in the federal district court for the Southern District of Florida. Zemba alleged that a former employee of ITG, Orestes Alegre was dispatched to her home in order to repair a cable television box located in her bedroom. While there, Alegre falsely imprisoned Zemba and performed inappropriate and unsolicited sexual acts in her presence. Zemba alleged that she called 305-COMCAST in order to schedule the repair, that Alegre arrived in a vehicle bearing the Comcast logo, that he was wearing a Comcast shirt, that he utilized a Comcast-issued identification card to gain access to her home, and that it was only after these events that Zemba learned Alegre was not an employee of Comcast, but of the defendant ITG.

The plaintiff's complaint alleged three counts: Count I, for negligent hiring, was leveled only at the defendant ITG; Counts II and III, for negligent hiring and negligent supervision, respectively, were leveled only at the defendant Comcast.

The plaintiff's negligent hiring claim against ITG was founded on the allegation that the background check ITG had performed on Alegre prior to his hiring was inadequate because it did not include any check whatsoever of his background prior to his arriving in the United States from Cuba. The negligent hiring claim against Comcast was founded on the allegation that Comcast (1) approved ITG's issuance to Alegre of the identification badge bearing the Comcast logo that enabled Alegre to gain access to the plaintiff's home, (2) had an agreement with ITG regarding qualifications and background checks for applicants to whom ITG would issue Comcast-approved identification cards, and (3) that Comcast therefore had a duty to ensure that ITG's background check was sufficient to both ensure safety of customers and to comply with the agreement on background checks alleged to exist between the defendants. The plaintiff's negligent supervision claim against Comcast was founded on the allegation that Comcast did not properly supervise ITG's background check procedures to ensure the safety of its customers.

The defendants moved to dismiss the plaintiff's complaint pursuant to Fed.R.Civ.P. 12(b)(6) on several grounds, all turning on the adequacy of the complaint's factual allegations. ITG's chief argument was that the plaintiff's complaint failed to state a claim for negligent hiring under Florida Law. "To state a claim for negligent hiring, plaintiff must allege facts showing that the employer was put on notice of the harmful propensities of the employee". The Florida Supreme Court has held that to bring a prima facie case for negligent hiring, a plaintiff must demonstrate that: (1) the employer was required to make an appropriate investigation of the employee and failed to do so; (2) an appropriate investigation would have revealed the unsuitability of the employee for the particular duty to be performed or for employment in general; and (3) it was unreasonable for the employer to hire the employee in light of the information he knew or should have known.

ITG contended that the plaintiff's complaint lacked any allegations related to the second element of the negligent hiring cause of action. The plaintiff did not allege any facts to show that any investigation in to Alegre's background in Cuba would have revealed Alegre's unsuitability for employ, and did not allege that anything in Alegre's background would have in fact rendered him unsuitable for employ.

The plaintiff did not respond to ITG's argument on this point at all. Instead, the plaintiff argued that she has pled enough facts to state some unspecified claim for negligence under a vicarious liability or agency theory, and that therefore her complaint should not be dismissed.

In her response to Comcast's motion to dismiss, the plaintiff claimed that her theory of liability changed from that found in the complaint, and that theory was not negligent hiring, retention, or supervision. Instead, the plaintiff claimed that the court should look to the facts alleged and not dismiss as long as those facts "would support some viable legal theory." The plaintiff cited to the *Restatement (Second) of Agency* for some undefined cause of action she would allege against Comcast.

**QUESTION:**

(13) On the defendant ITG's and Comcast's motions to dismiss the plaintiff's complaint pursuant to Fed.R.Civ.P. 12(b)(6) the federal district court should:

(a) Grant both defendants' motions to dismiss because the plaintiff failed to satisfy the pleading standards articulated by the Supreme Court in *Twombly* and *Iqbal*;

(b) Grant the defendant ITG's motion to dismiss, but deny Comcast's motion to dismiss based on a theory of agency and vicarious liability;

(c) Deny both defendants' motions to dismiss the plaintiff's complaint because she pleaded sufficient facts to allow the claims to go to trial;

(d) Deny both defendants' motions to dismiss because there was at least some set of facts upon which the plaintiff could prevail at trial;

(e) Deny both defendant's motions to dismiss because the facts the plaintiff pleaded would support some viable legal theory, and it would be unfair to dismiss her complaint so early in the proceedings.

\* \* \*

Timothy Siegel sued Blue Giant Equipment, LLC in the federal district court for the Northern District of Oklahoma, in a products liability litigation. The case arose out of the plaintiff's claims that a loading dock he was utilizing was "defective and unreasonably dangerous" and that Blue Giant "acted in reckless disregard to the rights of others and the safety of the using and consuming public." In the course of conducting discovery, the plaintiff requested information and documents pertaining to the "engineering, design, and technical drawings," documentation of the "installation, and/or manufacture" of the loading dock, and "any subsequent changes thereto." The defendant produced 241 pages of documents and had 29 additional pages that the defendant was willing to produce, but only pursuant to a court-entered protective order because the documents contained "internal information regarding ordering and configuration of the device at issue as well as specific engineering calculations and data, all of which was proprietary and trade secret information."

The defendant moved for a protective order pursuant to Fed.R.Civ.P. 26(b)(1) and the plaintiff opposed this request. The proposed protective order provided the plaintiff with a remedy to prevent and/or resolve any type of potential misuse. The parties were required to attempt to resolve any objection to a designation, but if unable to do so, the objecting party could file a motion with the court to resolve the dispute. The plaintiff complained that the defendant's proposed protective order would allow for unnecessary "wholesale designation of confidentiality of documents." The plaintiff contended that the protective order went against the common-law right of access to discovery information.

### Question:

(14) On the defendant Blue Giant's motion for a protective order pursuant to Fed.R.Civ.P. 26(c), the federal district court should:

(a) Grant the defendant's motion for a protective order because the public had no right of access to discovery materials;

(b) Grant the defendant's motion for a protective order because the defendant was only seeking to protect 29 pages out of 241 pages already disclosed, and had shown good cause for protection of these materials;

(c) Deny the defendant's motion for a protective order because the defendant has not carried its burden of showing good cause for issuance of the protective order;

(d) Deny the defendant's motion for a protective order because the defendant has just offered conclusory and stereotyped rationales for issuance of the protective order;

(e) Deny the defendant's motion for a protective order because the materials requested by the plaintiff are non-privileged and relevant to the plaintiff's claims.

* * *

Balasubramanian Ravishanker filed a lawsuit in Santa Clara County Superior Court against Mphasis Infrastructure Services, Inc. (MIS) asserting various state causes of action including whistleblower retaliation, wrongful termination in violation of public policy, and breach of contract. According to the complaint, the plaintiff worked at MIS as Associate Vice President of Sales, and during his employment, he discovered fraudulent misconduct committed by MIS. The plaintiff alleged he reported this misconduct and, consequently, was retaliated against and ultimately discharged.

MIS removed the case to the federal district court for the Northern District of California, claiming federal jurisdiction on the basis of diversity. The plaintiff moved to remand this case to state court contending that diversity jurisdiction did not exist, and sought attorneys' fees and costs due to improper removal. MIS opposed the motion.

In this case, there was no dispute that the amount in controversy exceeded $75,000 and that the plaintiff was a citizen of California. Instead, the parties disputed the state of citizenship of MIS. The parties agreed that MIS was incorporated in Delaware, but disagreed on MIS's principal place of business. The plaintiff argued that MIS's principal place of business was in Santa Clara, California because that was the location of its headquarters. He contended that during his tenure at MIS, he operated out of the Santa Clara office and every MIS executive he reported to or engaged with on a day-to-day basis also worked out of the Santa Clara office.

In response, MIS argued that MIS' principal place of business was in New York. MIS offered the declaration of Vijayakumar M., a Director of MIS, stating that "business conducted by MIS was managed and controlled from India or by individuals who direct the company from offices in New York."

### QUESTION:

(15) On the plaintiff's petition for remand of his case to California state court pursuant to 28 U.S.C. § 1447(c), the federal district court should:

(a) Grant the plaintiff's petition to remand his case to California state court pursuant to 28 U.S.C. § 1447(c) because the federal court should respect the presumption against removal;

(b) Grant the plaintiff's petition to remand his case to California state court pursuant to 28 U.S.C. § 1447(c) because both the plaintiff and the defendant were citizens of California;

(c) Deny the plaintiff's petition to remand his case to California state court pursuant to 28 U.S.C. § 1447(c) because MIS's principal place of business was New York;

(d) Deny the plaintiff's petition to remand of his case to California state court pursuant to 28 U.S.C. § 1447(c) because MIS's principal place of business was India;

(e) Deny the plaintiff's petition to remand of his case to California state court pursuant to 28 U.S.C. § 1447(c) because the plaintiff failed to carry his burden to show that diversity of citizenship was lacking.

\* \* \*

Michael S. Berman and Darrell B. Stapp filed suit in the federal district court for the Eastern District of California against defendants Edmund G. Brown, Jr., Governor of California, and Jeffrey A. Beard, Secretary of the California Department of Corrections and Rehabilitation (CDCR). The plaintiffs claimed that the defendants' exclusion of men from California's Alternative Custody Program (ACP), as authorized by the California Penal Code, violated the Equal Protection Clause of the Fourteenth Amendment to the United States Constitution. After Berman and Stapp filed their lawsuit, the court ordered that this case was related to *Sassman v. Brown*, a case in which William Sassman pursued identical challenges to those raised by Berman and Stapp. Subsequently, this court granted summary judgment in favor of Sassman and directed the defendants to permit male inmates to apply to the ACP.

In their litigation, Berman and Stapp filed a motion for summary judgment pursuant to Fed.R.Civ.P. 56, while the defendants filed a motion to stay proceedings. The plaintiffs sought an order of summary judgment because the court had already ruled in *Sassman* that the ACP's exclusion of male inmates did not pass constitutional scrutiny. The plaintiffs contended that the defendants were collaterally estopped from relitigating those issues here, in their lawsuit. The defendants disagreed, arguing that the plaintiffs should not be permitted to offensively invoke the collateral estoppel doctrine when they could easily have joined Sassman's action. They also contended that the court's decision in *Sassman* was not sufficiently firm because the defendants had noticed an appeal in that case.

## QUESTION:

(16) On the plaintiffs' Berman and Stapp's motion for summary judgment, the federal district court should:

(a) Grant the plaintiffs' motion for summary judgment because there are no credibility issues involved in their lawsuit;

(b) Grant the plaintiffs' motion for summary judgment because the defendants were parties to the *Sassman* action, they litigated issues identical to those raised here, and a final judgment was issued against them;

(c) Deny the plaintiffs' motion for summary judgment because the doctrine of collateral estoppel cannot be invoked on a summary judgment motion;

(d) Deny the plaintiffs' motion for summary judgment because the judgment in the *Sassman* case was on appeal;

(e) Deny the plaintiffs' motion for summary judgment because the application of offensive estoppel would be unfair to a defendant.

* * *

Victoria Urenia and Soeldad Corona filed a complaint against Bank of America, Public Storage, and Michael Anz. The claims in the original complaint against Public Storage were based on allegations that Bank of America had transferred the Original Plaintiff's personal property from Corona's home to a Public Storage unit. The plaintiffs sued the defendants under antitrust and unfair competition laws. Subsequently, the original plaintiffs filed a first amended complaint and joined three new plaintiffs: Catherine Hughes, Javier Hernandez, and Brenda Hernandez. The amended complaint did not include allegations against Public Storage that related to the Hernandezes, but only alleged that the Hernandezes' property was sent to "U.S. Public Storage."

Eventually, the original plaintiffs and Hughes were voluntarily dismissed from the case. After additional amendments and motion practice, the Hernandezes were ordered to file a third amended complaint that did not include allegations regarding the dismissed plaintiffs. Omitting references to the original plaintiffs, the third amended complaint nonetheless alleged that "in 1985 Public Storage, Inc. entered into a joint venture to form 'Westport Properties' which does business as 'U.S. Storage' (also referred to herein as U.S. Public Storage)." The third amended complaint also alleged that "Public Storage was holding plaintiffs' personal property that was transported to it by co-defendants without plaintiffs' consent." However, later factual allegations in the third amended complaint showed only that their property was held by "US Public Storage (Westport Properties)." Additionally, discovery documents showed that the Hernandezes were billed by "US Storage Centers-Mission Hills."

The defendant Public Storage alleged it sent the plaintiffs' counsel a letter on December 23, 2014, and again on January 12, 2015, informing her that the plaintiffs' allegations lacked factual support as to Public Storage, and that the third amended complaint therefore violated Rule 11. Public Storage alleged that it informed the plaintiffs' counsel it would seek sanctions if the plaintiffs' counsel did not dismiss Public Storage as a defendant in the litigation.

On February 6, 2015, Public Storage served upon the plaintiffs' counsel its motion for sanctions, starting the 21-day "safe harbor" period under Rule 11(c)(2). On March 2, 2015, Public Storage filed its Rule 11 motion with the court. The defendant moved for sanctions against the plaintiffs' counsel for: (1) filing claims that were factually baseless; and (2) filing claims without conducting reasonable inquiry.

The plaintiffs' claims for relief against Public Storage were based on the factual allegation that their belongings were stored at a Public Storage facility. The plaintiffs' third amended complaint contended that the Hernandezes' possessions were not placed in a Public Storage unit. Rather, the plaintiffs had a lease with U.S. Storage, affiliated with Westport Properties (invoice from U.S. Storage to Javier Hernandez).

The plaintiff's counsel asserted that Public Storage and Westport were in some kind of "joint venture." This assertion was based entirely on a *Los Angeles Times* article dated December 29, 1985. The article stated that Jim Warmington was entering into a venture with Barry Hoeven and Jon Pelmear to form Westport Properties to develop commercial real estate properties, and that Hoeven had previously developed business parks for Public Storage. The plaintiffs' counsel alleged that Hoeven was an executive for Public Storage at the time he joined the venture to form Westport, which then started to do business under the fictitious business name of U.S. Storage.

The *Times* article did not say that Hoeven was ever employed by Public Storage or at the time of the Westport deal. At oral argument, the plaintiffs' counsel stated that she had investigated the ownership of both companies, and that both were owned by insurance companies. The plaintiffs' counsel argued the *Times* article proved "independent inquiry" was made to assess the claims against Public Storage.

**QUESTION:**

(17) On the defendant Public Storage's motion for sanctions against the plaintiff's attorney pursuant to Fed.R.Civ.P. 11, the federal district court should:

    (a)  Grant the defendant's motion for Rule 11 sanctions against the plaintiff's attorney because the plaintiff's attorney failed to make a reasonable inquiry under the circumstances;

    (b)  Grant the defendant's motion for Rule 11 sanctions against the plaintiff's attorney because the plaintiff's attorney needlessly and vexatiously multiplied the proceedings;

    (c)  Deny the defendant's motion for Rule 11 sanctions against the plaintiff's attorney because the defense attorney failed to comply with the Rule 11 "safe harbor" provisions;

    (d)  Deny the defendant's motion for Rule 11 sanctions against the plaintiff's attorney because the plaintiff's attorney acted in good faith based upon a belief formed after a reasonable inquiry;

    (e)  Deny the defendant's motion for Rule 11 sanctions against the plaintiff's attorney because Rule 11 as amended in 1993 was not intended to be applied punitively.

* * *

Carlos David filed a seaman's complaint for damages in the federal district court for the Eastern District of Louisiana, following an accident aboard the

M/V MS. JANE which caused David injuries. David originally sued C and G Boats, Inc., alleging that C and G Boats owned and operated the M/V MS. JANE at the time of an accident in which David was injured. David subsequently amended his complaint, removing all references to C and G Boats and adding defendants M N M Boats, Inc., A & A Boats, Inc., and Chet Morrison Contractors, LLC.

David's complaint alleged that A & A Boats owned the M/V MS. JANE. David was employed by M N M Boats as a Jones Act seaman. At the time of the accident, M N M Boats operated and/or controlled the M/V MS. JANE. Chet Morrison Contractors was performing certain crane operations aboard the M/V MS. JANE at the time of David's accident. As a result of the accident, David injured his back, knee, and other parts of his body.

David alleged that A & A Boats, M N M Boats, and Chet Morrison Contractors were jointly negligent in causing his injuries and were therefore jointly liable for David's damages. As to A & A Boats and M N M Boats, David specifically alleged breach of the duty of reasonable care; failure to provide a reasonably safe place to work; failure to train and supervise; failure to take means or precautions to ensure their employees' safety; unseaworthiness; failure to provide minimum safety requirements; failure to provide adequate equipment; and failure to provide adequate personnel. As to Chet Morrison Contractors, David specifically alleged breach of the duty of reasonable care, including the operation of the crane used at the time of David's injury; failure to maintain control of the crane; failure to train and supervise its employees; failure to take means or precautions to ensure David's safety; failure to provide minimum safety requirements; failure to provide adequate equipment; failure to provide adequate personnel; and failure to adhere to the safety requirements specific in its contract regarding crane operations.

The defendants M N M Boats, Inc., and A & A Boats, Inc., moved the court to require David to more definitely state his claim for damages under Federal Rule of Civil Procedure 12(e). The defendants argued that David's complaint failed to comply with the pleading requirements of Federal Rule of Civil Procedure 8(a) and was so vague as to prevent a reasonable response. The defendants argued that David's complaint lacked sufficient information because he did not allege (1) the details of the accident, (2) the manner in which he believes the M/V MS. JANE, its equipment, or its crew were unseaworthy, or (3) the nature of his alleged physical injuries. David opposed the motion.

**QUESTION:**

(18) On the defendant's motion for a more definite statement pursuant to Fed.R.Civ.P. 12(e), the federal district court should:

    (a) Grant the defendant's motion for a more definite statement pursuant to Fed.R.Civ.P. 12(e) because the plaintiff's allegations are vague and ambiguous;

    (b) Grant the defendant's motion for a more definite statement pursuant to Fed.R.Civ.P. 12(e) because the defendant cannot frame a responsive pleading;

(c) Grant the defendant's motion for a more definite statement pursuant to Fed.R.Civ.P. 12(e) because the defendant should not be forced to use discovery to obtain the needed information;

(d) Deny the defendant's motion for a more definite statement pursuant to Fed.R.Civ.P. 12(e) because the defendant had sufficient notice of the claims;

(e) Deny the defendant's motion for a more definite statement pursuant to Fed.R.Civ.P. 12(e) because Rule 12(e) motions are disfavored.

\* \* \*

Debra Reichardt sued Emerson Electric Company, Katy Thomas, and State Farm Mutual Automobile Insurance Company in the federal district court for the Western District of Louisiana. The lawsuit arose from the collision of three vehicles at or near the intersection of Lake Street and Spring Street in downtown Shreveport, Louisiana.

In their statement of material facts on the summary judgment motion, the moving party cited the deposition testimony of four witnesses, which indicated the following: After being stopped at a red traffic light, Thomas testified that she began driving east on Lake Street through its intersection with Spring Street. At the same time, after being stopped at the opposing red light, Reichardt testified that she was traveling west on Lake Street through the Spring Street intersection. Reichardt's husband, Donald Reichardt, was a passenger in the vehicle. At the time the Thomas and Reichardt vehicles were traveling on Lake Street through the Spring Street intersection, the defendant Delon Wade, who was operating a truck owned by the defendant Emerson Electric Company, was traveling north through the intersection of Lake and Spring Streets. Wade asserted that he proceeded through the intersection with a green light.

Ultimately, two separate impacts occurred between these three vehicles; both impacts involved Wade's vehicle. The first collision involved the Wade and Thomas vehicles. According to the Reichardt's' testimony, Wade's vehicle collided first with the Thomas vehicle. Then, there was a second collision which involved the Wade and Reichardt vehicles. Wade, however, testified that his vehicle collided with only one vehicle, the Reichardts'. It was undisputed that the Thomas and Reichardt vehicles never collided with each other. Rather, they were each involved in separate collisions with the Wade vehicle.

Reichardt filed suit in federal court against Wade; Emerson Electric, Wade's employer and the owner of the truck he was driving on the date of the accident; Old Republic Insurance Company, Emerson Electric's insurer; Thomas; and State Farm, Thomas's insurer. Thomas and State Farm filed a motion for summary judgment pursuant to Fed.R.Civ.P. 56, contending that based on the undisputed facts, Reichardt cannot prove that Thomas's alleged negligence was the cause-in-fact of Reichardt's damages. Thomas and State Farm alleged that the plaintiff's personal injury suit against them lacked merit because the allegations and evidence failed to indicate fault on the part of Thomas. No party filed any pleading responsive to the Thomas and State Farm motion for summary judgment.

This personal injury dispute arose under Louisiana law. Under Louisiana's duty-risk analysis, a plaintiff asserting a negligence claim must establish:

> (1) proof that the defendant had a duty to conform his conduct to a specific standard (the duty element); (2) proof that the defendant's conduct failed to conform to the appropriate standard (the breach element); (3) proof that the defendant's substandard conduct was a cause-in-fact of the plaintiff's injuries (the cause-in-fact element); (4) proof that the defendant's substandard conduct was a legal cause of the plaintiffs injuries (the scope of liability or scope of protection element); and (5) proof of actual damages (the damages element).

## QUESTION:

(19) On the defendants Thomas and State Farm's motion for summary judgment pursuant to Fed.R.Civ.P. 56, the federal district court should:

(a) Grant the defendant's motion for summary judgment pursuant to Fed.R.Civ.P. 56 because the deposition testimony of all four witnesses revealed no indication of Thomas's responsibility for the accident between Reichardt and Wade;

(b) Grant the defendant's motion for summary judgment pursuant to Fed.R.Civ.P. 56 because the motion was unopposed;

(c) Deny the defendant's motion for summary judgment pursuant to Fed.R.Civ.P. 56 because there was a genuine issue of material fact concerning which party was the proximate cause of Reichardt's injuries;

(d) Deny the defendant's motion for summary judgment pursuant to Fed.R.Civ.P. 56 because the plaintiff should be permitted to have a jury decide whether Thomas's breach of a duty caused Reichardt's accident or her concomitant damages;

(e) Deny the defendant's motion for summary judgment pursuant to Fed.R.Civ.P. 56 because construing all facts and drawing all reasonable inferences in favor of the non-moving party, there was an issue of material fact as to whether the defendants were at least partially responsible for the plaintiff's injuries.

* * *

Precision Irrigation, Inc. was a Missouri corporation engaged in the business of designing, installing, and servicing commercial and residential lawn sprinkler systems. Precision employed Timothy Schmucker in the accounting department. Throughout his employment, Schmucker did not manage or supervise other employees, and his duties did not require him to exercise independent judgment or discretion. Schmucker routinely worked in excess of forty hours per work week. Precision knew that Schmucker worked hours beyond those that he recorded, and, in an attempt to circumvent its obligations to pay him overtime, manipulated his job title and classified him as an independent contractor. Precision also made improper deductions from his salary.

Schmucker filed suit against Precision in the federal district court for the Eastern District of Missouri, asserting willful failure to pay overtime wages in violation of the Fair Labor Standards Act and the Missouri Minimum Wage Law. Schmucker also asserted breach of the covenant of good faith and fair dealing. He sought to recover unpaid overtime wages and liquidated damages.

Precision filed an answer to the complaint and a counterclaim complaint, asserting claims for breach of fiduciary duty, professional negligence, and fraudulent and negligent misrepresentation. Precision alleged the following facts:

9. One of Schmucker's more specific responsibilities in his role as Accountant for Precision Irrigation included ensuring proper payments for the Company's bulk fuel purchases.

10. In late 2013, the Company discovered that, over the past approximately three years, Schmucker had been paying the fuel bills late and incurring excessive fees as a penalty for late payments. Upon discovery of these fees, the Company had accrued approximately $30,000 in penalties as a result of Schmucker's late payments.

11. Schmucker admitted to incurring the $30,000 in penalties. In lieu of termination, Schmucker agreed to pay the Company back for $15,000 of the total penalty amount. Schmucker indicated that he wanted to make payments by way of $75.00 deductions from his pay check per pay period. The Company agreed to this payment schedule.

12. To date, Schmucker has only repaid $1,575.00 of his original $15,000 repayment obligation. Accordingly, Schmucker still owes the Company $13,425.00 for the penalties he accrued.

Schmucker was also responsible for ensuring proper payment of housing costs, renewal or cancellation of apartment leases for Precision's seasonal workers, and payment of life insurance premiums for Precision's owners. Precision discovered that Schmucker had paid housing costs late, and had incurred penalties in the approximate amount of $4,500; that he had failed to give sufficient notice in order to terminate various housing leases, thereby forcing Precision to pay approximately $3,000 in rent for vacant apartments; and that he had failed to pay quarterly premiums for the owners' life insurance policies, causing the policies to lapse, and resulting in Precision paying approximately $2,000 more annually in premiums for a new policy. Precision also discovered that Schmucker had made multiple reimbursements to himself for unidentified expenses, totaling approximately $1,338.50.

In addition to declaratory relief and attorneys' fees, Precision sought judgment against Schmucker "for a sum that will adequately and completely compensate

Precision for the extent of its damages." Precision maintained that the court had supplemental jurisdiction over its counterclaims under 28 U.S.C. § 1367.

Schmucker moved to dismiss Precision's counterclaims for lack of jurisdiction, pursuant to Fed.R.Civ.P. 12(b)(1). Schmucker argued that supplemental jurisdiction did not exist because there was very little overlap in the evidence relevant to Schmucker's FLSA claim and the evidence relevant to Precision's counterclaims, as the former claim was a narrow and well defined claim for unpaid overtime, and the latter claims were not concerned with the number of hours Schmucker worked or his compensation. Precision contended that supplemental jurisdiction existed because the claims "derived from a common nucleus of operative facts"—namely, the nature and scope of Schmucker's employment duties, and the reason for the deductions from his salary—and would thus rely on the same evidence.

**QUESTION:**

(20) On the plaintiff's motion to dismiss Precision's counterclaims for lack of jurisdiction, pursuant to Fed.R.Civ.P. 12(b)(1), the federal district court should:

    (a)   Grant the plaintiff's motion to dismiss Precision's counterclaims for lack of jurisdiction pursuant to Fed.R.Civ.P. 12(b)(1) because there was no supplemental jurisdiction under 28 U.S.C. § 1367(b);

    (b)   Grant the plaintiff's motion to dismiss Precision's counterclaims for lack of jurisdiction pursuant to Fed.R.Civ.P. 12(b)(1) because the counterclaims were permissive;

    (c)   Grant the plaintiff's motion to dismiss Precision's counterclaims for lack of jurisdiction pursuant to Fed.R.Civ.P. 12(b)(1) because the counterclaims were not so related to the plaintiff's claims as to form one case or controversy;

    (d)   Deny the plaintiff's motion to dismiss Precision's counterclaims for lack of jurisdiction pursuant to Fed.R.Civ.P. 12(b)(1) because the plaintiff's claims and the defendant's counterclaims formed one constitutional case;

    (e)   Deny the plaintiff's motion to dismiss Precision's counterclaims for lack of jurisdiction pursuant to Fed.R.Civ.P. 12(b)(1) because federal courts can adjudicate state law counterclaims.

* * *

Leonetti's Frozen Foods, Inc., a southwest Philadelphia company, sued Crew, Inc. d/b/a Crew Marketing, Inc. in the Court of Common Pleas of Philadelphia County, Pennsylvania. The defendant removed the case to the federal district court for the Eastern District of Pennsylvania. The substantive legal issue concerned the effect of an errant 'reply-all' email sent by a Crew employee, which allegedly caused an unintended recipient/potential customer to stop working towards a business relationship with the Leonetti's Frozen Foods. Leonetti's developed frozen food products for sale to businesses under a private label and to consumers under its own label. Crew Marketing Inc. of Bentonville, Arkansas was a marketing services broker located near Walmart headquarters providing programs for the advertising, solicitation and marketing of products to club-format stores such as Sam's Club owned by Walmart.

Leonetti director Robert Ippaso met with a senior vice-president of Sam's Club. Ippaso and Sam's Club discussed developing a custom, ready-to-eat stromboli product for sale at Sam's Club's cafes. Leonetti proposed designing and testing the stromboli specifically for sale at Cafe Strombolis. Leonetti offered its own brand of frozen stromboli products for sale in Sam's Club's freezer section.

Leonetti's asked Crew to help it place its custom stromboli products in Sam's Club also headquartered in Bentonville. Crew already represented Leonetti with Costco warehouse stores. Leonetti and Crew limited their relationship to the Costco account and allowed additional accounts only if agreed in writing. As part of this on-going business relationship with Costco, Crew met with Leonetti in Philadelphia at unknown times. Leonetti never agreed, ether orally or in writing, to amend the Costco brokerage agreement to include the Sam's Club account.

The plaintiff's claims arose from the Arkansas defendant's agent sending a "reply-all" email with a copy to Sam's Club's agents in Arkansas, suggesting that the plaintiff might be selling stromboli to Sam's Club's lead competitor Costco. Sam's Club officials in Arkansas thereafter decided, for unknown reasons, to stop any further testing of the plaintiff's stromboli for placement in its stores.

Crew's Jeff Campigli represented Leonetti on the Costco account. Crew orally agreed at an unknown location to (1) represent Leonetti in interfacing with Sam's Club's head office and food buyers regarding Leonetti Cafe Stromboli and Frozen Stromboli products; (2) assist Leonetti with preparing forms and other paperwork required by Sam's Club in pitching and presenting the Cafe Stromboli and Leonetti Frozen Stromboli products; (3) assist Leonetti in the handling of the sampling, cutting and other product testing necessary to obtain Sam's Club's approval for the purchase of Leonetti Cafe Stromboli and Leonetti Frozen Stromboli products; and (4) maintain Leonetti product specifications and Sam's Club's respective product requirements for the Cafe Stromboli and Frozen Stromboli products in confidence as is standard within the industry.

Crew's Cindy Romines then represented Leonetti with Sam's Club. For six months, Leonetti developed the Cafe Stromboli under Sam's Club's specifications. Romines, along with other Crew staff, liaised with Sam's Club management and buying department regarding the status of Leonetti prototype Cafe Stromboli and Leonetti Frozen Stromboli products, in addition to presenting and cutting samples of Leonetti products for testing in Sam's Club's home office test kitchen and in-club testing. Sam's Club and Crew confirmed the Cafe Stromboli and Leonetti Frozen Stromboli products had been progressing favorably through development and testing.

On December 10, 2014, Sam's Club agreed to purchase Leonetti Frozen Stromboli subject to a final panel test in early January 2015. Sam's Club initially considered purchasing Leonetti Frozen Stromboli for sale at twenty-six stores in New Jersey, Pennsylvania, Delaware, and New York in the First Quarter 2015; if Leonetti Frozen Stromboli sold well, Sam's Club intended to expand the program nationwide. In early January 2015, Romines attended the final panel test of Leonetti Frozen Stromboli and told Leonetti the Frozen Stromboli tested beautifully per her conversation with the Sam's Club employee overseeing the panel's taste test. With the panel test complete, Sam's Club's appeared prepared to place orders for Leonetti Frozen Stromboli.

On December 16, 2014, Crew's Romines told Leonetti it had passed all tests to date for the Cafe Stromboli and the only remaining test before Sam's Club moved forward is the "hold test." Crew's Romines attended Sam's Club's "hold test" on January 14, 2015. On the same day, Romines emailed her summary of the hold test to "John and Jeremy" of Sam's Club:

> John and Jeremy good day! I completed the in-club testing this morning at the Bentonville Sam's Club. Test went extremely well. I used 8 Stromboli's in the test. The additional samples were used to determine where to start the pans as the temperature and times were not set at 485*—6 minutes. The ovens were set at 500*—6:30, club associate said they started the pizzas at the entrance of the oven and recommended we do the same. I found that the top oven cooked hotter than the 2nd and 3rd oven. While the top oven did not bum the Stromboli they were a little darker than we like to have. Attached is a recap of the testing. Please let me know if you have any questions and what our next steps will be.

Crew's Romines copied Leonetti and her colleague Campigli on her January 14, 2015 email to "John and Jeremy" of Sam's Club. Crew's Campigli "replied all" to Romines' January 14, 2015 email:

> Nice job Cindy. Robert and I could even use slides 2–5 in our Costco Presentation next week :)

Leonetti claimed "shock" to learn of Campigli's email sent to Sam's Club suggesting Leonetti would ever take part in using a confidential and proprietary stromboli developed for Sam's Club to sell to Costco, Sam's Club's largest competitor. The next day, Leonetti responded to Crew's Campigli and Romines: "Ouch Jeff. . . ."

Crew's Campigli responded: "I am so sorry guys . . . writing email to John now." Crew's Campigli immediately emailed John at Sam's Club:

> John, I AM SO SORRY. This was a very poor attempt at humor and meant for Cindy only. We would never share testing, conducted exclusively for you, with any customer . . . especially your #1 competitor. Cindy, Robert and Beth have worked so hard to meet your expectations. I can only hope that you won't hold this stupid, stupid error as a negative against a fantastic product and profitable program for Sam's Club.

> As the person responsible for the Costco account in our brokerage company, I'd like to assure you that the product Leonetti's has

developed with you over the past several years is exclusive to Sam's. Any work we have been asked to do for Costco does not include this specific product.

I'm traveling on Friday, but if you'd like to discuss this in further detail, please don't hesitate to contact me@ (Redacted)

Sam's Club responded furiously to Crew's Campigli's email, did not believe him and now believed Leonetti to be an untrustworthy business partner. Sam's Club concluded to not do business with Leonetti. In late January 2015, Sam's Club advised it would not purchase any of Leonetti stromboli. After learning of Sam's Club's decision, Crew's Romines called Leonetti and informed him the Cafe Stromboli passed the final test and Leonetti Frozen Stromboli performed exceptionally well at the focus group testing according to Sam's Club personnel present during the testing. Crew's Romines said Campigli's email was the only possible reason for Sam's Club's decision. Leonetti alleged CREW's Campigli's January 14, 2015 "reply-all" email was the sole reason for Sam's Club decision not to move forward.

Having lost the Sam's Club opportunity, Leonetti sued Crew in the Court of Common Pleas of Philadelphia County, Pennsylvania and the defendant Crew removed the case to the federal district court for the Eastern District of Pennsylvania for damages alleging professional negligence; breach of an oral contract; breach of a fiduciary duty; and, trade libel. Crew moved to dismiss arguing this court lacked personal jurisdiction or was otherwise an improper venue under Rules 12(b)(3).

## QUESTION:

(21) On the defendant's motion to dismiss for improper venue pursuant to Fed.R.Civ.P. 12(b)(3), the federal district court should:

    (a)  Grant the defendant's motion to dismiss for improper venue pursuant to Fed.R.Civ.P. 12(b)(3) because all the events giving rise to the litigation occurred in Arkansas;

    (b)  Transfer the case to federal court in the Western District of Arkansas because that it was a venue where the case could have been brought;

    (c)  Deny the defendant's motion to dismiss for improper venue because venue was proper under 28 U.S.C. § 1441(a);

    (d)  Deny the defendant's motion to dismiss for improper venue pursuant to Fed.R.Civ.P. 12(b)(3) because the Philadelphia federal court was a proper venue because it was the location of the plaintiff's business;

    (e)  Deny the defendant's motion to dismiss for improper venue pursuant to Fed.R.Civ.P. 12(b)(3) because Philadelphia was the place where the defendant suffered the effects of the defendant's conduct.

\* \* \*

Scott Butler was an employee of Allstate Insurance Company, where he served as a field vice president in the benefits department. His direct supervisor became Wayne Watkins. Butler believed that Watkins was violating the ethical rules of Allstate, when he learned that Watkins was carrying on an illicit relationship with a married woman who also had an insurance benefits business in New Orleans.

Butler discussed Watkins' alleged ethical violation with David Mueller, who worked in Allstate's corporate security office. Mueller was directed by Susan Rosborough, an in-house attorney for Allstate, to conduct an investigation into Watkins' alleged inappropriate conduct. Butler was terminated when human resources informed him that his production had not met the goals that Watkins had set for him.

Butler sued Allstate in the federal district court for the Eastern District of Texas, alleging a breach of contract claim, a wrongful termination claim, and a fraud claim. During discovery he filed a motion for compel, which the defendants opposed. The court entered an order regarding the plaintiff's motion to compel as follows:

> (1) Defendants must submit all documents regarding the Mueller investigation that they claim are privileged for an *in camera* inspection; (2) Defendants must produce to Plaintiff an un-redacted Settlement Agreement relating to the Steve Yang settlement; (3) Defendant must provide all other documents to Plaintiff by no later than September 16, 2015, at 5:00 p.m.

The defendants withheld documents claiming that both attorney-client privilege and the work-product doctrine barred production. The defendants asserted that the documents submitted to the court in its *in camera* review consisted of "internal email correspondences between Allstate's in-house counsel, or between Allstate's in-house counsel and Allstate's executives." The plaintiff alleged that there is "no indication . . . that Mr. Mueller was giving legal advice, only that he was conducting a fact finding investigation from which employment decisions regarding Watkins might be made."

Allstate alleged that the "only documents withheld by Allstate were (1) communications between and among attorneys for Allstate, and (2) communications between attorneys for Allstate and executives from Allstate, both categories of which were made for the purpose of those attorneys providing legal advice to Allstate." Allstate asserted that "Mueller was engaged by Allstate's in-house attorney, Sue Rosborough, to conduct an investigation for the purpose of enabling Allstate's legal department to render legal advice to Allstate regarding Butler's complaint." "The entire investigation was to be conducted at the direction of Rosborough, or at the direction of another member of the corporate legal team." Allstate alleged that Mueller was requested to assist with an investigation into a complaint made against Watkins and "Rosborough was required to provide legal advice to Allstate regarding what to do about the complaint and Watkins' continued employment with Allstate." Allstate "expected that if any disciplinary or termination action was taken against Watkins, he would likely file suit against Allstate."

As a part of his engagement, Mueller communicated with Allstate's in-house counsel and other employees of Allstate. Allstate alleged that these people were in a position to take advice from Allstate's attorney, and therefore, Mueller's communications were privileged and not subject to disclosure. "Mueller conferred with Rosborough regarding the investigation, and she relayed to Mueller what she needed, and whom he would need to initially interview." As the investigation was prompted by the plaintiff, Mueller interviewed the plaintiff first. During the interview, Allstate alleged that Mueller "told Plaintiff that because of in-house's direction, the investigation was attorney-client privileged."

The plaintiff alleged that "Defendants at no time have actually identified the 'legal advice' Mueller's communications relate to." The plaintiff argued that Mueller was "not providing legal advice to Allstate or Butler, but was acting as an investigator." According to Allstate, "at all times relevant, Mueller served in a legal capacity as he gathered the necessary information and documents so that the proper legal advice could be provided to Allstate."

### QUESTION:

(22) On the plaintiff Butler's motion to compel disclosure of the Mueller investigation documents, the federal district court should:

(a) Grant the plaintiff's motion to compel disclosure of the Mueller investigation documents because those materials were not privileged;

(b) Grant the plaintiff's motion to compel disclosure of the Mueller investigation documents because those materials were not attorney-work product;

(c) Grant the plaintiff's motion to compel disclosure of the Mueller investigation documents because the plaintiff needed the documents to prepare his case and could not obtain that information by other means;

(d) Deny the plaintiff's motion to compel disclosure of the Mueller investigation documents because Mueller was acting as an agent for Allstate's in house counsel when he conducted the investigation into Watkins;

(e) Deny the plaintiff's motion to compel disclosure of the Mueller investigation documents because Mueller failed to give Butler an *Upjohn* warning in connection with the interview, and therefore, attorney-client privilege did not attach to any evidence from Mueller's investigation.

\* \* \*

Johnny Edwards brought an action against defendants Mack Trucks, Inc. and M & K Quality Truck Sales of Summit, LLC d/b/a Chicago Mack, Center, Inc.

in the federal district court for the Northern District of Illinois. The plaintiff alleged breach of express warranty (Count I) and revocation of acceptance and cancellation of contract (Count II) against the defendant Mack Trucks. The plaintiff also alleged breach of implied warranty (Count III), revocation of acceptance and cancellation of contract (Count IV), and action to recover the price (Count V) against the defendant Chicago Mack.

Edwards bought a new 2014 Mack truck from the defendant Chicago Mack for $116,762.73. The truck was manufactured by the defendant Mack Trucks. The plaintiff received a copy of Mack Trucks' warranty coverage as part of his purchase. The coverage provided a limited warranty for certain component parts as part of a disclaimer of the implied warranty of merchantability or fitness for a particular purpose as a means of limiting consequential and incidental damages.

Up until the action commenced, the defendant Chicago Mack serviced the vehicle at least eleven times, primarily for issues relating to a severely left leaning ride but also for an illuminated engine system warning light, an oil leak, and a diesel exhaust fluid leak. Alleging that the malfunctions and defects had not been fixed, the plaintiff filed this action against the defendants seeking to cancel the contract and recover damages.

The defendant to dismiss Count II against defendant Mack Trucks for failure to state a claim under Rule 12(b)(6). The Illinois Commercial Code closely mirrors the Uniform Commercial Code and provides buyers with both a mechanism to revoke an acceptance to an offer, as well as a means to cancel a contract once an acceptance has been revoked in order to claim and recover damages. In Count II of the complaint, the plaintiff brought a revocation of acceptance claim against the defendant Mack Trucks. In Illinois, revocation of acceptance claims are not available against non-selling manufacturers. According to the Illinois Supreme Court, revocation of acceptance "contemplates a buyer-seller relationship" which would be "conceptually inapplicable" to a non-seller such as a manufacturer.

The plaintiff's Exhibit A showed that the only parties to the original contract were the plaintiff as buyer and the defendant Chicago Mack as seller. The defendant Mack Trucks was not listed as a party to the transaction. The defendant Mack Trucks was simply the manufacturer.

**QUESTION:**

(23) On the defendant Mack Trucks motion to dismiss Count II of the complaint pursuant to Fed.R.Civ.P. 12(b)(6), the federal district court should:

    (a)  Take all the plaintiff's allegations as true, and deny the defendant's motion to dismiss pursuant to Fed.R.Civ.P. 12(b)(6);

    (b)  View the pleadings and evidence in a light most favorable to the non-moving party, and consequently deny the defendant's motion to dismiss pursuant to Fed.R.Civ.P. 12(b)(6);

    (c)  Convert the defendant's motion to a summary judgment motion pursuant to Fed.R.Civ.P. 56;

(d)  Grant the defendant's motion to dismiss Count II because the plaintiff has failed to state a claim under Illinois law against Mack Trucks;

(e)  Deny the motion to dismiss Count II against Mack trucks to allow the plaintiff's revocation of acceptance claim to go to a jury.

\* \* \*

MoneyMutual, LLC, a Nevada corporation, operated a website that allowed individuals to apply for short-term loans, commonly known as "payday loans." Once an application was submitted, MoneyMutual offered the application to its lender network. After a lender selected the application, MoneyMutual notified the applicant via e-mail and received a fee from the lender. To promote its services, MoneyMutual advertised its website through television commercials. In addition, MoneyMutual e-mails marketing offers to people who had previously started or submitted a loan application.

Four Minnesota residents who used the MoneyMutual website to obtain loans filed a class-action complaint against MoneyMutual in state court in Minnesota. The plaintiffs alleged that MoneyMutual's website and advertising contained false and misleading statements, that MoneyMutual matched them with lenders that were unlicensed in Minnesota, and that their loans were illegal under Minnesota law. Plaintiffs claim that MoneyMutual violated Minnesota's consumer-protection statutes, breached its duty "not to engage in or facilitate illegal conduct," unjustly enriched itself, participated in a civil conspiracy, and aided and abetted unlicensed lenders.

MoneyMutual moved to dismiss the complaint for lack of personal jurisdiction and for failure to join indispensable parties. Minnesota's long-arm statute extends to the limits of due process. In response, the plaintiffs submitted additional evidence alleging that they submitted MoneyMutual applications with their Minnesota contact information from computers in Minnesota after seeing MoneyMutual advertisements in Minnesota. In addition, they submitted affidavits detailing MoneyMutual's advertising in Minnesota.

MoneyMutual argued that personal jurisdiction could be based on: (1) any contact it had with the plaintiffs because those contacts were based on the "fortuitous" presence of the plaintiffs in Minnesota; (2) its television commercials that aired in Minnesota because they were not targeted solely at Minnesota; or (3) its website, which was accessible from Minnesota, because it was not targeted solely at Minnesota. MoneyMutual argued that the district court relied on the plaintiff's contacts with Minnesota, not its own. MoneyMutual contended that its contacts with Minnesota were limited to the plaintiffs' fortuitous presence in the forum and unilateral activities. MoneyMutual also stated that each plaintiff initiated communication with MoneyMutual by visiting its website and submitting an application and that its e-mails responding to the applications were automated. Therefore, according to MoneyMutual, the plaintiffs acted unilaterally.

The plaintiffs were in Minnesota at all times: when they saw MoneyMutual advertising, when they interacted with MoneyMutual, when they submitted applications indicating they were Minnesota residents, and when MoneyMutual sold the plaintiffs' applications to lenders for profit. MoneyMutual received more than 1,000 loan applications from Minnesota residents. MoneyMutual was capable of blocking its advertisements from jurisdictions where it did not do business, and it did so in some jurisdictions.

The plaintiffs alleged targeting of the Minnesota market, alleging that MoneyMutual television commercials had been broadcast in Minnesota since at least 2010. MoneyMutual denied that it placed ads with any Minnesota-based or local stations, but did not deny using national advertising that includes Minnesota, that its services were available in Minnesota, or that its advertisements were intentionally broadcast in Minnesota. Finally, MoneyMutual argued that its website also was not expressly aimed at Minnesota and that basing personal jurisdiction on a website would subject website operators to "universal jurisdiction" because they could be sued anywhere the website was accessed.

### QUESTION:

(24) On the defendant MoneyMutual's motion to dismiss for a lack of personal jurisdiction by the Minnesota state court, the court should:

   (a)  Grant the defendant MoneyMutual's motion to dismiss for a lack of personal jurisdiction because it could not reasonably anticipate being haled into Minnesota court based on its website activities;

   (b)  Grant the defendant MoneyMutual's motion to dismiss for a lack of personal jurisdiction because the state court cannot based personal jurisdiction on the plaintiff's contacts with the state;

   (c)  Grant the defendant MoneyMutual's motion to dismiss for a lack of personal jurisdiction because the court cannot base personal jurisdiction on the plaintiff's unilateral activities in subscribing to the defendant's payday loan solicitations;

   (d)  Deny the defendant MoneyMutual's motion to dismiss for a lack of personal jurisdiction because the defendant was conducting business with contacts throughout the United States;

   (e)  Grant the defendant MoneyMutual's motion to dismiss for a lack of personal jurisdiction because the defendant had sufficient minimum contacts with Minnesota so that the assertion of personal jurisdiction over it did not offend due process.

*  *  *

Leroy Mckinnis filed an action in state court in Dallas, Texas against Digital Intelligence Systems Corporation (DISYS), which then removed the case to the federal district court for the Northern District of Texas. The plaintiff alleged that DISYS breached a contract with the plaintiff regarding the incentive compensation allegedly due to the plaintiff following the termination of his employment and discriminated against him during his employment on the basis of his race and age.

DISYS was a corporation organized under the laws of the state of Virginia, with its principal place of business in Virginia. McKinnis was hired as a Senior Account Executive at DISYS and entered into an employment agreement with DISYS to reflect the terms of his employment. Paragraph 9.7 of the employment agreement provided:

> Choice of Law/Jurisdiction. Employee acknowledges that this Agreement was made by the Parties in the Commonwealth of Virginia and shall be governed, construed and enforced in accordance with the laws of the Commonwealth of Virginia (without regard to its conflict of law principles). Employee acknowledges that the state and federal courts of the Commonwealth of Virginia shall be the exclusive forum for the resolution of any disputes concerning this Agreement or concerning Employee's employment with the Company, and that Employee agrees to submit to the jurisdiction of those courts, waiving the defenses of lack of personal jurisdiction or inconvenient forum.

In in his original petition, the plaintiff acknowledged that the employment agreement between the plaintiff and DISYS was a "valid and enforceable employment contract."

After removal, the defendant filed a motion to transfer venue pursuant to 28 U.S.C. § 1404(a), requesting that the court transfer the case to the Alexandria Division of the United States District Court for the Eastern District of Virginia. The defendant asserted that the plaintiff signed an employment agreement with the defendant, agreeing that the state or federal courts in Virginia had exclusive jurisdiction over any disputes concerning his employment agreement or concerning the plaintiff's employment with the defendant, and that the case should be transferred to the Eastern District of Virginia based on this explicit forum-selection clause.

The plaintiff opposed transfer on the basis that "this was an employment discrimination and breach of contract case arising from McKinnis's employment with Defendant in the State of Texas;" "McKinnis worked for Defendant at its offices in Dallas County, Texas for approximately five years before he was terminated in the spring of 2014" and that, "although the events giving rise to this action occurred in the State of Texas, Defendant now seeks to transfer venue to the Commonwealth of Virginia based upon a forum selection clause in McKinnis's employment contract with Defendant," but, "due to the nature of the facts and circumstances giving rise to this case in the State of Texas, this case presented extraordinary circumstances that should prevent transfer to Virginia," where "the relevant public interest factors established by federal courts weigh heavily against a transfer to the Commonwealth of Virginia."

The plaintiff asserted that all of the acts giving rise to his claims occurred in Texas and that he lived in Texas and was employed by the defendant for five years at its Dallas offices. The plaintiff contended that his claims were based on discriminatory employment actions committed by the defendant in Dallas County, Texas; that the employees and witnesses involved in the actions at issue were located in Texas; and that this court has a far greater local interest in deciding McKinnis's employment discrimination claims than did a Virginia court, where he has brought employment discrimination claims against the defendant under the Texas Labor Code. DISYS pointed out that the plaintiff no longer lived in the Northern District of Texas.

The plaintiff further asserted that, notwithstanding the employment agreement's choice-of-law clause, Texas law governed his statutory "discrimination claims, and the Texas court would be far more familiar with the protections provided in the Texas Labor Code, weighing heavily against transfer to Virginia."

Finally, the plaintiff asserted that the Northern District of Texas had an average of 284 fewer cases filed per division over a 12-month period, showing that the court congestion in the Eastern District of Virginia weighs against transfer of this case. DISYS provided statistics showing that the median time interval from filing to disposition in the Eastern District of Virginia's Alexandria Division—the so-called "rocket docket"—was lower than that in the Dallas Division of the Northern District of Texas.

### QUESTION:

(25) On the defendant DISYS's motion to transfer venue to the Eastern District of Virginia, the federal district court in Texas should:

 (a) Grant the defendant DISYS's motion to transfer venue to the Eastern District of Virginia because the parties' forum selection clause was valid and enforceable;

 (b) Grant the defendant DISYS's motion to transfer venue to the Eastern District of Virginia because the employment contract contained a choice of law provision;

 (c) Deny the defendant DISYS's motion to transfer venue to the Eastern District of Virginia because the private and public factors favored venue in Texas;

 (d) Deny the defendant DISYS's motion to transfer venue to the Eastern District of Virginia because Texas law applied to the plaintiff's claims;

 (e) Deny the defendant DISYS's motion to transfer venue to the Eastern District of Virginia the forum selection clause was unconscionable and unenforceable.

### END OF EXAM PROBLEMS #5

# CHAPTER 6
# ANSWER KEY FOR EXAM #1
# ANSWERS AND EXPLANATIONS

### PROBLEM #1. BEST ANSWER (D).

Problem #1 is based on *Biller v. Café Luna of Naples, Inc.*, 2015 WL 1648888 (M.D. Fla. April 13, 2015). This problem explores the proper assertion of affirmative defenses pursuant to Rule 8(d), the use of a Rule 12(f) motion to strike, and pleading requirements for affirmative defenses under Rule 8(b)(1)(A).

Under Fed.R.Civ.P. 12(f), "the Court may order stricken from any pleading any insufficient defense or redundant, immaterial, impertinent, or scandalous matter." Courts disfavor motions to strike and deny them unless the allegations have "no possible relationship to the controversy, may confuse the issues, or otherwise prejudice a party." *Reyher v. Trans World Airlines*, 881 F.Supp. 574, 576 (M.D.Fla.1995). "An affirmative defense is generally a defense that, if established, requires judgment for the defendant even if the plaintiff can prove his case by a preponderance of the evidence." *Wright v. Southland Corp.*, 187 F.3d 1287, 1303 (11th Cir.1999). Affirmative defenses must follow the general pleading requirements contained in Rule 8 of the Federal Rules of Civil Procedure. A party must "state in short and plain terms its defenses to each claim asserted against it." Fed.R.Civ.P. 8(b)(1)(A).

As with any pleading, an affirmative defense must provide "fair notice" of the nature of the defense and the grounds upon which it rests, *Bell Atl. Corp. v. Twombly,* 550 U.S. 544, 555 (2007), and state a plausible defense, *Ashcroft v. Iqbal,* 556 U.S. 662, 679 (2009). Thus, "while an answer need not include a detailed statement of the applicable defenses, a defendant must do more than make conclusory allegations. If the affirmative defense comprises no more than bare bones conclusory allegations, it must be stricken." *Microsoft Corp. v. Jesse's Computers & Repair, Inc.,* 211 F.R.D. 681, 684 (M.D.Fla.2002). The purpose of this pleading requirement "is simply to guarantee that the opposing party has notice of any additional issue that may be raised at trial so that he or she is prepared to properly litigate it." *Hassan v. U.S. Postal Serv.,* 842 F.2d 260, 263 (11th Cir.1988).

In this case, the plaintiff moved to strike defendants' affirmative defenses, which alleged in their entirety:

- Defendants invoke the defenses, protections and limitations of the Fair Labor Standards Act.

- Plaintiff's claims are barred in whole or in part by the doctrines of waiver, estoppel or laches.

- Plaintiff's claims are barred in whole or in part by accord and satisfaction, settlement or payment and release.

- Plaintiff has failed to exhaust all administrative remedies.

- Plaintiff has failed to mitigate her alleged damages.

- Defendants reserve the right to assert further affirmative defenses as discovery proceeds.

The first five of the challenged defenses are pled in the broadest possible terms and do not provide any information connecting them to plaintiff's claims. Such defenses fail to provide the plaintiff with adequate notice of the issue(s) defendants seek to raise and therefore are precisely the type of bare-bones conclusory allegations that must be stricken. *Microsoft*, 211 F.R.D. at 684. Moreover, the last of the challenged defenses is an attempt by the defendants to reserve their right to assert additional affirmative defenses in the future. It does not respond to the allegations of the complaint and does not raise any facts to vitiate plaintiff's claims. As such, it is not a proper affirmative defense and will be stricken. If, as discovery proceeds, the defendants wished to amend their answer to add additional affirmative defenses, they may seek to do so via an appropriate motion.

**ANSWER (A)** is incorrect because the defendants have not properly pled their affirmative defenses, for the reasons stated above. **ANSWER (B)** is incorrect because even though some of the affirmative defenses are listed in Rule 8(d), the defendants cannot simply list them without further information or detail. **ANSWER (C)** is incorrect because the mere use of labels to identify affirmative defenses is insufficient to give the plaintiff fair notice of the content of those defenses. **ANSWER (E)** is incorrect because there is no indication that the alleged affirmative defenses are impertinent or immaterial; this merely repeats the language and standard of Rule 12(f), but is not relevant to the assertion of these affirmative defenses.

### PROBLEM #2. BEST ANSWER (A).

This problem is based on *Bakken Waste, LLC v. Great American Ins. Co. of New York*, 2015 WL 4036190 (D. Colo. June 30, 2015). This requires application of Fed.R.Civ.P. 15(a), dealing with liberal amendment of pleadings.

In the Tenth Circuit, untimeliness alone may be a sufficient basis for denying a party leave to amend. *See Duncan v. Manager, Dep't of Safety*, 397 F.3d 1300, 1315 (10th Cir.2005); *Hayes v. Whitman*, 264 F.3d 1017, 1026 (10th Cir.2001). The important inquiry is not simply whether the plaintiff has delayed, but whether such delay is undue. *Minter*, 451 F.3d at 1206. Delay is undue "when the party filing the motion has no adequate explanation for the delay," *Frank v. U.S. West, Inc.*, 3 F.3d 1357, 1365–66 (10th Cir.1993), or when "the party seeking amendment knows or should have known of the facts upon which the proposed amendment is based but fails to include them in the original complaint." *Las Vegas Ice & Cold Storage Co. v. Far West Bank*, 893 F.2d 1182, 1185 (10th Cir.1990) (quoting *State Distribs., Inc. v. Glenmore Distilleries Co.*, 738 F.2d 405, 416 (10th Cir.1984)).

According to Rule 15, once a 21-day period after a responsive pleading to the complaint is filed lapses, a party may amend its pleading only by leave of the court or by written consent of the adverse party. Fed.R.Civ.P. 15(a). The grant or denial of leave is committed to the discretion of the court. *See Duncan*, 397 F.3d at 1315. The court must heed Rule 15's mandate that the "court should freely give leave when justice so requires." Fed.R.Civ.P. 15(a)(2); *see also Foman v. Davis*, 371 U.S. 178, 182 (1962); *Duncan*, 397 F.3d at 1315. "If the underlying facts or circumstances relied upon by a claimant may be a proper subject of relief, he ought to be afforded an opportunity to test his claim on the merits." *Foman*, 371 U.S. at 182. Leave to amend should be refused "only on a showing of undue delay, undue prejudice to the opposing party, bad faith or dilatory motive, failure to cure deficiencies by amendments previously allowed, or futility of amendment." *Duncan*, 397 F.3d at 1315; *see also Foman*, 371 U.S. at 182.

In the Tenth Circuit, the "most important . . . factor in deciding a motion to amend the pleadings . . . is whether the amendment would prejudice the nonmoving party." *Minter*, 451 F.3d at 1207. "Courts typically find prejudice only when the amendment unfairly affects the defendants 'in terms of preparing their defense to the amendment.'" *Id.* (citing *Patton v. Guyer*, 443 F.2d 79, 86 (10th Cir.1971)). "Most often, this occurs when the amended claims arise out of a subject matter different from what was set forth in the complaint and raise significant new factual issues." *Id.* (citations omitted). "As a general rule, a plaintiff should not be prevented from pursuing a valid claim . . . 'provided always that a late shift in the thrust of the case will not prejudice the other party in maintaining his defense upon the merits.'" *Evans v. McDonald's Corp.*, 936 F.2d 1087, 1090–91 (10th Cir.1991).

Here, the court did not believe that allowing the plaintiff to amend its complaint in the manner requested would cause undue delay or unduly prejudice the defendants at this stage in the litigation. Discovery was barely more than two months old at the time of the settlement conference and the discovery period would not end for another seven months. Therefore, the court held that in no respect was there undue or prejudicial delay here.

**ANSWER (B)** is incorrect because Fed.R.Civ.P. 15(c) is not applicable to these facts. There is no indication in the problem that the statute of limitations has run on the plaintiff's claims, necessitating recourse to Rule 15(c) to permit an amendment back to the original date of the filing of the complaint. **ANSWER (C)** is incorrect because, apart from the defendant's conclusory assertion of undue prejudice, there is no indication to support that prejudice, the case was in its early stages, and seven months remained to conduct discovery. **ANSWER (D)** is incorrect because there are no allegations of mistake in the fact pattern; moreover, the doctrine of mistake has relevance only in the context of a proposed Rule 15(c) amendment. **ANSWER (E)** is incorrect because even though the plaintiff sought to amend its complaint after 21 days from the last responsive pleading, the plaintiff still could seek such amendment with leave of the court under Fed.R.Civ.P. 15(a)(2).

PROBLEM #3. BEST ANSWER (B).

Problems 3 and 4 are based on *Ben v. Olvera-Arreola*, 2015 WL 5138263 (M.D. La. Aug. 28, 2015). This problem requires the student to understand the requirements for removal to federal court based on diversity jurisdiction, as well as the defendant's burden in establishing the requisite amount-in-controversy for the federal court to accept jurisdiction.

A defendant may remove "any civil action brought in a State court of which the district courts of the United States have original jurisdiction." 28 U.S.C. § 1441(a). When original jurisdiction is based on diversity of citizenship, the cause of action must be between "citizens of different states" and the amount in controversy must exceed the "sum or value of $75,000, exclusive of interest and costs." 28 U.S.C. § 1332(a)–(a)(1). Subject matter jurisdiction must exist at the time of removal to federal court, based on the facts and allegations contained in the complaint. *St. Paul Reinsurance Co., Ltd. v. Greenberg,* 134 F.3d 1250, 1253 (5th Cir.1998) ("jurisdictional facts must be judged as of the time the complaint is filed").

The removal statute, 28 U.S.C. § 1441, is strictly construed and any doubt as to the propriety of removal should be resolved in favor of remand. *Gasch v. Hartford Acc. & Indem. Co.,* 491 F.3d 278, 281–82 (5th Cir.2007). The removing party has the burden of proving federal jurisdiction and, if challenged, that the removal was procedurally proper. *Garcia v. Koch Oil Co. of Tex. Inc.,* 351 F.3d 636, 638 (5th Cir.2003). Remand is proper if at any time the court lacks subject matter jurisdiction. *See* 28 U.S.C. § 1447(c).

If removal is sought on the basis of diversity jurisdiction, then "the sum demanded in good faith in the initial pleading shall be deemed to be the amount in controversy." 28 U.S.C. § 1446(c)(2). If, however, the "State practice . . . does not permit demand for a specific sum" removal is proper "if the district court finds, by the preponderance of the evidence, that the amount in controversy exceeds 75,000." 28 U.S.C. § 1446(c)(2)(A)(ii)–(B). The burden of proof is on the removing defendant to establish that the amount in controversy has been satisfied. *Luckett v. Delta Airlines, Inc.,* 171 F.3d 295, 298 (5th Cir.1999). The defendant may make this showing by either (1) demonstrating that it is facially apparent that the claims are likely above $75,000, or (2) setting forth facts in controversy that support a finding of the jurisdictional minimum. *Id.* If the defendant can produce evidence sufficient to show by a preponderance that the amount in controversy exceeds the jurisdictional threshold, the plaintiff can defeat diversity jurisdiction only by showing to a legal certainty that the amount in controversy does not exceed $75,000. *See, e.g., St. Paul Mercury Indem. Co. v. Red Cab Co.,* 303 U.S. 283, 288–89 (1938); *Grant v. Chevron Phillips Chem. Co.,* 309 F.3d 864, 869 (5th Cir.2002); *De Aguilar v. Boeing Co.,* 47 F.3d 1404, 1412 (5th Cir.1995).

There is no dispute that there is complete diversity of citizenship. The only issue before the court is whether the amount in controversy was facially apparent, and if not, whether the ambiguity regarding the amount in controversy was resolved.

The plaintiff alleged that while he was sitting in his truck in traffic he was rear-ended by another truck driven by Mr. Olvera-Arreola. The Plaintiff alleged that "he sustained injuries that required medical treatment" and sought to recover past, present, and future physical pain and suffering, medical expenses, mental and emotional pain and suffering, lost wages, and loss of enjoyment of life. The plaintiff did not allege the severity of the collision or the nature of his physical injuries resulting from the collision. The plaintiff did not state whether he incurred medical and drug expenses, and did not identify the scope of the medical treatment he received or continued to receive as a result of the accident. Similarly, the plaintiff did not identify his profession or wages allegedly lost.

"Courts have routinely held that pleading general categories of damages, such as 'pain and suffering, disability, lost wages, loss of earning capacity, medical expenses, etc.,' without any indication of the amount of the damages sought, does not provide sufficient information for the removing defendant to meet his burden of proving that the amount in controversy is satisfied under the 'facially apparent' test." *See Davis v. JK & T Wings, Inc.,* No. 11–501–BAJ–DLD, 2012 WL 278728, at *3 (M.D. La. Jan. 6, 2012) (citing *Alderdice v. Lowe's Home Centers, Inc.,* 2010 WL 371027 (M.D. La. Jan. 29, 2010); *Nelson v. Wal-Mart Stores, Inc.,* 2009 WL 1098905 (W.D. La. Apr. 22, 2009), and numerous cases cited therein, *Fontenot v. Granite State Ins. Co.,* 2008 WL 4822283 (W.D. La. Nov. 3, 2008); and *Bonck v. Marriot Hotels, Inc.,* 2002 WL 31890932 (E.D. La. Dec. 30, 2002)), *report and recommendation adopted,* 2012 WL 278685 (M.D. La. Jan. 31, 2012). "When, as in the instant case, the petition is vague regarding the types of injuries incurred and any future problems resulting from the incident, 'the court must conclude that it was not "facially apparent" that the amount of damages would exceed $75,000.'" *Dunomes v. Trinity Marine Products, Inc.,* No. 14–1968, 2014 WL 7240158, at *4 (E.D. La. Dec. 19, 2014) (quoting *Broadway v. Wal-Mart Stores,* No. 00–1893, 2000 WL 1560167, at *2 (E.D. La. Oct. 18, 2000)).

In this case, the plaintiff's petition did not provide sufficient facts for determining the severity of his injuries. The plaintiff alleged various broad categories of damages commonly alleged in personal injury actions. The plaintiff did not allege the specific nature of his physical injuries or the treatment he sought or received. The plaintiff's vague allegation that "he sustained injuries that required medical treatment" indicated little more than potential soft tissue damage. There was no allegation that that the plaintiff had suffered fractures or other wounds that would require immediate medical attention. In the absence of additional factual assertions by the plaintiff regarding the extent or nature of the actual physical injuries suffered, the petition did not provide enough information for the court to conclude that the amount in controversy is facially apparent. *See Simon v. Wal-Mart Stores, Inc.,* 193 F.3d 848, 850 (5th Cir.1999).

The petition also did not allege that the plaintiff was seeking a jury trial. This suggested that the plaintiff believed his claims to be less than $50,000, which is the threshold for a right to a jury trial in Louisiana. Even if the plaintiff had requested a jury, given the vague injuries and categorical damages alleged in the petition, the court would give little weight to that request in establishing the amount in controversy.

The court concluded that in the absence of additional factual assertions by the plaintiff regarding the extent or nature of the actual physical injuries suffered, the petition did not provide enough information for the court to conclude that the amount in controversy was facially apparent.

In addition, State Auto provided no summary judgment type evidence in support of its removal indicating that the amount in controversy requirement was satisfied. At most, State Auto alleged, without supporting documentation, that the plaintiff's counsel advised it that the plaintiff "had undergone an MRI on his lumbar and/or cervical spine." Even if true, the cost of an MRI was insufficient for establishing the amount in controversy requirement. *See Donsereaux v. Hilbrenner,* No. 91–cv–1920, 1992 WL 125472, at *4 (E.D. La. May 20, 1992) (plaintiff's medical expenses listed cost of MRI scan as $610.00). There was no evidence in the record that the plaintiff had undergone, or plans to undergo, surgery as a result of the MRI's findings. For these reasons, the court concluded that State Auto had not met its burden of proving that the amount in controversy requirement was satisfied.

**ANSWER (A)** is incorrect because the facts clearly establish that there was diversity of citizenship among the parties. **ANSWER (C)** is incorrect because the case was removed to federal court based on diversity jurisdiction and if properly established, then the court may adjudicate state-based claims such as those alleged in the plaintiff's petition. The fact that the plaintiff pleaded state claims would not be a basis for remand in a properly removed case. The issue in this case entirely hinges on whether the defendant has carried its burden of establishing the requisite amount in controversy. **ANSWER (D)** is incorrect because the defendant has not satisfied the requirements for removal under 28 U.S.C. § 1441(a); the defendant has failed to carry its burden to demonstrate that the case is worth more than $75,000 in controversy. **ANSWER (E)** is incorrect because the defendant has failed to demonstrate that the amount in controversy exceeds $75,000 and this is not facially clear from the plaintiff's petition, for the reasons indicated above.

## PROBLEM #4. BEST ANSWER (C).

This problem is based on the same set of facts as Problem #3, and requires the student to understand when and how a defendant might be subject to sanctions for an improvident removal of a case. The plaintiff requested from State Auto "an award of costs and fees" pursuant to 28 U.S.C. § 1447(c) or Rule 11 of the Federal Rules of Civil Procedure. The plaintiff did not identify the costs and expenses incurred in light of State Auto's removal and the filing of the motion to remand. The court held that the plaintiff was entitled to costs and fees pursuant to 28 U.S.C.

Rule 11 specifically provides that "a motion for sanctions must be made separately from any other motion and must describe the specific conduct that allegedly violates Rule 11(b)." Fed.R.Civ.P. 11(c)(2). The present request for fees and costs fails to meet the procedural requirements of Rule 11(c)(2) because defendants failed to file a separate motion describing the specific conduct that allegedly violates Rule 11(b). Accordingly, the motion for sanctions pursuant to Rule 11 should be denied. *See Richard v. Louisiana Industries for the Disabled,* No. 10–426, 2011 WL 1527586, at \*3–4 (M.D. La. Apr. 20, 2011).

The court, however, awarded costs and fees pursuant to 28 U.S.C. § 1447(c). "An order remanding the case may require payment of just costs and any actual expenses, including attorney fees, incurred as a result of the removal." 28 U.S.C. § 1447(c). The award of costs and expenses under § 1447(c) is discretionary and should only be awarded where the removing party "lacked an objectively reasonable basis for seeking removal." *Martin v. Franklin Capital Corporation,* 546 U.S. 132, 141 (2005). The court must consider the propriety of the removing party's actions at the time of removal, based on an objective view of the legal and factual elements in each particular case, irrespective of the fact that it was ultimately determined that removal was improper. *Id.*; *Avitts v. Amoco Prod. Co.,* 111 F.3d 30, 32 (5th Cir.1997), *cert. denied,* 522 U.S. 977 (1997); *Miranti v. Lee,* 3 F.3d 925, 928–29 (5th Cir.1993). To be subject to an award of attorney's fees under § 1447(c), a defendant must have played a role in the decision to remove. *Avitts,* 111 F.3d at 32.

State Auto removed the action within 30 days of the filing of the lawsuit based solely on the allegations in the petition and an alleged representation by the plaintiff's counsel that the plaintiff had undergone an MRI. The petition was devoid of allegations that would support a finding that the amount in controversy was facially apparent. State Auto made no effort to oppose the plaintiff's motion to remand by providing summary judgment type evidence supporting a finding that the amount in controversy requirement was satisfied.

The court concluded that it was clear that State Auto removed the action within 30 days of receipt of the initial pleading without any objectively reasonable basis for removal. The Fifth Circuit has made it clear that "the thirty-day removal period is triggered only where the initial pleading '*affirmatively reveals on its face* that the plaintiff is seeking damages in excess of the minimum jurisdictional amount of the federal court.' " *Mumjrey v. CVS Pharmacy, Inc.,* 719 F.3d 392, 399 (5th Cir.2013) (quoting *Chapman v. Powermatic, Inc.,* 969 F.2d 160, 163 (5th Cir.1992)). This bright-line rule prevents "courts from expending copious time determining what a defendant should have known or have been able to ascertain at the time of the initial pleading" and is designed to prevent premature removals.

**ANSWER (A)** is incorrect because the plaintiff failed to comply with the requirements of Fed.R.Civ.P. 11, in order to seek recovery of costs under that provision, by not submitting a separate motion, as required by that rule. **ANSWER (B)** is incorrect because the facts do not indicate or suggest that the plaintiff sought recovery of costs and fees pursuant to 28 U.S.C. § 1927, a statute which permits recovery of costs and fees where litigants vexatiously multiply proceedings. **ANSWER (D)** is incorrect for similar reasons; the plaintiff did not invoke the court's inherent powers to discipline attorneys, and at any rate, the removal statute itself provides relief for improvidently granted removals. **ANSWER (E)** is incorrect because the court did find that the defendants had improvidently removed the case for the reasons stated above, and therefore the plaintiff was entitled to costs and fees under 28 U.S.C. § 1447(c).

## PROBLEM #5. BEST ANSWER (E).

Problems #5 and #6 are based on *Farley v. Cernak*, 2016 WL 162238 (E.D. Pa. Jan. 13, 2016). Problem #5 requires basic analysis of venue rules and the procedural means for properly asserting a venue challenge. In this instance, the defendants failed to raise a challenge to improper venue, and by failing to do so, waived any challenge to venue. Consequently, the court retained venue—even though it was improper.

In the plaintiffs' reply to the defendants' motion to dismiss, the plaintiffs requested, as "alternative relief," that this matter be transferred to the U.S. District Court for the District of Massachusetts for improper venue. Venue is proper:

> only in (1) a judicial district where any defendant resides, if all defendants reside in the same state, (2) a judicial district in which a substantial part of the events or omissions giving rise to the claim occurred, or a substantial part of property that is the subject of the action is situated, or (3) a judicial district in which any defendant may be found, if there is no district in which the action may otherwise be brought.

28 U.S.C. § 1391(b). Where venue is improper, the district court "shall dismiss, or if it be in the interest of justice, transfer such case to any district or division in which it should have been brought." 28 U.S.C. § 1406(a).

According to the plaintiffs' complaint, all the defendants resided in Massachusetts and the plaintiffs' complaint concerned a car accident that occurred in Pelham, Massachusetts. From a preliminary review, it would appear that venue was improper in the district court for the Eastern District of Pennsylvania.

However, the defendants failed to raise this issue in their motion to dismiss. The defendants' motion to dismiss only raised the issue of the statute of limitations. To preserve a challenge regarding improper venue, a defendant must raise the issue in the responsive pleading. Fed.R.Civ.P. 12(b)(3). A defendant has the burden of showing that the district in which the suit is brought is not the proper venue. *Kravitz v. Niezgoda*, 2012 WL 4321985, at *4 (E.D. Pa. 2012) (citing *Simon v. Ward*, 80 F.Supp.2d 464, 468 (E.D. Pa. 2000)). If the responsive pleading does not challenge improper venue, the defense is waived. Fed.R.Civ.P. 12(h). Thus, where a defendant does not "interpose timely and sufficient objection to the venue," the district court retains jurisdiction, even if the venue would otherwise be improper. 28 U.S.C. § 1406(b). The defendants did not move to dismiss or transfer this case due to improper venue. As such, the defendants waived their objection to improper venue.

Were the court to dismiss this case due to improper venue, the court would be doing so *sua sponte*. Case law is clear that such actions are disfavored. It is "inappropriate for the trial court to dispose of the case *sua sponte* on an objection to the complaint which would be waived if not raised by the defendant(s) in a timely manner." *Sinwell v. Shapp*, 536 F.2d 15, 19 (3d Cir.1976). "A district court may not dismiss a case *sua sponte* for improper venue absent extraordinary circumstances." *Fiorani v. Chrysler Grp.*, 510 F.App'x 109, 111 (3d Cir.2013) (quoting *Gomez v. USAA Fed. Sav. Bank*, 171 F.3d 794, 796 (2d Cir.1999)); *see also Day v. City of Galveston*, 480 F.App'x 119 (3d Cir.2012) (finding that it was error for a district court to *sua sponte* raise the issue of venue).

The court held that because the defendants waived any objections to the venue, and the Court found no extraordinary circumstances, it was inappropriate for the Court to *sua sponte* dismiss on the basis of improper venue. Likewise, given that the defendants' waiver made the improper venue into a proper venue, it was inappropriate for the court to transfer this case pursuant to 28 U.S.C. § 1406(a).

**ANSWERS (A), (B),** and **(C)** are tempting answers because venue actually is improper in Pennsylvania. But the best answer remains **(E)**. Venue properly could be laid in Massachusetts because it is the place where all the defendants resided, and it is the place where the accident occurred. However, this problem centers on the defendants' failure to object to venue in a timely responsive pleading, and their waiver of that objection as a consequence of that failure. This renders **(E)** the correct answer. **ANSWER (D)** is incorrect because it has no bearing on determination of venue under the statutory venue provisions, even though as a matter of common law, courts do give deference to a plaintiff's choice of forum.

### PROBLEM #6. BEST ANSWER (B).

This problem is a continuation of the fact pattern in Problem #5, and is based on the same facts. This problem explores both a Fed.R.Civ.P. 12(b)(6) motion to dismiss and the problem of applicable law—which law applies for the court to assess and decide the motion.

In deciding a motion to dismiss pursuant to Rule 12(b)(6), courts must "accept all factual allegations as true, construe the complaint in the light most favorable to the plaintiff, and determine whether, under any reasonable reading of the complaint, the plaintiff may be entitled to relief." *Phillips v. Cnty of Allegheny*, 515 F.3d 224, 233 (3d Cir.2008) (internal quotation and citation omitted). After the Supreme Court's decision in *Bell Atlantic Corp. v. Twombly*, 550 U.S. 544, 555 (2007), "threadbare recitals of the elements of a cause of action, supported by mere conclusory statements, do not suffice." *Ashcroft v. Iqbal*, 556 U.S. 662, 678 (2009). "A claim has facial plausibility when the plaintiff pleads factual content that allows the court to draw the reasonable inference that the defendant is liable for the misconduct alleged." *Id.* at 678 (citing *Twombly*, 550 U.S. at 556). This standard, which applies to all civil cases, "asks for more than a sheer possibility that a defendant has acted unlawfully." *Id.* at 678; *accord Fowler v. UPMC Shadyside*, 578 F.3d 203, 210 (3d Cir.2009) ("All civil complaints must contain more than an unadorned, the-defendant-unlawfully-harmed-me accusation.").

"Although the statute of limitations is an affirmative defense, it may be raised in a motion to dismiss where the plaintiff's failure to comply with the limitations period is apparent from the face of the pleadings." *Datto v. Harrison*, 664 F.Supp. 2d 472, 482 (E.D. Pa. 2009); *see also Oshiver v. Levin, Fishbein, Sedran & Berman*, 38 F.3d 1380, 1384 n. 1 (3d Cir.1994) (establishing that a statute of limitations may be raised in a motion to dismiss "where the complaint facially shows noncompliance with the limitations period and the affirmative defense clearly appears on the face of the pleading"); *Clark v. Sears, Roebuck & Co.*, 816 F.Supp. 1064, 1067 (E.D. Pa. 1993).

The issue before the court was whether the plaintiffs' claims were barred by the relevant statute of limitations. The parties did not dispute that the plaintiffs' injuries accrued starting on the day of the incident on December 6, 2012. They disputed whether Pennsylvania's or Massachusetts's statutes of limitations should apply.

Because this was a diversity case, and the court sits in the Eastern District of Pennsylvania, the court applied the choice of law rules of the forum state, Pennsylvania. *See Klaxon v. Stentor Electric Mfg. Co.*, 313 U.S. 487 (1941); *Maniscalco v. Brother Int'l (USA) Corp.*, 709 F.3d 202, 206 (3d Cir.2013). Generally, Pennsylvania courts apply the Pennsylvania statute of limitations except in cases in which the claim accrued in a foreign jurisdiction. *Ross v. Johns-Manville Corp.*, 766 F.2d 823, 826 n. 3 (3d Cir.1985). Here, the plaintiffs' claims accrued in Massachusetts. Because the plaintiffs' claims accrued in Massachusetts, but were filed in Pennsylvania, the Pennsylvania borrowing statute applied. *See Pac. Emp'rs Ins. Co. v. Global Reinsurance Corp. of Am.*, 693 F.3d 417, 432 (3d Cir.2012). The statute requires that:

> The period of limitation applicable to a claim accruing outside the Commonwealth shall be either that provided or prescribed by the law of the place where the claim accrued or by the law of this Commonwealth, whichever first bars the claim.

Pennsylvania provided a two year limitation for bringing personal injury claims. Massachusetts provided a three year limitation for bringing personal injury claims. The plaintiffs' complaint was timely filed under Massachusetts law, but not under Pennsylvania law. Pennsylvania's statute obviously bars the claim first. As such, Pennsylvania's statute applied.

**ANSWER (A)** is incorrect because the court found that the affirmative defense was adequately facially pleaded; the court did not address the adequacy of the plaintiffs' claims. **ANSWER (C)** is incorrect because Pennsylvania law applied under its borrowing statute for the reasons stated above; Massachusetts law did not apply to save the time-barred claims. **ANSWER (D)** is incorrect because Pennsylvania law, with the shorter statute of limitations, could not apply to save the claims. **ANSWER (E)** is incorrect because although granting Rule 12(b)(6) motions historically were disfavored because of the early stage of the proceedings, this is no longer true; in addition, the motion entails consideration of whether the defendant is entitled to a dismissal because the plaintiffs' claims are time-barred by the applicable statute of limitations.

## PROBLEM #7. BEST ANSWER (D).

Problems #7 and 8 are based on *Albritton v. CVS Caremark Corp.*, 2015 WL 7476186 (W.D. Ky. Nov. 23, 2015). Both these problems explore application of the doctrine of attorney-client privilege and motions to compel production of documents during discovery.

The court requested the documents to further examine two e-mails and case-status notes for attorney-client-privilege protection. The court found that attorney-client privilege protected the two e-mails, but not the case-status notes (*see* discussion below for Problem #8).

Pursuant to Sixth Circuit precedent, establishing attorney-client privilege under federal law requires proving eight elements: "(1) Where legal advice of any kind is sought (2) from a professional legal adviser in his capacity as such, (3) the communication relating to that purpose, (4) made in confidence (5) by the client, (6) are at his instance permanently protected (7) from disclosure by himself or by the legal adviser, (8) unless the protection is waived." *Reed v. Baxter*, 134 F.3d 351, 355–56 (6th Cir.1998) (*Fausek v. White*, 965 F.2d 126, 129 (6th Cir.1992)).

Both of the e-mails qualify as communications from the defendants' outside counsel to one of the defendants' employees, who worked in compliance operations. The outside counsel also carbon copied one of the two e-mails to an in-house paralegal and an in-house attorney of the defendants. Sixth Circuit precedent does not recognize an absolute privilege for communications sent from an attorney to his or her client. *Reed*, 134, 355 (stating the communications must be made by the client); *see e.g., Antoine v. Atlas Turner, Inc.*, 66 F.3d 105, 110 (6th Cir.1995) (stating that the privilege does not attach when an attorney conveys facts from third parties to his or her client).

The Supreme Court called the attorney-client privilege "the oldest of the privileges for confidential communications known to the common law." *Upjohn Co. v. United States*, 449 U.S. 383, 389 (1981). However, because the privilege shields relevant information from discovery and limits the truth-seeking function of our adversarial process, courts must narrowly construe its application. *Tenn. Laborers Health & Welfare Fund v. Columbia/HCA Healthcare Corp. (In re Columbia/HCA Healthcare Corp. Billing Practices Lit.)*, 293 F.3d 289, 294 (6th Cir.2002). For that reason, among others, courts have split as to the application of the privilege when an attorney sends a communication to a client. It appears that which rule applies remains an open question in both the Sixth Circuit and the Western District of Kentucky.

This court held that it did not need to determine which of the two constructions of the rule applies. Both emails either reveal or imply the defendants' communications to its outside counsel. The first e-mail gave outside counsel's legal analysis of facts provided by Defendants. The second e-mail appeared to contain no new information, but rather be a reply containing only copies of the communications previously sent to outside counsel. The first e-mail similarly contained copies of the prior communications from the client, albeit with additional text written by outside counsel. As such, attorney-client privilege protected both of these e-mails from discovery.

**ANSWER (A)** is incorrect because the emails were communicated among all attorneys covered by the attorney-client privilege. **ANSWER (B)** is incorrect because while facts are not privileged from discovery, the email communications contained the attorneys' analysis of facts—which communications are privileged from discovery. **ANSWER (C)** is incorrect because communication of the emails to the defendants' paralegal would not waive the attorney-client privilege. **ANSWER (E)** is incorrect because the First Amendment generally does not provide authority for protection from disclosure during discovery.

### PROBLEM #8. BEST ANSWER (A).

This variation of the fact scenario presented in Problem #7 presents a more difficult and closer call concerning whether the materials sought to be compelled were protected under attorney-client privilege, or not. The court decided that the case-status note(s) were not protected and therefore had to be produced to the plaintiffs.

The court requested an *in camera* review of two case-status notes because the privilege log stated they were "regarding correspondence with Sheila Bowe, Legal Coordinator," a non-attorney member of the defendants' in-house legal team. Upon *in camera* inspection, the note revealed only that the employee sent a copy of a file to the defendants' legal department. Not only did this note not amount to a communication with an attorney, but it in no way revealed the content of any communications to the legal department.

Defendants cannot use privilege to shield facts from disclosure. *Wright v. Firestone Tire & Rubber Co.*, 93 F.R.D. 491, 493 (W.D. Ky. 1982) ("Information itself is not protected by the privilege simply because it may have been conveyed to counsel."). Moreover, Rule 26 requires a party claiming privilege to "describe the nature of the documents or communications . . . not produced or disclosed—and do so in a manner that, without revealing information itself privileged or protected, will enable other parties to assess the claim." Fed.R.Civ.P. 26(b)(5)(A). To claim privilege concerning a communication, Defendants must, at a minimum, reveal that they sent the communication to their attorneys. *Id.*; 134 F.3d at 355–56. It would belie the discovery rules and law of attorney-client privilege if a party's internal note that he made an arguably privileged communication was itself privileged but the party had to reveal the same facts when claiming the privilege as to the communication itself.

The court therefore held that attorney-client privilege did not protect the case-status notes from discovery.

**ANSWER (B)** is incorrect because there are no facts in the problem that would suggest that the defendant had deliberately waived any privilege that might attach to the case-status note. **ANSWER (C)** is incorrect because there are absolutely no facts presented that would support assertion of the crime-fraud exception to attorney-client privilege. This basically is a red-herring answer. **ANSWER (D)** is incorrect because the mere fact that the file was sent to the defendants' legal department cannot be used to shield the case note from discovery, if it the note was not actually a communication to an attorney.

**ANSWER (E)** is incorrect because there are no facts suggesting that the case note embodied a privileged opinion of an attorney.

### PROBLEM #9. BEST ANSWER (B).

Problem #9 is based on *Henderson v. Boise Paper Holdings, LLC*, 2015 WL 6760483 (W.D. Tex. 2015). The problem involves application of Fed.R.Civ.P. 50(a) concerning judgments as a matter of law, or previously known as directed verdicts.

The court construed Boise's oral motion for a directed verdict as one for judgment as a matter of law pursuant to Federal Rule of Civil Procedure 50(a). Under Rule 50(a), a district court may grant judgment as a matter of law where "a party has been fully heard on an issue during jury trial and the court finds that a reasonable jury would not have a legally sufficient evidentiary basis to find for the party on that issue." Fed.R.Civ.P. 50(a). "A 'mere scintilla of evidence is insufficient to present a question for the jury' and 'there must be a conflict in substantial evidence to create a jury question.' " *DP Solutions, Inc. v. Rollins, Inc.*, 353 F.3d 421, 427 (5th Cir.2003) (quoting *Foreman v. Babcock & Wilcox Co.*, 117 F.3d 800, 804 (5th Cir.1997)). A court may grant a motion for judgment as a matter of law where "the facts and inferences point so strongly and overwhelmingly in favor of the moving party that reasonable jurors could not have arrived at a contrary verdict." *Homoki v. Conversion Servs., Inc.*, 717 F.3d 388, 395 (5th Cir.2013). In deciding a Rule 50(a) motion, the Court must "review all of the evidence in the record, draw all reasonable inferences in favor of the nonmoving party, and may not make credibility determinations or weigh the evidence." *Ellis v. Weasler Eng'g Inc.*, 358 F.3d 326, 337 (5th Cir.2001).

As indicated in the statement of facts, the FMLA prohibits an employer from interfering with, restraining, or denying the exercise or attempted exercise of an employee's right to take FMLA leave. 29 U.S.C. § 2615(a)(1). The FMLA also makes it unlawful for any employer to discharge or in any other manner discriminate against any individual for opposing the employer's unlawful FMLA practices. *Id.* § 2615(a)(2). An employee must actually qualify for FMLA leave or otherwise be protected under the statute in order to assert either an interference or a retaliation claim. *See, e.g., Lanier v. Univ. of Tex. Sw. Med. Ctr.*, 527 F.App'x 312, 316–317 (5th Cir.2013).

Under the FMLA, an eligible employee is entitled to up to twelve weeks of leave during any twelve-month period for a serious health condition that makes the employee unable to perform the functions of his or her position. 29 U.S.C. § 2612(1)(d). A "serious health condition" is defined as "an illness, injury, impairment, or physical or mental condition that involves ... continuing treatment by a healthcare provider." *Id.* § 2611. If scheduling planned medical treatment for a serious health condition, an employee must make a reasonable effort to schedule treatment so as not to disrupt the employer's operations and employees are generally expected to consult with their employers before scheduling treatment. 28 C.F.R. § 825.302(e). Employees should provide at least 30 days' notice in advance of treatment, but if 30 days is not possible, notice must be given as soon as practicable. *Id.*

§ 825.302(a). Notice need not expressly reference the FMLA, but it must indicate the request for time off is for a serious health condition and must convey the timing and duration of the leave. *Id.* § 825.302(c).

Boise argued it was entitled to judgment as a matter of law as to Henderson's FMLA claims because (1) Henderson did not qualify for protection within the meaning of the FMLA, and (2) even if Henderson did qualify, she had presented absolutely no evidence of any damages resulting from the alleged FMLA violations. The court agreed.

Henderson's own testimony established she did not qualify for FMLA leave and therefore could benefit from the statute's protections. Henderson testified she told her supervisor, Lena Lawrence, she would need time off for a previously scheduled neck surgery. Henderson further testified she asked an HR representative, Jennifer Crumley, for medical leave forms in passing in the parking lot while leaving work that same day. This did not qualify as adequate notice under the statute and corresponding regulations. Henderson did not indicate to her employer when she would need time off of work and for how long. On cross examination, Henderson could not recall the date she was planning to have the surgery, the precise nature of her medical condition, or the name of the doctor who was scheduled to perform the procedure. There was no evidence Henderson actually had a serious medical condition. Henderson admitted she never went to a doctor after being terminated to follow up on her neck injury and, to date, had never actually had the surgery she was allegedly scheduled to have. *See, e.g., Seaman v. CSPH, Inc.,* 179 F.3d 297, 302 (5th Cir.1999) (finding an employee had not sufficiently informed his employer of an FMLA-qualifying reason for leave where the employee did not actually seek treatment for the allegedly serious medical condition). Consequently, drawing all reasonable inferences in her favor, Henderson did not present sufficient evidence for a jury to find her eligible for protection under the FMLA.

Alternatively, even if the evidence presented at trial did demonstrate she qualified for FMLA leave, a jury still could not find for Henderson because she presented no evidence of damages. Henderson did not testify as to whether she experienced any actual damages in the form of lost wages, salary, employment benefits, or other compensation as required under the statute. 29 U.S.C. § 2617(a). Similarly, Henderson did not present any evidence of actual monetary losses sustained as a result of the alleged FMLA violations. *Id.* § 2617(a). Henderson's argument that she was entitled to nominal damages for violations of the FMLA is unavailing; the FMLA does not provide for nominal damages. *See Nero v. Indust. Molding Corp.,* 167 F.3d 921, 930 (5th Cir.1999) ("We hold that Nero's damages . . . are limited to an amount equal to the lost salary or wages, lost employment benefits, or any 'other compensation' that is indicative of a quid pro quo relationship between an employer and an employee . . . the FMLA does not provide for the recovery of general or consequential damages."); *see also Walker v. United Parcel Serv., Inc.,* 240 F.3d 1268, 1278 (10th Cir.2001); *Montgomery v. Maryland,* 72 F.App'x 17, 19 (4th Cir.2003). Having failed to present any evidence of actual damages or other actual monetary loss as required by the statute, no reasonable factfinder could have found for Henderson and therefore Boise was entitled to judgment as a matter of law as to each of Henderson's FMLA claims.

**ANSWER (A)** is incorrect because we cannot determine from the facts as to whether Henderson was a credible witness or not; but, at any rate, the defendant is entitled to a judgment as a matter of law because of the insufficiency of the evidence she presented—and failed to present—on her FMLA claims. **ANSWER (C)** is incorrect because the court determined that the plaintiff had failed to carry her burden of adducing sufficient evidence on her FMLA claim; there was no point in proceeding to hear the defendant's case in response. **ANSWER (D)** is incorrect because based on the insufficiency of the plaintiff's evidence, no reasonable inference could be drawn from this scant evidence to allow the plaintiff to go forward with her FMLA claims. **ANSWER (E)** is incorrect because the Supreme Court has held that directed verdicts pursuant to Fed.R.Civ.P. 50(a) do not violate the Seventh Amendment to the U.S. Constitution. *See Galloway v. United States.*

**PROBLEM #10. BEST ANSWER (D).**

Problem #10 is based on *Dupuis v. LRC Energy, LLC*, 2015 WL 8542871 (W.D. la. Dec. 9, 2015). This problem involves knowledge of the requirements for establishing federal diversity jurisdiction upon removal of a case from state court to federal court.

Federal courts exercise limited jurisdiction. For that reason, a suit is presumed to lie outside a federal court's jurisdiction until the party invoking federal-court jurisdiction establishes otherwise. Because "the effect of removal is to deprive the state court of an action properly before it, removal raises significant federalism concerns." The removal statute is therefore to be strictly construed, and any doubt about the propriety of removal must be resolved in favor of remand and against federal-court jurisdiction. Similarly, any ambiguities must be construed against removal. To determine whether jurisdiction is present for removal, the court must consider the claims in the state court petition as they existed at the time of removal. The party invoking the court's subject-matter jurisdiction has the burden of establishing the court's jurisdiction. Therefore, when a lawsuit is removed from state court, as this suit was, the removing party must bear that burden. Accordingly, Ms. Lisco, the removing party, had the burden of establishing that the court had subject-matter jurisdiction over this action.

Ms. Lisco removed the action under 28 U.S.C. § 1332, the statute concerning diversity jurisdiction. To remove a case based on diversity jurisdiction, a defendant must demonstrate "that all of the prerequisites of diversity jurisdiction contained in 28 U.S.C. § 1332 are satisfied."

Because the petition alleged that Ms. Lisco converted approximately $100,000 in money owed to LRC Energy, LLC, it was facially apparent that the amount-in-controversy requirement was satisfied in this case. Therefore, the court found that the monetary requirement for diversity jurisdiction was satisfied.

However, Ms. Lisco did not satisfy the statute's citizenship requirement. The jurisdictional statute that Ms. Lisco relied upon, 28 U.S.C. § 1332(a), requires complete diversity of citizenship; that is, a district court cannot exercise subject matter jurisdiction if any plaintiff shares the same citizenship as any defendant. The burden was on Ms. Lisco to prove the citizenship of each and every person or entity that was a party to the suit at the time of removal.

The lawsuit had four parties, one plaintiff—Casey Dupuis—and three defendants—LRC Energy, LLC, Erica Lisco, and Wells Fargo Bank, NA. The petition did not allege Ms. Dupuis's citizenship. In the removal notice, Ms. Lisco alleged that Ms. Dupuis was a Louisiana citizen. If this allegation was not refuted by Ms. Dupuis, it would be accepted by the court. The petition alleged that Ms. Lisco was a Florida resident. The citizenship of a natural person is determined by the state in which she is domiciled, and domicile is a combination of both a person's residence and her intent to remain there permanently. Therefore, "an allegation that a party is a resident of a certain state is not a sufficient allegation of his citizenship in that state." In the removal notice, however, Ms. Lisco alleged that she was a Florida citizen. This allegation was accepted by the court.

Defendant Wells Fargo Bank, N.A. consented to the removal of this action. In its consent, it represented that it was a national bank with its main office in South Dakota. The United States Supreme Court has determined that, for jurisdictional purposes, a national bank is a citizen of the state where it has its main office. Therefore, Wells Fargo is a citizen of South Dakota.

In the petition, it is alleged that LRC Energy, LLC was a limited liability company incorporated in the State of Louisiana with its principal place of business in St. Landry Parish, Louisiana. This is insufficient to establish the citizenship of the company. Although a corporation is a citizen of the state in which it was incorporated and the state in which it has its principal place of business, the rule regarding limited liability companies is different. A limited liability company is a citizen of every state in which any member of the company is a citizen, and "the citizenship of a LLC is determined by the citizenship of *all* of its members." Therefore, the diversity analysis for a limited liability company requires a determination of the citizenship of every member of the company. Ms. Dupuis contended that she was the sole member of LRC. If so, then LRC was a citizen of Louisiana only. But Ms. Lisco contended that she also was a member of LRC. If so, then LRC is a citizen of both Louisiana and Florida. In either case, LRC was not diverse in citizenship from the plaintiff. In the removal notice, Ms. Lisco failed to offer any explanation why LRC's lack of diversity should be overlooked. Furthermore, LRC did not consent to the removal of this action. "Any doubt about the propriety of removal must be resolved in favor of remand."

**ANSWER (A)** is incorrect because the defendant did not carry its burden establish valid diversity of citizenship under 28 U.S.C. § 1332(a). **ANSWER (B)** is incorrect because the case was removed under the court's diversity jurisdiction; the facts do not indicate that the case was removed within the court's "arising under" or federal question jurisdiction. **ANSWER (C)** is incorrect because it doesn't matter that Wells Fargo Bank has offices in all fifty states; the corporation's citizenship is determined by where its headquarters are located, in this instance, South Dakota. **ANSWER (E)** is incorrect because the plaintiff's petition states a claim for conversion in the amount of $100,000, which exceeds the $75,000 amount in controversy requirement for federal diversity jurisdiction.

**PROBLEM #11. BEST ANSWER (A).**

Problem #11 is based on *State of Louisiana v. Pfizer, Inc.*, 2015 WL 10012989 (M.D. La. Sept. 2, 2015). The problem involves knowledge about federal question jurisdiction and the court, holding that there was no good federal question jurisdiction and that the case should be remanded to state court, decided the issues based on the Supreme Court's decision in *Grable & Sons v. Darue* (discussed below).

The party invoking removal jurisdiction bears the burden of establishing federal jurisdiction over the state court suit. *Frank v. Bear Stearns & Company,* 128 F.3d 919, 921–22 (5th Cir.1997). To support removal the defendant must locate the basis of federal jurisdiction in the allegations necessary to support the plaintiff's claims, ignoring the defendant's own pleadings and notice of removal. *Gully v. First National Bank,* 299 U.S. 109, 111 (1936).

Absent jurisdiction under the diversity statute, removal is appropriate only for those claims within the district court's original jurisdiction. 28 U.S.C. § 1441(a). District courts have been granted original jurisdiction over "all civil actions arising under the Constitution, laws, or treaties of the United States," and "arising under any Act of Congress relating to patents." 28 U.S.C. §§ 1331 and 1338. It is well established that the "arising under" language of these sections has a narrower meaning than the corresponding language in Article III of the Constitution which defines the limits of the judicial power of the United States. The Supreme Court has interpreted the phrase "arising under" in both sections identically and has applied the precedents for both sections interchangeably. *Gunn v. Minton,* 133 S.Ct. 1059, 1064 (2013), citing, *Christianson v. Colt Indus. Operating Corp.,* 486 U.S. 800, 808–09 (1988).

Ordinarily, determining whether a case arises under federal law is governed by the well-pleaded complaint rule—a federal court has original or removal jurisdiction only if a federal question appears on the face of the plaintiff's well-pleaded complaint. Generally, there is no federal jurisdiction if the plaintiff properly pleads only state law causes of action, and the fact that federal law may provide a defense to a state law claim is insufficient to establish federal question jurisdiction. *Gutierrez v. Flores,* 543 F.3d 248, 251 (5th Cir.2008); *Terrebonne Homecare, Inc. v. SMA Health Plan, Inc.,* 271 F.3d 186, 188 (5th Cir.2001).

Federal question jurisdiction is generally invoked by the plaintiff pleading a cause of action created by federal law. Another well-established but less frequently encountered form of federal arising-under jurisdiction, is that in certain cases federal question jurisdiction will lie over state law claims that implicate significant federal issues. *Grable & Sons Metal Prods., Inc. v. Darue Eng'g & Mfg.,* 545 U.S. 308 (2005). Thus, a federal question exists only in "those cases in which a well-pleaded complaint establishes either that federal law creates the cause of action or that the plaintiff's right to relief necessarily depends on resolution of a substantial question of federal law." *Franchise Tax*

*Bd. v. Constr. Laborers Vacation Trust,* 463 U.S. 1, 27–28 (1983); *Singh v. Duane Morris LLP,* 538 F.3d 334, 337–38 (5th Cir.2008). As the Fifth Circuit observed in *Singh,* however, the Supreme Court in *Grable* warned that *Franchise Tax Board's* "necessary-resolution" language is no automatic test, and should be read as part of a carefully nuanced standard rather than a broad, simplistic rule.

> The fact that a substantial federal question is necessary to the resolution of a state-law claim is not sufficient to permit federal jurisdiction: *Franchise Tax Board* . . . did not purport to disturb the long-settled understanding that the mere presence of a federal issue in a state cause of action does not automatically confer federal-question jurisdiction. Likewise, the presence of a disputed federal issue is never necessarily dispositive. Instead, far from creating some kind of automatic test, *Franchise Tax Board* thus candidly recognized the need for careful judgments about the exercise of federal judicial power in an area of uncertain jurisdiction.

*Singh,* 538 F.3d at 338.

In *Grable* the Supreme Court summed up the standard for determining whether an embedded federal issue in a state law claim raises a substantial question of federal law: "The question is, does a state-law claim necessarily raise a stated federal issue, actually disputed and substantial, which a federal forum may entertain without disturbing any congressionally approved balance of federal and state judicial responsibilities." *Singh,* 538 F.3d at 338, citing, *Grable,* 545 U.S. at 314, 125 S.Ct. 2363.

The lack of a private cause of action under federal law is relevant to, but not dispositive of, the question of whether the right is substantial enough to satisfy the exercise of federal jurisdiction. The federal issue must be a substantial one that indicates a serious federal interest in claiming the advantages inherent in a federal forum. However, the presence of a disputed federal issue and the importance of a federal forum are never dispositive. The court must always assess whether the exercise of federal jurisdiction would be consistent with congressional judgment about the sound division of labor between state and federal courts governing the application of § 1331. *Grable,* 545 U.S. at 313, 125 S.Ct. at 2367, 2370.

One year after the *Grable* decision, the Supreme Court again addressed "arising under" jurisdiction in *Empire Healthchoice Assurance, Inc. v. McVeigh,* 547 U.S. 677 (2006), which involved a health insurer for federal employees. The health insurance carrier sued its former enrollee's estate in federal court under state contract law for reimbursement of the insurance benefits it had paid for the enrollee's medical care. The insurer and the government argued that the complaint raised a federal claim because it sought to vindicate a contractual right contemplated by a federal statute, the Federal Employees Health Benefits Act, and under *Grable* federal law was a necessary element of the insurer's state law claim.

The Court rejected both arguments and found that federal question jurisdiction was lacking, emphasizing that *Grable* exemplifies a "slim category" of cases. In its analysis, the Court made several observations about the circumstances in *Grable* which resulted in finding that the federal issue implicated by the state law claim was sufficient to find jurisdiction based on federal question:

> The dispute there (*Grable*) centered on the action of a federal agency (IRS) and its compatibility with a federal statute, the question qualified as substantial, and its resolution was both dispositive of the case and would be controlling in numerous other cases. Here, the reimbursement claim was triggered, not by the action of any federal department, agency, or service, but by the settlement of a personal-injury action launched in state court, and the bottom-line practical issue is the share of that settlement properly payable to Empire.

> *Grable* presented a nearly pure issue of law, one that could be settled once and for all and thereafter would govern numerous tax sale cases. In contrast, Empire's reimbursement claim, McVeigh's counsel represented without contradiction, is fact-bound and situation-specific.

*McVeigh*, 547 U.S. at 700–701.

Finally, in *Gunn v. Minton* the Supreme Court reaffirmed the standards and principles in *Grable* that the courts must use to identify the "special and small category" of cases in which arising under jurisdiction lies when a claim has its origins in state rather than federal law. *Gunn,* 133 S.Ct. at 1064–65.

With respect to cases "arising under" federal patent law, the Supreme Court has held that jurisdiction under § 1338 is not necessarily conferred by a well-pleaded claim alleging a single theory which requires the resolution of a patent-law question. *Christianson v. Colt Indus. Operating Corp.,* 486 U.S. 800, 810 (1988). Claims which can be supported by an alternative theory, not based on patent law, cannot confer jurisdiction under § 1338. *Id.,* citing *Franchise Tax Bd.,* 463 U.S. at 26, & n. 29. Stated another way, if "there are reasons completely unrelated to the provisions and purposes of federal patent law why petitioners may or may not be entitled to the relief they seek under their monopolization claim, . . . the claim does not arise under federal patent law." *Christianson*, 486 U.S. at 812.

**ANSWER (B)** is incorrect because the fact clearly indicates that the defendant removed the case based on federal question jurisdiction and the fact pattern supplies no information to determine whether diversity jurisdiction is or is not satisfied. **ANSWER (C)** is incorrect because the mere citation to or invocation of patent jurisdiction under 28 U.S.C. § 1338 is insufficient to confer such jurisdiction; resolution of the state-based claims does not turn on substantive patent law. **ANSWER (D)** is incorrect because the court did not find that remand to state court would interfere with federal prerogatives and therefore disturb federal-state comity. **ANSWER (E)** is incorrect because although federal courts do have discretion to hear state claims in validly removed cases, the court determined that it did not have good federal question jurisdiction on the removal (and therefore could not exercise discretion to hear state law claims).

**PROBLEM #12. BEST ANSWER (D).**

Problems #12, 13, and 14 are based on *Brookfield Global Relocation Services LLC v. Burnley*, 2016 WL 500110 (Feb. 9, 2016). Problem #12 presents a simple problem requiring analysis of the federal court's diversity jurisdiction, with a focus on the amount-in-controversy requirement of 28 U.S.C. § 1332.

The litigation invoked the court's jurisdiction under 28 U.S.C. § 1332, which provides "the district courts shall have original jurisdiction of all civil actions where the matter in controversy exceeds the sum or value of $75,000, exclusive of interest and costs, and is between—(1) citizens of different States." 28 U.S.C. § 1332 (a)(1). The Burnleys did not dispute that the parties are citizens of different states. The Burnleys contended, as their sole challenge to the court's subject matter jurisdiction, that the amount in controversy requirement was not met because Burnley's appeal of the judgment underlying the lien was still pending. The Burnleys did not dispute that the lien encumbered the property when the complaint was filed or that the amount of the lien is $89,948.18, plus interest. "In a federal diversity action, the amount alleged in the complaint will suffice unless it appears to a legal certainty that the plaintiff in good faith cannot claim the jurisdictional amount." *Klepper v. First American Bank*, 916 F.2d 337, 340 (6th Cir.1990), citing *St. Paul Mercury Indem. Co. v. Red Cab Co.*, 303 U.S. 283, 288–89 (1938). When determining whether the amount in controversy has been satisfied, the court examines the complaint at the time it was filed. *Id.*

In this matter there was no meaningful dispute as to the amount in controversy. The lien on the property more than satisfied the statutory threshold without reference to Brookfield's additional damage claims. Under Ohio law, the fact that the judgment that resulted in the lien was appealed did not alter the legal certainty of the operation of the lien at the time the complaint was filed. "When the party against whom a judgment is rendered appeals his cause, the lien of the opposite party on the real estate of the appellant that was created by judgment, shall not be removed or vacated. The real estate shall be bound in the same manner as if the appeal had not been taken until final determination of the cause." The defendants' challenge to the court's subject matter jurisdiction was meritless.

**ANSWER (A)** is incorrect because the court held that there was valid diversity jurisdiction; Brookfield and the Burnleys were citizens of different states, and the amount in controversy exceeded $75,000 (as discussed above). **ANSWER (B)** is incorrect for the same reason; the court found that the value of the outstanding lien—even though that judgment was on appeal—satisfied the $75,000 amount in controversy requirement. **ANSWER (C)** is incorrect because federal courts are capable of adjudicating state-based claims if the court has valid diversity jurisdiction; in this case, the court does, so the presence of state-based claims is not a basis for dismissal. **ANSWER (E)** is incorrect because the plaintiff is pursuing state contract claims and there is no indication in the fact pattern that any of the plaintiff's claims fall within a small category of cases in which the federal courts have an interest in supplying a uniform interpretation of federal law.

## PROBLEM #13. BEST ANSWER (E).

Problem #13 is a continuation of Problem #12, and is based on the same fact pattern. This question requires the student to apply principles relating to the state assertion of personal jurisdiction over non-resident defendants.

The court followed "state law in determining the bounds of its jurisdiction over persons." *Daimler AG v. Bauman*, 134 S.Ct. 746, 753 (2014) (citing Fed.R.Civ.P. 4(k)(1)(A)). Ohio's jurisdictional "long-arm" statute is "not coterminous with federal constitutional limits. Thus, 'to establish a prima facie case of personal jurisdiction, a plaintiff must demonstrate that (1) Ohio's long-arm statute has been satisfied and (2) exercising jurisdiction would comport with the Due Process Clause of the Fourteenth Amendment. *Schneider v. Hardesty*, 669 F.3d 693, 700 (6th Cir.2012) (quoting *Estate of Thompson*, 545 F.3d at 361). Under Ohio law, "a court may exercise personal jurisdiction over a non-resident defendant only if specific jurisdiction can be found under one of the enumerated bases in Ohio's long-arm statute." *Conn v. Zakharov*, 667 F.3d 705, 717–18. Ohio's long-arm statute provides:

(A) A court may exercise personal jurisdiction over a person who acts directly or by an agent, as to a cause of action arising from the person's:

(1) Transacting any business in this state;

. . .

(3) Causing tortious injury by an act or omission in this state;

(4) Causing tortious injury in this state by an act or omission outside this state;

. . .

(8) Having an interest in, using, or possessing real property in this state;

(9) Contracting to insure any person, property, or risk located within this state at the time of contracting.

(C) When jurisdiction over a person is based solely upon this section, only a cause of action arising from acts enumerated in this section may be asserted against him.

O.R.C. § 2307.382. The Burnley defendants did not dispute their ownership of real property in Ohio; they did not dispute that they entered a contract with Brookfield and conveyed the real property to Brookfield; nor do they dispute that they have failed to clear a defect in the title to the real property. Accordingly, this court, at a minimum, had personal jurisdiction over the defendants under part (8) of O.R.C. § 2307.382.

Having established an enumerated basis of personal jurisdiction under Ohio's long-arm statute, this court had to consider whether an exercise of jurisdiction in this instance satisfies the requirements of the Due Process Clause of the Fourteenth Amendment to the Constitution of the United States. *CompuServe v. Patterson*, 89 F.3d 1257, 1262 (6th Cir.1996). The Due Process Clause requires "that the defendant have sufficient 'minimum contacts' with the forum state so that finding personal jurisdiction does not 'offend traditional notions of fair play and substantial justice.' " *Conn, supra,* at 712. The Federal Due Process inquiry addresses two types of personal jurisdiction: "(1) general personal jurisdiction, where the suit does not arise from defendant's contacts with the forum state; and (2) specific jurisdiction, where the suit does arise from the defendant's contacts with the forum state." *Id.* at 712–713. This matter addresses specific jurisdiction insofar as the suit arises from the defendants' dealings with Ohio real property. A finding of specific jurisdiction in this instance satisfies all three elements of inquiry into jurisdiction identified by the Sixth Circuit:

> First, the defendant must purposefully avail himself of the privilege of acting in the forum state or causing a consequence in the forum state. Second, the cause of action must arise from the defendant's activities there. Finally, the acts of the defendant or consequences caused by defendant must have a substantial enough connection with the forum state to make the exercise of jurisdiction over the defendant reasonable.

*Id.* at 713. In this instance the plaintiff alleged that the defendants owned Ohio real property; they contracted to sell that real property to the plaintiff; and then breached that contract of sale by failing to clear a defect in the title to the property created by the judgment lien issued by an Ohio court for acts or omissions that occurred in Ohio. The defendants did not meaningfully challenge any of the facts alleged, but instead contend that the fact that they have relocated from Ohio to Florida extinguishes the court's jurisdiction. The defendants' argument had no basis in law. The state and federal law establishing long arm jurisdiction exists specifically to prevent individuals or entities from escaping liability by simply denying a relationship to the forum or leaving the forum in which the harm occurred. O.R.C. § 2307.382; *International Shoe Co. v. State of Wash.*, 326 U.S. 310 (1945). The defendants' challenge to the court's personal jurisdiction was meritless.

**ANSWER (A)** is incorrect because the defendants' contacts with the forum state Ohio were sufficient to confer specific jurisdiction under Ohio's long-arm statute. **ANSWER (B)** is incorrect because the court found that assertion of personal jurisdiction over the defendants would not violate Due Process principles (see discussion above). **ANSWER (C)** is incorrect because the plaintiffs have not asserted claims based in tort; the claims asserted are based in contract and property law. **ANSWER (D)** is incorrect because nothing in the fact pattern suggests that the basis for assertion of personal jurisdiction is based on the defendants' transient presence within Ohio.

### PROBLEM #14. BEST ANSWER (C).

Problem #14 is a continuation of the fact pattern in Problems #12 and 13. This problem addresses whether the plaintiff's choice of venue is proper under the federal venue statute. The court held that venue was proper, as against the defendants' challenges to that venue.

The defendants contended that venue in the Northern District of Ohio was improper because they were residents of Florida. The defendants also restated their argument concerning the amount in controversy, which is not relevant to venue.

Venue in federal district courts is governed generally by 28 U.S.C. § 1391, which provides:

**(b) Venue in general.**—A civil action may be brought in—

. . .

**(2)** a judicial district in which a substantial part of the events or omissions giving rise to the claim occurred, or a substantial part of the property that is the subject of the action is situated;

Venue within the Northern District of Ohio is governed specifically by Local Rule 3.8 which divides the district into Eastern and Western Divisions, and allows "all actions brought against a resident of a county within the Eastern Divisions" to be filed "at any of the offices within the Eastern Division." Local Rule 3.8 (a) and (b). The court was situated in the Eastern Division; the real property conveyed by the defendants Burnley was located in the Northern District, as was the court that issued the judgment and lien against the property. Therefore, venue was proper in the Northern District of Ohio.

**ANSWER (A)** is incorrect because venue is proper under 28 U.S.C. § 1391(b)(2), even though the defendants reside in Florida. **ANSWER (B)** is incorrect because, as indicated above, the amount-in-controversy requirement for federal diversity jurisdiction has no bearing on whether venue is properly laid in federal court. **ANSWER (D)** is incorrect because the convenience of the parties and witnesses is not a standard to determine threshold proper venue. **ANSWER (E)** is incorrect because what law applies to the litigation also has no bearing on determining whether venue is appropriate.

**PROBLEM #15. BEST ANSWER (A).**

As an alternative to their jurisdiction and venue arguments, the Burnley defendants, sought to "invoke the doctrine of *forum non conveniens*" because they were Florida residents. The defendants stated that continuing the matter in Ohio would present an "undue burden" on their resources. The Burnley defendants requested that the Court dismiss this matter under the doctrine, and instruct the plaintiff to refile in Florida.

"The principle of *forum non conveniens* is simply that a court may resist imposition upon its jurisdiction even when jurisdiction is authorized by the letter of a general venue statute." *Gulf Oil Corp. v. Gilbert*, 330 U.S. 501, 507 (1947). "Courts of equity and of law" may "occasionally decline, in the interest of justice, to exercise jurisdiction, where the suit is between aliens or nonresidents, or where for kindred reasons the litigation can more appropriately be conducted in a foreign tribunal." *Gilbert, supra* at 504. "The doctrine presupposes the availability of at least two forums in which the defendant may be sued; the defendant seeking a *forum non conveniens* dismissal must identify an alternative forum." *Dowling v. Richardson-Merrell,*

*Inc.*, 727 F.2d 608, 612 (6th Cir.1984). Although the doctrine was previously, as in *Gilbert*, applied to assess the relative appropriateness of alternate federal judicial districts, the doctrine is no longer applied to domestic venue disputes:

> *Gilbert* held that it was permissible to dismiss an action brought in a District Court in New York by a Virginia plaintiff against a defendant doing business in Virginia for a fire that occurred in Virginia. Such a dismissal would be improper today because of the federal venue transfer statute, 28 U.S.C. § 1404(a): 'For the convenience of parties and witnesses, in the interest of justice, a district court may transfer any civil action to any other district of division where it might have been brought.' . . . As a consequence, the federal doctrine of *forum non conveniens* has continuing application only in cases where the alternative forum is abroad.

*American Dredging Co. v. Miller*, 510 U.S. 443, 449 n.2 (1992). Accordingly, *forum non conveniens* had no application in this matter. As stated above, venue was proper in the Northern District of Ohio.

**ANSWER (B)**, while plausible, is not the best answer because forum non conveniens is not available for domestic disputes, and the defendant could request a transfer pursuant to 28 U.S.C. § 1406. **ANSWER (C)** is incorrect because it doesn't matter that Florida might be an adequate alternative forum; the doctrine of forum non conveniens simply does not apply to permit dismissal. Similarly, **ANSWER (D)** is incorrect because there is no support for the contention that a forum non conveniens dismissal would serve the interests of justice and, at any rate, as indicated, such a dismissal is not available for domestic cases. Finally, **ANSWER (E)** is incorrect because there is no need to conduct a weighing of private and public factors if a forum non conveniens dismissal is not available for domestic disputes.

### PROBLEM #16. BEST ANSWER (A).

Problem #16 is based *Center For Biological Diversity v. Gould*, 2015 WL 6951295 (E.D. Cal. Nov. 10, 2015). This problem requires analysis of intervention of right under Federal Rule of Civil Procedure 24(a). The district court permitted intervention as of right. Although the problem does not ask this, the court also permitted permissive intervention under Fed.R.Civ.P. 24(b).

The plaintiffs brought this action against defendants Dean Gould, the Sierra National Forest Supervisor, and the United States Forest Service, alleging that defendants violated the National Environmental Policy Act and the Administrative Procedure Act in approving the French Fire Recovery and Reforestation Project. Sierra Forest Products sought to intervene as a defendant pursuant to Federal Rule of Civil Procedure 24(a) or, in the alternative, Rule 24(b). The plaintiffs did not oppose the motion to intervene and federal defendants took no position.

A party may intervene as a matter of right under Rule 24(a) if the party seeking to intervene can demonstrate that (1) the motion is timely; (2) it has an interest relating to the property or transaction that is the subject of the action; (3) the disposition of the action may, as a practical matter, impair or impede the applicant's ability to protect its interest; and (4) the existing parties may not adequately represent the applicant's interest. Fed.R.Civ.P. 24(a); *Donnelly v. Glickman*, 159 F.3d 405, 409 (9th Cir.1998). In determining whether intervention is appropriate, the Ninth Circuit has held that courts are to be guided by practicable and equitable considerations, not technical distinctions. *Donnelly*, 159 F.3d at 409. Courts "generally interpret the requirements broadly in favor of intervention." *Id.*

The timeliness of a motion to intervene depends on three criteria: the current stage of the litigation, the possible prejudice to other parties, and the reason for any delay in moving to intervene. *United States v. Carpenter*, 298 F.3d 1122, 1125 (9th Cir.2002). All three factors weighed in favor of Sierra Forest Products' intervention in this case. The complaint was filed on August 31, 2015 and no substantive proceedings had yet occurred. Sierra Forest Products was awarded the government contract for the French Fire timber sale on September 29, 2015 and promptly filed its motion to intervene less than a month later. Sierra Forest Products agreed to follow the established summary judgment schedule and thus its intervention would not cause any delays.

Sierra Forest Products also had an interest related to the property or transaction challenged in this action and disposition of the action may, as a practical matter, impair or impede its ability to protect its interest. The Ninth Circuit has "taken the view that a party has a sufficient interest for intervention purposes if it will suffer a practical impairment of its interests as a result of the pending litigation." *Cal. ex. rel. Lockyer v. United States*, 450 F.3d 436, 441 (9th Cir.2006). "Whether an applicant for intervention as of right demonstrates sufficient interest in an action is a practical, threshold inquiry, and no specific legal or equitable interest need be established." *Citizens for Balanced Use v. Mont. Wilderness Ass'n*, 647 F.3d 893, 898 (9th Cir.2011).

Sierra Forest Products had contract rights that might be impacted by the resolution of the litigation. Sierra Forest Products was depending on the timber from the government contract to keep its mill fully operational through the winter and the court's findings on whether the French Fire Project complies with NEPA and the APA would determine whether its contract could be executed. Sierra Forest Products also had a broader interest in any litigation that might impede its ability to obtain timber from federal lands in the future. It wanted to ensure that NEPA continued to "achieve a balance between population and resource use," 42 U.S.C. § 4331(b)(5), and demonstrate that this timber harvest complies with the statute.

Lastly, there was a possibility that the existing government defendants would not adequately represent Sierra Forest Products' interests. "The burden of showing inadequacy is 'minimal,' and the applicant need only show that representation of its interests by existing parties 'may be' inadequate." *Sw. Ctr. for Biological Diversity v. Berg*, 268 F.3d 810, 823 (9th Cir.2001). The court considered: "(1) whether the interest of a present party is such that it will undoubtedly make all the intervenor's arguments; (2) whether the present party is capable and willing to make such arguments; and (3) whether the would-be intervenor would offer any necessary elements to the proceedings that other parties would neglect." *Id.* at 822. "The government's representation of the public interest may not be identical to the individual parochial interest of a particular group just because both entities occupy the same posture in the litigation." *Citizens for Balanced Use*, 647 F.3d at 899.

While the interests of Sierra Forest Products and the government were aligned to the extent they both believe the French Fire Project should proceed, Sierra Forest Products had unique economic and employment interests associated with this timber sale. Sierra Forest Products needed to obtain timber as quickly as possible in order to keep its mill in operation through the winter and provide full-time employment for its workers. It also had a strong interest in harvesting the timber before the value of the wood was lost due to decay. While the government wanted the timber removed and hoped to create economic opportunity, it did not have the same need for expedience. Moreover, the timber harvest was only one aspect of the government's project and it must ultimately do what is best for the public interest and most in line with federal regulations. While the two interests seemed to be running on parallel tracks, it was possible they could diverge as litigation proceeded. Accordingly, the court found that Sierra Forest Products may intervene as a matter of right.

**ANSWER (B)** is incorrect because courts do not liberally grant intervention as of right; courts apply the statutory criteria to determine whether a proposed intervenor satisfies those criteria to permit intervention. **ANSWER (C)** is incorrect because the court found that Sierra Products interests in its contract would be impaired or impeded if it was not permitted to intervene as of right to protect those interests (*see* discussion above). **ANSWER (D)** is incorrect because the court did not find that Sierra Products' presence in the lawsuit would needlessly complicate proceedings; to the contrary, it found Sierra Products willing to comply with the court's scheduling order. **ANSWER (E)** is simply incorrect; Sierra Products filed its motion very quickly after the plaintiff filed its initial lawsuit, and Rule 23 contains no deadlines concerning the timeliness of a motion to intervene.

### PROBLEM #17. BEST ANSWER (D).

Problem #17 is based on *Hankins v. Yellow Fin Marine Services, LLC*, 2015 WL 9004447 (E.D. La. Dec. 14, 2015). This problem involves analysis of whether a counterclaim is compulsory or permissive under Federal Rule of Civil Procedure 13(a) and (b), and the grounds for federal court jurisdiction over a counterclaim, as a consequence. The court held that the counterclaim was compulsory and federal jurisdiction was valid under the supplemental jurisdiction statute, 28 U.S.C. § 1367.

Hankins's motion argued that the court had to dismiss the defendant's counterclaim because it did not have subject-matter jurisdiction over the claim. The plaintiff's argument rested on the contentions that the claim was not a compulsory counterclaim under Rule 13 of the Federal Rules of Civil Procedure, and that it lacked an independent basis for subject-matter jurisdiction. Accordingly, the plaintiff maintained that the court had no jurisdiction over the counterclaim, and that it must be dismissed.

The defendant's contended that the court had independent subject-matter jurisdiction over the counterclaim because it fell within the Court's maritime jurisdiction under 28 U.S.C. § 1333. Yellow Fin argued that the claim fell within the court's maritime jurisdiction because it arose out of the maritime employment relationship. In the alternative, Yellow Fin asserted two other arguments. First, that even if this court deemed the claim outside the scope of 28 U.S.C. § 1333, it qualified as a compulsory counterclaim and thus fell within the court's jurisdiction. Second, that that even if it was not a compulsory counterclaim, it was a permissive counterclaim that fell within the court's supplemental jurisdiction. The defendant maintained that the court should deny the plaintiff's motion.

Rule 12(b)(1) of the Federal Rules of Civil Procedure permits the dismissal of a case or a particular claim for lack of subject-matter jurisdiction. "The standard of review applicable to motions to dismiss under Rule 12(b)(1) is similar to that applicable to motions to dismiss under Rule 12(b)(6)." *Powell v. Hunter*, 2012 WL 253105, No. 11–1640, at *2 (E.D. La. Jan. 25, 2012). However, when considering a motion to dismiss under Rule 12(b)(1), courts may look to: "(1) the complaint alone; (2) the complaint supplemented by undisputed facts evidenced in the record; or (3) the complaint supplemented by undisputed facts plus the court's resolution of disputed facts." *Ramming v. United States*, 281 F.3d 158, 161 (5th Cir.2001). "The burden of proof for a Rule 12(b)(1) motion to dismiss is on the party asserting jurisdiction." *Id.*

"Federal courts are courts of limited jurisdiction. They possess only that power authorized by Constitution and statute." *Kokkonen v. Guardian Life Ins. Co. of America*, 511 U.S. 375, 377 (1994). By statute, Congress has delineated two primary bases for original subject-matter jurisdiction in federal courts: federal question jurisdiction and diversity jurisdiction. 28 U.S.C. §§ 1331–1332. Additionally, in 1990, Congress enacted the supplemental jurisdiction statute, which provides in part: "in any civil action of which the district courts have original jurisdiction, the district courts shall have supplemental jurisdiction over all other claims that are so related to claims in the action within such original jurisdiction that they form part of the same case or controversy under Article III of the United States Constitution." 28 U.S.C. § 1367(a). Accordingly, certain claims may remain in federal court even if they do not meet the requirements for original jurisdiction so long as they form the same "case or controversy" as the claims with original jurisdiction.

The application of § 1367 is clear with respect to compulsory counterclaims. Compulsory counterclaims are those that "arise out of the transaction or occurrence that is the subject matter of the opposing party's claim" and must be plead or waived—outside of certain exceptions not relevant here. Fed.R.Civ.P. 13(a). A compulsory counterclaim by definition meets the "same transaction or occurrence" standard, meaning it also falls under the broader "case or controversy" standard of § 1367. Wright & Miller, et al, FEDERAL PRACTICE AND PROCEDURE § 3567.1 ("It is absolutely clear that the common nucleus concept encompasses claims that arise from the same 'transaction or occurrence' as the jurisdiction-invoking claim."). Accordingly, all compulsory counterclaims fall within the federal courts' supplemental jurisdiction. *CheckPoint Fluidic Systems Int'l, Ltd., v. Guccione*, 2012 WL 195533, No. 10–4505, at *4 (E.D. La. Jan. 23, 2012) ("When a counterclaim is compulsory it is within the supplemental jurisdiction of the court because by definition it must arise out of the same transaction or occurrence as the original claim.").

A permissive counterclaim, defined as any counterclaim that is not compulsory, is one that a party may, but is not required to, include in a pleading. Fed.R.Civ.P. 13(b). Prior to the passage of § 1367 in 1990, courts, including the United States Court of Appeals for the Fifth Circuit, required permissive counterclaims to have an independent jurisdictional basis. *See, e.g., Plant v. Blazer Fin. Servs., Inc. of Ga.*, 598 F.2d 1357, 1360 (5th Cir.1979). However, the plain language of § 1367 evidences an intent to do away with this distinction between compulsory and permissive counterclaims. The statute specifically states that it applies to *"all other claims* that are so related to claims in the action within such original jurisdiction that they form part of the same case or controversy." 28 U.S.C. § 1367(a).

Though the Fifth Circuit has yet to speak on the issue, the consensus among courts and commentators is that "Article III's case-or-controversy standard is the jurisdictional limit for counterclaims," not Rule 13's transaction-or-occurrence standard. *Global NAPs, Inc. v. Verizon New England, Inc.*, 603 F.3d 71, 87 (1st Cir.2010). *See also Jones v. Ford Motor Credit Co.*, 358 F.3d 205, 212 (2d Cir.2004); *Channel v. Citicorp Nat. Servs., Inc.*, 89 F.3d 379, 385 (7th Cir.1996); Wright & Miller, et al, FEDERAL PRACTICE AND PROCEDURE § 3567.1. Thus, the applicability of § 1367 turns on whether the counterclaim forms part of the same case or controversy, not whether it is compulsory or permissive. A compulsory counterclaim will always fall under § 1367 for the reasons delineated above, but a permissive counterclaim may or may not, depending on whether it is part of the same case or controversy as the claims invoking the court's original jurisdiction. If a permissive counterclaim does not fall within the parameters of § 1367, then it must have an independent jurisdictional basis. If it does not have an independent jurisdictional basis, then the Court must dismiss the claim for lack of subject-matter jurisdiction.

The parties' briefs placed significant emphasis on whether Yellow Fin's counterclaim was compulsory or permissive, but for the reasons enumerated above, the distinction is largely irrelevant for jurisdiction purposes. Regardless of whether the counterclaim is permissive or compulsory, the court has jurisdiction over the claim if it meets the case-or-controversy standard for supplemental jurisdiction.

The Supreme Court of the United States defined the case-or-controversy standard while explaining the outer limits of what was then known as "pendent jurisdiction" in *United Mine Workers of America v. Gibbs*, 383 U.S. 715 (1966). The Court defined a single case or controversy as one in which all the claims "derive from a common nucleus of operative fact," such that one would expect them to be tried in a single judicial proceeding. *Gibbs*, 383 U.S. at 725. "Legislative history makes clear that Congress intended to codify the result in *Gibbs*" with the passage of § 1367. Wright & Miller, et al, FEDERAL PRACTICE AND PROCEDURE § 3567.1. Since then, courts have found that a "loose factual connection between the claims is generally sufficient" to meet the common-nucleus standard. *Guccione*, 2012 WL 195533 at *3. Additionally, "a court's determination of whether to exercise supplemental jurisdiction is guided by considerations of judicial economy, convenience and fairness to litigants." *Id.*

Here, while different allegations form the bases of each of Hankins's claims and Yellow Fin's counterclaim, all of the allegations formed a common nucleus of facts. The main issues in this litigation are determining the events that took place and how those events impacted the physical and mental health of Hankins. At the center of at least one of Hankins' claims would be the causes of his emotional distress and the deterioration of his health, specifically: the causes of his depression and anxiety and the causes for the implementation of his pacemaker and cardiac defibrillator. While the plaintiff maintained that harassment by fellow crew members led to these issues, Yellow Fin contended that it was the stress from his arrests that caused Hankins's problems. Those arrests and the subsequent legal issues were what allegedly led Yellow Fin to loan Hankins money—the money they sought to recover via the counterclaim. Though litigation of the counterclaim would focus on why Yellow Fin lent Hankins the money, the parameters of the promissory note, and whether or not Hankins repaid the loan, the facts underlying those issues would also come up in the litigation over Hankins' claims against Yellow Fin.

Moreover, both claims stemmed from Hankins's employment with Yellow Fin. One would logically expect disputes between an employer and employee to be tried in a single proceeding, especially considering Yellow Fin's allegation that the loans were an advance on Hankins's regular wages. Deciding both sets of claims in a single proceeding would also facilitate judicial economy and convenience by avoiding redundant proceedings. Therefore, both sets of claims arose from a common nucleus of operative fact and Yellow Fin's counterclaim fell under the umbrella of this Court's supplemental jurisdiction. As such, this Court need not determine whether an independent jurisdictional basis existed for the counterclaim.

**ANSWER (A)** is incorrect because the court found that Yellow Fin's counterclaim did arise out of the same transactions and occurrences as the plaintiff's claims, and therefore the counterclaim was compulsory. **ANSWER (B)** is incorrect because the court did not find that the counterclaim was permissive, and also did not find any need to find an independent jurisdictional basis for the counterclaim, as that was provided by 28 U.S.C. § 1367. **ANSWER (C)** is incorrect because the court did have valid maritime jurisdiction pursuant to 28 U.S.C. § 1333. **ANSWER (E)** is incorrect because this problem does to involve or question whether Yellow Fin's counterclaim was well-pleaded under pleading standards; this is a red-herring answer.

**PROBLEM #18. BEST ANSWER (A).**

Problem #18 is based on *Bostic v. Glaxosmithkline, LLC*, 2015 WL 8486181 (E.D. Ky. Dec. 9, 2015). This problem entails analysis of the doctrine of fraudulent joinder in the diversity context, motions to sever under Federal Rule of Civil Procedure 21, and joinder of parties under Federal Rule of Civil Procedure 20. The court held that the Healthcare defendants were not fraudulently joined, and therefore the court would not sever them from the case. Consequently, the court lacked sufficient diversity jurisdiction, and ordered remand of the case to state court.

The Pharmaceutical defendants argued that the Healthcare defendants were fraudulently misjoined. Courts sometimes employ the controversial and relatively new doctrine of fraudulent misjoinder when a plaintiff joins a "valid, but unrelated, claim against a non-diverse defendant" to defeat diversity. *Murriel-Don Coal Co. v. Aspen Ins. UK Ltd.*, 790 F.Supp. 2d 590, 599 (E.D. Ky. 2011). For example, if a Kentucky plaintiff sues an Ohio driver for causing a car crash and then joins a Kentucky plastic surgeon for performing a botched facelift that occurred six months earlier, the surgeon is fraudulently misjoined. *Id.* Under the fraudulent misjoinder doctrine, the federal court could therefore sever the claim against the surgeon to obtain diversity jurisdiction. *Id.* Though the claim against the surgeon is "colorable, it is entirely unrelated to the claim against the Ohio driver." *Id.*

The Healthcare defendants are not fraudulently misjoined. Under both federal and Kentucky rules of civil procedure, there is no misjoinder "if the plaintiff's claims arise from the same" transaction or occurrence and a "question of law or fact common to all defendants will arise." (citing Fed.R.Civ.P. 20(a)(2) and Ky. R. Civ. P. 20.01). The Bostics' claims against the Healthcare defendants, DataBank, and the Pharmaceutical defendants meet those requirements. First, the same occurrence—D.B.'s death—gave rise to all of the Bostics' claims. The Bostics alleged that each defendant contributed to D.B.'s death. Second, a common question of fact arose as to all the defendants: did Zofran or its generic version cause D.B.'s death? True, some questions of fact or law are specific to the Healthcare Defendants, *e.g.*, was Dr. Wells negligent in prescribing Zofran to D.B.? But one common question is enough to show proper joinder, and here there is one. Fed.R.Civ.P. 20(a)(2); Ky. R. Civ. P. 20.01. Therefore, even if it could, the court would not sever the Healthcare Defendants using fraudulent misjoinder.

GlaxoSmithKline argues that, even if the defendants were not fraudulently misjoined, the Court should sever the Healthcare defendants and thereby preserve federal jurisdiction. Federal Rule of Civil Procedure 21 permits a court, in its discretion, to "sever any claim against a party," Fed.R.Civ.P. 21, as long as that party is not required under Rule 19. *Safeco Ins. Co. of Am. v. City of White House, Tenn.*, 36 F.3d 540, 546 (6th Cir.1994) (laying out requirements for necessary parties under Rule 19(a)); *Soberay Mach. & Equip. Co. v. MRF Ltd., Inc.*, 181 F.3d 759, 764 (6th Cir.1999) (outlining requirements for dispensable parties under Rule 19(b)).

Even when a party could be severed under Rule 21, however, the "authority to dismiss a dispensable nondiverse party . . . should be exercised sparingly." *Newman-Green, Inc. v. Alfonzo-Larrain*, 490 U.S. 826, 837 (1989). Courts should "carefully consider whether severance of a nondiverse party will prejudice any of the parties in the litigation." *Id.* at 838; *Hardaway v. Checkers Drive-In Restaurants, Inc.*, 483 Fed.Appx. 854, 855 (4th Cir.2012); *see also* 1 Fed. Proc., L. Ed. § 1:241 (stating that courts should consider prejudice to any party when deciding to sever a dispensable party).

Severance would prejudice the plaintiffs here. If the court severed the Healthcare defendants, the Bostics would have to litigate on two fronts: in state court against the Healthcare Defendants and in federal court against the Pharmaceutical defendants and DataBank. And the overlap between the two cases means the Bostics would have to duplicate their efforts. For example, the Bostics would have to prove in both cases that Zofran and its generic equivalent caused D.B.'s birth defects and death.

Moreover, a plaintiff is generally "the master of her complaint" and can choose who she wants to sue. *Lincoln Prop. Co. v. Roche*, 546 U.S. 81, 91 (2005). Here, the Bostics chose to sue all the defendants together in state court. All of the defendants were properly joined. There was a common nucleus of fact, involving one harm allegedly caused by multiple defendants. *See United Mine Workers of Am. v. Gibbs*, 383 U.S. 715, 724 (1966) ("Joinder of claims, parties, and remedies" is "strongly encouraged" under the Federal Rules of Civil Procedure.). There was no good reason to contravene the plaintiffs' decision here.

The Healthcare defendants were properly joined in this suit, and severing them would prejudice the Bostics. Because the Bostics and the Healthcare defendants shared Kentucky citizenship, the court lacked subject matter jurisdiction. Therefore, this case was remanded to state court.

**ANSWER (B)** is incorrect because the issue in this case and the grounds for the petition to remand concerned whether the federal court had good diversity jurisdiction and whether the Healthcare defendants had been misjoinder to defeat federal court jurisdiction on removal. The problem does not deal with the fact that the case involves state law issues, and so this answer is irrelevant to the question posed in the problem. **ANSWER (C)** is incorrect because there are no facts indicating whether all the defendants consented to the removal; the facts implicate the question of fraudulent joinder to defeat diversity jurisdiction. **ANSWER (D)** is incorrect because the court determined that the Healthcare defendants had not been improperly or fraudulently joined. **ANSWER (E)** is incorrect because the facts in the problem do not discuss or implicate any issue relating to the amount in controversy for federal diversity jurisdiction.

## PROBLEM #19. BEST ANSWER (C).

Problems #19 and 20 are based on *Boling v. Prospect Funding Holdings, LLC*, 2015 WL 5680418 (W.D. Ky. Sept. 24, 2015). Problem #19 requires simple application of Kentucky's long-arm statute. The federal court held that it had good person jurisdiction over the non-resident defendant prospect. To begin, the court determined that it has good diversity jurisdiction over the parties.

When sitting in diversity, federal courts apply the law of the state where it sits in determining whether personal jurisdiction exists over a nonresident defendant. *See Third Nat'l Bank v. WEDGE Grp., Inc.*, 882 F.2d 1087, 1089 (6th Cir.1989) (citing *Am. Greetings Corp. v. Cohn*, 839 F.2d 1164, 1167 (6th Cir.1988)). In determining whether personal jurisdiction exists, the Court must consider: "(1) whether the law of the state in which the district court sits authorizes jurisdiction, and (2) whether the exercise of jurisdiction comports with Due Process." *Brunner v. Hampson*, 441 F.3d 457, 463 (6th Cir.2006). At this stage of the litigation and because the court was addressing this issue based upon written submissions only, Boling "needed only make a prima facie showing of jurisdiction" to defeat Prospect's motion to dismiss. *Compuserve, Inc. v. Patterson*, 89 F.3d 1257, 1262 (6th Cir.1996).

In *Caesars Riverboat Casino, LLC v. Beach*, 336 S.W.3d 51 (Ky. 2011), the Kentucky Supreme Court clarified the scope of Kentucky's long-arm statute, KRS 454.210, which had been construed broadly by Kentucky courts. In *Beach*, the court explained the proper analysis of the long-arm statute:

> First, review must proceed under KRS 454.210 to determine if the cause of action arises from conduct or activity of the defendant that fits into one of the statute's enumerated categories. If not, then *in personam* jurisdiction may not be exercised. When that initial step results in a determination that the statute is applicable, a second step of analysis must be taken to determine if exercising personal jurisdiction over the non-resident defendant offends his federal due process rights.

*Id.* at 57.

In this case, the cause of action fell under KRS 454.210(2)(a), which provides that courts "may exercise personal jurisdiction over a person who acts directly or by an agent, as to a claim arising from the person's . . . transacting any business in this Commonwealth. . . ." In entering into the loan agreements with Kentucky residents, Prospect and CMG obtained an interest in the Bolings' potential personal injury recovery in a lawsuit pending in a federal court in Kentucky. Because the issues in the present case directly related to the enforceability of those loan agreements, the court concluded that Prospect and CMG transacted business in Kentucky for the purpose of its long-arm statute. *See Beach*, 336 S.W.3d at 59 ("If there is a reasonable and direct nexus between the wrongful acts alleged in the complaint and the statutory predicate for long-arm-jurisdiction, then jurisdiction is properly exercised.").

Even if Prospect's actions fell under KRS 454.210, the court must still determine whether the requirements of due process were met—"whether the facts of the case demonstrate that the nonresident defendant possesses such minimum contacts with the forum state that the exercise of jurisdiction would comport with 'traditional notions of fair play and substantial justice.'" *Theunissen v. Matthews*, 935 F.2d 1454, 1459 (6th Cir.1991) (quoting *Int'l Shoe Co. v. Washington*, 326 U.S. 310, 316 (1945)). Under Sixth Circuit precedent, this Court is to consider the following criteria in making that determination:

> First, the defendant must purposefully avail himself of the privilege of acting in the forum state or causing a consequence in the forum state. Second, the cause of action must arise from the defendant's activities there. Finally, the acts of the defendant or consequences caused by the defendant must have a substantial enough connection with the forum state to make the exercise of jurisdiction over the defendant reasonable.

*S. Mach. Co. v. Mohasco Indus., Inc.*, 401 F.2d 374, 381 (6th Cir.1968).

Considering the first criteria and taking all reasonable inferences in favor of Boling, the court found that Prospect purposefully availed itself of the privilege of transacting business in Kentucky. Prospect and CMG reached beyond their states of domicile and provided loans to Kentucky residents. These acts were more than just "random," "fortuitous," or "attenuated," but instead reflect deliberate and direct action by Prospect and CMG. *See Burger King Corp. v. Rudezewicz*, 471 U.S. 462, 475 (1985). As noted above, the loan agreements signed by Boling purported to assign an interest in the Kentucky litigation proceeds, the acceptance of which by Prospect and CMG was akin to owning property in the Commonwealth. Thus, Prospect and CMG should have reasonably anticipated that they would fall under a Kentucky court's jurisdiction. *See McGee v. Int'l Life Ins. Co.*, 355 U.S. 220, 223 (1957) (determining that the issuance of a single life insurance policy to a non-resident constituted purposeful availment). The second factor was also satisfied. Boling's claims against Prospect directly related to Prospect and CMG's contacts with Kentucky—the Bolings' loan agreements.

Finally, the court found that the actions of Prospect and CMG had a substantial enough effect on Kentucky to make jurisdiction reasonable. For loans totaling $30,000 plus fees, Prospect sought to recover more than $340,405, secured by the Bolings' claims pending in Kentucky for a personal injury occurring in Kentucky.

For these reasons, the court concluded that it could exercise personal jurisdiction over Prospect relating to Prospect and CMG's loan agreements with the Bolings. The court denied the motion to dismiss on this basis.

**ANSWER (A)** is incorrect because the court, on the facts, found to the contrary; that prospects contacts with Kentucky through the loans to the Bolings was sufficient to confer jurisdiction pursuant to Kentucky's long-arm statute and did not offend due process. **ANSWER (B)** is incorrect because the existence of a parallel lawsuit in New Jersey has no bearing on the Kentucky court's analysis whether it has good personal jurisdiction over the non-resident defendant Prospect. **ANSWER (D)** is incorrect because there is no indication in the facts that Prospect has nationwide contacts, and so this is irrelevant to an analysis of personal jurisdiction in this problem. **ANSWER (E)** is incorrect because, while a general statement of law, the plaintiff's choice of forum must give way to defendant's due process rights if the grounds for asserting personal jurisdiction are not present. The court denies the defendant's motion not because of deference to the plaintiff's choice of forum, but because the defendant has sufficient contacts with the state under Kentucky's long-arm statute and cases construing that statute.

### PROBLEM #20. BEST ANSWER (E).

Problem #20 is a continuation of the same fact pattern as in Problem #19. This problem involves a simple analysis of whether Mr. Boling's failure to join his wife as a party to his federal declaratory judgment action was a basis for dismissal under Federal Rule of Civil Procedure 19. The court held that Mrs. Boling was not an indispensable party to the litigation, and therefore denied the defendant's motion.

Prospect argued that the court should dismiss the complaint because Boling failed to include his ex-wife as a party in this action because she is a necessary party. Under Fed.R.Civ.P. 12(b)(7), the Court may "dismiss an action for failure to join a party in accordance with Rule 19." *Register v. Cameron & Barkley Co.*, 467 F.Supp. 2d 519, 530 (D.S.C. 2006). In ruling on whether to grant a motion on this basis, a court may consider "the allegations of the complaint and the affidavits and other proofs adduced in contradiction or support thereof." *Esters v. Shell Oil Co.*, 234 F.2d 847, 849 (5th Cir.1956).

In relevant part, Rule 19(a)(1) provides:

> A person who is subject to service of process and whose joinder will not deprive the court of subject-matter jurisdiction must be joined as a party if:
>
> (A)  in that person's absence, the court cannot accord complete relief among existing parties; or
>
> (B)  that person claims an interest relating to the subject of the action and is so situated that disposing of the action in the person's absence may:
>
> > (i)  as a practical matter impair or impede the person's ability to protect the interest; or
> >
> > (ii)  leave an existing party subject to a substantial risk of incurring double, multiple, or otherwise inconsistent obligations because of the interest.

As one court has explained:

> "One is not an indispensable party to a suit merely because he has a substantial interest in the subject matter of the litigation, nor is one an indispensable party even though one's interest in the subject matter of the litigation is such that his presence as a party to the suit is required for a complete adjudication in that suit of all questions related to the litigation."

*Ford v. Adkins*, 39 F.Supp. 472, 473–74 (D. Ill. 1941). Similarly, the term "necessary party" means " 'desirable parties' as distinguished from indispensable parties on the one hand and from proper parties on the other hand." *Bradley v. Sch. Bd. of City of Richmond*, 51 F.R.D. 139, 142 (E.D. Va. 1970).

Boling's ex-wife was not an indispensable party. In this lawsuit, Boling sought only to litigate his claims relating to the non-recourse loans. The absence of his ex-wife as a party did not preclude him from obtaining that relief; rather, it only meant that Prospect might still be entitled to seek enforcement of its loan agreements against her. Accordingly, the court denied the motion to dismiss pursuant to Rule 12(b)(7).

**ANSWERS (A)** and **(B)** are incorrect because the court found that Boling's wife was not a necessary nor an indispensable party to the litigation, therefore there were no grounds under Fed.R.Civ.P. 19 to grant the defendant's motion to dismiss the lawsuit under Fed.R.Civ.P. 12(b)(7). **ANSWER (C)** is incorrect because the court found there was good diversity jurisdiction; Mrs. Boling was a citizen of Kentucky as was her husband, and both were aligned as plaintiffs in their underlying litigation. Her addition to the declaratory judgment suit would not destroy diversity jurisdiction. **ANSWER (D)**, while a plausible reason for denying a motion to dismiss under Fed.R.Civ.P. 12(b)(7), did not come into play in this case because the court found that Mrs. Boling was not an indispensable party. Therefore, the court did not have to rely on Fed.R.Civ.P. 19(b) to allow the court to proceed.

### PROBLEM #21. BEST ANSWER (C).

Problem #21 is based on *National Feeds, Inc. v. United Pet Foods, Inc.*, 2015 WL 4496312 (N.D. Ohio July 23, 2015). This problem requires the student to understand the timing of a challenge to a court's assertion of personal jurisdiction, and the fact that a defendant can waive its right to challenge jurisdiction if the motion is not made in a timely fashion. In this instance the court denied the motion to dismiss for a lack of personal jurisdiction, holding that the defendant had waived its right to this challenge.

Fed.R.Civ.P. 12(b)(2) allows a defendant to contest the court's personal jurisdiction. The ability to challenge personal jurisdiction is not indefinite and can be waived if not pled at the correct time. *Gerber v. Riordan*, 649 F.3d 514, 518 (6th Cir.2011). To avoid waiver, a defendant must assert lack of personal jurisdiction in a responsive pleading. Fed.R.Civ.P. 12(h)(1). Moreover, a defendant may waive an objection to personal jurisdiction by actively participating in the litigation of the case. *Gerber*, 649 F.3d at 519; *Hamilton v. Atlas Turner, Inc.*, 197 F.3d 58, 60 (2d Cir.1999).

UPF argued that the court should dismiss the case for lack of personal jurisdiction and improper venue. The company argued it did not transact any business in Ohio throughout its relationship with NFI, and that it did not have sufficient minimum contact with Ohio to satisfy the Due Process Clause of the Fourteenth Amendment.

Plaintiffs contended that UPF has waived the defense of personal jurisdiction because UPF litigated the case on the merits for three years before seeking dismissal on jurisdictional grounds. The plaintiffs asserted that UPF's conduct gave them reason to believe UPF intended to defend the case on its merits.

Parties that choose to litigate a case actively on the merits surrender the right to object to the lack of personal jurisdiction and improper venue. *Days Inns Worldwide, Inc. v. Patel*, 445 F.3d 899, 905 (6th Cir.2006). Courts have held that the purpose of Rule 12(h) is to eliminate unnecessary delays by requiring parties to raise most Rule 12 defenses before the court undertakes adjudication of issues on the merits. *Plunkett v. Valhalla Inv. Servs. Inc.*, 409 F.Supp.2d 39, 41 (D.Mass.2006); *Yeldell v. Tutt*, 913 F.2d 533, 539 (8th Cir.1990).

During the three years between filing and UPF's motion to dismiss there was extensive discovery and considerable motion practice. UPF, moreover, entered a general appearance. By thus participating in the litigation for three years, UPF gave plaintiffs the reasonable impression that it would defend the case on the merits.

Because UPF waited so long before seeking dismissal under Rule 12(b)(2), and because it has actively participated in the litigation, the court concluded that UPF waived its personal jurisdiction defense. *Rates Tech. Inc. v. Nortel Networks Corp.,* 399 F.3d 1302, 1309 (Fed.Cir.2005).

By way of explanation for its delay, UPF claimed that its counsel was unaware of the ability to contest personal jurisdiction until only a few weeks before filing the pending motion. While UPF's counsel may only recently personally learned the names and addresses of all farmers who received tainted feed, it is undisputed that UPF itself had a nearly complete list of affected farmers as early in the litigation. What it knew, its lawyer should have learned. Had UPF raised its jurisdictional challenge in a timely manner, it might have been well taken.

For the same reasons, UPF waived the ability to contest the venue of this court. *See Rauch v. Day & Night Mfg. Corp.,* 576 F.2d 697, 700 (6th Cir.1978).

**ANSWERS (A)** and **(B)** are incorrect because the court never considers whether UPF had sufficient contacts with Ohio—or whether the contract was insufficient to support an assertion of personal jurisdiction, because the defendant waived its ability to bring this challenge. **ANSWER (D)** is incorrect for similar reasons; the court does not deny the motion based on a finding that the contract alone supports and assertion of personal jurisdiction. Again, **ANSWER (E)** is incorrect because the court does not conduct a due process analysis; it simply determines that it must deny the defendant's motion to dismiss for a lack of personal jurisdiction because this motion—three years into the litigation in which the defendant made a general appearance—is untimely and waived.

### PROBLEM #22. BEST ANSWER (A).

Problem #22 is based on *Grisett v. H.J. Baker Bros.,* 2015 WL 5734452 (S.D. Ala. Sept. 30, 2015). This problem focuses on pleading standards under Fed.R.Civ.P. 8(a)(2) and the Supreme Court pleading requirements in *Twombly* and *Iqbal.* The court here granted the defendant's motion to dismiss under Fed.R.Civ.P. 12(b)(6), for the failure of the plaintiff to satisfy pleading requirements.

To survive dismissal under Rule 12(b)(6), a complaint must first satisfy the pleading requirements of Rule 8(a)(2). *Bell Atlantic Corp. v. Twombly,* 550 U.S. 544, 555 (2007). "A pleading that states a claim for relief must contain . . . a short and plain statement of the claim showing that the pleader is entitled to relief. . . ." Fed.R.Civ.P. 8(a)(2). Rule 8 establishes a regime of "notice pleading." *Swierkiewicz v. Sorema N.A.,* 534 U.S. 506, 512, 513–14 (2002). It does not, however, eliminate all pleading requirements.

First, the complaint must address all the elements that must be shown in order to support recovery under one or more causes of action. "At a minimum, notice pleading requires that a complaint contain inferential allegations from which we can identify each of the material elements necessary to sustain a recovery under some viable legal theory." *Wilchombe v. TeeVee Toons, Inc.,* 555 F.3d 949, 960 (11th Cir.2009).

Pleading elements is necessary, but it is not enough to satisfy Rule 8(a)(2). The rule "requires more than labels and conclusions, and a formulaic recitation of the elements of a cause of action will not do" to satisfy that rule. *Twombly*, 550 U.S. at 555. There must in addition be a pleading of facts. Though they need not be detailed, "factual allegations must be enough to raise a right to relief above the speculative level. . . ." *Id.* That is, the complaint must allege "enough facts to state a claim for relief that is plausible on its face." *Id.* at 570. "A claim has facial plausibility when the plaintiff pleads factual content that allows the court to draw the reasonable inference that the defendant is liable for the misconduct alleged." *Ashcroft v. Iqbal*, 556 U.S. 662, 678 (2009). "The plausibility standard . . . asks for more than a sheer possibility that the defendant has acted unlawfully," and "where a complaint pleads facts that are merely consistent with a defendant's liability, it stops short of the line between possibility and plausibility of entitlement to relief." *Id.* A complaint lacking "sufficient factual matter, accepted as true, to state a claim to relief that is plausible on its face" will not "survive a motion to dismiss." *Id.* But so long as the plausibility standard is met, the complaint "may proceed even if it strikes a savvy judge that actual proof of those facts is improbable, and that a recovery is very remote and unlikely." *Twombly*, 550 U.S. at 556.

As noted, the plaintiff's claim was for hostile work environment. "To plead that claim the plaintiff was required to allege that: (1) he belongs to a protected group; (2) he was subjected to unwelcome harassment; (3) the harassment was based on his membership in the protected group; (4) it was severe or pervasive enough to alter the terms and conditions of employment and create a hostile or abusive working environment; and (5) the employer is responsible for that environment under a theory of either vicarious or direct liability." *Edwards v. Prime, Inc.*, 602 F.3d 1276, 1300 (11th Cir.2010). The Eleventh Circuit has indicated that, to satisfy *Twombly* and *Iqbal*, a complaint must set forth facts plausibly suggesting that the hostile environment experienced by the plaintiff was sufficiently severe and/or pervasive to satisfy the fourth element. The defendant argues the amended complaint fails to attain this standard.

The amended complaint alleged the following regarding the defendant's conduct towards the plaintiff (who is black): (1) falsely accusing him of forging and falsifying a transportation document; (2) placing him on leave (suspension) with pay; (3) terminating him (the only black office employee) and replacing him with a white male; (4) failing or refusing to take prompt remedial action in response to his complaints of being suspended and fired; and (5) failing or refusing to take prompt remedial action in response to the discrimination, hostile work environment and harassment of its managers.

"Discrete acts such as termination . . . must be challenged as separate statutory discrimination and retaliation claims" and cannot be considered part of a hostile work environment claim. *McCann v. Tillman*, 526 F.3d 1370, 1378–79 (11th Cir.2008). Under *McCann*, the plaintiff cannot complain of his termination or suspension under a hostile-work-environment rubric. Nor can he rest his claim on the allegation of forgery that allegedly prompted his termination and suspension. *Freeman v. City of Riverdale*, 330 Fed.Appx. 863, 865–66 (11th Cir.2009) (false accusations leading to termination had to be asserted as part of a separate termination claim, not as part of a hostile work environment claim). This leaves for consideration only the final two items on which the plaintiff relies.

"A hostile work environment claim under Title VII is established upon proof that the workplace is permeated with discriminatory intimidation, ridicule, and insult, that is sufficiently severe or pervasive to alter the conditions of the victim's employment and create an abusive working environment." *Miller v. Kenworth, Inc.*, 277 F.3d 1269, 1275 (11th Cir.2002). Simply failing to respond to the plaintiff's complaints of being placed on leave and being fired was not intimidating, ridiculing or insulting, much less to such a severe degree as to alter the terms and conditions of employment. And failing to correct a hostile work environment that does not exist cannot itself create a hostile work environment.

The amended complaint did state that the defendant "created a hostile work environment." "That broad statement, however, is merely a 'formulaic recitation of the elements' of a Title VII claim and, standing alone, does not satisfy the pleading standard of . . . Rule 8." *Edwards*, 602 F.3d at 1301 (quoting *Twombly*, 550 U.S. at 555). "An introductory conclusion cannot take the place of factual allegations in stating a plausible claim for relief." *Id.*

**ANSWER (B)** is incorrect because the fact pattern does not give rise to a problem implicating the well-pleaded complaint rule; as such, this possible answer is a red herring. **ANSWER (C)** is incorrect because the number of time a plaintiff might amend a complaint is not a basis for granting a Rule 12(b)(6) motion to dismiss; the question focuses on the sufficiency of the pleading before the court. **ANSWER (D)** is incorrect because the plaintiff's barebones, conclusory allegations do not permit the court to draw a conclusion as to the plausibility of the plaintiff's allegations, without more factual pleading to support the conclusory labels. **ANSWER (E)** is incorrect because while courts historically were more reluctant to grant Rule 12(b)(6) motions at the pleading stage, courts do so more often subsequent to the Supreme Court's holdings in Twombly and Iqbal, which standards have replaced the older liberal pleading regime.

## PROBLEM #23. BEST ANSWER (D).

Problems #23 and #24 are based on *Henman v. Indiana Harbor Belt Railroad Co.*, 2015 WL 6449693 (Oct. 22, 2015). This problem explores the scope of discovery under Fed.R.Civ.P. 26(b); motions to compel discovery; and motions for protective orders pursuant to Fed.R.Civ.P. 26(c). The court in this case denied the plaintiff's motion to compel the witness's testimony at his deposition, and granted the defendant's motion for a protective order to protect Jovanovich's testimony.

Federal Rule of Civil Procedure 26(b) provides, in relevant part: "Parties may obtain discovery regarding any non-privileged matter that is relevant to any party's claim or defense . . . Relevant information need not be admissible at the trial if the discovery appears reasonably calculated to lead to the discovery of admissible evidence." Fed.R.Civ.P. 26(b)(1). Relevancy is "construed broadly to encompass any matter that bears on, or that reasonably could lead to other matter that could bear on, any issue that is or may be in the case." *Oppenheimer Fund, Inc. v. Sanders*, 437 U.S. 340, 351 (1978) (citing *Hickman v. Taylor*, 329 U.S. 495, 501 (1947)). A party may seek an order to compel discovery when an opposing party fails to respond to discovery requests or provides evasive or incomplete responses. *See* Fed.R.Civ.P. 37(a). A party objecting to the discovery request bears the burden of showing why the request is improper. *See McGrath v. Everest Nat. Ins. Co.*, 625 F.Supp.2d 660, 670 (N.D.Ind.2008). The Court has broad discretion when deciding whether to compel discovery. *See Patterson v. Avery Dennison Corp.*, 281 F.3d 676, 681 (7th Cir.2002) (citing *Packman v. Chi. Tribune Co.*, 267 F.3d 628, 646–47 (7th Cir.2001); *Rennie v. Dalton*, 3 F.3d 1100, 1110 (7th Cir.1993)).

Federal Rule of Civil Procedure 26(c) also allows a court, for good cause, to issue an order to protect a party from discovery "from annoyance, embarrassment, oppression, or undue burden or expense," including "forbidding inquiry into certain matters." Fed.R.Civ.P. 26(c)(1)(D). Rule 26(c) "essentially operates to balance the public's interest in open proceedings against an individual's private interest in avoiding annoyance, embarrassment, oppression, or undue burden or expense." *Felling v. Knight*, 211 F.R.D. 552, 554 (S.D.Ind.2003). "The party moving for a protective order must establish that good cause exists for the Court to exercise its discretion in entering a protective order." *Nieves v. OPA, Inc.*, 948 F.Supp.2d 887, 891 (N.D.Ill.2013).

The plaintiff sought information from witness Jovanovich about whether he had ever been disciplined by IHB for events other than those that were the subject of the instant lawsuit. The defendant argued that any discipline of witnesses for events unrelated to the occurrence that gave rise to the plaintiff's injury was irrelevant, making the plaintiff's questions nothing more than a fishing expedition for prejudicial information. The plaintiff argued that if any railroad witness had been given favorable treatment in discipline history, that witnesses' credibility might be affected, and that the broad scope of discovery allowed for this kind of questioning. The counsel for the plaintiff admitted that he had no reason to think that there has been any exchange of favorable treatment for favorable testimony. At the deposition, Jovanovich was not asked whether there was any reason for him to give favorable testimony or if he had received any favorable treatment in exchange for his testimony; instead, the plaintiff's questions were targeted specifically to Jovanovich's discipline history and other personal employment issues.

The plaintiff is correct that the scope of discovery is broad, but it is not unlimited. Broad discovery rules "were never intended to be an excursion ticket to an unlimited exploration of every conceivable matter that captures an attorney's interest . . . and 'discovery of matter not reasonably calculated to lead to the discovery of admissible evidence is not within the scope of Rule 26(b)(1).' " *Miller UK Ltd. v. Caterpillar, Inc.*, 17 F.Supp.3d 711, 721 (N.D.Ill.2014) (quoting *Oppenheimer Fund*, 437 U.S. at 352). As the defendant argued, the plaintiff did not provide any reason to think that Jovanovich might be biased, and was asking him for personal information. The deponent was a witness to activities that occurred after the accident, and was being deposed in that role. Although the plaintiff argued broadly that he is entitled to determine whether there was any bias, counsel for the plaintiff admitted that he has no reason to think that Jovanovich might be biased. He did not seek any information in discovery about the witness's disciplinary history, and there was no apparent reason to suspect that he was biased at all, let alone that the bias was caused by IHB's treatment of him in disciplinary proceedings. His unsubstantiated desire to find anything in the background of Jovanovich, a person who was not a party to this case and was only testifying as to his role and observations in events that happened after the occurrence, did not justify such a personal fishing expedition into his background, did not appear to be calculated to lead to the discovery of admissible evidence, and was likely to invade his right to privacy. *See, e.g., Baker v. Town of Middlebury,* 753 N.E.2d 67, 72 (Ind.Ct.App.2001) (noting the important "public policy protecting the privacy rights of individuals with respect to sensitive personnel matters" when finding a right to private employee evaluations in Indiana).

The plaintiff also argued that lack of relevance was not a valid reason for counsel for the defendant to advise the deponent that he need not answer the questions. Although that is generally correct, "irrelevant questions, however, may unnecessarily touch sensitive areas or go beyond reasonable limits . . . and refusing to answer may be justified." *Eggleston v. Chi. Journeymen Plumbers' Local Union No. 130, U. A.,* 657 F.2d 890, 903 (7th Cir.1981). Likewise, Federal Rule of Civil Procedure 30 provides that "at any time during a deposition, the deponent or a party may move to terminate or limit it on the ground that it is being conducted in bad faith or in a manner that unreasonably annoys, embarrasses, or oppresses the deponent or party." Fed.R.Civ.P. 30(d)(3)(A).

Questions of employer discipline for events other than those related to the occurrence were not relevant to any claim or defense in this case, particularly where there was no reason to believe that there was any connection between disciplinary history and bias. "Before restricting discovery, the court should consider the totality of the circumstances, weighing the value of the material sought against the burden of providing it, and taking into account society's interest in furthering the truth-seeking function in the particular case before the court." *Patterson,* 281 F.3d at 681. In this case, the court concluded that there was no reason to think that the information being sought by the plaintiff—bias because of prior disciplinary treatment—existed. Instead, those questions were likely to cause unreasonable annoyance, embarrassment, and oppression of the deponent, as well as invading his privacy. Not only was it appropriate for the deposition to be limited, but the defendant had also shown good cause for a protective order barring inquiry into unrelated disciplinary matters of other IHB employees to be deposed in the case. *See, e .g., Matter of Ingram Barge Co.,* 306 F.R.D. 184, 187 (N.D.Ill.2014) (denying a motion to compel and granting a protective order upon a finding that a "personnel file and the draft workplace investigation report were not relevant" where they implicated privacy concerns and did not address the accident being litigated).

For the foregoing reasons, the court denied the plaintiff's motion to compel answers to deposition questions. The court granted the defendant's motion for a protective order and ordered that the plaintiff not question IHB employee witnesses regarding their disciplinary history unrelated to the occurrence that was the subject of this litigation.

**ANSWER (A)** is incorrect because the court concluded, on the facts, that the plaintiff had not shown good cause for the information it sought from the witness Jovanovich. **ANSWER (B)** is incorrect because even though the scope of discovery is broad, the court concluded that it was not without limits, and agreed with the defendant's counsel that the information sought by the plaintiff was largely irrelevant to the issues in the case. **ANSWER (C)** is incorrect because courts can compel witness testimony during a deposition, through a properly asserted motion to compel with a valid basis for the request. **ANSWER (E)** is incorrect because although the court denied the plaintiff's motion to compel, it did also grant the defendant's motion for a protective order. Therefore, **ANSWER (D)** the correct answer.

### PROBLEM #24. BEST ANSWER (B).

Problem #24 is a continuation of Problem #23, and requires the student to understand sanctions that are available under Fed.R.Civ.P. 37 for abusive attorney conduct during the discovery process. In this instance, the court ordered that the plaintiff's counsel, as the party moving for compelled testimony of the witness Jovanovich, pay the defendant's cost and expenses in opposing the motion.

Because the motion to compel was denied and a protective order entered, the court "must, after giving the opportunity to be heard, require the movant, the attorney filing the motion, or both to pay the party or deponent who opposed the motion its reasonable expenses incurred in opposing the motion, including attorney's fees" unless "the motion was substantially justified or other circumstances make an award of expenses unjust." Fed.R.Civ.P. 37(a)(5)(B). Accordingly, the court ordered the defendant to file an itemization of its costs and fees, including attorney's fees, incurred in opposing the motion to compel along with argument as to why those expenses are reasonable in this situation.

**ANSWER (A)** is incorrect because Fed.R.Civ.P. 11 governs truthfulness in pleadings and provides sanctions for violations of that rule. Discovery sanctions are provided in Fed.R.Civ.P. 37. **ANSWER (C)** is incorrect because 28 U.S.C. § 1927 is a federal statute that permits disciplining attorneys who needlessly and vexatiously multiple litigation proceedings; Rule 37 instead supplies the basis for sanctioning discovery abuse. Likewise, **ANSWER (D)** is incorrect because the court has no need to rely on its inherent powers to discipline attorney when there is a specific discovery rule providing for situations like the fact pattern in this case. Finally, **ANSWER (E)** is incorrect because the court concluded that the plaintiff's motion was not substantially justified to compel the deposition answers from the witness, and therefore the defendant was entitled to recover its costs and expenses in opposing the motion to compel.

### PROBLEM #25. BEST ANSWER (B).

Problem #25 is based on *Bishop v. Liberty Mutual Insurance Co.,* 2015 WL 6163246 (D.S.C. Oct. 19, 2015). The problem entails the burden on the defendant in seeking removal and the requirements for properly establishing federal court jurisdiction on removal under 28 U.S.C. § 1441. The court concluded that the defendant had failed to carry its burden of establishing diversity jurisdiction and therefore remand of the case to state court was proper.

The burden of demonstrating jurisdiction resides with "the party seeking removal." *Dixon v. Coburg Dairy, Inc.*, 369 F.3d 811, 816 (4th Cir.2004) (citing *Mulcahey v. Columbia Organic Chems. Co.*, 29 F.3d 148, 151 (4th Cir.1994)). District courts are obliged to construe removal jurisdiction strictly because of the "significant federalism concerns" implicated. *Id.* "If at any time before final judgment it appears that the district court lacks subject matter jurisdiction, the case shall be remanded." 28 U.S.C. § 1447(c). Therefore, "if federal jurisdiction is doubtful, a remand to state court is necessary." *Dixon*, 369 F.3d at 816; *see also Hartley v. CSX Transp., Inc.*, 187 F.3d 422, 425 (4th Cir.1999) ("Courts should 'resolve all doubts about the propriety of removal in favor of retained state court jurisdiction.' " (quoting *Marshall v. Manville Sales Corp.*, 6 F.3d 229, 232 (4th Cir.1993))).

The defendant removed this matter from state court pursuant to 28 U.S.C. §§ 1441 and 1446. Section 1441 provides that "any civil action brought in a State court of which the district courts of the United States have original jurisdiction, may be removed by the defendant or the defendants, to the district court of the United States for the district and division embracing the place where such action is pending." § 1441(a). Defendant averred that removal was proper in this instance because the district court had original jurisdiction to hear the plaintiff's case pursuant to 28 U.S.C. § 1332. Under § 1332, federal district courts have original jurisdiction over a case if the action involves citizens of different states and the amount in controversy exceeds $75,000, exclusive of interest and costs. § 1332(a). The complete diversity rule of § 1332 requires that the citizenship of each plaintiff be different from the citizenship of each defendant. *See Athena Auto., Inc. v. DiGregorio*, 166 F.3d 288, 290 (4th Cir.1999); *see also* § 1441(b)(2) ("A civil action otherwise removable solely on the basis of the jurisdiction under section 1332(a) of this title may not be removed if any of the parties in interest properly joined and served as defendants is a citizen of the State in which such action is brought.").

Additionally, "to invoke the original jurisdiction of a federal court under § 1332, courts require a corporate party to adequately demonstrate the existence of total diversity in light of its capacity for multiple residency under § 1332(c)." *Barnhill v. Ins. Co. of N. Am.*, 130 F.R.D. 46, 48 (D.S.C.1990). "In other words, Rule 8(a) has been applied in this context to require that a corporate party allege both its state of incorporation and its principal place of business in order to invoke federal diversity jurisdiction." *Id.* (citing *Equitable Life Assurance Soc'y v. Alexander Grant & Co.*, 627 F.Supp. 1023, 1025–26 (S.D.N.Y.1985) (diversity jurisdiction inadequately pled where corporate plaintiff fails to allege its principal place of business)); *see also Simmons v. Rosenberg*, 572 F.Supp. 823, 825 (E.D.N.Y.1983) (diversity jurisdiction must be alleged with detail and certainty); *Jizchak Bier Ltd. v. Wells, Inc.*, 310 F.Supp. 843, 843 (S.D.N.Y.1970) (jurisdictional averment patently insufficient under § 1332(c) where complaint does not contain, among other things, an allegation of the corporate party's principal place of business); *John Birch Soc'y v. Nat'l Broad. Co.*, 377 F.2d 194, 197 (2d Cir.1967) ("diversity of citizenship must be apparent from the pleadings"). "Because § 1441(a) provides only for removal of actions 'of which the district courts of the United States would have original jurisdiction,' . . . the court is constrained to apply these fundamental principles to Defendant's attempted removal of this matter on the basis of diversity jurisdiction." *Barnhill*, 130 F.R.D. at 49 (quoting § 1441(a)). Wright and Miller address the precise posture of this case in their treatise, stating, "a notice of removal that fails to contain an allegation of a defendant corporation's dual citizenship—its state of incorporation and the state of its principal place of business—is defective when complete diversity of citizenship is the basis for removal." 14C Charles Alan Wright, *et al.*, FEDERAL PRACTICE AND PROCEDURE § 3733 (4th ed.2013).

Here, the defendant failed to demonstrate the existence of complete diversity in its notice of removal. The defendant, a corporate party, failed to allege the state or states in which it was incorporated, as well as the state in which it maintained its principal place of business. The defendant's citizenship was briefly mentioned in its notice of removal and was also mentioned in the plaintiff's complaint. The defendant asserted in its notice of removal that the action was "between citizens of different states" and, "upon information and belief, exceeds the sum or value of $75,000.00, exclusive of interest and costs." The plaintiff's complaint merely stated that "Defendant is a corporation organized and existing under the laws of a state other than South Carolina, licensed to do business in South Carolina, solicits business in South Carolina, issue policies in South Carolina, and otherwise conducts business in South Carolina." Neither statement gave the court any guidance as to the defendant's citizenship. Thus, the defendant's failure to allege its state of incorporation and the state of its principal place of business was fatal to its attempt to remove the present action. Accordingly, the court did not need to address the amount in controversy. For the foregoing reasons, the court ordered that the plaintiff's motion to remand was granted.

**ANSWER (A)** is incorrect because there is no basis in the defendant's notice of removal that it is a citizen of South Carolina; the court concluded it could not determine the defendant's citizenship. **ANSWER (C)** is incorrect because the court determined that it need not discuss the amount-in-controversy requirement because the defendant had failed to establish diversity of citizenship. **ANSWER (D)** is incorrect because there is no "totality of the circumstances" test or standard to determine whether the federal court's jurisdiction on removal is satisfied. This is a red-herring answer. Likewise, **ANSWER (E)** is incorrect because there is no basis for a court taking "judicial notice" of a corporation's citizenship for the purpose of establishing valid removal jurisdiction.

END OF ANSWERS AND EXPLANATIONS TO EXAM #1

# CHAPTER 7
# ANSWER KEY FOR EXAM #2
# ANSWERS AND EXPLANATIONS

## PROBLEM #1. BEST ANSWER (A).

Problems #1 and 2 are based on *Bayan v. Sullivan*, 2015 WL 1780873 (D. Conn. April 20, 2015). These questions test the student's understanding of the motion for a judgment on the pleadings under Fed.R.Civ.P. 12(c), and the doctrine of *res judicata*. In this case, the court held that res judicata did not bar the federal suit, and therefore the court denied the defendant's motion to dismiss.

"The standard for granting a Rule 12(c) motion for judgment on the pleadings is identical to that of a Rule 12(b)(6) motion for failure to state a claim." *Patel v. Contemporary Classics of Beverly Hills*, 259 F.3d 123, 126 (2d Cir.2001). "In both postures, the district court must accept all allegations in the complaint as true and draw all inferences in the non-moving party's favor." *Id.* "The court will not dismiss the case unless it is satisfied that the complaint cannot state any set of facts that would entitle the plaintiff to relief." *Id.*

**ANSWER (B)** is incorrect because it misstates the standard governing a motion for a judgment on the pleadings; the opposite is true: the court must construe all inferences in the non-moving party's favor. **ANSWER (C)** is incorrect because there is no authority for the proposition that courts should "probe beyond the pleadings" on a Rule 12(c) motion to ascertain the "actual nature" of the case. **ANSWER (D)** is incorrect because courts can consider affirmative defenses if raised on a Rule 12(c) motion to dismiss. **ANSWER (E)** is incorrect because proper dismissals under Rule 12(c) do not violate a plaintiff's due process or jury trial rights.

## PROBLEM #2. BEST ANSWER (E).

Problem #2 is a continuation of Problem #1, and it requires analysis of the underlying challenge based on res judicata. The court held that res judicata did not bar the federal action as the prior state court decision was jurisdictional, and not a judgment on the merits.

Dr. Sullivan moved for judgment on the pleadings on the ground that Dr. Bayan's § 1983 claim is barred by *res judicata* because it could have been brought in the state court action. The application of that doctrine, however, required that her motion be denied. Under Connecticut law, the dismissal of the state court action on jurisdictional grounds was not a judgment on the merits and, therefore, the doctrine of *res judicata* did not preclude this current action.

Under the doctrine of *res judicata*, "a judgment on the merits in a prior suit bars a second suit involving the same parties or their privies based on the same cause of action." *Parklane Hosiery Co. v. Shore*, 439 U.S. 322, 326 n. 5 (1979).

State court judgments have *res judicata* effect in federal courts. *Migra v. Warren City Sch. Dist. Bd. of Educ.*, 465 U.S. 75, 81 (1984). Under the Full Faith and Credit Clause and its implementing statute, "a federal court must give to a state-court judgment the same preclusive effect as would be given that judgment under the law of the State in which the judgment was rendered." *Id.* The Supreme Court has held that state court judgments have preclusive effect as to subsequent § 1983 suits in federal court. *Id.* at 85 ("Section 1983 . . . does not override state preclusion law and guarantee petitioner a right to proceed to judgment in state court on her state claims and then turn to federal court for adjudication of her federal claims.").

When determining the preclusive effect of a state court judgment, federal courts may not "employ their own rules" but rather must "accept the rules chosen by the state from which the judgment is taken." *Kremer v. Chem. Const. Corp.*, 456 U.S. 461, 462 (1982); *Marrese v. Am. Acad. of Orthopaedic Surgeons*, 470 U.S. 373, 380 (1985) (federal court must "refer to the preclusion law of the State in which judgment was rendered."); *AmBase Corp. v. City Investing Co. Liquidating Trust,* 326 F.3d 63, 72 (2d Cir.2003) ("Where there is a final state court judgment, a federal court looks to that state's rules of res judicata to determine the preclusive effect of that judgment."). Because the judgment in the state court action was rendered by a Connecticut court, the court looked to Connecticut's law of *res judicata* to determine its preclusive effect.

In Connecticut, application of *res judicata* requires that there be a final judgment on the merits. *Weiss v. Weiss*, 998 A.2d 766, 775 (Conn.2010) ("The doctrine of res judicata provides that 'a valid, final judgment rendered on the merits by a court of competent jurisdiction is an absolute bar to a subsequent action between the same parties . . . upon the same claim or demand.'") (quoting *Gaynor v. Payne*, 804 A.2d 170, 177 (Conn.2002)); *Legassey v. Shulansky*, 611 A.2d 930, 933 (Conn.1992) ("Application of the doctrine of res judicata requires that there be a previous judgment on the merits.").

"A judgment on the merits is one which is based on legal rights as distinguished from mere matters of practice, procedure, jurisdiction or form." *Bruno v. Geller*, 46 A.3d 974, 988 (Conn .App.Ct.2012); *cf. Keller v. Beckenstein*, 46 A.3d 102, 107 (Conn.2012) ("A court lacks discretion to consider the merits of a case over which it is without jurisdiction."). Thus, the Supreme Court of Connecticut recently held that granting a motion to dismiss on jurisdictional grounds did not constitute a judgment on the merits for *res judicata* purposes. *Santorso v. Bristol Hosp.,* 63 A.3d 940, 947–51 (2013) (observing that because, in Connecticut, "a motion to dismiss . . . properly attacks the jurisdiction of the court," a court's determination of whether to grant a motion to dismiss "usually does not extend to the merits" and that "the granting of a motion to dismiss would not constitute a judgment on the merits"; holding that plaintiff's failure to satisfy condition precedent to wrongful death suit implicated personal jurisdiction, and that earlier judgment dismissing suit on that ground was therefore not on the merits).

The Appellate Court of Connecticut has recognized repeatedly that judgments based on lack of jurisdiction are not on the merits for *res judicata* purposes. *U.S. Bank, N.A. v. Foote*, 94 A.3d 1267, 1272 (Conn.App.Ct.2014) ("Judgments based on the following reasons are not rendered on the merits: want of jurisdiction. . . ."); *Bruno v. Geller*, 46 A.3d 974, 987 (Conn.App.Ct.2012) (same); *Legassey v. Shulansky*, 611 A.2d 930, 933 (Conn.App.Ct.1992) (same). Thus, trial courts in Connecticut have held that "dismissal of a complaint for lack of subject matter jurisdiction does not constitute a final judgment on the merits." *Braham v. Newbould*, No. NNHCV125034199S, 2012 WL 3870831, at *3 (Conn.Super.Ct. Aug. 3, 2012) (earlier decision granting motion to dismiss for lack of subject matter jurisdiction did not constitute final judgment on the merits because "the court's decision to grant the motion to dismiss was based on jurisdictional grounds, not the merits of the plaintiff's claim."); *Neylan v. Pinsky*, No. CV 950375368, 1997 WL 666780, at *2 (Conn.Super.Ct. Oct. 8, 1997) ("The dismissal of the plaintiffs' claim for lack of subject matter jurisdiction was not a judgment rendered on the merits. Thus, the plaintiffs' claim is not barred by the doctrine of res judicata."). Those holdings comport with the rule that only a final judgment on the merits by a court of competent jurisdiction has preclusive effect. *See Weiss*, 998 A.2d at 775 ("a valid, final judgment rendered on the merits by a court of competent jurisdiction is an absolute bar to a subsequent action between the same parties . . . upon the same claim or demand.").

In Connecticut, "sovereign immunity relates to a court's subject matter jurisdiction over a case. . . ." *Chief Info. Officer v. Computers Plus Ctr., Inc.*, 74 A.3d 1242, 1255 (Conn.2013). "Because sovereign immunity implicates subject matter jurisdiction . . . that doctrine is a basis for granting a motion to dismiss." *Gold v. Rowland*, 994 A.2d 106, 139 (Conn.2010); *Columbia Air Servs., Inc. v. Dep't of Transp.*, 977 A.2d 636, 641 (Conn.2009) ("The doctrine of sovereign immunity implicates subject matter jurisdiction and is therefore a basis for granting a motion to dismiss.").

The same is true for statutory immunity. *Martin v. Brady*, 802 A.2d 814, 817 (Conn.2002) ("The doctrine of statutory immunity implicates subject matter jurisdiction and is therefore a basis for granting a motion to dismiss."); *Lawrence v. Weiner*, 106 A.3d 963, 967 (Conn.App.Ct.2015) ("Claims involving the doctrines of common-law sovereign immunity and statutory immunity, pursuant to state employee immunity statute, implicate the court's subject matter jurisdiction.").

The judgment in the state court action did not bar Dr. Bayan's claims in the federal action because it was not a final judgment on the merits. The superior court entered judgment because it granted Dr. Sullivan's motion to dismiss for lack of subject matter jurisdiction. In Connecticut, a motion to dismiss challenges the court's jurisdiction. Conn. Practice Book § 10–30(b) ("Any defendant, wishing to contest the court's jurisdiction, shall do so by filing a motion to dismiss. . . ."); *Chief Info. Officer*, 74 A.3d at 1255 ("A motion to dismiss tests, inter alia, whether, on the face of the record, the court is without jurisdiction."). As explained *supra*, judgments based on lack of jurisdiction do not constitute final judgments for *res judicata* purposes in Connecticut. *See Santorso*, 63 A.3d 940, 947–51; *Foote*, 94 A.3d at 1272.

For the foregoing reasons, the defendant's motion for judgment on the pleadings was denied.

**ANSWER (A)** is incorrect because the federal court found that the state court dismissal was based on jurisdictional ground; therefore that court had not reached the merits of the case and res judicata would not bar assertion of the § 1983 claim in the subsequent federal case. **ANSWER (B)** is incorrect and is a red-herring answer. The plaintiff has the right to sue in both state and federal court and forum-shopping is not a ground for dismissing a lawsuit under Fed.R.Civ.P. 12(c). Likewise, **ANSWER (C)** is incorrect for similar reasons. Unless there was a prior adjudication of the plaintiff's claims on the merits, the plaintiff's subsequent federal lawsuit is not barred by the jurisdictional dismissal in the state court case. **ANSWER (D)** is incorrect because the bar of res judicata can be raised in a Rule 12(c) motion for a judgment on the pleadings.

### PROBLEM #3. BEST ANSWER (D).

Problem #3 is based on *Basch v. Knoll, Inc.*, 2015 WL 50099355 (W.D. Mich. Aug. 20, 2015). This problem requires application of two sanctioning provisions, Fed.R.Civ.P. 11 and 28 U.S.C. § 1927 to a set of facts relating to an attorney's conduct in litigation. The court held that the attorney was sanctionable under these provisions.

Rule 11 provides in pertinent part:

> By presenting to the court a pleading, written motion, or other paper—whether by signing, filing, submitting, or later advocating it—an attorney or unrepresented party certifies that to the best of the person's knowledge, information, and belief, formed after an inquiry reasonable under the circumstances:
>
> (1)   it is not being presented for any improper purpose, such as to harass, cause unnecessary delay, or needlessly increase the cost of litigation;
>
> (2)   the claims, defenses, and other legal contentions are warranted by existing law or by a non-frivolous argument for extending, modifying, or reversing existing law or for establishing new law;
>
> (3)   the factual contentions have evidentiary support or, if specifically so identified, will likely have evidentiary support after a reasonable opportunity for further investigation or discovery; and
>
> (4)   the denials of factual contentions are warranted on the evidence or, if specifically so identified, are reasonably based on belief or a lack of information.

Fed.R.Civ.P. 11(b).

Sanctions may be imposed under Rule 11 if "a reasonable inquiry discloses the pleading, motion, or paper is (1) not well grounded in fact, (2) not warranted by existing law or a good faith argument for the extension, modification or reversal of existing law, or (3) interposed for any improper purpose such as harassment or delay." *Merritt v. Int'l Ass'n of Machinists & Aerospace Workers*, 613 F.3d 609, 626 (6th Cir.2010) (quoting *Herron v. Jupiter Transp. Co.*, 858

F.2d 332, 335 (6th Cir.1988)). The standard for determining whether to impose sanctions is one of objective reasonableness. *Montell v. Diversified Clinical Servs., Inc.,* 757 F.3d 497, 510 (6th Cir.2014). Rule 11 "imposes on litigants a 'continuing duty of candor,' and a litigant may be sanctioned 'for continuing to insist upon a position that is no longer tenable.'" *Rentz v. Dynasty Apparel Indus., Inc.,* 556 F.3d 389, 395 (6th Cir.2009) (quoting *Ridder,* 109 F.3d at 293). "The plaintiff is impressed with a continuing responsibility to review and reevaluate his pleadings and where appropriate modify them to conform to Rule 11." *Merritt,* 613 F.3d at 626 (quoting *Runfola & Assocs., Inc. v. Spectrum Reporting II, Inc.,* 88 F.3d 368, 374 (6th Cir.1996)).

The defendant also requested sanctions pursuant to 28 U.S.C. § 1927 which provides:

> Any attorney or other person admitted to conduct cases in any court of the United States or any Territory thereof who so multiplies the proceedings in any case unreasonably and vexatiously may be required by the court to satisfy personally the excess costs, expenses, and attorneys' fees reasonably incurred because of such conduct.

28 U.S.C. § 1927. "The purpose of § 1927 is 'to deter dilatory litigation practices and to punish aggressive tactics that far exceed zealous advocacy.'" *Garner v. Cuyahoga Cnty. Juvenile Ct.,* 554 F.3d 624, 644 (6th Cir.2009) (quoting *Red Carpet Studios, Div. of Source Advantage, Ltd. v. Sater,* 465 F.3d 642, 646 (6th Cir.2006)). A court may sanction an attorney under § 1927, even in the absence of any "conscious impropriety" or "bad faith." *Hall v. Liberty Life Assur. Co. of Boston,* 595 F.3d 270, 275–76 (6th Cir.2010).

> However, there must be some conduct on the part of the subject attorney that trial judges, applying the collective wisdom of their experience on the bench, could agree falls short of the obligations owed by a member of the bar to the court and which, as a result, causes additional expense to the opposing party.

Rentz, 556 F.3d at 396. "Section 1927 sanctions 'require a showing of something less than subjective bad faith, but something more than negligence or incompetence.'" *Jordan v. City of Detroit,* 595 F.App'x 486, 488 (6th Cir.2014) (quoting *Red Carpet Studios,* 465 F.3d at 646). "'Thus, an attorney is sanctionable when he intentionally abuses the judicial process or knowingly disregards the risk that his actions will needlessly multiply proceedings.'" *Id.* (quoting *Red Carpet Studios,* 465 F.3d at 646).

The imposition of sanctions under either Rule 11 or § 1927 is discretionary. *See Hall,* 595 F.3d at 275 (noting that a decision to grant or deny sanctions under § 1927 or Rule 11 is reviewed under the abuse-of-discretion standard); Fed.R.Civ.P. 11(c)(1) (stating that the court "may impose" sanctions if it determines that Rule 11(b) has been violated); 28 U.S.C. § 1927 (stating that an attorney "may be" required to satisfy costs and fees).

Although the defendant was granted summary judgment on all of the plaintiff's claims, sanctions are not appropriate merely because Plaintiff pursued claims which were ultimately unsuccessful. *See Milner v. Biggs,* 566 F.App'x 410, 414 (6th Cir.2014). Here, the court's concern was not that the plaintiff's claims were ultimately unsuccessful, but that the plaintiff's counsel used a shot-gun approach in the complaint and failed to review the viability of the claims after the close of discovery. Even if, prior to discovery, counsel had a reasonable belief that all of the plaintiff's various claims had evidentiary support, counsel's failure to re-evaluate and pare down those claims after the close of discovery and after receiving notice from the defendant of the deficiencies of her claims, suggested that counsel failed in his continuing duty to assess the legal and factual support for the plaintiff's claims. This failure caused expense to the defendant who was forced to seek summary judgment on all nine claims. The court was not convinced that the plaintiff's counsel acted in bad faith, or that he acted for an improper purpose such as harassment or delay. Nevertheless, the counsel's failure to defend eight of the nine claims in response to the defendant's motion for summary judgment was strong evidence that he did not have a reasonable belief that the claims were warranted by the law or that they had evidentiary support.

Giving the plaintiff every benefit of the doubt, the plaintiff had an arguable basis for proceeding on her FMLA and disability claims. However, the same cannot be said with respect to the plaintiff's age and gender claims. Even under a most generous view of the pleadings, there were no factual allegations in the complaint with respect to the plaintiff's age and gender claims. The plaintiff's age and gender claims also lacked any arguable evidentiary support. The counsel's failures were particularly egregious with respect to the age and gender claims. The plaintiff's counsel's failure to withdraw the age and gender claims after the close of discovery fell far short of the obligations owed by a member of the bar to the court and are sanctionable under both Rule 11 and § 1927. *See Runfola & Associates, Inc. v. Spectrum Reporting II, Inc.,* 88 F.3d 368, 374 (6th Cir.1996) ("The district court was clearly within the parameters of Rule 11 when it imposed sanctions for plaintiff's failure to dismiss a factually meritless action.").

In determining what sanctions to impose, the court considered the purposes of Rule 11 and § 1927. "The purpose of Rule 11 sanctions is to deter rather than to compensate." Fed.R.Civ.P. 11 Advisory Committee Notes (1993 Amendments). Rule 11 sanctions must accordingly be "limited to what suffices to deter repetition of the conduct or comparable conduct by others similarly situated." Fed.R.Civ.P. 11(c)(4). "The purpose of § 1927 is 'to deter dilatory litigation practices and to punish aggressive tactics that far exceed zealous advocacy.'" *Garner,* 554 F.3d at 644 (quoting *Red Carpet Studios,* 465 F.3d at 646). As a general rule, in determining an appropriate sanction

> the court should consider the nature of the violation committed, the circumstances in which it was committed, the circumstances (including the financial state) of the individual to be sanctioned, and those sanctioning measures that would suffice to deter that individual from similar violations in the future. The court should also consider the circumstances of the party or parties who may have been adversely affected by the violation.

*Orlett v. Cincinnati Microwave, Inc.,* 954 F.2d 414, 420 (6th Cir.1992).

In its brief on summary judgment, the defendant argued that all of the plaintiff's discrimination and retaliation claims were deficient because the plaintiff failed to show an adverse employment action, because she failed to establish a *prima facie* case, and because she did not rebut the defendant's legitimate non-discriminatory reason for her termination. The defendant did not independently analyze the plaintiff's age and gender claims. Because the plaintiff's age and gender claims suffered from a complete lack of evidence, it did not appear that the defendant was required to devote a significant amount of time to independently analyzing or briefing these claims. The court was satisfied that a small monetary sanction would be sufficient to remind the plaintiff's counsel of his continuing responsibility to review and reevaluate his pleadings, and to deter counsel from failing to withdraw claims when it becomes apparent that they are patently frivolous. Accordingly, the court entered an order sanctioning the plaintiff's counsel in the amount of $2,000.

**ANSWER (A)** is incorrect because the court did not find that the plaintiff's counsel satisfied the god faith basis for pursuing all nine claims, especially after the close of discover. **ANSWER (B)** is incorrect because the defense counsel, in seeking Rule 11 sanctions, did comply with the notice and safe-harbor provisions of Rule 11 before seeking sanctions under the Rule. **ANSWER (C)** is incorrect because an attorney's duty to zealously advocate their client's interests is cabined by the Rule 11(b) requirements. **ANSWER (E)** is incorrect because, as the court indicated, the mere fact that a court grants summary judgment against a plaintiff's claims is not sufficient grounds, standing alone, to impose sanctions under the two provisions.

#### PROBLEM #4. BEST ANSWER (C).

Problem #4 is based on *Doughty v. Washington Metropolitan Area Transit Authority*, 2015 WL 9302946 (D. Md. Dec. 21, 2015). This problem involves application of the principles relating to the burdens of proof when a party moves for summary judgment pursuant to Fed.R.Civ.P. 56. The court granted the defendant's motion for summary judgment, concluding that the plaintiff failed to carry her burden of offering the court proof of a genuine issue of fact in her opposition to the defendant's motion for summary judgment.

A court may grant summary judgment "if the pleadings, depositions, answers to interrogatories, and admissions on file, together with the affidavits, if any, show that there is no genuine issue as to any material fact and that the moving party is entitled to a judgment as a matter of law." Fed.R.Civ.P. 56(c); *Celotex Corp. v. Catrett*, 477 U.S. 317, 322–23 (1986); *Felty v. Graves-Humphreys Co.*, 818 F.2d 1126, 1128 (4th Cir.1987). A court must construe the facts alleged and reasonable inferences in favor of the nonmoving party. *United States v. Diebold, Inc.*, 369 U.S. 654, 655 (1962).

To prevail on a motion for summary judgment, the moving party must demonstrate that no genuine issue of fact exists and that it is entitled to judgment as a matter of law. *Pulliam Inv. Co., Inc. v. Cameo Props.*, 810 F.2d 1282, 1286 (4th Cir.1987). The moving party bears the initial burden of "informing the district court of the basis for its motion, and identifying those portions of 'the pleadings, depositions, answers to interrogatories, and admissions on file, together with the affidavits, if any,' which it believes demonstrate the absence of a genuine issue of material fact." *Celotex Corp.*, 477 U.S. at 323. "The burden on the moving party may be discharged by 'showing'—that is, pointing out to the district court—that there is an absence of evidence to support the nonmoving party's case." *Id.* at 325.

"Once the moving party discharges its burden . . . , the nonmoving party must come forward with specific facts showing that there is a genuine issue for trial." *Kitchen v. Upshaw*, 286 F.3d 179, 182 (4th Cir.2002). Where the nonmoving party has the burden of proof, it is that party's responsibility to confront the motion for summary judgment with an affidavit or other similar evidence. *Anderson v. Liberty Lobby, Inc.*, 477 U.S. 242, 256 (1986). "The disputed facts must be material to an issue necessary for the proper resolution of the case." *Thompson Everett, Inc. v. Nat'l. Cable Adver., L.P.*, 57 F.3d 1317, 1323 (4th Cir.1995). There must be "sufficient evidence favoring the nonmoving party for a jury to return a verdict for that party." *Anderson*, 477 U.S. at 249–50.

Federal Rule of Civil Procedure 56 operates under a burden shifting framework, wherein the moving party has the burden to demonstrate that "there is no genuine issue as to any material fact." Fed.R.Civ.P. 56. If the moving party makes its motion properly, the burden shifts to the non-moving party, whose "response must . . . set out specific facts showing a genuine issue for trial." Fed.R.Civ.P. 56(e)(2). Unlike the moving party, the "opposing party may not rely merely on allegations or denials in its own pleadings; rather, its response must—by affidavits or as otherwise provided in this rule—set out specific facts showing a genuine issue for trial." *Id.* The opposing party must provide additional materials to successfully defend against summary judgment and those materials must include assurances to the Court that they are authentic and reliable.

Federal Rule of Civil Procedure 56 provides the types of materials that may be submitted for the court's consideration, and they include: pleadings, depositions, answers to interrogatories, admissions, and any affidavits. Fed.R.Civ.P. 56; *Celotex Corp.*, 477 U.S. at 323. Except for admissions, all of the materials Rule 56 allows in summary judgment are presented under oath. The oath, and the penalty of perjury which gives the oath its true power, gives the court strong reason to believe that the materials supporting the motion or the opposition are authentic.

The Rule 56 requirements for summary judgment "help assure the fair and prompt disposition of cases." *Orsi v. Kirkwood*, 999 F.2d 86, 91 (4th Cir.1993). "They also allow a district court to ascertain, through criteria designed to ensure reliability and veracity, that a party has real proof of a claim before proceeding to trial." *Id.*

Rule 56, though, "is not unfailingly rigid." *United States Dep't. of Housing and Urban Affairs v. Cost Control Mktg. & Sales Mgmt. of Virginia, Inc.*, 64 F.3d 920, 926 n.8 (4th Cir.1995). "Evidence appropriate for summary judgment need not be in a form that would be admissible at trial . . . Rule 56(e) permits a proper summary judgment motion to be opposed by any of the kinds of evidentiary materials listed in Rule 56(c), except the mere pleadings themselves." Celotex Corp., 477 U.S. at 324. *See also Global Policy Partners v. Yessin*, No. 1:09cv859, 2010 WL 675241, at *6 (E.D. Va. Feb. 18, 2010) ("It is clear that evidence not in a form admissible at trial may nonetheless be considered in summary judgment."); *Lorraine v. Markel Am. Ins. Co.*, 241 F.R.D. 534, 537–38 (D. Md. 2007). A "nonmoving party could defeat summary judgment with materials capable of being reduced to admissible evidence at trial." *Cost Control Mktg. & Sales Mgmt. of Virginia, Inc.*, 64 F.3d at 926 n.8 (citing *Celotex*, 477 U.S. at 327). While admissibility is important, authenticity is indispensable. The court must have confidence in the evidence it considers, particularly when it is contemplating a dispositive motion. Here, the Court had no confidence because there is no record evidence from the plaintiff.

It is clear that absent evidence of actual or constructive notice of the dangerous condition in sufficient time to warn or make safe, the defendant was entitled to judgment as a matter of law. The defendant pointed out, and the record evidence shows, that the plaintiff did not see anything on the escalator steps. Her claim was merely "that something bad happened." There was no record evidence to support the plaintiff's claim. There was no evidence that the defendant was aware of the condition of the escalator or that there was a substance on it. The defendant was entitled to judgment as a matter of law.

Thus, the court found that no genuine issue of material fact existed and that the defendant was entitled to judgment as a matter of law. For the foregoing reasons, the defendant WMATA's motion for summary judgment was granted.

**ANSWER (A)** is incorrect because under *Celotex*, the defendant satisfied its initial burden of production when it moved for summary judgment. **ANSWER (B)** is incorrect because the plaintiff failed to adduce evidence giving rise to a genuine issue of material fact that would have defeated the defendant's motion for summary judgment. **ANSWER (D)** is incorrect—it is a red herring—the plaintiff's photographs of her coat did not raise a genuine issue of material fact. **ANSWER (E)** is incorrect because the plaintiff had the responsibility in her opposition to adduce evidence giving rise to a genuine issue of material fact; there is no reason for the court to grant her additional discovery under Fed.R.Civ.P. 56(e).

### PROBLEM #5. BEST ANSWER (A).

Problem #5 is based on *Allen v. Bartholomew*, 2016 WL 311568 (E.D. La. Jan. 26, 2016). The problem entails an understanding of supplemental jurisdiction under 28 U.S.C. § 1367, especially in cases where original federal claims are settled in the lawsuit. The court held that in its discretion it would not exercise supplemental jurisdiction over the remaining state law claims.

The plaintiff conceded that only state law claims remained and did not argue that the court had any type of subject matter jurisdiction over his remaining claims other than supplemental jurisdiction. The plaintiff noted that R & S Towing had not participated in discovery, any negotiations, and "did not even participate in conference calls through this court and other counsels in this matter." The plaintiff's brief concluded with an unsupported assertion that "Plaintiff would be prejudice (sic) by State law prescription to address his state claim in this matter."

The essence of R & S Towing's argument was that the court should allow a state court to decide the matter because the court had not yet become familiar with the facts of the case or reached the merits of any argument in the case.

In determining whether to relinquish jurisdiction over pendent state law claims, district courts look to the statutory factors set forth by 28 U.S.C. § 1367(c) and to the common law factors of judicial economy, convenience, fairness, and comity. *Enochs v. Lampass Cty.*, 641 F.3d 155, 158–59 (5th Cir.2011); *see also Carnegie-Mellon Univ. v. Cohill*, 484 U.S. 343, 350 (1988) (setting forth the common law factors). The statutory factors are: "(1) whether the state claims raise novel or complex issues of state law; (2) whether the state claims substantially predominate over the federal claims; (3) whether the federal claims have been dismissed; and (4) whether there are exceptional circumstances or other compelling reasons for declining jurisdiction." *Id.* at 159 (citing 28 U.S.C. § 1367(c)). The "general rule" is to decline to exercise jurisdiction when all federal claims are dismissed or otherwise eliminated from a case prior to trial; however, this rule is neither mandatory nor absolute. *Smith v. Amedisys Inc.*, 298 F.3d 434, 446–47 (5th Cir.2002).

It is clear that this case falls within § 1367(c)(3), as the court had dismissed all of the plaintiff's claims that initially gave the court original jurisdiction. Furthermore, the court noted that there appeared to be a dearth of state court case law regarding the plaintiffs' claim. *Cf. Johnson v. Hardy*, 756 So. 2d 328, 333–34 (La. App. 1 Cir.1999); *see also Wilson v. T & T Auto Repair & Towing, LLC*, No. 50,095–CA, 2015 WL 5715454, at *2–4 (La. App. 2 Cir.2015).

Before following the general rule that would support declining to exercise supplemental jurisdiction on the plaintiff's remaining claims, the court turned to the common law factors of judicial economy, convenience, fairness, and comity. Judicial economy weighs in favor of declining to exercise supplemental jurisdiction, as the plaintiff conceded that he and R & S Towing have not engaged in discovery, nor had the court ruled on any motions regarding the merits of the plaintiff's claim against R & S Towing. The same goes for convenience, given that both the plaintiff and R & S Towing were apparently located in the same city and parish. As to comity and again because of the apparent lack of state court case law on the issue, there was at least some reason for the court to decline to exercise supplemental jurisdiction in favor of having a state court settle the dispute.

Similarly, fairness did not weigh in favor of continued supplemental jurisdiction.

**ANSWER (B)** is incorrect because the court originally did have good supplemental jurisdiction over the plaintiff's state law claims; the issue in this problem is whether the court should continue to exercise supplemental jurisdiction after the federal claims were settled and dismissed from the case. **ANSWER (C)** is incorrect because federal courts have the power to adjudicate state law claims in their valid supplemental jurisdiction. **ANSWER (D)** is incorrect because the question is not whether the court has good supplemental jurisdiction over the state law claims, but whether the court should dismiss those claims in its discretionary power under 28 U.S.C. § 1367(c).

**ANSWER (E)** is incorrect because it does make a difference that the federal claims were settled; this triggered the inquiry whether the court, in its discretion, should have continued to exercise jurisdiction over the state law claims.

**PROBLEM #6. BEST ANSWER (C).**

Problem #6 is based on *Collins v. Hagel*, 2015 WL 5691076 (N.D. Ga. Sept. 28, 2015). This problem involves analysis of two venue statutes, the general federal venue statute for cases involving suits against federal officers, and the specialized venue statute contained in Title VII of the Civil Rights Act. The court applied the special venue statute in Title VII and concluded that venue was improper.

28 U.S.C. § Section 1391(e)(1) provides:

> A civil action in which a defendant is an officer or employee of the United States or any agency thereof acting in his official capacity or under color of legal authority, or an agency of the United States, or the United States, may, except as otherwise provided by law, be brought in any judicial district in which (A) a defendant in the action resides, (B) a substantial part of the events or omissions giving rise to the claim occurred, or a substantial part of property that is the subject of the action is situated, or (C) the plaintiff resides if no real property is involved in the action.

In a civil action against an employee of the United States acting in his official capacity, whether venue is proper is determined under 28 U.S.C. § 1391(e), "except as otherwise provided by law." 28 U.S.C. § 1391(e)(1). Here, the plaintiff's claims arose under Title VII, which contains its own venue provision in 42 U.S.C. § 2000e–5(f)(3). "The venue provisions of § 2000e–5(f)(3) were intended to be the exclusive venue provisions for Title VII employment discrimination actions and that the more general provisions of § 1391 are not controlling in such cases." *Pinson v. Rumsfeld*, 192 F.App'x 811, 817 (11th Cir.2006) (citing *Stebbins v. State Farm Mut. Auto. Ins. Co.*, 413 F.2d 1100, 1102–1103 (D.C.Cir.1969)).

42 U.S.C. § 2000e–5(f)(3) provides, in relevant part, that the appropriate venue for a Title VII claim is:

> (1) in any judicial district in the State in which the unlawful employment practice is alleged to have been committed, (2) in the judicial district in which the employment records relevant to such practice are maintained and administered, or (3) in the judicial district in which the aggrieved person would have worked but for the alleged unlawful employment practice, but (4) if the respondent is not found within any such district, such an action may be brought within the judicial district in which the respondent has his principal office.

42 U.S.C. § 2000e–5(f)(3). "If the plaintiff brings suit in a jurisdiction that does not satisfy one of the venue requirements listed in 42 U.S.C. § 2000e–5(f)(3), venue is improper." *Buesgens v. Coates*, 435 F.Supp.2d 1, 3 (D.D.C.2006).

Here, the plaintiff did not allege any facts to support that venue was proper in the Northern District of Georgia. The plaintiff worked at Kadena Elementary School in Okinawa, Japan. The claimed Title VII violations—that the plaintiff was treated differently from her peers, and ultimately terminated, based on her race, gender and national origin—occurred in Okinawa, Japan, and the plaintiff would have continued to work in Okinawa, Japan, if the alleged discrimination had not occurred. Because this action could not be filed in Japan, venue could be based on the first or third criteria listed in § 2000e–5(f)(3).

The plaintiff did not allege that her employment records relevant to her termination were located in the Northern District of Georgia. Rather, the plaintiff's employment records were maintained by the DoDEA Human Resources Directorate, which was responsible for "overseeing recruitment and staffing, educator certification and recertification, classification and compensation, human capital record keeping, labor management relations, and data integrity" for DoDEA. The DoDEA Human Resources Directorate was located in Alexandria, Virginia. Finally, the principal office of Defendant Marilee Fitzgerald, the Director of DoDEA, was in Alexandria, Virginia, and the principal office of Defendant Chuck Hagel, the Secretary of Defense, was located at the Pentagon in Arlington, Virginia. Both Alexandria and Arlington, Virginia, were located within the Eastern District of Virginia.

Thus, under the second and fourth criteria listed in § 2000e–5(f)(3), venue was proper in the United States District Court for the Eastern District of Virginia, not the Northern District of Georgia. *See* 42 U.S.C. § 2000e–5(f)(3); *see also Lorenzo v. Rumsfeld*, No. CV05–00035, 2006 WL 1687772, at *2 (D. Guam June 13, 2006) (in Title VII action alleging DoDEA discriminated against plaintiff by denying him a teaching position in Okinawa, Japan, venue in District of Guam was improper because alleged discrimination took place in Okinawa, plaintiff would have continued to work in Okinawa but for alleged discrimination, and relevant employment records, and Secretary of Defense's principal office, were located within the Eastern District of Virginia; transferring action to Eastern District of Virginia); *Dawson v. Rumsfeld*, No. 8:04–cv–1251, 2005 WL 2850231 (M.D.Fla. Oct.31, 2005) (in Title VII action, venue was improper in Middle District of Florida because alleged discrimination occurred during employment with DoDEA in Germany, employment records were maintained at DoDEA headquarters in Arlington, Virginia, and plaintiff did not allege discrimination occurred in, or that but for discrimination, she would have worked in, the Middle District of Florida; transferring action to Eastern District of Virginia).

**ANSWER (A)** is incorrect because federal officers are subject to suit in federal court; this answer is a red-herring. **ANSWER (B)** is incorrect because Japan is simply not a possible venue; it is not part of the U.S. federal judicial system. **ANSWER (D)** is incorrect because the special venue provision in Title VII supersedes the general venue provision in 28 U.S.C. § 1391(e). **ANSWER (E)** is incorrect because a plaintiff must properly lay venue under the venue statutes; courts will not give deference to a plaintiff's choice of forum unless the court has proper jurisdiction and venue.

## PROBLEM #7. BEST ANSWER (D).

Problem #7 is based on *Hausman v. Holland-America Line-U.S.A.*, 2015 WL 8327934 (W.D. Wash. Dec. 9, 2015). This problem requires analysis of attorney work-product protection on a motion to compel production of documents. The court found that the materials requested were attorney opinion work product that was therefore protected from disclosure to the plaintiff. The court denied the motion to compel.

The attorney "work-product doctrine reflects the strong public policy against invading the privacy of an attorney's course of preparation." *In re Sealed Case*, 856 F.2d 268, 273 (D.C. Cir.1988) (citing *Hickman v. Taylor*, 329 U.S. 495 (1947)); *see also Admiral Ins. Co. v. United States District Court*, 881 F.2d 1486, 1494 (9th Cir.1989) (the purpose of the work-product rule is to "prevent exploitation of a party's efforts in preparing for litigation"). The work-product doctrine, therefore, serves to protect "written materials that lawyers prepare in anticipation of litigation." *United States v. Thompson*, 562 F.3d 387, 393 (D.C. Cir.2009); *Holmgren v. State Farm Mut. Auto. Ins. Co.*, 976 F.2d 573, 576 (9th Cir.1992) (same).

Although the attorney work-product doctrine protects an attorney's materials in a number of different circumstances, not "all written materials obtained or prepared by an adversary's counsel with an eye toward litigation are necessarily free from discovery in all cases." *Hickman*, 329 U.S. at 511. Rather, attorney work-product may be discoverable "if the party seeking discovery can make a sufficient showing of necessity." 8 Charles Alan Wright and Arthur R. Miller, FEDERAL PRACTICE AND PROCEDURE § 2025 (3d ed. 1998). Therefore, a party seeking work-product must show, at a minimum, a "substantial need of the materials in the preparation of the party's case and that the party is unable without undue hardship to obtain the substantial equivalent of the materials by other means." *Holmgren*, 976 F.2d at 576 (quoting Fed.R.Civ.P. Rule 26(b)(3)). However, if the work-product constitutes "opinion" work-product— *e.g.*, written materials prepared by counsel that reflect the attorney's "mental impressions, conclusions, opinions, or legal theories,"—such materials are "virtually undiscoverable." Rule 26(b)(3)(B); *Dir., Office of Thrift Supervision v. Vinson & Elkins, LLP*, 124 F.3d 1304, 1307 (D.C. Cir.1997); *see also Holmgren*, 976 F.2d at 577 ("A party seeking opinion work product must make a showing beyond the substantial need/undue hardship test required under Rule 26(b)(3) for non-opinion work product.").

Discovery of "opinion" work-product is therefore permissible only where a party has made "a far stronger showing of necessity and unavailability by other means" than would otherwise be sufficient for discovery of "fact" work product. *Upjohn Co. v. United States*, 449 U.S. 383, 402 (1981); *Holmgren*, 976 F.2d at 577 (suggesting that in the Ninth Circuit, in order to discover opinion work-product, the movant must establish that "mental impressions are *at issue* in a case" in addition to establishing that the need for "the material is compelling") (emphasis in original).

Therefore, when confronted with a motion to compel attorney work-product, the court must first determine if the work-product constitutes "fact" or "opinion" work-product. "The task of drawing a line between what is fact and what is opinion can at times be frustrating and perplexing." *Florida House of Representatives v. U.S. Dep't of Commerce*, 961 F.2d 941, 947 (11th Cir.1992). And, in the work-product analysis, the "fact" and "opinion" labels are even less useful because even if it can be agreed that a collection of statements constitute "facts," the collection itself might nonetheless reveal an attorney's mental impressions of the case, thereby converting the information into "opinion" work-product. *See, e.g., Dir., Office of Thrift Supervision*, 124 F.3d at 1308 ("At some point, . . . a lawyer's factual selection reflects his focus; in deciding what to include and what to omit, the lawyer reveals his view of the case."); *Better Gov. Bureau, Inc. v. McGraw*, 106 F.3d 582, 608 (4th Cir.1997) (concluding that information gained from a witness and memorialized in a typewritten summary "tended to indicate the focus of the attorney's investigation, and hence, her theories and opinions regarding this litigation").

As such, the Supreme Court has suggested that particular caution must be used in the event that an attorney is being asked to produce notes taken during an interview of a witness. *See Upjohn*, 449 U.S. at 399 ("Forcing an attorney to disclose notes and memoranda of witnesses' oral statements is particularly disfavored because it tends to reveal the attorney's mental processes."); *see also*, Notes of Advisory Committee on 1970 Amendment to Rules, 28 U.S.C.A. § 442 (noting that "the *Hickman* opinion drew special attention to the need for protecting an attorney against discovery of memoranda prepared from recollection of oral interviews.").

The plaintiff argued that he is entitled to a copy of Roberts' notes from her pre-trial interview of Mizeur. The plaintiff conceded that these notes constitute attorney work-product; nevertheless, he claimed that he was entitled to the notes because the defendants' motion to vacate is "based solely on what the defendants allege to be newly discovered evidence from Mizeur." According to the plaintiff, because the defendants implied that Mizeur lied to the defendants when they interviewed her before trial, the defendants had placed at issue the content of any interview the defendants had with her. At a minimum, the plaintiff argued, the defendants had to establish that Ms. Mizeur actually lied to them. This required a comparison between what she actually told them and what she then claimed to be the truth. As a result, the plaintiff alleged that any notes, recording, transcript, or other records of the defendants' contacts with Mizeur should be produced.

The court was not persuaded. The plaintiff misinterpreted the basis on which the motion to vacate rested. The motion was not, as the plaintiff alleged, based "solely" on a claim that Mizeur lied to the defendants during a pretrial interview. Rather, the motion raised a number of serious allegations, not the least of which was that the plaintiff allegedly failed to produce and/or destroyed relevant evidence in direct contravention of the Federal Rules of Civil Procedure and the court's orders. These allegations were raised by Mizeur with the defendants for the first time after the trial concluded. Therefore, it was not germane to the defendants' motion to vacate whether Ms. Mizeur's previous statement was truthful or untruthful.

Moreover, even if Mizeur's prior statement was germane to the motion to vacate, Roberts' written notes from Ms. Mizeur's pre-trial interview would constitute the exact type of opinion work-product that the Supreme Court cautioned must be zealously protected. *See Upjohn*, 449 U.S. at 399 (disclosure of notes of witnesses' oral statements is particularly disfavored because such work-product invariably reflects the attorney's impressions from the nature of what the attorney selected to memorialize). Further, even if an exception could be made to this general rule of non-disclosure, this was not the type of situation that would warrant such an exception.

For the foregoing reasons, the plaintiff's motion to compel production of the defendants' records of contact with witness Amy Mizeur was denied.

**ANSWER (A)** is incorrect because the court held that the defendant's motion to vacate did not place Mizeur's veracity in issue. **ANSWER (B)** is incorrect because the court did not find that the materials requested constituted ordinary work-product, which immunity can be overcome by the showing that the requesting party cannot obtain the materials by other means. **ANSWER (C)** is incorrect because the court held that the materials requested constituted protected attorney opinion work product. **ANSWER (E)** is incorrect because there is no evidence of the defendants' fraud to bring the plaintiff's request within the crime-fraud exception to the work product immunity.

### PROBLEM #8. BEST ANSWER (B).

Problems #8 and #9 are based *on Sinclair Cattle Company, Inc. v. Ward*, 2015 WL 6125269 (M.D. Pa. Oct. 16, 2015). These problems deal with the propriety of answers to allegation in a complaint under Fed.R.Civ.P. 8(b), and the pleading of affirmative defenses under Fed.R.Civ.P. (8)(c).

The problem also implicates the motion to strike under Fed.R.Civ.P. 12(f). The court granted the motion to strike the defendants' answers, but allowed the affirmative defenses (*see* Problem #9, below).

Under Federal Rule of Civil Procedure 12(f), the court may strike from a pleading "an insufficient defense or any redundant, immaterial, impertinent, or scandalous matter." Fed.R.Civ.P. 12(f). District courts have considerable discretion in resolving a Rule 12(f) motion. "Prejudice to one or more of the parties is the touchstone for deciding a motion to strike." *Fulton Fin. Advisors, Nat'l Ass'n v. NatCity Invs., Inc.*, No. 09–4855, 2013 WL 5635977, at *19 (E.D.Pa. Oct. 15, 2013); *see also Wincovitch v. Edwin A. Abrahamsen & Assoc.'s*, No. 3:12–CV–1846, 2013 WL 1909578, at *1 (M.D.Pa. May 8, 2013) (observing that courts have required a showing of prejudice before striking a pleading). A party is prejudiced when the challenged pleading "confuses the issues" or places an undue burden on the responding party. *Karpov v. Karpov*, 307 F.R.D. 345, 348 (D.Del.2015).

A Rule 12(f) motion to strike is the "primary procedure" for objecting to an insufficient affirmative defense. *See Wincovitch*, 2013 WL 1909578, at *1; 5C Charles Alan Wright & Arthur R. Miller, FEDERAL PRACTICE AND PROCEDURE § 1380 (3d ed.2015). A challenged affirmative defense must provide plaintiffs with "fair notice" of the grounds for the defense. *Mifflinburg Tel., Inc. v. Criswell*, 80 F.Supp.3d 566, 573 (M.D.Pa.2015). Fair notice is satisfied if the defense is "logically within the ambit of" the factual allegations in the litigation, but the pleading must contain "more than a mere rote recitation of generally available" affirmative defenses. *Id.* at 574. Further, courts "should not grant a motion to strike a defense unless the insufficiency of the defense is 'clearly apparent.'" *Ball v. Buckley*, No. 1:11–CV–1829, 2012 WL 6681797, at *1 (M.D.Pa. Dec. 21, 2012) (citing *Cipollone v. Liggett Grp., Inc.*, 789 F.2d 181, 188 (3d Cir.1986)); *see also Mifflinburg*, 80 F.Supp.3d at 572 (noting "general judicial agreement" that motions to strike should be denied unless the challenged allegations have no possible relation to the litigation's subject matter and may cause significant prejudice to a party).

SCC contended that the Wards' answer should be stricken in its entirety or in part because it failed to conform to the pleading requirements under Rule 8 of the Federal Rules of Civil Procedure. Specifically, SCC averred that the Wards' answer was replete with responses that did not comply with Rule 8(b), and that SCC's affirmative defenses did not comply with Rule 8(c).

SCC argued that the Wards circumvent the pleading requirements of Rule 8(b) by appending the generic phrase, "except those allegations constituting admissions against the interests of Sinclair Cattle and Smith, and each of them" to many of their responses. Consequently, SCC asserted it was "left trying to determine what facts Defendants have admitted." The Wards replied that their answer complies with Rule 8(b), and therefore should not be stricken.

Rule 8 of the Federal Rules of Civil Procedure sets forth general rules of pleading. Fed.R.Civ.P. 8. Rule 8(b) requires a party responding to a pleading to "admit or deny the allegations asserted against it by an opposing party." Fed.R.Civ.P. 8(b)(1)(B). A denial must "fairly respond to the substance of the allegation." Fed.R.Civ.P. 8(b)(2). Further, when a party intends to deny only a part of an allegation, it "must admit the part that is true and deny the rest." Fed.R.Civ.P. 8(b)(4).

The challenge that a pleading runs afoul of Rule 8(b) is not within the literal scope of a Rule 12(f) motion to strike. *See* Fed.R.Civ.P. 12(f) (targeting insufficient defenses and redundant, immaterial, impertinent, or scandalous matter). Courts have, however, applied Rule 12(f) beyond its specified categories, including to pleadings allegedly improper under Rule 8(b). *See, e.g., Ferraraccio v. Guardian Home and Cmty. Servs., Inc.*, No. 3:14–177, 2015 WL 518578, at *3–4 (W.D.Pa. Feb. 6, 2015) (evaluating under Rule 12(f) a response allegedly out of conformance with Rule 8(b)); *Dilmore v. Alion Sci. and Tech. Corp.*, No. 11–72, 2011 WL 2690367, at *2 (W.D.Pa. July 11, 2011) (presuming that a challenge to defendant's responses based on their purported noncompliance with Rule 8(b) operated under Rule 12(f)).

The phrases in the Wards' answer beginning with "except those allegations constituting . . . " were sufficiently violative of Rule 8(b) to prejudice SCC. These responses violated Rule 8(b) because the failure to identify the allegations excepted infects the entire response with ambiguity. Particularly in light of the sheer volume of offending responses in the Wards' answer, the equivocations so confused the matters in dispute and burdened SCC with ferreting out straightforward answers as to merit relief under Rule 12(f). *See Do It Best Corp. v. Heinen Hardware, LLC*, No. 1:13–CV–69, 2013 WL 3421924, at *4–6 (N.D.Ind. July 8, 2013) (striking "cryptic" responses denying "material allegations" because they failed to provide adequate guidance as to defendant's position on the allegations); *Reis Robotics USA, Inc. v. Concept Indus., Inc.*, 462 F.Supp.2d 897, 907–08 (N.D.Ill.2006) (striking from answer responses deemed "equivocal and serving to confuse the issues that are in dispute"). The Wards argued that they did not want to deny an allegation that would later prove to be an admission against the interest of SCC. The Federal Rules of Civil Procedure, however, contemplate admissions, denials, and effective denials through assertions of a lack of knowledge. *See* Fed.R.Civ.P. 8(b). A pleading model that obscures parties' positions on the bulk of the allegations against them until after discovery is neither permissible under the current rules, nor desirable. The therefore granted the plaintiff SCC's motion to strike the Wards' responses containing generic exceptions to denials.

**ANSWER (A)** is incorrect because technically the federal rules do not prohibit a defendant from issuing a general denial, but general denials are highly disfavored in federal court. At any rate, the defendants' answers were not general denials. **ANSWER (C)** is incorrect because the court held that the defendants had not sufficiently pleaded their answers under Fed.R.Civ.P. 8(b). **ANSWER (D)** is incorrect because the court faulted the form of the defendant's answers, which did not conform to the three possible ways of responding to allegations in a complaint. **ANSWER (E)**, while possibly true, is incorrect because Rule 12(f) can be used to strike insufficient answers in certain situations, as the court so held on these facts.

## PROBLEM #9. BEST ANSWER (E).

Problem #9 is a continuation of the fact pattern in Problem #8. This problem addresses the pleading of affirmative defenses under Fed.R.Civ.P. 8(c). The SCC argued that the Wards contravened the pleading requirements of Rule 8(c) by "presenting a laundry list of boilerplate, conclusory affirmative defenses" that fail to provide fair notice. The Wards contended that their affirmative defenses satisfied the fair notice standard because they were "logically related" to the litigation, and should therefore not be stricken.

Rule 8(c) requires that a party responding to a pleading must "affirmatively state any avoidance or affirmative defense." Fed.R.Civ.P. 8(c). Compliance with Rule 8(c) is not onerous for pleaders. In the instant case, all but one of the Wards' thirteen pleaded affirmative defenses were sufficiently compliant with Rule 8(c). The Wards' sparse pleading is non-exemplary, but SCC pointed to no specific affirmative defense that seems to transcend the logical ambit of the allegations within the parties' various pleadings. *See Mifflinburg*, 80 F.Supp.3d at 574 (stating that "fair notice" suggests the plaintiff "must be able to infer why an affirmative defense may be germane . . . based on some general allegations in the pleadings"). For example, given that some of the actions attributed to the Wards allegedly occurred in 2008, the Wards' assertion of time-bar defenses was at least not confusingly illogical. The same can be said for the Wards' assertion of unclean hands and estoppel considering the nature of their counterclaims against SCC and its sole shareholder. Accordingly, the court denied SCC's motion to strike the Wards' twelve affirmative defenses.

**ANSWERS (A)** and **(B)** are incorrect because even though the court decided that the pleading of the affirmative defenses was not exemplary, they nonetheless gave fair notice to the plaintiff of those defenses because they were within the logical ambit of the plaintiff's claims. **ANSWER (C)** is incorrect because it is irrelevant; there is no factual indication that the affirmative defenses are impertinent or immaterial. This is a red-herring answer parroting the language of Rule 12(f). **ANSWER (D)** is incorrect because the opposite is true: Rule 12(f) is the appropriate rule for addressing defects in pleading affirmative defenses.

### PROBLEM #10. BEST ANSWER (D).

Problem #10 is based on *Watts v. Smoke Guard, Inc.*, 2016 WL 26503 (D. Colo. Jan. 4, 2016). This problem entails analysis of the propriety of adding a party in an amended pleading after the applicable statute of limitations has run. The court held that the plaintiff satisfied the requirements of Fed.R.Civ.P. 15(c) to allow the amended party to relate back to the original pleading, circumventing the limitations problem. The court therefore denied the defendant's motion to dismiss.

Fed.R.Civ.P. 15(c)(1) governs the relation back of amendments. If the applicable statute of limitations has run, an amended complaint may relate back to the date of the timely filed original complaint when:

(A) the law that provides the applicable statute of limitations allows relation back;

(B) the amendment asserts a claim or defense that arose out of the conduct, transaction, or occurrence set out—or attempted to be set out—in the original pleading; or

(C) the amendment changes the party or the naming of the party against whom a claim is asserted, if Rule 15(c)(1)(B) is satisfied and if, within the period provided by Rule 4(m) for serving the summons and complaint (120 days from date of filing), the party to be brought in by amendment:

    (i) received such notice of the action that it will not be prejudiced in defending on the merits; and

    (ii) knew or should have known that the action would have been brought against it, but for a mistake concerning the proper party's identity.

Fed.R.Civ.P. 15(c)(1)(A–C). Rule 15(c)(1)(B) applies to an amendment asserting a claim or defense, and Rule 15(c)(1)(C) applies to an amendment changing a party or the naming of a party. *See Pierce v. Amaranto*, 276 Fed. Appx. 788, 792 (10th Cir.2008). The relation back doctrine's purpose is "to balance the interests of the defendant protected by the statute of limitations with the preference expressed in the Federal Rules of Civil Procedure . . . for resolving disputes on their merits." *Krupski v. Costa Crociere S.p.A.*, 560 U.S. 538 (2010).

The purpose of 15(c)(1)(B) is that "a party who has been notified of litigation concerning a particular occurrence has been given all the notice that statutes of limitations were intended to provide." *Baldwin Cnty. Welcome Ctr. v. Brown*, 466 U.S. 147, 149 n. 3 (1984). So long as there is a "factual nexus" between the original and amended complaints, the amended claim "is liberally construed to relate back to the original complaint if the defendant had notice of the claim and will not be prejudiced by the amendment." *Benton v. Bd. of Cnty. Comm'rs*, No. 06–cv–01406–PSF, 2007 WL 4105175, at *3 (D. Colo. Nov. 14, 2007), aff'd, 303 Fed. Appx. 625 (10th Cir.2008) (quoting *Grattan v. Burnett*, 710 F.2d 160, 163 (4th Cir.1983)). In *Benton*, the court summarized the law governing the application of the relation back doctrine as follows:

> As a general rule, amendments will relate back if they amplify the facts previously alleged, correct a technical defect in the prior complaint, assert a new legal theory of relief, or add another claim arising out of the same facts. For relation back to apply, there is no additional requirement that the claim be based on an identical theory of recovery. On the other hand, amendments generally will not relate back if they interject entirely different facts, conduct, transactions or occurrences. It is a matter committed to the district court's sound discretion to decide whether a new claim arises out of the same transaction or occurrence.

*Benton*, 2007 WL 4105175, at *3 (*quoting Kidwell v. Bd. of Cnty. Comm'rs of Shawnee Cnty.*, 40 F.Supp.2d 1201, 1217 (D. Kan. 1998)).

Rule 15(c)(1)(C) applies to relation back of an amended complaint that "changes the party or the naming of the party against whom a claim is asserted." Fed.R.Civ.P. 15(c)(1)(C). Thus, when a list of parties has "changed," Rule 15(c)(1)(C) governs the relation back to the original complaint. *See Garrett v. Fleming*, 362 F.3d 692, 696 (10th Cir.2004) (holding that the predecessor to Rule 15(c)(1)(C) governed relation back because the plaintiff's amendment "amounted to adding a new party"); *see also Bell v. City of Topeka, Kansas*, 279 Fed. Appx. 689, 692 (10th Cir.2008) (applying Rule 15(c)(1)(C) when a plaintiff adds a new party). Accordingly, Rule 15(c)(1)(C) applies to the addition of new parties after the statute of limitations has run on proposed new claims. *See VKK Corp. v. Nat'l Football League*, 244 F.3d 114, 128 (2d Cir.2001) ("if a complaint is amended to include an additional defendant after the statute of limitations has run, the amended complaint is not time barred if it 'relates back' to a timely filed complaint."). "Rule 15(c)(1) mandates relation back once the Rule's requirements are satisfied; it does not leave the decision whether to grant relation back to the district court's equitable discretion." *Krupski*, 130 S.Ct. at 2496.

In this litigation, on July 9, 2014, the plaintiff filed his original complaint. On July 15, 2015, the plaintiff filed his third amended complaint. In his third amended complaint, the plaintiff added the defendant LNA to the lawsuit, alleging a claim of negligence arising out of the same June 14, 2012 incident that caused the plaintiff's injuries. The applicable statute of limitations on the plaintiff's negligence claim was two years. Colo. Rev. Stat. § 13–80–102.

The plaintiff asserted various negligence claims arising out of the incident where he was hit on the head by a falling smoke detector. Because the plaintiff's negligence claim against LNA concerned the same incident with the smoke detector, the court found that it had a sufficient factual nexus between the original and amended complaints. Thus, the plaintiff's negligence claim against LNA related back to the original complaint, filed July 9, 2014, which was within the limitations period set forth for tort actions in Colorado. Colo. Rev. Stat. § 13–80–102.

The court next examined whether "within the period provided by Rule 4(m) for serving the summons and complaint, the party to be brought in by amendment: (i) received such notice of the action that it will not be prejudiced in defending on the merits; and (ii) knew or should have known that the action would have been brought against it, but for a mistake concerning the proper party's identity." Fed.R.Civ.P. 15(c)(1)(C). "Notice is satisfied when the parties are so closely related in their business operations or activities that the institution of an action against one serves to provide notice of the litigation to the other." *Laratta v. Raemisch*, No. 12–cv–02079–MSK, 2014 WL 1237880, at *16 (D. Colo. March 26, 2014).

The plaintiff asserted that LNA's notice was sufficient because LNA received such notice that it will not be prejudiced in its defense and knew or should have known that the action would have been brought against it, but for a mistake concerning the proper party's identity. In support, the plaintiff stated that such knowledge and notice was shown by the proximity and connection between LNA and an already named defendant, Little Nell Development ("LND"). LNA's Articles of Incorporation showed Brooke Peterson, as one of three members serving on the "Executive Board" of Little Nell Association. This same individual, as indicated by the Colorado Secretary of States' online website, served as the registered agent for Defendant LND when the action was commenced, and served as the registered agent for LNA. Peterson served as the registered agent for LND at the same time that she served for LNA as both its registered agent and Executive Board member. LNA did not filed any opposition to Plaintiff's argument.

Thus, based on the foregoing, the court found that notice was satisfied because LNA and LND were so closely related in their business operations, as evidenced by the role of Peterson in both entities, in that the institution of the action against LND served to provide constructive notice of the litigation to LNA. The court further that because it received such notice, LNA was not prejudiced in defending this suit. *See Krupski*, 130 S.Ct. at 2491–92.

Accordingly, the defendant LNA's motion to dismiss based on the applicable statute of limitations was denied pursuant to Fed.R.Civ.P. 15(c)(1).

**ANSWER (A)** is incorrect because even though the statute of limitation had run, the court permitted the plaintiff's amendment to relate back to the original proceeding pursuant to Fed.R.Civ.P. 15(c). **ANSWER (B)** is incorrect because the fact that the plaintiff's lawyer might have made a mistake in its original investigation does not undermine application of Rule 15(c) to save the amended pleading. **ANSWER (C)** is incorrect because the court found that, given the close relationship of the two corporate entities, LNA would have known of the lawsuit and would not be prejudiced by being added after the statute of limitations had run. **ANSWER (E)** is incorrect because Fed.R.Civ.P. (a) does not apply in this situation; this problem implicates Rule 15(c) because the statute of limitations has run out on the plaintiff's claim.

## PROBLEM #11. BEST ANSWER (B).

Problem #11 is based on *Zabic v. Cellco Partnership d/b/a Verizon Wireless*, 2015 WL 5921851 (M.D. Fla. Oct. 9, 2015). This problem involves the standards for establishing the amount-in-controversy in a federal diversity case on removal from state court. The court held that the defendant failed to carry its burden and therefore removal was improper. The court ordered remand to state court.

Under 28 U.S.C. § 1441, a defendant can remove an action to a United States district court if that court has original jurisdiction over the action. 28 U.S.C. § 1441(a). United States district courts have original jurisdiction over all civil actions between parties of diverse citizenship where the amount in controversy exceeds $75,000. *See* 28 U.S.C. § 1332(a). Removal is proper if the complaint makes it "facially apparent" that the amount in controversy exceeds $75,000. *Williams v. Best Buy, Co.,* 269 F.3d 1316, 1319 (11th Cir.2001). "If the jurisdictional amount is not facially apparent from the complaint, the court should look to the notice of removal and may require evidence relevant to the amount in controversy at the time the case was removed." *Id.*

In this case, it was undisputed that the parties are of diverse citizenship. The only question was whether the amount in controversy exceeds the $75,000 jurisdictional threshold. In both the initial complaint and the amended complaint, Zabic had not specified the precise amount of relief sought in the lawsuit, instead alleging damages "in excess of $15,000." Where, as here, "damages are unspecified, the removing party bears the burden of establishing the jurisdictional amount by a preponderance of the evidence." *Lowery v. Ala. Power Co.,* 483 F.3d 1184, 1208 (11th Cir.2007). "Removal statutes are construed narrowly; where plaintiff and defendant clash about jurisdiction, uncertainties are resolved in favor of remand." *Burns v. Windsor Ins. Co.,* 31 F.3d 1092, 1095 (11th Cir.1994).

As previously stated, the complaint alleged damages in excess of $15,000. Without any further specificity on damages, the defendants, as the removing parties, bore the burden of proving, by a preponderance of the evidence, that the amount in controversy was in excess of $75,000. *See Lowery,* 483 F.3d at 1208.

In the notice of removal, the defendants indicated: "Plaintiff's counsel has demanded $150,000 to settle the case" and "therefore, the amount in controversy exceeds $75,000.00, exclusive or interest and costs, as required for diversity jurisdiction in Federal Court." No further information regarding the amount in controversy was provided in the notice of removal.

A number of federal courts have held that settlement offers do not automatically establish the amount in controversy for purposes of diversity jurisdiction. *Lamb v. State Farm Fire Mut. Auto. Ins. Co.*, No. 3:10–CV–615–J–32JRK, 2010 WL 6790539, at *2 (M.D.Fla. Nov. 5, 2010); *Piazza v. Ambassador II JV, L.P.*, No. 8:10–CV–1582–T–23EAJ, 2010 WL 2889218, at *1 (M.D.Fla. July 21, 2010)("A settlement offer is relevant but not determinative of the amount in controversy.").

Instead, courts have analyzed whether demand letters merely "reflect puffing and posturing," or whether they provide "specific information to support the plaintiff's claim for damages" and thus offer a "reasonable assessment of the value of the claim." *Lamb*, 2010 WL 6790539, at *2 (quoting *Jackson v. Select Portfolio Servicing, Inc.*, 651 F.Supp.2d 1279, 1281 (S.D.Ala.2009)); *Piazza*, 2010 WL 2889218, at *1 ("a settlement demand provides only marginal evidence of the amount in controversy because the 'plaintiff's letter is nothing more than posturing by plaintiff's counsel for settlement purposes and cannot be considered a reliable indicator of the damages' sought by the plaintiff.").

Upon review the court found that Zabic's demand reflected mere posturing rather than a reasonable assessment of the value of her claim. The demand letter was factually detailed, but contained no analysis of why her claim was worth $150,000.00, or any other amount. Zabic's counsel correctly indicated in the demand letter: "This is not a claim in which the loss and damages suffered by Ms. Zabic can be quantified with any degree of precision." Rather than trying to zero-in on the amount of the loss, Zabic's counsel discussed only one other case:

> With respect to damages and what constitutes a reasonable amount, I commend your attention to the reported case styled *In re Thomas*, 254 B.R. 879 (S.C. Dist. Bkrtcy Ct.1999), a case arising in the context of a bankruptcy proceeding in which the debtor's finance (sic)—both private, non-celebrity citizens—was awarded $300,000 in compensatory damages, together with an additional $125,000 in punitive damages for the mailing of private, sexually explicit photographs of a girlfriend and the threat of publication.

The facts in the *Thomas* case were egregious and bore little resemblance to those presented here. To summarize, Hardy had a sexual relationship with Thomas and allowed Thomas to take photographs during various sexual acts. Hardy ended the relationship with Mr. Thomas and began a new romantic relationship with Prezioso, which led to an engagement to be married. Thereafter, Thomas mailed a copy of some of the sexually explicit photographs of Hardy to Prezioso and demanded money from Prezioso as well as the opportunity to have sex with Hardy once again. Unless these conditions were met, Thomas threatened to send the sexually explicit photos to Hardy's employer. Thomas was found guilty of criminal extortion and, in a trial brought by Prezioso, the court awarded $300,000 for intentional infliction of emotional distress as well as punitive damages. While the present case also involves provocative photographs, there were no other similarities.

Zabic's January 15, 2015, demand letter—attached to the notice of removal—failed to explain how Zabic arrived at the $150,000.00 figure and did not provide a discussion of the economic or non-economic damages she might be seeking with any particularity. *See Johnson v. Liberty Mut. Ins. Co.,* No. 8:13–cv–491, 2013 WL 1503109, at *4 (M.D.Fla. Apr. 12, 2013) (finding that the pre-suit demand letter was a general demand as it contained no specific information as to the amount of damages sustained by plaintiff); *Standridge v. Wal-Mart Stores,* 945 F.Supp. 252, 256 (N.D.Ga.1996)(holding that a pre-suit demand letter was "nothing more than posturing by plaintiff's counsel for settlement purposes and cannot be considered a reliable indicator of the damages plaintiff is seeking."). That Zabic offered to settle her case for more than $75,000.00 did not establish by a preponderance of the evidence that the amount in controversy requirement was met. *See Daniel v. Nationpoint,* No. 2:07–cv–640, 2007 U.S. Dist. LEXIS 93367, at *5, 2007 WL 4533121 (M.D.Ala. Dec. 19, 2007).

In addition, that the demand letter was presented months in advance of the initiation of this suit further eroded its value for the purposes of determining the amount in controversy. A number of courts have indicated that pre-suit demand letters (as opposed to offers to settle after the filing of the complaint), are often worthy of very little consideration. *See, e.g., Elder v. TFAL, Inc.,* 2007 U.S. Dist. LEXIS 82123, at *8, 2007 WL 4060230 (N.D.Ga. Oct. 31, 2007) (in the context of determining amount in controversy, giving "little weight" to a demand letter submitted prior to the filing of the complaint); *Saberton v. Sears Roebuck & Co.,* 392 F.Supp.2d 1358, 1360 (M.D.Fla.2005)("Although case law permits the use of post-suit demand letters in determining the amount in controversy requirement, a pre-suit demand letter will not be considered.").

Given that "uncertainties are resolved in favor of remand," *Burns,* 31 F.3d at 1095, the court found that the defendants had failed to prove that the amount in controversy exceeded $75,000. Consequently, the court determined that it lacked subject matter jurisdiction, and this case must be remanded to state court. *See* 28 U.S.C. § 1447(c) ("If at any time before final judgment it appears that the district court lacks subject matter jurisdiction, the case shall be remanded.").

**ANSWER (A)** is incorrect because federal courts can adjudicate state-based claims if they have proper diversity jurisdiction. **ANSWER (C)** is incorrect because the court determined that there was valid diversity of citizenship among the parties, and this was not challenged in the petition for remand. **ANSWER (D)** is incorrect because the court held that the plaintiff's settlement demand could not be used as a basis for determining whether the defendant carried its burden of establishing the requisite amount in controversy. **ANSWER (E)** is incorrect because the court found that citation to the Thomas case did not provide support for establishing the amount in controversy, because of the dissimilarity of facts between the two cases.

### PROBLEM #12. BEST ANSWER (D).

Problem #12 is based on *D & S Marine Transportation, L.L.C. v. S & K Marine, L.L.C.,* 2015 WL 5838220 (E.D. La. Oct. 7, 2015). This problem presents a question of applicable law in a federal diversity case. The court held that the Louisiana preemption doctrine constituted a state substantive right, and therefore under Erie doctrine, state law applied and not the Fed.R.Civ.P. 15(c). Consequently, the court overruled the magistrate judge's contrary ruling.

A federal court exercising diversity subject-matter jurisdiction over an action applies "state substantive law and federal procedural law." *Shady Grove Orthopedic Assocs., P.A. v. Allstate Ins. Co.*, 130 S.Ct. 1431, 1448 (2010) (quoting *Hanna v. Plumer*, 85 S.Ct. 1136, 1141 (1965)). Rule 15(c)(1)(B) of the Federal Rules of Civil Procedure provides that "an amendment to a pleading relates back to the date of the original pleading when . . . the amendment asserts a claim or defense that arose out of the conduct, transaction, or occurrence set out—or attempted to be set out—in the original pleading." The United States Court of Appeals for the Fifth Circuit has explained that this rule

> is a procedural provision to allow a party to amend an operative pleading despite an applicable statute of limitations in situations where the parties to litigation have been sufficiently put on notice of facts and claims which may give rise to future, related claims. The rationale of the rule is that, once litigation involving a particular transaction has been instituted, the parties should not be protected by a statute of limitations from later asserted claims that arose out of the same conduct set forth in the original pleadings. . . . This so-called "relation back" doctrine does not extend the limitations period, but merely recognizes that the purposes of the statute are accomplished by the filing of the initial pleading.

*Kansa Reinsurance Co., Ltd. v. Congressional Mortg. Corp. of Tex.*, 20 F.3d 1362, 1366–67 (5th Cir.1994). An amendment may be allowed after the statutory period has run even if it completely changes the legal theory of plaintiff's claim because "the federal rules shift the emphasis from state theories of law as to cause of action to the specified conduct of the defendant upon which plaintiff relies to enforce his claim." *Longbottom v. Swaby*, 397 F.2d 45, 48 (5th Cir.1968) "The purpose of the rule is accomplished if the initial complaint gives the defendant fair notice that litigation is arising out of a specific factual situation." *Id.*

La.Rev.Stat. § 1409(E) provides that an action under LUTPA "shall be prescribed by one year running from the time of the transaction or act which gave rise to the right of action." This is a preemptive period. *Glod v. Baker*, 899 S.2d 642, 646 (La.Ct.App.2005); *see also Naghi v. Brenner*, 17 So.3d 919, 923 (La.2009) (recognizing that when a statute creates a right of action and states the time in which it must be exercised, the time is a preemptive period). Louisiana Civil Code article 3458 defines preemption as "a period of time fixed by law for the existence of a right," and states that "unless timely exercised, the right is extinguished upon the expiration of the preemptive period." The Supreme Court of Louisiana has stated that the difference between prescription and preemption is that: "Statutes of prescription simply bar the remedy. Statutes of preemption destroy the cause of action itself. That is to say, after the time expires the cause of action no longer exists, it is lost." *Naghi,*

17 So.3d at 923 (quoting *Guillory v. Avoyelles Ry. Co.,* 28 So. 899, 901 (La.1900)). The Supreme Court of Louisiana has also explained that:

> Preemption differs from prescription in several respects. Although prescription prevents the enforcement of a right by legal action, it does not terminate the natural obligation (La.C.C. art. 1762(1)); preemption, however extinguishes or destroys the right (La.C.C. art. 3458). Public policy requires that rights to which preemptive periods attach are to be extinguished after passage of a specified period. Accordingly, nothing may interfere with the running of a preemptive period.

*Id.* (quoting *Hebert v. Doctors Mem'l Hosp.,* 486 So.2d 717, 723 (La.1986)). Citing these principles, the Supreme Court of Louisiana held that preempted claims cannot relate back to the filing of the original petition under Louisiana Code of Civil Procedure article 1153. *Id.* at 925–26.

Because the court must apply federal procedural rules, it is irrelevant whether a preempted claim would relate back under Louisiana Code of Civil Procedure article 1153. *See Shady Grove Orthopedic,* 130 S.Ct. at 1448. However, the Rules Enabling Act provides that the Federal Rules of Civil Procedure may not "abridge, enlarge or modify any substantive right." 28 U.S.C. § 2072(b). The Supreme Court of Louisiana has clearly stated that preemption is not merely a procedural bar to litigation, rather it destroys the existence of a substantive right. *See Naghi,* 17 So .3d at 923–26. Permitting relation back of a preempted claim under Rule 15(c) would expand a substantive right, which is prohibited by the Rules Enabling Act. *See Miguel v. Country Finding Corp.,* 309 F.3d 1161, 1165 (9th Cir.2002) (finding that the Rules Enabling Act prohibited the application of Rule 15(c) to a claim that was barred by a statute of repose because it would expand a substantive right). Therefore, D & S Marine's preempted LUTPA claims against Strafuss cannot relate back to the filing of the original petition, making the filing of the claim futile. The United States magistrate judge's order allowing the filing of those claims was overruled.

**ANSWER (A)** is incorrect because it is not true that the Federal Rules of Civil Procedure always apply in federal diversity cases; the court found to the contrary here. **ANSWER (B)** is incorrect because these facts do not implicate the application of federal common law; as such, this answer is a red herring. **ANSWER (C)** is incorrect because the court held the exact opposite: that application of the federal rule would violate the Rules Enabling Act. **ANSWER (E)** is incorrect because although appealing, the federal court held that it was irrelevant what Louisiana would permit or not under its own civil procedure code.

**PROBLEM #13. BEST ANSWER (E).**

Problems #13 and #14 are based on *Wichansky v. Zowine,* 2015 WL 5693521 (D. Ariz. Sept. 29, 2015). Problem #13 deals with application of the attorney-client privilege, and the court found that it was not applicable because the emails had been sent to and included a third-party non-attorney. The court further held, however, that the emails were protected by the work product doctrine. (*See* analysis for Problem #14, below).

The plaintiff's memorandum and the communications reviewed *in camera* made it clear that Prussin was a friend of the plaintiff's, as well as his father-in-law, and an individual from whom the plaintiff sought counsel. The submissions also made clear that Prussin discussed litigation strategy with the plaintiff and his counsel. The court could conclude, however, that this relationship brought Prussin within the attorney-client privilege. The following discussion from *United States v. Evans*, 113 F.3d 1457 (7th Cir.1997), was particularly relevant:

> The attorney-client privilege shields only those communications by a client to an attorney that were intended to be confidential. Thus as a general matter, the attorney-client privilege will not shield from disclosure statements made by a client to his or her attorney in the presence of a third party who is not an agent of either the client or attorney. *See* 8 Wigmore, Evidence § 2311 ("One of the circumstances by which it is commonly apparent that the communication is not confidential is the *presence of a third person* who is not the agent of either client or attorney."); *In re Walsh*, 623 F.2d 489, 495 (7th Cir.1980) (attorney required to testify about meetings with client at which third parties were present). As Wigmore explains, the presence of such a third party defeats the privilege even though the client may harbor a desire for confidentiality because the privilege "goes no further than is necessary to secure the client's subjective freedom of consultation. . . . The *presence of a third person* (other than the agent of either) is obviously unnecessary for communications to the attorney as such." 8 Wigmore, Evidence § 2311.

The court in *Evans* held that the presence of the defendant's friend, Holden, in communications with attorneys, resulted in waiver of the attorney-client privilege even though Holden was there to provide support and advice, to help locate a suitable criminal defense attorney, and was himself a lawyer. The Seventh Circuit found that "the critical inquiry" was whether Holden "was acting in his capacity as a professional legal advisor—as opposed to his capacity as a long-time friend who happens to be a lawyer." *Id.* at 1463. The court found that "Holden was present merely as a friend and potential character witness. This is plainly insufficient to establish the necessity of Holden's presence." *Id.* at 1465. Because Holden was not necessary to the communications, the attorney-client privilege did not apply.

Other cases are in accord. *See, e.g., Cavallaro v. United States*, 284 F.3d 236, 247–49 (1st Cir.2002) (finding communications between a party and an accounting firm not privileged where the firm was retained to provide accounting services, not to assist in providing legal services); *United States v. Ackert*, 169 F.3d 136, 139 (2d Cir.1999) (finding communications between a party's lawyer and an investment banker not privileged where the lawyer's purpose was "to gain information and to better advise his client"); *State v. Super. Ct., In & For Cnty. of Pima*, 586 P.2d 1313, 1315–16 (Ariz. Ct. App. 1978) (finding communications between a party and an insurance claims adjuster not privileged where the party lacked control over the claims adjuster, indicating the absence of an agency relationship).

The plaintiff relied on *Benedict v. Amaducci*, No. 92–cv–05239–KMW, 1995 WL 23555 (S.D.N.Y. Jan. 20, 1995), in which a plaintiff informally retained a close friend with financial expertise to act as a financial advisor and assist in preparing plaintiff for litigation. *Id.* at *1. The court found that the advisor became the functional equivalent of an independent contractor, and eventually entered into an oral agreement to receive compensation for his services. *Id.* The court held that the privilege protected only "those communications involving the advisor when he was acting as plaintiffs' representative with respect to litigation, impending or pending." *Id.* at *2.

Prussin is more like the friend in *Evans* than the friend in *Benedict*. The Court cannot conclude that Prussin acted as an independent contractor. The plaintiff did not identify any agreement that Prussin act in that capacity or be paid for his services. Prussin's actions were much like those of Holden in the *Evans* case—a friend helping to arrange counsel, providing support, and participating in attorney-client communications. As in *Evans*, the court concluded that Prussin was not necessary to the plaintiff's communications with his counsel and did not fall within the privilege.

The plaintiff's other cases were no more persuasive. Each involved a third person who was the functional equivalent of an agent or employee. *See Neighborhood Dev. Collaborative v. Murphy*, 233 F.R.D. 436, 440 (D. Md. 2005) (finding communications between a party and its financial consultant privileged where the consultant "essentially functioned as the plaintiff's employee with respect to the transaction at issue"); *Carte Blanche (Singapore) Pte. Ltd. v. Diners Club Int'l, Inc.*, 130 F.R.D. 28, 34 (S.D.N.Y. 1990) (finding communications between a party and its agent privileged based on "the existence of an agency relationship"); *Harkobusic v. Gen. Am. Transp. Corp.*, 31 F.R.D. 264, 266 (W.D. Penn. 1962) (finding communications between a party and his brother-in-law privileged where "plaintiff's brother-in-law was acting as plaintiff's agent in communicating with various attorneys").

**ANSWER (A)** is incorrect because it didn't matter that the plaintiff's attorney was included in the email communications; the problem was inclusion of the third-person that destroyed the privilege. **ANSWER (B)** is incorrect because it also didn't matter that the mail communications included litigation strategy; the privilege was breached when they were sent to the third person, non-attorney. **ANSWER (C)** is incorrect because the attorney-client privilege belongs to the attorney, not the client. **ANSWER (D)** is incorrect because emails may be protected by the attorney client privilege, if the privilege is properly invoked.

### PROBLEM #14. BEST ANSWER (D).

This problem, as continuation of Problem #13, requires the student to apply the principle relating to attorney work product immunity. In this instance, the court concluded that the work product doctrine shielded the email communications from disclosure.

Work product consists of "documents and tangible things that are prepared in anticipation of litigation or for trial by or for another party or its representative." Fed.R.Civ.P. 26(b)(3)(A). The protection thus applies to documents prepared "by" a party's representative, including his attorney, consultant, surety, indemnitor, insurer, or agent. *Id.* For reasons discussed above, the court concluded that Mr. Prussin does not fall into any of these categories. The protection also applies, however, to documents prepared "for" a party or his representative. *Id.* The list of persons in Rule 26(b)(3)(A)— attorney, consultant, surety, indemnitor, insurer, or agent—defines "representative," and thus identifies the persons "by or for" whom work product may be prepared. *Id.* It does not limit the persons who can prepare work product "for" a party or its representative.

The Ninth Circuit has identified only two requirements for the work product protection to apply to documents: "(1) they must be 'prepared in anticipation of litigation or for trial,' and (2) they must be prepared 'by or for the party seeking the protection or by or for that . . . party's representative.'" *In re Grand Jury Subpoena*, 357 F.3d 900, 907 (9th Cir.2004) (quoting Fed.R.Civ.P. 26(b)(3)). The emails written by Prussin satisfy both requirements. The emails were written in anticipation of litigation and for the plaintiff.

The work product protection applied not only to emails written by Prussin to the plaintiff and his counsel, but also to emails written to the plaintiff alone, so long as they were written in anticipation of litigation. As the Advisory Committee Note to Rule 26(b)(3) makes clear, a lawyer need not be party to a document for work product protection to apply: "Subdivision (b)(3) reflects the trend of the cases by requiring a special showing, not merely as to materials prepared by an attorney, but also as to materials prepared in anticipation of litigation or preparation for trial *by or for a party* or any representative acting on his behalf." Fed.R.Civ.P. 26(b)(3) advisory committee note (1970). Thus, "a lawyer need not be involved at all for the work product protection to take effect." *Goff v. Harrah's Operating Co., Inc.*, 240 F.R.D. 659, 660 (D. Nev. 2007) (quoting Roger Park et al., HORNBOOK ON EVIDENCE LAW § 8.09 (West 2d ed. 2004)).

The court concluded that emails written by Prussin satisfied the requirements for work product protection. They were written to a party in the litigation in anticipation of litigation.

The court also concluded that emails written by the plaintiff and his counsel in anticipation of litigation constituted work product, and that they retained this protection even though they were shared with Prussin. As many courts have recognized, unlike the more sensitive attorney-client privilege, waiver of work product protection does not occur simply because a document is shared with a third person:

> A disclosure to a third party waives the attorney-client privilege unless the disclosure is necessary to further the goal of enabling the client to seek informed legal assistance. Because the work-product doctrine serves instead to protect an attorney's work product from falling into the hands of an adversary, a disclosure to a third party does not necessarily waive the protection of the work-product doctrine. *Most courts hold that to waive the protection of the work-*

> *product doctrine, the disclosure must enable an adversary to gain access to the information.*

*Westinghouse Elec. Corp. v. Republic of Phil.*, 951 F.2d 1414, 1428 (3d Cir.1991) (emphasis added); *see also* 8 Charles Alan Wright, Arthur R. Miller & Richard L. Marcus, FEDERAL PRACTICE & PROCEDURE § 2024. Thus, as courts have recognized, "one may waive the attorney-client privilege without waiving the work product privilege." *Goff*, 240 F.R.D. at 661.

As other courts have explained, disclosure of work product to third persons "generally does not waive the work product immunity unless it has substantially increased the opportunities for potential adversaries to obtain the information." *Cal. Sportfishing Prot. All. v. Chico Scrap Metal, Inc.*, 299 F.R.D. 638, 645 (E.D. Cal. 2014). "Disclosure to a person with interests common to that of attorney or client is not inconsistent with intent to invoke work product doctrine's protection and would not amount to waiver." *Id.* (quoting *In re Doe*, 662 F.2d 1073, 1081 (4th Cir.1981)); *see also United States v. Stewart*, 287 F.Supp. 2d 461, 469 (S.D.N.Y. 2003) (finding no waiver of work product protection of an email between a party and her attorney after the party forwarded the email to her daughter).

Prussin was closely allied with the plaintiff in this litigation. His interests were aligned with the plaintiff's. The court could conclude that disclosure of work product to him substantially increased the opportunity for the defendants to obtain the information, or that it was otherwise inconsistent with the work product protection. The court concluded, therefore, that the disclosure did not waive the protection.

The defendants did not make a showing of substantial need under Rule 26(b)(3)(A)(ii). The defendants argued that the court should deem the work product protection waived as a discovery sanction. The court was not persuaded. The court ordered that emails written by Prussin, to the plaintiff or his counsel, in anticipation of litigation, were entitled to work product protection. Emails written by the plaintiff or his counsel in anticipation of litigation were also entitled to work product protection, even if they were shared with Prussin.

**ANSWER (A)** is incorrect because the court concluded the mails did constitute work product subject to the immunity. **ANSWER (B)** is incorrect because the court concluded that disclosure to a third-person non-attorney did not make a difference for application of the work product immunity doctrine. **ANSWER (C)** is incorrect because the fact pattern provides no evidence that the defendant made such a showing to overcome the immunity. **ANSWER (E)** in incorrect because the facts do not support a showing by the plaintiff of prejudice as a result of disclosure; this was not the basis for the court denying disclosure.

### PROBLEM #15. BEST ANSWER (A).

Problem #15 is based on *Tang v. Glocap Search LLC*, 2015 WL 5472929 (S.D.N.Y. Sept. 16, 2015). This problem involves application of the standards for a movant to be awarded a judgment as a matter of law after trial testimony. The court held that the jury rendered a reasonable verdict in favor of the defendants after trial testimony, and therefore the court denied the plaintiff's Rule 50 motion.

Rule 50 of the Federal Rules of Civil Procedure "imposes a heavy burden on a movant, who will be awarded judgment as a matter of law only when 'a party has been fully heard on an issue during a jury trial and the court finds that a reasonable jury would not have a legally sufficient evidentiary basis to find for the party on that issue.' " *Cash v. Cnty. of Erie*, 654 F.3d 324, 333 (2d Cir.2011) (quoting Fed.R.Civ.P. 50(a)(1)); *accord Bucalo v. Shelter Island Union Free Sch. Dist.*, 691 F.3d 119, 127–28 (2d Cir.2012). According to the Second Circuit, the "burden is particularly heavy where, as here, the jury has deliberated in the case and actually returned its verdict in favor of the non-movant." *Cash*, 654 F.3d at 333. In such circumstances, a court may set aside the verdict only if, viewing the evidence in the light most favorable to the non-movant, "there exists such a complete absence of evidence supporting the verdict that the jury's findings could only have been the result of sheer surmise and conjecture, or the evidence in favor of the movant is so overwhelming that reasonable and fair minded persons could not arrive at a verdict against it." *Id.; see also, e.g., Zellner v. Summerlin*, 494 F.3d 344, 371 (2d Cir.2007) (stating that a Rule 50 motion may be granted only if the court concludes that "a reasonable juror would have been compelled to accept the view of the moving party.").

Applying those standards, the court denied the plaintiff's motion. The court began with the plaintiff's argument that she was entitled to judgment as a matter of law on her city-law retaliation claim, which was brought pursuant to the New York City Human Rights Law. To prevail on her retaliation claim under the NYCHRL, the plaintiff was required to show, among other things, that she "engaged in a protected activity." There was no dispute that an employee's complaint about pregnancy discrimination—whether formal or informal—can constitute protected activity. For a complaint to qualify, however, the employee must also show that she had "a good faith, reasonable belief that the underlying challenged actions of the employer violated the law." As the plaintiff conceded, that showing involved "two components": first, that the plaintiff had subjective good faith belief "that her employer had violated the law and, second that the complaint was 'objectively reasonable.' " Thus, if a plaintiff complained, not in good faith, but rather to protect her job or extort money from her employer, the activity was not protected under the statute. *See, e.g., Sanders v. Madison Square Garden, L.P.*, 525 F.Supp.2d 364, 366 (S.D.N.Y.2007); *see also, e.g., Wolf v. Time Warner, Inc.*, No. 09–CV–6549 (RJS), 2011 WL 856264, at *8 (S.D.N.Y. Mar. 3, 2011) ("A retaliation claim is not a 'tactical coercive weapon that may be turned against the employer as a means for the asserted victims to advance their own retaliatory motives and strategies.' " ) (quoting *Spadola v. N.Y.C. Transit Auth.* 242 F.Supp.2d 284, 292 (S.D.N.Y.2003)).

Here, there was no question that the plaintiff complained to Zoia that she was subject to pregnancy discrimination. Nor, in the court's view, was there any reasonable question that her complaint was *objectively* reasonable, as the defendants admitted, by failing to respond to the plaintiff's requests for admissions, that in the weeks after the plaintiff revealed her pregnancy to

Zoia, he excluded her from certain discussions and decisions, reassigned some of her responsibilities to others, and asked her to transition to a compensation structure that would not include maternity leave. But one of the defendants' principal arguments at trial was that the plaintiff's complaint was made in bad faith: that she knew her job was on the line after her allegedly tepid response to a "crisis" at the company—a crisis that highlighted the problems of having a highly paid chief operating officer working from a different city—and that, days later, she told Zoia she was pregnant (despite not yet showing) and ultimately complained in a cynical effort to either keep her job or (in Zoia's words) "position" herself to file a lawsuit. And, viewed in the light most favorable to the defendants, the evidence was plainly sufficient for the jury to accept that argument.

For one thing, the jury was entitled to believe Zoia's testimony that he was "very happy for the Plaintiff" when he heard that she was pregnant and enthusiastically congratulated her. For another, the jury could infer that the plaintiff did not actually believe that Zoia's initial treatment of her was discriminatory from the fact that she continued to stay at his home while she was in New York, even after he purportedly reacted negatively to news of her pregnancy and asked her to take a pay cut for what she now alleges to be discriminatory reasons. Most compelling, however, there was evidence that three weeks after Zoia began treating Plaintiff differently (not, as the defendants asserted, because she was pregnant, but because she was absent in a time of crisis), she cynically generated a paper trail to support a later claim of discrimination by directing a subordinate who had called to ask why Zoia had reassigned some of the plaintiff's responsibilities to write her an e-mail as if they had not spoken and then responded by e-mail, again with no reference to their prior conversation, that she believed that Zoia was discriminating against her. To be sure, the jury was not compelled to accept the defendants' argument that, in creating that e-mail record, the plaintiff was merely "papering the file" and trying to "buy employment insurance by throwing up the pregnancy card", but it was certainly entitled to do so. Given that, the court could not say that a reasonable juror would have been compelled to find that Plaintiff had engaged in protected activity within the meaning of the New York City Human Rights Law.

In arguing otherwise, the plaintiff contended that Zoia himself admitted that the plaintiff had subjectively believed that she was being treated differently because of her pregnancy, pointing to his testimony that Plaintiff "felt she was being excluded from things" and that the email in which she complained to him about discrimination represented "a continuation of the sort of strange lack of understanding of what was really happening". But *Zoia's* opinion about the sincerity of the plaintiff's belief that she was discriminated against was arguably irrelevant; the jury was entitled to draw its own conclusions about the good faith or lack thereof of the plaintiff's belief based on its own assessment of her credibility and the other evidence in the record, including the evidence discussed above.

In any event, the premise of the plaintiff's argument was flawed. Viewed in context, Zoia's testimony could reasonably be construed (and certainly did not need to be viewed by the jury) as an admission about the sincerity of the plaintiff's belief in discrimination. Instead, according to Zoia, what the plaintiff failed to understand was "that Glocap was in the middle of this perilous crisis and she had to be flexible like everyone else." Similarly, while Zoia acknowledged that the plaintiff felt that she was being excluded, he testified that, if any exclusion occurred, it was because the plaintiff "just . . . wasn't there" when decisions were being made. Put simply, Zoia never linked the plaintiff's feelings to any perceived or actual discrimination. To the contrary, he explicitly testified that, upon receiving the plaintiff's alleged complaint of discrimination, he came to the conclusion that she was merely "positioning" to "protect her job."

In short, the jury was entitled to find that the plaintiff did not have a subjective good faith belief that the defendants had engaged in discrimination and therefore did not engage in "protected activity." It follows that her Rule 50 motion with respect to her New York City Human Rights claim was denied.

**ANSWER (B)** is incorrect because there is no indication on the facts whether the plaintiff moved for a directed verdict after she rested her case; therefore this is irrelevant to the issue before the court on a completed jury trial. **ANSWER (C)** is incorrect because the Supreme Court has ruled that Rule 50 motions do not violate a plaintiff or party's Seventh Amendment right to a jury trial. **ANSWER (D)** is incorrect because the jury found otherwise, and the court agreed that given the testimony, the jury reasonably could have reached the decision favorable to the defendants. **ANSWER (E)** is incorrect because the court, in analyzing whether the jury acted reasonably, took into account the reasonable inferences the jury could draw from the evidence, and concluded that their decision was reasonable.

### PROBLEM #16. BEST ANSWER (B).

Problem #16 is based on *Harrison v. Granite Bay Care, Inc.*, 2016 WL 147423 (1st Cir.2016). This problem involves determination of a corporation's citizenship for the purpose of establishing federal diversity jurisdiction pursuant to 28 U.S.C. § 1332(c). Relying on the Supreme Court's decision in *Hertz v. Friend*, the court determined that there was good diversity of citizenship because the corporation's principal place of business was New Hampshire, and the plaintiff was a citizen of Maine.

The court addressed whether it had diversity jurisdiction. *See* 28 U.S.C. § 1332(a)(1) (extending federal jurisdiction to civil actions between "citizens of different states"); *see also American Fiber & Finishing, Inc. v. Tyco Healthcare Group, LP,* 362 F.3d 136, 139 (1st Cir.2004) ("Federal courts are expected to monitor their jurisdictional boundaries vigilantly and to guard carefully against expansion by distended judicial interpretation.").

Harrison, a Maine citizen, filed her suit (which raises state law claims only) in Maine Superior Court. Granite Bay preferred to be in federal court and, invoking federal diversity jurisdiction, removed the action to the Maine district court. In doing so, Granite Bay held itself out as a New Hampshire corporation with a principal place of business in Concord, New Hampshire.

Granite Bay ran group homes and provided services for adults who have cognitive or physical disabilities. Granite Bay was a New Hampshire corporation, and it maintained its corporate headquarters in Concord. Nevertheless, its group homes were all in Maine and all of its clients were Maine residents. In addition to its Concord headquarters, Granite Bay had an administrative office in Portland, Maine.

Granite Bay was owned by two individuals, Kasai Mumpini and Caroletta Alicea, both of whom worked out of Concord. Mumpini served as the corporation's President, with Alicea as its Vice President. Mumpini and Alicea were Granite Bay's only two officers and the only corporate directors. Their role was to maintain a vision for the company and to set overall corporate policies.

Granite Bay's day-to-day operations—things like providing care to its clients and hiring, training, and supervising employees—were handled out of the Portland office. An employee with the title of state director directed operations in Maine. There have been two state directors, Gregory Robinson and Ken Olson, and there were no significant differences between how each one went about the job. Olson, the current State Director, divided his work week between the offices in Portland and Concord.

Although he had significant flexibility in managing Granite Bay, Olson nevertheless reported to Mumpini and Alicea. He communicated with them daily and met with them in person at least once per week. Olson kept the owners updated as to how Granite Bay was doing, and the owners directed him on the overall strategy he should employ in working towards the company's future goals. Furthermore, they gave Olson general financial parameters in which he was to operate, and they gave him different objectives to accomplish. The previous state director, Robinson, held that position for about seven years before becoming Granite Bay's Chief Operations Officer.

The court held Granite Bay was a citizen of New Hampshire. When it comes to questions of diversity jurisdiction, "a corporation shall be deemed to be a citizen of every State . . . by which it has been incorporated." 28 U.S.C. § 1332(c)(1). What we have to worry about is the location of its principal place of business. *See id.* (providing that a corporation is a citizen of the state where it has its principal place of business).

Because this case does not present a federal question, the parties' diversity of citizenship was the only basis for federal jurisdiction. *See* 28 U.S.C. § 1332(a). "For federal jurisdictional purposes, diversity of citizenship must be determined as of the time of suit." *Valentin v. Hospital Bella Vista*, 254 F.3d 358, 361 (1st Cir.2001).

Several years ago, the Supreme Court established beyond any doubt that federal courts must employ the "nerve center" test to determine the location of a corporation's principal place of business. *See Hertz Corp. v. Friend,* 559 U.S. 77, 80–81 (2010). The test is straightforward. A corporation's "nerve center" (i.e., its principal place of business) is the particular location from which its "officers direct, control, and coordinate the corporation's activities." *Id.* at 92–93. Generally speaking, this will "be the place where the corporation maintains its headquarters-provided that the headquarters is the actual center of direction, control, and coordination ... and not simply an office where the corporation holds its board meetings (for example, attended by directors and officers who have traveled there for the occasion)." *Id.* at 93.

The party seeking to establish diversity jurisdiction bears the burden of persuasion, and parties must support their jurisdictional allegations with "competent proof." *See id.* at 9697 (citing *McNutt v. General Motors Acceptance Corp.,* 289 U.S. 178, 189 (1936)). Although the Supreme Court did not go into depth about the exact quantum of proof required to meet the burden of persuasion, it made it clear that run-of-the-mill corporate filings—like a Form 10–K—are not enough on their own to satisfy it. *Id.* at 97.

The *Hertz* Court recognized that, "in this era of telecommuting, some corporations may divide their command and coordinating functions among officers who work at several different locations, perhaps communicating over the Internet." *Id.* at 95–96. But even when presented with such a situation, the nerve center test "nonetheless points courts in a single direction, towards the center of overall direction, control, and coordination." *Id.* at 96. Federal courts must also be on the lookout for attempts at "jurisdictional manipulation." *Id.* at 97. Therefore, "if the record reveals attempts at manipulation—for example, that the alleged 'nerve center' is nothing more than a mail drop box, a bare office with a computer, or the location of an annual executive retreat—the courts should instead take as the 'nerve center' the place of actual direction, control, and coordination, in the absence of such manipulation." *Id.*

The court held that the test may seem pretty simple, and it is. That's no accident. "Complex jurisdictional tests complicate a case, eating up time and money as the parties litigate, not the merits of their claims, but which court is the right court to decide those claims." *Id.* at 94. Complicated tests also engender appeals, "encourage gamesmanship, and ... diminish the likelihood that results and settlements will reflect a claim's legal and factual merits," not to mention demand the expenditure of judicial resources. *Id.* Accordingly, the test described by the Supreme Court is intended to be "relatively easier to apply" than others that could be imagined. *Id.* at 96.

At its heart, the nerve center test is an inquiry to find the one location from which a corporation is ultimately controlled. Put slightly differently, the federal court is to look for the place where the buck stops. And where it does, that's the corporation's nerve center and principal place of business.

The court held that the facts in the record were sufficient to determine that jurisdiction was proper. The competent evidence pointed towards Concord as Granite Bay's principal place of business.

Harrison did not contest (or seek to develop additional evidence to contest) that Granite Bay's owners, although they may be hands-off when it comes to day-to-day decisions, exercised "ultimate" control over Granite Bay, and that they did so from Concord. Granite Bay supported this assertion through affidavits and sworn deposition testimony showing that the owners set overall corporate policy and goals, plus advised and gave instructions to the state director as to how to make the owners' vision a reality.

Moreover, the uncontested evidence showed that the owners made the call as to just who exactly would be placed in what upper management position. This was a concrete example of the owners' actual exercise of control over Granite Bay. And all of the evidence indicated this ultimate control was wielded from Granite Bay's Concord headquarters.

In sum, the competent evidence in the record established that Granite Bay's principal place of business was in Concord, not Portland. Accordingly, the parties were diverse and the court had valid jurisdiction.

**ANSWER (A)** is incorrect because the two owners' citizenship is not in question; the citizenship of the company being sued by Harrison is the defendant and the entity whose citizenship is determinative of valid diversity jurisdiction. **ANSWER (C)** is incorrect because the location of Granite Bay's group home and clients was not determinative of its principal place of business. **ANSWER (D)** is incorrect for the same reason. **ANSWER (E)** is incorrect because the court determined that New Hampshire was the principal place of business for Granite Bay.

### PROBLEM #17. BEST ANSWER (A).

Problem #17 is based on *Troyer v. Johnson*, 2015 WL 5786794 (S.D.W. Va. Sept. 30, 2015). This problem involves application of principles relating to federal question jurisdiction pursuant to 28 U.S.C. § 1331. The court held that invocation of the federal Motor Carrier Safety Act was insufficient to confer federal question jurisdiction, and therefore remand to state court was proper.

United Financial claimed removal was appropriate and the court could exercise jurisdiction over the case because the complaint raised a federal question, vesting the court with original jurisdiction under 28 U.S.C. § 1331. As a defendant seeking removal, United Financial bore the burden of "demonstrating the court's jurisdiction over the matter." *Strawn v. AT & T Mobility LLC*, 530 F.3d 293, 296 (4th Cir.2008). And "if federal jurisdiction is doubtful, a remand is necessary." *Mulcahey v. Columbia Organic Chems. Co., Inc.*, 29 F.3d 148, 151 (4th Cir.1994).

Federal courts have federal question jurisdiction in cases "arising under the Constitution, laws, or treaties of the United States." 28 U.S.C. § 1331. When determining whether to exercise federal question jurisdiction, "a court must first discern whether federal or state law creates the cause of action." *Mulcahey*, 29 F.3d at 151. "The presence or absence of federal-question jurisdiction is governed by the 'well-pleaded complaint rule,' which provides that federal jurisdiction exists only when a federal question is presented on the face of the plaintiff's properly pleaded complaint." *Caterpillar Inc. v. Williams*, 482 U.S. 386, 392 (1987). If federal law creates the cause of action, federal question jurisdiction is unquestionable. *Mulcahey*, 29 F.3d at 151. But if state law creates the cause of action, "federal question jurisdiction depends on whether the plaintiff's demand 'necessarily depends on resolution of a substantial question of federal law.'" *Id.* (quoting *Franchise Tax Bd. v. Constr. Laborers Vacation Trust*, 463 U.S. 1, 28 (1983)).

The plaintiff did not state a cause of action arising under federal law. The only affirmative cause of action stated was the plaintiff's state law tort cause of action. Even if the complaint implicated the Motor Carrier Safety Act and its attendant regulations, it did not state an affirmative cause of action arising under the Act or the related regulations. In fact, it appeared—and United Financial did not argue otherwise—the Act and its attendant regulations did not provide a route for private enforcement.

Absent a federal cause of action, the jurisdictional inquiry turns on whether this case presents a substantial question of federal law. Put simply, it did not. United Financial argued that the case presented a substantial question of federal law because resolution of whether a federal regulation (i.e., 49 U.S.C. § 387) applied would resolve this case and might control the application of § 387 in other cases. Resolution of this case did not turn on coverage obligations; it turned on liability as defined by West Virginia tort law. Additionally, whether § 387 applies in this case is a fact-bound determination that will not govern the application of this regulation in other cases. Neither United Financial nor Johnson nor the plaintiff asked the court to interpret § 387. This was merely a matter of application, and the simple application of federal statute or regulation is not enough to support federal question jurisdiction. *Cf. Grable & Sons Metal Prods., Inc. v. Darue Eng'g & Mfg.*, 545 U.S. 308, 313 (2005) (noting movement away "from the expansive view that mere need to apply federal law in a state-law claim will suffice to open the 'arising under' door"). United Financial failed to demonstrate the application of § 387 alone was enough to warrant federal jurisdiction over this state law tort. There was no reason to doubt the ability of a state court to handle this matter. *See, e.g., Empire Healthchoice Assurance, Inc. v. McVeigh*, 547 U.S. 677, 701 (2006) ("The state court in which the personal-injury suit was lodged is competent to apply federal law, to the extent it is relevant. . . .").

Accordingly, United Financial failed to carry its burden to demonstrate that federal jurisdiction was appropriate and in the absence of federal jurisdiction, the plaintiff's motion to remand was granted.

**ANSWER (B)** is incorrect because there is no indication in the fact pattern that there is (or is not) an implied right of action under the federal Motor Carrier Safety Act; this is a red-herring answer. **ANSWER (C)** is incorrect because the federal Motor Carrier Safety Act does not confer federal question jurisdiction. **ANSWER (D)** is incorrect the court did not find that the question of application of the federal Motor Carrier Safety Act raised a substantial question of federal law requiring uniform interpretation by the federal court. **ANSWER (E)** is incorrect because the question of inter-system comity was not raised by the parties or the court. At any rate, comity concerns are appropriate where the federal court's assertion of jurisdiction might offend state court authority and prerogatives in adjudicating cases involving state law. Inter-state comity would not be served in this case by allowing the federal court to adjudicate largely state-based tort claims.

## PROBLEM #18. BEST ANSWER (E).

Problem #18 is based on *OKS Group, LLC v. Axtria Inc.*, 2015 WL 9694786 (D.N.J. Dec. 15, 2015). This problem involves the standards for granting a motion to dismiss on the grounds of the doctrine of forum non conveniens. The court held that the defendant had failed to demonstrate that India was an adequate alternative forum, and therefore the court denied the defendant's motion to dismiss on forum non conveniens ground.

An action may be dismissed on the basis of *forum non conveniens* when an adequate alternative forum exists and maintaining the action in the original forum would prove disproportionately oppressive or vexatious to the parties or problematic for court administrative purposes. *Windt v. Qwest Commc'ns Int'l, Inc.*, 529 F.3d 183, 192 (3d Cir.2008); *Tech. Dev. Co. v. Onischenko*, 174 F.App'x 117, 119 (3d Cir.2006); *Lony v. E.I. Du Pont de Nemours & Co.*, 886 F.2d 628, 632 (3d Cir.1989); *Lacey v. Cessna Aircraft Co.*, 862 F.2d 38, 42 (3d Cir.1988) (hereinafter *Lacey I*). Whether to grant dismissal on *forum non conveniens* grounds is left largely to the discretion of the district court. *Piper Aircraft Co. v. Reyno*, 454 U.S. 235, 257 (1981); *Windt*, 529 F.3d at 188, 192; *Lacey I*, 862 F.2d at 42.

Applicable case law makes clear that the showing of an available and adequate alternative forum is a prerequisite to considering the private and public interest factors that otherwise guide a *forum non conveniens* analysis. *Piper*, 454 U.S. at 254 n.22; *Windt*, 529 F.3d at 189–90; *Tech. Dev. Co.*, 174 F.App'x at 120; *Lacey v. Cessna Aircraft Co.*, 932 F.2d 170, 180 (3d Cir.1991) (hereinafter *Lacey II*); *Lacey I*, 38 F.2d at 45; *DeMateos v. Texaco, Inc.*, 562 F.2d 895, 899 (3d Cir.1977). A moving defendant bears the burden of demonstrating all factors in support of *forum non conveniens* dismissal, including the availability of an adequate alternative forum. *Bhatnagar v. Surrendra Overseas Ltd.*, 52 F.3d 1220, 1226 (3d Cir.1995) (affirming denial of a *forum non conveniens* dismissal motion as the defendant "did not make its threshold demonstration that an adequate alternative forum was available for the litigation"); *Lacey II*, 932 F.2d at 180; *Lacey I*, 862 F.2d at 43–44; *Gilbertson v. Hilton Worldwide, Inc.*, No. 12–5124(FLW), 2013 WL 1352146, at *5, 2013 U.S. Dist. Lexis 47654, at *14 (D.N.J. Apr. 2, 2013). A defendant generally may show the adequacy of an alternative forum by establishing that all defendants are amenable to process within its jurisdiction and that the plaintiff may pursue a satisfactory remedy pursuant to its laws. *See Piper*, 454 U.S. 254 n.22; *Bhatnagar*, 52 F.3d at 1227; *Lacey II*, 932 F.2d at 180; *see also Archut v. Ross Univ. Sch. of Veterinary Med.*, Civ. A. No. 10–1681(MLC), 2013 WL 5913675, at *4, 2013 U.S. Dist. Lexis 156024, at *12 (D.N.J. Oct. 30, 2013) (noting two conditions to demonstrate an adequate alternative forum: "(1) the defendant must be amenable to process in the alternative forum; and (2) the subject matter of the lawsuit must be cognizable in the alternative forum in order to provide the plaintiff appropriate redress."), *aff'd*, 580 F.App'x 90 (3d Cir.2014). Once the availability of an adequate alternative forum is demonstrated, the court then balances a number of private and public interest factors to determine whether the plaintiff's chosen forum is unsuitable in comparison to the defendant's proposed alternative. *See Windt*, 529 F.3d at 190; *Lacey II*, 932 F.2d at 180.

The defendant's motion to dismiss the action for *forum non conveniens* failed to meet the threshold requirement of demonstrating the existence of an adequate alternative forum. *See Bhatnagar*, 52 F.3d at 1226. The most basic test of the availability of an alternative forum, as articulated by the Supreme Court of the United States, was whether "the defendant is 'amenable to process' in the other jurisdiction." *Piper*, 454 U.S. at 254 n.22 (quoting *Gulf Oil Corp. v. Gilbert*, 330 U.S. 501, 507 (1947)). The defendant made no assertion that it was amenable to process in India, and thus fails to meet its burden of establishing an alternative forum. *See Lacey II*, 932 F.2d at 180. Indeed, when questioned on this point at oral argument, its counsel made clear that the defendant was neither representing itself as amenable to process there nor willing to consent to such process.

The defendant's contention that Axtria India was "the true party in interest" was not germane to the question of whether the plaintiff's action, currently asserted only against the defendant, a United States corporation, would be better heard in Indian courts. Simply put, the defendant's argument, though conceivably a colorable defense to its direct liability, was unsuited to a motion concerned with venue. For purposes of this motion, the court had top consider the amenability of the named defendant to suit in India, not the amenability of its nonparty subsidiary.

As the defendant failed to demonstrate that an adequate alternative forum existed for this action, the court did not need to weigh the other five factors that the defendant bore the burden to prove. Nevertheless, even had the defendant demonstrated the existence of an adequate alternative forum, the court observed that the defendant would have had a difficult time overcoming the "strong presumption of convenience" granted to a plaintiff's choice of forum, *Windt*, 529 F.3d at 190, particularly as the plaintiff commenced the action in the defendant's home forum, *see id.* at 191; *Tech. Dev. Co.*, 174 F.App'x at 122; *Lony*, 886 F.2d at 634.

For the reasons stated above, this court denied the defendant's motion to dismiss this action on the basis of *forum non conveniens*.

**ANSWER (A)** is incorrect because the court was not convinced that the fact that some events giving rise to the plaintiff's claims might have occurred in India overcame the threshold defect that India was not shown to be an adequate alternative forum. **ANSWER (B)** is incorrect because the court never analyzed the convenience and interests of justice, for the same reason as indicate in **ANSWER (A)**. **ANSWER (C)** is incorrect because the court held the opposite: that the defendant failed to carry its burden to show that India was an adequate alternative forum. **ANSWER (D)** is incorrect because the fact pattern gives no indication of what law would apply, or whether Indiana law was more or less favorable to either of the parties.

### PROBLEM #19. BEST ANSWER (D).

Problem #19 is based on *McCormick v. Maquet Cardiovascular U.S. Sales, LLC*, 2015 WL 6160701 (M.D. Tenn. Oct. 20, 2015). This problem addresses the proper means for enforcing a validly agreed-to forum selection clause. In this case, relying on the Supreme Court's decision in Atlantic Marine, the court denied the defendant's motion to dismiss the case and granted the plaintiff's motion to transfer the case to New Jersey.

The Supreme Court has held that a proper mechanism for enforcing a forum selection clause is 28 U.S.C. § 1404(a). _Atlantic Marine Constr. Co., Inc. v. U.S. Dist. Court for W. Dist. of Tx._, 134 S.Ct. 568, 581 (2013). When the parties have agreed to a valid forum-selection clause, a district court should ordinarily transfer the case to the forum specified in that clause. _Id._ Only under exceptional circumstances unrelated to the convenience of the parties should a Section 1404(a) motion be denied. _Id._

The court has previously found that Rule 12(b)(6) was not a proper mechanism for dismissing a case on improper venue grounds. _Carrillo v. Tifco Indus., Inc._, 2011 WL 4538079 at * 2 (M.D.Tenn. Sept.29, 2011). Although _Carrillo_ was decided before _Atlantic Marine_, nothing in _Atlantic Marine_ changes the Court's opinion as expressed in _Carrillo_. The _Atlantic Marine_ case involved Rule 12(b)(3), and the Court specifically did not address Rule 12(b)(6). _Atlantic Marine_, 134 S.Ct. at 580.

In _Atlantic Marine_, the Court found that a motion to dismiss for improper venue, pursuant to Rule 12(b)(3), was not the correct way to enforce a valid forum-selection clause. The Court found, however, that if the forum-selection clause pointed to a particular federal district, it may be enforced through a motion to transfer under Section 1404(a). _Atlantic Marine_, 134 S.Ct. at 579; _see also ACS Transport Solutions, Inc. v. Nashville Metropolitan Transit Authority_, 2014 WL 3565013 at * 2 (M.D.Tenn. July 18, 2014). Under those circumstances, a proper application of Section 1404(a) requires that a forum-selection clause be given controlling weight in all but the most exceptional cases. _Atlantic Marine_, 134 S.Ct. at 579; _see also Carrillo_. 2011 WL 4538079 at * 3.

By consenting to the forum selection clause, both the plaintiff and the defendant had agreed that New Jersey was a convenient forum. For these reasons, the court, in its discretion, pursuant to 28 U .S.C. § 1404(a) and in the interests of justice, found that the action should be transferred to the U.S. District Court for the District of New Jersey.

**ANSWERS (A), (B),** and **(C)** are each incorrect because after the Supreme Court's decision in _Atlantic Marine_, the proper means for enforcing a forum selection clause is through a transfer to the designated venue, under 28 U.S.C. § 1404(a). **ANSWER (E)** is incorrect because there are no facts in the problem description that would support an argument that the forum selection clause was unconscionable, and none of the litigants raised this issue.

### PROBLEM #20. BEST ANSWER (C).

Problems #20 and #21 are based on _Osage Producers Association v. Jewell_, 2016 WL 80660 (N.D. Okla. Jan. 7, 2016). These two problems involve application of the standards for intervention as of right under Fed.R.Civ.P. 24(a), and permissive intervention under Fed.R.Civ.P. 24(b). In both instances, the district court denied the motions to intervene, finding that the movant

Hayes had failed to satisfy the rule requirements for intervention. The court therefore denied both motions to intervene. (*See* discussion for Problem #21, below).

Rule 24(a)(2) entitles an applicant to intervene as of right if "(1) the application is timely, (2) the applicant claims an interest relating to the property or transaction which is the subject of the action, (3) the applicant's interest may be impaired or impeded, and (4) the applicant's interest is not adequately represented by existing parties." *Elliott Indus. Ltd. P'ship v. BP Am. Prod. Co.*, 407 F.3d 1091, 1103 (10th Cir.2005). This rule, "though speaking of intervention 'of right,' is not a mechanical rule." *San Juan Cty., Utah v. United States*, 503 F.3d 1163, 1199 (10th Cir.2007). Rather, as the Tenth Circuit has explained, "it requires courts to exercise judgment based on the specific circumstances of the case." *Id.*

Here, Hayes claimed an interest in this litigation based on the land "he owns in Osage County and the potential environmental harm that could" occur to his property as a result of this litigation. In particular, he contended that the government's failure to timely approve drilling permits was the result of BIA's efforts to comply with the National Environmental Policy Act, and that a ruling in OPA's favor could cause the government to shirk its duties under the statute. This interest, Hayes contended, was not adequately represented by the government because "the BIA could put up a weak defense to this action" so as to avoid complying with NEPA.

In response, the existing parties submitted that this case was about the government's alleged failure to approve drilling permits and that Hayes has failed to plead facts tying this dispute to the property in which he claimed an interest. In particular, the government contended that this case only concerned portions of the Osage Mineral Estate that were subject to pending permit applications and that Hayes had not shown that his property was so affected. Further, the parties asserted this action could impair Hayes's interest in ensuring NEPA compliance on his land because, regardless of the outcome here, the government must comply with NEPA.

The court agreed with the existing parties. Hayes did not have an interest in the subject of this litigation. This case concerned the government's processing of discrete permit applications, specifically those currently pending before the Superintendent. Hayes did not allege, nor was there any indication in the record, that his property was subject to a pending permit application. Thus, Hayes's claimed interest—ensuring NEPA compliance on this land—was *not* "related to the property or transaction that is the subject of this action." Fed.R.Civ.P. 24(a)(2).

Moreover, even if Hayes's land were implicated in this case, his interest in ensuring NEPA compliance could not be impaired or impeded by the litigation. OPA's complaint merely sought to compel agency action that, it contended, had been unlawfully withheld or unreasonably delayed, namely, the processing of pending drilling permits. Because this claim arose under the APA, the court might, at most, "compel the agency to act, but had no power to specify what the action must be." *Norton v. S. Utah Wilderness All.*, 542 U.S. 55, 64 (2004).

Any agency action ordered in this case, however, would, as a matter of law, had to comply with NEPA. Hayes's suggestion that such an order could cause the government to shirk its duties under the statute was speculative and, thus, insufficient to warrant intervention. *Cf. San Juan Cty.*, 503 F.3d at 1203 (noting that an "intervenor cannot rely on an interest that is wholly remote and speculative" (internal quotation marks omitted)). The government's obligations under NEPA were not a legal issue in this case. Hayes's intervention would only serve to inject legal issues collateral to the dispute between the existing parties. *See New York News, Inc. v. Kheel*, 972 F.2d 482, 486 (2d Cir.1992) (noting that "intervention under Rule 24(a)(2) . . . cannot be used as a means to inject collateral issues into an existing action").

Having determined that Hayes's motion failed on the interest and impairment elements, the court concluded that it did not need to consider whether his application was timely or whether his claimed interest was adequately represented by the existing parties. *See S.E.C. v. Kings Real Estate Inv. Trust*, 222 F.R.D. 660, 667 (D. Kan. 2004) ("All elements must be satisfied before an applicant can intervene as of right under Rule 24(a)(2)."). For these reasons, Hayes's motion to intervene as a matter of right was denied.

**ANSWER (A)** is incorrect because the court did not find that Hayes had a generalized interest in avoiding environment harm sufficient to satisfy the interest requirement of Rule 24(a). Similarly, **ANSWER (B)** is incorrect because the court did not find that Hayes had a property interest sufficient to satisfy the standard for intervention under Rule 24(a). **ANSWER (D)** is incorrect because courts may grant intervention even in cases where the plaintiff and defendants oppose the motion, provided that the movant satisfies the requirements of Rule 24(a). **ANSWER (E)** is incorrect because the court never considered whether the motion was untimely and the problem presents no facts to suggest this was a ground for denying intervention under Rule 24(a).

### PROBLEM #21. BEST ANSWER (C).

Problem #21 is a continuation of Problem #20 and is based on the same facts. This requires analysis of a motion to intervene permissively under Fed.R.Civ.P. 24(b). The court denied this motion as well, concluding that the movant Hayes had no satisfied the requirements for permissive intervention.

Rule 24(b)(1)(B) provides that a "court may permit anyone to intervene who . . . has a claim or defense that shares with the main action a common question of law or fact." "Once the threshold requirement of a common question is met, the decision to allow or deny permissive intervention lies within the discretion of the district court." *Am. Ass'n of People with Disabilities v. Herrera*, 257 F.R.D. 236, 259 (D.N.M. 2008). "In exercising its discretion, the court must consider whether the intervention will unduly delay or prejudice the adjudication of the original parties' rights." Fed.R.Civ.P. 24(b)(3).

Here, Hayes asserted that he "had claims and defenses relating to NEPA that he wished to present in the instant action" and that such "NEPA-related issues were central to the disposition of this" case. The court disagreed. As just discussed, the government's obligations under NEPA were not a legal issue in this case. Based on the claim asserted, the court could, at most, order the government "to take action on pending permit applications, without directing *how* it must act." *S. Utah Wilderness All.*, 542 U.S. at 64 . Any such action would, as a matter of law, have to comply with NEPA. The court could order relief requiring (or permitting) the government to ignore its duties under the statute. Hayes thus had not demonstrated the existence of a question of law or fact common both to the claim or defense he sought to raise and those involved in the present case.

In any event, even if Hayes had made this threshold showing, the court determined that it would deny his motion. Hayes's intervention would inject additional legal issues into this case that, in the court's view, would likely complicate the primary issues between the existing parties and severely delay the litigation. *See Edmondson v. State of Neb. ex rel. Meyer*, 383 F.2d 123, 127 (8th Cir.1967) (noting that such circumstances counsel against intervention). For these reasons, Hayes's request to intervene under Rule 24(b) was denied.

**ANSWER (A)** is incorrect because while the standard for permissive intervention is more liberal than under Rule 24(b), it is not without bounds, and movants must satisfy those standards for the court to grant permissive intervention. **ANSWER (B)** is incorrect for the same reasons. **ANSWER (D)** is incorrect because permissive intervention under Fed.R.Civ.P. 24(b) does not address whether the movant's interests are adequately represented or not; this is a standard for intervention as of right under Rule 24(a). **ANSWER (E)** while plausible, is not the best answer because there is no indication in the fact pattern that the court was going to allow Hayes to appear as an amicus curiae, as an alternative to intervention in the lawsuit.

### PROBLEM #22. BEST ANSWER (A).

Problem #22 is based on *Poehler v. Fenwick*, 2015 WL 7299804 (D. Ariz. Nov. 19, 2015). This problem involves analysis of a federal court's supplemental jurisdiction over permissive counterclaims under 28 U.S.C. § 1367(a). The court held that the counterclaims did not satisfy § 1367(a)'s requirement for one constitutional case, and therefore there was no basis for asserting supplemental jurisdiction over the counterclaims. Therefore the court granted the plaintiff's motion to dismiss the counterclaims.

Under Federal Rule of Civil Procedure 12(b)(1), a party may seek dismissal of an action for lack of subject matter jurisdiction. In order to survive a defendant's motion to dismiss, the plaintiff has the burden of proving jurisdiction. Where the defendant brings a facial attack on the subject matter of the district court, the court assumes the factual allegations in the plaintiff's complaint are true and draws all reasonable inferences in the plaintiff's favor. The court does not, however, accept the truth of legal conclusions cast in the form of factual allegations.

The parties agreed that the defendants' counterclaims were state law claims and were permissive, not compulsory, under Rule 13 of the Federal Rules of Civil Procedure. That is, the defendants conceded that their counterclaims for breach of contract and breach of fiduciary duty did not arise out of the same transaction or occurrence as the plaintiff's wage claims and that there was no independent basis for the court's jurisdiction over such claims. Where there is no independent basis for jurisdiction over a permissive counterclaim, the court may nonetheless exercise supplemental jurisdiction over such claim pursuant to 28 U.S.C. § 1367(a).

Under § 1367(a) the "court shall have supplemental jurisdiction over all other claims that are so related to the federal claims that they form part of the same case or controversy under Article III." Non-federal claims are part of the same case or controversy as federal claims when they "derive from a common nucleus of operative fact." The plaintiff argued that the defendants' counterclaims did not have any relationship to the hours she worked or the wages or overtime compensation she was paid and therefore were not part of the same common nucleus of operative fact. The defendants argued the two sets of claims had the requisite common nucleus because they both stemmed from "alleged monies owed to one another for one another's conduct during employment" and they both required common witnesses.

The court agreed with the plaintiff and concluded that the defendants' counterclaims should be dismissed for lack of subject matter jurisdiction because they did not have a common nucleus of operative fact with the plaintiff's FLSA claim. The allegations in the defendants' counterclaims involved the plaintiff's allegedly wrongful competition with CSS, while the plaintiff's federal wage claims concerned whether the defendants failed to pay overtime and minimum wages as required under FLSA. The two sets of claims clearly did not share a factual basis; that is, they were not "alternative theories of recovery for the same acts." The only connection between the defendants' contract claims and the plaintiff's FLSA claims was the existence of an employment relationship. Indeed, other federal courts considering the issue concluded that the mere existence of an employment relationship between plaintiffs and defendants were insufficient to establish supplemental jurisdiction over the defendants' counterclaims that had nothing to do with the underlying wage claims.

The defendants argued that the court should exercise supplemental jurisdiction in the interest of judicial economy, convenience, and fairness. They stressed that their "only recourse against the plaintiff for her breach of fiduciary duty and breach of contract would be bringing the defendants' counterclaims as a set off or recoupment" because the applicable statute of limitations on their state law claims has run. The defendants' counterclaims were not appropriate for set-off or recoupment in any event because, as admitted by the defendant, their claims did not arise out of the same transaction as the wage claims. *See Unispec Dev. Corp. v. Hardwood K. Smith & Partners*, 124 F.R.D. 211, 214 (D. Ariz. 1988) (noting that "recoupment is a reduction by the defendant of a part of plaintiff's claim because of a right in the defendant arising out of the same transaction.").

As noted by the plaintiff, however, such concerns did not "negate the court's additional obligation to ensure the existence of a common nexus." Moreover, the statute of limitations ran out through no fault of anyone but Defendants.

Even if the employment nexus was sufficient to confer jurisdiction, the court concluded that there were compelling reasons to decline supplemental jurisdiction under § 1367(c)(4) in this FLSA case. Federal FLSA policy presents a compelling reason for the court to refuse to exercise supplemental jurisdiction over the defendants' counterclaims. As noted by the Fifth Circuit, "the only economic feud contemplated by the FLSA involves the employer's obedience to minimum wage and overtime standards. To clutter these proceedings with the minutiae of other employer-employee relationships would be antithetical to the purpose of the Act." *See Brennan v. Heard*, 491 F.2d 1, 4 (5th Cir.1974) *rev'd on other grounds by McLaughlin v. Richland Shoe Co.*, 486 U.S. 128 (1988); *Martin v. Pepsiamericas, Inc.*, 628 F.3d 738 (5th Cir.2010) (affirming *Heard's* longstanding prohibition of set-offs claims in FLSA cases).

Based on the preceding discussion, the plaintiff's motion to dismiss the defendants' counterclaims was granted.

**ANSWER (B)** is incorrect because the court had good federal jurisdiction over the plaintiff's FSLA claim; the question in this case centered on jurisdiction over the defendant's state law counterclaims. **ANSWER (C)** is incorrect because even though the parties agreed that the counterclaims were permissive, the defendant still carried the burden of establishing that they came within supplemental jurisdiction under 28 U.S.C. § 1367(a). **ANSWER (D)** is incorrect because the court found the judicial economy and witness convenience would not be disserved by denying supplemental jurisdiction over the counterclaims. **ANSWER (E)** is incorrect because federal courts do not have automatic supplemental jurisdiction over permissive counterclaims.

**PROBLEM #23. BEST ANSWER (E).**

Problems #23, #24, and #25 are based on *Thorpe Design, Inc. v. Viking Corp.*, 2015 WL 5440792 (N.D. Cal. Sept. 15, 2015). These problems deal with removal jurisdiction, and motions to dismiss pursuant to Fed.R.Civ.P. 12(b)(6) and 12(b)(7).

In the actual case, the defendant's removal was not challenged. However, this problem probes the legitimacy of removal of a state-based claim that names "Doe" defendants who were alleged to be from the same state as the plaintiff. Removal jurisdiction in this case would have been predicated on 28 U.S.C. § 1441(a), which permits removal "of any civil action in a State court of which the district courts of the United States have original jurisdiction." The plaintiff, a California citizen, was diverse from the defendant, a Michigan corporation. The best answer is that removal jurisdiction was valid, because federal courts may ignore "Doe" defendants on removal. 28 U.S.C. § 1441(b)(1)("In determining whether a civil action is removable on the basis of the jurisdiction under section 1332(a) of this title, the citizenship of defendants sues under fictitious names shall be disregarded.").

**ANSWER (A)** is incorrect because the litigation was removed based on diversity jurisdiction and none of the claims in the plaintiff's complaint asserted federal claims. The court had valid diversity jurisdiction over the state-based claims. **ANSWER (B)** is incorrect because there is no information supplied in the fact pattern concerning whether the amount in controversy was satisfied; the problem in this case is the presence of the "Doe" defendants and whether they destroy diversity of citizenship. **ANSWER (C)** is incorrect because there was complete diversity of citizenship between the California plaintiff and the Michigan defendant, because on removal the court ignores the "Doe" defendants. **ANSWER (D)** is incorrect because the facts in this problem do not implicate the court's supplemental jurisdiction on removal; therefore this is a red-herring answer.

**PROBLEM #24. BEST ANSWER (B).**

Problem #24 is a continuation of the fact pattern in Problem #23, and is based on the same court decision. This problem requires the student to assess the sufficiency of a plaintiff's pleading a claim for relief, and whether insufficient pleading justifies a dismissal pursuant to Fed.R.Civ.P. 12(b)(6). In this case the court found the pleading of the product liability claim insufficiently vague and granted the defendant's motion to dismiss.

A complaint will survive a motion to dismiss if it contains "sufficient factual matter . . . to 'state a claim to relief that is plausible on its face.' " *Ashcroft v. Iqbal*, 129 S.Ct. 1937, 1949 (2009) (citing *Bell Atlantic Corp. v. Twombly*, 127 S.Ct. 1955, 1974 (2007)). The reviewing court's "inquiry is limited to the allegations in the complaint, which are accepted as true and construed in the light most favorable to the plaintiff." *Lazy Y Ranch LTD v. Behrens*, 546 F.3d 580, 588 (9th Cir.2008). A court need not, however, accept as true the complaint's "legal conclusions." *Iqbal*, 129 S.Ct. at 1949. "While legal conclusions can provide the framework of a complaint, they must be supported by factual allegations." *Id.* at 1950. Thus, a reviewing court may begin "by identifying pleadings that, because they are no more than conclusions, are not entitled to the assumption of truth." *Id.* Courts must then determine whether the factual allegations in the complaint "plausibly give rise to an entitlement of relief." *Id.* Though the plausibility inquiry "is not akin to a probability requirement," a complaint will not survive a motion to dismiss if its factual allegations "do not permit the court to infer more than the mere possibility of misconduct. . . ." *Id.* at 1949 & 1950. That is to say, plaintiffs must "nudge their claims across the line from conceivable to plausible." *Twombly*, 550 U.S. at 570.

The defendants first argued that the complaint failed to state a product liability or negligence claim because it did not identify which fire sprinkler product, part, component, system or model allegedly failed due to a defect in design or manufacture. To state a claim for products liability against a manufacturer or supplier of a defective product, plaintiff must allege that defendant placed the product on the market in the ordinary course of business, defendant knew the product was to be used without inspection for defects, the product was defective, plaintiff was injured by the product as a proximate result of the defect and plaintiff sustained injuries compensable in money. *See Nelson v. Superior Court*, 144 Cal.App.4th 689, 695 (2006).

The defendants argued that they designed and manufactured a number of different components and parts, and the vague allegations relating to the failure of a "fire sprinkler system" or "fire sprinkler" were insufficient to allow it to determine its applicable defenses. The plaintiff countered that it did not need to identify the specific component or model of the allegedly defective product, and that in any event the defendants had fair notice of the claims against them in light of paragraph 6, which stated: "Approximately five (5) years ago, Plaintiff began purchasing fire sprinkler systems designed, manufactured, and/or supplied by Defendants . . . including the Viking 457." Paragraph 31 of the complaint also mentioned the "Viking 457" but did not provide any explanation as to how or why it was defective.

The court concluded that the plaintiff's complaint was overly vague as to what product is at issue. Though there are two references to the Viking 457, the complaint was not limited to this product and generally referred to fire sprinklers or fire sprinkler systems throughout without any indication as to which portion of the systems were allegedly defective. The court granted the Rule 12(b)(6) motion with respect to these claims.

**ANSWER (A)** is incorrect because there was a legal basis for the plaintiff's claims; the failure here was to properly allege sufficient facts under *Twombly* and *Iqbal* to support assertion of those claims. **ANSWER (C)**, while a correct statement of the Rule 12(b)(6) standard, is not the best answer because the plaintiff's pleading of the claim still failed to satisfy the *Twombly* and *Iqbal* pleading requirements. And, the court granted the defendant's motion and did not deny it. For the same reasons, **ANSWER (D)** is not the best answer. **ANSWER (E)** is incorrect because the court concluded the exact opposite; that the plaintiff had failed to meet the *Twombly* and *Iqbal* pleading standards.

### PROBLEM #25. BEST ANSWER (C).

Problem #25 is a continuation of Problems #23 and #24, and is based on the same fact pattern and court decision. This problem requires the student to analyze whether the defendant is entitled to have the plaintiff's complaint dismissed under Fed.R.Civ.P. 12(b)(7), for failure to join parties needed for a just adjudication—in this case—the unnamed homeowners. The court held that the homeowners could not be named without defeating the court's diversity jurisdiction, and therefore denied the defendant's motion to dismiss under Rule 12(b)(7).

The defendants also moved to dismiss the complaint in its entirety pursuant to Fed.R.Civ.P. 12(b)(7) for failure to join a party under Rule 19. Rule 19 governs whether joinder of an absent party is essential in a particular case, and it requires a court to engage in "three successive inquiries." *EEOC v. Peabody W. Coal Co.,* 400 F.3d 774, 779 (9th Cir.2005). First, the court must determine whether the person or party to be joined is "necessary." *Id.* A party is necessary if (1) "in that person's absence, the court cannot accord complete relief among existing parties" or (2) "that person claims an interest relating to the subject of the action and is so situated that disposing of the action in the person's absence may . . . impair or impede the person's ability to protect the interest; or leave an existing party subject to a substantial risk of incurring double, multiple, or otherwise inconsistent obligations because of the interest." Fed.R.Civ.P. 19(a).

"If an absentee is a necessary party under Rule 19(a), the second stage is for the court to determine whether it is feasible to order that the absentee be joined." *Peabody W. Coal Co.,* 400 F.3d at 779. There are three circumstances in which joinder is not feasible under Rule 19(a): "when venue is improper, when the absentee is not subject to personal jurisdiction, and when joinder would destroy subject matter jurisdiction." *Id.; see also* Fed.R.Civ.P. 19(a). Third, if joinder is not feasible, "the court must determine . . . whether the case can proceed without the absentee, or whether the absentee is an 'indispensable party' such that the action must be dismissed." *Peabody W. Coal Co.,* 400 F.3d at 779. A party is indispensable "if in 'equity and good conscience,' the court should not allow the action to proceed in its absence." *Dawavendewa v. Salt River project Agric. Improvement and Power Dist.,* 276 F.3d 1150, 1161 (9th Cir.2002). In determining whether a party is indispensable, courts must balance the following four factors: "(1) the prejudice to any party or the absent party; (2) whether relief can be shaped to lessen prejudice; (3) whether an adequate remedy, even if not complete, can be awarded without the absent party; and (4) whether there exists an alternative forum." *Dawavendewa,* 276 F.3d at 1161–62; Fed.R.Civ.P. 19.

According to the defendants, the homeowners were necessary parties because there could be a final determination of rights and there was a substantial risk of multiple liability or inconsistent obligations if the homeowners were not joined because they might try to recover overlapping damages from the defendants. Though it was arguable whether the homeowners could be considered "necessary" parties because they might make claims directly against the defendants and disposing of this action without their involvement could potentially expose the defendants to multiple liability, these concerns could be addressed through an offset to any future damages recovered by homeowners in other actions. Further, joining the homeowners in this case was not feasible because it would destroy diversity given that they are alleged to be California homeowners and the plaintiff was a California corporation.

Therefore, the defendants' motion brought pursuant to Rule 12(b)(7) was denied.

**ANSWERS (A)** and **(B)** are incorrect because the court found that the homeowners were necessary parties but that the case could nonetheless proceed without them. **ANSWER (D)** is incorrect because the court never determined that the homeowners were indispensable parties; therefore the court did not rely on Fed.R.Civ.P. 15(b) in making its determination on the ruling. **ANSWER (E)** is incorrect because the court did not base its denial of the defendant's motion on considerations of judicial efficiency and economy.

#### END OF ANSWERS AND EXPLANATIONS TO EXAM #2

# CHAPTER 8
# ANSWER KEY FOR EXAM #3
# ANSWERS AND EXPLANATIONS

## PROBLEM #1. BEST ANSWER (B).

Problem #1 is based on *Kleinfeld v. Rand*, 2015 WL 2091255 (N.Y. Sup. April 30, 2015). This problem involves analysis of general personal jurisdiction under the New York statutes for assertion of personal jurisdiction. The court found that the defendant was not conducting business in New York sufficient to assert general jurisdiction over the defendant, and therefore the court granted the defendant's motion to dismiss.

It is well settled that plaintiff's complaint need not allege that the court has a basis for personal jurisdiction. *Fischbarg v. Doucet*, 9 N.Y.3d 375 (2007). However, when personal jurisdiction is challenged, the plaintiff has the burden of proving a basis of personal jurisdiction. *See, e.g., Arroyo v. Mountain School*, 68 A.D.3d 603 (1st Dept 2009).

The court found that the plaintiff failed to satisfy its burden of establishing a basis for personal jurisdiction over defendant under CPLR § 301. CPLR § 301, which is the codification of the common law concept of general personal jurisdiction, provides that "a court may exercise such jurisdiction over person, property, or status as might have been exercised heretofore." A defendant is subject to general personal jurisdiction in New York when it is "engaged in such a continuous and systematic course of 'doing business' here as to warrant a finding of its 'presence' in this jurisdiction." *McGowan v. Smith*, 52 N.Y.2d 268, 272 (1981). Here, the plaintiff contended that defendant was subject to general jurisdiction in New York as he made numerous visits over the years to BNB bank's offices in Manhattan to obtain financing for his real estate business. The court held that this contention was simply without merit. Making trips to a bank's New York offices was simply not the type of activity that would constitute such a continuous and systematic course of doing business within the state to confer general jurisdiction over the defendant, nor had plaintiff provided the court with any authority to support a finding to the contrary.

Additionally, the court also found that the plaintiff had failed to satisfy its burden of establishing a basis for personal jurisdiction over defendant under CPLR § 302(a)(1). CPLR 302(a)(1) provides in relevant part:

> As to a cause of action arising from any of the acts enumerated in this section, a court may exercise personal jurisdiction over any non-domiciliary, or his executor or administrator, who in person or through an agent:

1.  transacts any business within the state or contracts anywhere
    to supply goods or services in the state

"Whether a non-domiciliary is transacting business within the meaning of CPLR 302(a)(1) is a fact based determination, and requires a finding that the non-domiciliary's activities were purposeful and established 'a substantial relationship between the transaction and the claim asserted.'" *Paterno v. Laser Spine Institute*, 24 N.Y.3d 370, 376 (2014) (quoting *Fischbarg v. Doucet*, 9 N.Y.3d 375, 380 (2007)). "Purposeful activities are volitional acts by which the non-domiciliary 'avails itself of the privilege of conducting activities within the forum State, thus invoking the benefits and protections of its laws.'" *Id.* Indeed, "more than limited contacts are required for purposeful activities sufficient to establish that the non-domiciliary transacted business in New. York." *Id.*

In this case, the plaintiff failed to present facts establishing that the defendant engaged in sufficient purposeful activity in New York in connection with the subject guaranty to constitute transacting business here. The plaintiff asserted that defendant's attendance at two, perhaps three, meetings in New York to negotiate the essential terms of the Note, including defendant's personal guaranty, was sufficient to confer jurisdiction over defendant in this action to recover pursuant to the guaranty. However, the court found that two, maybe three, preliminary meetings in New York where defendant was negotiating the terms of the note, which was for the benefit of the corporate borrowers, was not sufficient to constitute that defendant, in his individual capacity, was transacting business in New York in connection with the subject guaranty. Rather, there was very limited connection between these alleged meetings in New York and the actual guaranty the plaintiff sought to recover under. Indeed, the note and alleged guaranty were both executed in New Jersey, not New York and both defendant and the borrowers were New Jersey residents. Thus, in the instant case, there simply was not a sufficient nexus between the defendant's alleged activities in New York in connection with the guaranty and the present action to confer personal jurisdiction over defendant pursuant to CPLR § 302(a)(1).

Based on the foregoing, the defendant's motion to dismiss for lack of personal jurisdiction was granted.

**ANSWER (A)** is incorrect because the fact pattern does not implicate the Full Faith and Credit Clause of the U.S. Constitution. As such, this is a red-herring answer. **ANSWER (C)** is incorrect because the jurisdictional inquiry is governed by New York's long-arm statute and whether the defendant was conducting systematic and continuous business in New York; the fact that the underlying events involved a loan agreement was not sufficient to confer general jurisdiction. **ANSWER (D)** is incorrect because although the state of New York has an interest in protecting its citizens from loan defaulters, the assertion of person jurisdiction over a non-resident defendant must comport with the requirements of its long-arm statutes. Similarly, **ANSWER (E)** is incorrect because even though banking is a highly regulated industry in New York, the assertion of person jurisdiction over a non-resident defendant must comport with the requirements of its long-arm statutes.

**PROBLEM #2. BEST ANSWER (A).**

Problems #2 and #3 are based on *Mikan v. Arbors at Fairlawn Care, LLC*, 2015 WL 5604666 (N.D. Ohio Sept. 23, 2015). These problems deal with the pleading of claims and defendant's motion to dismiss claims based on Fed.R.Civ.P. 12(b)(6). In Problem #2, the court found that Ohio law did not permit the plaintiff's Count Two because she had pleaded the same facts under her FMLA claim, and so the court granted the defendant's motion to dismiss the claim pursuant to Fed.R.Civ.P. 12(b)(6).

"Dismissal is appropriate when a plaintiff fails to state a claim upon which relief can be granted. Fed.R.Civ.P. 12(b)(6). The court assumes that the factual allegations in the complaint are true and construes the complaint in the light most favorable to the plaintiff." *Comtide Holdings, LLC v. Booth Creek Management Corp.*, 2009 WL 1884445 (6th Cir.July 2, 2009) (citing *Bassett v. Nat'l Collegiate Athletic Ass'n*, 528 F.3d 426, 430 (6th Cir.2008)). The Sixth Circuit explains:

> Federal Rule of Civil Procedure 8(a)(2) requires only 'a short and plain statement of the claim showing that the pleader is entitled to relief.' 'Specific facts are not necessary; the statement need only give the defendant fair notice of what the . . . claim is and the grounds upon which it rests.' *Erickson v. Pardus*, 551 U.S. 89, 93 (2007) (quoting *Bell Atlantic Corp. v. Twombly*, 550 U.S. 544, 555 (2007)). However, 'factual allegations must be enough to raise a right to relief above the speculative level' and to 'state a claim to relief that is plausible on its face.' *Twombly*, 550 U.S. at 555, 570. A plaintiff must 'plead factual content that allows the court to draw the reasonable inference that the defendant is liable for the misconduct alleged.' *Ashcroft v. Iqbal*, 556 U.S. 662, 678 (2009).

*Keys v. Humana, Inc.*, 684 F.3d 605, 608 (6th Cir.2012). The complaint must rise to the level of "plausibility" by containing "more than labels and conclusions;" a "formulaic recitation of the elements of a cause of action will not do." *Twombly*, 550 U.S. at 555, 564. The plausibility standard is not akin to a "probability requirement," but it asks for more than a sheer possibility that a defendant has acted unlawfully. *Iqbal*, 556 U.S. at 678 (2009). "Where a complaint pleads facts that are 'merely consistent with' a defendant's liability, it 'stops short of the line between possibility and plausibility of 'entitlement to relief." *Id.* The plaintiff is not required to include detailed factual allegations, but must provide more than "an unadorned, the-defendant-unlawfully-harmed-me accusation." *Id.* A pleading that offers legal conclusions or a simple recitation of the elements of a cause of action will not meet this pleading standard. *Id.*

With regard to Count Two, the defendant contended that the plaintiff was barred from simultaneously asserting a claim for wrongful discharge and/or punitive damages when she had set forth a claim under the FMLA. The court agreed that dismissal of count two was warranted. Count Two was predicated on the same facts as Count One, the FMLA claim. The plaintiff stated as the sole basis of her claim that she was wrongfully terminated in violation of public policy due to her attempt to exercise her rights under the FMLA. Ohio employment law did not recognize a separate cause of action for wrongful termination in violation of public policy if the statute establishing the policy contained its own remedy. The Ohio Supreme Court stated: "Simply put, there is no need to recognize a common-law action for wrongful discharge if there already exists a statutory remedy that adequately protects society's interests." *Wiles v. Medina Auto Parts*, 96 Ohio St.3d 240, 244, 773 N.E.2d 526 (2002). In *Wiles* the Ohio Supreme Court expressly declined to find a cause of action for wrongful discharge in violation of public policy based solely on an employer's violation of the FMLA. *Id.* at 240, 773 N.E.2d 526.

The court echoed the Sixth Circuit's acknowledgement of the Ohio Supreme Court's *Wiles* decision: "the Court concluded that because 'the statutory remedies in the FMLA adequately protect the public policy embedded in the FMLA,' a case alleging a violation of the FMLA could not establish the requisite elements of a claim of wrongful discharge in violation of public policy." *Morris v. Family Dollar Stores of Ohio, Inc.*, 320 Fed.Appx. 330, 341 (6th Cir.2009). Applying *Wiles* the court joined the Northern and Southern Districts of Ohio to find there was no cause of action in Ohio for wrongful discharge in violation of public policy based upon an alleged violation of the FMLA. *See e.g., James v. Diamond Prods.*, 1:14 CV 1138, 2014 WL 4285665 (N.D. Ohio, Aug. 27, 2014); *Morr v. Kamco Industries, Inc.*, 548 F.Supp.2d 472 (N.D.Ohio 2008); and *Johnson v. Honda of America Mfg., Inc.*, 221 F.Supp.2d 853 (S.D.Ohio 2002). Accordingly, Count Two of the complaint was dismissed.

**ANSWER (B)** is incorrect because whether the plaintiff can plausibly prove Count Two through some set of facts is irrelevant; Ohio law bars the second count, when the FMLA claim provides a remedy for the plaintiff. **ANSWER (C)** is incorrect because the problem is not addressing any challenge to the federal court's jurisdiction over the plaintiff's state law claims, and therefore the suggestion of supplemental jurisdiction is a red herring answer. **ANSWER (D)** is a possible answer, but not the best answer. Although a dismissal would be prejudicial to the plaintiff, she cannot pursue this claim according to Ohio law, because such a claim does not exist when redundant of a claim under a federal statute. **ANSWER (E)** is a possible answer, but not the best answer; although federal courts rarely grant Rule 12(b)(6) motions early in litigation, courts will grant those motions where appropriate under prevailing law (as here).

### PROBLEM #3. BEST ANSWER (C).

Problem #3 is a continuation of Problem #2 and is based on the same facts and court decision. This problem involves application of the Twombly/Iqbal pleading standards to the plaintiff's bare-bones allegation of a claim for emotional distress. The court held that the plaintiff had failed to allege her emotional distress claims sufficiently under Ohio law, and therefore the court granted the defendant's Rule 12(b)(6) motion to dismiss both the claims in Count Three.

Count three of the complaint made a generic claim for "emotional distress" without specifying the "conduct and/or actions" directed at the plaintiff, identifying outrageous behavior, or stating whether the cause was "deliberate, intentional, reckless and/or negligent." Ohio law recognizes two emotional distress torts: intentional infliction of emotional distress and negligent infliction of emotional distress. The plaintiff did not state whether she was claiming negligent or intentional infliction of emotional distress, but made an attempt to cover the elements of both offenses in her pleading. To the extent that the plaintiff stated a claim for negligent infliction of emotional distress, generally "Ohio courts do not recognize a separate tort for negligent infliction of emotional distress in the employment context." *Williams v. York Int'l Corp.*, 63 F.App'x 808, 814 (6th Cir.2003). *See also, Ray v. Libbey Glass, Inc.*, 133 F.Supp.2d 610, 620 (N.D.Ohio 2001). The complaint therefore failed to state a claim for negligent infliction of emotional distress on which relief can be granted.

The Ohio Supreme Court has "characterized" intentional infliction of emotional distress as involving "one who by extreme and outrageous conduct intentionally or recklessly causes serious emotional distress to another." *Hahn v. Star Bank*, 190 F.3d 708, 718 (6th Cir.1999), citing *Yeager v. Local Union 20 Teamsters Chauffers, Warehousemen, and Helpers of America*, 6 Ohio St.3d 369, 453 N.E.2d 666, 671 (Ohio 1983). The Ohio Supreme Court has identified three elements of an intentional infliction of emotional distress claim:

(1)  That the defendant intended to cause the plaintiff serious emotional distress,

(2)  That the defendant's conduct was extreme and outrageous, and

(3)  That the defendants conduct was the proximate cause of the plaintiff's serious emotional distress

Liability can only be found where conduct is 'so outrageous in character, and so extreme in degree, as to go beyond all possible bounds of decency, and to be regarded as atrocious, and utterly intolerable in a civilized community. *Burgess v. Fischer,* 735 F.3d 462, 480 (6th Cir.2013), citing *Phung v. Waste Mgmt., Inc.,* 71 Ohio St.3d 408, 644 N.E.2d 286, 289 (Ohio 1994), and *Yaeger, supra* at 671.

To the extent that the plaintiff made an intentional infliction of emotional distress, she did not plead facts establishing each element of the claim. Instead, what the Plaintiff pled was the exact "formulaic recitation of the elements" that "will not do" under *Twombley* without the factual content necessary to allow "the court to draw the reasonable inference that the defendant is liable for the misconduct alleged." *Iqbal, supra.* at 678. The complaint therefore failed to state a claim for intentional infliction of emotional distress. Accordingly, the Third Count of the complaint was dismissed.

**ANSWERS (A)** and **(B)** are incorrect because the correct answer is (c): both claims for emotional distress were defective under Ohio law and federal pleading standards and both were subject to dismissal (not one or the other). **ANSWER (D)** is incorrect because the court found that the plaintiff had not met the *Twombly/Iqbal* plausibility standard because she merely recited the elements of the claims without sufficient factual information. **ANSWER (E)** is incorrect because the plaintiff simply has failed to plead sufficient facts in her complaint; there was no need to permit her additional discovery, as the facts relating to a claim for intentional infliction of emotional distress were be in the plaintiff's possession and therefore should have been pled.

## PROBLEM #4. BEST ANSWER (B).

Problem #4 is based on *Matysik v. Judd Transportation, LLC*, 2016 WL 559217 (S.D. Ind. Feb, 12, 2016). This problem deals with the standards for seeking a protective order under Fed.R.Civ.P. 26(c), particularly with reference to medical records. The court held that the defendant Larsen had not placed his medical condition in issue and had not waived the physician-patient privilege as to his medical records, and therefore granted the defendant's motion for a protective order to protect these records from production to the plaintiff.

The court previously had held that the subpoenas seeking records relating to Larsen's DOT physical examination were relevant and discoverable. *See, e.g., Crowe v. Booker Transp. Servs., Inc.*, No. 11–690–CV–FJG, 2013 WL 394184, at *2–3 (W.D. Mo. Jan. 30, 2013) (granting motion to compel production of medical records from defendant driver's DOT physical examination); *Jackson v. Wiersema Charter Serv., Inc.*, No. 4:08 CV 27 JCH, 2009 WL 1798389, at *1 (E.D. Mo. June 24, 2009) (stating that "records pertaining to a commercial driver's license medical examination are not within the scope of the physician-patient privilege"); *State ex rel. Hayter v. Griffin*, 785 S.W.2d 590, 595–96 (Mo. Ct. App. 1990) (concluding that an examination which was for purposes of satisfying federal regulations and not for purposes of medical care or treatment was not protected and stating that the "physician-patient privilege extends only to information acquired by the physician for the purposes of prescribing and treatment"). Those courts applied Missouri privilege law, but the same result would obtain under Indiana law. *See Canfield v. Sandock*, 563 N.E.2d 526, 529 (Ind. 1990) (explaining "that the physician-patient privilege has been justified on the basis that its recognition encourages free communications and frank disclosure between patient and physician which, in turn, provide assistance in proper diagnosis and appropriate treatment") (quotation and citation omitted). Because the DOT physical examination was for purposes of meeting federal regulatory requirements and not for purposes of diagnosis and treatment, those examination records would not be protected by the physician-patient privilege.

However, the court held that the privilege extended to Larsen's other medical records. The physician-patient privilege provides that physicians "shall not be required to testify . . . as to matters communicated to them by patients, in the course of their professional business, or advice given in such cases." Ind. Code § 34–36–3–1(2); *see, e.g., Powell v. United Parcel Serv., Inc.*, No. 08–cv–1621–WTL–TAB, 2010 WL 1490029, at *2 (S.D. Ind. Apr. 13, 2010). The "privilege has been justified on the basis that it encourages free communication and frank disclosure between patient and physician and provides assistance in the proper diagnosis and appropriate treatment." *Vargas v. Shepherd*, 903 N.E.2d 1026, 1030 (Ind. Ct. App. 2009). The privilege is not absolute and can be waived. *Id.* If a party "places his mental or physical condition at issue in a lawsuit, he has impliedly waived the physician-patient privilege to that extent." *Id.*

The court found that Larsen had not expressly waived the privilege. Nor had he impliedly waived it. He had not placed his health at issue in the lawsuit. He claimed no personal injury; he had not raised his medical condition or health as a defense. Rather, Matysik was the one who placed Larsen's medical condition at issue by arguing that Larsen suffered from a condition that caused him to fall asleep at the wheel. Because Larsen had not waived the physician-patient privilege protecting his medical records, further inquiry into his medical records, specifically including but not limited to the information sought in the plaintiff's discovery requests, sought discovery of irrelevant and undiscoverable information.

Rule 26(c) of the Federal Rules of Civil Procedure provides that "the court, may for good cause, issue an order to protect a party ... from annoyance, embarrassment, oppression, or undue burden or expense." Fed.R.Civ.P. 26(c)(1). A court may enter an order "forbidding the disclosure of discovery" and "forbidding inquiry into certain matters, or limiting the scope of disclosure or discovery to certain matters. . . ." Fed.R.Civ.P. 26(c)(1)(A), (D).

The defendants had shown good cause for forbidding the plaintiff from further inquiry and discovery into the defendant Larsen's medical records, documents, images, bills, and prescription information. Accordingly, the court granted the defendants' motion for a protective order against discovery into Brett Larsen's medical history.

**ANSWER (A)** is incorrect because the Supreme Court has held that validly pursued discovery requests for medical records where a party places their medical condition in issue does not violate the litigant's privacy rights. **ANSWER (C)** is incorrect because the court found that Larsen had not waived the privilege protecting his other medical records by virtue of the earlier disclosure of his DOT physical examination records. **ANSWER (D)** is incorrect because the court found the opposite: Larsen had not placed his medical condition in issue, but Matysik had. **ANSWER (E)** is incorrect because the plaintiff had not shown good cause for disclosure of Larsen's medical records.

### PROBLEM #5. BEST ANSWER (D).

Problem #5 is based on *Omutiti v. Macy's Dept. Store*, 2015 WL 5311063 (S.D. Tex. Sept. 11, 2015). This problem examines the requirements for federal diversity jurisdiction, on removal, under 28 U.S.C. § 1441(a) 28 U.S.C. § 1331, and 28 U.S.C. § 1332(a), (c). The court held that it has both proper federal question and diversity jurisdiction and therefore denied the plaintiff's motion to remand to state court.

" 'Federal courts are courts of limited jurisdiction.' " *Gunn v. Minton*, 133 S.Ct. 1059, 1064 (2013) (quoting *Kokkonen v. Guardian Life Ins. Co. of Am.*, 511 U.S. 375, 377 (1994)); *Hotze v. Burwell*, 784 F.3d 984, 999 (5th Cir.2015); *Scarlott v. Nissan N. Am., Inc.*, 771 F.3d 883, 887 (5th Cir.2014). " 'They possess only that power authorized by Constitution and statute, which is not to be expanded by judicial decree' " *Gunn*, 133 S.Ct. at 1064 (quoting *Kokkonen*, 511 U.S. at 377). Any state court civil action over which the federal courts would have original jurisdiction may be removed by the defendant to federal court. *See* 28

U.S.C. § 1441(a); *Barker v. Hercules Offshore, Inc.,* 713 F.3d 208, 228 (5th Cir.2013).

District courts have both federal question jurisdiction and diversity jurisdiction. Federal question jurisdiction exists over "all civil actions arising under the Constitution, laws, or treaties of the United States." 28 U.S.C. § 1331. A district court has diversity jurisdiction over "civil actions where the matter in controversy exceeds the sum of $75,000, exclusive of interest and costs, and is between citizens of different States." 28 U.S.C. § 1332(a)(1). For the purposes of diversity jurisdiction, a corporation is a citizen of the state in which it was incorporated and the state in which it has its principal place of business. *See* 28 U.S.C. § 1332(c)(1); *Tewari De-Ox Sys., Inc. v. Mountain States/Rosen, LLC,* 757 F.3d 481, 483 (5th Cir.2014). A corporation's principal place of business is "the place where a corporation's officers direct, control, and coordinate the corporation's activities." *Hertz Corp. v. Friend,* 559 U.S. 77, 92–93 (2010); *Swindol v. Aurora Flight Sciences Corp.,* 2015 WL 5090578, *2 (5th Cir.2015); *see also MetroplexCore, L.L.C. v. Parsons Transp., Inc.,* 743 F.3d 964, 971 (5th Cir.2014).

The removing party bears the burden of establishing both the existence of federal subject-matter jurisdiction and that removal is otherwise proper. *Vantage Drilling Co. v. Hsin-Chi Su,* 741 F.3d 535, 537 (5th Cir.2014). "Jurisdictional facts are determined at the time of removal, and consequently post-removal events do not affect that properly established jurisdiction." *Spear Mktg., Inc. v. BancorpSouth Bank,* 791 F.3d 586, 592 (5th Cir.2015) (quoting *La. v. Am. Nat'l Prop. & Cas. Co.,* 746 F.3d 633, 636 (5th Cir.2014)). If a case is properly removed based on the petition at the time of removal, the federal court retains jurisdiction even if the federal claims are later abandoned by the plaintiff in an amended complaint. *See Spear,* 791 F.3d at 592.

The issue of federal subject matter jurisdiction was resolved based amended petition, which was the live pleading at the time of removal. In the amended petition, Omutiti included a claim based on an alleged violation of the FLSA, a federal statute. As a result, the court had federal question jurisdiction over Omutiti's FLSA claim, and had supplemental jurisdiction pursuant to 28 U.S.C. § 1367(a) over Omutiti's state law claims and over Chemali's claims. The plaintiffs' argument that they inadvertently included the FLSA claim was unavailing. The original petition and the amended petition included the FLSA claim, which was a live claim at the time of removal. The plaintiffs' attempt to dismiss that claim voluntarily post-removal did not affect the court's subject matter jurisdiction. *See id.*

In addition to federal question jurisdiction, the court had diversity jurisdiction over this dispute. It was undisputed that the plaintiffs were citizens of Texas. Macy's presented uncontroverted evidence that it was a New York corporation with its principal place of business in Ohio. The amount in controversy in the amended petition clearly exceeded $75,000.00, exclusive of interest and costs. Omutiti alleged that she was entitled to "at least $250,000.00 for her general and special damages." Chemali stated that she was seeking up to $200,000.00 as compensation for her injuries. Additionally, each plaintiff sought to recover exemplary damages and attorney's fees. Although the plaintiffs attempted to reduce the amount in controversy through the unfiled second amended petition, post-removal amendments do not destroy the court's removal jurisdiction. *See Spear*, 791 F.3d at 592.

The amended petition contained a federal FLSA claim over which the court would had original jurisdiction and over which the court had removal jurisdiction based on the existence of a federal question. Additionally, the amended petition established that there was complete diversity between plaintiffs and the defendant and, at the time of removal, the amount in controversy exceeded $75,000.00, exclusive of interest and costs. This provided the court with original and removal jurisdiction based on complete diversity of citizenship. Because the court had jurisdiction at the time of removal, the plaintiffs' purported second amended petition, attached to the motion for remand, did not affect the court's subject matter jurisdiction. The plaintiff's motion for remand was therefore denied.

**ANSWERS (A)** and **(B)** are incorrect because the court only considered the jurisdictional facts in the original and first amended petitions that existed at the time of removal; the plaintiffs' subsequent changes with regard to the FSLA claim and the amount in controversy were disregarded. **ANSWER (C)** is incorrect because the standard for determining the citizenship of a corporation for diversity jurisdiction is Hertz v. Friend, and the defendant Macy's satisfied the court that it was a citizen of Ohio. **ANSWER (E)** is a red-herring answer: there is no information provided that would allow the conclusion that FSLA claims are within the federal court's removal jurisdiction because these present issues of substantial federal interest for uniform interpretation by federal courts.

## PROBLEM #6. BEST ANSWER (A).

Problem #6 is based on *Jones v. Experian Information Solutions, Inc.*, 2015 WL 4095432 (D. Mass. July 7, 2015). This problem requires the student to apply principles of *res judicata* to determine whether a court should dismiss a plaintiff's lawsuit based on *res judicata*. In this case, the court determined that the facts satisfied the three criteria for application of *res judicata*, and therefore granted the defendant's motion to dismiss.

A Rule 12(b)(6) motion to dismiss challenges a party's complaint for failing to state a claim. In deciding such a motion, a court must " 'accept as true all well-pleaded facts set forth in the complaint and draw all reasonable inferences therefrom in the pleader's favor.' " *Haley v. City of Boston*, 657 F.3d 39, 46 (1st Cir.2011) (quoting *Artuso v. Vertex Pharm., Inc.*, 637 F.3d 1, 5 (1st Cir.2011)). When considering a motion to dismiss, a court "may augment these facts and inferences with data points gleaned from documents incorporated by reference into the complaint, matters of public record, and facts susceptible to judicial notice." *Id.* (citing *In re Colonial Mortg. Bankers Corp.*, 324 F.3d 12, 15 (1st Cir.2003)).

In order to survive a motion to dismiss under Rule 12(b)(6), the plaintiff must provide "enough facts to state a claim to relief that is plausible on its face." *Bell Atl. Corp. v. Twombly,* 550 U.S. 544, 570 (2007). The "obligation to provide the grounds of the plaintiff's entitlement to relief requires more than labels and conclusions, and a formulaic recitation of the elements of a cause of action will not do." *Id.* at 555. The "factual allegations must be enough to raise a right to relief above the speculative level," and to cross "the line from conceivable to plausible." *Id.* at 555, 570.

"A claim has facial plausibility when the plaintiff pleads factual content that allows the court to draw the reasonable inference that the defendant is liable for the misconduct alleged." *Ashcroft v. Iqbal,* 556 U.S. 662, 678 (2009) (citing *Twombly,* 550 U.S. at 556). However, the court is " 'not bound to accept as true a legal conclusion couched as a factual allegation.' " *Id.* (quoting *Twombly,* 550 U.S. at 555). Simply put, the court should assume that well-pleaded facts are genuine and then determine whether such facts state a plausible claim for relief. *See id.* at 679.

"Under the doctrine of *res judicata,* a final judgment on the merits of an action precludes the parties from relitigating claims that were or could have been raised in the prior action." *Haag v. United States,* 589 F.3d 43, 45 (1st Cir.2009) (citing *Gonzalez v. Banco Cent. Corp.,* 27 F.3d 751, 755 (1st Cir.1994)); *In re Colonial Mortg. Bankers Corp.,* 324 F.3d at 16. When analyzing the preclusive effect of a prior adjudication by a Massachusetts state court, a federal court will apply the Massachusetts law of *res judicata. See Atwater v. Chester,* 730 F.3d 58, 63 n. 3 (1st Cir.2013); *Kucharski v. Tribeca Lending Corp.,* 620 F.Supp.2d 147, 150 (D.Mass.2009). "Massachusetts *res judicata* law makes a valid, final judgment conclusive on the parties and their privies, and prevents relitigation of all matters that were or could have been adjudicated in the action." *Atwater,* 730 F.3d at 63 n. 3. In Massachusetts, *res judicata* requires three elements: " '(1) the identity or privity of the parties to the present and prior actions, (2) identity of the cause of action, and (3) prior final judgment on the merits.' " *Andrew Robinson Int'l v. Hartford Fire Ins. Co.,* 547 F.3d 48, 52 (1st Cir.2008) (quoting *Kobrin v. Board of Registration in Med.,* 444 Mass. 837, 832 N.E.2d 628, 634 (Mass.2005)).

In his state court action, Jones sued Bank of New York, challenging the foreclosure sale of his home on the theory that the assignment of his mortgage to Bank of New York was invalid, rendering the foreclosure improper. The Superior Court granted summary judgment for the Bank of New York, concluding that Jones's argument failed as a matter of law. That judgment was affirmed on appeal.

The first element of res judicata is " 'the identity or privity of the parties to the present and prior actions.' " *Andrew Robinson Int'l,* 547 F.3d at 52 (quoting *Kobrin,* 832 N.E.2d at 634). BANA, as the mortgage servicer, was Bank of New York's agent with regard to the mortgage at issue. *See Kogut v. Mortgage Elec. Registration Sys. Inc.,* 2014 WL 61345, at *2 (D.Mass.2014) ("The law is clear that a mortgage servicer acts as the agent of the mortgagee to effect collection of mortgage payments"). " 'Where one party acts for or stands in the place of another in relation to a particular subject matter, those parties are in privity' for purposes of preclusion." *Id.* (quoting *R.G. Fin. Corp. v. Vergara-Nunez,* 446 F.3d 178, 187 (1st Cir.2006)). In fact, courts have held that " 'it will be a rare case in which a mortgagee and mortgage servicer are not perfectly identical with respect to successive suits arising out of a single mortgage transaction.' "

*Id.* (quoting *R.G. Fin. Corp.,* 446 F.3d at 187). In this case, BANA was in privity with the Bank of New York with respect to lawsuits arising out of the mortgage transaction. On these facts, the first element of *res judicata* was met.

The second element of *res judicata* concerns the " 'identity of the cause of action.' " *See Andrew Robinson Int'l,* 547 F.3d at 52 (quoting *Kobrin,* 832 N.E.2d at 634). The proper inquiry for this element is whether "both sets of claims—those asserted in the earlier action and those asserted in the subsequent action—derive from a common nucleus of operative facts." *Haag,* 589 F.3d at 46; *accord Kogut,* 2014 WL 61345, at *2; *Kucharski,* 620 F.Supp.2d at 150–51; *Lynch v. Board of State Examiners of Electricians,* 218 F.Supp.2d 3, 8 (D.Mass.2002). "Put another way, 'as long as the new complaint grows out of the same transaction or series of connected transactions as the old complaint, the causes of action are considered to be identical.' " *Haag,* 589 F.3d at 46 (quoting *Kale v. Combined Ins. Co.,* 924 F.2d 1161, 1166 (1st Cir.1991)). This means that "Massachusetts courts bar the relitigation of any claims which the plaintiff had the full and fair opportunity to litigate in a prior action," even if he did not actually raise them. *Kucharski,* 620 F.Supp.2d at 151; *accord Lynch,* 218 F.Supp.2d at 7–8.

In his amended complaint, the plaintiff based his claims, in part, on the premise that Bank of New York lacked the authority to foreclose, and that the debt he allegedly owed BANA was "nonexistent." His entire claim under the FCRA was based on the premise that the foreclosure was invalid. These claims stemmed from the same nucleus of operative facts that gave rise to his state court complaint—namely, the validity of the assignment of the mortgage to Bank of New York and the validity of the foreclosure. For that reason, to the extent that the plaintiff's claims against BANA were based on Bank of New York's right to enforce the mortgage and the validity of the foreclosure, the second element of *res judicata* was satisfied.

Finally, the state court's decision on the merits of the claim, which was affirmed on appeal, satisfied the requirement for a final judgment on the merits. *See Mani v. United Bank,* 949 N.E.2d 948, at *2 & n. 6 (Mass.App.Ct.2011).

In summary, all elements for *res judicata* were met for the plaintiff's FCRA claim, and also for his other claims against BANA to the extent that they relied on the purported invalidity of the assignment foreclosure. These claims were thus precluded.

For the remainder of the plaintiffs' claims, BANA pointed to the first federal court action. Where a prior adjudication takes place in federal court, a court applies the federal law of *res judicata. See In re Colonial Mortg. Bankers Corp.,* 324 F.3d at 16 (citing *Massachusetts Sch. of Law at Andover, Inc. v. American Bar Ass'n,* 142 F.3d 26, 37 (1st Cir.1998)). The three elements of *res judicata* under federal law are essentially identical to those required under Massachusetts law: "(1) a final judgment on the merits in an earlier suit, (2) sufficient identicality between the causes of action asserted in the earlier and later suits, and (3) sufficient identicality between the parties in the two suits." *Gonzalez v. Banco Cent. Corp.,* 27 F.3d 751, 755 (1st Cir.1994); *accord In re Colonial Mortg. Bankers Corp.,* 324 F.3d at 16.

In his first federal action, the plaintiff sued Bank of New York and BANA, among others, challenging the assignment of the mortgage, the foreclosure sale, and debt collection practices. The district court dismissed Jones's federal claims under theories of collateral estoppel, failure to state a claim, time bar, and lack of jurisdiction. The plaintiff's appeal of this decision to the First Circuit remained pending.

As with the state court action, the current action and the federal action have common parties. In fact, BANA was a named party in the federal action, and so its identity as a party was not based solely on agency principles. Also, there was a final judgment on the merits on the plaintiff's federal claims in the first federal court case. Although Jones appealed the previous decision to the First Circuit, the district court's order dismissing the case was nevertheless a final decision on the merits for purposes of *res judicata. See Washington v. State Street Bank & Trust Co.,* 14 Fed. Appx. 12, 16 (1st Cir.2001); *Hutchins v. Zoli Med. Corp.,* 2007 WL 4986249, at *1 (D.Mass.2007); *see also AVX Corp. v. Cabot Corp.,* 424 F.3d 28, 32 & n. 2 (1st Cir.2005). As a result, two of the elements of *res judicata* were met.

"In considering whether the causes of action in two suits are sufficiently related to support claim preclusion, courts apply a 'transactional approach.'" *Silva v. City of New Bedford,* 660 F.3d 76, 79 (1st Cir.2011) (citing *Massachusetts Sch. of Law at Andover. Inc.,* 142 F.3d at 38). This approach "does not focus on the labels or sources for the plaintiff's causes of action but instead considers whether the underlying factual bases for the causes 'are related in time, space, origin or motivation.'" *Id.* (quoting *Airframe Sys., Inc. v. Raytheon Co.,* 601 F.3d 9, 15 (1st Cir.2010)). "In other words, we will find the required relationship if both sets of claims-those asserted in the earlier action and those asserted in the subsequent action-derive from a common nucleus of operative facts." *Id.*

In his first federal case, the plaintiff brought causes of action against Bank of New York and BANA under the FDCPA, the Real Estate Settlement Procedures Act, the Truth in Lending Act, and state unfair or deceptive practices laws, as well as a claim against BANA alone for violations of the FCRA. The district court found that, to the extent that the plaintiff's FDCPA claim was based on the validity of the assignment and the foreclosure, it was precluded under the doctrine of collateral estoppel because of the state court judgment. The court also dismissed the plaintiff's remaining allegations under the FDCPA, as well as his claims under RESPA, the TILA, and the FCRA, with prejudice, for failure to state a claim. The plaintiff's claims in the second federal lawsuit concerned BANA's debt collection practices, as did his prior claims under the FDCPA and RESPA. As a result, the claims arose out of a "common nucleus of operative facts," meeting the third element of res judicata. *See Silva,* 660 F.3d at 79.

In sum, the plaintiff's claims against BANA were barred under the doctrine of *res judicata*. For that reason, the court recommended that BANA's motion to dismiss be allowed, and that the plaintiff's claims against BANA be dismissed.

**ANSWER (B)** is incorrect because whether a claims are "frivolous" is not a standard for determining whether the doctrine of res judicata applies to require dismissal of a lawsuit. **ANSWER (C)** is incorrect because the court held that the Bank of New York and BANA were parties in privity for the purpose of applying res judicata. **ANSWER (D)** is incorrect because, as indicated above, the fact that Jones's first federal decision was on appeal did not detract from that court's order being a final judgment for the purpose of res judicata. **ANSWER (E)** is incorrect because the court found that all the claims shared a common nucleus of operative facts under its transactional test.

**PROBLEM #7. BEST ANSWER (D).**

Problem #7 is based on *Handy v. Logmein*, 2015 WL 1675445 (E.D. Cal. April 14, 2015). This problem involves application of the standards for imposition of sanctions pursuant to Fed.R.Civ.P. 11. In applying those standards, the court held that the plaintiff had satisfied the requirements of Rule 11, and therefore the defendant's motion for sanctions was denied.

Parties and their counsel have an obligation to file non-frivolous actions pursuant to Rule 11 of the Federal Rules of Civil Procedure, which "is intended to reduce the burden on district courts by sanctioning, and hence deterring, attorneys who submit motions or pleadings which cannot reasonably be supported in law or in fact." *Golden Eagle Distrib. Corp. v. Burroughs Corp.*, 801 F.2d 1531, 1536 (9th Cir.1986); *see also Cooter & Gell v. Hartmarx Corp.* 496 U.S. 384, 393, 110 S.Ct. 2447, 110 L.Ed.2d 359 (1990) ("the central purpose of Rule 11 is to deter baseless filings in District Court"). Specifically, Rule 11 provides:

> By presenting to the court a pleading, written motion, or other paper . . . an attorney or unrepresented party certifies that to the best of the person's knowledge, information, and belief, formed after an inquiry reasonable under the circumstances: (1) it is not being presented for any improper purpose, such as to harass, cause unnecessary delay, or needlessly increase the cost of litigation; (2) the claims, defenses, and other legal contentions are warranted by existing law or by a non-frivolous argument for extending, modifying, or reversing existing law or for establishing new law; (3) the factual contentions have evidentiary support or, if specifically so identified, will likely have evidentiary support after a reasonable opportunity for further investigation or discovery; and (4) the denials of factual contentions are warranted on the evidence or, if specifically so identified, are reasonably based on belief or a lack of information.

Fed.R.Civ.P. 11. The Ninth Circuit explained that "under the plain language of the rule, when one party files a motion for sanctions, the court must determine whether any provisions of subdivision (b) have been violated." *Warren v. Guelker*, 29 F.3d 1386, 1390 (9th Cir.1994). If Rule 11(b) was violated, the court "may" impose sanctions. *Id.* at 1390.

When, as here, the challenged pleading is a complaint, the court "must conduct a two-prong inquiry to determine (1) whether the complaint is legally or factually baseless from an objective perspective, and (2) if the attorney has conducted a reasonable and competent inquiry before signing and filing the complaint." *Holgate v. Baldwin*, 425 F.3d 671, 676 (9th Cir.2005) (quoting *Christian v. Mattel, Inc.*, 286 F.3d 1118, 1127 (9th Cir.2002)). Therefore, the Court may only find a complaint is "frivolous" and in violation of Rule 11 if it is " 'both baseless *and* made without a reasonable and competent inquiry.' " *Id.* (quoting *Moore v. Keegan Mgmt. Co.*, 78 F.3d 421, 434 (9th Cir.1996)). The inquiry requirement was satisfied if there is "*any* factual basis for an allegation." *Brubaker v. City of Richmond*, 943 F.2d 1363, 1377 (4th Cir.1991).

The defendant argued the initial complaint filed by the plaintiff lacked any objective factual basis. According to the defendant, the "Plaintiff's entire theory of liability rested upon the demonstrably false factual allegation that users who purchased the App no longer had access to it without paying an additional subscription fee." The defendant maintained that, contrary to the plaintiff's allegations, "all App users-to this day-still have full access to the App without paying any additional subscription fees." The defendant asserted the subscription fee applied to LogMeIn's separate and distinct premium service, LogMeIn Pro.

In addition, the defendant argued that the plaintiff's counsel failed to make a reasonable inquiry into the relevant facts prior to filing suit. The defendant asserted that it appeared that the plaintiff relied entirely upon a blog posted by LogMeIn on January 21, 2014, which "merely provided notice of upcoming changes to LogMeIn's suite of products, namely LogMeIn Pro, and alerted users to potential future developments, the details of which would be communicated to users in future messages." The defendant contended, "Even the most cursory investigation by Plaintiff at any point in time prior to the filing of the Complaint would have revealed that users could still access the App without paying any additional subscription fees."

Contrary to the defendant's position, the plaintiff's counsel, Matthew Loker, reported that he "spoke extensively with Plaintiff" prior to filing this action, and "Plaintiff informed Loker that Plaintiff was no longer able to use Defendant's App despite paying $29.99 for said App." Loker asserted that he also "conducted research regarding Defendant's App by visiting Defendant's website and reading online forums regarding the App." Loker reviewed the "FAQ about Changes to LogMeIn Free" prepared by the defendant, which stated in relevant part:

**Q:  How do I continue using remote access?**

**A:**  To continue using remote access, you will need to purchase an account-level subscription of LogMeIn Pro that meets your needs based on the number of computers you want to access. Log in at LogMeIn.com to see pricing details and a link to purchase.

**Q: What happens if I do not purchase an account-level subscription of LogMeIn Pro?**

**A:** Once your 7-day grace period is over, you will no longer be able to remotely access your Free-enabled computers. In order to access them, you will need to purchase an account-level subscription of LogMeIn Pro and choose a package that covers all the computers you want to access.

This same document informed users of the Ignition App that, "If you purchased the Ignition app, you will receive a special offer regarding an account-level subscription of LogMeIn Pro," thus implying the need to make an additional purchase. In addition, the plaintiff gave Loker a screenshot after attempting to login to the App which stated:

**You no longer have access to your computers.**

In order to continue using remote access, you'll need to purchase an account subscription of LogMeIn Pro. But you can still take advantage of discounted introductory pricing, with packages starting at **$49/year for two computers.**

Notably, this language was not restricted only to remote access from a non-mobile device and Loker declared that it was provided by Plaintiff as to the Ignition App.

Further, Loker asserted that before filing the original pleading he "found thousands of complaints by consumers on online forums." Loker determined "consumers were . . . quite dissatisfied with the forced migration and the effect it had on their ability to meaningfully utilize the Ignition App." Based upon his review of the websites and the screenshot provided by the plaintiff, Loker concluded the "pre-filing research established a violation of Cal. Bus. & Prof.Code § 17200."

Despite this recitation of investigatory effort, the defendant asserted that the allegations of the plaintiff's complaint appeared to be based only upon a blog post the company published in January 2014. However, as described above, Loker clarified that the facts and theories of the case were not based upon the review of only one post. Further, while the defendant contested the facts presented and the legal conclusions, the information contained on the website, the blog and the screenshot encouraged the belief that the plaintiff and others like him were not going to be able to use the App as they had in the part and would not have remote access to off-site computers. This was sufficient to provide a factual basis for the allegations that the defendant engaged in misleading business practices. *See Brubaker*, 943 F.2d at 1377 ("*any* factual basis for an allegation" will satisfy the requirements of Rule 11); *see also Cal. Architectural Bldg. Prods., Inc. v. Franciscan Ceramics, Inc.*, 818 F.2d 1466, 1472 (9th Cir.1987) (even weak and circumstantial evidence establishes a factual basis sufficient to avoid sanctions under Rule 11). Though the investigation did not yield the determination that, in fact, Ignition users continued to have access to the app, the evidence provided by Plaintiff's counsel demonstrates that the contrary conclusion was formed reasonably.

Consequently, the court did not find the complaint was factually baseless and found Loker conducted a reasonable and competent inquiry into the facts prior to filing the action on behalf of the plaintiff. The record did not establish that this is "one of the 'rare and exceptional' cases that warranted the extraordinary remedy of Rule 11 sanctions." *See Kelter v. Associated Fin. Group*, 382 Fed. App'x 632 (9th Cir.2010) (quoting *Operating Engineers Pension Trust v. A-C Co.*, 859 F.2d 1336, 1344 (9th Cir.1988)). Accordingly, the court ordered that the defendant's motion for sanctions under Rule 11 was denied.

**ANSWER (A)** is incorrect because the attorney Loker did not rely solely on his client's rendition of facts prior to filing his complaint. **ANSWER (B)** is incorrect because the court found that the attorney's investigation of the information online, along with his client's information, was a sufficient investigation under Rule 11 standards. **ANSWER (C)** is incorrect because the facts do not support a conclusion that the complaint was frivolous; based on his reasonable investigation, the attorney concluded there was a violation of the California business code provisions. **ANSWER (E)** is incorrect because the defense attorney did comply with the requirements of Rule 11 in seeking sanctions; this was not the reason the court denied sanctions, however.

PROBLEM #8. BEST ANSWER (E).

Problems #8 and #9 are based on *Cheese Depot, Inc. v. Sirob Imports, Inc.*, 2015 WL 7251949 (N.D. Ill. Nov. 17, 2015). Problem #8 deals with application of venue rules, and a motion to dismiss for improper venue under Fed.R.Civ.P. 12(b)(3), to a set of facts. In this instance the court held that venue was proper in the federal district court for the Northern District of Illinois because the events giving rise to contract formation and execution occurred in Chicago. Therefore, the court denied the defendant's motion to dismiss for improper venue,

In its motion to dismiss, Sirob argued that Illinois was not the proper venue for Cheese Depot's action. Although Sirob did not cite the rule in its motion to dismiss, Federal Rule of Civil Procedure 12(b)(3) governs dismissal for improper venue. In deciding a motion to dismiss for improper venue under Federal Rule of Civil Procedure 12(b)(3), all allegations are taken as true, unless contradicted by the defendant's affidavits, and the court may consider facts outside the pleadings. *See Faulkenberg v. CB Tax Franchise Sys., LP*, 637 F.3d 801, 806 (7th Cir.2011). Courts must resolve any conflicts in the affidavits regarding relevant facts in the plaintiff's favor. *Allstate Life Insurance Company v. Stanley W. Burns, Inc.*, 80 F.Supp.3d 870, 875 (N.D. Ill. 2015), *citing Purdue Research Found. v. Sanofi-Synthelabo, S.A.*, 338 F.3d 773, 782 (7th Cir.2003). The Seventh Circuit has cautioned that "once the defendant has submitted affidavits or other evidence in opposition to the exercise of jurisdiction, the plaintiff must go beyond the pleadings and submit affirmative evidence supporting the exercise of jurisdiction." *Purdue Research Found.*, 338F.3d at 783. When a defendant challenges venue, the plaintiff bears the burden of establishing proper venue. *Nat'l Tech v. Repcentric Solutions*, 2013 WL 3755052. at *5 (N.D. Ill. June 16, 2013). Cheese Depot had already met this burden.

In response to Sirob's original motion to dismiss, the court decided that Cheese Depot's argument that the Chicago agreement reflected the parties' intent to transfer the land to Sirob and that the Romanian agreement merely set forth when Sirob's payment obligations would begin was plausible. Therefore, Cheese Depot stated a colorable breach of contract claim. Further, because it was asserted that the Chicago agreement was negotiated in Chicago, executed in Chicago, and that payments were sent to Chicago, a "substantial part of the events or omissions giving rise to the claim" occurred in Chicago. *See Imperial Crane Servs., Inc. v. Cloverdale Equp. Co.*, 2013 WL 5904527, at *3 (courts will consider whether there was a failure to make a payment in a district pursuant to a contract); *MB Fin. Bank, N.A. v. Walker*, 741 F.Supp.2d 912, 917 (N.D. Ill. 2010) (courts will also consider where the contract was negotiated or executed).

The arguments presented in Sirob's motion to dismiss Cheese Depot's amended complaint, especially those concerning improper venue, closely mirrored the arguments in its motion to dismiss Cheese Depot's original complaint. Therefore, the court still found that Cheese Depot had stated a colorable breach of contract claim as Cheese Depot has adequately pled that a substantial part of the events giving rise to the claim occurred in Chicago. As a result, Sirob's motion to dismiss based on improper venue was denied.

**ANSWERS (A)** and **(B)** are incorrect because the court found that venue was proper in Illinois as the events giving rise to the plaintiff's claims arose in Chicago. The fact that the property and inventory was located in Romania did not affect the court's analysis. **ANSWER (C)** is incorrect because the court did not find that the Romanian agreement governed the litigation. **ANSWER (D)** is a red-herring answer; there are no facts to ascertain whether Illinois could or could not assert personal jurisdiction over the non-resident defendants.

## PROBLEM #9. BEST ANSWER (B).

Problem #9 is a continuation of the same facts as in Problem #8, and is based on the same case. Problem #9 addresses the issue of consolidation of motions under Fed.R.Civ.P. 12. The court held that a Rule 12(b)(6) motion can be presented at any time, and therefore the defendant's failure to raise and consolidate this motion with its previous motion to dismiss for improper venue was not fatal. On the merits, the court granted the defendant's Rule 12(b)(6) motion, holding that "Cheese Factory" was an improper party, and therefore the litigation could not proceed against this misnamed entity.

Sirob also sought to dismiss Cheese Depot's amended complaint pursuant to Rule 12(b)(6). To survive a motion to dismiss pursuant to Rule 12(b)(6), a complaint must "state a claim to relief that is plausible on its face." *Ashcroft v. Iqbal*, 556 U.S. 662, 678 (2009), *citing Bell Atl. Corp. v. Twombly*, 550 U.S. 544, 570 (2007). A claims satisfies this pleading standard when its factual allegations "raise a right to relief above the speculative level." *Twombly*, 550 U.S. at 555–56. For the purposes of a motion to dismiss, the court takes all facts alleged by the plaintiff as true and draws all reasonable inferences from those facts in the plaintiff's favor, although conclusory allegations that merely recite the elements of a claim are not entitled to this presumption of truth. *Virnich v. Vorwald*, 664 F.3d 206, 212 (7th Cir.2011).

In its motion to dismiss, Sirob argued that Cheese Depot was not the proper party to enforce the Chicago agreement. Sirob argued that the Chicago agreement was entered into by Nick Boboris and Nick Livaditis on behalf of an entity called "Cheese Factory." Cheese Depot argued that Federal Rule of Civil Procedure 12(g) bars Sirob from presenting this defense as Sirob failed to raise it in its original motion to dismiss.

Rule 12(g) bars a party from raising a defense or objection that was available to the party but omitted from its earlier motion. Fed.R.Civ.P. 12(g)(2). Cheese Depot argues that, because Sirob never raised the argument that Cheese Depot is an improper plaintiff in its original motion to dismiss, it is barred from doing so now pursuant to Rule 12(g)(2), as applied in *Muller v. Morgan*, 2013 WL 2422737 at *2 (N.D. Ill. June 3, 2013) and *Makor Issues & Rights, Ltd. v. Tellabs, Inc.*, 2008 WL 2178150 (N.D. Ill. May 22, 2008). However, Cheese Depot's reading of *Makor Issues & Rights, Ltd.* was inconsistent with the ruling in *Ennenga v. Starns*, 677 F.3d 766, 772–73 (7th Cir.2012). In *Ennenga*, the court ruled that Rule 12(h)(2) specifically excepts failure-to-state-a-claim defenses from the Rule 12(g) consolidation requirement. Therefore, Sirob is well within its right to assert that Cheese Depot has failed to state a claim because it is not the proper plaintiff.

Although Cheese Depot argues that "Cheese Factory" was a misnomer in its response to Sirob's motion to dismiss, it failed to allege as much in its amended complaint. Therefore, Sirob's motion to dismiss was granted on this basis. *Car Carriers, Inc. v. Ford Motor Co.*, 745 F.2d 1101, 1107 (7th Cir.1984) ("The court notes that it will not consider allegations made by plaintiff in its brief that do not appear in the complaint, as 'it is axiomatic that the complaint may not be amended by briefs in opposition to a motion to dismiss.' ").

**ANSWER (A)** is incorrect because the court did not base its decision to grant the defendant's motion on the plaintiff's failure to meet Twombly and Iqbal standards; on the merits, the court simply concluded that the plaintiff had failed to name the proper party. **ANSWER (C)** is incorrect because the defendant was not required to consolidate its Rule 12(b)(6) motion with its pervious Rule 12(b)(3) motion to dismiss for improper venue. **ANSWER (D)** is incorrect because a Rule 12(b)(6) motion is the proper procedural means for challenging an improperly named party. **ANSWER (E)** is incorrect because the Supreme Court has held that validly enforced Rule 12(b)(6) motions to dismiss do not violate a party's Seventh Amendment right to trial by jury.

**PROBLEM #10. BEST ANSWER (A).**

Problem #10 is based on *McLin v. Chiles*, 2016 WL208322 (S.D. Miss. Jan. 15, 2016). This problem requires the student to analyze a motion for summary judgment under Fed.R.Civ.P. 56, and the non-moving party's request for additional discovery under Fed.R.Civ.P. 56(d). The court granted the defendant's motion for summary judgment and in its discretion denied McLin, the non-moving party, additional discovery under Fed.R.Civ.P. 56(d).

Summary judgment is warranted under Rule 56(a) of the Federal Rules of Civil Procedure when evidence reveals no genuine dispute regarding any material fact and that the moving party is entitled to judgment as a matter of law. The rule "mandates the entry of summary judgment, after adequate time for discovery and upon motion, against a party who fails to make a showing sufficient to establish the existence of an element essential to that party's case, and on which that party will bear the burden of proof at trial." *Celotex Corp. v. Catrett*, 477 U.S. 317, 322 (1986).

The party moving for summary judgment "bears the initial responsibility of informing the district court of the basis for its motion, and identifying those portions of the record which it believes demonstrate the absence of a genuine issue of material fact." *Id.* at 323. The nonmoving party must then "go beyond the pleadings" and "designate 'specific facts showing that there is a genuine issue for trial.' " *Id.* at 324. In reviewing the evidence, factual controversies are to be resolved in favor of the non-movant, "but only when . . . both parties have submitted evidence of contradictory facts." *Little v. Liquid Air Corp.*, 37 F.3d 1069, 1075 (5th Cir.1994). When such contradictory facts exist, the court may "not make credibility determinations or weigh the evidence." *Reeves v. Sanderson Plumbing Prods., Inc.*, 530 U.S. 133, 150 (2000). Conclusory allegations, speculation, unsubstantiated assertions, and legalistic arguments have never constituted an adequate substitute for specific facts showing a genuine issue for trial. *TIG Ins. Co. v. Sedgwick James of Wash.*, 276 F.3d 754, 759 (5th Cir.2002); *Little*, 37 F.3d at 1075; *SEC v. Recile*, 10 F.3d 1093, 1097 (5th Cir.1993).

Title VII of the Civil Rights Act of 1964 prohibits discrimination based on gender. 42 U.S.C. § 2000e *et seq.* Generally speaking, plaintiffs seeking recovery under a failure-to-promote claim must "demonstrate that (1) she is a member of a protected class; (2) she sought and was qualified for an available employment position; (3) she was rejected for that position; and (4) the employer continued to seek applicants with the plaintiff's qualifications." *Scales v. Slater*, 181 F.3d 703, 709 (5th Cir.1999). Significantly, "failure to apply for a disputed promotion will bar a 'failure to promote' claim absent a showing that such an application would have been a futile gesture." *Irons v. Aircraft Serv. Int'l*, 392 Fed.Appx. 305, 312 (5th Cir.2010).

In the present case, McLin originally contended that JSU did not post the position of the Director of Clinical Training Ph.D. program before selecting Dr. Williams. On that basis the court allowed the claim to survive JSU's motion to dismiss. But JSU subsequently submitted competent record evidence that it did advertise the position, McLin was aware of it, and she did not apply.

McLin essentially conceded these facts in her response and supporting affidavit. *See also* Fed.R.Civ.P. 56(g) ("If a party . . . fails to properly address another party's assertion of fact . . . the court may . . . consider the fact undisputed for purposes of the motion."). But she raised two arguments to avoid summary judgment. First, she contended that she did not apply for the disputed position because it would have been futile. Second, she sought additional discovery. The court held that these arguments were somewhat related, and neither was sufficient to survive summary judgment.

The Fifth Circuit has stated that a plaintiff need not prove she applied for the position if doing so would have been a "futile gesture." *Irons*, 392 Fed.Appx. at

312. Here, McLin contended that she was deterred from applying based on JSU's history of systemically denying employment opportunities to women. The problem was that McLin never pleaded a futility case.

In her original *and* amended complaints, McLin premised this claim on the assertion that JSU never posted the disputed position. Faced with evidence to the contrary in JSU's summary-judgment motion, McLin pivoted to the futility claim. The two theories were not compatible.

As a general rule, "a claim which is not raised in the complaint, but, rather, is raised only in response to a motion for summary judgment is not properly before the court." *Cutrera v. Bd. of Supervisors of La. State Univ.*, 429 F.3d 108, 113 (5th Cir.2005). This rule is rooted in the need to provide adequate notice. As stated in *De Franceschi v. BAC Home Loans Servicing, L.P.*, "a properly pleaded complaint must give 'fair notice of what the claim is *and the grounds upon which it rests*.'" 477 Fed.Appx. 200, 204 (5th Cir.2012) (quoting *Ashcroft v. Iqbal*, 556 U.S. 662, 698–99 (2009)).

"Accordingly, district courts do not abuse their discretion when they disregard claims or theories of liability not present in the complaint and raised first in a motion opposing summary judgment." *Id.* This rule encompasses new factual theories supporting previously pleaded legal theories. *See, e.g., id.; see also Green v. JP Morgan Chase Bank, N.A.*, 562 Fed.Appx. 238, 240 (5th Cir.2014) (affirming refusal to consider new factual theory); *Benavides v. EMC Mortg. Corp.*, Civil Action No. 3–12–46, 2013 WL 416195, at \*4 (S.D. Tex. Jan. 31, 2013) (refusing to consider new factual theory supporting previously pleaded legal cause of action). Therefore, the court concluded that McLin's futility claim was not properly before the Court.

McLin essentially conceded the substance of JSU's motion, but contended that "if allowed to conduct discovery, she could establish a prima facie case." (invoking Rule 56(d)). The court denied this request on procedural and substantive grounds. To begin, the court found that McLin's request failed to comply with Rule 56(d)'s requirement that the movant support the need for discovery with "affidavit or declaration." Fed.R.Civ.P. 56(d).

The court might have afforded an opportunity to remedy those procedural issues had the request otherwise met Rule 56(d)'s substantive provisions. The decision to grant or deny a Rule 56(d) motion is within the sound discretion of the court. *Am. Family Life Assurance Co. of Columbus v. Biles*, 714 F.3d 887, 895 (5th Cir.2013). Under that rule, the Court to defer considering a summary-judgment motion or deny it when a non-movant "shows . . . that, for *specified reasons*, it cannot present facts essential to justify its opposition" to the motion. Fed.R.Civ.P. 56(d).

Although Rule 56(d) carries a policy favoring discovery, a party invoking the rule "may not simply rely on vague assertions that additional discovery will produce needed, but unspecified, facts." *Id.* (quoting *Raby v. Livingston*, 600 F.3d 552, 561 (5th Cir.2010)). "Instead, the non-moving party must 'set forth a plausible basis for believing that specified facts, susceptible of collection within a reasonable time frame, probably exist and indicate how the emergent facts, if adduced, will influence the outcome of the pending summary judgment motion.' " *Id.* (quoting *Raby*, 600 F.3d at 561); *see also Leatherman v. Tarrant Cnty. Narcotics Intelligence & Coordination Unit*, 28 F.3d 1388, 1396 (5th Cir.1994) (holding that "opposing party must demonstrate how the additional time will enable him to rebut the movant's allegations of no genuine issue of material fact"); *Washington v. Allstate Ins. Co.*, 901 F.2d 1281, 1285 (5th Cir.1990) (affirming denial of Rule 56(d) motion and noting that "non-movant may not simply rely on vague assertions that discovery will produce needed, but unspecified, facts"); *Fontenot v. Upjohn Co.*, 780 F.2d 1190, 1194 (5th Cir.1986) (same).

Here, McLin merely cited the rule and applicable cases without explaining the discovery she sought or how it would create a genuine fact issue. At most, McLin asserted that she "should be allowed to conduct discovery and complete the presentation of her case against JSU's motion for summary judgment." General statements of this nature are not sufficient. Moreover, her substantive response to JSU focused on the new futility argument which was not properly before the Court and would not warrant additional discovery. *See generally Cutrera*, 429 F.3d at 113.

For the reasons stated, the court held that defendant Jackson State University's motion for summary judgment should be granted.

**ANSWER (B)** is incorrect because the court did not make a determination in the merits that the plaintiff McLin's gender discrimination claim was frivolous. **ANSWER (C)** is incorrect because the court found that the plaintiff failed to carry her burden of demonstrating that there was a genuine issue of material fact relating to her claim of gender discrimination. Likewise, **ANSWER (D)** is incorrect because the court determined that the plaintiff McLin had failed to carry her burden alleging facts to show futility as a matter of law. **ANSWER (E)** is incorrect because the court, in its discretion, denied the plaintiff additional discovery under Fed.R.Civ.P. 56(d), for he reasons stated above.

### PROBLEM #11. BEST ANSWER (D).

Problem #11 is based on *Tolliver v. City of New Roads*, 2015 WL 5138258 (M.D. La. Aug. 28, 2015). This problem requires analysis of supplemental jurisdiction under 28 U.S.C. § 1367, in a removed case that embraces both federal and state law claims. The court denied the plaintiff's motion to remand the case in whole or to sever the state claims.

A defendant may remove "any civil action brought in a State court of which the district courts of the United States have original jurisdiction." 28 U.S.C. § 1441(a). This court has original subject matter jurisdiction "of all civil actions arising under the Constitution, laws, or treaties of the United States." 28 U.S.C. § 1331. "In any civil action of which the district courts have original jurisdiction, the district courts shall have supplemental jurisdiction over all other claims that are so related to claims in the action within such original jurisdiction that they form part of the same case or controversy under Article III of the United States Constitution." 28 U.S.C. § 1367(a). A district court may decline to exercise supplemental jurisdiction over a claim if "(1) the claim raises a novel or complex issue of State law, (2) the claim substantially predominates over the claim or claims over which the district court has original jurisdiction, (3) the district court has dismissed all claims over which it has original jurisdiction, or (4) in exceptional circumstances, there are other compelling reasons for declining jurisdiction." 28 U.S.C.A. § 1367(c).

As a preliminary matter, there was no dispute that this action was properly removed in light of the plaintiff s allegations pursuant to 42 U.S.C. § 1983, which provides the court with subject matter jurisdiction under 28 U.S.C. § 1331. Furthermore, there was no dispute that the court may exercise supplemental jurisdiction over the asserted state law claims pursuant to 28 U.S.C.A. § 1367. Accordingly, the only issue was whether the court should, in its discretion, exercise supplemental jurisdiction over the state law claims.

The plaintiff had not sought voluntary dismissal of his Section 1983 claim. Accordingly, this was not an action in which the federal court had to decide whether to exercise supplemental jurisdiction over a state law claim after all federal claims have been dismissed. Where federal claims are dismissed at the infancy of an action, a district court may abuse its discretion when it does not reconsider its supplemental jurisdiction over the remaining state law claims. *See Enochs v. Lampasas County,* 641 F.3d 155, 159 (5th Cir.2011) (district court abused its discretion in not remanding state law claims after federal claims were voluntarily amended away); *see also Savoy v. Pointe Coupee Parish Police Jury,* No. 15–128, 2015 WL 3773418, at *4 (M.D. La. June 16, 2015) (holding that, after voluntary dismissal of Section 1983 claim early in litigation, several factors—judicial economy, convenience, fairness, and comity—all weighed in favor of remanding the remaining claim pursuant to the Louisiana Whistleblower Statute).

Moreover, the plaintiff had not argued that his claims made pursuant to Louisiana law raised any novel or complex issues of state law or substantially predominated over the Section 1983 claims.

The plaintiff appeared to request the court to remand his state law claims on the basis that Louisiana courts and procedural law provided expedited adjudication of LWPA and PONR claims in Louisiana courts. The plaintiff went so far as to argue that requiring him to litigate these claims in federal court would violate his rights under the Louisiana Constitution.

The court concluded, however, that nothing prevented the plaintiff from seeking expedited adjudication of his claims in the federal court. Furthermore, the plaintiff provided no analysis of why the court's discretionary exercise of supplemental jurisdiction over his claims would result in a violation of Louisiana law.

Finally, it was appropriate for the court to exercise supplemental jurisdiction over the plaintiff's state law claims. The state law claims were so related to the federal claims for which the court has original jurisdiction that they "form part of the same case or controversy under Article III of the United States Constitution." *See* 28 U.S.C. § 1367(a). Furthermore, none of the statutory provisions for declining to exercise supplemental jurisdiction were applicable. *See* 28 U.S.C. § 1367(c).

There was no dispute that the court had original subject matter jurisdiction over the plaintiff s claims pursuant to 28 U.S.C. § 1441, and could exercise supplemental jurisdiction over the plaintiff's state law claims pursuant to 28 U.S.C. § 1367. If the plaintiff's federal claims were dismissed, either voluntarily or involuntarily, the court could reconsider whether to retain supplemental jurisdiction over any remaining state law claims.

**ANSWER (A)** is incorrect because the court determined that none of the statutory provisions for declining supplemental jurisdiction over the state claims were applicable, including that most of the claims were state claims. **ANSWER (B)** is incorrect because the court made no finding of exceptional circumstances under 28 U.S.C. § 1367(c) that warranted remand to state court. **ANSWER (C)** is incorrect because the court found no basis for retaining the federal claims and severing the state claims. **ANSWER (E)** is incorrect because the fact that the case included two federal questions was not the basis for the court retaining supplemental jurisdiction over the state claims, and for denying the motion to remand.

### PROBLEM #12. BEST ANSWER (C).

Problem #12 is based on *Northeast Landscape & Masonry Associates, Inc. v. State of Connecticut Department of Labor*, 2015 WL 8492755 (Dec. 10, 2015). This problem involves analysis of the proper venue in federal court under 28 U.S.C. § 1391, and a motion to dismiss for improper venue pursuant to Fed.R.Civ.P. 12(b)(3). The court held that venue was improper in the Southern District of New York, but ordered a transfer of venue to the District of Connecticut under 28 U.S.C. § 1406(a).

On a motion to dismiss a complaint under Rule 12(b)(3) for improper venue, "the plaintiff bears the burden of establishing that venue is proper." *Fedele v. Harris*, 18 F.Supp. 3d 309, 316 (E.D.N.Y. 2014); *see also Solow Bldg. Co. v. ATC Assocs., Inc.*, 175 F.Supp. 2d 465, 469 (E.D.N.Y. 2001) (same). "A court applies the same standard of review in Rule 12(b)(3) dismissals as Rule 12(b)(2) dismissals for lack of personal jurisdiction." *Fedele*, 18 F.Supp. 3d at 316 (citing *Gulf Ins. Co. v. Glasbrenner*, 417 F.3d 353, 355 (2d Cir.2005)). In analyzing a claim of improper venue, the court must view all facts in the light most favorable to the plaintiff. *Phillips v. Audio Active Ltd.*, 494 F.3d 378, 384 (2d Cir.2007). Thus, a "court must accept the facts alleged in the complaint and construe all reasonable inferences in the plaintiff's favor." *Matera v. Native Eyewear, Inc.*, 355 F.Supp. 2d 680, 681 (E.D.N.Y. 2005).

The permissible venue in this action was determined by the general venue provision for cases involving a federal question. *See* 28 U.S.C. § 1391(b). Under that statute, venue can be laid "in either (1) the district of the defendant's residence; (2) the district where 'a substantial part of the events giving rise to the claim occurred'; or (3) if neither of those can be applied, any district where a defendant is subject to personal jurisdiction." *Cooney v. Barry Sch. of Law*, 994 F.Supp. 2d 268, 271 (E.D.N.Y. 2014) (citing 28 U.S.C. § 1391(b)). "When a plaintiff relies on § 1391(b)(2) to defeat a venue challenge," a district court must engage in a two-step inquiry: first, "identify the nature of the claims and the alleged acts or omissions giving rise to the claims," and second, "determine whether a substantial part of the acts or omissions occurred in the district where the suit was filed." *Fedele*, 18 F.Supp. 3d at 316 (citing *Daniel v. Am. Bd. of Emergency Med.*, 428 F.3d 408, 432 (2d Cir.2005)). For venue to be proper under § 1391(b)(2), "*significant* events or omissions *material* to the plaintiff's claim must have occurred in the district in question, even if other material events occurred elsewhere." *Gulf Ins.*, 417 F.3d at 357; *see also Cottman Transmission Sys., Inc. v. Martino*, 36 F.3d 291, 294 (3d Cir.1994) (noting that "the current statutory language still favors the defendant in a venue dispute by requiring that the events or omissions supporting a claim be 'substantial' ").

"Substantiality for venue purposes is more a qualitative than a quantitative inquiry, determined by assessing the overall nature of the plaintiff's claims and the nature of the specific events or omissions in the forum, and not by simply adding up the number of contacts." *Daniel*, 428 F.3d at 432–33. Courts "are required to construe the venue statute strictly." *Gulf Ins.*, 417 F.3d at 357 (citing *Olberding v. Ill. Cent. R.R.*, 346 U.S. 338, 340 (1953)). Thus, "it would be error . . . to treat the venue statute's 'substantial part' test as mirroring the minimum contacts test employed in personal jurisdiction inquiries." *Id.* Rather, "only the events that directly give rise to a claim are relevant." *Fedele*, 18 F.Supp. 3d at 317 (quoting *Jenkins Brick, Co. v. Brenner*, 321 F.3d 1366, 1371 (11th Cir.2003)). Certainly, "venue can be proper in more than one district; that is, venue is not restricted to the district with the 'most substantial' connection to the events or omissions related to a claim." *See Prospect Capital*, 2009 WL 4907121, at *3 (citing *Daniel*, 428 F.3d at 432). However, the "substantial events or omissions" test limits proper venue in order "to protect the *defendant* against the risk that a plaintiff will select an unfair or inconvenient place of trial." *Id.* (quoting *Daniel*, 428 F.3d at 432).

Where venue is improper, a court "shall dismiss, or if it be in the interest of justice, transfer such case to any district or division in which it could have been brought." *Fedele*, 18 F.Supp. 3d at 319 (internal quotation marks omitted); *see also Daniel*, 428 F.3d at 435 (noting that a court must decide whether to "simply affirm dismissal on these improper venue grounds or, in the interest of justice, order transfer of the action to another district where jurisdiction and venue properly obtain"). Under 28 U.S.C. § 1406(a), a court has the discretion to cure a venue defect "in the interest of justice" by transferring case "to any district or division in which it could have been brought."

In this action, the defendants argued for dismissal pursuant to Federal Rule 12(b)(3) on the basis that "none of the requirements for venue in 28 U.S.C. § 1391 were met here." Specifically, the defendants emphasized that "the prevailing wage investigation and withholding of funds related thereto arose out of projects in Danbury, Connecticut," such that "the entirety of the property subject to this action, the funds withheld was located in the District of Connecticut." The plaintiff, on the other hand, asserted that venue was proper in the Southern District of New York under the provisions of § 1391(b)(2) because the "Plaintiff kept time and payroll records in the State of New York and those record keeping practices and the information contained in the Plaintiff's records were the root of this controversy." As noted above, the plaintiff bore the burden of showing that a substantial part of the events giving rise to its claims occurred in the Southern District of New York, *see Fedele*, 18 F.Supp.3d at 316, but the court "must accept the facts alleged in the complaint" as true, *Matera*, 355 F.Supp. 2d at 681. Following these guiding principles and analyzing the complaint under the two-part test discussed above, *see Fedele*, 18 F.Supp. 3d at 316, the court concluded the alleged facts were insufficient under § 1391(b)(2) to afford venue in the Southern District of New York.

The court's first task was to identify the nature of the plaintiff's claims and the alleged acts or omissions giving rise to those claims. *See Fedele*, 18 F.Supp. 2d at 316. Here, the relevant claim was the cause of action for a constitutional violation based on the defendants' prevailing wage investigation and related withholding of funds. According to the complaint, the acts constituting the alleged constitutional violation were the defendants' ongoing investigation and their withholding "from Plaintiff, funds due and owing in relation to projects located in Connecticut." The essence of the suit, therefore, was whether the defendants "deprived Plaintiff of their rights and property" without due process.

The second question to be addressed was whether the alleged acts of omissions occurred in this district. *See Fedele*, 18 F.Supp. 2d at 316. The plaintiff grounded its venue argument on the contention that its "record keeping practices and the information contained in Plaintiff's records were *located in New York*." Thus, the plaintiff argued that venue in this district was proper simply because the plaintiff's "time and payroll records . . . were maintained in the State of New York." However, the Second Circuit has made clear that the venue analysis "must focus on where the *defendant's* acts or omissions occurred." *Prospect Capital*, 2009 WL 4907121, at *3 (emphasis in original) (citing *Daniel*, 428 F.3d at 432); *see also Woodke v. Dahm*, 70 F.3d 983, 985–86 (8th Cir.1995) (explaining that "by referring to 'events or omissions giving rise to the claim,' Congress meant to require courts to focus on relevant activities of the defendant, not of the plaintiff"); *Cold Spring Harbor Lab. v. Ropes & Gray LLP*, 762 F.Supp. 2d 543, 558 (E.D.N.Y. 2011) (reaffirming "the Second Circuit's directive that the venue analysis should focus on the relevant activities of the defendants"); 17 James Wm. Moore et al., *Moore's Federal Practice* ¶ 110.04[1] (3d ed. 2013) (stating that, when engaging in the substantiality analysis, courts "ought not focus solely on the matters that gave rise to the filing of the action, but rather should look at the entire progression of the underlying claim"). The plaintiff's conduct, even as " 'a link in the chain of events,' simply did not constitute an event giving rise to" the claim that the defendants had arbitrarily withheld funds owed to the plaintiff. *TSIG Consulting, Inc. v. ACP Consulting, LLC*, No. 14–CV–2032, 2014 WL 1386639, at *4 (S.D.N.Y. Apr. 9, 2014).

The court then turned to the alleged acts and omissions of *defendants* to determine whether venue in this district is proper. Contrary to the plaintiff's conclusory assertions, the events giving rise to the plaintiff's claims all took place in the state of Connecticut. While the plaintiff conceded that "the work on the projects was performed in Connecticut," it was far more relevant that the defendants' investigation and subsequent withholding of funds relating to these projects occurred in Connecticut, pursuant to Connecticut state law. The plaintiff did not dispute this. As the defendants correctly explained, the plaintiff's claim was, in actuality, "directed to their procedures for conducting their investigation" rather than "the merits of the prevailing wage violations." The defendants further noted that this "Action focuses not on the location of Plaintiff's own payroll records in New York but on Defendants' investigation resulting in withholding of funds, conducted in Connecticut." Because § 1391(b) focuses on the activities of the defendants, *see I.M.D. USA, Inc. v. Shalit*, 92 F.Supp. 2d 315, 318 (S.D.N.Y. 2000); *see also Cold Spring Harbor*, 762 F.Supp. 2d at 558, the location of the plaintiff's records was not "sufficient to support venue because they do not concern the actions of Defendants that gave rise to the claims at issue," *TSIG Consulting*, 2014 WL 1386639, at \*3. Therefore, it was clear that the "events and omissions giving rise to the claim" of a due process violation occurred in the District of Connecticut, *not* in the Southern District of New York. *See Daniel*, 428 F.3d at 432.

The court also indicated that it was worth noting that any financial burden felt by the plaintiff as a result of the defendants' investigation and withholding of funds failed to support venue in this district. "While the locus of the harm suffered is a factor to consider, the case law does not support the theory that venue is proper on an economic-effects inquiry alone. . . ." *Astor Holdings, Inc. v. Roski*, No. 01–CV–1905, 2002 WL 72936, at \*9 (S.D.N.Y. Jan. 17, 2002). Simply put, "a plaintiff's economic harm felt in the original forum is not sufficient for a finding of proper venue under Section 1391(b)(2)." *Allstate Life Ins. Co. v. Stanley W. Burns, Inc.*, 80 F.Supp. 3d 870, 879 (N.D. Ill. 2015); *see also Golden Scorpio Corp. v. Steel Horse Bar & Grill*, 596 F.Supp. 2d 1282, 1287 n.4 (D. Ariz. 2009) (noting that "economic harm . . . is not a sufficient basis for conferring venue" under § 1391(b)(2)); *Fin. Mgmt. Serv., Inc. v. Coburn Supply Co, Inc.*, No. 02–CV–8928, 2003 WL 255232, at \*2 (N.D. Ill. Feb. 5, 2003) (finding the plaintiff's economic harm that resulted in the original forum from the defendant's alleged actions insufficient to satisfy venue under § 1391(b)(2)). As discussed above, the acts of the defendants, not the activities of or harm to the plaintiff, determine where venue properly lies. *See Woodke*, 70 F.3d at 985–86 (rejecting the plaintiff's contention "that venue lies in the district of his residency because that is the location of the ultimate effect of the defendants' actions"). Thus, because the defendants did not commit any of the alleged acts or omissions underlying the plaintiff's constitutional claim in the Southern District of New York, and any relevant economic injury suffered by the plaintiff was tangential to that claim, venue was not proper in this district.

Having concluded that venue was not proper in the Southern District of New York, the court had discretion to "dismiss, or if it be in the interest of justice, transfer such case to any district or division in which it could have been brought." 28 U.S.C. § 1406(a). Whether a transfer is in the interests of justice depends upon "whether the plaintiff has been diligent in pursuing his or her claim, whether the opposing party would be unduly prejudiced by the transfer, and whether the plaintiff's reason for bringing the case in the wrong forum is analogous to an 'erroneous guess' about an 'elusive fact.' " *Gibbons v. Fronton*, 661 F.Supp. 2d 429, 436 (S.D.N.Y. 2009). In light of the following analysis, the court found that transfer to a proper venue was the appropriate course. *See*

*Open Solutions Imaging Sys., Inc. v. Horn*, No. 03–CV–2077, 2004 WL 1683158, at *7 (D. Conn. July 27, 2004) ("In most cases of improper venue the courts conclude that it is in the interest of justice to transfer. . . ."); *see also Deskovic v. City of Peekskill*, 673 F.Supp. 2d 154, 172 (S.D.N.Y. 2009) (noting that "dismissal is a severe penalty").

First, the court fund that the plaintiff had been diligent in pursuing its claim, which has been pending in this district for over a year. The plaintiff filed the complaint in a timely fashion, albeit in the wrong forum. *See Gibbons*, 661 F.Supp.2d at 436 (concluding that "the equities weigh in . . . favor" of transfer where the plaintiff "filed his claims in a timely fashion, but in the wrong forum"). Second, given that the defendants resided in Connecticut, they would not be prejudiced by transferring the case there. *See Loos v. Mitcheltree*, No. 13–CV–69, 2013 WL 3759957, at *3 (W.D.N.Y. July 15, 2013) (finding "transfer to this district in which the defendants reside would not be prejudicial"). Because they remain able to defend the plaintiff's claim on the merits, transfer would not automatically result in an adverse judgment against the defendants. *See id.* (finding "transfer is not unduly prejudicial" where "transfer will not automatically result in an adverse judgment against the defendant"). Lastly, there were no allegations that the plaintiff exhibited any bad faith in bringing the action in the Southern District of New York. *See Deskovic*, 673 F.Supp.2d at 174–75 (finding "that it is in the interest of justice to transfer, rather than to dismiss, this case" where the "plaintiff has acted in good faith in all his pleadings"); *Pisani v. Diener*, No. 07–CV–5118, 2009 WL 749893, at *9 (E.D.N.Y. Mar. 17, 2009) (considering the absence of bad faith in transferring, rather than dismissing, plaintiff's case for improper venue).

Because the defendants were residents of Connecticut, venue was proper in the District of Connecticut, and, moreover, the defendants were subject to personal jurisdiction there. Accordingly, the court ordered transfer of the case to the District of Connecticut, a "district . . . in which it could have been brought." 28 U.S.C. § 1406(a). For the reasons stated above, the court concluded that venue in this district was improper, but that the case should be transferred to the District of Connecticut.

**ANSWERS (A)** and **(B)** are possible answers, but not the best answer because outright dismissal of the plaintiff's case for improper venue would be, as the court concluded, a harsh result for the plaintiff's choosing the wrong venue. Therefore, **ANSWER (C)** is the best answer because it both recognizes the improper venue, but offers the plaintiff the palliative remedy of transferring the case to the proper venue. **ANSWER (D)** is incorrect because, as noted above, courts will not consider the place of economic impact in determining proper venue. **ANSWER (E)** is incorrect because although courts do give deference to a plaintiff's choice of forum, the plaintiff still carries the burden of establishing proper jurisdiction under the venue statutes and this deference is not sufficient to override the legal obligation to properly lay venue.

### PROBLEM #13. BEST ANSWER (B).

Problems #13 and #14 are based on *Peterson v. Martin Marietta Materials, Inc.*, 310 F.R.D. 570 (N.D. Iowa 2015). Problem #13 addresses the applicability of the work product doctrine in the context of a motion to compel discovery. The court held that the requested Voicemail message was not ordinary work product, and therefore it was not subject to the work product immunity. Consequently, the court granted the defendant's motion to compel discovery. Problem #14 deals with the plaintiff's alternative request for a protective order under Fed.R.Civ.P. 26(c)(1), discussed below. The court denied that protective order.

Peterson raised two arguments in support of his refusal to produce the Voicemail Message. First, he contended that it was subject to the work product doctrine. Second, he contended that he was entitled to withhold the Voicemail Message because the individual who left the message was an MMM employee and was at risk of being retaliated against if MMM learns his identity. MMM denied that the work product doctrine applied and further argued that if it did apply, the defendants had shown a substantial need for the information and could secure the substantial equivalent without undue hardship. MMM also denied that the perceived risk of retaliation against a non-party was a valid basis to prevent discovery.

Fed.R.Civ.P. 26 includes the following limit on the scope of discovery:

> (3) Trial Preparation: Materials.
>
>   (A) *Documents and Tangible Things.* Ordinarily, a party may not discover documents and tangible things that are prepared in anticipation of litigation or for trial by or for another party or its representative (including the other party's attorney, consultant, surety, indemnitor, insurer, or agent). But, subject to Rule 26(b)(4), those materials may be discovered if:
>
>     (i) they are otherwise discoverable under Rule 26(b)(1); and
>
>     (ii) the party shows that it has substantial need for the materials to prepare its case and cannot, without undue hardship, obtain their substantial equivalent by other means.
>
>   (B) *Protection Against Disclosure.* If the court orders discovery of those materials, it must protect against disclosure of the mental impressions, conclusions, opinions, or legal theories of a party's attorney or other representative concerning the litigation.

Fed.R.Civ.P. 26(b)(3). Rule 26(b)(3) codifies the work product doctrine, which "was designed to prevent 'unwarranted inquiries into the files and mental impressions of an attorney,' and recognizes that it is 'essential that a lawyer work with a certain degree of privacy, free from unnecessary intrusion by opposing parties and their counsel.' " *Simon v. G.D. Searle & Co.,* 816 F.2d 397, 400 (8th Cir.1987) (quoting *Hickman v. Taylor,* 329 U.S. 495, 510–11 (1947)). To withhold information as work product, "the party seeking protection must show the materials were prepared in anticipation of litigation, *i.e.,* because of the prospect of litigation." *PepsiCo, Inc. v. Baird, Kurtz & Dobson, L.L.P.,* 305 F.3d 813, 817 (8th Cir.2002) (citing *Binks Mfg. Co. v. National Presto Indus., Inc.,* 709 F.2d 1109, 1118–19 (7th Cir.1983)). Thus, the party asserting work product protection must establish a factual basis supporting its applicability. *St. Paul Reinsurance Co., Ltd. v. Commercial Fin. Corp.,* 197 F.R.D. 620, 628 (N.D. Iowa 2000).

Federal courts recognize two types of work product—opinion work product and ordinary work product. Opinion work product consists of an attorney's mental impressions, conclusions, opinions or legal theories. *Baker v. General Motors Corp.,* 209 F.3d 1051, 1054 (8th Cir.2000). Opinion work product enjoys almost absolute protection against disclosure, making it discoverable in only very rare and extraordinary circumstances. *Id.; see also In re Murphy,* 560 F.2d 326, 336 (8th Cir.1977). Ordinary work product includes raw factual information and is discoverable only if the party seeking discovery has a substantial need for the information and cannot obtain it by other means. *Baker,* 209 F.3d at 1054; *see also* Fed.R.Civ.P. 26(b)(3)(A). Here, Peterson acknowledged that the recording at issue is not opinion work product but contended that it was ordinary work product.

Despite bearing the burden of establishing that the work product doctrine applies to the Voicemail Message, Peterson came forward with no evidence supporting that claim. The court could find no answers even to such basic questions as when the Voicemail Message was left and to whom it was directed. The description set forth in Peterson's initial disclosures was confusing, as it referred to a "recording from coworker from attorney investigating Petition." That choice of words conveyed virtually no information.

Peterson later stated in an interrogatory answer that the recording was of "a message left by an employee of Martin Marietta" and "was created in anticipation of litigation." Peterson also wrote: "Litigation was already pending and he understood that the message would likely be transmitted to Plaintiff's counsel and used by the Plaintiff and/or his counsel in preparation for litigation and/or trial." *Id.* However, Peterson presented no evidence supporting his allegation concerning the speaker's state of mind at the time the message was left.

Thus, the court concluded that the record contained no evidence of when the message was left, to whom it was directed or the speaker's motivation for leaving the message. While the court could guess, from context, that the unnamed employee may have directed the message to Peterson, and that Peterson then forwarded it to his attorney, the lack of evidence rendered this purely speculative. And, of course, Peterson's suggestion that the unnamed employee who left the message did so in preparation for litigation was even more speculative.

In short, the court concluded that Peterson had not come close to making the factual showing necessary to support his claim that the Voicemail Message constituted ordinary work product. Moreover, even if the court could assume (a) that the Voicemail Message was left for Peterson, (b) that Peterson forwarded it to his attorney and (c) that the unnamed employee who left the message did so for the purpose of providing assistance to Peterson, that scenario would not give rise to a valid work product argument. The purpose of the work product privilege is to:

> promote the adversary system . . . by protecting the confidentiality of papers prepared *by or on behalf of attorneys* in anticipation of litigation. Protecting attorneys' work product promotes the adversary system by enabling attorneys to prepare cases without fear that their work product will be used against their clients.

*Westinghouse Elec. Corp. v. Republic of Philippines*, 951 F.2d 1414, 1428 (3d Cir.1991); *see also Pittman v. Frazer,* 129 F.3d 983, 988 (8th Cir.1997) ("The work product privilege is designed to promote the operation of the adversary system by ensuring that a party cannot obtain materials *that his opponent has prepared* in anticipation of litigation."). The Voicemail Message was not "prepared" by either Peterson or his attorney. Nor did Peterson claim that the caller was a representative or agent of his attorney. *United States v. Nobles,* 422 U.S. 225, 238–39 (1975) (work product doctrine protects material prepared by agents of the attorney). Instead, it appeared to have been an unsolicited communication from a non-party to someone other than Peterson's attorney (probably Peterson). Even if Peterson then transferred that communication to his attorney, that transfer did not magically transform it into work product. *Petersen v. Douglas Cnty. Bank & Trust Co.,* 967 F.2d 1186, 1189 (8th Cir.1992) (citing *Shelton v. American Motors Corp.,* 805 F.2d 1323, 1328 (8th Cir.1986)). There was no evidence Peterson's attorney (or Peterson himself at the direction of his attorney) sought out the communication or did anything to cause it to occur. Thus, even the court could make assumptions about the Voicemail Message to cure Peterson's failure to supply evidence, those assumptions would not give rise to a work product claim.

The court concluded that Peterson failed to establish that the Voicemail Message constituted ordinary work product, and his work product objection was overruled and denied. Because the Voicemail Message was not work product, the court further indicated that it need not address MMM's argument that it had a substantial need for the message and could, without undue hardship, obtain its substantial equivalent by other means.

**ANSWER (A)**, while a possible answer, is not the best answer. There are no facts supplied to support this argument, and because the court concluded that the Voicemail Message was not ordinary work product, it did not address the defendant's argument based on need for the message. **ANSWER (C)** is incorrect because the court found that the Voicemail Message was neither ordinary nor opinion work product subject to that immunity from discovery. **ANSWER (D)** is incorrect because properly framed discovery requests do not constitute constitutional violations of privacy. **ANSWER (E)** is incorrect because there are no supported allegations for the court to make this finding.

## PROBLEM #14. BEST ANSWER (D).

Problem #14 is a continuation of Problem #13 and is based on the same facts and case. This problem addresses the propriety of the plaintiff's request for a protective order pursuant to Fed.R.Civ.P. 26(c)(1). The court denied the plaintiff's request for a protective order.

Peterson's alternative argument for withholding the Voicemail Message was that its disclosure to MMM would create a risk that MMM would retaliate against the employee who left the message. Peterson requested entry of a protective order pursuant to Fed.R.Civ.P. 26(c)(1) to protect that employee from annoyance, embarrassment, oppression.

The court found no legal basis to deprive MMM of otherwise-discoverable information because of speculation that MMM might take retaliatory action against a non-party. Peterson cited no authority for this proposition. Moreover, and as Peterson acknowledged, the MMM employee who left the message had legal protection against retaliatory conduct based on assisting or participating in an investigation, claim or proceeding. If MMM was foolish enough to take retaliatory action against that employee after receiving the Voicemail Message, the employee would have ample legal remedies. Therefore the court declined to enter a protective order, or otherwise prohibit discovery, based on speculation that MMM might break the law.

**ANSWER (A)** is incorrect because Peterson had not shown good cause for issuance of a protective order. **ANSWER (B)** is incorrect because, as the court noted, there is no authority for a plaintiff protecting non-parties to the litigation. **ANSWER (C)** is incorrect for similar reasons; there is no authority protecting privacy rights to non-parties to a litigation. **ANSWER (E)** because the fact that the non-party did not request the protective order was not the reason why the court denied the request.

**PROBLEM #15. BEST ANSWER (C).**

Problem #15 is based on *J & J Sports Prods. v. Olivo*, 2105 WL 3604457 (S.D. Cal. June 8, 2015). Problem #15 deals with a motion to strike answers to a complaint. The court held that the defendant's general denials to the plaintiff's allegations were insufficient under Fed.R.Civ.P. 8(b), but granted the defendant a right to amend its defective answers.

When responding to pleadings a party must "state in short and plain terms its defenses to each claim asserted against it" and when contesting an allegation "a denial must fairly respond to the substance of the allegation." Fed.R.Civ.P. 8(b)(1)–(2).

The plaintiff's motion to strike argued the defendants' answers (*i.e.,* responses to the allegations enumerated in the complaint) are invalid.

The plaintiff's complaint contained forty-eight allegations and included four separate counts. The first nineteen allegations addressed jurisdiction and the parties to the matter, as well as other allegations general to all counts. Beginning with the twentieth allegation, the complaint was broken into four counts, with all preceding allegations reincorporated into each count. In their answer to the complaint, the defendants listed four counts but merely stated that "Defendant denies each and every allegation of the complaint" by means of response to each of the counts.

The court held that the defendants' answers to the allegations of the complaint were insufficient.

Under Rule 8(b), parties may either respond to allegations individually or submit a general denial of the entire pleading. Fed.R.Civ.P. 8(b)(3). If a party wishes to submit a general denial, they must seek to deny all facets of the complaint, or deny all allegations except those specifically designated for admission. *Id.* at (c). Otherwise a party must address the substance of each allegation. *Id.* at (b). In this case, the defendants' answers satisfied neither requirement. Some allegations could not be disputed in good faith. For example, the defendants Martinez and Olivo were indeed identified on the liquor license issued to Club Caribe as alleged in the complaint. Therefore, a general denial was not valid. As the denials did not address the substance of any counts, the answers were also invalid as a response to individual allegations.

In light of these deficiencies, the court ordered that the defendants' answers were stricken with leave to amend. The court suggested that the defendants should take care to review the substance of the allegations before submitting an amended answer, and only deny those allegations which they intended to contest.

**ANSWER (A)** is incorrect because the federal rules do permit general denials, but just not in the circumstance of this pleading with multiple, detailed allegations. **ANSWER (B)** is a possible answer, but not the best answer; the plaintiff did not seek Rule 11 sanctions and the court did not sua sponte address whether the defendants' general denials violated Rule 11 pleading requirements. **ANSWER (D)** is incorrect for the same reasons indicated with regard to **ANSWER (A)**, above. **ANSWER (E)** is incorrect because a party may address insufficiently pleaded answers through a Rule 12 motion to strike.

## PROBLEM #16. BEST ANSWER (E).

Problem #16 is based on *Dominguez v. Crown Equipment Corp.*, 2015 WL 3477079 (C.D. Cal. June 1, 2015). This problem requires analysis of amendment to pleadings under Fed.R.Civ.P. 15(c), under the doctrine of "relation back" of amended pleadings. The court denied the plaintiff's motion to amend its pleadings under Fed.R.Civ.P. 15(c).

Fed.R.Civ.P. 15(a) requires courts to freely grant leave to amend pleadings "when justice so requires." Fed.R.Civ.P. 15(a)(2). In deciding whether to grant leave to amend, courts consider the following factors articulated by the Supreme Court in *Foman v. Davis,* 371 U.S. 178 (1962):

> undue delay, bad faith or dilatory motive on the part of the movant, repeated failure to cure deficiencies by amendments previously allowed, undue prejudice to the opposing party by virtue of allowance of the amendment, futility of amendment, etc.

*Id.* at 182; *see also Sharkey v. O'Neal,* 778 F.3d 767, 774 (9th Cir.2015).

"If after removal the plaintiff seeks to join additional defendants whose joinder would destroy subject matter jurisdiction, the court may deny joinder, or permit joinder and remand the action to the State court." 28 U.S.C. § 1447(e). While the permissive standard set forth in Fed.R.Civ.P. 15(a) usually governs a motion to amend, a motion to approve the post-removal joinder of a nondiverse defendant is governed by § 1447(e). *Boon v. Allstate Ins. Co.,* 229 F.Supp.2d 1016, 1020 (C.D.Cal.2002). Section 1447(e) commits the decision of whether to allow joinder to the court's discretion. *Newcombe v. Adolf Coors Co.,* 157 F.3d 686, 691 (9th Cir.1998). Section 1447(e) does not set forth standards guiding the exercise of this discretion. Instead, courts within the Ninth Circuit have considered a broad range of factors, including: "(1) whether the party sought to be joined is needed for just adjudication and would be joined under Fed.R.Civ.P. 19(a); (2) whether the statute of limitations would preclude an original action against the new defendants in state court; (3) whether there has been unexplained delay in requesting joinder; (4) whether joinder is intended solely to defeat federal jurisdiction; (5) whether the claims against the new defendant appear valid; and (6) whether denial of joinder will prejudice the plaintiff." *IBC Aviation Servs., Inc. v. Compania Mexicana de Aviacion, S.A. de C.V.,* 125 F.Supp.2d 1008, 1011 (N.D.Cal.2000).

Rule 15(c) (1)(B) allows an amendment to relate back to the original complaint if the amendment asserts a claim arising out of the "conduct, transaction, or occurrence set out—or attempted to be set out—in the original pleading." Fed.R.Civ.P. 15(c)(1) (B). Additionally, an amendment that changes the party or party's name relates back when "Rule 15(c)(1)(B) is satisfied and if, within the period provided by Rule 4(m) for serving the summons and complaint, the party to be brought in by amendment: (i) received such notice of the action that it will not be prejudiced in defending on the merits; and (ii) knew or should have known that the action would have been brought against it, but for a mistake concerning the proper party's identity." Fed.R.Civ.P. 15(c)(1) (C). Moreover, when the relevant limitations period derives from state law, Rule 15(c)(1)(A) requires the Court to examine both federal and state law and to apply the more permissive of the two relation back standards. *Butler v. Nat'l Cmty. Renaissance of California,* 766 F.3d 1191, 1200–01 (9th Cir.2014). The Ninth Circuit has held that an amendment to add the true identity of a "Doe" defendant does not relate back to the original complaint when the original complaint's description of the Doe defendant was "insufficient to identify anyone." *Lopez v. Gen. Motors Corp.,* 697 F.2d 1328, 1332 (9th Cir.1983).

The plaintiffs sought leave to amend the complaint by: (1) adding Cuevas as Dominguez's guardian ad litem; (2) adding several diverse defendants who designed, manufactured, or sold components of the allegedly defective safety equipment; (3) by adding claims against Crown pertaining to the allegedly defective shelving unit/rack; and (4) by joining nondiverse defendants which allegedly "designed, manufactured, fabricated, assembled, tested, marketed, installed, maintained, repaired, and/or sold" the purportedly defective shelving unit/rack. The plaintiffs did not assert any claim against Dominguez's employer and Dominguez's employer moved to a new warehouse facility.

The court previously granted Plaintiffs leave to add Cuevas as guardian *ad litem*. Additionally, Crown did not object to adding the diverse defendants who were involved in making and selling the allegedly defective safety equipment.

Instead, Crown objected to the assertion of a new shelving unit/rack claim against Crown and to the addition of the nondiverse defendants.

The plaintiffs claim that they did not discover the shelving unit/rack defect until February 20, 2015—when Dominguez's coworker informed them in deposition that a piece of plywood seen in photographs of the accident site wasn't added until after the accident. The coworker told the plaintiffs' counsel that this plywood blocks a roughly 40-foot hole through which Dominguez fell. Crown asserted that the plaintiffs were on notice about the factual basis for the shelving unit/rack claim as of December 2014, and thus unreasonably delayed bringing this claim because they did not move to amend until March 2015. According to Crown, not only was the relevant factual information contained in the OSHA report produced at the end of October 2014, but plaintiffs' counsel interviewed Dominguez's coworker in December 2014 (before the coworker's deposition) and then learned of the relevant facts. Both sides also accused each other of improperly withholding relevant information or evidence during discovery.

Given that Dominguez wasn't able to communicate since the accident, and when the plaintiffs saw the shelving unit the hole was blocked with plywood, it was reasonable that they did not know of the existence of the shelving unit/rack claim. Moreover, a four month delay between the earliest alleged date on which the plaintiffs should have known of the claim and the date of filing for leave to amend was not particularly long or unreasonable.

The most pressing issues raised by the plaintiffs' motion concerned the statute of limitations and relation back. In California, there is a two year statute of limitations for personal injury actions. The time for Dominguez to file a claim arising from his April 11, 2012 accident thus expired in April 2014—roughly one week after Dominguez filed his complaint in state court. Therefore, the new claims that the plaintiffs sought to assert in their amended complaint were time-barred unless they related back to the plaintiffs' original complaint.

Given the close factual relationship between the shelving unit/rack claim and safety equipment claim, the amendment asserting the shelving unit/rack claim against the existing defendants related back to the original complaint; these claims arose from the same conduct, transaction, or occurrence. Fed.R.Civ.P. 15(c)(1)(B). Moreover, any prejudice to Crown could be solved upon Crown's request by extending the time for discovery and (if necessary) continuing the trial date.

The plaintiff asserted that the claims against the nondiverse defendants related back because the plaintiffs originally named those defendants as Does in the original complaint. California law generally does not allow relation back of an amendment adding a party not named in the original complaint. *Butler*, 766 F.3d at 1201. However, "where an amendment does not add a new defendant, but simply corrects a misnomer by which an old defendant was sued, case law recognizes an exception to the general rule of no relation back." *Spitzer v. Aljoe*, No. 13–CV–05442–MEJ, 2015 WL 1843787, at *11 (N.D.Cal. Apr.6, 2015) (quoting *Hawkins v. Pac. Coast Bldg. Prods., Inc.*, 124 Cal.App.4th 1497, 1503, 22 Cal.Rptr.3d 453 (2004)). Thus, California Civil

Procedure Code § 474 allows "plaintiffs to substitute a fictional 'Doe' defendant in a lawsuit with a named defendant, so long as the plaintiff was unaware of the defendant's true identity at the time the prior complaint was filed." *Spitzer*, 2015 WL 1843787, at \*11. However, the plaintiff must "be 'genuinely ignorant' of the defendant's identity at the time the original complaint is filed." *Butler*, 766 F.3d at 1202 (quoting *Woo v. Superior Court*, 75 Cal.App.4th 169, 177, 89 Cal.Rptr.2d 20 (Cal.Ct.App.1999)). The § 474 relation-back doctrine applies even if the plaintiff's ignorance was the result of her own negligence. *Spitzer*, 2015 WL 1843787, at \*11 (citing *Woo*, 75 Cal.App.4th at 177, 89 Cal.Rptr.2d 20).

While the original complaint named Does 1–60, it did not describe any of the Doe defendants as being a designer, manufacturer, or installer of the shelving unit/rack. Thus, the complaint failed to adequately identify the nondiverse defendants which the plaintiffs sought to join. Therefore, the plaintiffs had not shown that this amendment simply sought to correct a misnomer. Thus, amendment would not be allowed under California law.

The Federal Rules of Civil Procedure are similarly unavailing to the plaintiffs. Under Rule 15(c)(1)(C), Plaintiffs must show that the defendants sought to be named either received notice of the action within the time for service of the complaint and summons or that they knew or should have known that the action would have been brought against them but for a mistake concerning the proper party's identity. The plaintiffs did not assert that the nondiverse proposed defendants received notice within the time for serving the complaint. Also, there was nothing about allegedly defective safety equipment that would have alerted them to a defect in their shelving unit/rack. Additionally, though the original complaint described Dominguez's injuries as being caused by a fall, it did not allege any facts pertaining to a hole or other defect in the shelving unit/rack. In fact, the use of safety equipment suggested that Dominguez already knew of the risk of falling and also that any such risk created by the shelving unit/rack was not due to a defect (because the risk could be allayed by properly functioning safety equipment). Moreover, there was nothing in the original complaint which would have put the nondiverse defendants on notice that they should have been named in the suit but for a mistake *concerning the proper party's identity*. The plaintiffs' original complaint did not assert any claim based on the shelving rack/unit. It thus appeared that the plaintiffs chose not to sue the nondiverse defendants for their involvement with the shelving rack/unit's design and manufacture; it did not appear that this failure was due to a mistake about the proper party's identity. *See Butler*, 766 F.3d at 1203.

The parties made several other arguments regarding the propriety of amendment. The plaintiffs argued that under California Code of Civil Procedure § 1431.2, liability for non-economic damages are several. Thus, the failure to include the nondiverse defendants might have prejudiced the plaintiffs by preventing them from obtaining a full recovery. However, any resulting inequity was diminished by the fact that the plaintiffs inexplicably delayed filing the action until just before the limitations period ran. Moreover, given that the plaintiffs knew Dominguez's injuries were caused by a fall, they likely could have anticipated a claim against the shelving unit/rack's manufacturer or installer relating to some form of gap or hole (even if they didn't know the precise details). Additionally, in their motion to amend and remand, the plaintiffs admitted that the nondiverse defendants were named on publicly recorded permit documents. The plaintiffs failed to explain why they apparently did not review those documents until March 2015.

In sum, the fact that the plaintiffs' claim against the nondiverse defendants would be time-barred if it did not relate back militated in favor of allowing amendment. The same is true of the possibility that the plaintiffs would not be able to recover their full noneconomic damages unless the nondiverse defendants were joined. However, it appeared that the claim against the nondiverse defendants would not be allowed under California law and did not actually relate back to the original complaint within the meaning of Rule 15(c)(1)(C).

For the aforementioned reasons, the court denied the plaintiffs' motion to amend as to the nondiverse defendants

**ANSWER (A)** is incorrect because the court held exactly the opposite: the plaintiffs had failed to satisfy the requirements of Rule 15(c) to allow the amendment to relater back to the original filing. **ANSWER (B)** is incorrect because the court rejected the plaintiff's economic harm argument in support of permitting the amendment to relate back. **ANSWER (C)** is incorrect because the court found that the plaintiff's conduct in failing to discover the additional defendants was not due to a reasonable mistake. **ANSWER (D)**, although a possible answer, is not the best answer because the plaintiffs simply failed to meet all the requirements for the relation-back doctrine of Rule 15(c) to apply.

### PROBLEM #17. BEST ANSWER (A).

Problem #17 is based on *Lewis v. Chubb & Sons, Inc.*, 2015 WL 5104825 (C.D. Cal. Aug. 31, 2015). This problem involves analysis of the amount-in-controversy requirement that the defendant carries on removal. In this case, the court held that the defendant failed to carry its burden in establishing the threshold $75,000 amount-in-controversy, and therefore the court granted the plaintiff's petition for remand to state court.

"Federal courts are courts of limited jurisdiction. They possess only that power authorized by Constitution and statute." *Kokkonen v. Guardian Life Ins. Co. of Am.*, 511 U.S. 375, 377 (1994). The courts are presumed to lack jurisdiction unless the contrary appears affirmatively from the record. *See DaimlerChrysler Corp. v. Cuno*, 547 U.S. 332, 342 n. 3, (2006). Federal courts have a duty to examine jurisdiction *sua sponte* before proceeding to the merits of a case, *see Ruhrgas AG v. Marathon Oil Co.*, 526 U.S. 574, 583 (1999), "even in the absence of a challenge from any party." *Arbaugh v. Y & H Corp.*, 546 U.S. 500, 501 (2006). Indeed, "if the court determines at any time that it lacks subject-matter jurisdiction, the court must dismiss the action." Fed.R.Civ.P. 12(h)(3); *see Snell v. Cleveland, Inc.*, 316 F.3d 822, 826 (9th Cir.2002) ("Federal Rule of Civil Procedure 12(h)(3) provides that a court may raise the question of subject matter jurisdiction, *sua sponte*, at any time during the pendency of the action, even on appeal.").

In general, "any civil action brought in a State court of which the district courts of the United States have original jurisdiction, may be removed by the defendant or the defendants, to the district court." 28 U.S.C. § 1441(a). A removing defendant bears the burden of establishing that removal is proper. *See Gaus v. Miles, Inc.*, 980 F.2d 564, 566–67 (9th Cir.1992) ("The strong presumption against removal jurisdiction means that the defendant always has the burden of establishing that removal is proper."); *Abrego v. The Dow Chem. Co.*, 443 F.3d 676, 684 (9th Cir.2006) (noting the "longstanding, near-canonical rule that the burden on removal rests with the removing defendant"). Moreover, if there is any doubt regarding the existence of subject matter jurisdiction, the court must resolve those doubts in favor of remanding the action to state court. *See Gaus*, 980 F.2d at 566 ("Federal jurisdiction must be rejected if there is any doubt as to the right of removal in the first instance."). Indeed, "if at any time before final judgment it appears that the district court lacks subject matter jurisdiction, the case shall be remanded." 28 U.S.C. § 1447(c); *see Kelton Arms Condo. Owners Ass'n, Inc. v. Homestead Ins. Co.*, 346 F.3d 1190, 1192 (9th Cir.2003) ("Subject matter jurisdiction may not be waived, and, indeed, we have held that the district court must remand if it lacks jurisdiction."); *Washington v. United Parcel Serv., Inc.*, 2009 WL 1519894, *1 (C.D. Cal. 2009) (a district court may remand an action where the court finds that it lacks subject matter jurisdiction either by motion or *sua sponte*).

The court's review of the notice of removal and the attached state court complaint made clear that this court did not have diversity jurisdiction over the matter. In other words, plaintiff could not have originally brought this action in federal court, as plaintiff did not competently allege facts supplying diversity jurisdiction. Therefore, removal was improper. *See* 28 U.S.C. § 1441(a); *Caterpillar, Inc. v. Williams*, 482 U.S. 386, 392 (1987) ("Only state-court actions that originally could have been filed in federal court may be removed to federal court by the defendant.").

Chubb bore the burden of proving by a preponderance of the evidence that the amount in controversy met that jurisdictional threshold. *See Valdez v. Allstate Ins. Co.*, 372 F.3d 1115, 1117 (9th Cir.2004); *Matheson v. Progressive Specialty Ins. Co.*, 319 F.3d 1089, 1090 (9th Cir.2003) ("Where it is not facially evident from the complaint that more than $75,000 is in controversy, the removing party must prove, by a preponderance of the evidence, that the amount in controversy meets the jurisdictional threshold. Where doubt regarding the right to removal exists, a case should be remanded to state court."). Here, there was no basis for diversity jurisdiction because the amount in controversy did not appear to exceed the diversity jurisdiction threshold of $75,000. *See* 28 U.S.C. § 1332.

Removal at this stage, *i.e.*, on the basis of the "initial pleading," must be ascertainable from an examination of the four corners of the Complaint. *See Harris v. Bankers Life and Cas. Co.*, 425 F.3d 689, 694 (9th Cir.2005) (Notice of removal under the first paragraph of § 1446(b) "is determined through examination of the four corners of the applicable pleadings, not through subjective knowledge or a duty to make further inquiry. . . . If no ground for removal is evident in the Complaint, the case is 'not removable' at that stage."). Here, the amount of damages plaintiff sought could be determined from the complaint, as the complaint did not set forth a specific amount.

Chubb contended that the amount in controversy threshold was met because at the time of plaintiff's resignation, plaintiff's hourly rate was $17.00, and calculating plaintiff's "lost income, earnings, and benefits on an annualized basis . . . Plaintiff seeks to recover $35,360 per annum," and when considering the date of any trial, "Plaintiff's unmitigated lost wages could amount to at least $88,400."

The court held that Chubb's conclusory and unsubstantiated assertions with respect to plaintiff's wages were insufficient for it to meet it burden of establishing, by a preponderance of the evidence, that the amount in controversy met or exceeded the diversity jurisdiction threshold. Chubb did not state or provide any evidence as to the basis for its calculations. For example, there was no indication as to the number of hours a week plaintiff worked, and whether she worked the same hours every week. Chubb's unsubstantiated assertions, untethered to any evidence, could satisfy the amount in controversy requirement of § 1332(a). *See Gaus,* 980 F.2d at 567 (remanding for lack of diversity jurisdiction where defendant "offered no facts whatsoever to overcome the strong presumption against removal jurisdiction, nor satisfy defendant's burden of setting forth . . . the underlying facts supporting its assertion that the amount in controversy exceeds the statutory threshold.").

While Chubb suggested that the court should consider plaintiff's lost wages through the time of trial in determining the amount in controversy, the court declined to project lost wages forward to some hypothetical trial date. "Jurisdiction depends on the state of affairs when the case begins; what happens later is irrelevant." *Gardynski-Leschuck v. Ford Motor Co.,* 142 F.3d 955, 958 (7th Cir.1998) (citing *St. Paul Mercury Indem. Co. v. Red Cab Co.,* 303 U.S. 283, 289–90 (1938)); *Soto v. Kroger Co.,* 2013 WL 3071267, *3 (C.D. Cal. 2013) (noting that "the guiding principle is to measure amount in controversy at the time of removal"). In measuring lost wages for purposes of the amount in controversy, other courts have cut off the calculation at the date of removal. *See, e.g., Soto,* 2013 WL 3071267, at *3 ("Jurisdiction based on removal depends on the state of affairs when the case is removed. Thus, Kroger is not persuasive when it argues that wages up until the present should be included in the amount in controversy."); *Haase v. Aerodynamics Inc.,* 2009 WL 3368519, *4 (E.D. Cal. 2009) ("The amount in controversy must be determined at the time of removal. At the time of removal, Plaintiff's lost wage claim, a special damage, totaled $21,830.").

Chubb's reliance on plaintiff's prayer for emotional distress damages, was similarly unpersuasive. Even if emotional distress damages were potentially recoverable, the plaintiff's complaint did not allege any specific amount for her emotional distress claims (or as general damages), and it would therefore have been speculative to include these damages in the total amount in controversy. *See Cable v. Merit Life Ins. Co.,* 2006 WL 1991664, *3 (E.D. Cal. 2006)

(Defendant's argument that emotional distress damages exceeded the jurisdictional threshold was insufficient when "defendant provided no reliable basis for determining the amount of emotional distress damages likely to be recovered in this case."). Further, Chubb failed to provide any analogous cases with substantially similar factual scenarios that might guide the court as to the amount of emotional distress damages that might be recovered in this case. *See Mireles v. Wells Fargo Bank, N.A.,* 845 F.Supp.2d 1034, 1055 (C.D. Cal. 2012) (remanding where defendants "proffered no evidence that the lawsuits and settlements alleged in the complaint are factually or legally similar to plaintiffs' claims."); *Dawson v. Richmond Am. Homes of Nevada, Inc.,* 2013 WL 1405338, *3 (D. Nev. 2013) (remanding where defendant "offered no facts to demonstrate that the proffered analogous suit is factually identical to plaintiffs' suit.").

Chubb also contended that the plaintiff sought punitive damages. While punitive damages may be included in the amount in controversy calculation, *see Gibson v. Chrysler Corp.,* 261 F.3d 927, 945 (9th Cir.2001), the plaintiff's request for such damages did not aid Chubb. "The mere possibility of a punitive damages award is insufficient to prove that the amount in controversy requirement has been met." *Burk v. Med. Sav. Ins. Co.,* 348 F.Supp.2d 1063, 1069 (D. Ariz. 2004); accord *Geller v. Hai Ngoc Duong,* 2010 WL 5089018, *2 (S.D. Cal. 2010); *J. Marymount, Inc. v. Bayer Healthcare, LLC,* 2009 WL 4510126, *4 (N.D. Cal. 2009). Rather, a defendant "must present evidence that punitive damages will more likely than not exceed the amount needed to increase the amount in controversy to $75,000." *Burk,* 348 F.Supp.2d at 1069. A removing defendant may establish "probable punitive damages, for example, by introducing evidence of jury verdicts in analogous cases." *Id.*

The court held that because Chubb had not provided evidence of punitive damages awards in factually similar cases, inclusion of punitive damages in the amount in controversy would be improper. *See Burk,* 348 F.Supp.2d at 1070 (defendant "failed to compare the facts of Plaintiff's case with the facts of other cases where punitive damages have been awarded in excess of the jurisdictional amount"); *Killion v. AutoZone Stores Inc.,* 2011 WL 590292, *2 (C.D. Cal. 2011) ("Defendants cite two cases . . . in which punitive damages were awarded, but make no attempt to analogize or explain how these cases are similar to the instant action. . . . Simply citing these cases merely illustrates that punitive damages are possible, but in no way shows that it is likely or probable in this case. Therefore, Defendants' inclusion of punitive damages in the calculation of the jurisdictional amount is speculative and unsupported.").

Finally, the plaintiff's complaint also included a claim for attorney's fees. "Where an underlying statute authorizes an award of attorneys' fees, either with mandatory or discretionary language, such fees may be included in the amount in controversy." *Lowdermilk v. U.S. Bank Nat'l Ass'n,* 479 F.3d 994, 1000 (9th Cir.2007). "Courts are split as to whether only attorneys' fees that have accrued at the time of removal should be considered in calculating the amount in controversy, or whether the calculation should take into account fees likely to accrue over the life of the case." *Hernandez v. Towne Park, Ltd.,*

2012 WL 2373372, *19 (C.D. Cal. 2012); *see Reames v. AB Car Rental Servs., Inc.*, 899 F.Supp.2d 1012, 1018 (D. Or. 2012) ("The Ninth Circuit has not yet expressed any opinion as to whether expected or projected future attorney fees may properly be considered 'in controversy' at the time of removal for purposes of the diversity-jurisdiction statute, and the decisions of the district courts are split on the issue."). The court was persuaded that "the better view is that attorneys' fees incurred after the date of removal are not properly included because the amount in controversy is to be determined as of the date of removal." *Dukes v. Twin City Fire Ins. Co.*, 2010 WL 94109, *2 (D. Ariz. 2010) (citing *Abrego*, 443 F.3d at 690). Indeed, "future attorneys' fees are entirely speculative, may be avoided, and are therefore not 'in controversy' at the time of removal." *Dukes*, 2010 WL 94109 at *2; accord *Palomino v. Safeway Ins. Co.*, 2011 WL 3439130, *2 (D. Ariz. 2011).

Here, Chubb provided no evidence of the amount of attorney's fees that were incurred at the time of removal. Chubb had not shown by a preponderance of the evidence that the inclusion of attorney's fees in the instant case would cause the amount in controversy to reach the $75,000 threshold. *See Walton v. AT & T Mobility*, 2011 WL 2784290, *2 (C.D. Cal. 2011) (declining to reach the issue of whether future attorney's fees could be considered in the amount in controversy because the defendant "did not provide any factual basis for determining how much attorney's fees have been incurred thus far and will be incurred in the future, and bald assertions are simply not enough.").

In sum, given that any doubt regarding the existence of subject matter jurisdiction must be resolved in favor of remanding the action to state court, *see Gaus*, 980 F.2d at 566, the court was not persuaded, under the circumstances here, that Chubb had met its burden of proving by a preponderance of the evidence that the amount in controversy meets the jurisdictional threshold. *See Matheson*, 319 F.3d at 1090 ("Where it is not facially evident from the complaint that more than $75,000 is in controversy, the removing party must prove, by a preponderance of the evidence, that the amount in controversy meets the jurisdictional threshold. Where doubt regarding the right to removal exists, a case should be remanded to state court.") *Valdez*, 372 F.3d at 1118. Therefore, there was no basis for diversity jurisdiction.

The court ordered that action should be remanded to the Superior Court of the State of California for the County of Los Angeles, for lack of subject matter jurisdiction pursuant to 28 U.S.C. § 1447(c).

**ANSWER (B)** is incorrect because the fact pattern explicitly states that the diversity of citizenship of the parties was satisfied; this problem addresses only whether the amount-in-controversy requirement was satisfied. **ANSWERS (C)** and **(D)** are incorrect because the court, under prevailing precedent, concluded that the removing defendant failed to offer proof that lost wages, emotional distress, punitive damages, or attorney fees should be counted to satisfy the threshold amount-in-controversy requirement. **ANSWER (E)** is incorrect because there is no indication that the plaintiff has improperly pleaded damages under California law for her state complaint. On removal, the burden to prove the requisite amount in controversy is on the removing defendant.

### PROBLEM #18. BEST ANSWER (D).

Problem #18 is based on *Cuprite Mine Partners LLC v. Anderson*, 809 F.3d 548 (9th Cir.2015). This problem involves a question of applicable law, and involves an analysis of Erie doctrine when a state and federal rule are in conflict. The Ninth Circuit upheld the district court's summary judgment determination, holding the sale by partition was procedural and Fed.R.Civ.P. 56 applied, rather than the conflicting Arizona state rule.

The defendants contended that the summary judgment order should be reversed because a trial was required in an Arizona partition action. The court acknowledged that section 12–1218(B) of the Arizona Code contemplated partition by sale "on the trial of the action." It was not clear to the court whether this language meant that summary judgment was never appropriate in a partition action under Arizona law.

Like the federal rules, the Arizona rules of procedure allowed for summary judgment when there were no genuine disputes of material fact. Ariz. R. Civ. P. 56(a). And the partition statute states that the rules of procedure "which govern all other civil actions shall govern actions for partition when not in conflict with the proceedings provided by this article." Ariz. Rev. Stat. § 12–1224(B). The defendants urged the court to conclude that the "trial" language from section 12–1218(B) conflicted with Fed.R.Civ.P. Rule 56, making it inapplicable to partition actions. Arizona courts did not appear to take this view. In *Register v. Coleman*, the Arizona Supreme Court held that it was appropriate to order partition by sale on summary judgment, but without specifically addressing the "trial" referenced in section 12–1218(B). 130 Ariz. 9, 633 P.2d 418, 421 (1981).

However, the court concluded that it did not need to decide whether the statute required Arizona state courts to conduct a trial in all partition by sale cases. Regardless of whether an Arizona state court would have been required to hold a trial, the district court correctly resolved the summary judgment motion according to the Federal Rules of Civil Procedure.

Under the *Erie* doctrine, federal courts sitting in diversity apply state substantive law and federal procedural rules. *Gasperini v. Ctr. for Humanities, Inc.*, 518 U.S. 415, 427 (1996). The "procedural aspects of summary judgment" are governed by the Federal Rules of Civil Procedure, and "the law of the forum controls the substantive issues." *Caesar Elecs., Inc. v. Andrews*, 905 F.2d 287, 290 n. 3 (9th Cir.1990). The court held that even if Arizona state law prohibited summary judgment and instead required a trial in a suit for partition by sale, such a requirement was procedural in nature and a federal court sitting in diversity was required to follow federal, not state, procedural rules. *See e.g. Maroules v. Jumbo, Inc.*, 452 F.3d 639, 645–46 (7th Cir.2006) ("Federal courts may ... grant summary judgment under Rule 56 upon concluding that no reasonable jury could return a verdict for the party opposing the motion, even if the state would require the judge to submit an identical case to the jury.").

In determining whether a state law is substantive or procedural, courts ask whether the law is outcome determinative; in other words, whether it would "significantly affect the result of a litigation for a federal court to disregard a law of a State that would be controlling in an action upon the same claim by the same parties in a State court." *Gasperini*, 518 U.S. at 427 (quoting *Guaranty Trust Co. v. York*, 326 U.S. 99, 109 (1945)). Courts do not apply this test mechanically, but rather, guided by "the twin aims of the *Erie* rule: discouragement of forum-shopping and avoidance of inequitable administration of the laws." *Id.* at 428 (quoting *Hanna v. Plumer*, 380 U.S. 460, 468 (1965)).

Even if Arizona courts required trials in suits for partition by sale, that would not be outcome determinative here. According to the facts as presented on summary judgment, the outcome—partition by sale—would have been identical even if the district court had held a trial. There were no material disputed facts that would suggest that Cuprite was not entitled as a matter of law to partition by sale. Cuprite had an interest in the property and wished to end its co-tenancy with the defendants. The defendants speculated, without a genuine basis, that a more beneficial result could have been achieved by not ordering partition, ordering partition in kind, or ordering sale by auction, but nothing in the record suggested that those issues needed to be elucidated in a trial for the district court to apply the appropriate legal standards.

The Ninth Circuit concluded that the district court properly applied Fed.R.Civ.P. 56(a) in granting relief on summary judgment where there was no genuine dispute of material fact to be resolved at trial.

**ANSWER (A)** is incorrect because both the district court and the Ninth Circuit, applying Erie doctrine, concluded that Fed.R.Civ.P. 56 applied and not the Arizona statutory provision. **ANSWER (B)** is incorrect because the court concluded that the federal summary judgment order was appropriate and the defendants therefore had not been denied a jury trial right. **ANSWER (C)** is incorrect for the same reason; on the merits, the court found that a jury trial would not have resulted in a different and more favorable outcome for the defendants on the merits of their claims. **ANSWER (E)** is incorrect because it misstates the reason for the Ninth Circuits' conclusion: the court found the partition by sale to be procedural, not substantive (see discussion above).

### PROBLEM #19. BEST ANSWER (B).

Problems #19 and #20 are based on *Gillespie v. Charter Communications*, 2015 WL 5638055 (E.D. Mo. Sept. 24, 2015). Problem #19 deals with application of principles relating to the attorney client privilege. Problem #20 addresses the attorney work product doctrine. In both instances the court held that neither the attorney-client privilege nor the attorney work product doctrine applied, so the court granted the plaintiff's motion to compel production of the document without the "Attorney Eyes Only" designation.

"Parties may obtain discovery regarding any non-privileged matter that is relevant to any party's claim or defense." Fed.R.Civ.P. 26(b)(1). The federal attorney-client privilege affords a client the right to refuse to disclose "communications between attorney and client made for the purpose of obtaining legal advice." *Carr v. Anheuser-Busch Cos.*, 791 F.Supp.2d 672, 674 (E.D.Mo.2011). Similarly, Missouri's attorney-client privilege "prohibits the discovery of confidential communications, oral or written, between an attorney and his client with reference to litigation pending or contemplated." *State ex rel. Koster v. Cain,* 383 S.W.3d 105, 116 (Mo.Ct.App.2012). Under both Missouri and federal law, the party asserting the privilege has the burden of proof to demonstrate that the privilege applies to the documents at issue. *See In re Advanced Pain Ctrs. Poplar Bluff v. Ware*, 11 F.Supp.3d 967, 973 (E.D.Mo.2014); *State ex rel. Ford Motor Co. v. Westbrooke*, 151 S.W.3d 364, 367 (Mo.2004).

In the context of corporate attorney-client communications, the United States Supreme Court has clarified that the privilege applies when: (1) the document or communication was provided by agents of the corporate client to counsel, acting as counsel, at the direction of their corporate superiors; (2) the information was necessary for the provision of legal advice; (3) the agents were aware that their communication was made for the purpose of obtaining legal advice for the corporation; and (4) the communication was treated as confidential. *See Upjohn Co. v. United States*, 449 U.S. 383, 394–95 (1981).

Here, the c determined that it need not address whether federal or state law governs Charter's assertion of privilege in this case, as the court found that Charter had not met its burden under either law to show that the privilege applied to the documents at issue. Charter failed to show that the incident report was created to obtain legal advice, and that the corporate agents involved knew that the document was prepared so that Charter could obtain such advice. Both Missouri and the Eighth Circuit agree that a corporate document is not protected by the attorney-client privilege solely because an attorney was one of its recipients. *See, e.g., Diversified Indus., Inc. v. Meredith*, 572 F.2d 596, 602 (8th Cir.1977) ("In order for the privilege to be applicable, the parties to the communication in question must bear the relationship of attorney and client. . . . A communication is not privileged simply because it is made by or to a person who happens to be a lawyer."); *Bd. of Registration for Healing Arts v. Spinden*, 798 S.W.2d 472, 476 (Mo.Ct.App.1990) (holding that in-house counsel's "mere involvement in the investigation does not shield the investigative reports from discovery"). The court recognized that information of this type could be privileged if it was communicated to counsel for the purpose of obtaining legal advice, but Charter had not met its burden to establish such facts in this case.

Charter's reliance on *Geller*, 2011 WL 5507572, for the proposition that the incident report was privileged is unpersuasive. In that non-binding case, unlike here, the documents at issue (the defendant's internal investigative documents concerning the plaintiff's complaint that she was subjected to a hostile work environment) were created by the defendant's corporate compliance officer only after the defendant had received a notice from the plaintiff's counsel that the plaintiff was bringing claims against the employer for sexual discrimination and harassment, and after the defendant had retained counsel as a result. *Id.* at *2–3. In this case, unlike *Geller*, the incident report was not prepared in response to any pending litigation, and the Director of Human Resources who prepared the report did so as an agent of Charter's entire corporate compliance team, rather than a single defense attorney as was the case in *Geller*. Therefore, the court found that the attorney-client privilege did not apply to either the EthicsPoint complaint or the incident report.

**ANSWER (A)** is incorrect because there are no facts provided that would indicate the defendant Charter had waived its privilege, therefore this was not the basis for the court granting the plaintiff's motion to compel. **ANSWER (C)** is incorrect because the court did not base its grant of the motion based on this broad generalization. **ANSWER (D)** is incorrect because the court found that the privilege for corporate communications did not apply on these facts. **ANSWER (E)** is incorrect because the court made no finding of inappropriate behavior by the plaintiff with regard to the prior protective order.

### PROBLEM #20. BEST ANSWER (B).

Problem #20 is a continuation of Problem #19 and is based on the same facts and court decision. This problem addresses whether the documents sought by the plaintiff were protected under attorney work product immunity. The court held not, and therefore granted the plaintiff's motion for compelled production.

"Historically, a lawyer's mental impressions, conclusions, opinions, and legal theories have been afforded substantial protection in order to secure the lawyer's effective advocacy and representation of his or her clients' interests." *In re Grand Jury Proceedings, G.S., F.S.,* 609 F.3d 909, 916 (8th Cir.2010). This doctrine protects from discovery materials "prepared in anticipation for litigation or for trial." Fed.R.Civ.P. 26(b)(3). There are two types of protected work product. Non-opinion work product is only given qualified protection, and "is generally discoverable upon a showing of substantial need and an inability to secure the substantial equivalent of the materials by alternate means without undue hardship." *In re Grand Jury Proceedings,* 609 F.3d at 913. Opinion work product, "which encompasses a lawyer's opinions, conclusions, mental impressions, and legal theories," is afforded "substantially more protection." *Id.* The mere possibility that litigation may result is not sufficient to trigger the protection of the work product doctrine. *See Diversified Indus., Inc.,* 572 F.2d at 604. As with claims of attorney-client privilege, the party claiming protection under this doctrine bears the burden of establishing that it exists. *See Hickman v. Taylor,* 329 U.S. 495, 512 (1947).

In this case, it was undisputed that the incident report contained no opinions or mental impressions of Charter's attorneys. And as discussed above, it appeared to the court, based on the record before it, that the documents in question were not prepared in anticipation of litigation, but were rather generated in the ordinary course of Charter's business. Indeed, Charter made clear that the EthicsPoint reporting system, and the process of investigating claims made within this system, were part of an ongoing compliance program instituted by Charter. Though it is always possible that internal corporate complaints may result in litigation, such speculative possibilities were insufficient to establish that the documents were prepared in anticipation of litigation.

Moreover, even if the work product doctrine did apply, the court found that the plaintiff had sufficiently showed his substantial need for documents, which might have demonstrated that the defendants had a history of discriminating or retaliating in a similar fashion to what the plaintiff alleged here, and that the plaintiff had no other means to obtain these documents. Therefore, the court found that the EthicsPoint complaint and Charter's incident report were not protected from discovery by the work product doctrine. *See Diversified Indus., Inc.,* 572 F.2d at 604 (finding that there was no work product immunity for documents prepared in the ordinary course of business); *Love v. Sears, Roebuck and Co.,* No. 3–13–CV–402–S, 2014 WL 1092270, at *2 (W.D.Ky. Mar. 14, 2014) (holding that incident reports were not prepared in anticipation of litigation because they were prepared as part of general policy to record alleged incidents rather than specifically in anticipation of litigation).

Therefore the court ordered that the plaintiff's motion to compel the production of documents without the "Attorneys' Eyes Only" designation was granted.

**ANSWER (A)** is incorrect because there are no facts that would indicate or support the conclusion that the defendants had engaged in criminal or fraudulent conduct so as to override the attorney work product protection. This is a red-herring answer. **ANSWER (C)** is incorrect because the defendants failed to carry their burden of convincing the court that attorneys were involved in the compliance program or had reviewed the documents in anticipation of litigation. **ANSWER (D)** is incorrect because the court made no finding that the documents constituted ordinary work product subject to protection. **ANSWER (E)** is incorrect because the defendant Charter made no such showing, and this in and of itself would not be a ground for invoking the attorney work product immunity.

### PROBLEM #21. BEST ANSWER (A).

Problems #21 and #22 are based on *Ela v. Destefano,* 2015 WL 7839723 (M.D. Fla. Dec. 12, 2015). Both problems deal with Fed.R.Civ.P. 50(a) motions for judgment as a matter of law, sought by the plaintiff and defendant at the conclusion of the plaintiff's case-in-chief at trial. In Problem #20, the court granted the plaintiff's motion for a Rule 50(a) judgment, and in Problem #21, the court granted the sheriff defendant's Rule 50(a) motion (*see* discussion below).

Fed.R.Civ.P. 50(a) governs motions for judgment as a matter of law. Such a motion may be granted against a party "if a party has been fully heard on an issue during a jury trial and the court finds that a reasonable jury would not have a legally sufficient evidentiary basis to find for the party on that issue." Fed.R.Civ.P. 50(a). But, entry of judgment as a matter of law is appropriate "only if the facts and inferences point overwhelmingly in favor of one party, such that reasonable people could not arrive at a contrary verdict." *Action Marine. Inc. v. Cont'l Carbon Inc.,* 481 F.3d 1302, 1309 (11th Cir.2007). In considering Rule 50(a) motions, a court must review all evidence in the record and draw all reasonable inferences in favor of the nonmoving party; however, a court may not make credibility determinations or weigh the evidence, as those are solely functions of the jury. *Cleveland v. Home Shopping Network,*

*Inc.*, 369 F.3d 1189, 1193 (11th Cir.2004). Even under this generous standard, the nonmoving party is obligated to come forward with some evidence indicating that reasonable jurors could reach different verdicts. *Campbell v. Rainbow City, Ala.*, 434 F.3d 1306, 1312 (11th Cir.2006).

The DPPA is enforceable under its own terms, but it also creates a statutory right to privacy that is enforceable under § 1983. *See Collier v. Dickinson*, 477 F.3d 1306, 1309–10 (11th Cir.2007). It generally provides that except when carrying out an official governmental or law enforcement function "a person who knowingly obtains, discloses or uses personal information, from a motor vehicle record . . . shall be liable to the individual to whom the information pertains." 18 U.S.C. §§ 2721(b), 2724(a). To "obtain" personal information under the DPPA, a defendant need only access and observe the data. *McDonough v. Anoka Cty.*, 799 F.3d 931, 944 (8th Cir.2015). Also, each "access" of a person's personal information is a separate "obtainment" and thus an additional violation of the DPPA. *See Rollins v. City of Albert Lea*, 79 F.Supp. 3d 946, 974 (D. Minn. 2014). Accordingly, Destefano violated the DPPA each time she accessed the plaintiff's personal information, even when the accesses occurred in close succession to one another.

In this case, the unrefuted testimony elicited during trial established that Destefano violated the DPPA and the plaintiff's statutory right to privacy. Destefano admitted that while she was on duty as a law enforcement officer she accessed driver's license databases to view the plaintiff's personal information. Except for one instance where Destefano claimed to view the plaintiff's information for a law enforcement purpose—an instance about which she could recall no details—Destefano testified that she viewed the data for an improper purpose. Based on this testimony, Destefano violated the DPPA and the plaintiff's statutory right to privacy as a matter of law.

**ANSWER (B)** is incorrect because the "egregiousness" of the alleged violation was not at issue and not part of the standard for evaluating whether a Rule 50(a) judgment as a matter of law was appropriate on the trial evidence. **ANSWER (C)** is incorrect because, based on the trial testimony, the court concluded that the plaintiff had carried her burden of establishing a violation of the DPPA statute and there was no triable issue for a jury to determine. **ANSWER (D)** is incorrect because the plaintiff carried her burden of establishing a facial violation of the DPPA statute; there was no point in a jury hearing the defendant's rebuttal case (if any). **ANSWER (E)** is incorrect because the fact that the judge may or may not have granted summary judgment prior to trial has no bearing on an assessment of the evidence presented at trial, and the appropriateness of a Rule 50(a) motion.

**PROBLEM #22. BEST ANSWER (B).**

Problem #22 is a continuation of Problem #21, and is based on the same set of facts and case. In this variation, the court granted the defendant sheriff's motion for a Rule 50(a) judgment as a matter of law, applying the same legal standards to the evidence adduced at trial during the plaintiff's case-in-chief.

In Count III, the plaintiff attempted to hold the sheriff accountable in his official capacity for Destefano's conduct under § 1983 based on inadequate training or supervision. In doing so, the plaintiff could not rely on the doctrine of respondeat superior. *Gold v. City of Miami*, 151 F.3d 1346, 1350 (11th Cir.1998). Instead, a municipality may only be liable under § 1983 if its policy directly causes a violation. *Am. Fed'n of Labor & Cong, of Indus. Orgs, v. City of Miami*, 637 F.3d 1178, 1187 (11th Cir.2011). The plaintiff did not claim or prove the sheriff's policy on its face violated federal law or that it directed its employees to do so; thus, the only question is whether the plaintiff presented sufficient evidence that would allow the jury to conclude that there was a direct causal connection between the sheriff's policy and the alleged violation.

To prove that the sheriffs' office caused a violation, the plaintiff had to show that the sheriff had in place a policy or custom that amounted to a deliberate indifference to the plaintiff's rights, *Id.* at 1189. This required evidence that the sheriff had notice of a need to train or supervise his employees. *Id.* The notice requirement could be satisfied by a pattern of similar constitutional violations by untrained employees or through a single prior incident. *Id.* In some cases, even without a prior incident it may be so obvious that without training, drivers' rights under the DPPA would be violated. *Id.* The plaintiff also had to establish that, once the sheriff had notice of a violation, he "made a deliberate choice not to train his employees." *Id.* In this case, the plaintiff utterly failed to meet this rigorous standard.

The plaintiff did not present evidence of a single prior violation of the DPPA by a sheriff's employee, let alone evidence upon which a reasonable jury could conclude that misuse of law enforcement databases was so "widespread" that the sheriff was on notice of the need to correct it. To be widespread, the violation would have to be " 'obvious, flagrant, rampant and of continued duration.' " *Holloman ex rel. Holloman v. Harland*, 370 F.3d 1252, 1294 (11th Cir.2004) (quoting *Brown v. Crawford*, 906 F.2d 667, 671 (11th Cir.1990)).

One of the sheriff's employees testified that there may have been one or two investigations per year into instances of improper use of DAVID, but he could not recall the specifics of a single such investigation, nor could he identify a single violation of the DPPA on the part of the sheriff's employees. If indeed such investigations did occur, it was entirely possible that they resulted in findings of "no violation." The testimony of Toni Dow supported the conclusion that there were no violations. Dow was the terminal agency coordinator and in charge of DAVID user management during the relevant time period. Dow testified that she was unaware of any sheriff's employee misusing the DAVID system. There was no evidence in the record to the contrary.

Even if the plaintiff had satisfied the notice requirement, there was no evidence that the sheriff made a deliberate choice not to train or supervise his employees. *See Am. Fed'n of Labor*, 637 F.3d at 1187. In fact, the evidence showed just the opposite—that the sheriff ensured that his employees understood that the databases were to be used only for law enforcement purposes. As a condition for use of DAVID, deputies were required to sign an acknowledgment of the Memorandum of Understanding making it clear that DAVID was to be used only for official law enforcement purposes. The acknowledgment also put deputies on notice that unauthorized use could result in criminal and civil liability. The Memorandum itself further contained an attachment listing every exception from the DPPA. Destefano signed at least one acknowledgment form during the time period at issue in this case.

Additionally, deputies were reminded each time they accessed the DAVID database that their use was authorized only for law enforcement purposes. Both the current and former terminal agency coordinators, Anne Howard and Dow, respectively, testified that before each separate access of DAVID, officers were required to enter through the criminal justice information system portal, which prompted the user to agree to use the database solely for law enforcement purposes. If an officer did not register agreement, he or she was denied access to the system. The objective of these training efforts was met— Destefano unequivocally testified that each time she accessed the plaintiff's personal information she knew she was misusing DAVID in violation of the Sheriff's policy, but she did so anyway.

It is difficult to imagine what else the sheriff might have done to prevent Destefano from viewing the plaintiff's personal information in violation of the DPPA. Additional supervision would have been hugely expensive and likely ineffective. Dow testified that technically there was no way to discern whether a search query made by an officer was for a lawful or unlawful purpose. Other than having a supervisor look over the shoulder of each officer as they made their searches, the only way the sheriff could know of DAVID misuse was to observe and track every DAVID transaction made by every DAVID user to detect suspicious searching trends. As the sheriff oversaw 1,254 active DAVID users, such a task would have been unreasonable.

In sum, the plaintiff failed to present evidence upon which a reasonable jury could infer that the sheriff had a policy indifferent to rights established by the DPPA. Therefore, as a matter of law, the sheriff was not liable to the plaintiff under § 1983.

**ANSWER (A)** is incorrect because the problem does not raise any issues relating to the sheriff's immunity from suit; this is a red-herring answer. **ANSWER (C)** is incorrect because the court held that the plaintiff presented no evidence to support a finding of a direct causal connection between the sheriff's policies and practices for a jury to conclude there was a violation of the law. **ANSWER (D)** is incorrect because granting the motion would not deny the plaintiff of a jury trial right; she failed to present evidence that the sheriff was liable under § 1983, and therefore there would be no point to a jury trial as a matter of law. **ANSWER (E)** is incorrect because the testimony of one or two possible prior violations was insufficient to overcome a finding that the sheriff was not liable under § 1983, as a matter of law.

## PROBLEM #23. BEST ANSWER (E).

Problem #23 is based on *Turner v. The Paul Revere Life Ins. Co.,* 2015 WL 5097805 (D. Nev. Aug. 28, 2015). This problem deals with the scope of discovery under Fed.R.Civ.P. 26(b), and motions to compel disclosure of information pursuant to Fed.R.Civ.P. 37. The court denied the plaintiff's motion for disclosure of three of the categories of requested information, but ordered disclosure of the employee performance records.

Fed.R.Civ.P. 26(b)(1) governs the scope of discovery. Information falls within the scope of discovery if two elements are satisfied. The rule states that "parties may obtain discovery regarding any non-privileged matter" if the information is both (1) "relevant to any party's claim or defense" and (2) "proportional to the needs of the case." Fed.R.Civ.P. 26(b)(1); 26(b)(2)(C)(iii); *see also* 26(b)(1), Advisory Comm. Notes (2015).

A party may no longer obtain information because it is "relevant to the subject matter involved in the action." In 1999, Rule 26(b)(1) stated that "parties may obtain discovery regarding any matter, not privileged, which is relevant to the subject matter involved in the pending action, whether it relates to the claim or defense of the party seeking discovery or to the claim or defense of any other party." 26(b)(1) (1999). In 2000, the rule was amended to curb overbroad discovery. *See* Fed.R.Civ.P. 26(b)(1), Advisory Comm. Notes (2000). It required a party to show "good cause" before obtaining discovery that is "relevant to the subject matter involved in the action." Fed.R.Civ.P. 26(b)(1). In December of 2015, the rule will be amended again. Fed.R.Civ.P. 26(b)(1), Advisory Comm. Notes (2015). The new rule will limit the scope of discovery to information that is (1) "relevant to any party's claim or defense" and (2) "proportional to the needs of the case." *Id.* These principles are currently codified in Rules 26(b)(1) and 26(b)(2)(C)(iii).

The 2015 amendments to Rule 26(b)(1) "restore the proportionality factors to their original place in defining the scope of discovery, and reinforce the Rule 26(g) obligation of the parties to consider these factors in making discovery requests, responses, or objections." Fed.R.Civ.P. 26(b)(1), Advisory Comm. Notes (2015).

To be "relevant to any party's claim or defense," the requested information "need not be admissible in evidence." *Id.* To be "proportional to the needs of the case," the court examines the requested information in light of six factors: "(1) the importance of the issues at stake in the action, (2) the amount in controversy, (3) the parties' relative access to relevant information, (4) the parties' resources, (5) the importance of the discovery in resolving the issues, and (6) whether the burden or expense of the proposed discovery outweighs its likely benefit." Fed.R.Civ.P. 26(b)(1); 26(b)(2)(C)(iii); Fed.R.Civ.P. 26(b)(1), Advisory Comm. Notes (2015).

When a party signs a discovery request, response, or objection, it certifies that it has considered and complied with these factors. *See* Fed.R.Civ.P. 26(b)(1), Advisory Comm. Notes (2015). Rule 26(g) states that a signature certifies that the request, response, or objection is "neither unreasonable nor unduly burdensome, considering the needs of the case, prior discovery in the case, the amount in controversy, and the importance of the issues at stake in the action." Fed.R.Civ.P. 26(g)(1)(B)(iii). These provisions provide for "liberal discovery," *see Seattle Times, Co. v. Rhinehart*, 467 U.S. 20, 34 (1984), and echo the Supreme Court's mandate that courts and litigations must resolve civil matters fairly but without undue cost. *Brown Shoe Co. v. United States*, 370 U.S. 294, 306 (1962).

If, as here, a party resists discovery, the requesting party may file a motion to compel. *See* Fed.R.Civ.P. 37(a)(1). A facially valid motion to compel has two components. First, the motion must certify that the movant has "in good faith conferred or attempted to confer" with the party resisting discovery. Fed.R.Civ.P. 37(a)(1); LR 26–7(b); *ShuffleMaster, Inc. v. Progressive Games, Inc.,* 170 F.R.D. 166, 171 (D.Nev.1996). Second, the motion must include a threshold showing that the requested information falls within the scope of discovery under Rule 26. *See Hofer v. Mack Trucks, Inc.,* 981 F.2d 377, 380 (8th Cir.1992) (citing *Oppenheimer Fund, Inc. v. Sanders,* 437 U.S. 340, 352 (1978)).

If the requesting party makes these showings, the resisting party carries a "heavy burden" of demonstrating why discovery should be denied. *Blankenship v. Hearst Corp.,* 519 F.2d 418, 429 (9th Cir.1975). The resisting party must specifically detail the reasons why each request is improper. *Beckman Indus., Inc. v. Int'l Ins. Co.,* 966 F.2d 470, 472–73 (9th Cir.1992) ("Broad allegations of harm, unsubstantiated by specific examples or articulated reasoning, do not satisfy the Rule 26(c) test."); *Serrano v. Cintas Corp.,* 699 F.3d 884, 901 (6th Cir.2012) ("To justify a protective order, one of Rule 26(c)(1)'s enumerated harms must be illustrated 'with a particular and specific demonstration of fact, as distinguished from stereotyped and conclusory statements.' ").

Dr. Turner's motion was denied because he failed to demonstrate that the requested information falls within the scope of discovery under Rule 26. The motion seeks "(1) prior testimony/deposition transcripts and/or affidavits from employees who handled Plaintiff's claim; (2) employee training documents from Defendant's training session entitled 'Defining the Scope of the Insured's Own or Regular Occupation,'; (3) employee performance reviews from employees who handled Plaintiff's claims; and (4) Defendant's corporate ethics manual."

None of these requests were both "relevant to any party's claim or defense" and "proportional to the needs of the case." Fed.R.Civ.P. 26(b)(1); 26(b)(2)(C)(iii). The first category of information seeks discovery regarding other lawsuits. This information was irrelevant to Dr. Turner's claim and only tangentially related to the subject-matter of the action. Under current Rule 26(b)(1), a party may seek information that is "relevant to the subject-matter of the action" upon a showing that "good causes" exists to warrant the discovery.

Dr. Turner's motion did not argue that good cause existed to expand the scope of discovery. Instead, he relied on unpublished decisions involving other actions that are allegedly analogous to this case. It was unnecessary for the court to consider other cases that might be analogous when Dr. Turner did not demonstrate that his discovery requests were relevant to his claims and proportional to the needs of this case.

The court also found that Dr. Turner's second and fourth discovery requests were not "proportional to the needs of the case." *See* Fed.R.Civ.P. 26(b)(2)(C)(iii). He sought training manuals and related training documents. He argued that this information was discoverable because a party may obtain "*all* responsive training documents." This was incorrect. Paul Revere had already provided its employee Code of Conduct and a Benefits Center Manual.

And, Rule 26 directs the court to limit discovery that is "unreasonably cumulative or duplicative." Fed.R.Civ.P. 26(b)(2)(C)(i). Dr. Turner did not demonstrate how the requested discovery was not unreasonably cumulative or duplicative in light of the needs of the case and Paul Revere's prior discovery. This was what Rules 26(b) and 26(g) required.

The court reached a different conclusion with regard to Dr. Turner's fourth discovery request, which sought "employee performance reviews from employees who handled Plaintiff's claims." This information was facially relevant to Dr. Turner's claim and "proportional to the needs of the case" in light of "the issues at stake in the action." Fed.R.Civ.P. 26(b)(1); 26(b)(2)(C)(iii). The gravamen of Dr. Turner's complaint was that Paul Revere failed to honor its policy when it should have. Performance reviews by employees who handled Dr. Turner's claim might contain probative information.

In opposition, Paul Revere contended that employee performance reviews were not discoverable because they were privileged in Massachusetts, where Paul Revere was headquartered, and in Nevada, where this diversity action was pending. This argument was unpersuasive. It was unnecessary for the court to choose between upholding a party's right to discovery and denying a non-party's right to privacy. These competing interests were easily reconciled by redaction. Paul Revere was ordered to produce the employee performance reviews and redact all of the employee's personal identifiers. This would ensure that the employee's information remained private while permitting Dr. Turner to obtain relevant information.

For good cause shown, the court ordered that Dr. Turner's motion to compel was granted in part and denied in part; that Dr. Turner's motion to compel was granted with regard to "employee performance reviews from employees who handled the plaintiff's claims." Paul Revere was directed to redact the performance reviews and remove all personal identifiers from the performance reviews. The court further ordered that Dr. Turner's motion to compel was denied with regard to all other discovery requests.

**ANSWER (A)** is incorrect because the court held that three of the plaintiff's discovery requests were not within the scope of discovery under Fed.R.Civ.P. 26, for the detailed reasons delineated above. **ANSWER (B)** is incorrect because the facts do not raise issues of attorney-client privilege or work product immunity; these were not challenges asserted by the defendant in opposition to disclosure. **ANSWERS (C)** and **(D)** are incorrect because the court did not make findings that the discovery requests were burdensome or for the purpose of harassment, but rather not within the scope of discovery (not relevant to the claims and defenses, or duplicative and cumulative), and not proportional under the amended 2015 rule.

### PROBLEM #24. BEST ANSWER (C).

Problem #24 is based on *Stringer v. Volkswagen Group of America, Inc.,* 2015 WL 5898326 (S.D. Ala. Oct. 8, 2015). This problem requires analysis of the requirements for a federal court's diversity jurisdiction under 28 U.S.C. § 1332(a) and (c). The court found that the plaintiff had failed to properly plead its own citizenship, and also had defectively pleaded the nature of the entities

Volkswagen AG and Audi AG. As such, the court could not determine whether it had good diversity jurisdiction based on the pleadings.

"It is . . . axiomatic that the inferior federal courts are courts of limited jurisdiction. They are 'empowered to hear only those cases within the judicial power of the United States as defined by Article III of the Constitution,' and which have been entrusted to them by a jurisdictional grant authorized by Congress." *Univ. of S. Ala. v. Am. Tobacco Co.*, 168 F.3d 405, 409 (11th Cir.1999) (quoting *Taylor v. Appleton*, 30 F.3d 1365, 1367 (11th Cir.1994)). Accordingly, "it is well settled that a federal court is obligated to inquire into subject matter jurisdiction *sua sponte* whenever it may be lacking." *Id.* at 410. "A court should inquire into whether it has subject matter jurisdiction at the earliest possible stage in the proceedings." *Id.*

The complaint alleged diversity of citizenship under 28 U.S.C. § 1332(a) as the sole basis for the court's subject matter jurisdiction over the claims in the action. When federal jurisdiction is invoked based upon diversity, the plaintiff's allegations must include the citizenship of each party, so that the court is satisfied that no plaintiff is a citizen of the same state as any defendant. *Triggs v. John Crump Toyota, Inc.*, 154 F.3d 1284, 1287 (11th Cir.1998) ("Diversity jurisdiction requires complete diversity; every plaintiff must be diverse from every defendant."). Without such allegations, district courts are constitutionally obligated to dismiss the action altogether if the plaintiff does not cure the deficiency. *Stanley v. C.I.A.*, 639 F.2d 1146, 1159 (5th Cir.Unit B Mar. 1981); *see also DiMaio v. Democratic Nat'l Comm.*, 520 F.3d 1299, 1303 (11th Cir.2008) ("Where dismissal can be based on lack of subject matter jurisdiction and failure to state a claim, the court should dismiss on only the jurisdictional grounds.") That is, if a complaint's factual allegations do not assure the court it has subject matter jurisdiction, then the court is without power to do anything in the case. *See Goodman ex rel. Goodman v. Sipos*, 259 F.3d 1327, 1331, n.6 (11th Cir.2001) (" 'A district court must dismiss a case without ever reaching the merits if it concludes that it has no jurisdiction.' " (quoting *Capitol Leasing Co. v. FDIC*, 999 F.2d 188, 191 (7th Cir.1993))); *see also Belleri v. United States*, 712 F.3d 543, 547 (11th Cir.2013) ("We may not consider the merits of a complaint unless and until we are assured of our subject matter jurisdiction."); *Travaglio v. Am. Exp. Co.*, 735 F.3d 1266, 1268 (11th Cir.2013). *See also, e.g., Ray v. Bird & Son & Asset Realization Co., Inc.*, 519 F.2d 1081, 1082 (5th Cir.1975) ("The burden of pleading diversity of citizenship is upon the party invoking federal jurisdiction . . . " (citing *Mas v. Perry*, 489 F.2d 1396 (5th Cir.1974)).

The plaintiff, as the party invoking the court's jurisdiction, bore the initial burden of pleading sufficient facts establishing jurisdiction. The plaintiff properly alleged that § 1332(a)'s requisite amount in controversy was satisfied by claiming that damages sought are "in excess of $75,000 exclusive of interest and costs." *See, e.g., Federated Mut. Ins. Co. v. McKinnon Motors, LLC*, 329 F.3d 805, 807 (11th Cir.2003) ("In order to invoke a federal court's diversity jurisdiction, a plaintiff must claim, among other things, that the amount in controversy exceeds $75,000." (citing 28 U.S.C. § 1332)). They also properly alleged the citizenships of corporate Defendant Volkswagen Group of America,

Inc. (a citizen of New Jersey and Virginia, by alleging the states under whose laws it was incorporated and where it has its principal places of business). *See* 28 U.S.C. § 1332(c)(1). However, the plaintiff failed to properly plead facts establishing the citizenships of itself and the foreign defendants.

The plaintiff, a natural person, alleged that he was a "resident of the state of Alabama." The Eleventh Circuit has repeatedly stressed that "citizenship, not residence, is the key fact that must be alleged to establish diversity for a natural person." *See also Travaglio*, 735 F.3d at 1269 ("As we indicated in remanding this case for jurisdictional findings, the allegations in Travaglio's complaint about her citizenship are fatally defective. Residence alone is not enough."); *Molinos Valle Del Cibao, C. por A. v. Lama*, 633 F.3d 1330, 1342 n.12 (11th Cir.2011) ("Ordinarily, the complaint must allege the citizenship, not residence, of the natural defendants."); *Corporate Mgmt. Advisors, Inc. v. Artjen Complexus, Inc.*, 561 F.3d 1294, 1297 (11th Cir.2009) ("If a party fails to specifically allege citizenship in their notice of removal, the district court should allow that party to cure the omission."); *Beavers v. A.O. Smith Elec. Prods. Co.*, 265 Fed.Appx. 772, 778 (11th Cir.2008) ("The plaintiffs' complaint alleges only the residence of the nearly 100 plaintiffs, not their states of citizenship. Because the plaintiffs had the burden to affirmatively allege facts demonstrating the existence of jurisdiction and failed to allege the citizenship of the individual plaintiffs, the district court lacked subject matter jurisdiction on the face of the complaint."); *Crist v. Carnival Corp.*, 410 Fed.Appx. 197, 200 (11th Cir.2010) ("The allegation that Crist is a 'resident' of Florida is insufficient for diversity jurisdiction purposes because residency is not the equivalent of citizenship.").

"Citizenship is equivalent to 'domicile' for purposes of diversity jurisdiction. A person's domicile is the place of his true, fixed, and permanent home and principal establishment, and to which he has the intention of returning whenever he is absent therefrom." *McCormick v. Aderholt*, 293 F.3d 1254, 1257–58 (11th Cir.2002). *See also Travaglio*, 735 F.3d at 1269 (" 'Citizenship is equivalent to "domicile" for purposes of diversity jurisdiction.' And domicile requires both residence in a state and 'an intention to remain there indefinitely' " (quoting *McCormick*, 293 F.3d at 1257–58); *Mas*, 489 F.2d at 1399 ("For diversity purposes, citizenship means domicile; mere residence in the State is not sufficient.").)

The court therefore held that if the plaintiff wished to adequately plead diversity, he had to allege his own state of citizenship/domicile as a natural person.

Regarding Defendants Volkswagen AG and Audi AG, the plaintiff alleged only that each of them was "a corporation created and existing pursuant to the laws of the nation of Germany." This was not even nominally adequate for an American corporation, as no allegation was made about each entity's principal place of business. Moreover, the plaintiff made no attempt to explain what the suffix "AG" means or to plead to the court how it should be treated for purposes of diversity.

Generally, "a corporation shall be deemed to be a citizen of every State and foreign state by which it has been incorporated and of the State or foreign state where it has its principal place of business, "28 U.S.C. § 1332 (c)(1). However, a court should not "assume that a foreign state has business entities that enjoy corporate status as the United States understands it," as "not even the United Kingdom has a business form that is exactly equal to that of a corporation." *White Pearl Inversiones S.A. (Uruguay) v. Cemusa, Inc.*, 647 F.3d 684, 686 (7th Cir.2011). "Deciding whether a business enterprise based in a foreign nation should be treated as a corporation for the purpose of § 1332 can be difficult. Businesses in other nations may have attributes that match only a subset of those that in the United States distinguish a 'corporation'—a business with indefinite existence, personhood (the right to contract and litigate in its own name), limited liability for equity investors, and alienable shares, among other features—from forms such as the limited liability company, the limited partnership, and the business trust." *Fellowes, Inc. v. Changzhou Xinrui Fellowes Office Equip. Co.*, 759 F.3d 787, 788 (7th Cir.2014) (vacating district court's judgment and remanding with instructions to dismiss for want of subject-matter jurisdiction where, on appeal, the defendant business established under the law of China was found to be "closer to a limited liability company than to any other business structure in this nation," thus defeating diversity where both the plaintiff and a member of the defendant entity were citizens of Illinois). *See also BouMatic*, 759 F.3d at 791 ("Classification of a foreign business entity can be difficult, because other nations may use subsets of the characteristics that distinguish corporations from other business entities in the United States.").

"In *Carden v. Arkoma Assocs.*, 494 U.S. 185, 195–96 (1990), the Supreme Court held that for purposes of diversity of citizenship, a limited partnership is a citizen of each state in which any of its partners, limited or general, are citizens. In reaching this holding, the Court noted the long-standing rule that the citizenship of an artificial, unincorporated entity generally depends on the citizenship of all the members composing the organization." *Rolling Greens*, 374 F.3d at 1021. Thus, "the Court in *Carden* provided a general rule: every association of a common-law jurisdiction other than a corporation is to be treated like a partnership. That rule applies without regard to the corporation-like features or other business realities of the artificial entity." *Underwriters at Lloyd's, London v. Osting-Schwinn*, 613 F.3d 1079, 1087 (11th Cir.2010). Moreover, "if it is hard to determine whether a business entity from a common-law nation is equivalent to a 'corporation,' it can be even harder when the foreign nation follows the civil-law tradition." *White Pearl Inversiones*, 647 F.3d at 686 ("Uruguay has at least three forms of limited-liability businesses: sociedad anónima (S.A.), sociedad anónima financiera de inversión (S.A.F.I.), and sociedad responsabilidad limitada (S.R.L.). White Pearl did not say which kind it is, and its lawyers did not analyze whether that kind of business organization should be treated as a corporation. They simply assumed that Uruguay has such a beast as a 'corporation' and that White Pearl is one. The lawyers for Cemusa made the same assumption.").

The court held that if the plaintiff wished to adequately plead diversity, he had to allege what kind of entity the defendants Volkswagen AG and Audi AG were—that is, whether each was a corporate or unincorporated entity. If they were to be treated as corporations, the plaintiff had to allege "every State and foreign state by which each has been incorporated and the State or foreign state where it had its principal place of business." § 1332(c)(1). If they were to be treated as unincorporated entities, the plaintiff had to allege the citizenships of each of its members. *Rolling Greens, MHP, L.P. v. Comcast SCH Holdings, L.L.C.*, 374 F.3d 1020, 1022 (11th Cir.2004).

**ANSWER (A)** is incorrect because there is an insufficient factual basis to conclude whether the parties to the litigation satisfied or failed to satisfy the complete diversity rule. **ANSWER (B)** is incorrect because foreign corporations can and are subject to American federal court jurisdiction, if such jurisdiction is properly established. **ANSWER (D)** is incorrect because the court in the case could not determine whether there was good diversity jurisdiction, because of the pleading defects with regard to the parties' citizenship and status. **ANSWER (E)** is incorrect because pendant party jurisdiction was not raised on these facts, and so this is a red-herring answer.

**PROBLEM #25. BEST ANSWER (B).**

Problem #25 is based on *Trust v. Staab*, 2015 WL 8493925 (C.D. Cal. Dec. 9, 2015). This problem involves a simple analysis of whether a federal court has good removal jurisdiction based on federal question jurisdiction, where a defendant relies on a federal defense. The court held there was no valid federal question and therefore granted the plaintiff's petition for remand to state court.

Christiana Trust filed an unlawful detainer action against Staab in Riverside County Superior Court. The Staabs filed a notice of removal under 28 U.S.C. § 1441 on the basis of federal question jurisdiction. Trust then petitioned for remand back to state court.

Under 28 U.S.C. § 1441(a), a defendant may remove a civil action from state court to federal court if original jurisdiction would lie in federal court. *City of Chicago v. Int'l College of Surgeons*, 522 U.S. 56, 163 (1997). The removing party has the burden of showing removal was proper, *i.e.*, there are grounds for federal jurisdiction and the removing party complied with all procedural requirements for removal. *Emrich v. Touche Ross & Co.*, 846 F.2d 1190, 1195 (9th Cir.1988). The removing party may show that removal was proper by submitting summary-judgment-type evidence. *Matheson v. Progressive Specialty Ins. Co.*, 319 F.3d 1089, 1090 (9th Cir.2003). Conclusory allegations and speculative assertions are insufficient to meet this burden, however. *See, e.g., Matheson*, 319 F.3d at 1090–91; *Conrad Assocs. v. Hartford Accident & Indem. Co.*, 994 F.Supp. 1196, 1198 (N.D. Cal. 1998). In any event, the Ninth Circuit has directed that courts must "strictly construe the removal statute against removal jurisdiction," and that "any doubt as to the right of removal" is resolved in favor of remanding the case to state court. *Gaus v. Miles, Inc.*, 980 F.2d 564, 566 (9th Cir.1992).

Under 28 U.S.C. § 1331, federal jurisdiction is proper if the case arises under federal law. *See* 28 U.S.C. § 1331. When the removing party asserts federal question jurisdiction under 28 U.S.C. § 1331, the federal question generally must appear on the face of the initial complaint. *See Okla. Tax Comm'n v. Graham*, 489 U.S. 838, 840 (1989). Defenses and counterclaims based on federal law may not normally serve as the jurisdictional basis for removal. *Holmes Grp., Inc. v. Vornado Air Circulation Sys., Inc.*, 535 U.S. 826, 831–32 (2002).

The court determined that it must remand the case because it lacked federal question jurisdiction over the action. Although the Staabs asserted that the court had federal question jurisdiction under 28 U.S.C. § 1331, Christiana Trust's unlawful detainer action under Cal. Civ. Proc. Code §§ 1161 et seq. raised no question of federal law. The Staabs' defense under 12 U.S.C. § 5201 did not by itself make removal proper. *Vornado Air*, 535 U.S. at 831. Accordingly, removal was improper for lack of federal question jurisdiction.

For the reasons stated above, the court granted the motion and remanded the case to Riverside County Superior Court.

**ANSWER (A)** is incorrect because the court did not order the remand because the plaintiff had only pleaded a single state law claim, but because the federal defense did not confer federal question jurisdiction on the court. **ANSWER (C)** is incorrect because there was no assertion of supplemental jurisdiction as a basis for the removal; the court would first have to determine it had good federal question jurisdiction before it could assess any claims of supplemental jurisdiction. **ANSWER (D)** is incorrect because the opposite is true: the well-pleaded complaint rule would not allow jurisdiction based on the defendant's pleading a federal defense. **ANSWER (E)** is incorrect because 28 U.S.C. § 1441(c) does not apply to these facts and is not, on these facts, a basis for establishing federal question removal jurisdiction.

**END OF ANSWERS AND EXPLANATIONS TO EXAM #3**

# CHAPTER 9
# ANSWER KEY FOR EXAM #4
# ANSWERS AND EXPLANATIONS

## PROBLEM #1. BEST ANSWER (D).

Problems #1 and #2 are based on *Kellerman v. Inter-Island Launch d/b/a Price of Whales Whale Watching*, 2015 WL 6620604 (Oct. 30, 2015). Problem #1 concerns a motion to dismiss for improper venue under Fed.R.Civ.P. 12(b)(3), to enforce a forum selection clause. The court held that the forum selection clause was not enforceable because in absence of seeing the clause, the plaintiffs could not have assented to it. Problem #2, discussed below, deals with the defendant's alternative motion to dismiss on the grounds of forum no conveniens. The court dismissed this motion, as well. (*See* discussion below).

A motion to dismiss pursuant to a forum selection clause is treated as a motion to dismiss for improper venue under Fed.R.Civ.P. 12(b)(3). *Doe 1 v. AOL LLC*, 552 F.3d 1077, 1081 (9th Cir.2009). When considering a motion to dismiss for improper venue, the pleadings need not be accepted as true and the court may consider facts outside the pleadings. *Id.* (citing *Argueta v. Banco Mexicano, S.A.*, 87 F.3d 320, 323 (9th Cir.1996)); *Kukje Hwajae Ins. Co. v. M/V Hyundai Liberty*, 294 F.3d 1171, 1174 (9th Cir.2002). However, "in the context of a Rule 12(b)(3) motion based upon a forum selection clause, the trial court must draw all reasonable inferences in favor of the non-moving party and resolve all factual conflicts in favor of the non-moving party." *Murphy v. Schneider Nat'l Inc.*, 362 F.3d 1133, 1138 (9th Cir.2003); *see also Peterson v. Boeing Co.*, 715 F.3d 276, 279 (9th Cir.2013).

The defendants asserted that this suit must be dismissed because the plaintiffs agreed to the forum selection clause that required that any suit be brought in British Columbia. The defendants insist that the plaintiffs were aware of the forum selection clause because its employees were required to physically open all pages of the booklet and ask passengers to read the entire booklet before signing it. Moreover, the defendants argued that the plaintiffs' signatures on the third page of the booklet indicated that they understood and agreed to the entire booklet, including the forum selection clause.

The plaintiffs responded that they are not bound by the forum selection clause because they were never shown it (*i.e.*, it was not included on the one-page document they alleged they signed) and therefore could not have manifested their assent to the clause. According to the plaintiffs, they believed they were signing a single page disclosure of medical conditions and contact information (page three of the booklet). The plaintiffs argued that page three of the booklet reasonably appeared to be a stand-alone document because it did not include references to prior pages nor did it have any pagination to indicate it was the third page of a three-page document. Finally, the plaintiffs pointed to declarations by three of the plaintiffs' co-passengers that corroborated their version of events: namely, that Inter-Island employees did not show the passengers the entire booklet or explain that they should read it all, but rather hastily urged the passengers to sign a one-page document in a crowded and hectic office.

In their reply, the defendants contended that the one-page document signed by the plaintiffs did indeed refer to the booklet's prior pages. More specifically, the defendants noted that the bottom of page three included an indemnification clause for the parents/guardians of children which contained an acronym that was earlier defined on page one of the booklet. Additionally, the defendants insisted that the passengers' decision to complete the waiver quickly should not invalidate the enforceability of the waiver.

To determine the enforceability of a forum selection clause, a federal court must ask whether a contract existed under state law. *See San Diego Police Officers' Ass'n v. San Diego City Emps. Ret. Sys.,* 568 F.3d 725, 737 (9th Cir.2009) ("Federal courts look to state law to determine the existence of a contract."). Under Washington state law, the proponent of the contract bears the burden of proving the existence of a contract. *Keystone Land & Dev. Co. v. Xerox Corp.,* 152 Wash.2d 171, 94 P.3d 945, 949 (Wash.2004). Of particular relevance here, "it is essential to the formation of a contract that the parties manifest to each other their mutual assent to the same bargain at the same time." *Yakima Cty. (W.Valley) Fire Prot. Dist. No.12 v. Yakima,* 122 Wash.2d 371, 388, 858 P.2d 245 (Wash.1993). Mutual assent can be shown by a party's signature on a contract, even if that party did not read it. *Id.* (citing *Skagit State Bank v. Rasmussen,* 109 Wash.2d 377, 381–84, 745 P.2d 37 (1987)). However, mutual assent is lacking if a party is "deprived of the opportunity to read the contract." *Id.*

Here, the defendants failed to demonstrate that the plaintiffs gave their mutual assent to the forum selection clause. Despite the defendants' claim that its employees were required to show the entire waiver booklet to passengers and urge them to read all three pages, the plaintiffs provided declarations by three of the other eight passengers on the tour supporting the plaintiffs' claim that the defendants' employees did not follow such policy on the day of the plaintiffs' whale-watching tour. Moreover, the plaintiffs asserted that they had no knowledge of the first two pages of the booklet because only the third page was presented to them on a flat surface (like a clipboard or a desk), and, therefore, they believed that they were signing a single page document which only asked them for a disclosure of medical and contact information.

Accepting the plaintiffs' representation of the facts as this court was required to do, the court found that the plaintiffs' belief was reasonable given that the third page of the booklet did not contain any language or information referencing the two prior pages and lacked pagination or anything else that would suggest there was more than one page to the document. The court was unpersuaded by the defendants' argument that the indemnification section on the third page used acronyms that were defined in prior pages and, therefore, the plaintiffs should have known that there were additional pages. Not only was the indemnification provision crossed out in the plaintiffs' waivers, but the provision was also located at the very bottom of the page, several lines below the signature line.

In addition, the plaintiffs were not required to initial or confirm in any way that they had agreed to the first and second page of the booklet. The plaintiffs' signatures on the third page could definitively prove that they assented to the contractual terms located on the second page of the booklet, when it was questionable whether the plaintiffs knew that a second page even existed. Under these circumstances and drawing all reasonable inferences to the plaintiff (as the court must given the procedural posture of this case), the defendants failed to demonstrate that the plaintiffs manifested their assent to the forum selection clause which was located on the second page of the booklet.

**ANSWER (A)** is incorrect because the court held that the forum selection clause was unenforceable. **ANSWER (B)** is incorrect because the presence of a choice of law clause was not argued as a ground for enforcing the forum selection clause; at any rate, on the facts the plaintiffs most likely were unaware of the choice of law clause, as well. **ANSWER (C)** is incorrect because the court decided that notwithstanding the fact that the plaintiffs signed page three, this could not be taken as a knowing assent to the forum selection clause earlier in the document. **ANSWER (E)** is incorrect because the court did not base its decision to deny the improper venue motion on the grounds that the defendants' employees failed to review the document with the whale watching clients that day.

## PROBLEM #2. BEST ANSWER (D).

Problem #2 is a continuation of Problem #1, and is based on the same facts and case as Problem #1. The court found that, weighing the public and private interest factors on a *forum non conveniens* motion, that these factors weighed in favor of the Seattle forum. Therefore the court denied the defendant's alternative motion to dismiss the cased on forum non conveniens grounds.

"The doctrine of forum non conveniens is based on the inherent power of the courts to decline jurisdiction in exceptional circumstances." *Paper Operations Consultants Intn'l, Ltd. v. SS Hong Kong Amber*, 513 F.2d 667, 670 (9th Cir.Cal.1975). More specifically, the doctrine is used by federal courts to refuse jurisdiction of cases that "should have been brought in a foreign jurisdiction, rather than in than in the United States." *Id.* "The ultimate question to be decided in determining whether the doctrine of *forum non conveniens* is applicable is whether 'the forum chosen by the plaintiff is so completely inappropriate and inconvenient that it is better to stop the litigation in the place where brought and let it start all over again somewhere else.' " *Id.* (quoting *Norwood v. Kirkpatrick*, 349 U.S. 29, 31 (1955)).

"To prevail on a motion to dismiss based upon *forum non conveniens*, a defendant bears the burden of demonstrating an adequate alternative forum, and that the balance of private and public interest factors favors dismissal." *Carijano v. Occidental Petroleum Corp.*, 643 F.3d 1216, 1224 (9th Cir.2011). Therefore, the court analyzed the private and public interest factors with respect to this case.

The defendants argued that the private factors favor dismissal because the defendants, the witnesses, and the evidence were located in British Columbia, making travel to that forum more convenient and less costly. The plaintiffs argued that, as the plaintiffs, they had the right to choose the forum within which to bring their case and Washington was no less convenient as a forum than British Columbia. Finally, the plaintiffs urged that a judgment secured in the Western District of Washington would be readily enforced in Canada.

The following private interest factors are considered when deciding a motion for *forum non conveniens:* "(1) the residence of the parties and the witnesses; (2) the forum's convenience to the litigants; (3) access to physical evidence and other sources of proof; (4) whether unwilling witnesses can be compelled to testify; (5) the cost of bringing witnesses to trial; (6) the enforceability of the judgment; and (7) all other practical problems that make trial of a case easy, expeditious and inexpensive." *Bos. Telecomm. Grp., Inc. v. Wood*, 588 F.3d 1201, 1206–07 (9th Cir.2009) (citing *Lueck v. Sundstrand Corp.*, 263 F.3d 1137, 1145 (9th Cir.2001)).

The parties and the witnesses were located in two countries. The defendants resided in Canada, whereas the plaintiffs resided in the United States. The witnesses resided in various provinces throughout Canada. The cost of flying witnesses for depositions or flying them to trial was relatively the same whether the trial is held in Victoria, British Columbia or Seattle, Washington, given that the two cities are not far from one another. Moreover, there was also no indication that there would be unwilling witnesses that would require a court's subpoena power in order to compel testimony.

With respect to the location of evidence in this case, the plaintiffs indicated that the only evidence they intended to present were documents. Modern technology easily allows for the transfer of such documents from one location to another. Although the defendants raised the possibility that the *Countess* would need to be inspected, the plaintiffs reassured the court that they had no desire to inspect the *Countess* and the defendants did not otherwise persuade the court that such an inspection would become critical to the case. As for the enforceability of any future judgment, there was no reason to question that a Canadian court would enforce a judgment entered in a United States court. *Cf. Morguard Invs. Ltd. v. De Savoye* (1990) 3 S.C.R.

The defendants argued that the public factors favored dismissal because Washington's interest in resolving this dispute was minimal, the burden on juries would be great, the Western District of Washington had a full docket, and the Washington court did not regularly preside over Canadian maritime law. In response, the plaintiffs emphasized that Washington and the people in the Seattle community were interested in resolving tort actions where the alleged accident and treatment occurred in Washington.

The public interest factors considered when deciding whether to dismiss a case include: "(1) administrative difficulties flowing from court congestion; (2) imposition of jury duty on the people of a community that has no relation to the litigation; (3) local interest in having localized controversies decided at home; (4) the interest in having a diversity case tried in a forum familiar with the law that governs the action; and (5) the avoidance of unnecessary problems in conflicts of law." *Creative Tech., Ltd. v. Aztech Sys. Pte., Ltd.,* 61 F.3d 696, 703–04 (9th Cir.1995).

The court agreed that Washington state and the people from the Seattle community who may end up serving on a jury in this case had a significant interest in adjudicating this dispute. Not only did the accident allegedly occur in Washington waterways, but the *Countess* also docked in a Washington port where local Emergency Medical Services evaluated Ms. Kellerman and then airlifted her to Harborview Medical Center in Seattle. Furthermore, the court did not anticipate any unusual "administrative difficulties flowing from court congestion," and there was no indication that the court system in British Columbia was any less busy than this district court. Nor was the court persuaded by the defendants' bald assertions regarding this court's lack of familiarity with the governing law, whatever that law may be. As such, the public factors did not tip in favor of dismissal.

In conclusion, even if Canada was an adequate alternative forum, the balance between public and private factors did not strongly favor dismissal. *See Paper Operations Consultants International, Ltd. v. SS Hong Kong Amber,* 513 F.2d 667, 671 (9th Cir.Cal.1975) ("The plaintiff's choice of forum should rarely be disturbed unless the balance is strongly in favor of adjudicating the matter in another forum.").

Accordingly, the defendants' motion to dismiss for improper venue and *forum non conveniens* was denied.

**ANSWER (A)** is incorrect because the court evaluated the *forum non conveniens* motion based on an assessment of both the private and public factors; the location of the injuries was but one factor in this analysis, and did not outweigh all the other factors. **ANSWER (B)** is incorrect because the court never made a finding that the Canadian courts were an adequate alternative forum; even assuming they were, the court still held that the private and public factors weighed in favor of the Washington forum. **ANSWER (C)** sounds like a possible answer, but it is not the best answer; this does not reflect a weighing of all the private and public factors in a *forum non conveniens* analysis. **ANSWER (E)** is a possible answer, but not the best answer. Although it is true and the court acknowledged that courts give deference to a plaintiff's choice of forum, the basis for the court's decision was the complete analysis of the private and public factors involved in a *forum non conveniens* determination.

### PROBLEM #3. BEST ANSWER (E).

Problem #3 is based on *Virginia Uranium, Inc. v. McAuliffe,* 2015 WL 6143105 (W.D. Virginia Oct. 19, 2015). This problem deals with the Dan River Basin Association's and the Roanoke River Basin Association's motion to intervene under Fed.R.Civ.P. 24(a). The court held that the proposed intervenors were adequately represented by the defendants and therefore the court denied the motion.

A motion to intervene "must state the grounds for intervention and be accompanied by a pleading that sets out the claim or defense for which intervention is sought." Fed.R.Civ.P. 24(c). "Liberal intervention is desirable to dispose of as much of a controversy 'involving as many apparently concerned persons as is compatible with efficiency and due process.' " *Feller v. Brock,* 802 F.2d 722, 729 (4th Cir.1986) (quoting *Nuesse v. Camp,* 385 F.2d 694, 700 (D.C.Cir.1967)); *see also Spring Constr. Co. v. Harris,* 614 F.2d 374, 377 (4th Cir.1980). Accordingly, a "district court must accept as true the non-conclusory allegations of the motion and accompanying pleading." *Lake Inv'rs Dev. Grp ., Inc. v. Egidi Dev. Grp.,* 715 F.2d 1256, 1258 (7th Cir.1983).

Intervention is "a procedure by which an outsider with an interest in a lawsuit may come in as a party though the outsider has not been named as a party by the existing litigants." 7C Charles Alan Wright, Arthur R. Miller & Mary Kay Kane, *Federal Practice and Procedure* § 1901, at 257 (2007). "Rule 24 creates two intervention alternatives, . . . Rule 24(a) governs 'Intervention of Right,' while Rule 24(b) addresses 'Permissive Intervention.' " *Alt v. EPA,* 758 F.3d 588, 590 n. 2 (4th Cir.2014). The basin associations invoke them both.

> On timely motion, the court must permit anyone to intervene who . . . claims an interest relating to the property or transaction that is the subject of the action, and is so situated that disposing of the action may as a practical matter impair or impede the movant's ability to protect its interest, unless existing parties adequately represent that interest.

Fed.R.Civ.P. 24(a)(2). The plaintiffs contested only the last element.

A would-be intervenor generally bears a "minimal" burden of showing that an existing party inadequately represents its interests, *see Virginia v. Westinghouse Elec. Corp.,* 542 F.2d 214, 216 (4th Cir.1976), but presumptions may arise against such a finding. "When the party seeking intervention has the same ultimate objective as a party to the suit, a presumption arises that its interests are adequately represented, against which the petitioner must demonstrate adversity of interest, collusion, or nonfeasance." *Id.* That presumption strengthens when one seeks to intervene on the side of a government party defending a law of the polity; there, a would-be intervenor "must mount a strong showing of inadequacy." *Stuart v. Huff,* 706 F.3d 345, 351–52 (4th Cir.2013).

The court held that the strong presumption arose that the defendants adequately represented the basin associations' interests. Both were ultimately concerned that the court hold that the AEA did not preempt Va. Code Ann. § 45.1–283. The basin associations principally contended that their interests might diverge from the defendants' on a question of injunctive relief.

Although their respective motions to dismiss opposed injunctive relief, the defendants had not briefed the subject to the same extent, or along the same argument, that the basin associations had. The court held that these differences revealed neither nonfeasance nor adversity of interests. The defendants were diligently and zealously defending against the suit, and the court had no reason to doubt that they were litigating, and would continue to litigate, in good faith and as fully as they deemed appropriate. The court held that the basin associations' "disagreement over how to approach the conduct of the litigation was not enough to rebut the presumption of adequacy." *See id.* at 353.

The court also found that the basin associations were incorrect insofar as they suggested a potential adversity of interests respecting a possible decision on injunctive relief. At this stage, the court noted, it seemed that, whatever the court's decision on declaratory relief, the decision on injunctive relief would follow from it. Moreover, the basin associations had no role in implementing Va. Code Ann. § 45.1–283 and, therefore, could be enjoined neither "from complying with Virginia's ban on uranium mining" nor "to accept and process Plaintiffs' applications for . . . permits and licenses. . . ." Therefore, the court concluded, it was doubtful that a question of such relief would bring their hardships into issue.

Thus, the court concluded that the basin associations had not shown that the defendants inadequately represented their interests. At bottom, they offered the litigation a local position that merged with the defendants'. The strong presumption of adequate representation withstands.

"On timely motion, the court may permit anyone to intervene who . . . has a claim or defense that shares with the main action a common question of law or fact." Fed.R.Civ.P. 24(b)(1)(B). "In exercising its discretion, the court must consider whether the intervention will unduly delay or prejudice the adjudication of the original parties' rights." Fed.R.Civ.P. 24(b)(3). Plaintiffs focus the Court on undue delay or prejudice, the most important consideration in this inquiry. *See Hill v. W. Elec. Co.,* 672 F.2d 381, 386 (4th Cir.2003).

Weighing the benefits and burdens of a permitted intervention, a court should ensure that the litigation will not "become unnecessarily complex, unwieldy or prolonged." *See United States v. Pitney Bowes, Inc.,* 25 F.3d 66, 69 (2d Cir.1994). "Where . . . intervention as of right is decided based on the government's adequate representation, the case for permissive intervention diminishes or disappears entirely." *Tutein v. Daley*, 43 F.Supp.2d 113, 131 (D.Mass.1999). " 'Where he presents no new questions, a third party can contribute usually most effectively and always most expeditiously by a brief amicus curiae and not by intervention.' " *Bush v. Viterna*, 740 F.2d 350, 359 (5th Cir.1984) (quoting *Crosby Steam Gage & Valve Co. v. Manning, Maxwell & Moore, Inc.,* 51 F.Supp. 972, 973 (D.Mass.1943)).

The court concluded that "the benefit, fairly perceived, from the basin associations' intervention did not justify the burden. The defendants adequately represented the basin associations' interests, and the basin associations' motion to dismiss merged, in substance, with the defendants". The court held that at this stage, it seemed that intervention would require additional rounds of responsive briefs, overlapping with matters raised in the motions already extensively briefed. The basin associations seemed to want, most of all, to share their views, and the court held that the associations could do so as amicus curiae. The scales weighed against intervention.

In sum, the defendants adequately represented the interests of the basin associations, which had no right to intervene. Because the accompanying burden outweighed the benefit, the court would not permit intervention. The court, however, granted the basin associations leave to file briefs, as amicus curiae, in further proceedings.

**ANSWER (A)** is incorrect because the only part of Fed.R.Civ.P. 24(a) that was contested was whether the defendants were adequately representing the interests of the proposed intervenors. No party challenged whether the associations had a property interest in the action. **ANSWER (B)** is incorrect because the court held exactly the opposite: that the defendants did adequately represent the interests of the proposed intervenors. **ANSWER (C)** is incorrect because while factually correct, the fact that the defendants did not oppose the intervention is not part of an analysis of whether intervention meets the standards under Rule 24(a). **ANSWER (D)** is incorrect for similar reasons; it doesn't matter that the plaintiffs opposed the motion to intervene.

### PROBLEM #4. BEST ANSWER (D).

Problem #4 is based on *Espinoza v. Mex-Am Café, LLC*, 2015 WL 5431949 (M.D. N.C. 2015). This problem deals with compulsory counterclaims under Fed.R.Civ.P. 13(a) and jurisdiction over such counterclaims. The court held that the counterclaims were compulsory and denied the plaintiff's motion to dismiss these claims.

Rule 13(a) of the Federal Rules of Civil Procedure describes a compulsory counterclaim as follows:

> A pleading shall state as a counterclaim any claim which at the time of serving the pleadings the pleader has against any opposing party, if it arises out of the transaction or occurrence that is the subject matter of the opposing party's claim.

Fed.R.Civ.P. 13(a). Section 1367(a) "confers supplemental jurisdiction over 'all other claims that are so related to claims in the action within original jurisdiction that they form part of the same case or controversy'" *United Capitol Ins. Co. v. Kapiloff*, 155 F.3d 488, 492 (4th Cir.1998). Accordingly, "compulsory counterclaims under Fed.R.Civ.P. 13(a) always satisfy § 1367(a)'s same case or controversy standard because they must satisfy the more stringent requirement that the counterclaim arise out of the same 'transaction or occurrence' as the jurisdiction invoking claim." *Smith v. James C. Hormel Sch. of Va. Inst. of Autism*, No. 3:08–CV–00030, 2010 WL 1257656, at *19 (W.D. Va. Mar. 26, 2010).

The defendants alleged that Espinoza returned to the restaurant and, without authorization from Galvan or Casares, removed three plasma televisions and plants from the restaurant. According to the defendants, "the facts involved in determining whether Espinoza was the owner of the plasma televisions and plants largely related to whether Espinoza was an owner or member/manager of Mex-Am or an employee." The defendants' argument suggested that Espinoza's removal of the items from the restaurant might not amount to conversion if he was deemed a member/manager. Indeed, if Espinosa was deemed a member/manager, he might have an interest in the fixtures in the restaurant. Certainly the claim of conversion would be affected by a determination of Espinosa's employment status.

The defendants' counterclaim for breach of contract also "arose out of the transaction or occurrence that was the subject matter of the opposition party's claim" so as to be considered compulsory under Rule 13(a). The defendants alleged that Galvan, Espinoza, and Casares entered into an agreement whereby they would operate the restaurant "as partners and co-owners", that, pursuant to that agreement, "Galvan, Espinoza, and Casares held interests of 70%, 15% and 15%, respectively". Espinoza severed all ties with the restaurant, and Espinoza and Casares failed to contribute their proportional share of the debts of Mex-Am, "forcing Galvan to incur the costs of all debts owed by Mex-Am". Thus, as the defendants noted, resolution of this claim would overlap directly with the inquiry required of their defense to Espinoza's FLSA claim—*i.e.,* that "Espinoza was not entitled to any recovery from the defendants, because at all times relevant hereto, Espinoza was a member and manager of Mex-Am, with a primary duty of managing the restaurant's 'front of the house', including, but not limited to, operating the cash register and overseeing all waiters, waitresses and hostesses, and hiring and firing employees."

The court applied four factors outlined in *Painter v. Harvey,* 863 F.2d 329, 331 (1988), to determine whether a counterclaim is compulsory. This analysis also led the court to conclude that the defendants' breach of contract claim was compulsory:

> (1) Are the issues of fact and law raised in the claim and counterclaim largely the same? (2) Would res judicata bar a subsequent suit on the party's counterclaim, absent the compulsory counterclaim rule? (3) Will substantially the same evidence support or refute the claim as well as the counterclaim? and (4) Is there any logical relationship between the claim and the counterclaim.

"A court need not answer all these questions in the affirmative for the counterclaim to be compulsory. Rather, the tests are less a litmus, more a guideline." *Id.* "Where . . . the same evidence will support or refute both the claim and counterclaim, the counterclaim will almost always be compulsory." *Id.* at 332.

First, as to whether issues of fact and law raised in the claim and counterclaim were largely the same, inquiry into the single issue of Espinoza's employee status would support or refute the claim under the FLSA, as well as the breach of contract claim and possibly the conversion claim. For example, if it was determined that Espinosa was a member/manager of the LLC and that part of this contribution to the business was the purchase of the three televisions, then the plaintiff's FLSA claim failed, the defendant's breach of contract claim might succeed if it was further shown that Espinosa breached the terms of the contract, and the conversion claim would fail assuming Espinosa was entitled to take back items he contributed as a member of the LLC. While resolution of Mr. Espinoza's FLSA claim would require inquiry primarily into the number of hours worked and payment received and resolution of the defendants' breach of contract claim would, in contrast, be analyzed according to the contractual obligations of the parties, the issue of Espinosa's employee status might be determinative as a threshold matter of either claim.

Similarly, as to the second prong of the test, the breach of contract and conversion claims depended upon whether Espinoza was an employee or a member/manager in the LLC. A finding that he was a member/manager in the LLC could create the contractual obligations necessary to have a cognizable breach of contract claim, while a finding that he was an employee could foreclose the breach of contract claim but perhaps allow the conversion claim. On the other hand, the conversion claim might not be successful if it is shown that Espinoza had an ownership interest in the fixtures in the restaurant.

As to the third and fourth elements of the test, evidence showing Espinoza was, in fact, a member of the LLC would also refute his claim that he was entitled to FLSA damages and would affect whether he could be held liable for breach of contract and conversion. Thus, substantially the same evidence would support or refute the claim as well as the counterclaim, and there was a logical relationship between the claim and the counterclaim. *See Whyte v. PP & G, Inc.,* No. WMN–13–2806, 2014 WL 1340194, *5 (D.Md. Apr. 2, 2014); *Taylor v. PP & G, Inc.,* No. WMN–13–3706, 2014 WL 1340210, *5 (D.Md. Apr. 2, 2014) (finding defendant's "counterclaims are intertwined with the issues set forth in the plaintiff's FLSA claims").

**ANSWER (A)** is incorrect because the court held that the counterclaims were compulsory under Fed.R.Civ.P. 13(a), and not permissive under Fed.R.Civ.P. 13(b). **ANSWER (B)** is incorrect because, having determined that the counterclaims were compulsory, the court had automatic valid federal jurisdiction over the counterclaims pursuant to 28 U.S.C. § 1367(a). **ANSWER (C)** is incorrect because the fact that the counterclaims were state-based is not a reason to dismiss them, nor was the assertion that the counterclaims were alleged in retaliation a basis for granting the plaintiff's motion to dismiss them. **ANSWER (E)** is incorrect because the court did not make any findings of whether the counterclaims were pleaded in good faith, and this is not part of an analysis of whether counterclaims are compulsory or permissive.

### PROBLEM #5. BEST ANSWER (C).

Problem #5 is based on *Broadstone v. Sherman's Place, Inc.,* 2016 WL 199395 (C.D. Ill. Jan. 15, 2016). This problem deals with the joinder of parties and claims pursuant to Fed.R.Civ.P. 20(a). The court determined that the parties and claims were properly joined under the joinder standards in Rule 20(a), and therefore the court denied the defendant's motion to sever the claims of the Boeschs.

Fed.R.Civ.P. 20 provides, in relevant part, that persons may join in one action as plaintiffs if: 1) they assert any right to relief jointly, severally, or in the alternative with respect to or arising out of the same transaction, occurrence, or series of transactions or occurrences; and 2) any question of law or fact common to all plaintiffs will arise in the action. Fed.R.Civ.P. 20(a)(1)(A), (B). Misjoinder occurs when the parties seeking joinder fail to satisfy either of the two requirements set forth in Rule 20(a)(1). *Hawkins v. Groot Industries, Inc.,* 210 F.R.D. 226, 229–30 (N.D. Ill. 2002). "Federal policy favors joinder." *Id.* at 230.

"In ascertaining whether a particular factual situation constitutes a single transaction or occurrence for purposes of Rule 20, a case-by-case approach is generally pursued because no hard and fast rules have been established." *Bailey v. Northern Trust Co.*, 196 F.R.D. 513, 515 (N.D. Ill. 2000). Courts often consider the following factors to determine whether the requirement of Rule 20(a)(1)(A) is met:

> The time period during which the alleged acts occurred, whether the acts of discrimination are related, whether there were differing types of adverse employment actions, whether more than one type of discrimination is alleged, whether the same supervisors were involved, whether employees worked in the same department, whether employees were at different geographical locations, and whether a company-wide policy is alleged.

*McDowell v. Morgan Stanley & Co., Inc.*, 645 F.Supp. 2d 690, 694 (N.D. Ill. 2009).

Here, the defendant argued that the time period of each alleged occurrence was different, that the individuals allegedly responsible for each of the adverse actions complained of by the plaintiffs were different, that the events underlying each of the adverse actions complained of by the plaintiffs were different, and that the witnesses required to testify varied significantly for each plaintiffs' claims. Thus, the defendant argued that there was no logical connection between the alleged events and so they did not arise out of the same transaction, occurrence, or series of transactions or occurrences. The plaintiffs countered that the standard for joinder of parties was a liberal one construed as broadly as possible to promote judicial economy.

The court held that the defendant was not incorrect that there are some differences between each of the plaintiff's claims. However, the differences are not so distinct or significant to preclude a finding that the plaintiffs' claims arise out of the same transaction, occurrence, or series of transactions or occurrences. A span of little more than twelve months was involved, and the underlying events of two of the plaintiffs' claims happened within less than a month of each other. While two of the plaintiffs alleged that they were terminated by the defendant and one alleged she resigned from her position, they all alleged sex discrimination and retaliation for complaining of sex discrimination based upon events that occurred within twelve of each other. Moreover, there was overlap between the individuals involved in the events leading up to Broadstone's and Julie Boesch's terminations and Renee Boesch's resignation. For instance, Assistant Sales Manager Jim Torok was identified as playing a role in the underlying events pertaining to plaintiffs Broadstone and Julie Boesch, and President Paul Sherman was identified as playing a role in the underlying events pertaining to plaintiffs Julie Boesch and Renee Boesch. Though the supervisors that were involved in each instance were not exactly the same, the same individuals were identified in more than one of the plaintiffs' claims.

The court further held that an inescapable fact in this case was that the plaintiffs alleged incidents that occurred at just one location—the Sherman's store in Peoria, Illinois, and there was nothing in the record to suggest that the store was so large, or had such different departments of workers and supervisors as to render each plaintiff's claim a separate transaction or occurrence. To the contrary, as the court had already discussed, the same individuals reappeared in different counts of the complaint, two of the plaintiffs held the position of salesperson, and all of the plaintiffs worked at the same geographical location. For these reasons, it was not fatal to the plaintiffs' joinder that there were different alleged particular events that led to two of the plaintiffs' terminations and the other plaintiff's resignation. The court therefore found that at this stage of the case, each of the plaintiff's claims arose out of "the same transaction, occurrence, or series of transactions or occurrences." Fed.R.Civ.P. 20(a)(1)(A).

As for the second requirement of Rule 20, that there exist any question of law or fact common to all plaintiffs that will arise in the action, the defendant again argued that the plaintiffs' claims involved alleged discrete acts by Sherman's, undertaken by different individuals during different time periods and the only similarity the plaintiffs' claims share was that they all alleged unlawful gender discrimination and retaliation. The defendant further argued that the complaint alleged violations of the Illinois Sales Representative Act for only two of the three plaintiffs, thereby also precluding a finding of a common question of law or fact as to all the plaintiffs. The plaintiffs argued, as they did in regard to the first requirement of Rule 20, for the liberal application of Rule 20 and that the second requirement was satisfied where they alleged Sherman's discriminated against them in the workplace and terminated their employment when they complained.

The court found that the second requirement of Rule 20 was satisfied given that all three of the plaintiffs alleged sex discrimination and retaliation against the same defendant based upon alleged underlying events which involved common individuals in the same geographical location during the same general time period. The defendant's additional argument that the inclusion of claims for violations of the Illinois Sales Representatives Act by only two of the three plaintiffs precluded a commonality finding as to *all* the plaintiffs went nowhere; Rule 20(a)(1)(B) only requires that there be *any* question of law or fact common to all plaintiffs that will arise in the action.

Finally, the defendant argued that the court might consider, in addition to the two requirements of Rule 20(a), whether joinder would prejudice any party or result in needless delay. In *Chavez v. Illinois State Police*, the Seventh Circuit Court of Appeals explained that the discretion allowed a trial court concerning the joinder of parties under Rule 20 also included "other relevant factors in a case in order to determine whether the permissive joinder of a party will comport with the principles of fundamental fairness." 251 F.3d 612, 632 (7th Cir.2001). Accordingly, if joinder would create prejudice, expense, or delay a court may deny the motion. *Id.*

Here, the court found that at this stage of the litigation, severance of the individual plaintiffs' claims into three separate lawsuits would lead to judicial inefficiency and potentially cause additional expense to the parties. There was sufficient overlap between the alleged underlying events that there would almost certainly be overlap in the discovery that was conducted, particularly in regard to the witnesses to be deposed and the information to be gathered regarding employment at Sherman's.

The court noted that the defendant's motion to sever for misjoinder presents a close question, but in ruling as it does, the Court is guided by the notion that the tests of Rule 20(a) are "to be read as broadly as possible whenever doing so is likely to promote judicial economy." *see United Mine Workers of America v. Gibbs*, 383 U.S. 715, 724 (1966) ("Under the Rules, the impulse is toward entertaining the broadest possible scope of action consistent with fairness to the parties; joinder of claims, parties and remedies is strongly encouraged"); *Elmore v. Henderson*, 227 F.3d 1009, 1012 (7th Cir.2000) ("The purpose of Rule 20(a) in permitting joinder in a single suit of persons who have separate claims, albeit growing out of a single incident, transaction, or series of events, is to enable economies in litigation."). Insofar as the defendant's expressed concerns over the judicial inefficiency of three mini-trials within one action and the risk of confusion and prejudice towards Sherman's should this case proceed to a single trial involving all three of the plaintiffs' claims, there were safeguards available to the court and the parties to mitigate any unfairness to the parties that might result from the denial of the defendant's motion to sever for misjoinder. *See, e.g.*, Fed.R.Civ.P. 20(b) ("The court may issue orders—including an order for separate trials—to protect a party against embarrassment, delay, expense, or other prejudice that arises from including a person against whom the party asserts no claim and who asserts no claim against the party"). Lastly, the parties were given leave to file a properly supported motion for separate trials pursuant to whichever applicable, suitable authority the parties so chose at the appropriate time.

For the foregoing reasons, the defendant's motion to sever for misjoinder and to require individual suits was denied.

**ANSWER (A)** is incorrect because the court found the opposite: that the claims of the three plaintiffs sufficiently overlapped so as to satisfy the requirement under Rule 20(a). **ANSWER (B)** is incorrect because there were no facts in the problem discussing joint or several liability, which would only pertain to multiple defendants. **ANSWER (D)** is incorrect because it implies an improper motive on the defendant's part, in seeking the severance. A party's motive in seeking severance for misjoinder is not relevant. **ANSWER (E)** is incorrect because the court assessed possible prejudice to the defendant as a consequence of denying the motion to sever; the court did not assess any possible prejudice to the plaintiffs.

## PROBLEM #6. BEST ANSWER (E).

Problem #6 is based on *Giampietro v. Viator, Inc. and TripAdvisor LLC*, 2015 WL 5729244 (Sept. 29, 2015). This problem requires analysis of a motion to join parties needed for a just adjudication under Fed.R.Civ.P. 19. The court held that Piaggio and Florencetown Vespa were not necessary parties, and did not need to be joined. Because the court determined that they were not necessary parties under Fed.R.Civ.P. 19(a), the court determined that it did not have to evaluate whether they were indispensable parties under Fed.R.Civ.P. 19(b).

TripAdvisor and Viator contended that Florencetown Vespa, the tour operator, and Piaggio & C. S.p.a., the manufacturer of Vespa, were indispensable parties whom the Giampietros had failed to join. The Giampietros responded that the defendants' advertisements and solicitations for the tour did not mention either Florencetown Vespa or Piaggio.

The court had to first determine whether these absent parties were necessary under Fed.R.Civ.P. 19(a). If they are not, we need inquire no further. *See, e.g., Hall v. National Serv. Indus., Inc.*, 172 F.R.D. 157, 159 (E.D.Pa.1997). If they were necessary and should have been joined, but their joinder was not feasible because joinder would defeat diversity or deprive the court of subject-matter jurisdiction, then the court would next have to determine whether the absent parties were indispensable under Fed.R.Civ.P. 19(b). *See, e.g., General Refractories Co. v. First State Ins. Co.*, 500 F.3d 306, 312 (3d Cir.2007).

If a party who is required to be joined if feasible under Fed.R.Civ.P. 19(a) cannot be joined, then "the court must determine whether, in equity and good conscience, the action should proceed among the existing parties or should be dismissed." Fed.R.Civ.P. 19(b). Courts consider several factors, including: (1) the extent to which a judgment rendered in the person's absence might prejudice that person or the existing parties; (2) the extent to which any prejudice could be lessened or avoided by protective provisions in the judgment, shaping the relief, or other measures; (3) whether a judgment rendered in the person's absence would be adequate; and (4) whether the plaintiff would have an adequate remedy if the action were dismissed for non-joinder. Fed.R.Civ.P. 19(b)(1)–(4).

Further, an absent tortfeasor that is jointly liable to the claimant is not a Rule 19 indispensable party. *Bank of America Nat'l Tr. & Sav. Ass'n v. Hotel Rittenhouse Assocs.*, 844 F.2d 1050, 1054 (3d Cir.1988) (citing *Gold v. Johns-Mansville Sales Corp.*, 723 F.2d 1068, 1076 (3d Cir.1983)). *See, e.g., Cushman & Wakefield, Inc. v. Backos*, 129 B.R. 35, 37 (E.D.Pa.1991) (defendant's right to contribution or indemnity from an absent party does not render the absent party indispensable under Rule 19); *Carter v. Dover Corp., Rotary Lift Div.*, 753 F.Supp. 577, 579 (E.D.Pa.1991) (absent tortfeasors who may be jointly liable to the plaintiff are not indispensable parties under Rule 19); *Ospina v. Department of Corr., State of Del.*, 749 F.Supp. 572, 581 (D.Del.1990) (plaintiff's failure to join healthcare providers in his suit against the prison where he was injured was not fatal to suit because the healthcare providers, as joint tortfeasors, were not indispensable parties).

Fed.R.Civ.P. 19(a)(1)(A) provides: "A person who is subject to service of process and whose joinder will not deprive the court of subject-matter jurisdiction must be joined as a party if . . . in that person's absence, the court cannot accord complete relief among existing parties." It is not necessary for all joint tortfeasors to be named as defendants in a single lawsuit. *Temple v. Synthes Corp, Ltd.*, 498 U.S. 5, 7 (1990). The Advisory Committee Notes to Rule 19 explain that the rule "is not at variance with the settled authorities holding that a tortfeasor with the usual 'joint-and-several' liability is merely a permissive party to an action against another with like liability." *See also* Temple, 498 U.S. at 7 (explaining that the 1966 revision to Rule 19 did not change this principle).

The court first turned to consider whether Piaggo was a necessary party. The court concluded that the defendants made much of Megan Giampietro's allegation that "As a result of the stalled Vespa, Plaintiff sustained various burns, injuries and damages as set forth below." The defendants neglected, however, to quote ¶ 26 in full, which continued, "Plaintiff's burns, injuries and damages were the direct and proximate result of Defendants' negligence." But that was the extent of Megan Giampietro's complaint about the Vespa. There were no allegations of defective design or manufacture implicating the Vespa's manufacturer. It was the defendants who alleged that "it was clear that a defective part or manufacturing process by the Vespa manufacturer might have jointly or proximately caused or could be the superseding/intervening cause of Plaintiff's injuries and resulting damages." The court held that might be the defendants' theory, but it was not in the complaint. Furthermore, the court held that it could accord complete relief among the existing parties—the Giampietros, TripAdvisor, and Viator—without joining Piaggio, as Megan Giampietro's claims pertained to Viator's recommendation of the Vespa tour, not any defect in her Vespa. The court therefore found that Piaggio was not a necessary party under Fed.R.Civ.P. 19(a).

Turning to Florencetown Vespa, the court considered whether Florencetown Vespa was a necessary party. A fair reading of the complaint suggested that Count I was Megan Giampietro's negligence claim against TripAdvisor and Viator and Count II was Samuel Giampietro's derivative claim for loss of consortium. Megan Giampietro alleged that Viator and TripAdvisor were negligent for failing to use reasonable care in selecting a local tour provider; failing to warn her of the unsafe conditions and dangers of the tour; failing to select a competent provider for the tour; negligent misrepresentation; failing to provide proper control and supervision of the tour; failing to exercise reasonable care under the circumstances; negligently selecting Florencetown Vespa as the tour provider; failing to investigate the operations and conduct of the tour provider; and continuing to place its customers with the tour provider after learning of problems with its operations, vehicles, and where the tour was conducted. The defendants argued that Florencetown Vespa was necessary party because the Giampietros "must first prove as a threshold matter that it was the negligence or carelessness of Florencetown Vespa that proximately caused her injuries."

The court held that this was not the test of Fed.R.Civ.P. 19(a), which asks whether, without the absent party, the court can accord complete relief among the existing parties, or whether the absent party is situated such that disposing of the action without it will either impair its ability to protect its interest in the subject of the action or leave an existing party subject to substantial risk of incurring double, multiple, or otherwise inconsistent obligations. Fed.R.Civ.P. 19(a)(1). While Florencetown Vespa's conduct might be relevant to establishing a causal chain as an evidentiary matter,

Florencetown Vespa itself did not need to be a party in this action to accord relief among the existing parties—the Giampietros, TripAdvisor, and Viator. Nor did Florencetown Vespa's absence subject an existing party to a substantial risk of double, multiple, or otherwise inconsistent obligations. *See, e.g., Manufacturers & Traders Tr. Co. v. Minuteman Spill Response, Inc.*, 999 F.Supp.2d 805, 815–16 (W.D.Pa.2013) (explaining that even though the Commonwealth's absence from a case might pose "unusual challenges" in according relief among the existing parties, the Commonwealth was not a necessary party because relief could be accorded).

Because the court concluded that Piaggio and Florencetown Vespa were not necessary parties, the court held that it need not consider whether their joinder was feasible and, as they were not necessary, they could not be indispensable. Therefore, the court denied the defendants' motion to dismiss on that basis.

**ANSWERS (A)** and **(B)** are incorrect because the court determined that Piaggio and Florencetown Vespa were neither necessary nor indispensable parties, for the reasons stated above. **ANSWER (C)** is incorrect because the court did not make a determination that it would be feasible to join Piaggio and Florencetown Vespa, and there are no facts in the fact pattern to support this conclusion. **ANSWER (D)** is incorrect because the court did not reach the conclusion that Piaggio and Florencetown Vespa needed to be joined in the litigation; the court concluded that they were not necessary parties.

### PROBLEM #7. BEST ANSWER (B).

Problems #7 and #8 are based on *Pullar v. Cappelli*, 2015 WL 352019 (R.I. Super May 29, 2015). Problem #7 requires an analysis of the timeliness of a motion to dismiss for a lack of personal jurisdiction. The court held that the defendant's motion was timely, as he had raised the lack of personal jurisdiction as an affirmative defense it its answer, which preserved this objection. Problem #8 addressed the merits of the motion. This problem requires an analysis of whether a state court in Rhode Island could validly assert person jurisdiction over the defendant Cappelli in the lawsuit. The Rhode Island court held that it lacked personal jurisdiction over the defendant, and granted the defendant's motion to dismiss.

The court treated the defendant's motion for summary judgment as a motion to dismiss for want of personal jurisdiction pursuant to Super. R. Civ. P. 12(b)(2). "The question of personal jurisdiction is a mixed question of law and fact, in which the trial justice must first make 'a determination as to the minimum contacts that will satisfy the requirements of due process'—a finding that depends on the facts of each case." *Cassidy v. Lonquist Mgmt. Co.*, 920 A.2d 228, 232 (R.I. 2007). It is well settled "that to withstand a defendant's Rule 12(b)(2) motion to dismiss a complaint for lack of *in personam* jurisdiction, a plaintiff must allege sufficient facts to make out a *prima facie* case of jurisdiction." *Cerberus Partners, L.P. v. Gadsby & Hannah, LLP*, 836 A.2d 1113, 1118 (R.I. 2003). To determine if a plaintiff has made a *prima facie* showing of jurisdiction, the court must examine the pleadings, accepting all facts alleged in the complaint as true and resolving factual conflicts in the plaintiff's favor. *Id.* at 1117. "A *prima facie* case of jurisdiction is established when the requirements of Rhode Island's long-arm statute."

The defendant argued that the court had no personal jurisdiction over him because he, in his individual capacity, did not have sufficient contacts with Rhode Island. The defendant insisted that the only contacts with Rhode Island related to Helios as a corporation. However, since Helios was not a party to this suit, nor had an alter-ego form of liability been pled in the complaint, the contacts of Helios with Rhode Island could be imputed to the defendant personally. Additionally, the defendant argued that the plaintiff could obtain personal jurisdiction over the defendant through invocation of the alter-ego doctrine when he had not named Helios as a defendant nor even alleged the existence of personal jurisdiction over Helios.

The plaintiff countered that the defendant waived personal jurisdiction by failing to raise the issue in a timely manner, waiting until discovery was completed and the plaintiff had requested that the case be set down for a trial. The plaintiff argued that the issue of personal jurisdiction had been waived.

Rule 12(h) of the Rhode Island Superior Court Rules of Civil Procedure provides in relevant part that "a party waives all defenses and objections which the party does not present either by motion as hereinbefore provided or, if the party has made no motion, in the party's answer or reply. . . ." *See* Super. R. Civ. P. 12(h). The defenses enumerated in Super. R. Civ. P. 12(b)—including that of lack of jurisdiction over the person—"whether made in a pleading or by motion . . . shall be heard and determined before the trial on application of any party. . . ." *See* Super. R. Civ. P. 12(d); *See also* Super. R. Civ. P. 12(b). A defendant does not waive his right to challenge personal jurisdiction so long as he either raises it in an affirmative defense in his answer or files an appropriate motion. *See Hall v. Kuzenka*, 843 A.2d 474, 478 (R.I. 2004); *see also R.I. Hosp. Trust Nat'l Bank v. de Beru*, 553 A.2d 544, 547 (R.I. 1989) (to preserve objections to personal jurisdiction, a party must raise them by motion or in his answer).

Here, the defendant raised the defense of lack of subject matter jurisdiction in his answer as an affirmative defense. Since the plaintiff initiated the action, the defendant had maintained that Rhode Island lacked personal jurisdiction over him. By raising this defense in his answer, he had satisfied the requirements of Super. R. Civ. P. 12(h), and by filing a motion prior to trial, he had satisfied any timing requirements imposed by Super. R. Civ. P. 12(d). Therefore, the defendant did not waive his lack of personal jurisdiction defense.

**ANSWER (A)** is incorrect because it is not true that a motion to dismiss may be raised at any time; to preserve the ability to raise that challenge later in proceedings, a defendant must have asserted the lack of personal jurisdiction in its answer as an affirmative defense. **ANSWERS (C)** and **(D)** are incorrect because the court determined that the defendant had properly preserved his right to challenge personal jurisdiction even after discovery and when a trial date was set, by virtue of having raised the challenge as an affirmative defense in its answer to the plaintiff's complaint. **ANSWER (E)** is incorrect because there is no indication of what prior motions the defendant might have pursued; it doesn't matter because he preserved his right to object to personal jurisdiction by initially raising that defense in his answer.

## PROBLEM #8. BEST ANSWER (A).

Problem #8 is a continuation of Problem #7, and is based on the same facts and case as Problem #7. This problem asks the student to assume that the court finds the motion to dismiss timely (which the court did). This problem requires an analysis of whether a state court in Rhode Island could validly assert person jurisdiction over the defendant Cappelli in the lawsuit. The Rhode Island court held that it lacked personal jurisdiction over the defendant, and granted the defendant's motion to dismiss.

Alternatively, the plaintiff argued that the contacts of Helios should be attributed to the defendant. The plaintiff insisted that Helios was the defendant's alter-ego, justifying the piercing of its corporate veil and imputing the contacts of Helios with Rhode Island to the defendant.

Rhode Island's long-arm statute, provided in part that:

> "every foreign corporation, every individual not a resident of this state . . . and every partnership or association, composed of any person or persons not such residents, that shall have the necessary minimum contacts with the state of Rhode Island, shall be subject to the jurisdiction of the state of Rhode Island . . . in every case not contrary to the provisions of the constitution or laws of the United States."

As interpreted by the Rhode Island Supreme Court, Rhode Island's long-arm statute permitted the exercise of jurisdiction over nonresident defendants "to the fullest extent allowed by the United States Constitution." *Rose v. Firstar Bank*, 819 A.2d 1247, 1250 (R.I. 2003) (citing *McKenney v. Kenyon Piece Dye Works, Inc.*, 582 A.2d 107, 108 (R.I. 1990)).

"To ensure constitutional due process to a nonresident defendant, certain minimum contacts with the forum state are required such that the maintenance of the suit does not offend 'traditional notions of fair play and substantial justice.'" *Kalooski v. Albert-Frankenthal AG*, 770 A.2d 831, 832–33 (R.I. 2001) (quoting *Int'l Shoe Co. v. Washington*, 326 U.S. 310, 316 (1945)). The minimum contacts requirement protects defendants from the burden of having to litigate in an inconvenient forum and it ensures that states "do not reach out beyond the limits imposed on them by their status as coequal sovereigns in a federal system." *World-Wide Volkswagen Corp. v. Woodson*, 444 U.S. 286, 292 (1980). "A determination as to the minimum contacts that will satisfy the requirements of due process will depend upon the facts of each particular case." *Ben's Marine Sales v. Sleek Craft Boats*, 502 A.2d 808, 810 (R.I. 1985). "The fundamental question here is, thus, whether 'the Defendant's conduct and connection with Rhode Island are such that he should reasonably anticipate being hauled into court here.'" *See Bendick v. Picillo*, 525 A.2d 1310, 1312 (R.I. 1987).

A court "possesses personal jurisdiction over a nonresident defendant when a plaintiff alleges and proves the existence of either general or specific personal jurisdiction." *Cerberus Partners*, 836 A.2d at 1118. The court held that the plaintiff had not alleged any connection between his breach of contract claim and the State of Rhode Island. This precluded a finding of specific jurisdiction. *See id.* Therefore, the Court's analysis will focus on general jurisdiction. "To justify the exercise of general jurisdiction, (1) the defendant must have sufficient contacts with the forum state, (2) those contacts must be purposeful, and (3) the exercise of jurisdiction must be reasonable under the circumstances." *Cossaboon v. Me. Med. Ctr.*, 600 F.3d 25, 32 (1st Cir.2010). A defendant's contacts with the forum must be "continuous and systematic" and "purposeful" such that it will not offend the "traditional notions of fair play and substantial justice" to subject them to the forum's jurisdiction. *Id.* The contacts must be purposeful, in that the defendant purposefully avails himself of the privilege of conducting activities within the forum state, thus invoking the benefits and protections of its laws. *Id.* Lastly, the exercise of jurisdiction must be "reasonable under the circumstances." *Id.* at 33.

"The forum-state contacts of a corporation may be attributed to an individual who is an officer, director, or shareholder of the corporation when evidence is presented that shows that the corporation is the alter ego of the individual, or where other circumstances permit the court to pierce the corporate veil." *N. Laminate Sales, Inc. v. Matthews*, 249 F.Supp. 2d 130, 139 (D.N.H. 2003). In Rhode Island, to invoke the equitable alter-ego doctrine "there must be a concurrence of two circumstances: (1) there must be such a unity of interest and ownership that the separate personalities of the corporation and the individual no longer exist, viz., the corporation is, in fact, the alter ego of one or a few individuals; and (2) the observance of the corporate form would sanction a fraud, promote injustice, or an inequitable result would follow." *Heflin v. Koszela*, 774 A.2d 25, 30 (R.I. 2001) (*quoting Transamerica Cash Reserve, Inc. v. Dixie Power & Water, Inc.*, 789 P.2d 24, 26 (Utah 1990)). The second prong of the alter-ego test "is addressed to the conscience of the court, and the circumstances under which it will be met will vary with each case." *Id.* However, to satisfy the second prong, "it must be shown that the corporation itself played a role in the inequitable conduct at issue." *Id.*

The court held that the complaint failed to "properly allege a claim for alter ego liability." *See Chunghwa Telecom Global, Inc. v. Medcom, LLC*, No. 5:13–CV–02104 HRL, 2013 WL 5688941, at *4 (N.D. Cal. Oct. 16, 2013) (motion to dismiss for lack of personal jurisdiction appropriate where plaintiff did not properly allege a claim for alter-ego liability in complaint but sought to impute the contacts of the corporation on the individual). The plaintiff did not allege in the complaint that the defendant should be held personally liable for the alleged breach of contract based on any alter-ego doctrine. *Compare Skydive Ariz., Inc. v. Quattrochi*, No. CV 05–2656–PHX–MHM, 2006 WL 2460595, at *7–8 (D.Ariz. Aug. 22, 2006) (finding plaintiff failed to state a claim against defendants where complaint simply alleged the alter-ego theory with no factual basis), *with Whitney v. Wurtz*, No. C–04–5232 PVT, 2006 WL 83119, at *2 (N.D. Cal. Jan. 11, 2006) (finding complaint established a cognizable alter-ego theory by alleging individual defendants "used assets of the corporation for their personal use," "controlled, dominated and operated" corporation "as their individual business and alter ego" without "holding of director's or shareholder's meetings," and "caused monies to be withdrawn from the funds of defendant corporation and distributed to themselves without any consideration to the corporation").

The court held that the plaintiff could seek to establish jurisdiction over a non-resident defendant by arguing a theory—here alter-ego—that he had not pled in his complaint. *See Medcom*, WL 5688941, at *4. Furthermore, this court could consider Helios, a foreign corporate entity which was not a party to this suit, as the alter-ego of the defendant for purposes of establishing jurisdiction over the defendant. *See Wilson v. Metals USA, Inc.*, No. CIV. S–12–0568 LKK, 2013 WL 4586919, at *5 (E.D. Cal. Aug. 28, 2013) (court may not exercise personal jurisdiction over an individual shareholder and officer of a corporation under an alter-ego theory if the corporation itself is not a party to the action).

Therefore, the court determine that it need not decide whether Helios' corporate veil should be pierced and its contacts with Rhode Island attributed to the defendant personally for purposes of establishing jurisdiction. Without considering Helios' contacts with Rhode Island, it was clear and undisputed that the defendant's contacts alone were not "continuous and systematic" and "purposeful" to support Rhode Island's exercise of general personal jurisdiction over him. *See Cossaboon*, 600 F.3d at 32. In examining the pleadings, and accepting all facts alleged by the plaintiff as true, the court found that the plaintiff had failed to establish a *prima facie* showing of jurisdiction.

For the reasons set forth, the court granted the defendant's motion to dismiss. The plaintiff had failed to establish a *prima facie* showing of the court's jurisdiction over the defendant.

**ANSWER (B)** is incorrect because maritime jurisdiction deals with a court's subject matter jurisdiction; the question in this problem addresses personal jurisdiction. This answer is a red-herring answer. **ANSWERS (C)** and **(D)** are incorrect because the court determines that there is no specific or general jurisdiction over the only named defendant Cappelli, and because it will not allow the theory of alter-ego to apply, the court refuses to impute Helios contacts to Cappelli. Even if the court had accepted the theory of alter-ego, it still would have found insufficient contacts of Helios with Rhode Island to impose personal jurisdiction over Cappelli. **ANSWER (E)** is incorrect because the court never makes this finding; because the plaintiff failed to plead the theory of alter-ego, the court declined to apply it to the facts.

### PROBLEM #9. BEST ANSWER (B).

Problems #9 and #10 are based on *Strizic v. Northwestern Corp.*, 2015 WL 1275404 (D. Montana March 19, 2015). Problem #9 deals with a motion to dismiss for failure to state a claim under Fed.R.Civ.P. 12(b)(6). The court granted the motion and ordered that the defendant Lowney be dismissed from the suit. Problem #10, discussed below, deals with the plaintiff's petition to remand the case. With the defendant Lowney dismissed from the case, the

## PROBLEM #10. BEST ANSWER (D).

Problem #10 is a continuation of Problem #9 and is based on the same set of facts and decision. This problem requires the student to consider a plaintiff's petition for remand to state court after a defendant's removal to federal court. As indicated above, with the defendant Lowney dismissed from the case, the federal court retained good diversity jurisdiction under 28 U.S.C. § 1332(a) and (c), and good removal pursuant to 28 U.S.C. § 1441. Courts also can ignore the citizenship of defendants who are fraudulently joined to defeat diversity jurisdiction.

Strizic's motion for remand asserted that the plaintiff properly joined Lowney as a defendant because there was a "possibility" that an unfair trade practices claim could be proven against Lowney. However, a possibility of a claim is not enough. Under the *Iqbal* standard, the claim must be plausible on its face. *Iqbal*, 556 U.S. at 678 (quoting *Twombley*, 550 U.S. at 570). "The plausibility standard . . . asks for more than a sheer possibility that a defendant has acted unlawfully." *Id.* Plaintiff must plead "factual content that allows the court to draw the reasonable inference that the defendant is liable for the misconduct alleged." *Iqbal*, 129 S.Ct. at 1949. Strizic merely alleged that Lowney was doing her job for Northwestern when she provided inaccurate information to Standard. Strizic did not state any fact from which the court could infer that Lowney's acts were outside the scope of her employment, that Lowney's acts were of such frequency as to indicate general business practice, or that Lowney's acts were for her own pecuniary benefit and against the best interests of the corporation. The closest the plaintiff could come was an allegation that Lowney "desired to prevent Strizic from obtaining disability benefits." (This unremarkable factual allegation that the employee intended the consequences of her actions was insufficient to reasonably infer any fact that would support a plausible claim against an employee of a corporation who was otherwise protected from suit by Montana public policy.) *See Phillips*, 610 P.2d at 157. "One public policy consideration is that the officers, directors, employees and agents of a corporation must be shielded from personal liability for acts taken on behalf of the corporation, including the breaching of contracts in furtherance of corporate goals, policies, and business interests." *Id.*

Strizic intended to amend his complaint to assert a negligence claim against Lowney. It was unclear to the court how such a claim would be feasible in light of Montana law and *Crane Creek Ranch,* 103 P.3d at 538; *Bottrell,* 773 P.2d at 70809; and *Phillips,* 610 P.2d at 158. However, Strizic "might well develop facts showing that Peggy Lowney provided inaccurate information to Standard Insurance Company to prevent employees from successfully making claims under the short-term disability plan," Until Strizic discovered such facts, that claim did not yet exist. In the meantime, the defendants had demonstrated that removal was proper, so the court determined that the motion for remand must be denied.

**ANSWER (A)** is incorrect because the court dismissed Lowney from the case, or could have ignored her citizenship as fraudulently joined. **ANSWER (B)** is incorrect because the court is not in the business of providing litigants with opportunities to go back to state court to add claims; the only question before the court was whether it had good federal diversity jurisdiction on the removal. Similarly, **ANSWER (C)** is incorrect because the court had to apply federal pleading rules to the removal; there was no reason to allow the plaintiff a remand to state court to take advantage of more liberal pleading rules. **ANSWER (E)** is incorrect because there was no argument for federal court jurisdiction presented by the defendant based on supplemental jurisdiction; this is a red-herring answer.

## PROBLEM #11. BEST ANSWER (C).

Problem #11 is based on *The Boyd Group v. D'Orazio*, 2015 WL 5445751 (N.D. Ill. Sept. 15, 2015). This problem deals with a non-party intervenor's motion for a protective order under Fed.R.Civ.P. 26(c), and requires application of the principles relating to issuance of a protective order. The court held that PPG had failed to establish good cause for issuance of the protective order, and therefore declined to grant the non-party intervenor's request for a protective order.

"In order to establish that information should be subject to a protective order, the party seeking protection bears the burden of establishing that: 1) the information is in fact a trade secret or confidential commercial information and 2) there is good cause to protect the information." *Culinary Foods, Inc. v. Raychem Corp.*, 151 F.R.D. 297, 300 (N.D.Ill.1993). To establish "good cause" under Federal Rule of Civil Procedure 26(c), the moving party must show that the "disclosure 'will work a clearly defined and very serious injury' to its business." *Id.* at 300 n.1 (quoting *United States v. IBM Corp.*, 67 F.R.D. 40, 46 (S.D.N.Y.1975)). However, "broad allegations of harm unsubstantiated by specific examples of articulated reasoning do not satisfy the Rule 26(c) test." *Id.* Where the allegations of injury stemming from disclosure of confidential information are speculative, courts in this circuit have found that good cause does not exist. *See Harrisonville Telephone Co. v. Illinois Commerce Comm'n*, 472 F.Supp.2d 1071, 1078 (S.D.Ill.2006). Courts must also balance the moving party's interest in privacy with the non-moving party's need to adequately and fully prepare its case.

The court held that PPG had failed to establish good cause for the protective order it seeks. First, PPG was incorrect that a protective order was appropriate "regardless of whether specific evidence presently exists" that D'Orazio might disclose the proprietary information. In fact, "courts have insisted on particular and specific demonstration of fact, as distinguished from stereotyped and conclusory statements, in order to establish good cause." 8A Charles Alan Wright, Arthur R. Miller, and Richard L. Marcus, *Federal Practice and Procedure* § 2035 (3d ed.2010) (collecting cases). PPG failed to meet this requirement.

Moreover, D'Orazio was not a competitor of PPG. PPG asserted that D'Orazio was once a customer of PPG, but that was no longer true. In fact, it was D'Orazio's sale of his company and subsequent exit from the relevant industry that gave rise to the underlying suit in the case. The only evidence that PPG could conjure supporting its argument was that D'Orazio was involved in the relevant industry for a long time and "undoubtedly" had contact with participants in the industry. However, PPG failed to identify who these participants were, or provide any evidence that D'Orazio was, in fact, in contact with them. In short, there was no immediate danger to PPG in allowing D'Orazio to see the relevant documents, and PPG had not articulated any harm other than a generalized, unsubstantiated, speculative fear that D'Orazio might divulge them to PPG's current competitors or customers. This was not sufficient to meet the "good cause" requirement pursuant to Rule 26(c). Therefore, for the reasons discussed above, PPG's motion for a protective order was denied.

**ANSWER (A)** is incorrect because the court found that PPG had failed to meet the good cause test for issuance of a protective order, therefore it did not matter whether the material was claimed to be proprietary, or not. For similar reasons, **ANSWER (B)** is incorrect. **ANSWER (D)** is incorrect because non-party intervenors are able to seek protective orders if they can meet the standards in Rule 26(c). **ANSWER (E)** is incorrect because it doesn't make sense, and it is irrelevant if the plaintiff could protect the defendant's interest in the documents.

### PROBLEM #12. BEST ANSWER (A).

Problem #12 is based on *American Homes 4 Rent Properties Eight, LLC v. Green*, 2015 WL 504 3222 (S.D. Ga. Aug. 25, 2015). This problem addresses a plaintiff's motion to remand a case to state court pursuant to 28 U.S.C. 1447(c), after the defendant's removal of a case to federal court. The court found that there was no valid federal question or diversity jurisdiction, and therefore ordered that the case be remanded to state court, and that the defendant pay costs and expenses to the plaintiff as a result of the improper removal.

On a motion to remand, the burden of establishing federal jurisdiction is placed upon the party seeking removal. *Williams v. Best Buy Co., Inc.*, 269 F.3d 1316, 1319 (11th Cir.2001). It is well established that removal jurisdiction is construed narrowly with all doubts resolved in favor of remand. *Mann v. Unum Life Ins. Co. of Am.*, 505 Fed.Appx. 854, 856 (11th Cir.2013) ("We strictly construe removal statutes, resolving all doubts in favor of remand."); *Univ. of S. Ala. v. Am. Tobacco Co.*, 168 F.3d 405, 411 (11th Cir.1999) (citing *Shamrock Oil & Gas Corp. v. Sheets*, 313 U.S. 100, 108–09 (1941)); *Burns v. Windsor Ins. Co.*, 31 F.3d 1092, 1094 (11th Cir.1994) ("Removal statutes are construed narrowly."). A district court considering whether removal is proper "has before it only the limited universe of evidence available when the motion to remand is filed—i.e., the notice of removal and accompanying documents." *Lowery v. Ala. Power Co.*, 483 F.3d 1184, 1214 (11th Cir.2007). If that evidence is insufficient to establish removal, "neither the defendants nor the court may speculate in an attempt to make up for the notice's failings." *Id.* at 1214–15.

To have removal jurisdiction, a federal court must have original jurisdiction over the subject matter. 28 U.S.C. § 1441(a). A federal district court has original jurisdiction over two types of civil actions: (1) those arising under federal law ("federal question jurisdiction") and (2) those involving diversity of citizenship ("diversity jurisdiction"). 28 U.S.C. §§ 1331, 1332.

Removal jurisdiction based on a federal question is governed by the well-pleaded complaint rule. *Taylor v. Anderson*, 234 U.S. 74, 75–76 (1914); *Cmty. State Bank v. Strong*, 651 F.3d 1241, 1251 (11th Cir.2011); *Ervast v. Flexible Products Co.*, 346 F.3d 1007, 1012 (11th Cir.2003); *Kemp v. Int'l Bus. Machs. Corp.*, 109 F.3d 708, 712 (11th Cir.1997) (citing *Franchise Tax Bd. v. Constr. Laborers Vacation Trust*, 463 U.S. 1, 11 (1983)). In plain terms, unless the face of a plaintiff's complaint states a federal question, a defendant may not remove a case to federal court on this basis. *Kemp*, 109 F.3d at 712. As a result, neither a party's defenses nor its counterclaims can give rise to federal question jurisdiction. *Vaden v. Discover Bank*, 556 U.S. 49, 60 (2009).

In this case, the dispossessory eviction action filed by the plaintiff did not involve a federal question. *See Nguyen v. Hinton*, No. 1:15–CV–1292, 2015 WL 3407856, at *2 (N.D.Ga. May 26, 2015) (stating that a dispossessory action is "fundamentally a matter of state law"); *Citimortgage, Inc. v. Dhinoja*, 705 F.Supp.2d 1378, 1381 (N.D.Ga.2010) (holding that a dispossessory claim is "exclusively a matter of state law"). However, in her petition for removal, the defendant alleged violations of three federal provisions: 15 U.S.C. § 1692, Federal Rule of Civil Procedure 60, and the Due Process Clause of the Fourteenth Amendment. Although federal in nature, these claims were not present on the face of the plaintiff's complaint and thus could not be considered for purposes of federal question jurisdiction. Accordingly, the court held that the case presented no federal question.

Federal courts may exercise diversity jurisdiction over all civil actions where the amount in controversy exceeds $75,000, exclusive of interest and costs, and the action is between citizens of different states. 28 U.S.C. § 1332(a)(1). In the removal context, when diversity jurisdiction is invoked, two additional conditions must be met. 28 U.S.C. §§ 1441(b)(2), 1446(c)(1). First, no defendant can be a citizen of the state in which the case was brought. 28 U.S.C. § 1441(a)(2). Second, a case cannot be removed more than one year after it was filed in state court. 28 U.S.C. § 1446(c)(1).

To meet the diversity of citizenship requirement, a defendant's notice of removal "must distinctly and affirmatively allege each party's citizenship." *Seven Oaks Constr., L.L.C. v. Talbot Constr., Inc.*, No. 2:11cv140, 2011 WL 1297971, at *1 (N.D.Ala. Apr. 5, 2011) (citing *McGovern v. Am. Airlines, Inc.*, 511 F.2d 653, 654 (5th Cir.1975)). If one of the parties is a limited liability company, the notice must allege " 'the citizenships of all the company's members.' " *Seven Oaks*, 2011 WL 1297971, at *1 (quoting *RollingGreens MHP, L.P. v. Comcast SCH Holdings, L.L.C.*, 374 F.3d 1020, 1022 (11th Cir.2004)). Here, the defendant had not alleged either party's citizenship, much less the citizenships of all the plaintiff's members. Nevertheless, there seemed to be no dispute that the defendant was a citizen of Georgia. The record contained no evidence that the defendant was a citizen of another state, and the defendant's address for service—a Georgia address—was the same address for the premises at issue here. Therefore, because 28 U.S.C. § 1441(a)(2) bars federal courts from exercising diversity jurisdiction in cases removed by an in-state defendant, diversity jurisdiction did not exist in this matter. *See Federal Home Loan Mortg. Corp. v. Lipai*, No. 1:11–CV–2386, 2011 WL 4436493 (N.D.

Ga. Aug. 3, 2011) (holding that where the record is devoid of any information suggesting that the defendant is a citizen of another state and the defendant "has listed a Georgia address as her address for service, the same address as the premises that are the subject of the dispossessory action," removal on diversity jurisdiction grounds is improper).

Moreover, the court held that the defendant had not satisfied the amount-in-controversy requirement of 28 U.S.C. § 1332(a). A dispossessory claim seeking ejectment "cannot be reduced to a monetary sum for purposes of determining the amount in controversy." *Novastar Mortg., Inc. v. Bennett,* 173 F.Supp. 2d 1358, 1361–62 (N.D.Ga.2001), *aff'd,* 35 Fed.Appx. 858 (11th Cir.2001). Consequently, the amount-in-controversy requirement could not be met.

Because no federal jurisdiction existed, the court held that it was proper to consider the plaintiff's request for costs and attorney's fees incurred pursuant to removal. 28 U.S.C. § 1447(c) provides that "an order remanding the case may require payment of just costs and any actual expenses, including attorney's fees, incurred as a result of removal." Because the defendant did not act with a reasonable belief that removal was proper, the court required the defendant to pay the plaintiff's reasonable removal costs.

For the reasons above, the court found that the defendant has not met her burden of establishing federal jurisdiction, and granted the plaintiff's motion to remand.

**ANSWER (B)** is incorrect because the basis for granting the remand motion was the lack of diversity jurisdiction. Federal courts may adjudicate state claims if the court has valid diversity jurisdiction. **ANSWER (C)** is incorrect because the court cannot establish federal question jurisdiction based on claims asserted by the defendant; this violates the well-pleaded complaint rule. There were no federal questions pleaded on the fact of the plaintiff's complaint. **ANSWER (D)** is incorrect because there were no grounds for the court's exercise of supplemental jurisdiction based on these facts. **ANSWER (E)** is incorrect because it is simply wrong; the court did not have valid diversity jurisdiction.

### PROBLEM #13. BEST ANSWER (D).

Problems #13 and #14 are based on *Horne v. Lightning Energy Services, LLC,* 123 F.Supp.3d 839 (N.D. W.Va. Aug. 12, 2015). Problem #13 deals with the issue whether the court has valid diversity jurisdiction over the parties, or whether the citizenship of the alleged defendant Lightning Trucking and Lightning Energy should be disregarded under the doctrine of fraudulent joinder. The court concluded that because of the minority stake of one of the limited liability partners, there was no diversity jurisdiction and Lightning had been fraudulently joined. Problem #14 deals with whether res judicata barred the plaintiff's second lawsuit (*see* discussion of Problem #14, below).

Turner contended that if either Lightning Trucking or Lightning Energy had West Virginia citizenship due to Hamrick's minority interest, the citizenship of Lightning Trucking and Lightning Energy should be disregarded under the doctrine of fraudulent joinder because the same claims had been tried already, resulting in a verdict against Horne.

When an action is removed from state court, a federal district court must determine whether it has original jurisdiction over the plaintiff's claims. *Kokkonen v. Guardian Life Ins. Co. Of Am.*, 511 U.S. 375, 377 (1994). "Federal courts are courts of limited jurisdiction. They possess only that power authorized by the Constitution and statute, which is not to be expanded by judicial decree." *Id.* at 377.

Federal courts have original jurisdiction primarily over two types of cases, (1) those involving federal questions under 28 U.S.C. § 1331, and (2) those involving diversity of citizenship under 28 U.S.C. § 1332. When a party seeks to remove a case based on diversity of citizenship under 28 U.S.C. § 1332, that party bears the burden of establishing "the amount in controversy exceeds the sum or value of $75,000, exclusive of interests and costs, and is between citizens of different states." 28 U.S.C. § 1332. Courts should resolve any doubt "about the propriety of removal in favor of retained state court jurisdiction." *Marshall v. Manville Sales Corp.*, 6 F.3d 229, 232–33 (4th Cir.1993).

The doctrine of fraudulent joinder is a narrow exception to the complete diversity requirement. *Jackson v. Allstate Ins. Co.*, 132 F.Supp.2d 432, 433 (N.D.W.Va.2000). If the doctrine applies, the court can exercise removal jurisdiction even though a non-diverse party is a defendant. *Id.* (citing *Mayes v. Rapoport*, 198 F.3d 457, 461 (4th Cir.1999)). The court can disregard the citizenship of and dismiss the non-diverse defendant, thereby retaining jurisdiction over the case. *Mayes*, 198 F.3d at 461.

The removing party bears the "heavy burden of showing that there is no possibility of establishing a cause of action against a non-diverse party" by clear and convincing evidence. *Jackson*, 132 F.Supp.2d at 433 (citing *Hartley v. CSX Transp. Inc.*, 187 F.3d 422, 424 (4th Cir.1999)); *Clutter v. Consolidation Coal Co.*, No. 1:14CV9, 2014 WL 1479199, at *4 (N.D. W.Va. Apr. 15, 2014). In the alternative, the removing party can establish that "there has been outright fraud in the plaintiff's pleading of jurisdictional facts." *Pritt v. Republican Nat. Committee*, 1 F.Supp.2d 590, 592 (S.D.W.Va.1998). "Fraudulent joinder claims are subject to a rather black-and-white analysis in this circuit. Any shades of gray are resolved in favor of remand." *Adkins v. Consolidation Coal Co.*, 856 F.Supp.2d 817, 820 (S.D.W.Va.2012).

The court must resolve all issues of fact and law in the plaintiff's favor, but, in doing so, "is not bound by the allegations of the pleadings." *Marshall*, 6 F.3d at 232–33; *AIDS Counseling and Testing Ctrs. v. Grp. W Television, Inc.*, 903 F.2d 1000, 1004 (4th Cir.1990). Instead, the Court can consider "the entire record, and determine the basis of joinder by any means available." *AIDS Counseling*, 903 F.2d at 1004 (quoting *Dodd v. Fawcett Publ'ns, Inc.*, 329 F.2d 82, 85 (10th Cir.1964)). The standard for fraudulent joinder is more favorable to the plaintiff than the standard for a Rule 12(b)(6) motion to dismiss. *Mayes*, 198 F.3d at 464.

When ruling on a motion to remand based on fraudulent joinder, the court cannot consider post-removal filings "to the extent that they present new causes of action or theories not raised in the controlling petition filed in state court." *Griggs v. State Farm Lloyds*, 181 F.3d 694, 700 (5th Cir.1999). A plaintiff cannot " 're-plead the complaint after removal in an attempt to divest this court of jurisdiction by hindsight.' " *McCoy v. Norfolk S. Ry. Co.,* 858 F.Supp.2d 639, 642 n. 1 (S.D.W.Va.2012) (quoting *Justice v. Branch Banking & Trust Co.,* No. 2:08–230, 2009 WL 853993, at *7 (S.D. W.Va. Mar. 24, 2009)). The court must determine removal jurisdiction "on the basis of the state court complaint at the time of removal, and . . . a plaintiff cannot defeat removal by amending it." *Cavallini v. State Farm Mut. Auto Ins. Co.,* 44 F.3d 256, 265 (5th Cir.1995). Nonetheless, "if at any time before final judgment it appears that the district court lacks subject matter jurisdiction, the case shall be remanded." 28 U.S.C. § 1447(c).

According to the defendants, if the court found that either Lightning Trucking or Lightning Energy was a West Virginia citizen due to Hamrick's minority interest in Lightning Energy, it should disregard the citizenship of the LLCs under the doctrine of fraudulent joinder because "because the . . . same claims asserted in the instant lawsuit were previously tried against Lightning Energy and Lightning Trucking and resulted in a verdict of no liability.".

Pursuant to 28 U.S.C. § 1332, a federal district court has original jurisdiction over all civil actions between citizens of different states where the amount in controversy exceeds $75,000. *See* 28 U.S.C. § 1332(a)(1). Generally, § 1332 requires complete diversity among parties, which means that the citizenship of all defendants must be different from the citizenship of all plaintiffs. *See Caterpillar, Inc. v. Lewis,* 519 U.S. 61, 68 (1996). For the purposes of diversity jurisdiction, the citizenship of a limited liability company is determined by the citizenship of *all* of its members, regardless of the characterization of that membership. *Gen. Tech. Applications, Inc. v. Exro Ltda,* 388 F.3d 114, 121 (4th Cir.2004); *see, e.g., Carden v. Arkoma, Assocs.,* 494 U.S. 185, 192 (1990) ("We have never held that an artificial entity, suing or being sued in its own name, can invoke the diversity jurisdiction of the federal courts based on the citizenship of *some* but not *all* of its members."); *Fadal Machining Ctrs., LLC v. Mid-Atl. CNC, Inc.,* 464 Fed.Appx. 672, 673–74 (9th Cir.2012) (holding that the characterization of a membership as being a minority interest is irrelevant when determining citizenship, as citizenship is determined by *all* members).

The defendants admitted that Charles Hamrick, a West Virginia citizen, was a member of Lightning Energy. Regardless of how minor Hamrick's interest was, the citizenship of an LLC was determined by the citizenship of *all* of its members. Lightning Energy was the sole member of Lightning Trucking. Accordingly, both Lightning Energy and Lightning Trucking were West Virginia citizens for the purposes of diversity jurisdiction. The court therefore was bound to remand the case unless the doctrine of fraudulent joinder applied. *See Mayes,* 198 F.3d at 464.

**ANSWER (A)** is incorrect because the court found that the defendants were not completely diverse, taking into account the citizenship of the individual members of the limited liability corporation. **ANSWER (B)** is incorrect for the same reason; the minority shareholder of one of the four entities was a citizen of West Virginia, which destroyed diversity jurisdiction. **ANSWER (C)** is incorrect because the court held that it could not disregard the citizenship of the minority shareholder. **ANSWER (E)** because plaintiffs may limit the amount in controversy in a state court complaint; this was not the reason for the court finding a lack of diversity jurisdiction.

## PROBLEM #14. BEST ANSWER (A).

Problem #14 is a continuation of problem #13 and is based on the same fact pattern and judicial decision. This problem entails an analysis of the doctrine of res judicata. Applying the principles of res judicata, the court determined that the plaintiff's second lawsuit was barred by the first litigation, and therefore the court dismissed the case.

The doctrine of res judicata precludes relitigation of the same claim. *See Sattler v. Bailey,* 184 W.Va. 212, 400 S.E.2d 220, 225 (1990). Under res judicata, "a judgment on the merits in a prior suit bars a second suit involving the same parties or their privies based on the same cause of action." *Porter v. McPherson,* 198 W.Va. 158, 479 S.E.2d 668, 676 (1996) (quoting *Parklane Hosiery Co., Inc. v. Shore,* 439 U.S. 322, 326, n. 5 (1979)).

Under West Virginia law, res judicata is comprised of three elements:

> First, there must have been a final adjudication on the merits in the prior action by a court having jurisdiction of the proceedings. Second, the two actions must involve either the same parties or persons in privity with those same parties. Third, the cause of action identified for resolution in the subsequent proceeding either must be identical to the cause of action determined in the prior action or must be such that it could have been resolved, had it been presented, in the prior action.

*Blake v. Charleston Area Medical Center, Inc.,* 201 W.Va. 469, 498 S.E.2d 41, 44 (1997).

Turner must first establish that there was a final adjudication on the merits by a court having jurisdiction. "A final decision is one that ends the litigation on the merits and leaves nothing more for the court to do but execute the judgment." *Green Tree Fin. Corp. v. Randolph,* 531 U.S. 79, 86, 121 S.Ct. 513, 519–20, 148 L.Ed.2d 373 (2000). "An erroneous ruling of the court will not prevent the matter from being *res judicata.*" *Conley v. Spillers,* 171 W.Va. 584, 301 S.E.2d 216, 217 (1983). Furthermore, "it is not essential that the matter should have been formally put in issue in a former suit, but it is sufficient that the *status* of the suit was such that the parties might have had the matter disposed of on its merits." *Blake,* 498 S.E.2d at 48.

It is undisputed that there was a final judgment on the merits in the first action by a court having jurisdiction of the proceedings. Horne's claims were litigated in the Circuit Court of Harrison County, and at the end of trial, the jury returned a verdict against him on all counts.

Turner also had to establish that the cause of action identified for resolution in the instant suit is identical to the cause of action in the prior litigation. *See Blake,* 498 S.E.2d at 44. A "cause of action" is "the fact or facts which establish or give rise to a right of action, the existence of which affords a party a right to judicial relief." *Id.* at 48. "The test to determine if the . . . cause of action involved in the two suits is identical is to inquire whether the same evidence would support both actions or issues." *Id.* "If the two cases require substantially different evidence to sustain them, the second cannot be said to be the same cause of action and barred by res judicata." *Id.; see also Slider v. State Farm Mut. Auto. Ins. Co.,* 210 W.Va. 476, 557 S.E.2d 883, 888 (2001) (when the claims are not identical, courts must apply the "same evidence" test to determine "whether two claims should be deemed to be the same for purposes of claim preclusion.").

The court found that Horne's alleged causes of action were virtually identical. Both complaints alleged: (1) abuse of process, (2) defamation, and (3) violation of W. Va. § 21–5–4(b). In the first complaint, Horne asserted that the "decision of the defendants, including, but not limited to, the individual defendant, Charles Hamrick, is being done with a malicious purpose and is an abuse of the legal process.". In the second complaint, Horne similarly asserted that the "decision of the defendants, including, but not limited to, the individual defendant, Tracy S. Turner, is being done with a malicious purpose and is an abuse of the legal process.". This claim, and the others, were nearly identical in both form and substance, with mere omissions and substitutions of names. The prayer for relief in both complaints was also virtually identical, beyond the addition of requests for "compensation for unpaid wages" and "judicial determination that the plaintiff is the owner of an equity interest in one or both of the limited liability company defendants." Furthermore, the facts alleged in both complaints were virtually identical, with no substantive changes beyond the removal or substitution of references to Charles Hamrick and August Schultes, defendants from the first action.

These were the precise issues and facts on which Horne received a jury verdict of no liability in the first action, and as such, Turner satisfied the second element of res judicata.

Finally, the state court action must have involved the same parties, or persons in privity with those parties. "Privity is not established . . . from the mere facts that persons may happen to be interested in the same question or in proving the same facts." *State v. Miller,* 194 W.Va. 3, 459 S.E.2d 114, 124 (1995). Rather, "the key consideration for its existence is the sharing of the same legal right by the parties allegedly in privity, so as to ensure that the interest of the party *against whom* preclusion is asserted have been adequately represented." *West Virginia Human Rights Comm'n v. Esquire Grp., Inc.,* 217 W.Va. 454, 618 S.E.2d 463, 469 (2005).

Privity "is merely a word used to say that the relationship between one who is a party on the record and another is close enough to include that other within the res judicata." *Rowe v. Grapevine Corp.,* 206 W.Va. 703, 527 S.E.2d 814, 826 (1999). Virtual representation is a variety of privity that "precludes relitigation of any issue that has once been adequately tried by a person sharing a substantial identity of interests with a nonparty." *Galanos v. Nat'l Steel Corp.,* 178 W.Va. 193, 358 S.E.2d 452, 454 (1987). "The privity concept is fairly elastic under West Virginia law, as elsewhere." *Gribben v. Kirk,* 195 W.Va. 488, 466 S.E.2d 147, 157 n. 21 (1995).

As an initial matter, the defendants Lightning Energy and Lightning Trucking were named in both complaints in identical capacities, and as such are bound as the same parties from the prior action. *Esquire Grp.*, 618 S.E.2d at 469. The remaining defendant, Turner, was not a party in the first action at the time of the jury verdict, having been dismissed for lack of service of process. He did, however, satisfy the primary concern on which the privity requirement focuses, fairness towards the party against whom res judicata is raised. Horne was a party to the first action and received a full opportunity to litigate these same claims.

Furthermore, the court found that Turner had such significant interest of identity with Lightning Trucking and Lightning Energy as to trigger virtual representation. *Galanos v. Nat'l Steel Corp.*, 358 S.E.2d at 454. As alleged by Horne in both actions, Turner was the "manager and/or director of the defendant, Lightning Energy Services, LLC, and at all times relevant hereto was a principal decision maker of the defendant, Lightning Trucking Services, LLC." Turner shared a substantial identity of interest with August Schultes and Charles Hamrick, as the claims alleged against these parties all arose out of the same factual circumstance, that is, their roles as managers, directors, or principal decision makers of the respective LLCs. Additionally, the same legal interests defended in the prior litigation by Lightning Energy and Lightning Trucking were implicated in the second action. The nature of the claims, seeking unpaid wages stemming from Horne's termination, indicated that Horne was seeking recovery from Turner in his capacity as a representative or member of the LLCs. This matter was resolved in the prior action, and furthermore, there has been no divergence in legal interests between this action and the prior action.

Accordingly, the court held that Turner was in privity with the defendants from the prior action. Horne's claims therefore were barred by the principles of res judicata. Horne had no possibility of recovery against any of the named defendants, who invoked the doctrine of fraudulent joinder. *Jackson,* 132 F.Supp.2d at 433. Based on that, the court granted Turner's motion to dismiss.

**ANSWER (B)** is incorrect because although the doctrine of res judicata is based on underlying values of judicial efficiency and economy, these were not the bases upon which the court granted the motion to dismiss. **ANSWER (C)** is incorrect because the court held that there was an adjudication on the merits in the prior action. **ANSWER (D)** is incorrect because the court found that the two actions were virtually identical. **ANSWER (E)** is incorrect because the court found that the parties were in privity from the first to the second action.

**PROBLEM #15. BEST ANSWER (D).**

Problem #15 is based on *Bodenheimer v. Williams*, 2015 WL 4528910 (E.D. La. Oct. 20, 2015). This problem deals with a motion for sanctions and fees pursuant to 28 U.S.C. § 1927, and the relationship of that provision to Fed.R.Civ.P. 11. The court found that the plaintiff remediated his complaint within the safe harbor provision of Rule 11, and therefore denied the defendant's motions for sanctions independently under 28 U.S.C. § 1927.

Under 28 U.S.C. § 1927, an attorney who "so multiples the proceedings in any case unreasonably and vexatiously may be required by the court to satisfy personally the excess costs, expenses, and attorneys' fees reasonably incurred because of such conduct." The Fifth Circuit has held that the district court must find that an attorney multiplied the proceedings both "unreasonably" and "vexatiously" under § 1927 to shift reasonable fees. *Edwards v. Gen. Motors Corp.*, 153 F.3d 242, 246 (5th Cir.1998); *FDIC v. Calhoun*, 34 F.3d 1291, 1297 (5th Cir.1994). Section 1927 sanctions are not to be awarded lightly. *Gonzalez v. Fresenius Med. Care N. Am.*, 689 F.3d 470, 479 (5th Cir.2012). "To prevent the courts from dampening 'the legitimate zeal of an attorney in representing her client,' *Browning v. Kramer*, 931 F.2d 340, 344 (5th Cir.1991), the Fifth Circuit has interpreted § 1927 as penal and construes it in favor of the sanctioned party, *FDIC v. Conner*, 20 F.3d 1376, 1384 (5th Cir.1994)." *Id.* at 526. Awarding sanctions under section 1927 thus "requires that there be evidence of bad faith, improper motive, or reckless disregard of the duty owed to the court." *Edwards*, 153 F.3d at 246.

"The standards for bad faith are necessarily stringent," and the court must exercise its inherent power to levy fees for bad faith with restraint. *Batson v. Neal Spelce Associates, Inc.*, 805 F.2d 546, 550 (5th Cir.1986). "A party should not be penalized for maintaining an aggressive litigation posture," but "advocacy simply for the sake of burdening an opponent with unnecessary expenditures of time and effort clearly warrants recompense for the extra outlays attributable thereto." *Id.* Courts support imposing sanctions where an attorney used repeated filings despite warnings from the court, or other proof of excessive litigiousness. *Procter & Gamble Co.*, 280 F.3d at 525–26 (citing *Nat'l Ass'n of Gov't Employees v. Nat'l Fed'n of Fed. Employees*, 844 F.2d 216, 224 (5th Cir.1988)). However, sanctions will not be imposed for mere negligence of counsel. *See Hahn v. City of Kenner*, 1 F.Supp.2d 614, 617–18 (E.D.La.1998).

The court can shift fees "only to counsel, not to parties." *Procter & Gamble Co. v. Amway Corp.*, 280 F.3d 519, 525 (5th Cir.2002). "By its terms § 1927 does not authorize the wholesale reimbursement of a party for all of its attorneys' fees or for the total costs of the litigation." *Browning v. Kramer*, 931 F.2d 340, 344–45 (5th Cir.1991). "Except when the entire course of proceedings were unwarranted and should neither have been commenced nor persisted in, an award under § 1927 may not shift the entire financial burden of an action's defense." *Id.* (citing *Lewis v. Brown & Root, Inc.*, 711 F.2d 1287, 1292 (5th Cir.1983), *clarified on reconsideration*, 722 F.2d 209 (5th Cir.1984)). Instead, under § 1927, only those fees and costs associated with "the persistent prosecution of a meritless claim" may be awarded. *Id.* (citing *Thomas v. Capital Sec. Serv., Inc.*, 836 F.2d 866, 875 (5th Cir.1988)).

The court noted that the defendants' Rule 11 argument was not ripe for review—as the defendants conceded—and would consider only the request for fees under section 1927. Upon review, the court found that the plaintiff's counsel has not acted in bad faith nor "unreasonably" or "vexatiously" multiplied the proceedings in this matter. The defendants relied almost exclusively on their contention that the plaintiff's claims were time-barred and therefore meritless in asserting that the plaintiff's counsel acted in bad faith. Assuming *arguendo*, that at least some of the plaintiff's claims were time-barred and meritless, the plaintiff's counsel nevertheless acted within the scope of the Rule 11 safe-harbor provision in amending the complaint and removing any claims that he might have believed were prescribed. Moreover, while miscommunication occurring informally between counsel may have frustrated the defendants' efforts, such conduct did not rise to the level of "bad faith" or evidence any improper motive such that sanctions should be levied against the plaintiff's counsel. Indeed, the plaintiff's counsel would not have had the opportunity to file for entry of preliminary default had any responsive pleading been filed by the defendants and only made such filing after issuance of the court's call docket lest his action be dismissed for inaction.

Under similar facts, the Fifth Circuit has explained why such conduct such as the plaintiff's counsel's in this case did not merit sanctions:

> Of course, under Rule 11, plaintiff's counsel should have investigated his case before filing it. Such an investigation would usually include obtaining documentary proof supporting, or disproving, his client's allegations prior to or soon after filing suit. Had Plaintiff's counsel been more diligent, this litigation might have ended sooner, sparing the costs expended by the plaintiff, defendant, district court, and this court. But § 1927, unlike Rule 11, is not about mere negligence. *See Schwartz v. Millon Air, Inc.,* 341 F.3d 1220, 1225 (11th Cir.2003). Rule 11, with its lower standard of culpability that permits sanctions for failure to conduct a reasonable inquiry, provides a "safe harbor" during which an attorney may correct his actions by withdrawing or correcting the challenged paper, claim, defense, contention or denial. *See* Fed.R.Civ.P. 11(c)(2). Here, Plaintiff's counsel took corrective action once his good faith belief in his client's allegations was challenged by the lack of documentary evidence-he did not further multiply the litigation nor persist in a meritless claim. The whole point of Rule 11's "safe harbor" is to allow an attorney who is mistaken about the merits of his claim to withdraw it. Section 1927, by contrast, is about the intentionally wrongful or reckless counsel, not the one who is merely negligent or lacking in diligence.

*Vanderhoff v. Pacheco*, 344 F.App'x 22, 28 (5th Cir.2009). In sum, in light of the above and construing § 1927 strictly in favor of the plaintiff's counsel, it appears that the plaintiff's counsel had not persisted in pursing frivolous claims nor have the defendants shown that the plaintiff's counsel knowingly persisted in pursuing meritless claims.

Accordingly, the defendants' motion for fees and costs pursuant to 28 U.S.C. § 1927 was denied.

**ANSWER (A)** is incorrect because the court did not find that the plaintiff had needless or vexatiously multiplied the proceedings. **ANSWER (B)** is incorrect because the court did not find that the plaintiff had acted in bad faith. **ANSWER (C)** is incorrect because the court found that once the defendant communicated with the plaintiff, the plaintiff remedied the defects in its complaint within the safe harbor period afforded by Rule 11. **ANSWER (E)** is a possible answer, but not the best answer; the court found that even though the Rule 11 motion for sanctions was not ripe, it could still rule on the motion for sanctions under 28 U.S.C. § 1927.

## PROBLEM #16. BEST ANSWER (C).

Problems #16 and #17 are based on *Allen v. Antal*, 2015 WL 5474080 (S.D.N.Y. Sept. 15, 2015). Problem #16 addresses the conversion of a motion for a judgment on the pleadings under Fed.R.Civ.P. 12(c) to a summary judgment motion, while Problem #17 deals with the merits of the summary judgment motion under Fed.R.Civ.P. 56. In problem #16, the court held that the motion for a judgment on the pleadings was converted into a summary judgment motion. On the merits of the summary judgment motion, the court granted summary judgment to the defendant. (*See* discussion below).

Under Fed.R.Civ.P. 12(c), "after the pleadings are closed—but early enough not to delay trial—a party may move for judgment on the pleadings." Fed.R.Civ.P. 12(c). "To survive a Rule 12(c) motion, the complaint must contain sufficient factual matter to 'state a claim to relief that is plausible on its face.' " *Graziano v. Pataki*, 689 F.3d 110, 114 (2d Cir.2012) (quoting *Bell Atl. Corp. v. Twombly*, 550 U.S. 544, 570 (2007)). The standard for analyzing a motion for judgment on the pleadings under Rule 12(c) is identical to the standard for a motion to dismiss for failure to state a claim under Rule 12(b)(6). *Cleveland v. Caplaw Enters.*, 448 F.3d 518, 521 (2d Cir.2006); *see also* Fed.R.Civ.P. 12(b)(6).

In ruling on a motion to dismiss, a "court may consider the facts as asserted within the four corners of the complaint together with the documents attached to the complaint as exhibits, and any documents incorporated in the complaint by reference." *Peter F. Gaito Architecture, LLC v. Simone Dev. Corp.*, 602 F.3d 57, 64 (2d Cir.2010). Courts may also consider "matters of which judicial notice may be taken" and "documents either in plaintiffs' possession or of which plaintiffs had knowledge and relied on in bringing suit." *Brass v. Am. Film Techs., Inc.*, 987 F.2d 142, 150 (2d Cir.1993).

Conversely, when documents are included on a motion to dismiss that do not fall into these categories, "a district court must either exclude the additional material and decide the motion on the complaint alone or convert the motion to one for summary judgment . . . and afford all parties the opportunity to present supporting material." *Friedl v. City of N.Y.*, 210 F.3d 79, 83 (2d Cir.2000). Rule 12(d) provides:

> If, on a motion under Rule 12(b)(6) or 12(c), matters outside the pleadings are presented to and not excluded by the court, the motion must be treated as one for summary judgment under Rule 56. All parties must be given a reasonable opportunity to present all the material that is pertinent to the motion.

Fed.R.Civ.P. 12(d). Accordingly, a district court acts properly in converting a motion for judgment on the pleadings into a motion for summary judgment when the motion presents matters outside the pleadings, as long as the Court gives "sufficient notice to an opposing party and an opportunity for that party to respond." *Groden v. Random House, Inc.*, 61 F.3d 1045, 1052 (2d Cir.1995).

Ordinarily, formal notice is not required where a party "should reasonably have recognized the possibility that the motion might be converted into one for summary judgment and was neither taken by surprise nor deprived of a reasonable opportunity to meet facts outside the pleadings." *Villante v. Dep't of Corrections of City of New York,* 786 F.2d 516, 521 (2d Cir.1986) (quoting *In re G. & A. Books, Inc.,* 770 F.2d 288, 295 (2d Cir.1985)). *Hernandez v. Coffey,* 582 F.3d 303, 307 (2d Cir.2009).

In this case, the court determined that because the defendant has presented matters outside the pleadings, which the court did not exclude, and because the plaintiff was timely apprised of the possibility that this motion could be treated as a motion for summary judgment and had the opportunity to present supporting material, the court hereby therefore defendant's motion as one for summary judgment.

**ANSWER (A)** is incorrect because it does not properly state the standard for a judgment on the pleadings under Fed.R.Civ.P. 12(b)(6). **ANSWER (B)** is a possible answer, but not the best answer because the facts indicate that the defendant supplied information in addition to the pleadings, which converted the motion to a summary judgment motion. **ANSWER (D)** is incorrect because Fed.R.Civ.P. 56 imposes a different standard than Fed.R.Civ.P. 12(c), but this is not a reason for a court to decline to convert the motion. **ANSWER (E)** is incorrect because it doesn't matter whether converting the motion to a summary judgment motion would prejudice the defendant; the defendant by its conduct in supplying materials in addition to the pleadings was responsible for triggering the conversion of the motion to a summary judgment motion.

## PROBLEM #17. BEST ANSWER (A).

Problem #17 is a continuation of Problem #16, and is based on the same fact pattern and judicial decision. This problem requires analysis of the defendant's motion for summary judgment under the standards of Fed.R.Civ.P. 56. The court granted the defendants motion because the court concluded that there was no genuine issue of material fact whether attorney Atwell's negligence was the proximate cause of the plaintiff's injuries. Therefore, there would be no purpose for a trial and the defendant was entitled to a judgment as a matter of law.

Rule 56 of the Federal Rules of Civil Procedure governs motions for summary judgment. The Rule states, in pertinent part: "The court shall grant summary judgment if the movant shows that there is no genuine dispute as to any material fact and the movant is entitled to judgment as a matter of law." Fed.R.Civ.P. 56(a). The moving party bears the initial burden of pointing to evidence in the record, "including depositions, documents . . . and affidavits or declarations," Fed.R.Civ.P. 56(c)(1)(A), "which it believes demonstrates the absence of a genuine issue of material fact." *Celotex Corp. v. Catrett,* 477 U.S. 317, 323 (1986). The moving party may also meet its initial burden that there is no genuine dispute by "showing . . . that the adverse party cannot produce admissible evidence to support the fact." Fed.R.Civ.P. 56(c)(1)(B); *Hill v. Melvin,* No. 05 Civ. 6645, 2006 WL 1749520, at *4 (S.D.N.Y. June 27, 2006) ("The movant may discharge this burden by demonstrating to the Court that there is an absence of evidence to support the non-moving party's case on an issue on which the non-movant has the burden of proof."); *Fuertado v. City of New York,* 337 F.Supp.2d 593, 599 (S.D.N.Y.2004) ("The moving party may use a memorandum or brief to 'point to' the absence of evidence and thereby shift to the non-movant the obligation to come forward with admissible evidence supporting its claim.").

If the moving party fulfills its preliminary burden, the onus shifts to the non-movant to prove or raise the existence of a genuine issue of material fact. Fed.R.Civ.P. 56(c)(1)(A). The party asserting that a fact is genuinely disputed must identify "specific facts showing that there is a genuine issue for trial." *Anderson v. Liberty Lobby, Inc.,* 477 U.S. 242, 248 (1986) (quoting Fed.R.Civ.P. 56); *Bennett v. Watson Wyatt & Co.,* 136 F.Supp.2d 236, 244 (S.D.N.Y.2001). The non-movant must support their assertion by "citing to particular parts of materials in the records" or "showing that the materials cited do not establish the absence . . . of a genuine dispute." Fed.R.Civ.P. 56(c)(1). "Statements that are devoid of any specifics, but replete with conclusions, are insufficient to defeat a properly supported motion for summary judgment." *Bickerstaff v. Vassar Coll.,* 196 F.3d 435, 452 (2d Cir.1999); *see also Matsushita Elec. Indus. Co. v. Zenith Radio Corp.,* 475 U.S. 574, 586 (1986) (nonmoving party "must do more than simply show that there is some metaphysical doubt as to the material facts"); *F.D.I.C. v. Great Am. Ins. Co.,* 607 F.3d 288, 292 (2d Cir.2010) (nonmoving party "may not rely on conclusory allegations or unsubstantiated speculation" (quoting *Scotto v. Almenas,* 143 F.3d 105, 114 (2d Cir.1998))). Summary judgment should be granted when a party "fails to make a showing sufficient to establish the existence of an element essential to that party's case, and on which that party will bear the burden of proof at trial." *Celotex Corp.,* 477 U.S. at 322.

A genuine dispute of material fact exists when "the evidence is such that a reasonable jury could return a verdict for the nonmoving party." *Anderson, All* U.S. at 248; *accord Benn v. Kissane,* 510 F.App'x 34, 36 (2d Cir.2013); *Gen. Star Nat'l Ins. Co. v. Universal Fabricators, Inc.,* 585 F.3d 662, 669 (2d Cir.2009); *Roe v. City of Waterbury,* 542 F.3d 31, 35 (2d Cir.2008). Courts must "construe the evidence in the light most favorable to the non-moving party and draw all reasonable inferences in its favor." *Fincher v. Depository Trust & Clearing Corp.,* 604 F.3d 712, 720 (2d Cir.2010) (quoting *Allianz Ins. Co. v. Lerner,* 416 F.3d 109, 113 (2d Cir.2005)). In reviewing the record, "the judge's function is not himself to weigh the evidence and determine the truth of the matter," nor is it to determine a witness's credibility. *Anderson,* 477 U.S. at 249; *see also Kaytor v. Elec. Boat Corp.,* 609 F.3d 537, 545 (2d Cir.2010) ("The function of the district court in considering the motion for summary judgment is not to resolve disputed questions of fact"). Rather, "the inquiry performed is the threshold inquiry of determining whether there is the need for a trial." *Anderson,* 477 U.S. at 250.

In order to prove a claim for legal malpractice under New York law, a plaintiff must establish: (1) an attorney-client relationship, (2) attorney negligence, (3) that the attorney's negligence is the proximate cause of plaintiff's loss or injury, and (4) actual damages. *See Decker v. Nagel Rice LLC*, No. 09 Civ.

9878(SAS), 2010 WL 2346608, at *3 (S.D.N.Y. May 28, 2010); *Hoffenberg v. Meyers*, No. 99 Civ. 4674, 2002 WL 57252 (S.D.N.Y.2002) (plaintiff must show "that an attorney-client relationship existed, that a duty was owed, that there was a wrongful act or omission which was the proximate cause of the damages, and the measure of those damages."); *Brooks v. Lewin*, 21 A.D.3d 731, 734–35, 800 N.Y.S.2d 695 (N.Y.App.Div.2005) ("An action for legal malpractice requires proof of three elements: (1) that the attorney was negligent; (2) that such negligence was a proximate cause of plaintiff's losses; and (3) proof of actual damages."). To establish negligence, a plaintiff must show that the attorney's conduct "fell below the ordinary and reasonable skill and knowledge commonly possessed by a member of the profession." *Decker*, No. 09 Civ. 9878(SAS), 2010 WL 2346608, at *3. To establish the proximate cause and actual damages elements, a plaintiff must show that "but for the attorney's negligence, what would have been a favorable outcome was an unfavorable outcome." *Id.*

The court held that regardless of whether Atwell was negligent, the plaintiff's legal malpractice claim failed because he could show that Atwell's actions (or failure to act) proximately caused his damages.

"The rule in a legal malpractice action is that a plaintiff must demonstrate not only that actual damages have been sustained, but also that counsel's negligence was the proximate cause of the loss." *Zarin v. Reid & Priest*, 184 A.D.2d 385, 387, 585 N.Y.S.2d 379 (N.Y.App.Div.1992) (citing *O'Brien v. Spuck,* 99 A.D.2d 910, 911, 472 N.Y.S.2d 514 (N.Y.App.Div.1984)). "To prove the proximate cause element, 'a plaintiff must demonstrate that but for the attorney's negligence, she would have prevailed in the underlying matter or would not have sustained any ascertainable damages.'" *Law Practice Mgmt. Consultants, LLC v. M & A Counselors & Fiduciaries, LLC,* 599 F.Supp.2d 355, 359 (E.D.N.Y.2009) (quoting *Brooks,* 21 A.D.3d at 734, 800 N.Y.S.2d 695); *Stonewell Corp. v. Conestoga Title Ins. Co.,* 678 F.Supp.2d 203, 209 (S.D.N.Y.2010) ("The plaintiff must show that but for the attorney's negligence, what would have been a favorable outcome was an unfavorable outcome."); *Dawson v. Schoenberg,* 129 A.D.3d 656, 657–58 (N.Y.App.Div.2015). "A failure to establish that an attorney's conduct proximately caused harm requires dismissal of the malpractice action, regardless of whether the attorney was in fact negligent." *Stonewell Corp.,* 678 F.Supp.2d at 211–12 (collecting cases); *Decker*, No. 09 CIV. 9878(SAS), 2010 WL 2346608, at *3; *Law Practice Mgmt. Consultants, LLC*, 599 F.Supp.2d at 359.

The court found that this case involved a unique set of circumstances in that the plaintiff was not alleging that the defendant Atwell was negligent in his representation of the plaintiff during the underlying criminal proceedings, but rather that Atwell's failure occurred after he actually secured a reversal of the plaintiff's conviction, when he allegedly failed to notify the plaintiff that his conviction was vacated and failed to follow up to ensure that his rapsheet was cleared. The court held that what the plaintiff failed to note, however, was that the plaintiff's own actions and the actions of other non-parties were intervening causes responsible for the injury that he suffered.

"Where the record in a professional malpractice case demonstrates that an intervening cause was responsible for the injury, summary judgment will be granted to the defendant." *Brooks*, 21 A.D.3d at 734–35, 800 N.Y.S.2d 695; *see also Hoffenberg v. Meyers*, No. 99 Civ. 4674 RWS, 2002 WL 57252, at *4 (S.D.N.Y. Jan.16, 2002)(dismissing malpractice claim where plaintiff's plea, not defendant's representation, proximately caused plaintiff's damages); *D.D. Hamilton Textiles v. Estate of Mate*, 269 A.D.2d 214, 215, 703 N.Y.S.2d 451 (N.Y.App.Div.2000) (malpractice claim against accountant dismissed where proximate cause of injury was plaintiffs own financial distress); *Phillips Smith Specialty Retail Group II, L.P. v. Parker Chapin Flattau & Klimpl, L.L.P.,* 265 A.D.2d 208, 210, 696 N.Y.S.2d 150 (N.Y.App.Div.1999) (malpractice claim dismissed where connection between plaintiff's injuries and alleged malpractice was purely speculative); *Senise v. Mackasek*, 227 A.D.2d 184, 185, 642 N.Y.S.2d 241 (N.Y.App.Div.1996) ("The record establishes the damages sustained by plaintiff in that action were proximately caused by plaintiff's own conduct in violating . . . the New York State Insurance Law . . . , rather than due to any legal malpractice on the part of defendants as appellate counsel.").

Here, the damages that the plaintiff alleged in the complaint—his arrest for violating the terms of his supervised release, his re-incarceration, the costs of the drug treatment program he attended, etc.—were proximately caused by intervening actions, or failures to act, on the part of the plaintiff and other non-parties, rather than by any negligence on the part of Atwell as his attorney. The court held that the plaintiff could not show that "but for" Atwell's alleged failure to fulfill his duties to his client, he would not have been arrested for violating his release terms and made to suffer other consequent injuries. One intervening cause was the plaintiff's own conduct, in failing the drug test and admitting to the violation of the terms of his post-release supervision. More important, however, was the intervening cause of the trial court clerk's failure to notify the division of criminal justice services and clear the plaintiff's rapsheet. New York law provides that:

> Upon the termination of a criminal action or proceeding against a person in favor of such person . . . , the record of such action or proceeding shall be sealed and the clerk of the court wherein such criminal action or proceeding was terminated shall immediately notify the commissioner of the division of criminal justice services and the head of all appropriate police departments and other law enforcement agencies that the action has been terminated in favor of the accused, and unless the court has directed otherwise, that the record of such action or proceeding shall be sealed.

N.Y.Crim. Proc. Law § 160.50; *see also People v. Alien*, 89 A.D.3d 742, 742, 932 N.Y.S.2d 142 (N.Y.App.Div.2011) ("Ordered that the judgment is reversed, on the law, . . . the indictment is dismissed, and the matter is remitted to the County Court, Dutchess County, for the purpose of entering in its discretion pursuant to CPL 160.50"). Thus, it is undisputed that it was the clerk of the trial court who bore the responsibility of notifying the division of criminal justice services and appropriate law enforcement agencies that the action had been terminated in the plaintiff's favor, and it was the clerk's ultimate failure to do so that serves as an intervening cause of the plaintiff's damages. Regardless of whether the defendant had notified the plaintiff of the final disposition of his case, in accordance with his responsibilities as appellate counsel, the clerk's failure to notify the division of criminal justice services breaks any proximate cause link between the defendant's alleged failure to notify the plaintiff and the plaintiff's damages. Thus, the plaintiff's damages were not a "direct or reasonably foreseeable result of the defendant's conduct." *Pension Comm. of Univ. of Montreal Pension Plan v. Banc of America Secs. LLC*, 568 F.3d 374, 381 (2d Cir.2009); *see Fin. Freedom Senior Funding Corp. v. Bellettieri, Fonte & Laudonio, P.C.,* 852 F.Supp.2d 430, 437–38 (S.D.N.Y.2012) ("It is well-established that one element of proximate causation is foreseeability."). Explained another way, it was the clerk's failure to act that was the true "but for" cause of the plaintiff's injury, not Atwell's alleged negligence.

The court concluded that the plaintiff's failure to establish proximate causation, or any questions of material fact that remain in dispute as to proximate causation, doomed his claim regardless of Atwell's negligence or lack thereof. *See D'Jamoos v. Griffith,* 340 F.App'x 737, 739–40 (2d Cir.2009) ("Although Griffith's representation of D'Jamoos raises concerns, . . . plaintiff has failed to put forth evidence that would permit a rational fact-finder to conclude that Griffith's conduct proximately caused damages to plaintiff."); *Law Practice Mgmt. Consultants, LLC,* 599 F.Supp.2d at 359 ("At this stage, construing the complaint in the light most favorable to the Plaintiffs, the Court is willing to accept the fact that Defendant may have been negligent. . . . However, the Plaintiffs' legal malpractice claim necessarily fails as a matter of law because they cannot establish proximate causation.").

For the foregoing reasons, the defendant Atwell's motion for summary judgment was granted in favor of defendant.

**ANSWER (B)** is incorrect because there is no requirement that a litigant move for a Rule 12(c) judgment on the pleadings in order to move for a motion for summary judgment later in the litigation. **ANSWER (C)** is incorrect because there was no reason to send the case to the jury on the malpractice issue; the court determined that there was no genuine issue of material fact and therefore the defendant was entitled to a judgment as a matter of law. **ANSWER (D)** is incorrect because Atwell's credibility was not at issue in this case and therefore this did not serve as a basis for denying the defendant's summary judgment motion. **ANSWER (E)** is incorrect because the facts do not present any basis for allowing a jury to draw inferences from the evidence in the case.

## PROBLEM #18. BEST ANSWER (B).

Problem #18 is based on *Hooks v. Auto Field Corp.,* 2015 WL 8042241 (E.D.N.Y. Dec. 3, 2015). This problem deals with the issue whether a federal court should exercise supplemental jurisdiction over state-based claims in a lawsuit with a good federal question jurisdictional basis. The court determined that it would not exercise supplemental jurisdiction over the state claims under 28 U.S.C. § 1367 and dismissed the state claims but retained jurisdiction over the federal TILA claim.

Under 28 U.S.C. § 1367(c), a federal district court has discretion to decline to exercise supplemental jurisdiction for a number of reasons. Included among those reasons is that the state law claims "substantially predominate over the claim or claims over which the district court has original jurisdiction." This consideration is derived from the Supreme Court's seminal decision in *United Mineworkers v. Gibbs*, 383 U.S. 715 (1966). There, the Supreme Court gave three examples of when state law claims could be found to substantially predominate over federal claims: "in terms of proof, of the scope of the issues raised, or of the comprehensiveness of the remedy sought. . . ." *Id.* at 727.

The court held that the mere enumeration of plaintiff's eight state law claims, as set forth above, was sufficient to show that they met all of these criteria. The alleged defects in plaintiff's vehicle, the issue of whether plaintiff gave defendant a reasonable opportunity to effect repairs, the quality of the repairs done by the BMW dealership, and the remedy that plaintiff seeks for the alleged defect—full restitution—all presented issues requiring substantial discovery that had nothing to do with her technical non-disclosure claim under TILA. And the TILA claim could hardly be more straightforward—the simple question was whether a $95 charge was properly disclosed. The main remedy if it wasn't was double damages, not restitution. The TILA claim could be resolved in a matter of weeks on cross-motions for summary judgment, with limited, if any, discovery, whereas the state law claims would require months of discovery and likely a trial. The court held that if there was ever a case where the federal law tail was wagging a state law dog, this was it.

The court indicated that numerous courts have recognized that when state law claims overshadow federal claims to the extent they did here, it was appropriate for the court to decline to exercise supplemental jurisdiction. *See Feezor v. Tesstab Operations Group, Inc.*, 524 F.Supp. 2d 1222, 1224 (S.D. Cal. 2007) ("Given the disparity in terms of comprehensiveness of the remedy sought, state law claims substantially predominate over the ADA for purposes of 28 U.S.C. § 1367(c)(2)."); *Szendrey-Ramos v. First BanCorp*, 512 F.Supp. 2d 81, 86 (D. P.R. 2007) (dismissing local law discrimination claims despite original jurisdiction over federal discrimination claims, because "not only do the P.R. law claims far outnumber the federal claims, but their scope also exceeds that of the federal claims. . . . and although some of the P.R. law claims mimic the federal claims . . . the remaining P.R. law claims . . . are distinct and each has its own elements of proof; proof that is not necessary to establish the Title VII claims."); *Semi-Tech Litigation LLC v. Bankers Trust Company*, 234 F.Supp. 2d 297, 301 (S.D.N.Y. 2002) ("The factual and legal questions unique to the common law claims against the moving defendants simply overwhelm any questions common to the federal claims."); *Craig Lyle Ltd. Partnership v. Land O'Lakes, Inc.*, 877 F.Supp. 476 (D. Minn. 1995) (declining to exercise supplemental jurisdiction over state law nuisance and trespass claim based on original jurisdiction over federal Resource Conservation and Recovery Act claim).

Indeed, the distinction in issues and proof between the plaintiff's TILA claim and her state law claims was so dramatic that it was questionable whether the court even had supplemental jurisdiction to begin with under 28 U.S.C. § 1367. Subsection (a) states that a federal district court shall have jurisdiction over state law claims when they are "so related to claims in the action within such original jurisdiction that they form part of the same case or controversy under Article III of the United States Constitution." 28 U.S.C. § 1367(a). The plaintiff argued that it did because all of the claims arose out of the same "transaction," which she defined as the sale of the car. But the court found that was an awfully broad definition of the case. Defining the "case" as did the *Gibbs* Court—as deriving from "a common nucleus of operative fact," 383 U.S. at 725—made apparent the distinction between the plaintiff's federal claim and her numerous state law claims. The plaintiff's alleged TILA violation occurred when the defendant provided her with the allegedly inadequate disclosure document; her state law claims accrued some time thereafter, when defendant failed to adequately address her alleged problems with the BMW. If defendant had adequately addressed the plaintiff's alleged problems with the car, she would still have her TILA claim, and the circumstances surrounding that claim would remain unaltered. There is thus very little overlap between those two nuclei of fact. *See Semi-Tech*, 234 F.Supp. 2d at 301 (original jurisdiction over Trust Indenture Act claim against trustee in giving inaccurate certifications did not confer supplemental jurisdiction tort claims against officers whose conduct made the certifications false).

The court noted that the plaintiff pointed out that, by declining supplemental jurisdiction, she would have to bring two claims in two forums. That was only technically true. It presumed that the plaintiff was actually interested in pursuing her $198 TILA claim for economic reasons as opposed to merely using it as means of bringing her $45,000 state law claims in federal court. If plaintiff did not want to pursue her federal claim, she did not have to. It would only cost her a fraction of what this controversy is really about.

The federal court concluded that "this court does not sit as a state court." Congress did not intend TILA to supply a $95 federal "hook" to turn it into one. Thus, the court determined that Counts 2 through 9 of the complaint were dismissed without prejudice to recommencement in state court.

**ANSWER (A)** is incorrect because the court did not dismiss the entire case, but only the state law claims. **ANSWER (C)** is incorrect because the court found it was dubious that the federal and state law claims could be characterized as constituting "one constitutional case." **ANSWER (D)** is incorrect because even though federal courts do have jurisdiction to exercise supplemental jurisdiction over state law claims, this was not an appropriate case to exercise that supplemental jurisdiction. **ANSWER (E)** is incorrect because although courts generally will pay deference to a plaintiff's choice of forum, the judge in this case clearly indicated that he would not allow the plaintiff to forum shop seven state based claims into federal court by bootstrapping those claims onto a federal TILA claim.

**PROBLEM #19. BEST ANSWER (E).**

Problem #19 is based on *Okereke v. Allen*, 2015 5508888 (S.D.N.Y. July 29, 2015). This problem requires a simple analysis of the federal venue statute at 28 U.S.C. § 1391(b). The court determined that venue was not proper in the Southern District of New York, because the plaintiff could not rely on his own activities as a basis for laying venue there.

Under 28 U.S.C. § 1391(b), venue in a diversity action may arise (1) from a defendant's residence in the forum state; (2) from the occurrence of a "substantial part of the events or omissions giving rise to the claim" or the presence of a substantial part of the property at issue in the forum state; or (3) "if there is no district in which the action may otherwise be brought," from the fact that a defendant is subject to personal jurisdiction in the forum state. *D.H. Blair & Co. v. Gottdiener*, 462 F.3d 95, 105–06 (2d Cir.2006). "Once an objection to venue has been raised, the plaintiff bears the burden of establishing that venue is proper." *French Transit, Ltd. v. Modern Coupon Systems, Inc.*, 858 F.Supp. 22, 25 (S.D.N.Y.1994); *accord Bank of America, N.A. v . . Wilmington Trust FSB*, 943 F.Supp.2d 417, 421 (S.D.N.Y.2013). In deciding a claim of improper venue, a "Court must accept the facts alleged in the complaint and construe all reasonable inferences in the plaintiff's favor." *Matera v. Native Eyewear, Inc.*, 355 F.Supp.2d 680, 681 (E.D.N.Y.2005).

Venue in this action did not arise from the defendant's residence in the forum state under 28 U.S.C. § 1391(b)(1), as it is undisputed that Mr. Allen is a resident of New Jersey. Nor does the fact that Dr. Okereke lives in this district support venue; indeed, in 1990 Congress amended Section 1391 primarily to remove the plaintiff's residence from consideration for purposes of venue. *See* 14D Charles Alan Wright *et al.*, FEDERAL PRACTICE AND PROCEDURE § 3806.1 (4th ed.2015); *MB Financial Bank, N.A. v. Walker*, 741 F.Supp.2d 912, 918 (N.D.Ill.2010); *accord Cold Spring Harbor Laboratory v. Ropes & Gray LLP*, 762 F.Supp.2d 543, 559 (E.D.N.Y.2011).

Venue in the Southern District of New York was also not proper under 28 U.S.C. § 1391(b)(2). "When a plaintiff relies on Section 1391(b)(2) to defeat a venue challenge, a two-part inquiry is appropriate." *Daniel v. American Board of Emergency Medicine*, 428 F.3d 408, 432 (2d Cir.2005). First, a court must "identify the nature of the claims and the acts or omissions that the plaintiff alleges give rise to the claims." *Id.* In referring to the "acts or omissions giving rise to the claims," Congress intended for courts to examine the activities of the defendant and not of the plaintiff. *Prospect Capital Corp. v. Bender*, No. 09 Civ. 826, 2009 WL 490712, at *3 (S.D.N.Y. Dec. 21, 2009) (citing *Daniel*, 428 F.3d at 432). Second, a court should "determine whether a substantial part of those acts or omissions occurred in the district where suit was filed." *Daniel*, 428 F.3d at 432. " 'Substantiality' for venue purposes is more a qualitative than a quantitative inquiry, determined by assessing the overall nature of the plaintiff's claims and the nature of the specific events or omissions in the forum, and not by simply adding up the number of contacts." *Id.* at 432–33.

The court held that Okereke's argument for venue under U.S.C. § 1391(b)(2) failed under both prongs of the inquiry. First, while the complaint articulated specific acts of the defendant that gave rise to the legal malpractice claim, it identified none that would support venue in the Southern District of New York. Rather, Okereke based his claim for venue on his own conduct.

Second, even if the acts Okereke cited in support of venue could be attributed to Allen, they did not constitute a substantial part of the events or omissions that give rise to the malpractice claim. When analyzing venue in legal malpractice cases, most courts have found that events must relate to "the alleged malpractice and, not the entire attorney-client relationship" or the underlying action. *Cold Spring Harbor Laboratory*, 762 F.Supp.2d at 555 (listing cases). Furthermore, incidental events "that have only some tangential connection with the dispute in litigation are not enough" to support venue. *Loeb v. Bank of America*, 254 F.Supp.2d 581, 587 (E.D.Pa.2003).

Okereke bases his claim for venue on telephone conversations in connection with the underlying action, execution of the retainer with Allen, and review of court documents. But, while the telephone conversations likely provided Allen with information to pursue the case against RUSM, Okereke did not articulate how those calls contributed to any specific acts of malpractice. *See Trico Bancshares & Subsidiaries v. Rothgerber Johnson & Lyons LLP*, No. 09 CV 1700, 2009 WL 3365855, at *3 (E.D.Cal. Oct. 15, 2009); *Cold Spring Harbor Laboratory*, 762 F.Supp.2d at 556. Similarly, Okereke had not shown how signing the retainer or reviewing the court documents were substantially related to the claims of professional negligence, and not merely to the general underlying action. *Trico Bancshares & Subsidiaries*, 2009 WL 3365855, at *3.

Lastly, venue in the Southern District of New York was not supported under 28 U.S.C. § 1391(b)(3) because there was another district in which this action might be otherwise brought pursuant to 28 U.S.C. § 1391(b)(1) and (2). As a result, there was no basis for venue in the Southern District of New York.

In conclusion, the court granted the defendant's motion to dismiss the case pursuant to Rule 12(b)(3) for improper venue, but ordered that case should be transferred to the District of New Jersey for further proceedings pursuant to 28 U.S.C. § 1406.

**ANSWER (A)** is incorrect because venue was not proper in the Southern District of New York because the plaintiff's residence cannot serve as a basis for laying venue. **ANSWER (B)** is incorrect because the court determined that the relevant transactions and events relating to the malpractice claim occurred in New Jersey, and not New York. **ANSWER (C)** is incorrect because the fact pattern does not supply sufficient information to conclude whether Allen would be subject to personal jurisdiction in New York. **ANSWER (D)** is a possible answer, but not the best answer. Venue was proper in New Jersey because the defendant Allen resided and worked there; but the court found that venue was improper in New York because the plaintiff was relying on his activities to satisfy the 'transaction and occurrence' test for laying venue. Because the court concluded that the plaintiff's activities could not be used to satisfy venue, the court held that this was the basis for finding venue improper.

## PROBLEM #20. BEST ANSWER (A).

Problems #20 and #21 are based on *Le v. Diligence, Inc. and Nice Glide Fishing LLC*, 2015 WL 8483253 (D. Mass. Dec. 9, 2015). Problem #20 deals with the issue of a party's request for an additional deposition beyond what the federal rules permit. The court held that because of the newly discovered evidence relating to the wind gauge, the plaintiffs could take a second deposition of the ship captain. Problem #21, discussed below, deals with the defendant's invocation of the work product immunity to shield production of photographs from discovery, which immunity protection the court denied.

A party who wishes to depose a person more than once must seek and obtain prior leave of court, absent the parties' written stipulation. Fed.R.Civ.P. 30(a)(2)(A). Although the decision is discretionary, courts have generally allowed re-opening a deposition where, as here, new information is unearthed only after the initial deposition. *See, e.g., Quality Aero Tech., Inc. v. Telemetrie Elektronik GmbH*, 212 F.R.D. 313, 319 (E.D.N.C.2002) (allowing second 30(b)(6) deposition, finding that "newly-discovered information is sufficient for a finding of good cause under Rule 30"), *Dixon v. Certainteed Corp.*, 164 F.R.D. 685, 692 (D.Kan.1996) (second deposition warranted where plaintiff was unaware of, and thus could not inquire about, statements in the first deposition), *and Keck v. Union Bank of Switzerland*, No. 94–4912, 1997 WL 411931, at *1 (S.D.N.Y. July 22, 1997) ("a second deposition is often permitted, where new information comes to light triggering questions that the discovering party would not have thought to ask at the first deposition"). Here, the defendants failed to disclose the maintenance invoices concerning the wind station until one year after their initial discovery response, when pressed by the plaintiff to supplement. The court held that the defendants provided no reason for the delayed disclosures, and it was only fair that the plaintiff should not be penalized for their lack of promptness.

The defendants argued that a second deposition would be cumulative and duplicative because the plaintiff's counsel questioned Captain Larsen about the wind station during the first deposition. Reviewing the prior deposition testimony, the court found that the brief wind gauge questioning constituted the entire extent of the wind station discussion. At the time of this deposition, the plaintiff's counsel did not have access to the maintenance invoices provided in the defendants' supplemental discovery response. He was unaware that the weather sensor malfunctioned and was removed, that a new upgraded weather sensor was installed after the accident and that within a month after the accident a technician may have performed work on the electronic connection between the weather sensor and the display in the wheelhouse. Therefore, at the first deposition, the plaintiff's attorney could not have questioned Captain Larsen about these topics. Because none of these topics were covered previously, the court held that allowing a second deposition to probe Captain Larsen's knowledge of the wind station would not be cumulative or duplicative.

The defendants also asked the court to limit the deposition in "time, location, and scope of inquiry." Although Fed.R.Civ.P. 31(d) generally limits depositions to 7 hours, it also provides that "the court must allow additional time . . . if needed to fairly examine the deponent . . . " The court held that because the second deposition was necessitated by the newly-revealed documents and information, the court found that more time was warranted.

**ANSWER (B)** is a possible answer, but not the best answer. While it is true that the plaintiff might have been prejudiced by not being able to take the second deposition of the ship captain, the essential reason for granting the motion for the second deposition was because of the newly-discovered evidence. **ANSWER (C)** is incorrect because the court found that the second deposition would not be duplicative or cumulative of the information obtained in the first deposition. **ANSWER (D)** is incorrect because although the rule limits deposition testimony to seven hours, a court may extend this time limitation in circumstances such as those in this case, where there is newly discovered evidence that would necessitate another deposition. **ANSWER (E)** is incorrect because there is no indication on the facts that the plaintiffs did not diligently conduct their discovery before the first deposition; the problem arose because the defendants delayed in sending proper information to the plaintiffs about the wind gauge.

PROBLEM #21. BEST ANSWER (A).

Problem #21 is a continuation of Problem #20, and is based on the same fact pattern and judicial decision. This problem requires an analysis of the attorney work product immunity, and its application to the facts in this case. The court held that the photographs were ordinary work product, and because the plaintiff had substantial need for the photos and could not obtain them by other means, that the work product immunity was overcome, and the defendant had to produce the photos to the requesting plaintiff.

The defendants asserted that the photographs were taken in anticipation of litigation, and were therefore exempt from discovery as work product. This was a federal question case, so the federal common law of privilege applies. Fed. R. Evid. 501, *and see In re Keeper of Records (Grand Jury Subpoena Addressed to XYZ Corp.)*, 348 F.3d 16, 22 (1st Cir.2003). The defendants, who invoked the privilege, bore the burden of establishing that the privilege applied. *State of Maine v. United States Dep't of the Interior*, 298 F.3d 60, 71 (1st Cir.2002). The work-product doctrine, codified in Fed.R.Civ.P. 26(b)(3), is intended to preserve a "zone of privacy" within which a lawyer can prepare and develop legal theories and strategy "with an eye toward litigation." *Hickman v. Taylor*, 329 U.S. 495, 510–11 (1947); *United States v. Textron, Inc. and Subsidiaries*, 577 F.3d 21, 25 (1st Cir.2009). Documents and tangible things prepared by or for a party or its representative, in preparation for trial or in anticipation of litigation, are not discoverable absent a showing of substantial need, undue hardship, and inability to obtain their substantial equivalent by other means. Fed.R.Civ.P. 26(b)(3).

Here, the photographs met the work-product criteria of Rule 26(b)(3), as they are tangible things prepared in anticipation of litigation by the defendants or their agents. However, because the plaintiff had shown substantial need for the photographs and no means of obtaining equivalent images, they fell under the exemption in Rule 26(b)(3)(A)(ii). "Courts have generally allowed discovery of photographs and diagrams which were made at the time of an accident because of the inherent inability of a party to reproduce these materials . . . Photographs which are taken at the scene long after the occurrence of the accident may not be the substantial equivalent of photographs which were taken at an earlier date." *Reedy v. Lull Eng'g Co.*, 137 F.R.D. 405, 407 (M.D.Fla.1991). This was especially true here, where the vessel and wind station had been altered significantly since the incident, so that the plaintiff could simply take photographs today. The plaintiff had also requested the insurance survey photographs from the relevant years, but none were available. There did not appear to be any other means for him to access photographs of the vessel as it appeared at the time of the accident.

The facts here were also similar to other cases involving substantial injuries. *See, e.g., Trejo v. Alter Scrap Metal, Inc.*, No. 08–257, 2009 WL 2634485, at *1 (S.D.Miss. Aug. 24, 2009) (photographs discoverable where plaintiff's head injuries meant that he had no memory of the event and could not communicate his recollection of the scene), *and Martinsen v. Lykes Bros. Steamship Co.*, No. 86–1514, 1987 WL 6692, at *2 (E.D.Pa. Feb. 12, 1987) (plaintiff could not have obtained contemporaneous photographs of accident scene because he left vessel shortly after his injuries and had no right to re-board until filing suit). Here, the plaintiff had no memory of the incident, was airlifted off the vessel to receive medical care, and suffered a severe traumatic brain injury. The photographs might help to fill in the information missing from the plaintiff's recollection.

The defendants included an affidavit from counsel asserting that none of the photographs showed a location where the wind station would have been visible. However,

> A verbal description of a given area cannot substitute for photographs of the location. The description may omit relevant information such as whether certain signs were posted or whether certain items were present. Further, an expert may be unable to reach conclusions that may be of aid to the jury as to the composition of materials and construction at the location from incomplete verbal descriptions. Finally, a picture is certainly worth a thousand words to a jury, as well as to witnesses who may be unable to separate their recollection of the site as it appeared then from the present appearance of the site.

*Zoller v. Conoco, Inc.*, 137 F.R.D. 9, 10 (W.D.La.1991). The court concluded that giving full credit to defense counsel's assurances that the photographs did not show the presence or absence of the wind station, there might be other valuable information that the plaintiff could gain from viewing them. The plaintiff might be able to use the photographs to question witnesses, to seek expert opinions, or to pursue alternate theories of his case. Because the photographs were necessary to depict the condition of the vessel at the time of the incident, and are otherwise unavailable, the defendants were ordered to produce them.

For the reasons above, the plaintiff's motion to compel a second 30(b)(6) deposition and production of the photographs is was granted.

**ANSWER (B)** is incorrect because parties are not simply entitled to all materials in the opposing party's possession and control; the statement is an overbroad characterization of the discovery process. **ANSWER (C)** is incorrect because although the court found that the photographs were ordinary work product, this immunity can be overcome on a showing of substantial need by the requesting party, coupled with an inability to obtain the materials by other means. **ANSWER (D)** is incorrect because the photos were not the attorney's opinion work product, and not such claim was made by the defendant. **ANSWER (E)** is incorrect because the court found that the photos could provide useful to the plaintiff in finding additional witnesses, developing expert testimony, or developing additional legal theories of the case.

### PROBLEM #22. BEST ANSWER (E).

Problem #22 is based on *Revocable Living Trust of Stewart I v. Lake Erie Utilities Co.,* 2015 WL 209 7738 (N.D. Ohio May 5, 2015). This problem deals with the standards for pleading answers to a plaintiff's allegation in a complaint under Fed. Rule Civ. P. 8, coupled with a motion for a judgment on the pleadings pursuant to Fed.R.Civ.P. 12(c). The court held that the defendant's answers did not comport with the requirements of Rule 8, but did not grant the plaintiff's motion for a judgment on the pleadings. Instead, the court granted the defendant leave to amend its answers to comply with the rule.

Motions for judgment on the pleadings under Rule 12(c) of the Federal Rules of Procedure are analyzed using the same standard employed for a motion to dismiss under Rule 12(b)(6). *Tucker v. Middleburg-Legacy Place,* 539 F.3d 545, 549 (6th Cir.2008). "For purposes of a motion for judgment on the pleadings, all well-pleaded material allegations of the pleadings of the opposing party must be taken as true, and the motion may be granted only if the moving party is nevertheless clearly entitled to judgment." *JP Morgan Chase Bank, N.A. v. Wignet,* 510 F.3d 577, 582 (6th Cir.2007) (quoting *Southern Ohio Bank v. Merrill Lynch, Pierce, Fenner & Smith, Inc.,* 479 F.2d 478, 480 (6th Cir.1973)). A Rule 12(c) motion "is granted when no material issue of fact exists and the party making the motion is entitled to judgment as a matter of law." *Paskvan v. City of Cleveland Civil Serv. Comm'n,* 946 F.2d 1233, 1235 (6th Cir.1991).

Pursuant to Rule 12(f), "a court may strike from a pleading an insufficient defense or any redundant, immaterial, impertinent, or scandalous matter." A defense is insufficient if "as a matter of law, the defense cannot succeed under any circumstances." *Swift v. City of Detroit,* No. 10–12911, 2012 WL 32683, \*2 (E.D.Mich. Jan.6, 2012). But "the action of striking a pleading should be sparingly used by the courts," because "it is a drastic remedy" and only to be used when "the pleading to be stricken has no possible relation to the controversy." *Felts v. Cleveland Hous. Auth.,* 821 F.Supp.2d 968, 981 (E.D.Tenn.2011) (quoting *Brown & Williamson Tobacco Corp., v. U.S.,* 201 F.2d 819, 822 (6th Cir.1953)).

Rule 8 establishes the rules of pleading, including the form it should take and a party's responsibilities in answering a claim asserted against it. Fed.R.Civ.P. 8(b) and (d); *Felts,* 821 F.Supp.2d at 980. First and foremost, allegations in any pleading "must be simple, concise, and direct." Fed.R.Civ.P. 8(d)(1). With respect to responses, a party is required to do two things: (1) "state in short and plain terms its defenses to each claim asserted against it," and (2) "admit or deny the allegations asserted against it by an opposing party." Fed.R.Civ.P. 8(b)(1)(A) and (B). Rule 8 provides for only three possible responses to allegations in a civil complaint: (1) admit the allegation; (2) deny the allegation; or (3) state that there is insufficient knowledge or information to form a belief about the truth of the allegation. Fed.R.Civ.P. 8(b)(1)(5). In the event of a denial, a party must "fairly respond to the substance of the allegation." Fed.R.Civ.P. 8(b)(2).

"The corollary to Rule 8 is the liberal amendment policies embodied in Rule 15." *U.S. v. Vehicle 2007 Mack 600 Dump Truck, et al.,* 680 F.Supp.2d 816, 826 (E.D.Mich.2010). Pertinent here, Rule 15 allows a party to amend with the opposing party's written consent or the court's leave, which the court "should freely give leave when justice so requires." Fed.R.Civ.P. 15(2). Granting or denying leave to amend is within the trial court's discretion. *Foman v. Davis,* 371 U.S. 178 (1962).

In this case, the defendants' answers did not flatly deny or admit the allegations in the plaintiff's amended complaint, nor did they indicate insufficient knowledge to form a belief. Instead, the defendants "neither admit nor deny" and demanded that the plaintiff prove their case, or the defendants deny the allegations of a particular paragraph "in the manner and form alleged."

The court held that as to the former, the defendants failed to present an answer in any of the three approved forms required by Rule 8. Moreover, "answers that neither admit nor deny but simply demand proof of the plaintiff's allegations . . . are insufficient to constitute denial." *U.S. v. Vehicle 2007,* 680 F.Supp.2d at 826. As to the latter, the defendants' denial of an allegation as to "the manner and form alleged" violated Rule 8(b)(2)'s requirement that a denial fairly respond to the substance of the allegation. A defendant who cannot in good faith deny an allegation in its entirety must parse the allegation and "admit the part that is true and deny the rest." Fed.R.Civ.P. 8(b)(4). Thus, the defendants' duet of responses failed to meet the pleading requirements of Rule 8(b), and was not helpful in framing the issues.

The court found that it strained credibility to suggest that the defendants were not in a position to address the factual background of certain matters, such as the state of incorporation of the defendants' Lake Erie Utilities Co. and Burgundy Bay Association, the location of their respective offices and places of business, the names of their respective trustees and officers, the location of Burgundy Bay subdivision, its purpose and function, and the existence of recorded deeds restrictions.

The court noted that the consequences of deficient pleading include striking or deeming certain answers admitted. But in light of Rule 15 and cautionary directives regarding striking pleadings, the court afforded the defendants an opportunity to properly answer the amended complaint. Thus, the court held that in their amended answers, the defendants had admit, deny, or state that they lacked sufficient knowledge or information to form a belief about the truth of an allegation. If the defendants denied an allegation, the "denial must fairly respond to the substance of the allegation" as required by the federal rules. Fed.R.Civ.P. 8(b)(2).

For the reasons stated above, the plaintiff's motion for judgment on the pleadings and its alternative motion to strike were denied. The defendants were required to amend their answer within 21 days of the court's order to cure the deficiencies described and provide a more definite statement.

**ANSWER (A)** is incorrect because although the court found that the defendant's answers did not conform to the requirements of Rule 8, the court declined to grant the plaintiff's motion for a judgment on the pleadings. **ANSWER (B)** is incorrect because the plaintiff did not request that the defendant be sanctioned under Rule 11, and the court sua sponte did not raise the possibility of non-conformance with the requirements of Rule 11. **ANSWER (C)** is a possible answer, but not the best answer. Although the court found the defendant's answers deficient, the relief the court ordered was for the defendant to amend its answers pursuant to Rule 15. **ANSWER (D)** is incorrect because the court found the opposite: that the defendant's answers failed to comply with the requirements of Rule 8.

### PROBLEM #23. BEST ANSWER (D).

Problem #23 is based on *Wadis v. Norristown State Hospital*, 617 Fed.Appx 133 (3d Cir.2015). This problem deals with the amendment of a complaint pursuant to Fed.R.Civ.P. 15(c) and the doctrine of relation-back of pleadings after a statute of limitations has expired. In this case, the Third Circuit Court of Appeals affirmed the district court's conclusion that the plaintiff failed to satisfy the requirements of Rule 15(c), and therefore did not permit the amendment to add new parties to the original complaint.

In this case, the statute of limitations had expired by the time Wadis filed his motion to amend the complaint. His proposed amendment would therefore be futile unless it could be deemed to "relate back" to his original complaint pursuant to Rule 15(c). Wadis named eighteen additional defendants in his amendment, all of whom he alleged were employees of the Hospital. He claimed that these defendants were part of an ongoing conspiracy to victimize him by tampering with his food, forcing drugs on him, and stealing his mail. He also alleged that he was subject to "serious life threatening abuses" within the Philadelphia prison system. Relevant here, an amendment "relates back to the date of the original pleading" when it "asserts a claim . . . that arose out of the conduct, transaction, or occurrence set out . . . in the original pleading." Fed.R.Civ.P. 15(c)(1)(B). Wadis' allegations of new abuses did not appear to arise out of the 2012 beating at the Hospital, and at least one of them did not even concern the Hospital. "Amendments 'that significantly alter the nature of a proceeding by injecting new and unanticipated claims' " are treated with great caution for relation back purposes. *Glover v. FDIC*, 698 F.3d 139, 146 (3d Cir.2012) (quoting *United States v. Hicks*, 283 F.3d 380, 388 (D.C.Cir.2002)). Here, Wadis' amendment set forth new claims that did not "relate back" to his original complaint.

Even if the reference to employees being influenced to "possibly attack" Wadis could be read to implicate the new defendants in the 2012 beating, there was no evidence that those defendants received notice of the lawsuit, or had reason to believe that Wadis intended to sue them, as required by Rule 15(c)(1)(C). Although notice under Rule 15(c) may be a complex inquiry in certain circumstances, the court noted that this was not a case where the plaintiff made a "mistake concerning the proper party's identity." Fed.R.Civ.P. 15(c)(1)(C)(ii). Wadis did not seek to substitute a named defendant for a John Doe defendant in the original complaint. *See Singletary v. Pa. Dep't of Corr.,* 266 F.3d 186, 200–01 (3d Cir.2001) (noting that Rule 15(c)(1)(C)(ii) may be satisfied in such circumstances). Instead, he explicitly stated that he could not discover the last names of "Theodore" and "Isaiah"—the Hospital employees alleged to have beaten him—so he sought to add numerous other individuals who he claimed worked in the building where he was attacked. This did not amount to a mistake concerning the proper parties such that relation back should be permitted.

Under these circumstances, the Court of Appeals held that it was not an abuse of discretion for the district court to deny Wadis' motion, and the appellate court affirmed its judgment. In light of this disposition, the court denied the motion Wadis filed in the appellate court seeking leave to file an amended complaint.

**ANSWER (A)** is incorrect because the facts present an amendment problem requiring application of Fed.R.Civ.P. 15(c), not Rule 15(a), because the statute of limitations had run on the plaintiff's claims. **ANSWER (B)** is incorrect because even if this is true, the plaintiff failed to satisfy the other requirements of Rule 15(c) in order for the court to allow the amendment to relate back to the original complaint. **ANSWER (C)** is incorrect because the court found exactly the opposite; that the plaintiff's proposed amendment could not satisfy the requirements for relation back under Rule 15(c). **ANSWER (E)** is incorrect because it basically is gibberish and a red-herring; the concept of conforming pleadings to the proof is the basis for an amendment under Rule 15(b), but at the time of the attempt to amend his complaint, there had been no trial.

### PROBLEM #24. BEST ANSWER (A).

Problem #24 is based on *Squyres v. United Airlines*, 2015 WL 9604255 (M.D. La. Dec. 14, 2015). This problem addresses the amount in controversy requirement for federal removal jurisdiction. The court held that the defendant failed its burden on removal of proving that the amount in controversy exceeded $75,000, and ordered a remand to state court. The court further ordered that the defendant pay the plaintiff his costs and expenses in defending against the improper removal.

A defendant may remove "any civil action brought in a State court of which the district courts of the United States have original jurisdiction." 28 U.S.C. § 1441(a). When original jurisdiction is based on diversity of citizenship, the cause of action must be between "citizens of different States" and the amount in controversy must exceed the "sum or value of $75,000, exclusive of interest and costs." 28 U.S.C. § 1332(a)–(a)(1). Subject matter jurisdiction must exist at the time of removal to federal court, based on the facts and allegations contained in the complaint. *St. Paul Reinsurance Co., Ltd. v. Greenberg*, 134 F.3d 1250, 1253 (5th Cir.1998) ("jurisdictional facts must be judged as of the time the complaint is filed"). Remand is proper if at any time the court lacks subject matter jurisdiction. *See* 28 U.S.C. § 1447(c). The removal statute, 28 U.S.C. § 1441, is strictly construed and any doubt as to the propriety of removal should be resolved in favor of remand. *Gasch v. Hartford Acc. & Indem. Co.*, 491 F.3d 278, 28182 (5th Cir.2007).

If removal is sought on the basis of diversity jurisdiction, then "the sum demanded in good faith in the initial pleading shall be deemed to be the amount in controversy." 28 U.S.C. § 1446(c)(2). If, however, the "State practice . . . does not permit demand for a specific sum" removal is proper "if the district court finds, by the preponderance of the evidence, that the amount in controversy exceeds $75,000." 28 U.S.C. § 1446(c)(2)(A)(ii)–(B). In Louisiana state court, plaintiffs are generally prohibited from alleging a specific monetary amount of damages sought in their petitions. La.Code Civ. P. art. 893(A)(1). This prohibition on alleging a specific amount of damages, however, "is not applicable to a suit on a conventional obligation, promissory note, open account, or other negotiable instrument . . . " La.Code Civ. P. art. 893(B).

The burden of proof is on the removing defendant to establish that the amount in controversy has been satisfied. *Luckett v. Delta Airlines, Inc.*, 171 F.3d 295, 298 (5th Cir.1999). The defendant may make this showing by either (1) demonstrating that it is facially apparent that the claims are likely above $75,000, or (2) setting forth facts in controversy that support a finding of the jurisdictional minimum. *Id.* If the defendant can produce evidence sufficient to show by a preponderance that the amount in controversy exceeds the jurisdictional threshold, the plaintiff can defeat diversity jurisdiction only by showing to a legal certainty that the amount in controversy does not exceed $75,000. *See, e.g., St. Paul Mercury Indem. Co. v. Red Cab Co.*, 303 U.S. 283, 288–89 (1938); *Grant v. Chevron Phillips Chem. Co.*, 309 F.3d 864, 869 (5th Cir.2002); *De Aguilar v. Boeing Co.*, 47 F.3d 1404, 1412 (5th Cir.1995).

As the parties did not dispute that there is complete diversity, the only issue with regard to diversity jurisdiction was whether the amount in controversy has been satisfied under 28 U.S.C. § 1332(a). The court first considered whether it was facially apparent from the petition that the plaintiff's claims were likely to exceed $75,000. If not, the court considered whether the defendant set forth any facts in controversy supporting a finding of the jurisdictional minimum.

The court found that the plaintiff's failure to include any allegations regarding the amount in controversy to support federal jurisdiction, as required by Louisiana Civil Code of Procedure article 893(A)(1), was not dispositive. *See Weber v. Stevenson*, No. 07–595, 2007 WL 4441261 (M.D.La. Dec. 14, 2007). Plaintiff does allege, however, that he is not entitled to recover damages in excess of $50,000. (Petition, ¶ 15). It appeared that the plaintiff made this allegation to clarify that he was not seeking a jury trial. *See* La. C.C.P. art. 1732(1) ("A trial by jury shall not be available in . . . a suit where the amount of no individual petitioner's cause of action exceeds fifty thousand dollars exclusive of interest and costs."). This allegation was a factor considered for determining whether the amount in controversy was facially apparent. *See Brown v. Richard*, No. 00–1982, 2000 WL 1653835, at \*4 (E.D.La. Nov. 2, 2000).

The court concluded that it was not facially apparent that the amount in controversy requirement was satisfied. The plaintiff's requests for reimbursement of the cost of his first-class airline ticket and hotel expenses were not likely to exceed $5000. There was nothing in the petition indicating that the mental damages alleged by the plaintiff were worth the remainder necessary to meet the federal jurisdictional requirement. The plaintiff did not allege that he suffered any physical injuries, that he had obtained any medical treatment, that he had been prescribed any medication, or that he had suffered lost wages or capacity to work. The court held that the plaintiff had certainly not alleged that he sought recovery for such damages.

As the amount in controversy requirement was not facially apparent, the court turned to whether the defendant has set forth any facts in controversy supporting a finding of the jurisdictional minimum. The defendant had not submitted any arguments or evidence indicating that the damages sought by the plaintiff would likely exceed the jurisdictional amount.

Rather than attempting to meet its own burden, the defendant merely harped on the fact that the plaintiff did not submit a pre-removal binding stipulation that the amount in controversy was not satisfied. There is was requirement that the plaintiff must do so.

The court concluded that the defendant had not established that the amount in controversy requirement was satisfied based on any facts in controversy. Indeed, the defendant made no argument that the damages sought by the plaintiff exceeded the jurisdictional amount. Accordingly, the court found that it was of no event that the plaintiff did not enter into a pre-removal binding stipulation. To hold otherwise would result in a finding of jurisdiction in every case, no matter how insignificant the amount in controversy might be, simply because the plaintiff failed to execute such a stipulation within a timeframe deemed appropriate by the defense. In short, the plaintiff's failure to enter into such a stipulation did not relieve the removing party of its burden to establish that the jurisdictional minimum is satisfied. *Lowe*, 2008 WL 906311, at \*2.

"An order remanding the case may require payment of just costs and any actual expenses, including attorney fees, incurred as a result of the removal." 28 U.S.C. § 1447(c). The award of costs and expenses under § 1447(c) is discretionary and should only be awarded where the removing party "lacked an objectively reasonable basis for seeking removal." *Martin v. Franklin Capital Corporation*, 546 U.S. 132, 141 (2005). The court must consider the propriety of the removing party's actions at the time of removal, based on an objective view of the legal and factual elements in each particular case, irrespective of the fact that it was ultimately determined that removal was improper. *Id.; Avitts v. Amoco Prod. Co.*, 111 F.3d 30, 32 (5th Cir.1997); *Miranti v. Lee*, 3 F.3d 925, 928–29 (5th Cir.1993). To be subject to an award of attorney's fees under § 1447(c), a defendant must have played a role in the decision to remove. *Avitts*, 111 F.3d at 32.

The court determined to award costs and expenses to the plaintiff pursuant to 28 U.S.C. § 1447(c). The defendant removed the action on the basis that the amount in controversy requirement was satisfied. The petition was devoid of allegations that would support a finding that the amount in controversy was facially apparent. The defendant did not allege that it requested a binding stipulation prior to removal and the plaintiff refused to enter into such a stipulation. Instead, the defendant simply stated that the plaintiff did not unilaterally provide such a stipulation. The defendant had presented no argument or evidence to support its burden of proving that the amount in controversy requirement was satisfied.

For the foregoing reasons, the court did not have subject matter jurisdiction under 28 U.S.C. § 1332(a) because the amount in controversy requirement had not been satisfied. The plaintiff's motion to remand was granted and the case was remanded to Louisiana state court. It was further recommended that pursuant to 28 U.S.C. § 1447(c), the defendant United Airlines Inc. should be ordered to pay to the plaintiff costs and expenses incurred as a result of the removal in the amount of $500, within 14 days of the ruling on the motion to remand or within such time as the district judge may direct.

**ANSWER (B)** is incorrect because the diversity of citizenship of the parties was not contested; the only issued presented in the problem focused on whether the amount in controversy for diversity jurisdiction was satisfied. **ANSWER (C)** is incorrect because the court found that the plaintiff's lack of stipulating to the amount in controversy was not relevant; the plaintiff was not required to agree to such a stipulation. **ANSWER (D)** is incorrect because courts do not use a "common sense" approach to evaluating the amount in controversy for jurisdictional purposes; the amount must be satisfied either facially on the complaint, or by evidence presented by the removing defendant. **ANSWER (E)** is incorrect because it misstates the party who carries the burden of proof on the amount in controversy on removal; the defendant carries that burden.

### PROBLEM #25. BEST ANSWER (D).

Problem #25 is based on *Sun v. Ikea U.S. West, Inc.*, 2015 WL 6734480 (N.D. Cal. Nov. 4, 2015). This problem deals with a motion to compel disclosure of a corporate accident report. The problem focuses on whether the defendant, seeking to prevent disclosure, had waived its ability to invoke the attorney client privilege or work product immunity, by its dilatory conduct in responding to the plaintiff's initial requests for disclosure. Based on the facts, the court held that the defendant had not waived its right to challenge the compelled disclosures.

Fed.R.Civ.P. 26 provides that a party may obtain discovery "regarding any non-privileged matter that is relevant to any party's claim or defense." Fed.R.Civ.P. 26(b)(1). "Relevant information need not be admissible at the trial if the discovery appears reasonably calculated to lead to the discovery of admissible evidence." *Id.* A court "must limit the frequency or extent of discovery otherwise allowed by the Federal rules" if "(i) the discovery sought is unreasonably cumulative or duplicative, or can be obtained from some other source that is more convenient, less burdensome, or less expensive; (ii) the party seeking discovery has had ample opportunity to obtain the information by discovery in the action; or (iii) the burden or expense of the proposed discovery outweighs its likely benefit, considering the needs of the case, the amount in controversy, the parties' resources, the importance of the issues at stake in the action, and the importance of the discovery in resolving the issues." Fed.R.Civ.P. 26(b)(2)(C).

"The court may, for good cause, issue an order to protect a party or person from annoyance, embarrassment, oppression, or undue burden or expense," including by (1) prohibiting disclosure or discovery; (2) conditioning disclosure or discovery on specified terms; (3) preventing inquiry into certain matters; or (4) limiting the scope of disclosure or discovery to certain matters. Fed.R.Civ.P. 26(c)(1). "Rule 26(c) confers broad discretion on the trial court to decide when a protective order is appropriate and what degree of protection is required." *Seattle Times Co. v. Rhinehart*, 467 U.S. 20, 36 (1984).

As a threshold matter, the court had to determine whether the defendant waived its right to object to the plaintiff's request. Any party served with a request for production "must respond in writing within thirty days after being served." Fed.R.Civ.P. 34(b)(2)(A). "It is well established that a failure to object to discovery requests within the time required constitutes a waiver of any objection." *Richmark Corp. v. Timber Falling Consultants*, 959 F.2d 1468, 1473 (9th Cir.1992). A privilege, however, is not waived "per se" if a party fails to assert the privilege in its initial response. *Burlington N. & Santa Fe Ry. Co. v. D. of Mont.*, 408 F.3d 1142, 1149 (9th Cir.2005). "Although Rule 34 does not contain an express provision that untimely objections are waived, the courts have interpreted the rule regarding waiver consistent with Rule 33." *Liguori v. Hansen*, 2012 WL 760747, at *11 (D. Nev. Mar. 6, 2012); *see* Fed.R.Civ.P. 33(b)(4) ("Any ground not stated in a timely objection is waived unless the court, for good cause, excuses the failure.")

Accordingly, courts have broad discretion to excuse an untimely response based on a case-by-case determination. *Burlington*, 408 F.3d at 1149. Factors that establish good cause include "(1) the length of the delay; (2) the reason for the delay; (3) the existence of bad faith; (4) the prejudice to the party seeking the disclosure; (5) the nature of the request; and (6) the harshness of imposing the waiver." *Lam v. City & Cty. of S.F.*, 2015 WL 4498747, at *3 (N.D. Cal. July 23, 2015). "Minor procedural violations, good faith attempts at compliance, and other such mitigating circumstances militate against finding waiver." *Bess v. Cate*, 2008 WL 5100203, at *4 (E.D. Cal. Nov. 26, 2008).

In this case, the court found good cause to excuse the defendant's failure to respond in a timely manner. Although the defendant was five days late in its initial response to the plaintiff's request for the incident report, it explained it was unable to locate the report "after performing a reasonable and diligent search," but would continue to search. Once the defendant located the incident report, the defendant's counsel informed the plaintiff "that an amended . . . response would be sent, including additional objections." The defendant served an amended response thirty-three days after the plaintiff first alerted it that the incident report was not included in the initial request. Based on its initial response and subsequent communications with the plaintiff, the court found that the defendant made a good faith effort to respond in a timely manner. *See Jumping Turtle Bar & Grill v. San Marcos*, 2010 WL 4687805, at *3 (S.D. Cal. Nov. 10, 2010) (finding defendant's untimely response—approximately one and one half months after the initial response was due—reasonable given the parties' constant communication clarifying the scope of discovery and reviewing the documents responsive to the requests for production).

The plaintiff rejected the defendant's explanation, arguing that the "Defendant produced extensive documentation of company policies and procedures regarding the preparation of incident reports." The plaintiff added that the defendant's "employee manual provides eight pages on the company's Incident Reporting System, as well as a sample incident report." The plaintiff argued these policies, along with the fact that the plaintiff remained on the store floor after the incident until paramedics arrived, made it reasonably apparent that an incident report likely existed. However, while the defendant did produce general policy documents responsive to the plaintiff's request, it maintained it was unable to locate the specific incident report, and there was no evidence that the defendant did so in bad faith. *See Moe v. Sys. Transp., Inc.*, 270 F.R.D. 613, 623 (D. Mont. 2010) ("Waiver of a privilege . . . is a harsh sanction reserved generally for unjustified, inexcusable, or bad faith conduct. . . ."); *see also E.E.O.C. v. Safeway Store, Inc.*, 2002 WL 31947153, at *2 (N.D. Cal. Sept. 16, 2002) ("Finding that a party has waived its right to assert a privilege objection due to its conduct (or lack thereof) is a harsh sanction utilized where that party has unjustifiably delayed discovery.").

Further, the plaintiff did not argue she suffered prejudice as a result of the delay, and given that the case was in the early stages of litigation, the court found that the slight delay did not prejudice her. *See Karr v. Napolitano*, 2012 WL 1965855, at *6 (N.D. Cal. May 31, 2012) ("Perhaps most significantly, plaintiff has not expressed that he has been prejudiced in any way by the delay, and the court does not see how he would have been. And without any prejudice, the court believes that a complete waiver of Defendant's objections would be a disproportionately harsh result.").

Considering the totality of the circumstances, the court found good cause to excuse the defendant's untimely objections.

**ANSWER (A)** is incorrect because the court did not find that the defendant had acted in bad faith in its delayed production. **ANSWER (B)** is incorrect because although the court agreed that the defendant's response was technically untimely, it concluded that the amount of time in the delayed response was minimal, and not sufficient to trigger a waiver of objections. **ANSWER (C)** is incorrect because the court was unpersuaded that the defendant's prior disclosure of company documents and manuals was sufficient to trigger a waiver of objections based on the defendant's late production of the incident report. **ANSWER (E)** is incorrect because under certain circumstances (not including the facts here), a party may waive its privileges and immunity by a failure to comply with the discovery rules and deadlines.

**END OF ANSWERS AND EXPLANATIONS TO EXAM #4**

# CHAPTER 10
# ANSWER KEY FOR EXAM #5
# ANSWERS AND EXPLANATIONS

<u>PROBLEM #1. BEST ANSWER (D).</u>

Problems #1 and #2 Problem #1 are based on *Williams v. Fico*, 2015 WL 3759737 (N.D. Ill. June 15, 2015). Problem #1 deals with a motion for a judgment as a matter of law after a jury verdict, pursuant to Fed.R.Civ.P. 50(b). Problem #1 addresses the procedural requirement that a party seeking to make a Rule 50(b) motion must have previously made a motion for a directed verdict under Fed.R.Civ.P. 50(a). Because the plaintiff failed to do this, the court held that the plaintiff's subsequent Rule 50(b) motion was procedurally defective. Problem #2, discussed below, discusses the merits of the Rule 50(b) motion, if the court had considered it based on the evidence at trial.

Rule 50(a)(2) of Federal Rules of Civil Procedure provides: "A motion for judgment as a matter of law may be made at any time before submission of the case to the jury. The motion must specify the judgment sought and the law and facts that entitle the movant to the judgment." Rule 50(b) explains that if a Rule 50(a) motion made at the close of all the evidence is denied by the court, the movant may then renew the motion within 28 days after the entry of judgment. Fed.R.Civ.P. 50(b). The movant may also include an alternative or joint request for a new trial under Rule 59. *Id.*

Rule 50 "allows a district court to enter judgment against a party who has been fully heard on an issue during a jury trial if 'a reasonable jury would not have a legally sufficient evidentiary basis to find for the party on that issue.'" *Passananti v. Cook County*, 689 F.3d 655, 659 (7th Cir.2012) (citing Fed.R.Civ.P. 50(a)). "In deciding a Rule 50 motion, the court construes the evidence strictly in favor of the party who prevailed before the jury and examines the evidence only to determine whether the jury's verdict could reasonably be based on that evidence." *Id.* In so doing, the court does not weigh the evidence or make credibility determinations. *Tart v. Illinois Power Co.*, 366 F.3d 461, 478 (7th Cir.2004) (citing *Reeves v. Sanderson Plumbing Prods., Inc.*, 530 U.S. 133, 150–51 (2000)). Furthermore, while the court reviews the entire record, "it must disregard all evidence favorable to the moving party that the jury was not required to believe." *Reeves*, 530 U.S. at 151.

"Overturning a jury verdict is not something that a court does lightly." *Massey v. Blue Cross-Blue Shield of Ill.*, 226 F.3d 922, 925 (7th Cir.2000). A court will do so only if "the moving party can show that no rational jury could have brought in a verdict against it." *Hossack v. Floor Covering Assoc. of Joliet, Inc.*, 492 F.3d 853, 859 (7th Cir.2007).

The court noted at the outset a considerable impediment to Brown's ability to bring his Rule 50(b) motion: Brown's failure to first raise his arguments pursuant to a Rule 50(a) motion made prior to submission of the case to the jury. As clarified in the 2006 amendment to Rule 50, a Rule 50(b) motion is simply a renewal of a pre-verdict Rule 50(a) motion:

> Rule 50(b) is amended to permit renewal of any Rule 50(a) motion for judgment as a matter of law, deleting the requirement that a motion be made at the close of all the evidence. Because the Rule 50(b) motion is only a renewal of the pre-verdict motion, it can be granted only on grounds advanced in the pre-verdict motion. The earlier motion informs the opposing party of the challenge to the sufficiency of the evidence and affords a clear opportunity to provide additional evidence that may be available.

Fed.R.Civ.P. 50, advisory committee note (2006 amend.); *see also Prod. Specialties Group, Inc. v. Minsor Systems, Inc.,* 513 F.3d 695, 699 n. 1 (7th Cir.2008).

Brown asserted that the language of Rule 50 need not be applied rigidly where the moving party made its arguments clear in previously presented documents, such as motions *in limine* and trial briefs. Brown directed the court to *Petit v. City of Chicago,* 239 F.Supp.2d 761, 767 (N.D.Ill.2002), and *Urso v. United States,* 72 F.3d 59, 61 (7th Cir.1995), for the proposition that a Rule 50(a) motion need not always serve as a prerequisite to a Rule 50(b) motion. While Brown's position may have had support in the case law at one time, the Seventh Circuit has explained that the 1991 amendments to Rule 50 eliminated the practice of using other documents to stand in the place of a Rule 50(a) motion. *Laborers' Pension Fund v. A & C Envtl., Inc.,* 301 F.3d 768, 775–76 (7th Cir.2001); Fed.R.Civ.P. 50 advisory committee note (1991 amend.) (stating that "the revision thus alters the result in cases in which courts have used various techniques to avoid the requirement that a motion for a directed verdict be made as a predicate to a motion for judgment notwithstanding the verdict"); *see also U.S. E.E.O.C. v. AIC Sec. Investigations, Ltd.,* 55 F.3d 1276, 1286 (7th Cir.1995) (signaling an end to a lenient application of Rule 50, as the 1991 amendments make clear that "only a proper Rule 50(a) motion preserves the issue for later review"). Moreover, neither of the cases the plaintiffs cite applies directly to the factual situation raised here, where there is a complete absence of a Rule 50(a) motion. The court thus rejected Brown's position that the failure to file a Rule 50(a) motion might be cured by using other filings such as motions *in limine* or motions for summary judgment to clarify the movant's position.

The purpose of requiring a timely Rule 50(a) motion as a prerequisite to a Rule 50(b) motion "is to afford the opposing party an opportunity to cure any defect in its case before the jury retires." *Laborers Pension Fund,* 301 F.3d at 775. Brown waived the opportunity to seek relief pursuant to a Rule 50(b) motion because he failed to preserve his arguments pursuant to a Rule 50(a) motion. *See Savino v. C.P. Hall Co.,* 199 F.3d 925, 931 (7th Cir.1999) ("A party who wants to challenge the propriety of submitting a given claim or defense to the jury is obliged to make a motion under Fed.R.Civ.P. 50(a) at some time prior to the submission of the case to the jury. Failure to make such a motion waives the sufficiency of the evidence point on appeal").

**ANSWER (A)** is incorrect because the rules require the opposite; a party making a Rule 50(b) motion after trial must have previously sought a Rule 50(a) motion for a judgment as a matter of law. **ANSWER (B)** is incorrect because the court noted that courts have rejected this prior position that evidence in earlier motions and papers could substitute for a Rule 50(a) motion. **ANSWER (C)** is incorrect because Brown can only challenge the jury's verdict if he had made a prior Rule 50(a) motion, which he did not. **ANSWER (E)** is incorrect because a losing party may make a Rule 50(b) motion, if properly perfected, and such a motion does not prejudice the jury's verdict.

### PROBLEM #2. BEST ANSWER (A).

Problem #2 is a continuation of Problem #1, and is based on the same facts and judicial opinion. In this problem the student is asked to evaluate the merits of the Rule 50(b) motion, if the court had allowed consideration of it (even though the court in Problem #1 found the motion to be procedurally deficient. Applying the standards for a Rule 50(b) motion and evaluating the trial testimony, the court concluded that Brown would not have been entitled to a judgment as a matter of law because the jury reasonably could have found for the defendants on the competing evidence.

The court concluded that even if Brown had not forfeited his ability to move for judgment as a matter of law pursuant to Rule 50(b), he still would not be entitled to the relief he sought. The jury in this case was entrusted with the role of weighing the evidence, making credibility determinations, and drawing reasonable inferences from the facts. *Anderson v. Liberty Lobby, Inc.,* 477 U.S. 242, 255 (1986). The court found no reason to disturb the jury's determination in favor of the defendants and against Brown. With the exception of conflicting testimony regarding Officer Cervantes having hit Mr. Brown in the face, the jury heard no testimony from Brown specifically identifying John Frano, Wayne Frano, and/or Nicholas Cervantes as the officers who searched his body and then handcuffed him.

Moreover, the evidence allowed a jury rationally to conclude that the detention of Brown was neither degrading nor unduly prolonged. The police officers were searching for marijuana in the second floor apartment when Mr. Brown was found; but, at the same time, officers were searching for weapons in the basement apartment of the same building. A jury reasonably could have concluded that handcuffing and securing Mr. Brown was reasonable under these circumstances, and that the length of the cuffing was reasonable in light of the activities occupying the officers in the other rooms of the second floor and basement apartments.

In addition, the jury was shown a picture of Brown sitting on the living room couch in his boxer shorts, which were no more revealing of his body than a pair of gym shorts. At bottom, it was for the jury to assess the evidence and the credibility of the witnesses who testified about the events at issue. The fact that Brown disagreed with the credibility determinations of the jury provided no basis for disturbing the verdict. The totality of the evidence was sufficient to permit the jury to conclude that Brown failed to establish that his detention was unreasonable under the circumstances.

For the reasons set forth above, the court denied Brown's Rule 50(b) motion for judgment as a matter of law and, alternatively, Rule 59 motion for a new trial.

**ANSWER (B)** is incorrect because the jury did weigh the credibility of the police officers and apparently found their testimony to be credible to support a favorable verdict. **ANSWER (C)** is incorrect because the jury found the opposite, which the court believed that it reasonably and rationally good find that the officer's behavior was not degrading nor unduly prolonged. **ANSWER (D)** is incorrect because granting a Rule 50(b) does not usurp the province of the jury as fact finder. **ANSWER (E)** is incorrect because the possible conflict with Brown's prior deposition testimony was not the basis for the court's concluding that he was not entitled to a Rule 50 judgment as a matter of law; the actual basis was that the jury reasonably and rationally could render the verdict based on the trial evidence.

## PROBLEM #3. BEST ANSWER (A).

Problem #3 is based on *Wertz v. GEA Heat Exchangers Inc.*, 2015 WL 8959408 (M.D. Pa. Dec. 16, 2015). This problem deals with the scope and limits of discovery, in particular, a plaintiff's request for depositions in excess of the number limited by the discovery rules. The problem asks the student to apply the standards relating to proportionality in discovery. The court granted the plaintiff's requests for additional depositions.

The general scope of discovery is outlined by Fed.R.Civ.P. 26(b)(1):

> Parties may obtain discovery regarding any non-privileged matter that is relevant to any party's claim or defense and proportional to the needs of the case, considering the importance of the issues at stake in the action, the amount in controversy, the parties' relative access to relevant information, the parties' resources, the importance of the discovery in resolving the issues, and whether the burden or expense of the proposed discovery outweighs its likely benefit. Information within this scope of discovery need not be admissible in evidence to be discoverable.

Issues relating to the scope of discovery permitted under Rule 26 rest in the sound discretion of the court. *Wisniewski v. Johns-Manville Corp.*, 812 F.2d 81, 90 (3d Cir.1987). Thus, a court's decisions regarding the conduct of discovery, and whether to compel disclosure of certain information, will be disturbed only upon a showing of an abuse of discretion. *Marroquin-Manriquez v. I.N.S.*, 699 F.2d 129, 134 (3d Cir.1983).

Rule 26 establishes a liberal discovery policy. *Clemens v. N.Y. Cent. Mut. Fire Ins. Co.*, 300 F.R.D. 225, 226–27 (M.D. Pa. 2014); *Great West Life Assurance Co. v. Levithan*, 152 F.R.D. 494, 497 (E.D. Pa. 1994). Discovery is generally permitted of any items that are relevant or may lead to the discovery of relevant information. *Hicks v. Big Brothers/Big Sisters of Am.*, 168 F.R.D. 528, 529 (E.D. Pa. 1996); *Stabilus v. Haynsworth, Baldwin, Johnson, & Greaves, P.A.*, 144 F.R.D. 258, 265–66 (E.D. Pa. 1992) (when there is no doubt about relevance a court should tend toward permitting discovery). Moreover, discovery need not be confined to items of admissible evidence but may encompass that which appears reasonably calculated to lead to the discovery of admissible evidence. *Callahan v. A.E.V., Inc.*, 947 F.Supp. 175, 177 (W.D. Pa. 1996); *Momah v. Albert Einstein Medical Ctr.*, 164 F.R.D. 412, 417 (E.D. Pa. 1996). Although "the scope of relevance in discovery is far broader than that allowed for evidentiary purposes, it is not without its limits." *Stabilus*, 144 F.R.D. at 265. A court will not permit discovery where a request is made in bad faith, unduly burdensome, irrelevant to the general subject matter of the action, or relating to confidential or privileged information. *S.S. Fretz, Jr., Inc. v. White Consol. Indus., Inc.*, No. 90–1731, 1991 WL 21655, at *2 (E.D. Pa. Feb. 15, 1991).

These factors are retained in revised Fed.R.Civ.P. 26(b)(1), reflecting "their original place in defining the scope of discovery." Fed.R.Civ.P. 26 advisory committee's note to 2015 amendment. The revised Rule 26(b)(1) factors are as follows: the importance of the issues at stake in the action, the amount in controversy, the parties' relative access to relevant information, the parties' resources, the importance of the discovery in resolving the issues, and whether the burden or expense of the proposed discovery outweighs its likely benefit. The present amendment restores the proportionality factors to their original place in defining the scope of discovery, but does not change any of the existing responsibilities of the court or the parties in considering proportionality:

> This change reinforces the obligation of the parties to consider these factors in making discovery requests, responses or objections. Restoring the proportionality calculation to Rule 26(b)(1) does not change the existing responsibilities of the court and the parties to consider proportionality, and the change does not place on the party seeking discovery the burden of addressing all proportionality considerations. Nor is the change intended to permit the opposing party to refuse discovery simply by making a boilerplate objection that it is not proportional. The parties and the court have a collective responsibility to consider the proportionality of all discovery and consider it in resolving discovery disputes.

Fed.R.Civ.P. 26 advisory committee's note to 2015 amendment.

The plaintiff sought to exceed the ten deposition limit imposed by the Federal Rules of Civil Procedure. Specifically, the plaintiff sought to take one additional deposition over the ten permitted by the rules and the case management order in place. Rule 30(a)(2)(A) of the Federal Rules of Civil Procedure states that "a party must obtain leave of court, and the court must grant leave to the extent consistent with Rule 26(b)(1) and (2): (A) if the parties have not stipulated to the deposition and:(i) the deposition would result in more than 10 depositions being taken under this rule. . . ." Fed.R.Civ.P. 30(a)(2)(A). When determining whether leave to conduct additional depositions is warranted, the Court must consider the factors outlined in Rule 26(b)(2), which provides:

> On motion or on its own, the court must limit the frequency or extent of discovery otherwise allowed by these rules or by local rule if it determines that: (i) the discovery sought is unreasonably cumulative or duplicative, or can be obtained from some other source that is more

convenient, less burdensome, or less expensive; (ii) the party seeking discovery has had ample opportunity to obtain the information by discovery in the action; or (iii) the proposed discovery is outside the scope permitted by Rule 26(b)(1).

Fed.R.Civ.P. 26(b)(2)(C)(i)–(iii); *see also* Notes of Advisory Committee on 1993 Amendments ("Leave to take additional depositions should be granted when consistent with the principles of Rules 26(b)(2), and in some cases the ten-per-side limit should be reduced in accordance with those same principles."). "In other words, a party seeking more than ten depositions must overcome this presumptive limit by demonstrating that the additional depositions are reasonable and necessary." *Alaska Elec. Pension Fund v. Pharmacia Corp.*, No. CIV.A. 03–1519 (AET), 2006 WL 6487632, at *3 (D.N.J. Aug. 22, 2006) (citing Fed.R.Civ.P. 26(b)).

The court found that the plaintiff had made a particularized showing as to why one additional deposition was reasonable and necessary, thus satisfying the standard promulgated in Federal Rules 30(a)(2)(A) and (26)(b)(2). While averring that a case is "complex" alone is insufficient to justify deviation from the presumptive number of depositions, the court was persuaded by the plaintiff's proffered rationale that the nature of this case required the one additional deposition. The court was further persuaded by the plaintiff's argument that the information sought through the proposed deposition of Ambrose was information only in the possession of the defendants, as he was a current employee of the defendant. Additionally, the plaintiff submitted that this deposition would likely be a few hours in length. The plaintiff had identified with specificity for the court the relevance of Ambrose's likely testimony. *Compare with Whittingham v. Amherst Coll.*, 163 F.R.D. 170, 171 (D. Mass. 1995) (denying plaintiff's motion for leave to exceed the deposition limit on the basis that plaintiff's "failure to indicate the number and/or names of the additional depositions sought made it difficult for the court to measure the appropriateness of plaintiff's motion"). Accordingly, counsel for the plaintiff had demonstrated that the discovery sought is not unreasonably cumulative or duplicative, or that the information sought could be obtained from a more convenient source. *See Alaska Elec. Pension Fund*, 2006 WL 6487632, at *5 (finding that while plaintiff's description of the likely testimony qualified as adequately "particularized," plaintiff failed to show how each deposition would be necessary to their case). The court held that the plaintiff had not had an ample opportunity to obtain the information he sought without the additional deposition, and in fact, had proactively sought leave from the court early in the discovery phase. Moreover, the cost would not likely outweigh the likely benefit of the additional deposition, as the plaintiff's attorney represented to the court that they expected the deposition to be limited to two hours. The court concluded that as the plaintiff had justified the departure from the presumptive limit, the court would permit Plaintiff to conduct the additional deposition.

The plaintiff also sought to take the depositions of Shirey and Stauch. The plaintiff submitted that the deposition of Shirey was relevant to impeach defendant Brubaker's testimony, because she worked on the plaintiff's FMLA requests, attendance tracking, and re-certification under defendant Brubaker's supervision. The plaintiff submitted that the deposition of Stauch was relevant to whether defendant Lutz and Lee were aware of the plaintiff's reading disability. The defendants objected to these depositions as speculative. The defendants further submitted that these depositions were disproportionate to the needs of the case, and that the burden and the expense of the depositions outweighed any relevance they may have.

As stated in the advisory committee's note to the 2015 amendment to the rules, it was the court's responsibility, using the information provided by the parties, to consider both the ways in which the information sought bears on the issues and the burden or expense required to provide the information. Having considered the factors related to proportionality, and specifically, the importance of the issues at stake in the action, the amount in controversy, the parties' relative access to relevant information, the parties' resources, the importance of the discovery in resolving the issues, and whether the burden or expense of the proposed discovery outweighs its likely benefit, the court found that the plaintiff should be permitted to depose Shirey and Stauch. The court found that those depositions should not be unduly burdensome to the defendant, and that the information sought through the testimony was important to the issues at stake in the case.

In conclusion, based on the foregoing, and having considered the parties' arguments, and the factors in Rule 26, the court found that the plaintiff would be permitted to take the deposition of Ambrose, in excess of the ten permitted in the current case management order, and further, would be permitted to take the depositions of Sandra Shirey and Dave Stauch.

**ANSWER (B)** is a possible answer, but not the best answer, because even if the proposed depositions were within the scope of relevancy, the court still needed to make a proportionality analysis before it could allow additional depositions. **ANSWER (C)** is incorrect because applying the proportionality factors, the courts did not find that the requests were disproportionate to the needs of the case. Similarly, **ANSWER (D)** is incorrect because the court made no finding that the additional depositions would be unduly burdensome or expensive. Finally, **ANSWER (E)** is incorrect because the facts give no indication that the additional depositions would be cumulative of other testimony, and the court did not find this.

### PROBLEM #4. BEST ANSWER (E).

Problem #4 is based on *OHM Hotel Group LLC v. Dewberry Consultants, LLC*, 2015 WL 5920663 (E.D. Mo. Oct. 9, 2015). This problem concerns a simple application of the rules for determining diversity of citizenship on removal of a case from state court to federal court, involving limited liability corporations as both the plaintiff and defendant. Because the court could not, based on the notice of removal, determine the citizenship of the parties, it could not assert valid federal removal jurisdiction.

This matter was before the court on review following removal. "Courts have an independent obligation to determine whether subject-matter jurisdiction exists." *Hertz Corp. v. Friend,* 559 U.S. 77, 94 (2010). "Federal courts are courts of limited jurisdiction. The requirement that jurisdiction be established as a threshold matter springs from the nature and limits of the judicial power of the United States and is inflexible and without exception." *Kessler v. National Enters., Inc.,* 347 F.3d 1076, 1081 (8th Cir.2003). Statutes conferring diversity jurisdiction are to be strictly construed, *Sheehan v. Gustafson,* 967 F.2d 1214, 1215 (8th Cir.1992), as are removal statutes. *Nichols v. Harbor Venture, Inc.,* 284 F.3d 857, 861 (8th Cir.2002).

OHM Hotel Group, LLC initially filed suit in the Circuit Court of St. Louis County, State of Missouri. The petition alleged a state law claim for breach of contract. Defendant Dewberry Consultants, LLC removed the action to the federal court based on diversity of citizenship pursuant to 28 U.S.C. §§ 1332(a), 1441(b) and 1446.

In removal cases, the district court reviews the petition pending at the time of removal to determine the existence of jurisdiction. *St. Paul Mercury Indem. Co. v. Red Cab Co.,* 303 U.S. 283 (1938). The district court may also look to the notice of removal to determine its jurisdiction. 28 U.S.C. § 1446(c)(2)(A)(ii); *Ratermann v. Cellco P'ship,* 2009 WL 1139232, at *3 (E.D.Mo. Apr. 28, 2009). The removing defendant, as the party invoking jurisdiction, bears the burden of proving that all prerequisites to jurisdiction are satisfied. *Central Iowa Power Co-op. v. Midwest Indep. Transmission Sys. Operator, Inc.,* 561 F.3d 904, 912 (8th Cir.2009). "All doubts about federal jurisdiction must be resolved in favor of remand." *Id.*

The diversity jurisdiction statute, 28 U.S.C. § 1332, requires complete diversity of citizenship between plaintiffs and defendants. *Buckley v. Control Data Corp.,* 923 F.2d 96, 97, n.6 (8th Cir.1991). "Complete diversity of citizenship exists where no defendant holds citizenship in the same state where any plaintiff holds citizenship." *OnePoint Solutions, LLC v. Borchert,* 486 F.3d 342, 346 (8th Cir.2007). To establish complete diversity of citizenship, a complaint must include factual allegations of each party's state of citizenship, including allegations of any corporate party's state of incorporation and principal place of business. *Sanders v. Clemco Industries,* 823 F.2d 214, 216 (8th Cir.1987); *see* 28 U.S.C. § 1332(a). In a removed action, diversity must exist both when the state petition is filed and when the petition for removal is filed. *Ryan ex rel. Ryan v. Schneider Nat'l Carriers, Inc.,* 263 F.3d 816, 819 (8th Cir.2001) (citing 28 U.S.C. § 1447(e)).

In *Carden v. Arkoma Associates,* 494 U.S. 185, 195–96 (1990), the Supreme Court held that for diversity purposes, the citizenship of a limited partnership is the citizenship of each of its partners, both general and limited.

Both the plaintiff and defendant in this case were limited liability companies. The citizenship of an LLC is not determined in the same way as that of a corporation. "An LLC's citizenship, for purposes of diversity jurisdiction, is the citizenship of each of its members." *E3 Biofuels, LLC v. Biothane, LLC,* 781 F.3d 972, 975 (8th Cir.2015). Thus, for LLCs such as plaintiff and defendant, the court had to examine the citizenship of each member of the LLC to determine whether it had diversity jurisdiction. *GMAC Commercial Credit LLC v. Dillard Dep't Stores, Inc.,* 357 F.3d 827, 829 (8th Cir.2004). For any members of LLCs that are limited liability companies, partnerships, limited partnerships or trusts, facts concerning their underlying members, partners, trustees or beneficiaries must be alleged in accordance with the rules applicable to each such type of entity, through however many layers of ownership there may be. The defendant must plead facts as to the state(s) of citizenship of all of its members, and its member's members, both at the time of filing and of removal.

The petition alleged only that plaintiff OHM was a Missouri limited liability company and defendant Dewberry was a Virginia limited liability company. The petition therefore did not establish the parties' citizenship for purposes of diversity jurisdiction. The defendant Dewberry's removal notice alleged that plaintiff OHM was an LLC organized under Missouri law, and alleged "on information and belief" that OHM's principal place of business was in Missouri and that none of its members were citizens of Virginia. Thus, defendant Dewberry's only factual allegation relevant to plaintiff OHM's citizenship, made on information and belief, was that none of its unnamed members were citizens of Virginia.

This allegation was insufficient to establish the plaintiff's citizenship. Defendant Dewberry did not identify plaintiff OHM's members or their state(s) of citizenship at the time of filing and the time of removal, as required by the Eighth Circuit's decisions in *GMAC* and *Ryan*. The Supreme Court held long ago that an assertion in a removal notice that the defendant was a citizen of a particular state and the plaintiffs were not citizens of that state was insufficient to confer federal diversity jurisdiction. *Cameron v. Hodges*, 127 U.S. 322. 324–25 (1888). *Cameron* remains good law. *D.B, Zwirn Special Opportunities Fund, L.P. v. Mehrotra,* 661 F.3d 124, 126 (1st Cir.2011) (discussing *Cameron,* holding allegation in notice of removal that defendant was a citizen of Rhode Island and the plaintiff was not considered a citizen of Rhode Island was insufficient to invoke federal diversity jurisdiction); *see also Mullins v. Testamerica Inc.,* 300 Fed.Appx. 259, 260 (5th Cir.2008) (allegation that removing defendant limited partnership believed to the best of its knowledge that all of its limited partners' members, partners or trustees were of diverse citizenship from the plaintiffs, without factual specificity, was not sufficient to establish diversity jurisdiction); *Affordable Communities of Mo. v. EF & A Capital Corp.,* 2008 WL 4966731, at *3 (E.D.Mo. Nov. 19, 2008) (removing defendants' allegation in notice of removal that none of the unnamed members of an LLC defendant shared Nevada citizenship with the plaintiff was insufficient to establish diversity of citizenship).

With respect to defendant Dewberry's own citizenship, the notice of removal alleged Dewberry was a limited liability company organized under the laws of Virginia with its principal place of business in Virginia, and that its sole member was The Dewberry Companies, LC, also a limited liability company organized under the laws of Virginia. "An LLC is not necessarily a citizen of its state of organization but is a citizen of each state in which its members are citizens." *OnePoint Solutions,* 486 F.3d at 346. Defendant Dewberry's removal notice failed to identify the members of its sole member The Dewberry Companies, LC, and did not allege facts concerning each such member's citizenship. To properly plead its citizenship, defendant Dewberry had to allege facts concerning the citizenship of the underlying members of The Dewberry Companies, LC, through all layers of its membership structure, at the time of filing and removal.

Thus, the court held that the defendant Dewberry's notice of removal was procedurally defective because it did not allege sufficient facts to establish the citizenship of either party. As a result, the existence of federal diversity jurisdiction over this matter was unclear.

**ANSWERS (A), (B),** and **(C)** are each incorrect because the court could not determine from the statement of facts in the defendant's notice of removal the actual citizenship of each of the limited liability companies. Therefore, the allegations were not sufficient for the court to make a finding that it had valid removal jurisdiction. **ANSWER (D)** is incorrect and a red herring answer; the fact that the plaintiff had alleged a single state law claim in its state petition had no bearing on whether the court had diversity of citizenship jurisdiction on removal.

### PROBLEM #5. BEST ANSWER (D).

Problem #5 is based on *Tanner v. Kaiser Foundation Health Plan, Inc.*, 2015 WL 6081771 (N.D. Cal. Oct. 15, 2015). This problem requires the student to assess whether the federal district court had federal question jurisdiction on removal, when a state court plaintiff pleaded a combination of federal and state claims. The federal court denied the plaintiff's petition for remand to state court, holding that the court had good federal question jurisdiction based on the plaintiff having pleaded multiple claims under federal law.

"A motion to remand is the proper procedure for challenging removal." *Moore-Thomas v. Alaska Airlines, Inc.*, 553 F.3d 1241, 1244 (9th Cir.2009). The court may order remand either for defects in the removal procedure or lack of subject matter jurisdiction. *See* 28 U.S.C. § 1447(c). "Removal statutes are strictly construed against removal." *Luther v. Countrywide Home Loans Servicing*, LP, 533 F.3d 1031, 1034 (9th Cir.2008). "The presumption against removal means that 'the defendant always has the burden of establishing that removal is proper.'" Moore-Thomas, 553 F.3d at 1244. As such, any doubts regarding the propriety of the removal favor remanding the case. *See Gaus v. Miles, Inc.*, 980 F.2d 564, 566 (9th Cir.1992).

The plaintiff contended removal was improper because "exclusive federal question jurisdiction" was lacking. The plaintiff argued that, although he asserted claims arising under federal law, he did so in the alternative to claims arising under state law. The plaintiff further argued that he was the "master" of his own complaint, and may defeat removal by abjuring any and all federal claims. The court found that the plaintiff's arguments were misguided.

A defendant may remove an action filed in state court if "the case originally could have been filed in federal court." *In re NOS Commc'ns, MDL No. 1357*, 495 F.3d 1052, 1057 (9th Cir.2007) (citing 28 U.S.C. § 1441(a), (b)). "The basic statutory grants of federal-court subject-matter jurisdiction are contained in 28 U.S.C. §§ 1331 and 1332." *Arbaugh v. Y & H Corp.*, 546 U.S. 500, 513 (2006). Section 1331 confers federal question jurisdiction in "all civil actions *arising under* the Constitution, laws, or treaties of the United States." The " 'arising under' qualification" of Section 1331 confers upon district courts the jurisdiction to hear only those cases in which a well-pleaded complaint establishes either that: (1) federal law creates the cause of action; or (2) the plaintiff's right to relief necessarily depends on resolution of a substantial question of federal law. *Armstrong v. N. Mariana Islands*, 576 F.3d 950, 954–55 (9th Cir.2009).

On its face, the plaintiff's complaint stated causes of action arising under both federal and state law, setting forth such allegations in the conjunctive, not the disjunctive. Specifically, the second through seventh causes of action allege violations of the Age Discrimination in Employment Act of 1967, 29 U.S.C. § 621 et seq.; the Americans with Disabilities Act of 1990, 42 U.S.C. § 12111 et seq.; and the Civil Rights Act of 1964, 42 U.S.C. §§ 2000e–2, 2000e–3. As the plaintiff argued, he was the "master of his own complaint," and could have "avoided federal jurisdiction by exclusive reliance on state law." *Caterpillar Inc. v. Williams*, 482 U.S. 386, 392 (1987). This, however, the plaintiff did not do. Consequently, the action was removable based on federal question jurisdiction. *See Vaden v. Discover Bank*, 556 U.S. 49, 59–60 (2009) (a suit arises under federal law when "the plaintiff's statement of his own cause of action shows that it is based upon federal law"); *Abada v. Charles Schwab & Co.*, 300 F.3d 1112, 1118 (9th Cir.2002) ("The presence or absence of federal-question jurisdiction is governed by the 'well-pleaded complaint rule,' which provides that federal jurisdiction exists only when a federal question is presented on the face of the plaintiff's well-pleaded complaint.") (quoting *Caterpillar*, 482 U.S. at 392–93).

The plaintiff nonetheless argued that federal law served only as "an alternative" to state law, and relies on *Rains v. Criterion Sys., Inc.*, 80 F.3d 339 (9th Cir.1996) for the proposition that federal question jurisdiction does not attach unless it is exclusive. This argument is without merit. When a *state* law claim "can be supported by alternative and independent *theories*—one of which is a state law theory and one of which is a federal law theory—federal question jurisdiction does not attach because federal law is not a necessary element of the claim." *Rains*, 80 F.3d at 345–46. Where, as here, the complaint stated both state and federal law *claims*, however, Rains' holding was inapposite. The question was not whether the plaintiff's state law claims necessarily raised a substantial federal question, but whether the plaintiff alleged independent federal law claims. He did, as evidenced by the plaintiff's request for damages under the various federal statutes listed above. Furthermore, contrary to the plaintiff's contention, federal question jurisdiction need not be exclusive. *See* 28 U.S.C. § 1441(a) (requiring only "original jurisdiction"); *see also Mims v. Arrow Fin. Servs., LLC*, 132 S.Ct. 740, 748 (2012) (recognizing the presumption in favor of "concurrent" jurisdiction). In view of the foregoing, the plaintiff's motion for remand was denied.

**ANSWER (A)** is incorrect because although it states a proper principle of law, the federal court still had to determine whether it had valid federal question jurisdiction—which the court determined that it did. **ANSWER (B)** is incorrect for the same reason: although some courts recognize a presumption against removal, this presumption will be overcome upon a proper showing of valid federal court jurisdiction. **ANSWER (C)** is incorrect because the presence of state claims in a complaint does not defeat removal, and federal courts may exercise removal jurisdiction over cases with federal claims in the court's concurrent jurisdiction. **ANSWER (E)** is a possible answer, but not the best answer; the overwhelming number of federal claims and the court's ability to exercise concurrent jurisdiction were the basis for the court denying remand to state court.

## PROBLEM #6. BEST ANSWER (B).

Problem #6 is based on *Wenzel v. Marriott Int'l, Inc.,* 2015 WL 6643262 (2d Cir.2015). This problem deals with appellate review of a district court's grant of a defendant's forum non conveniens motion. The court held that Aruba was an adequate alternative forum, and that the private and public factors of the forum non conveniens analysis supported the district court's decision to dismiss the case on forum non conveniens grounds. The court affirmed the trial court's decision.

"The decision to dismiss a case on *forum non conveniens* grounds lies wholly within the broad discretion of the district court and may be overturned only when we believe that discretion has been *clearly abused*." *Iragorri v. United Tech. Corp.,* 274 F.3d 65, 72 (2d Cir.2001). Clear abuse occurs only when the district court's "decision (1) rests either on an error of law or on a clearly erroneous finding of fact, or (2) cannot be located within the range of permissible decisions, or (3) fails to consider all the relevant factors or unreasonably balances those factors." *Norex Petroleum Ltd. v. Access Indus., Inc.,* 416 F.3d 146, 153 (2d Cir.2005). Under this deferential standard, we conclude that the district court did not abuse its discretion when it dismissed this case on *forum non conveniens* grounds.

In reaching its conclusion, the district court considered the three relevant factors necessary to making such a decision: (1) the degree of deference accorded to the plaintiff's choice of forum; (2) the adequacy of the alternative forum proposed by the defendants; and (3) the balance of the private and public interests in the forum choice. *See id.* As for the first factor, the district court explained that "generally, a plaintiff's choice of forum is entitled to greater deference when the plaintiff has chosen the home forum. However, many courts have held that where none of the operative facts of the action occurred in the plaintiff's chosen forum, the choice is afforded less weight." *Wenzel v. Marriott Int'l, Inc.,* No. 13–cv–8335, 2014 WL 6603414, at *3 (S.D.N.Y. Nov.17, 2014) Here, as the district court correctly reasoned, although the Wenzels lived in New York and Patti Wenzel was treated for her injuries there such that their choice of New York as the forum deserves some level of deference, the deference owed to their choice was nevertheless limited by the fact that the "lawsuit lacked a substantial connection to New York, as the alleged negligence and injury occurred in Aruba." *Id.* Moreover, as the district court properly emphasized, "the operative facts of this action took place outside of the Southern District of New York." *Id.*

On the second factor, the district court concluded that Aruba provided an adequate alternative forum for the plaintiffs' suit. The Second Circuit agreed. The Wenzels argued that Aruba was an inadequate forum because tort cases there are decided by judges, pretrial discovery was more limited, and the potential recovery was less than if the case proceeded in the United States. Yet, in reality none of these factors demonstrated that Aruba constituted an inadequate forum. As explained on prior occasions, "some inconvenience or the unavailability of beneficial litigation procedures similar to those available in the federal district courts does not render an alternative forum inadequate," *Borden, Inc. v. Meiji Milk Prods. Co.*, 919 F.2d 822, 829 (2d Cir.1990), nor does "the fact that a plaintiff might recover less in an alternate forum . . . render that forum inadequate," *Figueiredo Ferraz E Engenharia de Projeto Ltda. v. Republic of Peru*, 665 F.3d 384, 391 (2d Cir.2011). Rather, as the district court correctly explained, "the adequacy of an alternative forum does not require the causes of action, procedures, or remedies that are available to be identical to those in the United States." *Wenzel*, 2014 WL 6603414, at *5. Instead, the "forum must be one in which defendants are amenable to service of process and which permits litigation of the dispute. . . ." *Id.* (quoting *Abdullahi v. Pfizer, Inc.*, 562 F.3d 163, 189 (2d Cir.2009)). As the district court reasonably concluded that service of process on these defendants would be possible were the Wenzels to bring their suit in Aruba and litigation of this sort was permitted in that jurisdiction, the Second Circuit agreed that Aruba represented an adequate alternative forum.

As for the third factor, the district court concluded that both the private interests and public interests pointed to Aruba as the proper forum, and the Second Circuit found no error in this conclusion. First, the fact that "the premises, equipment, employees, and other sources of proof relevant to establishing liability were, with the exception of the plaintiffs themselves, located entirely in Aruba" demonstrated that the private benefits supported trying the case in Aruba. *Id.* at *6. Second, the public interests such as the busy Southern District of New York docket, the difficulty of applying foreign law, and the importance of the hotel and tourism industry to Aruba supported Aruba as the forum. Ultimately, because the Second Circuit did not find fault in the district court's analysis of each of those relevant factors, nor with its relative weighting of these factors, the appellate court affirmed the district court's dismissal of the case on the grounds of *forum non conveniens*.

**ANSWER (A)** is incorrect because "forum shopping" is not a ground for approving or disapproving of a motion for *forum non conveniens* dismissal. **ANSWER (C)** is incorrect because the district and appellate courts did not think that the procedural differences between the courts rendered Aruba an inadequate alternative forum. Similarly, **ANSWER (D)** is not correct because the court found that Aruba's substantive law allowed for pursuit of the plaintiff's claims, and did not think that the plaintiff's claims of less advantageous Aruban law merited keeping the case in New York. **ANSWER (E)** is incorrect because the court decided that the lawsuit had more of a connection with Aruba, and therefore the private and public factors weighed in favor of the *forum non conveniens* dismissal.

### PROBLEM #7. BEST ANSWER (A).

Problem #7 is based on *Danganan v. Guardian Protection Services*, 2015 WL 6103386 (E.D. Pa. Oct. 16, 2015). This problem deals with the enforceability of a forum selection clause in a consumer contract. The court held that the clause was enforceable under the Supreme Court's precedent in *Carnival Cruise Lines v. Shute*, and therefore granted the defendant's motion that the case be transferred to the Western District of Pennsylvania.

Since the lawsuit was brought against Guardian, the forum selection clause required it to be filed in a state or federal court "where Guardian's principal place of business is located." It was undisputed that Guardian's principal place of business was located in Allegheny County, Pennsylvania. Allegheny County lies within the Western District of Pennsylvania. Thus, Guardian argued, the lawsuit belonged in that district pursuant to the forum selection clause. The plaintiff countered that the forum selection clause should not be honored because the agreements with Guardian's customers were contracts of adhesion.

Guardian relied primarily on the Supreme Court's decision in *Atlantic Marine Construction Co. v. U.S. District Court*, 134 S.Ct. 568 (2013). There, the Court explained that if venue is proper, as it was here, a decision to transfer because of a forum selection clause in a contract must be made under 28 U.S.C. § 1404(a). Under these circumstances, however, the usual § 1404(a) balancing-of-interest analysis does not apply. No weight is to be given to plaintiff's choice of forum, the parties' private interests, or the original venue's choice of law rules as articulated in *Van Dusen v. Barrack*, 376 U.S. 612 (1964). Cf. *Jumara v. State Farm Ins. Co.*, 55 F.3d 873, 880 (3d Cir.1995). The court may only consider public interest factors. *Atlantic Marine*, 134 S.Ct. at 581–83. As the Supreme Court concluded, "in all but the most unusual cases, 'the interest of justice' is served by holding parties to their bargain." *Id.* at 583; *see also Bremen v. Zapata Off-Shore Co.*, 407 U.S. 1, 4 n.4 (1972).

The plaintiff sought to distinguish *Atlantic Marine* on the ground that the construction contract in that case was between two sophisticated parties. He argued that this court should apply the usual balancing of interests under § 1404(a) because the plaintiff here was a consumer who signed a form contract and realistically had no opportunity to negotiate over its terms. The plaintiff pointed out that *Atlantic Marine* quotes from a concurring opinion of Justice Kennedy in *Stewart Organization, Inc. v. Rico Corp.*, "The enforcement of valid forum-selection clauses, bargained for by the parties, protects their legitimate expectations and furthers vital interests of the justice system." 467 U.S. 22 (1988).

The Supreme Court had before it, in *Carnival Cruise Lines v. Shute*, 499 U.S. 585 (1991), the question of the enforcement of a forum selection clause in a consumer agreement. In that case, a passenger on a cruise ship slipped and fell while the ship was in international waters off the Mexican coast. She had purchased the ticket in the state of Washington and boarded the ship in Los Angeles. The ticket had a provision that required her to pursue any lawsuit against the cruise line in a court in the state of Florida. Instead, she filed suit in the United States District Court for the Western District of Washington. The passenger argued to the Supreme Court that the forum selection clause should not be enforced because "the clause was not the product of negotiation, and enforcement effectively would deprive the passenger of her day in court." *Id.* at 590. The Supreme Court disagreed.

The Court first rejected the ruling of the Court of Appeals that "a non-negotiated forum-selection clause in a form ticket contract is never enforceable simply because it is not the subject of bargaining." *Id.* at 593. It recognized that the cruise line had a special interest in limiting the fora in which it could be sued. Without a forum selection clause, it would be subject to suit in many places. Such a clause also provides clarity so as to avoid pretrial litigation over venue and, thus, the unnecessary expenditure of time and money by the parties and the waste of scarce judicial resources. Furthermore, it was reasonable, the Court wrote, to conclude that charges for cruises are reduced because of the requirement that lawsuits against the cruise line be heard in one forum.

The Supreme Court emphasized that "forum-selection clauses contained in form passage contracts are subject to judicial scrutiny for fundamental fairness." *Id.* at 595. It found no evidence that the forum selection clause was designed to discourage passengers from pursuing legitimate claims. It noted that bad faith in choosing the forum was not an issue since the cruise line had its principal place of business in Florida and many of its cruise ships departed from Florida. In addition, there was no evidence of "any fraud or overreaching."

The court in this case found the similarities between *Carnival* were striking. Both involved a non-negotiated consumer contract. Both forum selection clauses required legal actions against the corporate defendant to be filed where it maintained its principal place of business. In this case, the principal place of business of Guardian was in Allegheny County, Pennsylvania. Here, the designated place for the lawsuit was much closer to Washington, D.C., where the plaintiff lived at the time he signed the Guardian agreement than Florida was to the state of Washington, the scenario in *Carnival*. Both defendants had customers in many different locations. There is also no bad faith since both defendants have their principal places of business where suit must be brought and conduct business there. Nor had fraud or overreaching been shown in either action. As in *Carnival*, the plaintiff here could have rejected the agreement if he did not like its terms.

Significantly, the convenience of the passenger or her choice of forum were not relevant considerations to the Supreme Court in *Carnival*. In this case, plaintiff initially brought suit in the state court in Philadelphia which had absolutely no connection to plaintiff or his claim for relief. There was no assertion, for example, that any witnesses or documents were located in this district. If anything, it seemed reasonable that more records and witnesses were in Allegheny County than in any other specific location. The Eastern District of Pennsylvania was merely where plaintiff's attorney was located. Indeed, the plaintiff currently resided in San Francisco, California, which was approximately 300 miles closer to Pittsburgh, the county seat of Allegheny

County, where the Western District of Pennsylvania sits than to Philadelphia where the Eastern District of Pennsylvania sits.

In *Jumara v. State Farm Ins. Co.*, 55 F.3d 873 (3d Cir.1995), where a forum selection clause existed in an automobile insurance policy, the Third Circuit Court of Appeals, without citing *Carnival*, identified several private and public factors for the court to consider in determining whether movant had met its burden for transfer under § 1404(a). *Id.* at 879. The private interests included: "plaintiff's forum preference as manifested in the original choice; the defendant's preference; whether the claim arose elsewhere; the convenience of the parties as indicated by their relative physical and financial condition; the convenience of the witnesses—but only to the extent that the witnesses may actually be unavailable for trial in one of the fora; and the location of books and records (similarly limited to the extent that the files could not be produced in the alternative forum)." *Id.*

The public interests included: "the enforceability of the judgment; practical considerations that could make the trial easy, expeditious, or inexpensive; the relative administrative difficulty in the two fora resulting from court congestion; the local interest in deciding local controversies at home; the public policies of the fora; and the familiarity of the trial judge with the applicable state law in diversity cases." *Id.*

The Court of Appeals, in *Jumara*, observed that a forum selection clause is a "private expression of the parties venue preference" and while not dispositive, is "entitled to substantial consideration." *Id.* at 880. It cited the Supreme Court decision in *Bremen v. Zapata Off-Shore Co.*, 407 U.S. 1 (1972) for the proposition that absent "fraud, influence, or overweening bargaining power," the plaintiff bears the burden of proof to show why it should not be bound by the forum selection clause to which the plaintiff had agreed. *Jumara*, 55 F.3d at 880; *Bremen*, 407 U.S. at 12–13. The Supreme Court reiterated in *Atlantic Marine* that where the plaintiff is "the party defying the forum-selection clause, the plaintiff bears the burden of establishing that transfer to the forum for which the parties bargained is unwarranted." *Atlantic Marine*, 137 S.Ct. at 581.

Here, plaintiff chose Philadelphia as his preferred forum while the defendant preferred Pittsburgh. The claim did not arise in either place. It was certainly not more convenient for the plaintiff to have this action in Philadelphia rather than Pittsburgh, which was closer to his home in California. On this record, as noted above, there was no evidence that the convenience of the witnesses or the location of books and records favored the Eastern District of Pennsylvania.

As to the public interests, the enforcement of any judgment was a non-issue. Expense was not a realistic consideration and court congestion was not a factor. There were no special local interests or public policies favoring one district over another. The plaintiff alleged only violations of Pennsylvania law. The judges in the Western District of Pennsylvania were as familiar with the laws of the Commonwealth as the judges in this district.

Finally, although the plaintiff alleged that the forum selection clause was the product of fraud or overreaching, the plaintiff had not offered any supporting evidence. Rather, the record indicated to the contrary. The forum selection clause contained reciprocal terms. When a customer initiates suit, the clause required that suit be brought in the place encompassing Guardian's principal place of business. However, if Guardian initiated suit, the clause required the suit to be brought in a forum where the customer resided.

The court concluded that it not need decide whether *Atlantic Marine* applied to consumer contracts, for the result here was the same under the test developed by the Supreme Court in *Carnival*. That test rests ultimately on the question whether the forum selection clause was fundamentally fair. The plaintiff had not met his burden of proof to establish that there was fundamental unfairness to the enforcement of the forum selection clause and to holding the parties to the terms of their agreement. If the forum selection clause in *Carnival* passed muster, the clause in this case passed muster.

Accordingly, the court ordered transfer of the action to the United States District Court for the Western District of Pennsylvania.

**ANSWER (B)** is incorrect because the parties to the contract were not both sophisticated parties; the plaintiff was a consumer and the defendant a corporation. The motion for transfer was granted under the authority of the Supreme Court's decision in *Carnival Cruise Lines* (*see* discussion above). **ANSWER (C)** is incorrect because the court did not find the forum selection clause to be unconscionable or a contract of adhesion. **ANSWER (D)** is incorrect because the court determined to enforce the forum selection clause, which overrode the plaintiff's choice of forum. **ANSWER (E)** is incorrect because the legal enforceability of a forum selection clause does not depend on whether the clause favors one party or the other.

## PROBLEM #8. BEST ANSWER (C).

Problems #8 and #9 are based on *Breech v. Liberty Mutual Fire Ins. Company*, 2015 WL 6859676 (S.D. Ohio Nov. 9, 2015). Problem #8 requires the student to analyze whether the court should grant a non-party's motion to intervene under Fed.R.Civ.P. 24(a). The court denied this motion. Problem #9 deals with the non-party's alternative motion to be joined as a party pursuant to Fed.R.Civ.P. 19, which the court also denied (*see* discussion of Problem #9 below).

The movant sought to intervene as a matter of right. Generally, Fed.R.Civ.P. 24, which governs interventions, is "broadly construed in favor of potential intervenors." *Purnell v. Akron*, 925 F.2d 941, 950 (6th Cir.1991).

Fed.R.Civ.P. 24(a) governs intervention of right. In pertinent part, Rule 24(a) provides as follows:

    (a)  Intervention of Right. On timely motion, the court must permit anyone to intervene who:

             \* \* \*

        (2)  claims an interest relating to the property or transaction which is the subject of the action, and is so situated that disposing of the action may as a practical matter impair or

> impede the movant's ability to protect its interest, unless
> existing parties adequately represent that interest.

The United States Court of Appeals for the Sixth Circuit has interpreted Rule 24(a)(2) as requiring the movant to establish each of the following four elements: (1) the application was timely filed; (2) the applicant possesses a substantial legal interest in the case; (3) the applicant's ability to protect its interest will be impaired without intervention; and (4) the existing parties will not adequately represent the applicant's interest. *See Blount-Hill v. Zelman*, 636 F.3d 278, 283 (6th Cir.2011) (citing *Grutter v. Bollinger*, 188 F.3d 394, 397–98 (6th Cir.1999)). "Failure to satisfy any one of the elements will defeat intervention under the Rule." *Id.* (citing *United States v. Michigan*, 424 F.3d 438, 443 (6th Cir.2005) and *Grubbs v. Norris*, 870 F.2d 343, 345 (6th Cir.1989)).

The court found that the movant had not established that it is entitled to intervene as a matter of right. Timeliness was not disputed, but the movant had not established the remaining three elements. Turning to the second factor, the court found that the movant had not articulated a substantial legal interest in the action. The court was mindful that the Sixth Circuit had endorsed "a 'rather expansive notion of the interest sufficient to invoke intervention of right.' " *Grutter*, 188 F.3d at 398 (quoting *Miller*, 103 F.3d at 1245). Indeed, "an intervenor need not have the same standing necessary to initiate a lawsuit in order to intervene in an existing district court suit where the plaintiff has standing." *Providence Baptist Church v. Hillandale Comm., Ltd.*, 425 F.3d 309, 315 (6th Cir.2005).

The substantial legal interest required to intervene under Rule 24 must relate "to the property or transaction that is the subject of the action." Fed.R.Civ.P. 24(a)(2). The property that is the subject of this action was the plaintiff's insured property; the transaction that was the subject of this action was the contract relationship arising out of the homeowner's insurance policy purchased by the plaintiff from the defendant. The movant had a substantial legal interest in its agreement with the plaintiff to receive fourteen percent of the proceeds of her claim. The movant, however, had no substantial legal interest in either the transaction between the plaintiff and the defendant or the insured property.

The movant was not a party to the insurance policy. The movant did not assent or agree to anything and had no duties under the plaintiff's insurance policy. The movant, therefore, was not a party to the insurance policy contract.

The court further found that the plaintiff did not assign her interest in the insurance policy to the movant. Under Ohio law, "an insurance policy is a contract between an insured and the insurer." *Pilkington N. Am., Inc. v. Travelers Cas. & Sur. Co.*, 2006–Ohio–6551, ¶ 31, 112 Ohio St. 3d 482, 487, 861 N.E.2d 121, 126 (Ohio 2006.) Post-loss assignments of rights under an insurance policy, however, are valid in Ohio, even where the underlying policy contains an anti-assignment clause. *Id.* at ¶ 43, 861 N.E.2d 121. "An assignment, no matter how informal, may be found when there is intent on the part of the assignor to assign the rights in question, an intent on the part of the assignee to be assigned the rights in question, and valuable consideration exchanged." *Eberhard Architects, L.L.C. v. Schottenstein, Zox & Dunn Co., L.P.A.*, 2015–Ohio–2519 at ¶ 29, No. 102088 2015 WL 3899367 at *7 (Ohio Ct. App. June 25, 2015) (quoting *Acme Co. v. Saunders & Sons Topsoil*, 2011–Ohio–6423, ¶ 82–83, No. 10 MA 93, WL 6230529 (Ohio Ct. App. Dec. 7, 2011)). The contract between the movant and the plaintiff did not demonstrate any intent on the part of the plaintiff to assign her rights under the insurance policy. That the contract calculated the amount of payment in terms of some possible future recovery by the plaintiff did not demonstrate the plaintiff's intent to assign any rights under the policy. The movant has not provided the court with any additional facts or legal arguments that would tend to demonstrate such intent. Accordingly, the court found that the movant was not an assignee of any rights under the insurance policy. The movant's substantial legal interest, therefore, was merely a contract right to payment for services enforceable against the plaintiff.

The court further found that the movant had not satisfied the impairment prong of Rule 24(a). This element required the movant to "show only that impairment of its substantial legal interest is possible if intervention is denied." *Miller*, 103 F.3d at 1247 (citing *Purnell*, 925 F.2d at 948). The Sixth Circuit repeatedly described this burden as "minimal." *Id.*; *Grutter*, 188 F.3d at 399; *N.E. Ohio Coal. for the Homeless & Serv. Emp. Int'l Union, Local 1199 v. Blackwell*, 467 F.3d 999, 1007 (6th Cir.2006). Here, the outcome of this case would have no effect on the movant's ability to protect its interest. As explained above, the movant's interest sounded in contract as between it and the plaintiff. The movant's interest was enforceable, if at all, against the plaintiff personally. Although the amount of any eventual recovery might affect the plaintiff's ability to pay the movant, it did not affect any legal obligation she might have to pay under the contract. The movant's ability to protect its interest, therefore, was not impaired in the absence of intervention.

Because all four prongs must be met in order to meet Rule 24(a)'s requirements, failure to show either a substantial legal interest or impairment of the movant's ability to protect that interest was fatal to a motion to intervene as of right. *Coal. to Defend Affirmative Action v. Granholm*, 501 F.3d 775, 779 (6th Cir.2007). Accordingly, the court found that the movant had not established that it was entitled to intervene as a matter of right.

**ANSWER (A)** is incorrect because the court did not find that the movant had a property interest in the case in chief. **ANSWER (B)** is incorrect because the court—since it did not find that the movant had an interest in the litigation—did not determine that the movant's interest would be adequately or inadequately protected by the parties to the litigation. **ANSWER (D)** is incorrect the court made no determination about whether the intervention would needless complicate the proceedings; the four requirements for intervention simply were not satisfied by the movant. **ANSWER (E)** is incorrect because the court also denied permissive intervention under Rule 24(b).

### PROBLEM #9. BEST ANSWER (C).

Problem #9 is a continuation of Problem #8 and is based on the same facts and judicial decision. The non-party movant alternatively asked the court to be joined as a party under Fed.R.Civ.P. 19. The court determined that the movant was neither a necessary or indispensable party and therefore declined the request to join the party under Rule 19.

Federal Rule of Civil Procedure 19(a) states:

> (a)   Persons Required to Be Joined if Feasible
>
> > (1)   Required Party. A person who is subject to service of process and whose joinder will not deprive the court of subject-matter jurisdiction must be joined as a party if:
> >
> > > (A)   in that person's absence, the court cannot accord complete relief among existing parties; or
> > >
> > > (B)   that person claims an interest relating to the subject of the action and is so situated that disposing of the action in the person's absence may:
> > >
> > > > (i)    as a practical matter impair or impede the person's ability to protect the interest; or
> > > >
> > > > (ii)   leave an existing party subject to a substantial risk of incurring double, multiple, or otherwise inconsistent obligations because of the interest.

A "necessary" party must be joined if feasible—if they are "subject to service of process" and would "not deprive the court of subject-matter jurisdiction." Fed.R.Civ.P. 19(a). If a court determines that a party is not "necessary" under Rule 19(a), "joinder, as well as further analysis, is unnecessary." *Local 670, et al. v. Int'l Union, et al.*, 822 F.2d 613, 618 (6th Cir.1987). The burden is on the moving party to establish that a party is necessary for purposes of Rule 19(a). *Marshall v. Navistar Intern. Transp. Corp.*, 168 F.R.D. 606, 611 (E.D. Mich.1996). "The moving party may satisfy this burden through the production of affidavits or other relevant extra-pleading evidence." *Lewis v. Ceralvo Holdings, LLC*, No. 4:11–CV–55–JHM, 2012 WL 32607 at *8 (W.D. Ky. Jan. 6, 2012) (citing *Potawatomi Indian Tribe of Okla. v. Collier*, 17 F.3d 1292, 1293 (10th Cir.1994)). *See* 5C CHARLES A. WRIGHT AND ARTHUR R. MILLER, FEDERAL PRACTICE AND PROCEDURE § 1359 (3d ed. 2013) ("To discharge this burden, it may be necessary to present affidavits of persons having knowledge of these interests as well as other relevant extra-pleading evidence").

The court found that the movant had not met its burden here. The movant's Rule 19 analysis consisted of legal conclusions unsupported by facts or legal argument. The movant asserted that it is a necessary party without providing an explanation of why it was, in fact, a necessary party. The movant's Rule 19 analysis consisted entirely of the conclusory argument that "it is axiomatic that under Rule 19 the movant and its claim must be allowed to intervene and to deny such an intervention would deprive the movant of the ability to protect its interest." The movant directed the court to its contract with the plaintiff, presumably to imply that it supported the movant's argument, and nothing more. The movant neither cited case law nor presented facts that would support the court making such an inference. Moreover, the court found that no facts supported a conclusion that the movant was a required party. Accordingly, the court found that the movant had not established that it was entitled to joinder as required party under Rule 19.

**ANSWERS (A)** and **(B)** are incorrect because the court found that the movant had not supplied any evidence or argument to support that it was a necessary or indispensable party under Rule 19. **ANSWER (D)** is incorrect because the court simply determine that the movant's request to be joined would be denied; it made no finding under Rule 19(b) to allow the case to go forward without the movant, in equity and good conscience. **ANSWER (E)** is incorrect because the fact pattern does not supply sufficient information to draw any conclusions whether the movant's joined to the lawsuit would affect the court's diversity jurisdiction.

### PROBLEM #10. BEST ANSWER (A).

Problem #10 is based on *Nehrlich v. JLW-TW Corp.*, 2016 WL 127584 (S.D. Cal, Jan. 11, 2016). This problem requires the student to make an assessment whether claims in the removed lawsuit were barred because they were compulsory counterclaims in the Ohio litigation. The court held that they were compulsory counterclaims, and therefore granted the plaintiff's motion to dismiss the federal case.

In moving to dismissing the plaintiff's complaint, Suntan argued the claims filed in the federal lawsuit were compulsory counterclaims that should have been filed in the Ohio action. The question of whether the plaintiff's claims were compulsory counterclaims which should have been pleaded in the Ohio action was a question of state law. *Pochiro v. Prudential Ins. Co. of Am.*, 827 F.2d 1246, 1249 (9th Cir.1987). The earlier action was brought in Ohio state court, accordingly Ohio law applies.

The Ohio rule governing compulsory counterclaims, Ohio Civ. R. 13, which was modeled on Rule 13 of the Federal Rules of Civil Procedure, states, in relevant part:

> A pleading shall state as a counterclaim any claim which at the time of serving the pleading the pleader has against any opposing party, if it arises out of the transaction or occurrence that is the subject matter of the opposing party's claim and does not require for its adjudication the presence of third parties of whom the court cannot acquire jurisdiction. But the pleader need not state the claim if (1) at the time the action was commenced the claim was the subject of another pending action, or (2) the opposing party brought suit upon his claim by attachment or other process by which the court did not acquire jurisdiction to render a personal judgment on that claim, and the pleader is not stating any counterclaim under this Rule 13.

The Supreme Court of Ohio applies a two-prong test for determining whether there is a compulsory counterclaim: "(1) does the claim exist at the time of serving the pleading; and (2) does the claim arise out of the transaction or occurrence that is the subject matter of the opposing claim." *Rettig Enters., Inc. v. Koehler*, 68 Ohio St. 3d 274, 277 (1994).

If both prongs are met, then the present claim was "a compulsory counterclaim in the earlier action and is barred by virtue of Civ. R. 13(A)." *Id.*; *see also Pochiro*, 827 F.2d at 1253 (state law governs the preclusive effect of the failure to raise a compulsory counterclaim in an earlier state court action); *Corbett v. Beneficial Ohio, Inc.*, 847 F.Supp. 2d 1019, 1025 (S.D. Ohio 2012) (citing *Forney v. Climbing Higher Enters., Inc.*, 158 Ohio App.3d 338, 344 (2004)) (Under Ohio law, "if a party fails to assert a compulsory counterclaim, he or she is barred from litigating it in a subsequent action."); *Rettig Enters.*, 68 Ohio St.3d at 277; *Polymer Indus. Prods. Co. v. Bridgestone/Firestone, Inc.*, 211 F.R.D. 312, 317 (N.D. Ohio 2002); *McConnell v. Applied Performance Techs., Inc.*, 2002 WL 32882707, at *8–9, n. 4 (S.D. Ohio Dec. 11, 2002).

As the plaintiff pointed out in his opposition, the claims in this matter arose prior to or at the same time as Suntan's claims in the Ohio action. Therefore, the claims existed at the time the plaintiff served his answer in the Ohio action. As the first prong is met, the court turned to examine whether the claims in this action arose out of the same transaction or occurrence that was the subject matter of the claims in the Ohio action.

"In determining whether claims arise out of the same transaction or occurrence, courts most frequently utilize the 'logical relation' test." *Rettig Enters., Inc.*, 68 Ohio St. 3d at 278. "Under this test, a compulsory counterclaim is one which is logically related to the opposing party's claim where separate trials on each of their respective claims would involve a substantial duplication of effort and time by the parties and the courts." *Id*. The logical relation test is intended to be flexible and "comports with the object and purpose of Rule 13(A), *viz.*, to avoid a multiplicity of actions and to achieve a just resolution by requiring in one lawsuit the litigation of all claims arising from common matters." *Id*. at 278–79. "Multiple claims are compulsory counterclaims where they 'involve many of the same factual issues, or the same factual and legal issues, or where they are offshoots of the same basic controversy between the parties.'" *Id*. at 279 (quoting *Great Lakes Rubber Corp. v. Herbert Cooper Co.*, 286 F.2d 631, 634 (3d Cir.1961)). "Ohio courts employ a liberal construction favoring compulsory counterclaims under Civ. R. 13(A)." *Sherman v. Pearson*, 110 Ohio App. 3d 70, 73 (1996).

In the Ohio action, the issues involve whether the plaintiff breached his employment agreement with Suntan and whether he was truthful about Suntan's failure to pay wages under his employment agreement to both the California Labor Commission and the JK Group. In this federal case, the issues involved whether Suntan breached its employment agreement with the plaintiff and whether Suntan was engaged in illegal activities that forced the plaintiff to resign. Implicitly at issue in both lawsuits were the terms of the plaintiff's employment, whether the employment agreement was violated, the circumstances of the plaintiff's resignation, and whether the illegal activities alleged by the plaintiff were actually engaged in by Suntan. Because the factual and legal issues presented in both lawsuits had a logical relationship and arose out of the same basic controversy between the parties, the court found that the claims brought in the federal lawsuit were compulsory counterclaims to the Ohio action.

Because the court found that the claims in this lawsuit are compulsory counterclaims to the Ohio action and the plaintiff has failed to establish that an exception applies, the Court granted Suntan's motion to dismiss the plaintiff's complaint.

**ANSWER (B)** is incorrect because the legal issue in the problem requires an analysis of whether the plaintiff's claims could be characterized as compulsory counterclaims in the Ohio action. The court concluded that they were; it granted the motion to dismiss on that basis, and not because the claims were "redundant." **ANSWER (C)** is incorrect because the pleading of claims and counterclaims in Ohio was relevant to the California federal litigation. **ANSWER (D)** is incorrect because the federal court could apply Ohio state law with regard to the pleading of compulsory counterclaims there. **ANSWER (E)** is incorrect because the plaintiff was subject to the procedural rules of Ohio, as it was named as a defendant there, and could not avoid the force of the Ohio compulsory counterclaim rule by suing as a plaintiff in California.

### PROBLEM #11. BEST ANSWER (D).

Problems #11 and #12 are based on *SPM Thermo-Shield, Inc. v. SICC*, 2015 WL 7076692(M.D. Fla. Nov. 13, 2015). Both problems deal with the ability of the federal court to assert personal jurisdiction over non-resident defendants. Problem #11 deals with so-called tag jurisdiction, but the court held that it could not assert personal jurisdiction over the defendant Walczok because he had been fraudulently induced into the jurisdiction. Problem #12, discussed below, requires a conventional minimum contacts analysis to assess whether the court could assert personal jurisdiction over the non-resident corporation. The court concluded that it had good jurisdiction under the Florida long-arm statute, and that the assertion of personal jurisdiction did not offend constitutional due process. (*See* discussion below).

Walczok argued that the complaint must be dismissed as to him because the court lacked personal jurisdiction. A court is obligated to dismiss an action against a defendant over which it has no personal jurisdiction. *Posner v. Essex Ins. Co.*, 178 F.3d 1209, 1214 n.6 (11th Cir.1999). Whether a court has personal jurisdiction over a defendant in a diversity case is governed by a two-part analysis. *Mutual Serv. Ins. Co. v. Frit Indus.*, 358 F.3d 1312, 1319 (11th Cir.2004). The court must first determine whether the exercise of jurisdiction is appropriate under the law of the forum state. *Future Tech. Today, Inc. v. OSF Healthcare Sys.*, 218 F.3d 1247, 1249 (11th Cir.2000) (citing *Sculptchair, Inc. v. Century Arts*, 94 F.3d 623, 626 (11th Cir.1996)). If the court determines that the forum state permits the exercise of personal jurisdiction, it must then determine "whether the extension of jurisdiction comports with the due process requirements of the Fourteenth Amendment." *Meier v. Sun Int'l Hotels, Ltd.*, 288 F.3d 1264, 1269 (11th Cir.2002) (citing Posner, 178 F.3d at 1214).

Walczok was a German citizen and a non-resident of Florida. Under Florida law, "a plaintiff seeking the exercise of personal jurisdiction over a nonresident defendant bears the initial burden of alleging in the complaint sufficient facts to make out a prima facie case of jurisdiction." *United Techs. Corp. v. Mazer*, 556 F.3d 1260, 1274 (11th Cir.2009). The complaint did not contain any specific allegation concerning personal jurisdiction over Walczok, although it did allege that Walczok "directed, controlled, ratified, participated in or was the moving force behind SICC's wrongful activity," and that SPM was harmed in Florida as a result. Accordingly, the complaint presumably intended to allege that Walczok was subject to personal jurisdiction via Florida's long-arm statute as a result of the alleged "wrongful activity" he committed against SPM, a Florida corporation. The defendants made the same assumption, as the motion to dismiss argued that neither Walczok nor SICC had Florida contacts sufficient to permit the exercise of long-arm personal jurisdiction. However, in its response to the motion to dismiss, SPM eschewed that argument and instead contended that the court had personal jurisdiction over Walczok because he was personally served in Naples, Florida as he was leaving a business meeting with SPM.

"As a general rule, Florida courts have personal jurisdiction over nonresidents when that nonresident is properly served with service of process while voluntarily present in the state." *Keveloh v. Carter*, 699 So. 2d 285, 288 (Fla. 5th DCA 1997). So-called "tag jurisdiction" also satisfies the Fourteenth Amendment's due process requirements because "jurisdiction based on physical presence alone is one of the continuing traditions of our legal system that define the due process standard of traditional notions of fair play and substantial justice." *Burnham v. Superior Court of California*, 495 U.S. 604, 619 (1990). Simply put, if personal service upon Walczok in Florida was "proper," the court possessed personal jurisdiction over him. Walczok argued that service was improper because the plaintiff lured him into the Middle District under false pretenses for the purpose of effectuating service.

"Service of process is void if obtained by enticing a defendant into the court's territorial jurisdiction through fraud or deceit, or under the pretense of settlement, whether the matter of settlement was first broached by plaintiff or defendant." *Coca-Cola Co. v. Empresa Comercial Int'l de Frutas S.A.*, No. 96–CV–358, 1996 WL 378856, at *1 (M.D. Fla. July 1, 1996); *see also Lisa, S.A. v. Gutierrez*, 806 So. 2d 557, 558 (Fla. 3d DCA 2002) (quashing service where non-resident defendants "entered the jurisdiction solely to attend a meeting where, in good faith, they would attempt to provide the financial information which plaintiff had been seeking and thereby avert litigation" and plaintiff's "elaborate preparations to serve the defendants at the meeting belie any good faith"); *Citrexsa, S.A. v. Landsman*, 528 So. 2d 517, 518 (Fla. 3d DCA 1988) (quashing service where non-resident defendants "arranged the conference in Florida in a good faith attempt to settle their dispute with appellees" and plaintiffs' conduct "including filing the complaint, causing the summons to be issued, changing the location of the meeting, and arranging service prior to the start of the settlement conference, clearly demonstrated that plaintiffs never intended to participate in good faith settlement negotiations"); *Mallin v. Sunshine Kitchens, Inc.*, 314 So. 2d 203, 204 (Fla. 3d DCA 1975) (quashing service where after "plaintiffs had secured an undertaking by defendant to come to this jurisdiction they then proceeded to file a complaint, caused process to issue, and arranged to have it served during the good faith settlement conference").

The parties each submitted affidavits concerning the events surrounding the business meeting that brought Walczok to Florida. In early 2015 SPM commenced a trademark infringement lawsuit against SICC in Turkey. On July 3, 2015, an SICC employee emailed Peter Spiska (Spiska), President of SPM, regarding the Turkish lawsuit and suggested that Spiska and Walczok meet in New York "to discuss the possibilities of a peaceful co-existence and successful business development in the future." In reply, Spiska expressed interest in meeting with Walczok and offered to host the meeting in Naples, Florida at his country club. SICC accepted the offer and the parties agreed to meet in Naples on July 23rd. Walczok averred that the sole reason he entered Florida was to attend the meeting and that he would not have attended had he known SPM intended to serve him while he was in Florida.

On July 22nd, the day before the meeting, SPM commenced this lawsuit. The summons issued in connection with the lawsuit listed SICC's address as 4784 Naples Lake Boulevard, which was the address of Spiska's country club. The meeting took place at the country club on July 23rd as planned. According to Walczok, while the meeting was ongoing "it appeared that SPM's representatives received a text message and immediately after receiving this alert they suddenly terminated the meeting and left the room." Walczok then left the meeting room and was served with process in the parking lot of the country club as he was walking to his car. Although Spiska averred that he "entered the meeting in good faith, but realistic of the potential that out disputes would not be resolved," neither he nor SPM took issue with Walczok's description of the events immediately preceding service of process.

The following facts gleaned from the parties' affidavits supported Walczok's contention that SPM lured him into Florida under false pretenses: (1) SPM requested that settlement discussions take place in Florida; (2) SPM waited until the day before the meeting to file suit; (3) SPM made advanced preparations to serve Walczok at Spiska's country club; and (4) Walczok was served immediately following SPM's decision to abruptly conclude the meeting. Based on these facts, "the inference could be drawn that the plaintiff's purpose in continuing the meeting until the Marshal could serve process was not to conduct good faith negotiations, but rather was an artifice to obtain service on the defendant." *Sunshine Kitchens, Inc. v. Alanthus Corp.*, 65 F.R.D. 4, 5–6 (S.D. Fla. 1974); *see also Coca-Cola*, 1996 WL 378856, at *1; *Lisa*, 806 So. 2d at 558; *Citrexsa*, 528 So. 2d at 518; *Mallin*, 314 So. 2d at 204.

Accordingly, the court concluded that Walczok was enticed into the court's jurisdiction under false pretenses. Therefore, personal service of process upon Walczok was quashed and, as a result, the court lacked personal jurisdiction over Walczok on the basis of "tag jurisdiction." As SPM did not assert any alternative basis for jurisdiction over Walczok, all claims against him were dismissed.

**ANSWER (A)** is incorrect because Walczok did not voluntarily appear in the jurisdiction to defend against the suit. **ANSWER (B)** is incorrect because although tag jurisdiction provides a good basis for a court's jurisdiction, a defendant cannot be fraudulently induced into the forum in order to be served or tagged. **ANSWER (C)** is incorrect because Walczok did not consent to the jurisdiction of the court. **ANSWER (E)** is incorrect because Walczok did not make either a special or a general appearance in the jurisdiction, so the answer is gibberish.

### PROBLEM #12. BEST ANSWER (E).

Problem #12 is a continuation of Problem #11 and is based on the same facts and judicial decision. In this problem, the student is required to conduct a conventional personal jurisdiction analysis concerning the non-resident German corporation. On the facts, the court held that Florida could assert personal jurisdiction over the defendant SICC under Florida's long-arm statute and that this assertion of personal jurisdiction did not offend constitutional due process.

The reach of Florida's long-arm statute is a question of Florida law and federal courts must construe it as would the Florida Supreme Court. *Mazer*, 556. F.3d at 1274. Under Florida law, "a plaintiff seeking the exercise of personal jurisdiction over a nonresident defendant bears the initial burden of alleging in the complaint sufficient facts to make out a prima facie case of jurisdiction." *Mazer*, 556F.3d at 1274 (citing *Posner*, 178 F.3d at 1214). In assessing the sufficiency of the jurisdictional allegations, the Court must accept the factual allegations in the complaint as true. *Licciardello v. Lovelady*, 544 F.3d 1280, 1284 n.3 (11th Cir.2008). If the plaintiff's factual allegations are sufficient to support the exercise of personal jurisdiction, the burden then shifts to the defendant to challenge the allegations with affidavits or other evidence to the contrary. *Meier*, 288 F.3d at 1269. The burden then shifts back to the plaintiff to produce evidence supporting jurisdiction. *Id.*

SPM alleged that the court had personal jurisdiction over SICC because SICC's misleading advertising, Lanham Act violations, unfair competition, and deceptive and unfair trade practices were committed in Florida. In relevant part, Florida's long-arm statute provides for personal jurisdiction over defendants who commit "a tortious act" within Florida. Fla. Stat. § 48.193(1)(a)(2). Florida courts have interpreted this provisions expansively, concluding that it encompasses a "nonresident defendant who commits a tort outside of the state that causes injury inside the state." *Licciardello*, 544 F.3d at 1283. Furthermore, an out-of-state defendant's physical presence in Florida was not necessarily required. Rather, a nonresident defendant can commit a tortious act in Florida "through the nonresident defendant's telephonic, electronic, or written communications into Florida," as long as the cause of action arises from those communications. *Wendt v. Horowitz*, 822 So. 2d 1252, 1260 (Fla. 2002).

Here, SPM alleged that SICC knowingly and intentionally misappropriated SPM's studies, test results, certifications, and photographs. SPM further alleged that SICC used those marketing materials to tout SICC's competing products on SICC's publicly-available website and in sales presentations given in the United States. Finally, SPM alleged that its products competed with

SICC's in the United States and, therefore, SICC's alleged misappropriation of SPM's marketing materials caused SPM injury in Florida. These allegations placed SICC squarely in the category of a "nonresident defendant who commits a tort outside of the state that causes injury inside the state" and, therefore, were sufficient to invoke the Florida long-arm statute. *Licciardello*, 544 F.3d at 1283 (non-resident defendant's creation of a website which used Florida plaintiff's likeness without permission satisfied long-arm statute because "the alleged infringement clearly also occurred in Florida by virtue of the website's accessibility in Florida.").

Once the Florida long-arm statute had been satisfied, the court must then determine if exercising personal jurisdiction over the defendant would comport with the due process requirements of the Fourteenth Amendment. *See, e.g., Meier*, 288 F.3d at 1269. To do so, the court had to consider two things. First, the court had to determine whether the defendant had purposefully established such constitutionally significant contact with the state of Florida that he could have reasonably anticipated that he might be sued here in connection with those activities. If the defendant had done so, the court must then determine whether the forum's interest in the dispute and the plaintiff's interest in obtaining relief were outweighed by the burden of the defendant having to defend himself in a Florida court. *Licciardello*, 544 F.3d at 1284.

In cases involving intentional torts, a defendant will be found to have constitutionally significant contact with a forum state if he "(1) committed an intentional tort (2) that was directly aimed at the forum, (3) causing an injury within the forum that the defendant should have reasonably anticipated." *Oldfield v. Pueblo De Bahia Lora, S.A.*, 558 F.3d 1210, 1221 n.28 (11th Cir.2009). When performing this analysis, the court must keep in mind that "it is an inescapable fact of modern commercial life that a substantial amount of business is transacted solely by mail and wire communications across state lines, thus obviating the need for physical presence within a State in which business is conducted." *Burger King Corp. v. Rudzewicz*, 471 U.S. 462, 476 (1985). Accordingly, "so long as a commercial actor's efforts are 'purposefully directed' toward residents of another State, we have consistently rejected the notion that an absence of physical contacts can defeat personal jurisdiction there." *Id.* Indeed, intentional torts "may support the exercise of personal jurisdiction over the nonresident defendant who has no other contacts with the forum." *Licciardello*, 544 F.3d at 1285.

Here, SICC was alleged to have (1) intentionally misappropriated SPM's marketing materials; (2) used them to tout its competing products in the United States; and (3) injured SPM in Florida as a result. Taking these allegations as true, SICC's conduct established constitutionally significant contact with Florida. *See Licciardello*, 544 F.3d at 1288 ("The Constitution is not offended by the exercise of Florida's long-arm statute to effect personal jurisdiction over defendant" where defendant "used plaintiff's trademarked name and picture on a website accessible in Florida in a manner to imply plaintiff's endorsement of defendant and his products.").

Even where a defendant has purposefully established constitutionally significant contacts within the forum state, jurisdiction must further be evaluated in light of several other factors to determine "whether the extension of jurisdiction comports with traditional notions of fair play and substantial justice under the principles established in International Shoe and its progeny." *Meier*, 288 F.3d at 1276 (citing *Posner*, 178 F.3d at 1221); *see also Licciardello*, 544 F.3d at 1284. In determining whether jurisdiction would comport with traditional notions of fair play and substantial justice, the court looks at factors such as: the burden on the defendant of litigating in the forum, the forum state's interest in adjudicating the dispute, the plaintiff's interest in obtaining convenient and effective relief, the interstate judicial system's interest in obtaining the most efficient resolution of controversies, and the shared interest of the several states in furthering fundamental substantive social policies. *Meier,* 288 F.3d at 1276; *see also Burger King*, 471 U.S. at 476; *Licciardello*, 544 F.3d at 1288. "Where these factors do not militate against otherwise permitted jurisdiction, the Constitution is not offended by its exercise." *Licciardello*, 544 F.3d at 1284 (citing *World-Wide Volkswagen Corp. v. Woodson*, 444 U.S. 286, 292 (1980)). In sum, the Court must "consider whether the forum's interest in this dispute and the plaintiff's interest in obtaining relief are outweighed by the burden on the defendant of having to defend himself in a Florida court." *Licciardello*, 544 F.3d at 1284.

The court found that Florida had an interest in resolving the alleged misappropriation of a Florida company's trademarks and marketing materials. The law was clear that "Florida has a very strong interest in affording its residents a forum to obtain relief from intentional misconduct of nonresidents causing injury in Florida." *Licciardello*, 544 F.3d at 1288. While the court recognized that there was some burden placed on non-resident defendants required to litigate in Florida, and that the burden was especially great for an international defendant, *Asahi Metal Indus. Co. v. Superior Court of California*, 480 U.S. 102, 114–15 (1987), such a burden could largely be eliminated by the use of telephonic hearings and conferences. *See Robinson v. Giarmarco & Bill, P.C.*, 74 F.3d 253, 259 (11th Cir.1996) ("The burden on the defendants occasioned by litigating outside of Michigan is not slight, but modern methods of transportation and communication reduce this burden significantly."). Moreover, any burden to SICC was offset by the burden to SPM should it be required to litigate in Germany. Indeed, the Eleventh Circuit had held that a "Florida plaintiff, injured by the intentional misconduct of a nonresident expressly aimed at the Florida plaintiff, is not required to travel to the nonresident's state of residence to obtain a remedy." *Licciardello*, 544 F.3d at 1288; *see also Calder v. Jones*, 465 U.S. 783, 790 (1984) ("An individual injured in California need not go to Florida to seek redress from persons who, though remaining in Florida, knowingly cause the injury in California."). Accordingly, on balance the court found that constitutional concerns of fair play and substantial justice were not offended by the exercise of personal jurisdiction over SICC.

**ANSWER (A)** is incorrect because the court held the opposite: that SICC's conduct within Florida fell under the Florida long-arm statute. **ANSWER (B)** is incorrect because the court found otherwise; that the defendant's activities in the forum reasonably subjected them to the court's jurisdiction. **ANSWER (C)** is incorrect because the court found no constitutional due process infirmity in asserting personal jurisdiction over the German corporation. **ANSWER (D)** is incorrect because the court did not base its assertion of personal jurisdiction over the German corporation based on a contractual relationship with the plaintiff.

## PROBLEM #13. BEST ANSWER (A).

Problem #13 is based on *Zemba v. Comcast Corp.*, 2015 WL 3540068 (S.D. Fla. June 3, 2015). This problem requires the student to evaluate the pleading requirements under the Supreme Court's decisions in *Twombly* and *Iqbal*, on a defendant's motion to dismiss a complaint pursuant to Fed.R.Civ.P. 12(b)(6). The court held that the plaintiff's pleadings failed these requirements and therefore granted the both of the defendants' motions to dismiss the plaintiff's complaint.

A complaint must contain short and plain statements of the grounds for the court's jurisdiction, of the cause of action, and of the relief sought. Fed.R.Civ.P. 8(a). Under the heightened pleading standards set forth by the Supreme Court in *Ashcroft v. Iqbal*, 556 U.S. 662 (2010) and *Bell Atl. Corp. v. Twombley*, 550 U.S. 544 (2007), there must be "enough facts to state a claim to relief that is plausible on the face" of the complaint. *Twombley*, 550 U.S. at 570. A plaintiff must plead sufficient facts to show entitlement to relief and must plead "more than labels and conclusions. A formulaic recitation of the elements of a cause of action will not do." *Id.* "Only a complaint that states a plausible claim for relief survives a motion to dismiss." *Iqbal*, 556 U.S. at 678. "A claim has facial plausibility when the plaintiff pleads factual content that allows the court to draw the reasonable inference that the defendant is liable for the misconduct alleged." *Id.*

In deciding a motion to dismiss, the court must accept a complaint's well-pled allegations as true. *Erickson v. Pardus*, 551 U.S. 89, 94 (2007). Such allegations must be construed in the light most favorable to the plaintiff. *Am. Dental Ass'n v. Cigna Corp.*, 605 F.3d 1283, 1288 (11th Cir.2010). "In analyzing the sufficiency of the complaint, the Court limits its consideration to the well-pleaded factual allegations, documents central to or referenced in the complaint, and matters judicially noticed." *La Grasta v. First Union Sec., Inc.*, 358 F.3d 840, 845 (11th Cir.2004).

ITG's chief argument in its motion to dismiss was that the plaintiff's complaint failed to state a claim for negligent hiring under Florida Law. "To state a claim for negligent hiring, plaintiff must allege facts showing that the employer was put on notice of the harmful propensities of the employee" *Ure v. Oceania Cruises, Inc.*, 2014 WL 5523122 *3 (S.D.Fla. Oct.31, 2014). Further, the Florida Supreme Court has held that to bring a prima facie case for negligent hiring, a plaintiff must demonstrate that: (1) the employer was required to make an appropriate investigation of the employee and failed to do so; (2) an appropriate investigation would have revealed the unsuitability of the employee for the particular duty to be performed or for employment in general; and (3) it was unreasonable for the employer to hire the employee in light of the information he knew or should have known. *Malicki v. Doe*, 814 So.2d 347, 362 (Fla.2002).

ITG pointed to the complete absence from plaintiff's complaint of any allegations related to the second element of the negligent hiring cause of action. The plaintiff did not allege any facts to show that any investigation in to Alegre's background in Cuba would have revealed Alegre's unsuitability for employ, and did not allege that anything in Alegre's background would have in fact rendered him unsuitable for employ. In short, the plaintiff alleged no facts showing that the employer was put on notice of any harmful propensities of the employee, or that they would have been had they conducted a more thorough check.

The plaintiff did not respond to ITG's argument on this point at all. Instead, the plaintiff argued that she has pled enough facts to state some unspecified claim for negligence under a vicarious liability or agency theory, and that therefore her complaint should not be dismissed.

The court agreed with ITG both that the plaintiff's failure to plead facts to support her negligent hiring claim was fatal to that claim, and that the plaintiff's abandonment of that claim in failing to respond to ITG's argument warranted dismissal of that claim. *See West Coast Life Ins. Co. v. Life Brokerage Partners LLC*, 2009 WL 2957749 (S.D.Fla.2009).

The court further held that the plaintiff's complaint suffered from similar deficiencies in Counts II and III against Comcast. First, as the plaintiff's claim for negligent hiring as against Comcast was based entirely on the same facts, in shotgun fashion, as the facts underlying the plaintiff's claim against ITG, the complaint failed to state a claim against Comcast for negligent hiring for the same reason that claim failed against ITG. Further, because the plaintiff's negligent supervision claim against Comcast rested on the theory that Comcast inadequately supervised ITG's background check procedures, and the plaintiff could state a claim for negligent hiring based on those procedures, the plaintiff's negligent supervision claim must fail.

Moreover, the court found that the plaintiff had conceded that her complaint failed to state either of these causes of action against Comcast. In her response to Comcast's motion to dismiss, the plaintiff claimed that her theory of liability had changed from that found in the complaint, and that theory "was not negligent hiring, retention, or supervision—defendants are right about that." Instead, and in attempt to save the facts of the complaint as alleged, the plaintiff claimed that the court should look to the facts alleged and not dismiss as long as those facts "would support some viable legal theory." *Id.*

The court rejected the plaintiff's attempt to amend the complaint through her responses to the defendants' motions to dismiss. As plead, the plaintiff's complaint failed to state a claim for negligent hiring against either defendant, and failed to state a claim for negligent supervision against Comcast. Accordingly, the court ordered that the plaintiff's complaint be dismissed.

**ANSWER (B)** is incorrect because the court found that the plaintiff's pleadings on all counts were deficient as to both of the defendants, and ordered dismissal as to both. **ANSWER (C)** is incorrect because the court found the plaintiff's pleadings insufficient on the face of the complaint, and therefore there was no need to allow the plaintiff to take the case to trial. **ANSWER (D)**

is incorrect because it mischaracterizes the standard for evaluating the sufficiency of a plaintiff's pleading under *Twombly* and *Iqbal*. **ANSWER (E)** is incorrect because a plaintiff cannot simply suggest to the court that its pleading would support recovery on "some viable legal theory"; the plaintiff must present facts sufficient to show a plausibility of recovery on the pleaded claims.

### PROBLEM #14. BEST ANSWER (B).

Problem #14 is based on *Siegel v. Blue Giant Equipment, LLC*, 2015 WL 7272216 (N.D. Okla. Nov. 17, 2015). This problem presents a simple discovery problem relating to the issuance of a protective order. The court found that the defendant requesting the protective order pursuant to Fed.R.Civ.P. 26(c) had shown the "good cause" required by the rule, and therefore the court granted the request for a protective order.

Rule 26(b)(1) of the Federal Rules of Civil Procedure allows a party to obtain information concerning "any non-privileged matter that is relevant to any party's claim or defense." Rule 26(c)(1) provides that upon a showing of good cause, the court "may issue an order to protect a party or person from annoyance, embarrassment, oppression, or undue burden or expense." Fed.R.Civ.P. 26(c)(1). This may include protection of trade secret, or other confidential research, development, or commercial information. Fed.R.Civ.P. 26(c)(1)(G). The moving party bears the burden of demonstrating "good cause" and requires a particular and specific demonstration of fact as distinguished from conclusory or stereotyped statements. *Gen. Dynamics Corp. v. Selb Mfg. Co.*, 481 F.2d 1204, 1212 (8th Cir.1973); *Samson Resources Co. v. J. Aron & Co.*, 2009 WL 1606564, *1 (N.D. Okla. June 8, 1999). However, the "good cause" standard of Rule 26(c) is "highly flexible, having been designed to accommodate all relevant interests as they arise." *Rohrbough v. Harris*, 549 F.3d 1313, 1321 (10th Cir.2008). Trial courts have broad discretion in managing discovery matters and are subject to review only for abuse of discretion. *WN Petroleum Corp. v. OK-Tex Oil & Gas Inc.*, 998 F.2d 853, 858 (10th Cir.1993); *see also Seattle Times Co. v. Rhinehart*, 467 U.S. 20, 36 (1984) (trial courts have broad discretion in deciding when to issue a protective order and in deciding the appropriate degree of protection).

The plaintiff complained that the defendant's proposed protective order would allow for unnecessary "wholesale designation of confidentiality of documents." The plaintiff contended that the protective order goes against the common-law right of access to discovery information.

The court disagreed, noting that the Tenth Circuit had approved the issuance of protective orders, such as the proposed one in this case, to expedite discovery documents, noting that at the discovery stage of litigation, "those documents have not been filed with the court and certainly have not satisfied threshold tests of relevancy and admissibility. They therefore are not available to the public generally." *Id. See also Burke v. Glanz*, 2013 WL 211096, at *2, *4–5 (N.D. Okla. Jan. 18, 2013) (noting the frequent practice of entering into "blanket" or "umbrella" protective orders and observing the distinction between materials produced in discovery and admissible materials). Thus, despite the plaintiff's insistence, the public has no right to access discovery material, which was what the proposed protective order sought to protect.

To establish good cause under Rule 26(c)(1)(H), the defendant must demonstrate that the information sought constitutes a trade secret, or other confidential research, development, or commercial information and then demonstrate that its disclosure might be harmful. *Centurion Indus., Inc. v. Warren Steurer & Assocs.*, 665 F.2d 323, 325 (10th Cir.1981). The defendant sought to protect only 29 pages (out of 270 pages) of responsive documents containing proprietary and trade secret information. The court found that the defendant had met its burden of demonstrating good cause for the issuance of a protective order.

For these reasons, the defendant's motion for a protective order was granted.

**ANSWER (A)** is incorrect because this was not the reason the court granted the defendant's request for a protective order, although the court noted that the public did not have a right to access to discovery materials at an early stage of litigation. **ANSWER (C)** is incorrect because the court found that the defendant had carried its burden to show good cause for issuance of the protective order. **ANSWER (D)** is incorrect because although this states a principle for denying a request for a protective order, the court did not find that the defendant violated this in its request. **ANSWER (E)** is incorrect because the court did not consider questions of privilege or relevancy on the motion for the protective order.

### PROBLEM #15. BEST ANSWER (B).

Problem #15 is based on *Ravishanker v. Mphasis Infrastructure Services, Inc.*, 2015 WL 6152779 (N.D. Cal. Oct. 20, 2015). This problem deals with establishing diversity of citizenship on removal jurisdiction, and a plaintiff's petition for remand to state court pursuant to 28 U.S.C. § 1447(c). Citing *Hertz Corp. v. Friend*, the federal district court held that the corporate defendant was a citizen of California, and therefore the court lacked diversity removal jurisdiction. The court granted the plaintiff's petition for remand of the case to California state court.

Removal jurisdiction is a creation of statute. *See Libhart v. Santa Monica Dairy Co.*, 592 F.2d 1062, 1064 (9th Cir.1979) ("The removal jurisdiction of the federal courts is derived entirely from the statutory authorization of Congress."). In general, only those state court actions that could have been originally filed in federal court may be removed. 28 U.S.C. § 1441(a) ("Except as otherwise expressly provided by Act of Congress, any civil action brought in a State court of which the district courts of the United States have original jurisdiction, may be removed by the defendant."); *see also Caterpillar, Inc. v. Williams*, 482 U.S. 386, 392 (1987) ("Only state-court actions that originally could have been filed in federal court may be removed to federal court by defendant."). Accordingly, the removal statute provides two basic ways in which a state court action may be removed to federal court: (1) the case presents a federal question, or (2) the case is between citizens of different states and the amount in controversy exceeds $75,000. 28 U.S.C. § 1441(a), (b).

On a motion to remand, it is the removing defendant's burden to establish federal jurisdiction, and the court must strictly construe removal statutes against removal jurisdiction. *See Hunter v. Philip Morris USA*, 582 F.3d 1039, 1042 (9th Cir.2009) ("The strong presumption against removal jurisdiction means that the defendant always has the burden of establishing that removal is proper, and that the court resolves all ambiguity in favor of remand to state court.").

To invoke diversity jurisdiction, the complaint must allege that the amount in controversy exceeds $75,000 and that the matter in controversy is between citizens of different states. 28 U.S.C. § 1332(a)(1). As to diversity of citizenship, there must be complete diversity in which each of the plaintiffs must be a citizen of a different state than each of the defendants. *Caterpillar, Inc. v. Lewis*, 519 U.S. 61, 68 (1996). Here, there was no dispute that the amount in controversy exceeded $75,000 and that the plaintiff was a citizen of California. Instead, the parties disputed the state of citizenship of MIS.

For purposes of diversity jurisdiction, a corporation is a citizen of the state in which it is incorporated and the state where its principal place of business is located. *Lightfoot v. Cendant Mortg. Corp.*, 769 F.3d 681, 698 (9th Cir.2014). As to the principal place of business, the Supreme Court has concluded that it refers "to the place where a corporation's officers direct, control, and coordinate the corporation's activities." *Hertz Corp. v. Friend*, 559 U.S. 77, 92–93 (2010). Such location "should normally be the place where the corporation maintains its headquarters—provided that the headquarters is the actual center of direction, control, and coordination, i.e., the 'nerve center,' and not simply an office where the corporation holds its board meetings." *Id.* at 93.

Here, the parties agreed that MIS was incorporated in Delaware, but disagreed on MIS's principal place of business. The plaintiff argued that MIS's principal place of business was in Santa Clara, California because that was the location of its headquarters. He contended that during his tenure at MIS, he operated out of the Santa Clara office and every MIS executive he reported to or engaged with on a day-to-day basis also worked out of the Santa Clara office. In response, MIS argued that MIS' principal place of business was in New York, and focused its argument on the plaintiff's inability to establish Santa Clara as the principal place of business. To support its argument, MIS offered the declaration of Vijayakumar M., a Director of MIS, stating that "business conducted by MIS is managed and controlled from India or by individuals who direct the company from offices in New York."

The court found that MIS's argument was unpersuasive for several reasons. First, as the party asserting federal jurisdiction, MIS had the burden of establishing diversity jurisdiction. But, MIS attempted to place the burden on the plaintiff by challenging the plaintiff's inability to establish California as MIS's principal place of business. *See Gaus v. Miles, Inc.*, 980 F.2d 564, 566 (9th Cir.1992) ("The strong presumption against removal jurisdiction means that the defendant always has the burden of establishing that removal is proper."). Such an argument was without merit and could not be considered.

Second, to show diversity jurisdiction, MIS had offered only a self-serving declaration by one of its directors. It has failed, however, to provide any other evidence that could corroborate the statements made in the declaration. The Supreme Court established that the party asserting diversity jurisdiction has the burden of persuasion and must support its allegations by competent proof. *See Hertz Corp.*, 559 U.S. at 96. The party must justify his jurisdictional allegations by a preponderance of the evidence. *See Gaus*, 980 F.2d at 567. Moreover, "California district courts have found that reliance on a single piece of evidence is insufficient for a party to prove the location of its headquarters under the nerve center test." *L'Garde, Inc. v. Raytheon Space & Airborne Sys.*, 805 F.Supp. 2d 932, 940 (C.D. Cal. 2011). In the instant case, reliance on a single declaration by one of MIS's directors was insufficient to support its claim for diversity jurisdiction.

Third, as the Supreme Court has found, the "principal place of business" is the one location that is the main or leading place of operation, located within a state. *Hertz Corp.*, 559 U.S. at 93. If not California, MIS failed to identify the one location either in India or New York that was presumably the principal place of business.

In sum, MIS failed to meet its burden of establishing diversity jurisdiction. Given the absence of objective evidence showing that MIS's "nerve center" was somewhere other than Santa Clara, California, MIS failed to overcome the strong presumption against removal. Thus, the court concluded that the case had to be remanded to state court. *See Gaus*, 980 F.2d at 566 ("Federal jurisdiction must be rejected if there is any doubt as to the right of removal in the first instance.").

Based on the foregoing, the court granted the plaintiff's motion to remand to state court.

**ANSWER (A)** is incorrect because although there is a presumption against removal, the reason for the remand was the lack of diversity of citizenship of the plaintiff and defendant. **ANSWERS (C)** and **(D)** are incorrect because MIS failed in its burden to establish that it principal place of business was somewhere other than California (and not New York or India). **ANSWER (E)** is incorrect because it misstates which party carries the burden of proving federal court jurisdiction on removal; that burden rests with the defendant removing the case.

## PROBLEM #16. BEST ANSWER (B).

Problem #16 is based on *Berman v. Brown*, 2015 WL 8780634 (E.D. Cal. Dec. 15, 2015). This problem presents a simple problem dealing with the application of collateral estoppel. The court found that, applying the principles of collateral estoppel, the plaintiffs Berman and Stapp could assert collateral estoppel to prevent relitigation of issues previously decided in the Sassman litigation. Therefore, the court granted their motion for summary judgment as against the same defendants.

The plaintiffs sought an order of summary judgment because the court had already ruled in *Sassman* that the ACP's exclusion of male inmates did not pass constitutional scrutiny. Accordingly, the plaintiffs contended that the defendants were collaterally estopped from relitigating those issues here. The defendants disagreed, arguing that the plaintiffs should not be permitted to offensively invoke the collateral estoppel doctrine when they could easily have joined Sassman's action. They also contended that this court's decision in *Sassman* was not sufficiently firm because the defendants had noticed an appeal in that case. The court concluded that the plaintiffs had the better arguments.

Reliance on collateral estoppel as a bar to further litigation "is appropriate only if (1) there was a full and fair opportunity to litigate the identical issue in the prior action; (2) the issue was actually litigated in the prior action; (3) the issue was decided in a final judgment; and (4) the party against whom issue preclusion is asserted was a party or in privity with a party to the prior action." *Syverson v. Int'l Bus. Machs. Corp.*, 472 F.3d 1072, 1078 (9th Cir.2007). "Trial courts have broad discretion to determine when offensive collateral estoppel should be applied." *Parklane Hosiery Co., Inc. v. Shore*, 439 U.S. 322, 331 (1979). "The general rule should be that in cases where a plaintiff could easily have joined in the earlier action or where the application of offensive estoppel would be unfair to a defendant, a trial judge should not allow the use of offensive collateral estoppel." *Id.*

In this case, the court ruled that collateral estoppel barred the defendants from defending against the plaintiffs' action. The defendants were parties to the *Sassman* action, where they litigated issues identical to those raised here, and a final judgment was issued against them. Moreover, despite the defendants' arguments to the contrary, it was not clear to the court that the plaintiffs in this action could easily have joined the *Sassman* proceedings. By the time the plaintiffs contacted counsel to initiate this action, the court was preparing to rule on the *Sassman* motions for summary judgment. Regardless, the court failed to see how the plaintiffs in this case would have gained much tactical advantage by taking a "wait and see" approach with regard to the *Sassman* proceedings. Had the court ruled against *Sassman* on what were essentially purely legal issues, the plaintiffs' claims would have fallen as well. It was thus implausible that the plaintiffs could have maneuvered themselves into a position to take another bite at the apple simply by waiting for a ruling in the related case. Furthermore, the defendants identified no prejudice they would suffer by entry of judgment in this case, when the court had already ruled that all eligible male inmates must be considered for the ACP. Finally, the defendants' argument that this court's decision was not "sufficiently firm" was rejected. The defendants cited no authority for the proposition that a pending appeal renders a judgment less final. To the contrary, appeals do not affect the firmness of district court decisions. *See Robi v. Five Platters, Inc.*, 838 F.2d 318, 327 (9th Cir.1988). The court held that the plaintiffs were entitled to summary judgment, and the defendants' request for a stay was moot.

**ANSWER (A)** is incorrect because the court did not address or consider whether credibility issues affected the analysis of whether collateral estoppel applied to bar relitigation of the same claims resolved in the *Sassman* case. **ANSWER (C)** is incorrect because the opposite is true: collateral estoppel can be invoked as a basis for seeking and granting a summary judgment motion.

**ANSWER (D)** is incorrect because the fact that the defendants had appealed the *Sassman* decision did not render collateral estoppel inapplicable. **ANSWER (E)** is incorrect because it is not true; it also is an overbroad statement of the consequences of application of collateral estoppel when the doctrine legitimately applies.

### PROBLEM #17. BEST ANSWER (A).

Problem #17 is based on *Urenia v. Public Storage*, 2015 WL 3378247 (C.D. Cal. May 7, 2015). This problem deals with a defendant's motion for sanctions pursuant to Fed.R.Civ.P. 11 and it requires the student to assess whether the attorney's conduct violated the requirements of Rule 11. The problem also raises questions whether the defendant properly sought sanctions pursuant to Rule 11. The court held that the defendant complied with the Rule 11 requirements for seeking sanctions, and granted the defendant's motion for sanctions.

Fed.R.Civ.P. 11 permits a court to impose sanctions upon attorneys, law firms, or parties that violate the rule's requirements regarding representations to the court. Fed.R.Civ.P. 11(c). The Ninth Circuit has held sanctions should be imposed if (1) "after reasonable inquiry, a competent attorney could not form a reasonable belief that the pleading is well grounded in fact and is warranted by existing law" or if (2) "a pleading has been interposed for any improper purpose." *Golden Eagle Distributing Corp. v. Burroughs Corp.*, 801 F.2d 1531 (9th Cir.1986). When a "complaint is the primary focus of Rule 11 proceedings, a district court must conduct a two-prong inquiry to determine (1) whether the complaint is legally or factually baseless from an objective perspective, and (2) if the attorney has conducted a reasonable and competent inquiry before signing and filing it." *Holgate v. Baldwin,* 425 F.3d 671, 676 (9th Cir.2005).

As an initial matter, the plaintiff's counsel argued that Public Storage failed to comply with Rule 11(c)(2)'s "safe harbor" provision requiring the moving party to first serve the motion on the attorney to give her an opportunity to withdraw the challenged paper or claim before filing it with the court. Public Storage did serve the plaintiff's counsel with the motion, but it revised its motion before filing with the court to include statements made by Judge Wistrich and the plaintiffs' counsel.

Rule 11(c)(2) says that "the motion must be served but it must not be filed. . . ." This plain language does suggest that the motion served must be at least substantively the same as the motion ultimately filed. On the other hand, Public Storage cited to a case from the Northern District of Iowa that held that the filed motion need not be "identical" to the served motion, as long as *"the grounds* for sanctions asserted in the draft Rule 11 motion served . . . are the same as the grounds asserted in the Motion For Sanctions ultimately filed." *Ideal Instruments, Inc. v. Rivard Instruments, Inc.,* 243 F.R.D. 322, 339 (N.D.Iowa 2007). The Second Circuit has held that the motion initially served "need not be accompanied by supporting papers such as a memorandum of law or affidavits." *Star Mark Mgmt., Inc. v. Koon Chun Hing Kee Soy & Sauce Factory, Ltd.,* 682 F.3d 170, 176 (2d Cir.2012). And the Seventh Circuit has gone so far as to say that the requirement may be satisfied by a letter stating the party's intent to seek sanctions. *Matrix IV, Inc. v. Am. Nat. Bank & Trust Co. of Chicago,* 649 F.3d 539, 552 (7th Cir.2011). In other words, courts have tended to emphasize the importance of adequate notice, not identical form or language.

Although the memorandum and exhibits accompanying the motion for sanctions varied somewhat from the versions initially served (chiefly in presenting additional evidence, such as bill from U.S. Storage Centers—Mission Hills), the grounds on which sanctions were sought are the same, and most of the language was identical. The plaintiffs' counsel was informed, during the "safe harbor" period, of the alleged grounds for sanctions, the authority under which sanctions were sought, and nature of the requested relief. This provided sufficient notice for her to make a decision as to whether to withdraw the filing. The defendant Public Storage substantially complied with the 21-day "safe harbor" provision.

A factual assertion is baseless and violates Rule 11(b)(3) if there is no evidentiary support for it and such support is not "likely" to be developed by discovery. Fed.R.Civ.P. 11.

The plaintiffs' claims for relief against the defendant Public Storage were based on the factual allegation that their belongings were stored at a Public Storage facility. But the plaintiffs' own third amended complaint contended that the Hernadezes' possessions were not placed in a Public Storage unit. Rather, the plaintiffs had a lease with U.S. Storage, affiliated with Westport Properties.

The plaintiff's counsel appeared to assert that Public Storage and Westport were in some kind of "joint venture." But this assertion was based entirely on a *Los Angeles Times* article. The article stated that Jim Warmington was entering into a venture with Barry Hoeven and Jon Pelmear to form Westport Properties to develop commercial real estate properties, and that Hoeven had previously developed business parks for Public Storage. The plaintiffs' counsel appeared to allege that Hoeven was an executive for Public Storage at the time he joined the venture to form Westport which then started to do business under the fictitious business name of U.S. Storage.

However, the *Times* article did not say that Hoeven was ever employed by Public Storage, much less at the time of the Westport deal. Even if it did say so, that would not, by itself, show that Westport was involved in any kind of "joint venture" with Public Storage. And even if the two companies were engaged in a joint venture that would not show that U.S. Storage facilities actually belonged to Public Storage, or that Public Storage could be held liable for actions taken by Westport/US Storage. In short, the *Times* article was several logical leaps short of showing that there was any factual basis for allegations of liability against Public Storage.

At oral argument, the plaintiffs' counsel also stated that she had investigated the ownership of both companies, and that both were owned by insurance companies. But this, too, was not evidence that the companies were related, much less that Public Storage shared any liability for the acts of Westport/US

Storage. On the record before the court, the third amended complaint's allegations against Public Storage were factually baseless.

The second question in the Rule 11 analysis is whether "an attorney, after conducting an objectively reasonable inquiry into the facts and law, would have found the complaint to be well-founded." *Holgate v. Baldwin,* 425 F.3d 671, 677 (9th Cir.2005).

The plaintiffs' counsel argued the *Times* article proved "independent inquiry" was made to assess the claims against Public Storage. To the "extent that a newspaper article corroborated the plaintiff's own investigation and provided detailed factual allegations, it could at least in combination with plaintiff's investigative efforts be a reasonable source of information." *In re McKesson HBOC, Inc. Sec. Litig.,* 126 F.Supp.2d 1248, 1272 (N.D.Cal.2000). However, as discussed above, that article provided no support for the allegations against Public Storage. Even crediting her claim to have searched public records for some sign of a relationship between the two companies that search also turned up nothing. Proceeding with the allegation anyway was not acting on a belief formed after a reasonable inquiry. This was not a case where a reasonable inquiry turned up facts that appeared to support the allegation but were later revealed to be false. In this case, the inquiry revealed no supporting facts, but the plaintiff's counsel proceeded with the allegation anyway.

The court concluded that the plaintiffs' counsel had violated Rule 11. To deter the repetition of this conduct in the future, the court found that it was necessary to sanction the plaintiffs' counsel by ordering her personally to partially reimburse defendant for the unnecessary legal fees incurred as a result of her sanctionable conduct.

**ANSWER (B)** is incorrect because this restates the standard for imposing sanctions pursuant to 28 U.S.C. § 1927, which was not at issue in this problem. Therefore, this was not the basis upon which the court granted Rule 11 sanctions. **ANSWER (C)** is incorrect because the court held that the defense attorney had properly complied with the requirements of Rule 11 in seeking sanctions. **ANSWER (D)** is incorrect because the court found the opposite. **ANSWER (E)** is incorrect because it embodies a public policy reason for the 1993 amendment to Rule 11, but the underlying rationale will not serve to overcome a violation of the rule, as the case here demonstrates.

### PROBLEM #18. BEST ANSWER (D).

Problem #18 is based on *David v. C and G Boats, Inc.,* 2015 WL 5553668 (E.D. La. Sept. 18, 2015). This problem presents a simple issue relating to a defendant's motion for a more definite statement pursuant to Fed.R.Civ.P. 12(e). The court found that the plaintiff's allegations were sufficient to give the defendant notice of his claims, and therefore the court denied the defendant's Rule 12(e) motion.

A district court will grant a motion for a more definite statement pursuant to Rule 12(e) when the pleading at issue "is so vague or ambiguous that a party cannot reasonably be required to frame a responsive pleading." Fed.R.Civ.P. 12(e). The motion must state the defects in the pleading and the details desired. *See id.* A party, however, may not use a Rule 12(e) motion as a substitute for discovery. *Mitchell v. E-Z Way Towers, Inc.,* 269 F.2d 126, 132 (5th Cir.1959). Given the liberal pleading standard set forth in Rule 8, Rule 12(e) motions are disfavored. *See Mitchell,* 269 F.2d at 132; *Gibson v. Deep Delta Contractors, Inc.,* No. 97–3791, 2000 WL 28174, at *6 (E.D.La. Jan. 14, 2000). At the same time, the Supreme Court has noted that "if a pleading fails to specify the allegations in a manner that provides sufficient notice," then a Rule 12(e) motion may be appropriate. *Swierkiewicz v. Sorema N.A.,* 534 U.S. 506, 514 (2002). In deciding whether to grant a Rule 12(e) motion, the trial judge is given considerable discretion. *Newcourt Leasing Corp. v. Regional Bio-Clinical Lab, Inc.,* No. 99–2626, 2000 WL 134700, at *1 (E.D.La. Feb. 1, 2000).

The court found David's complaint sufficient to withstand defendants' Rule 12(e) motion. A complaint is considered inadequate under the "notice" pleading requirements of Rule 8(a) only if it wholly fails to "(1) provide notice of circumstances which give rise to the claim, or (2) set forth sufficient information to outline the elements of the claim or permit inferences to be drawn that these elements exist." *Beanal v. Freeport-McMoran, Inc.,* 197 F.3d 161, 164 (5th Cir.1999) (citing *Gen. Star Indem., Co. v. Vesta Fire Ins., Corp.,* 173 F.3d 946, 950 (5th Cir.1999)). The defendants argued that David's complaint lacked sufficient information because he did not allege (1) the details of the accident, (2) the manner in which he believes the M/V MS. JANE, its equipment, or its crew were unseaworthy, or (3) the nature of his alleged physical injuries. The court held that while David's complaint was not a model of clarity, this information could be readily obtained through discovery. Because a party may not use a Rule 12(e) motion as a substitute for discovery, and because Rule 12(e) motions are disfavored, the court denied the defendants' motion for a more definite statement.

**ANSWER (A)** is incorrect because the court found that the plaintiff's allegations were legally sufficient to put the defendant on notice of the claims. Similarly, **ANSWER (B)** is incorrect because the court found the plaintiff's allegations sufficient to permit the defendant to frame answers and defenses to the plaintiff's claims. **ANSWER (C)** is incorrect because the court clearly believed that the defendant could subsequently obtain additional information through discovery, and therefore the court held that the defendant could not use a Rule 12(e) motion as a substitute for later discovery. **ANSWER (E)** is a possible answer, but not the best answer. As a policy matter, Rule 12 motions are disfavored—which the court noted—but the primary reason for denying the defendant's Rule 12(e) was the sufficiency of the plaintiff's allegations in his complaint.

### PROBLEM #19. BEST ANSWER (A).

Problem #19 is based on *Reichardt v. Emerson Electric Co.,* 2015 WL 5608203 (W.D. La. Sept. 23, 2015). This problem requires analysis of the standards for a summary judgment motion pursuant to Fed.R.Civ.P. 56. Applying those standards, the court held that there was no genuine issue of material fact with regard to the defendant's causation or liability for the plaintiff's injuries, and therefore granted the defendants' motion for summary judgment.

Under Fed.R.Civ.P. 56, summary judgment is proper "if the movant shows that there is no genuine dispute as to any material fact and the movant is entitled to judgment as a matter of law." Fed.R.Civ.P. 56(a); *Celotex Corp. v. Catrett*, 477 U.S. 317, 322 (1986). To determine whether there exists any genuine factual dispute, parties are empowered to submit to a court materials within the record for support, "including depositions, documents, electronically stored information, affidavits or declarations, stipulations (including those made for purposes of the motion only), admissions, interrogatory answers, or other materials." Fed.R.Civ.P. 56(c)(1)(a).

The plain text of Rule 56 requires that, after an appropriate time for discovery, a motion for summary judgment should be entered against an opposing party "who fails to make a showing sufficient to establish the existence of an element essential to that party's case, and on which that party will bear the burden of proof at trial." *Celotex Corp.*, 477 U.S. at 322. If the movant fails to satisfy their burden of showing that there is no genuine dispute of material fact with the motion for summary judgment, such a motion must be denied, regardless of the response by the non-movant. *See Little v. Liquid Air Corp.*, 37 F.3d 1069, 1075 (5th Cir.1994). Conversely, if the movant satisfies this initial burden, the non-movant must demonstrate that there is, in fact, a genuine factual issue for dispute at trial by going "beyond the pleadings" and designating specific facts for support. *Id.* (citing *Celotex Corp.*, 477 U.S. at 323–25). "A dispute as to a material fact is 'genuine' if the evidence is such that a reasonable jury could return a verdict for the nonmoving party." *Boudreaux v. Swift Transp. Co.*, 402 F.3d 536, 540 (5th Cir.2005) (citing *Anderson v. Liberty Lobby, Inc.*, 477 U.S. 242, 250–51 (1986)). The failure of the party bearing the initial burden at trial to demonstrate there is a genuine factual dispute to an essential element of their case renders any remaining facts immaterial. *See Celotex Corp.*, 477 U.S. at 322–23.

Additionally, Local Rule 56.1 requires the moving party to file a statement of material facts as to which it contends there is no genuine issue to be tried. Pursuant to Local Rule 56.2, the party opposing the motion for summary judgment must set forth a "short and concise statement of the material facts as to which there exists a genuine issue to be tried." All material facts set forth in the statement required to be served by the moving party "will be deemed admitted, for purposes of the motion, unless controverted as required by this rule." Local Rule 56.2.

When considering a motion for summary judgment, courts are to construe all facts and make inferences in the light most favorable to the nonmoving party. *Cooper Tire & Rubber Co. v. Farese*, 423 F.3d 446, 454 (5th Cir.2005) (citing *Murray v. Earle*, 405 F.3d 278, 284 (5th Cir.2005)). However, both the United States Supreme Court and the Fifth Circuit Court of Appeals maintain satisfying this burden on the part of the nonmoving party requires the presentation of supporting evidence. As the Fifth Circuit explained in *Little:*

> This burden is not satisfied with "some metaphysical doubt as to the material facts," by "conclusory allegations," by "unsubstantiated assertions," or by only a "scintilla" of evidence. We resolve factual controversies in favor of the nonmoving party, but only when there is

an actual controversy, that is, when both parties have submitted evidence of contradictory facts. *We do not, however, in the absence of any proof, assume that the nonmoving party could or would prove the necessary facts.*

*Little,* 37 F.3d at 1075. While a court is not to weigh the evidence or evaluate witness credibility, courts should grant summary judgment where the critical evidence in support of the non-movant is so weak and tenuous that it could not support a judgment in their favor. *Id.; Boudreaux,* 402 F.3d at 540.

Significantly, the instant motion for summary judgment was unopposed. However, summary judgment cannot be granted simply because there is no opposition to its entry. Rather, the court may only grant summary judgment "if the motion and supporting materials-including the facts considered undisputed-show that the movant is entitled to it. . . ." Fed.R.Civ.P. 56(e)(3). Because Reichardt failed to file an opposition and statement of contested material facts, Thomas's and State Farm's statement of uncontested material facts was deemed admitted for purposes of the instant motion.

This personal injury dispute arose under Louisiana law. Under Louisiana's duty-risk analysis, a plaintiff asserting a negligence claim must establish:

> (1) proof that the defendant had a duty to conform his conduct to a specific standard (the duty element); (2) proof that the defendant's conduct failed to conform to the appropriate standard (the breach element); (3) proof that the defendant's substandard conduct was a cause-in-fact of the plaintiff's injuries (the cause-in-fact element); (4) proof that the defendant's substandard conduct was a legal cause of the plaintiffs injuries (the scope of liability or scope of protection element); and (5) proof of actual damages (the damages element).

*Boykin v. Louisiana Transit Co.,* 96–1932 (La.3/4/98); 707 So.2d 1225, 1230. All of the elements must be satisfied in order to impose liability. *See Richard v. Swiber,* 98–1515 (La.App. 1 Cir.1999); 760 So.2d 355, 359.

The court first considered the cause-in-fact element of the test. *See id.* "Cause-in-fact usually is a 'but for' inquiry which tests whether the accident would or would not have happened but for the defendant's substandard conduct." *Id.* "When there are concurrent causes of an accident which nevertheless would have occurred in the absence of one of the causes, the proper inquiry is whether the conduct under consideration was a substantial factor in bringing about the accident." *Id.* at n. 10.

Thus, in the present case, the appropriate inquiry was whether Thomas's actions were a substantial factor in bringing about the Wade-Reichardt accident. Reichardt admitted that her vehicle never collided with the Thomas vehicle. Reichardt failed to present any other factual allegation that would suggest that Thomas's manner of driving was a substantial factor in causing the accident between Reichardt and Wade. The deposition testimony of all four witnesses revealed no indication of Thomas's responsibility for the accident between Reichardt and Wade. There was no allegation or even a mere suggestion that Wade's collision with the Thomas vehicle was a substantial factor in causing the accident between Wade and Reichardt. In short, there was nothing to suggest Thomas's breach of a duty caused Reichardt's accident or her concomitant damages. Reichardt had not identified any facts which would support a finding of Thomas's liability for the Wade-Reichardt accident. Thus, even in a light most favorable to the plaintiff, the evidence supported the finding that there was no genuine dispute of material fact as to whether Thomas was the "cause-in-fact" of the Wade-Reichardt collision.

For the foregoing reasons, the court granted the motion for summary judgment filed by Thomas and State Farm and the dismissed the plaintiff's claims against Thomas and State Farm with prejudice.

**ANSWER (B)** is a possible answer, but not the best answer. As the court indicated, even though the defendant's summary judgment was unopposed, the court still had to assess whether the material presented by the defendant's summary judgment motion was a sufficient basis upon which to grant the motion. **ANSWER (C)** is incorrect because viewing the deposition testimony of the four witnesses, the court concluded that there was no genuine issue of a material fact to go to a jury. For the same reasons, **ANSWERS (D)** and **(E)** are incorrect. *See* discussion above.

### PROBLEM #20. BEST ANSWER (C).

Problem #20 is based on *Schmucker v. Precision Irrigation, Inc.*, 2015 WL 6438351 (E.D. Mo. Oct. 22, 2015). This problem requires analysis of whether a defendant's counterclaims are within a federal court's supplemental jurisdiction pursuant to 28 U.S.C. § 1367. On the plaintiff's motion to dismiss for lack of supplemental jurisdiction, the court agreed that the counterclaims did not constitute one constitutional case, and therefore the court did not have good supplemental jurisdiction over the counterclaims.

Pursuant to section 1367, "in any civil action of which the district courts have original jurisdiction, the district courts shall have supplemental jurisdiction over all other claims that are so related . . . that they form part of the same case or controversy under Article III of the United States Constitution." 28 U.S.C. § 1367(a). Claims are part of the same case or controversy if they "derive from a common nucleus of operative fact." *City of Chi. v. Int'l Coll. of Surgeons*, 522 U.S. 156, 164–65 (1997) (citing *United Mine Workers of Am. v. Gibbs*, 383 U.S. 715, 725 (1966)). "A plaintiff's claims derive from a common nucleus of operative fact if the claims are such that he would ordinarily be expected to try them all in one judicial proceeding." *OnePoint Solutions, LLC v. Borchert*, 486 F.3d 342, 350 (8th Cir.2007).

A federal court may, in its discretion, decline to exercise supplemental jurisdiction over a state law claim if the claim involves complex issues of state law; state law claims predominate over federal claims; all federal claims have been dismissed; or, under exceptional circumstances, a compelling reason exists to decline supplemental jurisdiction. *See* 28 U.S.C. § 1367(c); *Innovative Home Health Care, Inc. v. P.P.-O.T. Assocs. of the Black Hills*, 141 F.3d 1284, 1287 (8th Cir.1998).

Schmucker argued that supplemental jurisdiction did not exist, in part because "there was very little overlap" in the evidence relevant to Schmucker's FLSA claim and the evidence relevant to Precision's counterclaims, as the former claim was a narrow and well defined claim for unpaid overtime, and the latter claims were not concerned with the number of hours Schmucker worked or his compensation. Precision contended that supplemental jurisdiction existed because the claims "derived from a common nucleus of operative facts"—namely, the nature and scope of Schmucker's employment duties, and the reason for the deductions from his salary—and will thus rely on the same evidence.

The court found that Schmucker's FLSA claim and Precision's counterclaims did not derive from a common nucleus of operative fact. Schmucker's FLSA claim would require consideration of evidence related to the scope of Schmucker's employment duties, the number of hours he worked, and his compensation, or lack thereof, for any overtime he worked. Precision's counterclaims would require consideration of evidence primarily related to Schmucker's performance of his employment duties, the alleged deficiencies of which bore no relationship to the numbers of hours he worked or Precision's wage and hour policies. *See Herbst v. Ressler & Assocs. Inc.,* No. 4:13–CV–2327 CAS, 2014 WL 4205294, at *4–5 (E.D.Mo. Aug. 22, 2014) (supplemental jurisdiction did not exist over fraud counterclaim to extent it related to plaintiff's alleged concealment of information, because it did not "involve plaintiff's duties or hours of work"). This was not a case where the defendant employer's allegations related to the number of hours the plaintiff worked, or the plaintiff's compensation; Precision had not alleged, for example, that Schmucker perpetrated fraud by falsifying his time records. *Cf. Herbst,* 2014 WL 4205294 at *4–5 (supplemental jurisdiction existed over fraud counterclaim to extent it related to allegations that defendant was entitled to recover compensation it had paid to plaintiff for time he claimed he was working but actually was not; both claims required "a determination whether plaintiff actually worked when he claimed to have worked, and what he was paid"); *Ahle v. Veractiy Research Co.,* 641 F.Supp.2d 857, 863 (D.Minn. July 28, 2009) (supplemental jurisdiction existed over counterclaims for breach of duty of loyalty and intentional or negligent misrepresentation, where defendant alleged that plaintiffs falsified time and mileage reports and failed to perform required duties while being compensated by defendant).

The court therefore concluded that the claims were not so related that they form part of the same case or controversy. Furthermore, even if the court found that Precision's counterclaims were so related to Schmucker's FLSA claim that they formed part of the same case or controversy, the court would decline to exercise supplemental jurisdiction because of the concern that the state law claims would substantially predominate over Schmucker's FLSA claim. *See* 28 U.S.C. § 1367(c); *Innovative Home Health Care,* 141 F.3d 1284 at 1287.

Therefore, Precision's counterclaims would be dismissed for lack of subject matter jurisdiction, pursuant to Fed.R.Civ.P. 12(b)(1).

**ANSWER (A)** is incorrect because the facts do not implicate possible supplemental jurisdiction under 28 U.S.C. § 1367(b); this is a red-herring answer. **ANSWER (B)** is incorrect because the court made no threshold analysis concerning whether the counterclaims were compulsory or permissive; as permissive counterclaims, these would need a supplemental jurisdictional base under 28 U.S.C. § 1367, which the court found did not find applicable. **ANSWER (D)** is incorrect because the court held the opposite; it concluded that the plaintiff's claims and the defendant's counterclaims were not so factually related as to constitute one constitutional case or controversy to allow supplemental jurisdiction over the counterclaims. **ANSWER (E)** is incorrect because it begs the threshold jurisdictional problem; federal courts can adjudicate state based claims or counterclaims, provided the court has valid jurisdiction—which in this case, the court concluded it did not.

### PROBLEM #21. BEST ANSWER (B).

Problem #21 is based on *Leonetti's Frozen Foods, Inc. v. Crew, Inc. d/b/a Crew Marketing, Inc.*, 2015 WL 5769228 (Sept. 30, 2015). This problem addresses a defendant's motion for dismissal for improper venue under Fed.R.Civ.P. 12(b)(3). The court granted the motion finding that venue was improper, but ordered a transfer of the case to the Western District of Arkansas because it was a district where the case could have been brought.

Crew removed the case from the Court of Common Pleas of Philadelphia County, Pennsylvania in this District. Venue was presumptively proper here. Section 1441(a) expressly provides that the proper venue of a removed action is 'the district court of the United States for the district and division embracing the place where such action is pending.' *Polizzi v. Cowles Magazines, Inc.*, 345 U.S. 663, 666 (1953) (*citing* 28 U.S.C. § 1441). While Leonetti and Crew discussed the factors under 28 U.S.C. § 1391, those factors were not relevant in a removed case.

The court held that despite the presumptive propriety of venue, the court could transfer the case after carefully applying the factors in *Jumara v. State Farm Ins. Co.* 55 F.3d 873, 879 (3d Cir.1995). Pursuant to 28 U.S.C. § 1404(a), a district court for the convenience of parties and witnesses, in the interest of justice, may transfer any civil action to any other district or division where it might have been brought or to any district or division to which all parties consented. "Section 1404(a) is intended to place discretion in the district court to adjudicate motions for transfer according to an individualized, case-by-case consideration of convenience and fairness." *Stewart Org., Inc. v. Ricoh Corp.*, 487 U.S. 22, 29 (1988); *see also Jumara*, 55 F.3d at 879.

Section 1404(a) requires the alternate venue to be one in which the case might have been brought. 28 U.S.C. § 1404(a). Crew was an Arkansas corporation, retained by Leonetti to liaise with Sam's Club in the same town in Arkansas. A substantial part of the events giving rise to Leonetti claims occurred in the Western District of Arkansas, even though a Pennsylvania company experienced the harm of conduct emanating from California but not effected until a decision by Sam's Club in the Western District of Arkansas. As Crew was located in the Western District of Arkansas, general personal jurisdiction might be invoked over it there. This action could have been properly brought in the Western District of Arkansas. *See id.*

In ruling on § 1404(a) motions, courts have not limited their consideration to the three enumerated factors in § 1404(a) (convenience of parties, convenience of witnesses, or interests of justice). *Jumara*, 55 F.3d at 879. Beyond the three enumerated factors, courts consider private and public interest factors to determine whether to transfer venue. *Id.*

Leonetti focused almost entirely on its harm felt in this District. The court appreciated that a Pennsylvania company's loss of a possible relationship allegedly was caused by an unfortunate email sent by an Arkansas company to another Arkansas company. Leonetti focused on this email and Sam's Club's reasons to not work with Leonetti. The court could not find authority categorically mandating venue in the Pennsylvania district court when the only connection to the district was a Pennsylvania plaintiff seeking recovery for an errant email causing an Arkansas company to make a business decision to not work with the Pennsylvania company, particularly when there was no directed activity to harm the Pennsylvania citizen. Instead, the court decided it had to apply *Jumara's* private and public interest factors in determining whether a transfer serves the convenience of the parties and witnesses and the interests of justice.

The private interests have included: (1) plaintiffs forum preference as manifested in the original choice; (2) the defendant's preference; (3) whether the claim arose elsewhere; (4) the convenience of the parties as indicated by their relative physical and financial condition; (5) the convenience of the witnesses-but only to the extent that the witnesses may actually be unavailable for trial in one of the fora; and (6) the location of books and records (similarly limited to the extent that the files could not be produced in the alternative forum). *Jumara*, 55 F.3d at 879.

Leonetti preferred its home forum in the Eastern District of Pennsylvania, and Crew preferred its home forum in the Western District of Arkansas. The court noted that it was black letter law that a plaintiffs choice of a proper forum is a paramount consideration in any determination of a transfer request, and that choice should not be lightly disturbed. *Shutte v. Armco Steel Corp.*, 431 F.2d 22, 25 (3d Cir.1970) (citing *Ungrund v. Cunningham Brothers, Inc.*, 300 F.Supp. 270, 272 (S.D.Ill.1969)).

The claim for breach of contract might have arisen in the Eastern District of Pennsylvania or the Western District of Arkansas. The breach occurred in an email sent from California to Arkansas and Pennsylvania. The breach, if any, was of Crew's oral agreement (admittedly not permitted under their written agreement) reached in an unknown location to represent Leonetti in the Western District of Arkansas.

The tort claims for professional negligence, breach of fiduciary duty, and trade libel weighed in favor of transfer, as they all arose outside of Pennsylvania. The convenience of the parties was neutral as one party would need to travel to the other forum regardless of which was selected. The convenience of witnesses appeared neutral, although the Sam's Club representatives making the decisions and the Crew agents were located in, or worked from, Arkansas. There was no basis to find any witness from either party was not available for a trial in Arkansas but third party witnesses from Sam's Club were located in the Western District of Arkansas. The location of books and records, particularly in this electronic age, was not dispositive as the records could be produced and transferred with ease from either venue. If anything, the key documents and emails involved Sam's Club's internal decision to not hire Leonetti. Those original records and their custodians, along with CREW's records, were headquartered in the Western District of Arkansas.

The public interests have included: (1) the enforceability of the judgment; (2) practical considerations that could make the trial easy, expeditious, or inexpensive; (3) the relative administrative difficulty in the two fora resulting from court congestion; (4) the local interest in deciding local controversies at home; (5) the public policies of the fora; and (6) the familiarity of the trial judge with the applicable state law in diversity cases. *Jumara*, 55 F.3d at 879–80.

A judgment rendered by the district court in Western Arkansas was as equally enforceable as a judgment from the Pennsylvania district, although Leonetti's potential judgment in Arkansas might be procedurally easier to execute upon local company Crew rather than a transferred judgment from Pennsylvania. The court was not aware of any Crew assets in this Pennsylvania but Leonetti conceded Crew was located in the Western District of Arkansas. Practical considerations weighed in favor of transfer as all witnesses to Sam's Club's decision to cease discussions with Leonetti were located in Western Arkansas.

The court was also mindful, while it did not rule upon personal jurisdiction, that Leonetti had a difficult argument to sustain specific personal jurisdiction over CREW for its professional negligence, breach of fiduciary duty and trade libel claims in Pennsylvania. The court held that it was likely this court might only retain personal jurisdiction over Leonetti's breach of contract claim. Conversely, Leonetti was unlikely to face challenges to either general or specific personal jurisdiction over Crew in its home district; transferring the whole action to a single forum with unquestioned personal jurisdiction rather than requiring two trials on largely the same facts in two fora would make trial easier, more expeditious, and less expensive for all parties.

Applying the remaining public interest factors, the court found that the factors were either neutral or weighed in favor of the Western District of Arkansas. The parties did not offer comparisons of case processing between this district and the Western District of Arkansas but, absent some extraordinary fact, the court expected that the jurists in the Western District of Arkansas who reviewed cases involving Walmart matters would similarly move this matter to prompt resolution. The interest in resolving local controversies at home might have weighed in favor of retaining venue if the majority of witnesses were not located in Arkansas. Here, the controversy only affected a Pennsylvania citizen. All facts and witnesses relating to the errant reply-all email, and its alleged harmful affect upon Sam's Club, were local in the Western District of Arkansas. The court found that the public policies of both Pennsylvania and Arkansas recognized the impact of mistaken reply-all emails and their effect upon an innocent party. The court also recognized that the district judge in either state could apply the applicable law of either Arkansas or Pennsylvania and this factor was also neutral.

Taken as a whole, the court concluded that the private and public interest factors weighed in favor of transferring venue to the Western District of

Arkansas. While Leonetti's choice of venue was not lightly disturbed particularly given it felt the effects of Crew's actions in Pennsylvania, the court found that the all of the remaining factors relating to the convenience and location of witnesses relating to Sam's Club's decision based on Crew's representation arose in, and were more directly related to, the Western District of Arkansas. The court ordered transfer of venue to the Western District of Arkansas.

**ANSWER (A)** is incorrect because the court analyzed all the factors implicated in a possible transfer under 28 U.S.C. § 1404(a); the place where the events arose was only one factor. Also, it is not factually correct that all the events giving rise to the plaintiff's claims arose in Arkansas; arguably, some of the events occurred in Pennsylvania. **ANSWER (C)** is incorrect because venue was technically proper initially in Pennsylvania pursuant to the removal statute; the court then had to make the determination whether to transfer the case to Arkansas. **ANSWER (D)** is incorrect because the court was not persuaded that the fact that the plaintiff's business was located in Pennsylvania was sufficient to permit the court to retain venue, as most of the events giving rise to the action occurred in Arkansas. **ANSWER (E)** is incorrect because the place where the effects of the defendant's conduct was felt was not dispositive of the venue determination.

**PROBLEM #22. BEST ANSWER (D).**

Problem #22 is based on *Butler v. American Heritage Life Insurance Company*, 2016 WL 367314 (E.D. Texas Jan. 29, 2016). This problem deals with a plaintiff's motion to compel disclosure of documents created by a corporate employee at the direction of the company's legal department. The court ruled that the documents were protected by attorney-client privilege, and therefore denied the plaintiff's request for disclosure of the documents.

The defendants withheld documents claiming that both attorney-client privilege and the work-product doctrine barred production. The attorney-client privilege is "the oldest and most venerated of the common law privileges of confidential communications and serves an important interest in our judicial system." *U.S. v. Edwards*, 303 F.3d 606, 618 (5th Cir.2002); *Upjohn Co. v. United States*, 449 U.S. 383, 389 (1981). "Its purpose is to encourage full and frank communication between attorneys and their clients and thereby promote broader public interests in the observance of law and administration of justice." *Upjohn*, 449 U.S. 383, 389 (1981).

The parties agreed that Texas law governed the resolution of the privilege issue in this diversity case. *See* Fed. R. Evid. 501; *Seibu Corp. v. KPMG LLP*, No. 3–00–CV–1639–X, 2002 WL 87461, at *1 (N.D. Tex. Jan. 18, 2002). Under Texas law, the elements of the attorney-client privilege are: (1) a confidential communication; (2) made for the purpose of facilitating the rendition of professional legal services; (3) between or amongst the client, lawyer, and their representatives; and (4) the privilege has not been waived. Tex. R. Evid. 503(b); *Huie v. DeShazo*, 922 S.W.2d 920, 925 n.4 (Tex. 1996).

The burden is on the party asserting the privilege to demonstrate how each document or communication satisfies each element. *Navigant Consulting, Inc.*

*v. Wilkinson*, 220 F.R.D. 467, 473 (N.D. Tex. 2004); *see Hodges, Grant & Kaufmann v. U.S. Gov't, Dep't of the Treasury, I.R.S.*, 768 F.2d 719, 721 n.7 (5th Cir.1985). General allegations of privilege are insufficient to meet this burden. *Navigant*, 220 F.R.D. at 473; *see Nutmeg Ins. Co. v. Atwell, Vogel & Sterling A Div. of Equifax Servs., Inc.*, 120 F.R.D. 504, 510 (W.D. La. 1988); *Saxholm AS v. Dynal, Inc.*, 164 F.R.D. 331, 333 (E.D.N.Y. 1996). Instead, "a clear showing must be made which sets forth the items or categories objected to and the reasons for that objection." *Navigant*, 220 F.R.D. at 473 (quoting *Caruso v. Coleman Co.*, 1995 WL 384602, at *1 (E.D. Pa. Jun. 22, 1995)). "The proponent must provide sufficient facts by way of detailed affidavits or other evidence to enable the court to determine whether the privilege exists." *Id.* "Although a privilege log and an *in camera* review may assist the court in conducting its analysis, a party asserting the privilege still much provide 'a detailed description of the materials in dispute and state specific and precise reasons for their claim of protection from disclosure.' " *Id.* at 473–474 (quoting *Pippenger v. Gruppe*, 883 F.Supp. 1201, 1212 (S.D. Ind. 1994); *see also Greene, Tweed of Del., Inc. v. DePont Dow Elastomers, L.L.C.*, 202 F.R.D. 418, 423 (E.D. Pa. 2001); *Diamond State Ins. Co. v. Rebel Oil Co., Inc.*, 157 F.R.D. 691, 699 (D. Nev. 1994)).

The defendants asserted that the documents submitted to the court in its *in camera* review consisted of "internal email correspondences between Allstate's in-house counsel, or between Allstate's in-house counsel and Allstate's executives." The plaintiff alleged that there is "no indication that Mr. Mueller was giving legal advice, only that he was conducting a fact finding investigation from which employment decisions regarding Watkins might be made."

Allstate alleged that the "only documents withheld by Allstate were (1) communications between and among attorneys for Allstate, and (2) communications between attorneys for Allstate and executives from Allstate, both categories of which were made for the purpose of those attorneys providing legal advice to Allstate." Allstate asserted that "Mueller was engaged by Allstate's in-house attorney, Sue Rosborough, to conduct an investigation for the purpose of enabling Allstate's Legal Department to render legal advice to Allstate regarding Butler's complaint." "The entire investigation was to be conducted at the direction of Rosborough, or at the direction of another member of the Corporate Legal team." Allstate alleged that Mueller was requested to assist with an investigation into a complaint made against Watkins and "Rosborough was required to provide legal advice to Allstate regarding what to do about the complaint and Watkins' continued employment with Allstate." Allstate "expected that if any disciplinary or termination action was taken against Watkins, he would likely file suit against Allstate."

As a part of his engagement, Mueller communicated with Allstate's in-house counsel and other employees of Allstate. Allstate alleged that these people were in a position to take advice from Allstate's attorney, and therefore, Mueller's communications were privileged and not subject to disclosure. "Mueller conferred with Rosborough regarding the investigation, and she relayed to Mueller what she needed, and whom he would need to initially interview." As the investigation was prompted by the plaintiff, Mueller interviewed the plaintiff first. During the interview, Allstate alleged that Mueller "told plaintiff that because of in-house's direction, the investigation was attorney-client privileged."

Tex. R. Evid. 503(b) precludes the discovery of communications between attorney and client. "A client has the privilege to refuse to disclose and prevent any other person from disclosing confidential communications made for the purpose of facilitating the rendition of legal services to the client." *IMC Fertilizer, Inc. v. O'Neill*, 846 S.W.2d 590, 592 (Tex. App.—Houston [14th Dist.] 1993, orig. proceeding) (citing Tex. R. Evid. 503(b)). The privilege applies to communications between:

> (1) the client's representative and the attorney or the attorney's representative; (2) the attorney and the attorney's representative; (3) the client, his representative, his attorney and an attorney representing another party in the pending action and concerning a matter of common interest; (4) representatives of the client, and the client and his representatives; (5) attorneys and their representatives representing the same client.

Tex. R. Evid. 503(b). "A representative of the lawyer is a person employed by the lawyer to assist the lawyer in the rendition of professional legal services." *IMC Fertilizer, Inc.*, 846 S.W.2d at 592 (citing Tex. R. Evid. 503(a)(4)).

> Although the attorney-client privilege extends to communications between 'representatives of the client,' a party invoking the privilege must show that each person privy to the communication: (1) had the authority to obtain professional legal services on behalf of the client; (2) had authority to act on legal advice rendered to the client; or (3) made or received the confidential communication while acting within the scope of his employment for the purpose of effectuating legal representation to the client.

*Navigant*, 220 F.R.D. at 475 (quoting *Seibu*, 2002 WL 87461, at *2) (citing Tex. R. Evid. 503(a)(2)(A)–(B)).

"The attorney-client privilege protects confidential communications between a lawyer and a client or their respective representatives made to facilitate the rendition of professional legal services to the client." *In re Tex. Farmers Ins. Exch.*, 990 S.W.2d 337, 340 (Tex. App.—Texarkana 1999, orig. proceeding [mand. denied]) (citing Tex. R. Evid. 503(b)). Although the privilege is not limited to communications made in anticipation of litigation, it does not apply if the attorney is acting in a capacity other than that of an attorney. *In re Tex. Farmers Ins. Exch.*, 990 S.W.2d at 340; *Harlandale Indep. Sch. Dist. v. Cornyn*, 25 S.W.3d 328, 332 (Tex. App—Austin 2000, pet. denied); *see Clayton v. Canida*, 223 S.W.2d 264, 266 (Tex. App.—Texarkana 1949, no writ) (attorney acting as an accountant); *Pondrum v. Gray*, 298 S.W. 409, 412 (Tex. Comm'n App. 1927, holding approved)(communications to attorney acting as scrivener not privileged). But in appropriate circumstances, "the privilege may bar disclosures made by a client to non-lawyers who had been employed as agents of an attorney." *United States v. Pipkins*, 528 F.2d 559, 562 (5th Cir.1976) (citing *United States v. Kovel*, 296 F.2d 918, 921 (2d Cir.1961); *Burlington Indus. v. Exxon Corp.*, 65 F.R.D. 26, 40 (D.Md. 1974); *United States v. Schmidt*, 360 F.Supp. 339, 346 (M.D.Pa. 1973)).

"The privilege recognizes that sound legal advice or advocacy serves public ends and that such advice or advocacy depends upon the lawyer's being fully informed by the client." *Upjohn*, 449 U.S. at 389. However, "the privilege only protects disclosure of communications; it does not protect disclosure of the underlying facts by those who communicated with the attorney." *Dunn v. State Farm Fire & Cas. Co.*, 122 F.R.D. 507, 509 (W.D. Miss. 1988) (quoting *Upjohn*, 449 U.S. at 395). In *Upjohn*, the Supreme Court found that attorney-client privilege applied for investigative inquiries because,

> . . . the privilege exists to protect not only the giving of professional advice . . . but also the giving of information to the lawyer to enable him to give sound and informed advice . . . The first step in the resolution of any legal problem is ascertaining the factual background and sifting through the facts with an eye to the legally relevant.

*In re LTV Sec. Litig.*, 89 F.R.D. 595, 601 (N.D. Tex. 1981). However, "the privilege does not protect documents and other communications simply because they result from an attorney-client relationship." *Navigant*, 220 F.R.D. at 473; *see Seibu*, 2002 WL 87461, at \*2. Additionally, "documents are not privileged merely because they are prepared by and sent to an attorney." *Navigant*, 220 F.R.D. at 475; *see Thurmond v. Compaq Comput. Corp.*, 198 F.R.D. 475, 479 (E.D. Tex. 2000).

The court found that Mueller was acting as an agent for Allstate's in house counsel when he conducted the investigation into Watkins. At all times relevant to the investigation, Mueller reported to Rosborough or someone else within the legal department of Allstate, and conducted his investigation in order to provide legal advice to Allstate's in-house counsel. The court found that the undisclosed emails were communications made to Mueller to aid in the providing the needed legal advice. Additionally, the emails were made either to a lawyer within Allstate's in-house department or to Allstate representatives who were acting within the scope of their employment when they sent and received communications from Mueller. *See Navigant*, 220 F.R.D. at 475 (quoting *Seibu*, 2002 WL 87461, at \*2) (citing Tex. R. Evid. 503(a)(2)(A)–(B)). Therefore, the documents were covered by attorney-client privilege, and may remain protected and did not need to be disclosed to the plaintiff in the pending action.

Finally, the plaintiff asserted that Mueller failed to give Butler an *Upjohn* warning in connection with the interview, and therefore, attorney-client privilege did not attach to any evidence from Mueller's investigation. Allstate asserted that Mueller "very clearly" explained the reason for the interview. The court agreed with Allstate that Mueller gave the plaintiff adequate warning that he was not representing the plaintiff. First, Mueller stated that he was conducting an investigation on behalf of Allstate. Furthermore, Mueller told Plaintiff, "Ok and just a reminder that the investigation I'm doing is being done at the direction of a lawyer here at Allstate and so it is subject to the attorney/client privilege." It also appeared that during the interview the plaintiff was not confused that he was represented by Mueller or by Allstate's in-house counsel. It did not appear that the plaintiff sought legal counsel from Mueller during the interview; in fact, the plaintiff appeared to understand throughout the interview that he was testifying regarding the complaint he made against Watkins. The court found that the plaintiff was not confused as to Mueller's role in the investigation, and therefore, attorney-client privilege did not attach to the plaintiff from the interview.

**ANSWER (A)** is incorrect because the court held the opposite: that the requested documents were protected by attorney-client privilege. **ANSWER (B)** is incorrect because the court did not find that the documents were not protected by attorney work product immunity. **ANSWER (C)** is incorrect because the question focuses on the defendant's invocation of attorney client privilege, which is absolute. The fact that a party may have need of documents to prepare for its case is not a ground for overcoming the attorney-client privilege, if it exists. **ANSWER (E)** is incorrect because the court found that Mueller correctly apprised Butler that their conversation was not privileged under the Supreme Court's holding in Upjohn; in other words, the court found that Mueller gave Butler a proper Upjohn warning.

### PROBLEM #23. BEST ANSWER (D).

Problem #23 is based on *Edwards v. Mack Trucks, Inc., and M & K Quality Truck Sales of Summit, LLC, d/b/a Chicago Mack, Center, Inc.*, 310 F.R.D. 382 (N.D. Ill. Aug. 26, 2015). This problem deals with a defendant's motion to dismiss a count in a complaint against it, under Fed.R.Civ.P. 12(b)(6), for failure to state a claim against it. The court found the claim deficient under applicable Illinois substantive law, and therefore granted the defendant's motion to dismiss Count II against it.

A motion to dismiss under Rule 12(b)(6) does not test the merits of a claim; rather, it tests the sufficiency of the complaint. *Gibson v. City of Chicago,* 910 F.2d 1510, 1520 (7th Cir.1990). In deciding a 12(b)(6) motion, the court accepts all well-pleaded facts as true, and draws all reasonable inferences in favor of the plaintiff. *Id.* at 1521. To survive a 12(b)(6) motion, "a complaint must contain sufficient factual matter, accepted as true, to state a claim to relief that is plausible on its face." *Ashcroft v. Iqbal,* 556 U.S. 662, 678 (2009). "A claim has facial plausibility when the plaintiff pleads factual content that allows the court to draw the reasonable inference that the defendant is liable for the misconduct alleged." *Id.* "While legal conclusions can provide the framework of a complaint, they must be supported by factual allegations." *Id.* at 679.

The Illinois Commercial Code closely mirrors the Uniform Commercial Code and provides buyers with both a mechanism to revoke an acceptance to an offer, as well as a means to cancel a contract once an acceptance has been revoked in order to claim and recover damages. In Count II of the complaint, the plaintiff brought a revocation of acceptance claim under Illinois statutes against Defendant Mack Trucks.

In Illinois, however, revocation of acceptance claims are not available against non-selling manufacturers. Although some other states allow this type of remedy, *see, e.g., Volkswagen of Am., Inc. v. Novak*, 418 So.2d 801, 804 (Miss.1982), Illinois does not. *Mydlach v. DaimlerChrysler Corp.*, 226 Ill.2d 307, 327, 314 Ill. Dec. 760, 875 N.E.2d 1047 (2007); *see also Kutzle v. Thor Indus., Inc.*, No. 03 C 2389, 2003 WL 21654260 (N.D. Ill. July 14, 2003). In *Mydlach*, the Illinois Supreme Court considered whether a plaintiff who bought a used vehicle from a dealership could bring a suit to recover damages against the car's manufacturer, using the warranty as a basis for his claim. *Mydlach*, 226 Ill.2d at 309, 314 Ill. Dec. 760, 875 N.E.2d 1047. According to the court, revocation of acceptance "contemplates a buyer-seller relationship" which would be "conceptually inapplicable" to a non-seller such as a manufacturer. *Id.* at 332, 314 Ill Dec. 760, 875 N.E.2d 1047. Although the car in *Mydlach* was a used vehicle and the truck in this case is a new vehicle, the court's reasoning in *Mydlach* applied here. According to *Mydlach*, revocation of acceptance claims are not available to non-selling manufacturers—and this rule can be applied regardless of whether the car is new or used.

Here, the plaintiff lacked the requisite buyer-seller relationship with the defendant Mack Trucks that was required for a claim of revocation of acceptance. Much like the plaintiff in *Mydlach*, the plaintiff bought a vehicle from a dealership without any direct connection to the manufacturer. In fact, the plaintiff's Exhibit A plainly showed that the only parties to the original contract were the plaintiff as buyer and the defendant Chicago Mack as seller. The defendant Mack Trucks was not listed as a party to the transaction. *Id.* The defendant Mack Trucks was simply the manufacturer, and based on the pleadings, the plaintiff had not established the requisite buyer-seller relationship upon which a revocation of acceptance claim must be brought.

Because the plaintiff failed to state a claim under Illinois law, the court dismissed Count II of the complaint with prejudice.

**ANSWER (A)** is incorrect because the court held the opposite and granted the defendant's motion to dismiss under Rule 12(b)(6). Similarly, **ANSWER (B)** is incorrect because even viewing the allegations in a light most favorable to the non-moving party, *i.e.*, the plaintiff, the court still held that the defendant was entitled to have its motion to dismiss granted. **ANSWER (C)** is incorrect because Rule 12(b)(6) motions typically are not converted to summary judgment motions; this procedural possibility occurs when a party moves for a judgment on the pleadings pursuant to Rule 12(c). **ANSWER (E)** is incorrect because having concluded that Count II was legally insufficient under Illinois law, there was no point in allowing the case to proceed to a jury trial, where the jury could not have found against the defendant truck manufacturer.

## PROBLEM #24. BEST ANSWER (E).

Problem #24 is based on *Rilley v. MoneyMutual, LLC*, 863 N.W.2d 789 (App. Minn. Aug. 22, 10215). This problem deals with the question whether the state of Minnesota could assert personal jurisdiction over the non-resident defendant corporation MoneyMutual, based on its contacts with the state. The Minnesota court held that the defendant had sufficient contacts with Minnesota to assert personal jurisdiction, and rejected the defendant's arguments to the contrary.

MoneyMutual argued that the district court erred by denying its motion to dismiss for lack of personal jurisdiction. The court reviewed *de novo* whether personal jurisdiction existed. *Volkman v. Hanover Invs., Inc.*, 843 N.W.2d 789, 794 (Minn.App.2014). To establish personal jurisdiction, the plaintiff must make a prima facie showing of jurisdiction, and the complaint and supporting evidence will be taken as true. *Hardrives, Inc. v. City of LaCrosse*, 307 Minn. 290, 293, 240 N.W.2d 814, 816 (Minn.1976). The court must view the evidence in the light most favorable to the plaintiff. *Fastpath, Inc. v. Arbela Techs. Corp.*, 760 F.3d 816, 820 (8th Cir.2014). Doubts should be resolved in favor of retaining jurisdiction. *Hardrives*, 307 Minn. at 296, 240 N.W.2d at 818.

A Minnesota court may exercise personal jurisdiction over an out-of-state defendant as long as jurisdiction is authorized by the long-arm statute and comports with the constitutional due-process requirement. *Juelich v. Yamazaki Mazak Optonics Corp.*, 682 N.W.2d 565, 570 (Minn.2004). Because Minnesota's long-arm statute extends to the limits of due process, the inquiry turns on whether the defendant has sufficient minimum contacts with Minnesota so that exerting personal jurisdiction over the defendant "does not offend traditional notions of fair play and substantial justice," *Int'l Shoe Co. v. Washington*, 326 U.S. 310, 316 (1945). Because the court's ultimate conclusion depended on the Due Process Clause of the United States Constitution, the court applied federal case law in examining this issue. *Valspar Corp. v. Lukken Color Corp.*, 495 N.W.2d 408, 411 (Minn.1992).

To exercise personal jurisdiction consistent with due process, the out-of-state defendant must have purposefully availed itself of the privilege of conducting activities within the forum state. *Burger King Corp. v. Rudzewicz*, 471 U.S. 462, 475 (1985). A court must focus "on the relationship among the defendant, the forum, and the litigation." *Griffis v. Luban*, 646 N.W.2d 527, 532 (Minn.2002). To determine if minimum contacts exist, a court considers five factors: (1) the quantity of the defendant's contacts with Minnesota; (2) the nature and quality of the defendant's contacts with Minnesota; (3) the connection between the claims and the defendant's contacts; (4) Minnesota's interest in providing a forum; and (5) the convenience of the parties. *Volkman*, 843 N.W.2d at 795. The first three factors are given greater weight than the last two. *Id.*

The third factor determines which form of personal jurisdiction may exist. General jurisdiction exists when the defendant's contacts are "continuous and systematic," so the forum may assert jurisdiction regardless of whether the claims are related to the contacts. *Id.* at 795. For specific jurisdiction to exist, the defendant must have "purposefully directed" its actions at the forum state, and the claims must "arise out of or relate to" the contacts. *Burger King*, 471 U.S. at 472. The plaintiffs asserted that specific jurisdiction existed because MoneyMutual conducted business activities in Minnesota and their claims arose from those activities.

MoneyMutual argued that personal jurisdiction could be based on: (1) any contact it had with the plaintiffs because those contacts are based on the "fortuitous" presence of the plaintiffs in Minnesota; (2) its television commercials that aired in Minnesota because they were not targeted solely at Minnesota; or (3) its website, which is accessible from Minnesota, because it is not targeted solely at Minnesota. The court agreed that personal jurisdiction would not exist if the court disregarded these items; however, the court was not persuaded by MoneyMutual's contention that the court had to ignore the plethora of contacts alleged by the plaintiffs.

MoneyMutual first argued that the district court relied on the plaintiffs' contacts with Minnesota, not its own. MoneyMutual contended that its contacts with Minnesota were limited to the plaintiffs' fortuitous presence in the forum and unilateral activities. MoneyMutual's argument appeared to be that any contact involving a plaintiff could not also be a contact of the defendant's, but the court held that one did not preclude the other. Case law made clear that when a resident of a forum state leaves that state, his residency alone cannot establish personal jurisdiction. *Walden v. Fiore*, 134 S.Ct. 1115, 1122–23 (2014). But this was not one of those cases. Here, MoneyMutual reached into Minnesota through its advertising and communications. The plaintiffs were in Minnesota at all times: when they saw MoneyMutual advertising, when they interacted with MoneyMutual, when they submitted applications indicating they were Minnesota residents, and when MoneyMutual sold the plaintiffs' applications to lenders for profit. Mere residency of the plaintiffs was not the sole basis for personal jurisdiction here; rather, MoneyMutual's efforts to reach the plaintiffs and conduct business with them were the bases.

MoneyMutual also stated that each plaintiff initiated communication with MoneyMutual by visiting its website and submitting an application and that its e-mails responding to the applications were automated. Therefore, according to MoneyMutual, the plaintiffs acted unilaterally. This argument failed. First, it disregarded MoneyMutual's active solicitation of Minnesota residents, without which the plaintiffs might never have become aware of MoneyMutual or its services. Second, MoneyMutual disregarded its own actions to ensure that a loan was created, such as encouraging inquiring customers via phone conversations and e-mail to submit an application online. The interaction between the plaintiffs, MoneyMutual, and the lenders was better described as a three-sided transaction with each party taking action before the loan was made, rather than a series of unilateral acts by the plaintiffs. In order to obtain a loan, plaintiffs submitted applications to MoneyMutual. MoneyMutual then offered each application to its lender network. Each time a lender selected an application, MoneyMutual notified the plaintiff who had submitted the application via e-mail and received a fee from the lender. Given this business model, the contacts were not based on the plaintiffs' unilateral acts; MoneyMutual took independent action by selling the contact information to lenders *after* it knew that the applicant was a Minnesota resident, thus generating its own profit in the second step of the overall transaction.

Additionally, MoneyMutual analyzed each named plaintiff separately, giving no weight to the allegation that MoneyMutual received more than 1,000 loan applications from Minnesota residents. The sheer volume of loan applications indicated that MoneyMutual's contacts with Minnesota were not limited to those who "fortuitously" happened to be Minnesota residents, but rather the result of a business strategy that included a Minnesota market. *See Zippo Mfg. Co. v. Zippo Dot Com, Inc.,* 952 F.Supp. 1119, 1126 (W.D.Pa.1997) (theorizing that it would be "fortuitous" if a subscription-based Internet news service with no Pennsylvanian subscribers found itself sued in Pennsylvania because an Ohio subscriber downloaded a message and forwarded it to a Pennsylvanian). Furthermore, MoneyMutual was capable of blocking its advertisements from jurisdictions where it does not do business, and it had done so in some jurisdictions. MoneyMutual's e-mails also indicated that its services might not be available in all areas, implying that its automated replies connecting applicants with lenders confirmed that the resident lived in a market where MoneyMutual offered its services. *See Lakin v. Prudential Sec., Inc.,* 348 F.3d 704, 712 (8th Cir.2003) (holding that a website that accepts online loan applications and provides electronic responses may form the basis of personal jurisdiction if the plaintiffs demonstrate that forum residents actually accessed the website).

MoneyMutual also argued that specific jurisdiction did not exist because its advertisements were not "expressly aimed" at Minnesota. When an intentional tort is at issue, a court may exert personal jurisdiction over a foreign defendant if the effects of the tort were felt in the forum state. *Calder v. Jones*, 465 U.S. 783, 789–90 (1984). The Minnesota Supreme Court has adopted a three-prong effects test requiring the plaintiff to show that:

> (1) the defendant committed an intentional tort; (2) the plaintiff felt the brunt of the harm caused by that tort in the forum such that the forum was the focal point of the plaintiff's injury; and (3) the defendant expressly aimed the tortious conduct at the forum such that the forum state was the focal point of the tortious activity.

*Griffis*, 646 N.W.2d at 534.

The court held that the plaintiffs alleged sufficient targeting of the Minnesota market. First, the plaintiffs alleged that MoneyMutual television commercials had been broadcast in Minnesota since at least 2010. MoneyMutual denied that it placed ads with any Minnesota-based or local stations, but did not deny using national advertising that included Minnesota, that its services were available in Minnesota, or that its advertisements were intentionally broadcast in Minnesota. MoneyMutual appeared to argue that advertising was not expressly aimed at Minnesota unless it specifically mentioned Minnesota, airs only in Minnesota, or was otherwise customized to the Minnesota market. But the court affirmed a finding of personal jurisdiction based on national advertising and marketing where the intended market merely included Minnesota. *See, e.g., State by Humphrey v. Granite Gate Resorts, Inc.,* 568 N.W.2d 715, 719–20 (Minn.App.1997), *aff'd*, 576 N.W.2d 747 (Minn.1998).

Moreover, MoneyMutual's communications with the plaintiffs evinced a willingness to offer its services to Minnesota residents. The plaintiffs alleged that when one Minnesota resident called MoneyMutual from her Minnesota phone number after seeing a television commercial broadcast in Minnesota, a MoneyMutual representative directed her to its website to complete a loan application. Then, after plaintiffs submitted applications confirming that they were Minnesota residents, MoneyMutual e-mailed plaintiffs to notify them that MoneyMutual had matched them with a lender. In addition, MoneyMutual sent follow-up e-mails, called "offers," encouraging past Minnesota customers to use its services again.

Finally, MoneyMutual argued that its website also was not expressly aimed at Minnesota and that basing personal jurisdiction on a website would subject website operators to "universal jurisdiction" because they could be sued anywhere the website was accessed. MoneyMutual's "universal jurisdiction" argument was somewhat hyperbolic because personal jurisdiction continues to be bounded by due process, even when based on Internet contacts. For example, a website that can be accessed from anywhere cannot provide the sole basis for personal jurisdiction if it has never been visited by a forum resident. *Johnson v. Arden*, 614 F.3d 785, 797 (8th Cir.2010).

Furthermore, the court found it unwise to disregard contacts through an openly accessible website given the increased tendency for commerce to take place via the Internet, particularly when the website is used to circumvent Minnesota law. Minnesota expressed a clear intent to regulate payday lending and to protect its residents from predatory practices by enacting statutes that govern not just lenders, but also those who arrange payday loans. *See* Minn. Stat. §§ 47.60–.601 (2014). Moreover, Minnesota's long-arm statute extended to the limits of due process, and nothing here would "offend traditional notions of fair play and substantial justice." *Int'l Shoe*, 326 U.S. at 316. The MoneyMutual website contributed to the required minimum contacts because it was a commercial website that was visited repeatedly by customers known by MoneyMutual to be Minnesotans to submit applications for payday loans. When considered alongside MoneyMutual's advertising, acceptance of and profit from more than 1,000 loan applications from Minnesotans, and e-mail communications with Minnesota residents, the court held that the district court did not err when it denied MoneyMutual's motion to dismiss for lack of personal jurisdiction.

**ANSWER (A)** is incorrect because the court upheld assertion of personal jurisdiction over the defendant MoneyMutual, finding that the defendant's business contacts with the state were sufficient to subject it to the jurisdiction of the court. **ANSWER (B)** is incorrect because the court rejected this argument presented by the defendant; the court's personal jurisdiction analysis focused on the defendant's contacts with the state, and not the plaintiffs' contacts or activities. **ANSWER (C)** is incorrect for similar reasons; the court did not consider the plaintiffs' unilateral activities as a basis for asserting or denying personal jurisdiction over the defendant. **ANSWER (D)** is incorrect because the court did not base its assertion of personal jurisdiction over the defendant on its possible contacts with other states.

### PROBLEM #25. BEST ANSWER (A).

Problem #25 is based on *McKinnis v. Digital Intelligence Systems Corp.*, 2015 WL 7424778 (N.D. Tex. Nov. 23, 2015). This problem deals with a defendant's motion to transfer a case pursuant to a forum selection and choice of law clause in an employment contract. Under the authority of the Supreme Court's decision in Atlantic Marine, the court upheld the enforceability of the clause and ordered that the case be transferred to the Eastern District of Virginia, from the federal district court in Texas.

28 U.S.C. § 1404(a) provides that, "for the convenience of parties and witnesses, in the interest of justice, a district court may transfer any civil action to any other district or division where it might have been brought." In applying Section 1404(a), the court must first determine "whether the judicial district to which transfer is sought would have been a district in which the claim could have been filed." *In re Volkswagen AG*, 371 F.3d 201, 203 (5th Cir.2004). Once this initial determination is made, the court

> turns to the language of § 1404(a), which speaks to the issue of "the convenience of parties and witnesses" and to the issue of "in the interest of justice." The determination of "convenience" turns on a number of private and public interest factors, none of which is given dispositive weight. The private concerns include: (1) the relative ease of access to sources of proof; (2) the availability of compulsory process to secure the attendance of witnesses; (3) the cost of attendance for willing witnesses; and (4) all other practical problems that make trial of a case easy, expeditious and inexpensive. The public concerns include: (1) the administrative difficulties flowing from court congestion; (2) the local interest in having localized interests decided at home; (3) the familiarity of the forum with the law that will govern the case; and (4) the avoidance of unnecessary problems of conflict of laws of the application of foreign law.

*Id.*

Transfer of venue under Section 1404(a) is generally at the court's discretion, considering " 'all relevant factors to determine whether or not on balance the litigation would more conveniently proceed and the interests of justice be better served by transfer to a different forum.' " *El Chico Restaurants of Texas, Inc. v. Carroll*, No. 3:09–cv–2294–L, 2010 WL 2652286, at *2 (N.D. Tex. June 29, 2010) (quoting *Peteet v. Dow Chem. Co.*, 868 F.2d 1428, 1436 (5th Cir.1989)).

A plaintiff's original choice of forum is generally entitled to some deference, which dictates that the moving party must "demonstrate that the transferee venue is clearly more convenient." *In re Volkswagen of America, Inc.*, 545 F.3d 304, 315 (5th Cir.2008). But, while a plaintiff's choice of forum "should be respected" unless "the transferee venue is clearly more convenient," Plaintiff's "choice of forum is not an independent factor within the § 1404(a) analysis." *Id.* at 314 n.10, 315. Rather, "a plaintiff's choice of venue is to be treated as a burden of proof question." *Id.* at 314 n.10.

A forum selection clause may be enforced by a motion to transfer venue under Section 1404(a). *Atlantic Marine Constr. Co., Inc. v. U.S. Dist. Ct. for the Western Dist. of Texas*, 134 S.Ct. 568, 574, 579 (2013). A valid forum selection clause is " 'given controlling weight in all but the most exceptional cases,' " and, when the parties have agreed to a valid forum selection clause, a district court should ordinarily transfer the case to the forum specified in that clause. *Id.* at 581 (quoting *Stewart Org., Inc. v. Ricoh Corp*, 487 U.S. 22, 33 (1988)).

In *Atlantic Marine*, the United States Supreme Court held that "the presence of a valid forum-selection clause requires district courts to adjust their usual § 1404(a) analysis in three ways." *Id.* "First, the plaintiff's choice of forum merits no weight," because "the plaintiff has effectively exercised its 'venue privilege' before the dispute arises" through the forum selection clause agreement. *Id.* at 581–82. Second, "arguments about the parties' private interests" must not be considered, since, by agreeing to the forum selection clause, the parties effectively "waive the right to challenge" any private inconvenience that the "preselected forum" may create. *Id.* at 582. Accordingly, the court "must deem the private-interest factors to weigh entirely in favor of the preselected forum," and only "arguments about public-interest factors" may be considered when deciding whether to transfer under Section 1404(a) to the contractually-specified venue. *Id.* But "those factors will rarely defeat a transfer motion," with "the practical result is that forum-selection clauses should control except in unusual cases." *Id.* And "the party acting in violation of the forum-selection clause must bear the burden of showing that public-interest factors overwhelmingly disfavor a transfer." *Id.* at 583; *see also In re Rolls Royce Corp.*, 775 F.3d 671, 674–83 (5th Cir.2014) (discussing *Atlantic Marine*); *Cline v. Carnival Corp.*, No. 3:13–cv–1090–B, 2014 WL 550738, at *6 (N.D. Tex. Feb. 12, 2014) (same).

As an initial matter, DISYS's removal of this action to this court from state court did not prohibit DISYS from then invoking a forum-selection clause and moving to transfer the case to another federal district. *See generally Sharpe v. AmeriPlan Corp.*, 769 F.3d 909, 914, 918–19 (5th Cir.2014); *Baumgart v. Fairchild Aircraft Corp.*, 981 F.2d 824, 835 (5th Cir.1993); *Benz v. Recile*, 778 F.2d 1026, 1028 (5th Cir.1985); *Aguacate Consolidated Mines, Inc., of Costa Rica v. Deeprock, Inc.*, 566 F.2d 523, 525 (5th Cir.1978); *Icepiece, Inc. v. Wells Fargo Bank, N.A.*, No. 3:14–cv–3528–BN, 2015 WL 524202, at *2 (N.D. Tex. Feb. 9, 2015); *Quality Custom Rail & Metal, LLC v. Travelers Cas. and Sur. Co. of Am.*, No. 3:13–cv–3587–D, 2014 WL 840046, at *2 (N.D. Tex. Mar. 4, 2014).

And the *Atlantic Marine* analytical framework applied here where the parties' employment agreement contained a mandatory, not permissive, forum-selection clause—which the plaintiff did not dispute. *Waste Mgmt. of La., L.L.C. v. Jefferson Parish ex rel. Jefferson Parish Council*, 594 F.App'x 820, 820–22 (5th Cir.2014); *UNC Lear Services, Inc. v. Kingdom of Saudi Arabia*, 581 F.3d 210, 219 (5th Cir.2009) ("Mandatory forum-selection clauses that require all litigation to be conducted in a specified forum are enforceable if their language is clear.").

Further, DISYS had shown that the employment agreement's forum-selection clause was valid and applied to this action, which the plaintiff, again, did not dispute. Indeed, Plaintiff does not argue that the employment agreement's forum-selection clause is invalid or inapplicable. *See generally Ginter ex rel. Ballard v. Belcher, Prendergast & Laporte*, 536 F.3d 439, 441 (5th Cir.2008) ("Under federal law, forum-selection clauses are presumed enforceable, and the party resisting enforcement bears a 'heavy burden of proof.'"); *Braspetro Oil Servs. Co. v. Modec (USA), Inc.*, 240 F.App'x 612, 615 (5th Cir.2007) ("Such clauses are prima facie valid and should be enforced unless enforcement is shown by the resisting party to be unreasonable under the circumstances."); *Steve Silver Co., Inc. v. Manna Freight Sys., Inc.*, No. 3:14–cv–2601–D, 2014 WL 5286624, at *2–*4 (N.D. Tex. Oct. 15, 2014).

When a court is presented with a valid, applicable, mandatory forum-selection clause, the Supreme Court has instructed that "only under extraordinary circumstances unrelated to the convenience of the parties should a § 1404(a) motion be denied." *Atlantic Marine*, 134 S.Ct. at 581. *Atlantic Marine* dictates that the Court should enforce such a forum-selection clause unless public-interest factors overwhelming disfavor a transfer. *See Atlantic Marine*, 134 S.Ct. at 581–82; *Cline*, 2014 WL 550738, at *6. And the plaintiff bore the burden to show that public-interest factors overwhelmingly disfavored DISYS's request for a transfer. *See Atlantic Marine*, 134 S.Ct. at 583.

Recognizing this, the plaintiff opposed transfer on the basis that "this was an employment discrimination and breach of contract case arising from McKinnis's employment with Defendant in the State of Texas;" "McKinnis worked for Defendant at its offices in Dallas County, Texas for approximately five years before he was terminated in the spring of 2014" and that, "although the events giving rise to this action occurred in the State of Texas, Defendant now seeks to transfer venue to the Commonwealth of Virginia based upon a forum selection clause in McKinnis's employment contract with Defendant," but, "due to the nature of the facts and circumstances giving rise to this case in the State of Texas, this case presents extraordinary circumstances that should prevent transfer to Virginia," where "the relevant public interest factors established by federal courts weigh heavily against a transfer to the Commonwealth of Virginia."

As to the factor relating to the local interest in having localized interests decided at home, the plaintiff asserted that all of the acts giving rise to his claims occurred in Texas and that he lived in Texas and was employed by Defendant for five years at its Dallas offices. The plaintiff contended that his claims are based on discriminatory employment actions committed by Defendant in Dallas County, Texas; that the employees and witnesses involved in the actions at issue are located in Texas; and that this court had a far greater local interest in deciding McKinnis's employment discrimination claims than did a Virginia court, where he has brought employment discrimination claims against the defendant under the Texas Labor Code.

The court was not persuaded that these facts showed that this public-interest factor overwhelming disfavored a transfer. The facts regarding witnesses related to arguments about the parties' private interests that the Supreme

Court had directed must not be considered in this context. *See Atlantic Marine*, 134 S.Ct. at 582. And, as DISYS pointed out, the plaintiff no longer lived in the Northern District of Texas.

Finally, the plaintiff's other arguments as to this factor otherwise, "at most, set forth facts to establish that this court has a local interest in considering the case because the alleged acts of discrimination occurred in Texas and Defendant maintains an office in Texas." *Henry v. Covenant Transp. Inc.*, No. 3:13–cv–1926–L, 2014 WL 2217336, at *3 (N.D. Tex. May 29, 2014). The court found that—even including any local interest in having the Texas court apply Texas law—"was insufficient to sustain the plaintiff's heavy burden to demonstrate that public interest factors 'overwhelmingly disfavor' transfer under the forum selection clause." *Id.* Were it otherwise, merely filing a lawsuit alleging conduct in a district sufficient to establish venue there under 28 U.S.C. § 1391(b)(2) and alleging violations of the forum state's law would also be sufficient to make any such action one of those "most unusual cases" in which the public interest overwhelmingly disfavored transfer. *Atlantic Marine*, 134 S.Ct. at 583. The court could square this logical conclusion of the plaintiff's approach with the Supreme Court's guidance that the public-interest "factors will rarely defeat a transfer motion" based on a forum-selection clause. *Id.* at 582.

As to the factor relating to the familiarity of the forum with the law that will govern the case, the plaintiff asserted that, notwithstanding the employment agreement's choice-of-law clause, Texas law governed his statutory "discrimination claims, and the Texas court would be far more familiar with the protections provided in the Texas Labor Code, weighing heavily against transfer to Virginia." The court found that even assuming that the plaintiff was correct as to this choice-of-law issue, the plaintiff has also asserted a breach of contract claim to which Virginia law undisputedly would apply under the choice-of-law clause. For that reason alone, in this case presenting two causes of action, the court could find that this public-interest factor overwhelmingly disfavored transfer.

Finally, as to the factor relating to the administrative difficulties flowing from court congestion, the plaintiff asserted that the Northern District of Texas had an average of 284 fewer cases filed per division over a 12-month period, showing that the court congestion in the Eastern District of Virginia weighed against transfer of this case. But, as DISYS correctly pointed out in reply, judges in this district have reasoned that, "when considering this factor, the real issue is not whether transfer will reduce a court's congestion but whether a trial may be speedier in another court because of its less crowded docket." *Siragusa v. Arnold*, No. 3:12–cv–4497–M, 2013 WL 5462286, at * 7 (N.D. Tex. Sept. 16, 2013) (quoting *USPG Portfolio Two, LLC v. John Hancock Real Estate Fin., Inc.*, No. 3:10–cv–2466–D, 2011 WL 1103372, at *5)(N.D. Tex. Mar. 25, 2011). "Accordingly, the median time interval from case filing to disposition is a better statistic for this analysis." *Id.* And DISYS provided statistics showing that the median time interval from filing to disposition in the Eastern District of Virginia's Alexandria Division—the so-called "rocket docket"—was lower than that in the Dallas Division of the Northern District of Texas. Under these circumstances, the court could find that this public-interest factor overwhelmingly disfavored transfer.

Because the plaintiff had not met his burden to show that this was one of those "most unusual cases" in which the public interest overwhelmingly disfavored transfer and that therefore presented extraordinary circumstances that should prevent transfer to the Eastern District of Virginia, the court found that " 'the interest of justice,' " as defined in Section 1404(a), "was served by holding the plaintiff to his bargain" by way of transfer to the parties' agreed-upon venue. *Atlantic Marine*, 134 S.Ct. at 581, 583.

The Court granted defendant Digital Intelligence Systems Corporation's motion to transfer venue and ordered that the case be transferred to the United States District Court for the Eastern District of Virginia, Alexandria Division pursuant to 28 U.S.C. § 1404(a).

**ANSWER (B)** is a possible answer, but not the best answer. The court enforced the forum selection agreed to by the parties; the court did not base its decision on the presence of a choice of law provision in the same contract. **ANSWER (C)** is incorrect because, assessing the private and public interest factors, the court concluded that these factors weighed in favor of transfer to Virginia. **ANSWER (D)** is incorrect because the court determined that the Virginia court might apply Virginia law to the breach of contract claim, but where there were two different causes of action, this might disfavor transfer. However, on balance of all relevant public and private factors, the problem of applicable law was not sufficient to overcome the factors favoring transfer. **ANSWER (E)** is incorrect because the court did not consider or make any rulings about the unconscionability of the forum selection clause. As indicated above, the plaintiff did not challenge the clause on that basis. The plaintiff had conceded that the clause was valid and enforceable.

END OF ANSWERS AND EXPLANATIONS TO EXAM #5

## ANSWER SHEET EXAM #1

Problem #1   A ◯   B ◯   C ◯   D ◯   E ◯
Problem #2   A ◯   B ◯   C ◯   D ◯   E ◯
Problem #3   A ◯   B ◯   C ◯   D ◯   E ◯
Problem #4   A ◯   B ◯   C ◯   D ◯   E ◯
Problem #5   A ◯   B ◯   C ◯   D ◯   E ◯
Problem #6   A ◯   B ◯   C ◯   D ◯   E ◯
Problem #7   A ◯   B ◯   C ◯   D ◯   E ◯
Problem #8   A ◯   B ◯   C ◯   D ◯   E ◯
Problem #9   A ◯   B ◯   C ◯   D ◯   E ◯
Problem #10  A ◯   B ◯   C ◯   D ◯   E ◯
Problem #11  A ◯   B ◯   C ◯   D ◯   E ◯
Problem #12  A ◯   B ◯   C ◯   D ◯   E ◯
Problem #13  A ◯   B ◯   C ◯   D ◯   E ◯
Problem #14  A ◯   B ◯   C ◯   D ◯   E ◯
Problem #15  A ◯   B ◯   C ◯   D ◯   E ◯
Problem #16  A ◯   B ◯   C ◯   D ◯   E ◯
Problem #17  A ◯   B ◯   C ◯   D ◯   E ◯
Problem #18  A ◯   B ◯   C ◯   D ◯   E ◯
Problem #19  A ◯   B ◯   C ◯   D ◯   E ◯
Problem #20  A ◯   B ◯   C ◯   D ◯   E ◯
Problem #21  A ◯   B ◯   C ◯   D ◯   E ◯
Problem #22  A ◯   B ◯   C ◯   D ◯   E ◯
Problem #23  A ◯   B ◯   C ◯   D ◯   E ◯
Problem #24  A ◯   B ◯   C ◯   D ◯   E ◯
Problem #25  A ◯   B ◯   C ◯   D ◯   E ◯

## Answer Sheet Exam #2

Problem #1    A ⬭    B ⬭    C ⬭    D ⬭    E ⬭
Problem #2    A ⬭    B ⬭    C ⬭    D ⬭    E ⬭
Problem #3    A ⬭    B ⬭    C ⬭    D ⬭    E ⬭
Problem #4    A ⬭    B ⬭    C ⬭    D ⬭    E ⬭
Problem #5    A ⬭    B ⬭    C ⬭    D ⬭    E ⬭
Problem #6    A ⬭    B ⬭    C ⬭    D ⬭    E ⬭
Problem #7    A ⬭    B ⬭    C ⬭    D ⬭    E ⬭
Problem #8    A ⬭    B ⬭    C ⬭    D ⬭    E ⬭
Problem #9    A ⬭    B ⬭    C ⬭    D ⬭    E ⬭
Problem #10   A ⬭    B ⬭    C ⬭    D ⬭    E ⬭
Problem #11   A ⬭    B ⬭    C ⬭    D ⬭    E ⬭
Problem #12   A ⬭    B ⬭    C ⬭    D ⬭    E ⬭
Problem #13   A ⬭    B ⬭    C ⬭    D ⬭    E ⬭
Problem #14   A ⬭    B ⬭    C ⬭    D ⬭    E ⬭
Problem #15   A ⬭    B ⬭    C ⬭    D ⬭    E ⬭
Problem #16   A ⬭    B ⬭    C ⬭    D ⬭    E ⬭
Problem #17   A ⬭    B ⬭    C ⬭    D ⬭    E ⬭
Problem #18   A ⬭    B ⬭    C ⬭    D ⬭    E ⬭
Problem #19   A ⬭    B ⬭    C ⬭    D ⬭    E ⬭
Problem #20   A ⬭    B ⬭    C ⬭    D ⬭    E ⬭
Problem #21   A ⬭    B ⬭    C ⬭    D ⬭    E ⬭
Problem #22   A ⬭    B ⬭    C ⬭    D ⬭    E ⬭
Problem #23   A ⬭    B ⬭    C ⬭    D ⬭    E ⬭
Problem #24   A ⬭    B ⬭    C ⬭    D ⬭    E ⬭
Problem #25   A ⬭    B ⬭    C ⬭    D ⬭    E ⬭

# ANSWER SHEET EXAM #3

Problem #1    A ◯    B ◯    C ◯    D ◯    E ◯
Problem #2    A ◯    B ◯    C ◯    D ◯    E ◯
Problem #3    A ◯    B ◯    C ◯    D ◯    E ◯
Problem #4    A ◯    B ◯    C ◯    D ◯    E ◯
Problem #5    A ◯    B ◯    C ◯    D ◯    E ◯
Problem #6    A ◯    B ◯    C ◯    D ◯    E ◯
Problem #7    A ◯    B ◯    C ◯    D ◯    E ◯
Problem #8    A ◯    B ◯    C ◯    D ◯    E ◯
Problem #9    A ◯    B ◯    C ◯    D ◯    E ◯
Problem #10   A ◯    B ◯    C ◯    D ◯    E ◯
Problem #11   A ◯    B ◯    C ◯    D ◯    E ◯
Problem #12   A ◯    B ◯    C ◯    D ◯    E ◯
Problem #13   A ◯    B ◯    C ◯    D ◯    E ◯
Problem #14   A ◯    B ◯    C ◯    D ◯    E ◯
Problem #15   A ◯    B ◯    C ◯    D ◯    E ◯
Problem #16   A ◯    B ◯    C ◯    D ◯    E ◯
Problem #17   A ◯    B ◯    C ◯    D ◯    E ◯
Problem #18   A ◯    B ◯    C ◯    D ◯    E ◯
Problem #19   A ◯    B ◯    C ◯    D ◯    E ◯
Problem #20   A ◯    B ◯    C ◯    D ◯    E ◯
Problem #21   A ◯    B ◯    C ◯    D ◯    E ◯
Problem #22   A ◯    B ◯    C ◯    D ◯    E ◯
Problem #23   A ◯    B ◯    C ◯    D ◯    E ◯
Problem #24   A ◯    B ◯    C ◯    D ◯    E ◯
Problem #25   A ◯    B ◯    C ◯    D ◯    E ◯

## ANSWER SHEET EXAM #4

Problem #1   A ◯   B ◯   C ◯   D ◯   E ◯
Problem #2   A ◯   B ◯   C ◯   D ◯   E ◯
Problem #3   A ◯   B ◯   C ◯   D ◯   E ◯
Problem #4   A ◯   B ◯   C ◯   D ◯   E ◯
Problem #5   A ◯   B ◯   C ◯   D ◯   E ◯
Problem #6   A ◯   B ◯   C ◯   D ◯   E ◯
Problem #7   A ◯   B ◯   C ◯   D ◯   E ◯
Problem #8   A ◯   B ◯   C ◯   D ◯   E ◯
Problem #9   A ◯   B ◯   C ◯   D ◯   E ◯
Problem #10   A ◯   B ◯   C ◯   D ◯   E ◯
Problem #11   A ◯   B ◯   C ◯   D ◯   E ◯
Problem #12   A ◯   B ◯   C ◯   D ◯   E ◯
Problem #13   A ◯   B ◯   C ◯   D ◯   E ◯
Problem #14   A ◯   B ◯   C ◯   D ◯   E ◯
Problem #15   A ◯   B ◯   C ◯   D ◯   E ◯
Problem #16   A ◯   B ◯   C ◯   D ◯   E ◯
Problem #17   A ◯   B ◯   C ◯   D ◯   E ◯
Problem #18   A ◯   B ◯   C ◯   D ◯   E ◯
Problem #19   A ◯   B ◯   C ◯   D ◯   E ◯
Problem #20   A ◯   B ◯   C ◯   D ◯   E ◯
Problem #21   A ◯   B ◯   C ◯   D ◯   E ◯
Problem #22   A ◯   B ◯   C ◯   D ◯   E ◯
Problem #23   A ◯   B ◯   C ◯   D ◯   E ◯
Problem #24   A ◯   B ◯   C ◯   D ◯   E ◯
Problem #25   A ◯   B ◯   C ◯   D ◯   E ◯

# ANSWER SHEET EXAM #5

Problem #1    A ◯    B ◯    C ◯    D ◯    E ◯

Problem #2    A ◯    B ◯    C ◯    D ◯    E ◯

Problem #3    A ◯    B ◯    C ◯    D ◯    E ◯

Problem #4    A ◯    B ◯    C ◯    D ◯    E ◯

Problem #5    A ◯    B ◯    C ◯    D ◯    E ◯

Problem #6    A ◯    B ◯    C ◯    D ◯    E ◯

Problem #7    A ◯    B ◯    C ◯    D ◯    E ◯

Problem #8    A ◯    B ◯    C ◯    D ◯    E ◯

Problem #9    A ◯    B ◯    C ◯    D ◯    E ◯

Problem #10    A ◯    B ◯    C ◯    D ◯    E ◯

Problem #11    A ◯    B ◯    C ◯    D ◯    E ◯

Problem #12    A ◯    B ◯    C ◯    D ◯    E ◯

Problem #13    A ◯    B ◯    C ◯    D ◯    E ◯

Problem #14    A ◯    B ◯    C ◯    D ◯    E ◯

Problem #15    A ◯    B ◯    C ◯    D ◯    E ◯

Problem #16    A ◯    B ◯    C ◯    D ◯    E ◯

Problem #17    A ◯    B ◯    C ◯    D ◯    E ◯

Problem #18    A ◯    B ◯    C ◯    D ◯    E ◯

Problem #19    A ◯    B ◯    C ◯    D ◯    E ◯

Problem #20    A ◯    B ◯    C ◯    D ◯    E ◯

Problem #21    A ◯    B ◯    C ◯    D ◯    E ◯

Problem #22    A ◯    B ◯    C ◯    D ◯    E ◯

Problem #23    A ◯    B ◯    C ◯    D ◯    E ◯

Problem #24    A ◯    B ◯    C ◯    D ◯    E ◯

Problem #25    A ◯    B ◯    C ◯    D ◯    E ◯

# NOTES